I0596995

PRIMEROS MEMORIALES

by Fray Bernardino de Sahagún

PALEOGRAPHY OF NAHUATL TEXT AND ENGLISH TRANSLATION

by Thelma D. Sullivan

Completed and Revised, with Additions,
by H. B. Nicholson, Arthur J. O. Anderson,
Charles E. Dibble, Eloise Quiñones Keber,
and Wayne Ruwet

Published by the
UNIVERSITY OF OKLAHOMA PRESS,
Norman, Oklahoma,
in Cooperation with the
Patrimonio Nacional
and the
Real Academia de la Historia, Madrid

This volume follows the manuscript order reconstructed for the *Primeros Memoriales* by Francisco del Paso y Troncoso in his 1905–1907 facsimile edition of the collection of Sahaguntine manuscripts he called the *Códices Matritenses*. Published with the assistance of the National Endowment for the Humanities, a federal agency which supports the study of such fields as history, philosophy, literature, and language, and of the Program for Cultural Cooperation Between Spain's Ministry of Culture and United States' Universities.

Library of Congress Cataloging-in-Publication Data

Sahagun, Bernardino de, d. 1590.
[Primeros memoriales. Nahuatl & English]
Primeros memoriales / by Bernardino de Sahagun : paleography of Nahuatl text and English translation by Thelma D. Sullivan : completed and rev., with additions, by H. B. Nicholson . . . [et al.].
p. cm. — (The civilization of the American Indian series : 200, pt. 2)
Includes index.

ISBN 978-0-8061-5749-8 (paper)

1. Aztecs. 2. Paleography. Nahuatl. 3. Nahuatl language—Texts. I. Sullivan, Thelma D. H Nicholson, H.B. (Henry B.) III. Title. IV. Series.
F1219.73.S2416 1997
497'.45211— DC21 96-45377
CIP

Primeros Memoriales: Paleography of Nahuatl Text and English Translation is volume 200, part two, in The Civilization of the American Indian Series.

The paper in this book meets the guidelines for permanence and durability of the Committee on Production Guidelines for Book Longevity of the Council on Library Resources, Inc. ∞

Copyright © 1997 by the University of Oklahoma Press, Norman, Publishing Division of the University All rights reserved. Paperback published 2017. Manufactured in the U.S.A.

Primeros Memoriales

PALEOGRAPHY OF NAHUATL TEXT
AND ENGLISH TRANSLATION

THE CIVILIZATION OF THE AMERICAN INDIAN SERIES

Contents

Figures

Following Page 20

TABLES

Following Page 37

PREFACE

This volume realizes a project that, sad to say, could not be finished by the scholar who initiated it. Fortunately, she was able to finish most of it, which made it possible for others to carry it through to completion. The late Thelma D. Sullivan, born and educated in New York, resided in Mexico for many years (see Sullivan's summary biography, with her bibliography, in Dakin and Heyden 1988). With her interest and training in languages and literature, she became fascinated by the culture of the final period of pre-Hispanic Central Mexico, usually called Aztec, and especially by its dominant language, the rich and expressive Nahuatl. She studied the latter assiduously, mainly under Miguel León-Portilla and Angel M. Garibay K. The latter was the leading Nahuatl scholar in Mexico until his death in 1971. He was the author, among many other works, of two classic contributions to this field, *Llave de Náhuatl* (1940; second, enlarged edition, 1961) and *Historia de la Literatura Náhuatl* (1971 [1954–1955]).

In 1963, Thelma's first translation into English of a Classical Nahuatl text appeared in *Estudios de Cultura Náhuatl.* After a warm personal tribute to her mentor, Garibay, she published the paleography of the Nahuatl text and English translation of the proverbs, conundrums, and metaphors in the final chapters (42–43) of the Nahuatl column of Book 6 of the *Florentine Codex* version of Sahagún's *Historia General (Universal) de las Cosas de (la) Nueva España.* During the next few years she published a number of significant articles on aspects of Aztec culture, as well as translations into both English and Spanish of additional Nahuatl texts. She soon earned an international reputation as one of the most accomplished modern "Nahuatlatos," a reputation capped by the 1976 publication, by the Instituto de Investigaciones Históricas of the Universidad Nacional Autónoma de México, of her *Compendio de la Gramática Náhuatl*—which in 1988 was posthumously published, somewhat modified by Wick Miller and Karen Dakin, in an English version by the University of Utah Press.

Thelma was always particularly interested in the monumental corpus of Nahuatl texts compiled, with extensive native assistance, by the greatest of the sixteenth-century Spanish missionary-ethnographers active in New Spain, Fray Bernardino de Sahagún. Most of her translations were of Sahaguntine texts, including various paragraphs of the document published in this volume, the *Primeros Memoriales.* By 1967 she had also completed a translation into English of the entire Spanish text of Sahagún's encyclopedic account of Aztec culture contained in the *Historia General.* This translation is still unpublished.

I first met Thelma in Mexico in 1970. Shortly before, I had written an article on Sahagún's *Primeros Memoriales* that was in press in volume 13 of *The Handbook of Middle American Indians* (it appeared in 1973). In that article I emphasized that only a limited portion of the *Primeros Memoriales* had been included by Sahagún in the final version of his *Historia.* While recognizing that most of its paragraphs had been paleographized and translated into Spanish, English, or German, I pointed out that these publications had appeared in widely scattered outlets and indicated the obvious desirability of a unitary publication of the *Primeros Memoriales,* with complete Nahuatl text and translation into a modern language. When I discovered that Thelma Sullivan had already paleographized the Nahuatl and translated into English a considerable portion of the

Primeros Memoriales, working from the rare 1905 photoreproduction edited by Francisco del Paso y Troncoso, I strongly urged her to complete the task and seek an outlet for its publication, offering her my help and support.

After considerable further discussion and cogitation, Thelma, now a full-time researcher with the Centro de Investigaciones Superiores of the Instituto Nacional de Antropología e Historia, decided to undertake the project. In 1979 she applied for a grant to the National Endowment for the Humanities (Arthur J. O. Anderson, Charles E. Dibble, and I wrote letters of support), which she received early the following year. She also contracted with the University of Oklahoma Press to publish the work upon its completion. Thelma devoted most of her time and energy to this project from the spring of 1980 until shortly before her untimely death from cancer on August 7, 1981. By the onset of her final illness, she had completed much of the paleography and translation and many of the notes, although all of it was in preliminary form.

Not long after Thelma Sullivan's passing, I contacted four of her friends and colleagues in Mexico—Karen Dakin, Doris Heyden, and Nicholas Hopkins and Kathryn Josserand Hopkins—inquiring whether it might be possible to obtain the manuscript drafts of Thelma's *Primeros Memoriales* project. It was my hope that the project could be completed with the aid of two of her most esteemed fellow Nahuatlatos and Sahagún scholars, Arthur Anderson and Charles Dibble. With their encouragement and cooperation, and with the invaluable help of the executrix of Thelma's estate, Rita Wilensky, that September I traveled to Mexico City, accompanied and aided by Wayne Ruwet of the UCLA Powell Library, and we obtained the necessary materials. Anderson and Dibble agreed to review Thelma's paleography and translation and to complete the sections she had left unfinished. I applied to the National Endowment for the Humanities to assume the primary responsibility for coordinating the completion of Thelma's project, requesting allocation of the remaining funds to help defray the expenses, and this was generously granted. The University of Oklahoma Press was also contacted and expressed interest in seeing the project through if it could be satisfactorily completed.

Finally, after many unavoidable delays owing mainly to previous commitments on the part of the project participants, we present the first complete paleography of the Nahuatl text and English translation of the *Primeros Memoriales* of Fray Bernardino de Sahagún. As Volume 200, part two, in The Civilization of the American Indian Series, it constitutes the companion volume to *Primeros Memoriales by Fray Bernardino de Sahagún: Facsimile Edition,* Volume 200, part one, in the same series (Sahagún 1993). The completion of Thelma Sullivan's project was very much a joint effort. Arthur J. O. Anderson and Charles E. Dibble, the editors and translators of the monumental, thirteen-volume edition of the profusely illustrated *Florentine Codex* version of Sahagún's *Historia General* (University of Utah Press, 1950–1982), with their unrivaled knowledge of Sahaguntine matters and the Classical Nahuatl language, played an indispensable role. Anderson assumed the chief responsibility for reviewing and modifying, where necessary, the paleography and English translation of the portion Thelma had finished and for completing the portion she had left unfinished. Dibble reviewed these revisions and additions and suggested various modifications and changes. Anderson also contributed to the linguistic aspect of the notes, the chief overall responsibility for the completion of which I assumed. Art historian Eloise Quiñones Keber, who worked with the original manuscript of the *Primeros Memoriales* in Madrid in 1986, contributed a description of its physical aspects and an introduction to its illustrations, discussing their sources, artists, and relationships to the texts. Wayne Ruwet assisted in various capacities in addition to participating in the initial retrieval of Sullivan's drafts. He inspected the Madrid manuscripts in 1983, aided in the correspondence, and undertook the lengthy and laborious task of typing onto the computer diskettes, in double-column format, both the preliminary and final versions of the paleography of the Nahuatl text and English translation. I revised and greatly enlarged the notes and contributed the general introduction. The latter is intended to provide a cultural and historical context for the *Primeros Memoriales*, to place it accurately within the development of Sahagún's overall long-term ethnographic-linguistic project, and to provide a basic notion of its contents. I also had the opportunity of working with the original manuscript in Madrid on three occasions, in 1968 (Academy portion), 1976, and 1986, recording the watermarks and studying in a preliminary way its structural features.

We attempted to complete the project following as closely as possible Thelma Sullivan's original intentions, revealed to me in numerous conversations and letters. She wished to produce an "eminently readable" translation of the *Primeros Memoriales*. As Anderson (personal communication) has expressed it, "I think she favored a considerably freer translation of the P.M. than what Charles and I produced in the *Florentine Codex*. In revising her work on the P.M. I did not change her free style except when it seemed to me that there were accidental or perhaps unwarranted omissions, or incorrect translations."

If we have succeeded in achieving most of Thelma Sullivan's aims, it is owing to the help and cooperation of many persons and institutions. Special thanks must be extended to the National Endowment for the Humanities—above all to Susan A. Mango, program officer, Translations Program, Division of Research Programs—for its original financial support of the project and, particularly, its willingness to reassign it, with the unexpended funds, to the undersigned and to grant the necessary temporal extensions. We appreciate the willingness of the University of Oklahoma Press to honor the original contract to publish the work and, particularly, the considerable patience and interest in the project displayed by the editor-in-chief, John Drayton, throughout the long delay in completing it. We would also like to express our sincere appreciation to Karen Dakin, Nicholas Hopkins and Kathryn Josserand Hopkins, Doris Heyden, and especially Rita Wilensky, who initially made it all possible by facilitating our acquisition of Sullivan's *Primeros Memoriales* manuscript. Particular thanks is owed to the directors and staff members of the libraries of the Palacio Real (Patrimonio Nacional) and Real Academia de la Historia in Madrid, who made available for our inspections the original manuscript of the *Primeros Memoriales* and who granted permission for the publication of its color photoreproduction as part one of the set of which this book is part two. Finally, we would like to acknowledge our special debt to Thelma Sullivan herself, to whose memory, of course, we dedicate this work. Her ability and her energy in the final period of her tragically truncated life have resulted in the first unitary publication of one of the most valuable accounts ever compiled concerning the indigenous civilization of Central Mexico at the time of the Spanish Conquest.

H. B. Nicholson
University of California—Los Angeles

Editorial Note

ARTHUR J. O. ANDERSON

Concerning the extent of additions to and revisions of the Thelma Sullivan paleography and English translation of the Nahuatl text of the *Primeros Memoriales*, with comment on paleographical aspects of the manuscript:

1. Sullivan's transcription of the Nahuatl text was carefully reviewed and, where necessary, modified for correctness and consistency. Her English translation was reviewed throughout for consistency and correctness and was modified where necessary. Otherwise her style was not changed.

2. The following sections, left untranslated by Thelma Sullivan, I translated with the aid of Charles E. Dibble: Chapter III, Paragraphs 4–10; and Chapter IV, Paragraphs 10 and 11.

The following sections were translated preliminarily by Thelma Sullivan but not always completely: Chapter I, Paragraph 14; Chapter II, Paragraphs 6 and 7; Chapter III, Paragraphs 1–3 and 11–17; Chapter IV, Paragraphs 1–7 and 9. With the aid of Charles E. Dibble, I filled in the blanks and often considerably revised the translations. (Chapter IV, Paragraph 9, particularly required revision.)

The entire manuscript is in the exceptionally legible script one associates with Sahagún's scribes, except for a few scrawled pages (e.g., Chapter I, Paragraph 4; Chapter IV, Paragraph 9) never copied in a clearer hand. Anyone familiar with the mysteries of Nahuatl spelling in the sixteenth century and the grammatical conventions observed in the *Florentine Codex* will find nothing new or unusual in the *Primeros Memoriales*, except the perhaps more frequent use of the abbreviation transcribed here as *-qz* (for *-que*), the occasional omission of final nasalizations (e.g., *tepito* for *tepiton*), and the occasional use of *t* for the affricative *tz (o)*.

Primeros Memoriales

PALEOGRAPHY OF NAHUATL TEXT
AND ENGLISH TRANSLATION

INTRODUCTION

H. B. NICHOLSON

A figure of landmark importance in the conveyance of an exceptionally detailed account of major aspects of the indigenous culture of Central Mexico at the time of the Conquest and in the early colonial period was the Spanish Franciscan, Fray Bernardino de Sahagún, who served as a missionary in New Spain from 1529 to 1590. He has often been designated "the father of modern ethnography." Although his proselytizing motive was quite distinct from that of the modern ethnographer, the aptness of this label derives from his use of a technique for obtaining information about the native culture that remarkably anticipated what is currently recognized as one of the most effective methods of recording accurate ethnographic data. This technique involved the collecting from his informants, following a structured interrogatory, of extensive texts in Nahuatl, the dominant language of Central Mexico.

Sahagún's vigorous program of compiling these texts, however, was not just for ethnographic purposes. After mastering Nahuatl himself, he sought to transmit his knowledge of this idiom, the principal communicative tool of the conversion program, to his fellow missionaries as effectively as possible through these lengthy texts (plus other aids, such as a grammar and a Spanish-Nahuatl dictionary, which he also prepared). Entirely apart from its immense ethnographic value, therefore, the Sahaguntine corpus provides an invaluable body of linguistic information concerning the most important and widespread of the Mesoamerican native languages. As Sahagún (1950–1982, Part I: 47) himself expressed it: "This work is like a dragnet to bring to light all the words of this language with their exact and metaphorical meanings, and all their ways of speaking, and most of their ancient practices, the good and evil."

SAHAGÚN'S ETHNOGRAPHIC-LINGUISTIC PROJECT

Although Sahagún compiled two substantial Nahuatl texts (which became Books 6 [rhetorical orations] and 12 [history of the Conquest]) some years earlier, it was not until 1558 that he was officially commissioned by the Provincial of his order, Fray Francisco de Toral, to undertake a systematic investigation of the native culture by compiling in Nahuatl what would be "useful for the indoctrination, the propagation and perpetuation of the Christianization of these natives of this New Spain, and as a help to the workers and ministers who indoctrinate them" (Sahagún 1950–1982, Part I: 53). Accompanied by four Indian assistants—the famous "trilinguals" (Nahuatl-Spanish-Latin)[1]—whom he had earlier taught as a member of the faculty of the Colegio de Santa Cruz in Tlatelolco, he moved to the Franciscan convent in Tepepolco, about fifty miles northeast of Mexico City. There he assembled a group of knowledgeable local informants, including the native ruler and ten or twelve community elders. Aided by a "minuta, o

1. Sahagún (1950–1982, Part I: 55) identified them as Antonio Valeriano of Azcapotzalco, Alonso Vegerano and Pedro de San Buenaventura of Cuauhtitlan, and Martín Jacobita of Tlatelolco.

memoria" of all the topics to be investigated, he systematically interrogated these members of the Tepepolcan nobility for nearly two years. He described how they supplied him with relevant pictorial materials, beneath which the trilingual assistants wrote down the explanations in Nahuatl. These labors resulted in the manuscript whose text and English translation is published in the present work and which Francisco del Paso y Troncoso dubbed the *Primeros Memoriales.*

This first stage of Sahagún's project terminated in 1561, when he and his investigative team moved to the Colegio de Santa Cruz in Tlatelolco. There he gathered a similar group of high-born local informants and obtained from them more extensive information covering a substantial number of the same ethnographic categories he had investigated in Tepepolco. The results of these investigations in Tlatelolco are contained in the *Manuscrito de Tlatelolco,* presently divided, as is the manuscript of the *Primeros Memoriales,* between the libraries of the Real Academia de la Historia and the Real Palacio in Madrid.

The next significant stage took place in the convent of San Francisco in Mexico Tenochtitlan, where Sahagún completed, in 1569, the final organization of the Nahuatl text, in twelve books, of his encyclopedic *Historia General (Universal) de las Cosas de (la) Nueva España.* During this process, additional informants from Tenochtitlan "amended and added many things to the twelve books when they made a clear copy" (Sahagún 1950–1982, Part I: 55). This manuscript of 1569, containing all twelve books of the Nahuatl text, is apparently lost. Only a small portion of the information collected in Tepepolco was included in this final version of the *Historia,* which was later translated, paraphrastically, into Spanish, mostly during the period 1575–1577.

A massive (1,223 folios), lavishly illustrated version of the *Historia,* with the Nahuatl and Spanish text in double-column format, was prepared under Sahagún's supervision apparently during 1578–1580. Sent to Spain, by unknown means it reached Florence, Italy, probably no later than 1588, where, known as the *Florentine Codex,* it resides today in the Biblioteca Medicea Laurenziana (ms. 218–220, Col. Palatina). A slightly modified version of the Spanish column, whose date and exact relation to the *Florentine Codex* are still uncertain, was reported in 1732–1733 in the Franciscan convent of Tolosa in northern Spain. It is from this version of the *Historia,* the "Manuscrito de Tolosa," now in the library of the Real Academia de la Historia, Madrid (Ms. 9-4812; Colección de Muñoz, vol. 50), that until recently all modern editions, through copies, beginning in 1829–1830, have been derived.

TEPEPOLCO

Tepepolco, "Place of the Large Hill," was a sizable but not otherwise particularly prominent community near the northeast rim of the Basin of Mexico. The choice of this community rather than one of the principal Central Mexican native metropolitan centers for the initiation of Sahagún's formal ethnographic-linguistic project has given rise to some speculation. The reasons for Sahagún's assignment at this time to the Tepepolco convent—apparently founded about 1530–1533, possibly by another famous Franciscan missionary-ethnographer-linguist, Fray Andrés de Olmos—are unknown. Dibble (in Sahagún 1950–1982, Part I: 10) speculated that he might have chosen this place owing to his possibly having resided there in 1547, when the rhetorical orations that later constituted Book 6 of the final *Historia* were compiled, at which time he could have established "an earlier working relationship with native leaders." Kirchhoff (1959: 81) conjectured that Tepepolco had enjoyed a certain reputation in pre-Hispanic times as a culture center and that this had influenced Sahagún's choice. Perhaps practical administrative exigencies of the Franciscan missionary program constituted the real determining factor in Sahagún's assignment to this provincial center. In any case, Tepepolco appears to have been culturally typical of most of the larger Central Mexican native communities and probably served Sahagún's ethnographic-linguistic purposes about as well as any other comparable town.

A certain amount of archaeological and ethnohistorical information is available concerning Tepepolco. Located near major obsidian sources and adjacent to a strategic corridor of communication leading northeast from the Basin of Mexico, during the Terminal Preclassic and Classic periods (ca. 200 B.C.–A.D. 750) the Tepepolco area appears to have been a major center for the obsidian tool industry (Charlton 1978). For the Late Postclassic period, various primary sources, including Tepepolco's 1581 *relación geográfica,* the *Códice Xolotl,* and the works of Alva Ixtlilxochitl and Torquemada, describe Tepepolco's founding by valiant "Chichimec" chieftains. These sources permit the reconstruction of a local dynasty of at least four sequent rulers, commencing probably in the twelfth century, before the imposition in 1435 of a steward by Nezahualcoyotl, *huey tlatoani* of Tetzcoco, capital from 1433–1434 onward of the megaprovince of Acolhuacan. Earlier, Tepepolco seems to have been subject to various other polities at different times: Coatlinchan (original capital of Acolhuacan), Xaltocan, possibly (historic) Teotihuacan, and Azcapotzalco (capital of the Tepanec empire of Tezozomoc and Maxtla, ca. 1350–1428). There is also evidence for an early movement into the area of immigrants from Colhuacan, in the southwest Basin of Mexico, probably during the second half of the fourteenth century. Colhuacan had maintained with particular vigor the Toltec dynastic and cultural tradition, and these Colhuaque settlers probably exerted a strong "civilizing" influence on "Chichimec" Tepepolco and its neighbors.

According to Alva Ixtlilxochitl, in late pre-Hispanic times this whole region, comprising a major sector of northern Acolhuacan, was known as "las provincias de la campiña." Various of Tepepolco's neighbors, in addition to their obligations to Tetzcoco, were also tributary to Mexico Tenochtitlan. Whether this included Tepepolco itself is uncertain. In any case, Mexica influence was obviously quite strong. It was especially evident in the religious-ritual system, as the data in the *Primeros Memoriales* abundantly indicate.

Nahuatl was clearly dominant in the zone, but Otomi speakers were also present in some numbers. A possible third language, "Chichimeca," is also mentioned in some sources. If this was not just a more rustic dialect of Nahuatl or Otomi, it may have represented a survival of the tongue spoken by the original "Chichimec" settlers of the area.

At European contact, Tepepolco was a populous and thriving *cabecera* (chief city) with a large number of dependencies. Its territory bordered the powerful superprovince of Tlaxcallan to the southeast, and near this boundary was located one of the *xochiyaoyotl,* or "flowery war," fields where the young elite warriors of the Triple Alliance (Mexico Tenochtitlan-Tetzcoco-Tlacopan) met periodically to engage in ritualized combat with their Tlaxcalteca counterparts. The extensive section on elite warrior costumes contained in the *Primeros Memoriales* might well reflect this proximity, for young Tepepolcan manhood would almost certainly have participated in these combats. Motolinia mentioned the large size of the principal temple of Tepepolco at the time of the Conquest, and there can be little doubt—judging from the extensive data concerning religion in the *Primeros Memoriales*—that the rich, complex religious-ritual system that played such a pervasive role in late pre-Hispanic Central Mexican culture functioned actively and importantly in this community.[2]

2. See Nicholson 1974 for an overview of pre-Hispanic and early colonial Tepepolco, with specific citations of all sources mentioned in the preceding paragraphs.

THE *PRIMEROS MEMORIALES:* DISCOVERY AND PUBLICATION

Fortunately, nearly the complete manuscript containing the final, systematically organized version of the ethnographic information, in Nahuatl, collected by Sahagún and his four trilingual native assistants in Tepepolco has survived. It constitutes a significant portion of an extensive Sahaguntine manuscript corpus, the *Códices Matritenses*, that is divided between two Madrid repositories, the libraries of the Real Palacio (Palacio del Oriente) (Ms. 3280) and the Real Academia de la Historia (Ms. 9-5524).[3] How and when the two parts of this corpus first reached Madrid is unknown. They may have been sent to Spain in the period 1577–1578 in response to orders sent to the viceroy of New Spain, Martín de Enríquez, by King Philip II and the Council of the Indies to send to the home country all of Sahagún's manuscripts, both drafts and more finished versions, that related to his *Historia* project.[4] The date the Royal Palace acquired its portion of the *Códices Matritenses* is unknown. It was referred to in an 1867 study (not published until 1885) by the pioneer Mexican historian José Fernando Ramírez of the Royal Academy of History's portion of the corpus. In his article, Ramírez referred to a document that indicated that the Academy acquired its portion in 1762 from a Madrid book dealer.

Francisco del Paso y Troncoso, director of the Mexican National Museum, was sent by the Porfirian government in 1892 to supervise the installation of the large Mexican display at the major international exposition mounted in Madrid that year to celebrate the four-hundredth anniversary of the European encounter with the Americas. He remained in Europe until his death in 1916, serving as "Director on Mission in Europe," locating, transcribing, and photographing in various repositories documents relating to Mexican history, with special attention to the Sahaguntine manuscripts in Madrid and Florence (Zavala 1939; Cline 1973: 391–403). As an accomplished Nahuatl scholar himself, Paso y Troncoso recognized the great value of the extensive Nahuatl texts derived from the Tepepolco and Tlatelolco stages of Sahagún's ethnographic project, contained in what he called the *Códices Matritenses.* Apparently, sometime between 1903 and 1907 he arranged to have excellent large photocopies made in Madrid of all folios with text or pictures, rearranging these folios into what he considered appropriate categories relating to the history of the overall Sahaguntine project.

One of these he labeled "Primeros Memoriales," reflecting his recognition that these folios belonged to the ethnographic material Sahagún and his native assistants had obtained during the first stage of his project in Tepepolco. Out of the 645 folios of the total *Códices Matritenses* corpus, Paso y Troncoso selected 88 that he believed could be assigned to the Tepepolco materials. Fifty-four (fols. 250r–303v) were from the Palace manuscript and thirty-four (51r–85v) were from the Academy manuscript. His reconstruction resulted in a continuous, nearly complete work containing four chapters divided into forty-nine numbered paragraphs (Nicholson 1973: Tables 5–8). Although they were not part of the integrated chapter-paragraph structure of the *Primeros Memoriales,* he in-

3. See Ballesteros-Gaibrois 1964 and Gibson and Glass 1975: 362–366 for modern descriptions of the *Códices Matritenses.* The former includes transcriptions of all Spanish annotations; a chart correlating the material in the Madrid codices (including the *Manuscrito de Tolosa*) with the *Florentine Codex;* a partial lexicon of Nahuatl words, with Spanish translations, contained in the *Códices Matritenses;* a catalogue of the illustrations (confined to the *Primeros Memoriales*), correlating them with those in the *Florentine Codex;* and a brief discussion of watermarks, with copies of a representative sample (Forty-three examples) of the four types found in the Madrid manuscripts. The latter includes a table specifying the distribution of materials and their foliation in the two *Códices Matritenses.* See also the recent study by Bustamante García (1990:247–305).

4. See Nicolau d'Olwer 1987: 72–77 for coverage of this "confiscatory period" in the history of the Sahaguntine ethnographic-linguistic project, with citations of the original documentation.

cluded, after Academy Ms. folio 69r, which concludes Chapter IV, Paragraph 8B, devoted to warrior costumes, folios 72r–80r of the same manuscript, which also contain illustrations of warrior costumes and devices, with brief texts and labels. On the basis of identity of subject matter, he also inserted, after folio 69, which contains Chapter IV, Paragraph 9, devoted to an itemization of diseases and their cures, folio 81, which is written in a distinct, more cursive hand and which concludes with a chapter heading that does not fit the *Primeros Memoriales* sequence.

Paso y Troncoso had the photocopy of each folio printed on a large, folio-sized page, continuously paginated 1–175, with the specification of the chapter and paragraph (including paragraph subsections with alphabetical designations) and his Spanish titles for them printed at the top of each page. He had the original manuscript foliation of both the Palace and the Academy portions of the work printed at the foot of each page. The Mexican artist Genaro López copied the *Primeros Memoriales* illustrations, and Paso y Troncoso had color lithographs of them printed by Alejandro Ruffoni in Florence, grouped on twenty-seven separate, large, folio-sized pages (Estampas I–XXVII).

These printed pages, constituting Cuadernos 2 and 3 of Volume VI of his projected fifteen-volume publication of the whole European Sahaguntine corpus, were apparently still unbound at the time of Paso y Troncoso's death in Florence in 1916. Finally obtained, with some difficulty, by the Mexican government, Cuaderno 2 (which also included what Paso y Troncoso labeled "Memoriales con Escolios," prepared under Sahagún's direction later in Tlatelolco) was bound and distributed in the mid-1920s. The title page, dated 1905, featured Paso y Troncoso's title for the whole series, "Historia General de las Cosas de Nueva España de Fr. Bernardino de Sahagún." Part I was entitled "Primeros Memoriales compilado por el autor en cuatro capítulos como fundamento para escribir la obra general en doce libros y cuatro volúmenes."

A Cuaderno 1, "Descripción de los códices," was to have been included in this volume, but if written, it was never found and had to be omitted. Paso y Troncoso's own exposition of the steps he followed in reconstructing the *Primeros Memoriales*, therefore, is unavailable—although it can be generally understood from the reconstruction itself and the titles he employed for the chapters and paragraphs.

Cuaderno 3, the twenty-seven plates containing the Genaro López color lithographs of the *Primeros Memoriales* illustrations, was also bound and distributed at this time. It is often bound with Volume VI, where it belongs, but sometimes with Volume V, devoted to color lithographs of all of the *Florentine Codex* illustrations.

Paso y Troncoso's great German contemporary in Mexicanist studies, Eduard Seler, who had earlier, in 1889, worked in Madrid with the *Códices Matritenses*, had also recognized the Tepepolco derivation of what his Mexican colleague was to denominate the *Primeros Memoriales* (e.g., Seler 1890). To Paso y Troncoso, however, belongs the credit of selecting the relevant folios, arranging them in proper order, having them photographed, and labeling, in Spanish, the various chapters and paragraphs of the work. Although not really published in his lifetime, it was Paso y Troncoso's careful preparatory labors that led to the eventual publication and distribution of the high-quality photoreproduction of this priceless source some years after his death. Thus, if Fray Bernardino de Sahagún must be considered the father of the *Primeros Memoriales*, this outstanding turn-of-the-century Mexican scholar should be recognized as its prime resuscitator and disseminator.

Before the distribution in the 1920s by the Mexican government of Paso y Troncoso's "1905" photoreproduction, only scholars such as Eduard Seler and Daniel Brinton, who had had the opportunity to work with the original manuscript in its Madrid repositories, were able to publish transcriptions and translations of parts of the *Primeros Memo-*

riales. After it became more generally available in major libraries and private collections, other scholars could utilize it, too, and during the following half century or so, most of its paragraphs were paleographized and translated into German, Spanish, and/or English. In 1973 a concise discussion of the *Primeros Memoriales* appeared in volume 13 of the *Handbook of Middle American Indians* as one of the articles in the three-part entry devoted to the ethnographic, linguistic, and evangelical writings of Fray Bernardino de Sahagún (Nicholson 1973). It included four tables listing the forty-nine numbered paragraphs of the work, with specification of all known paleographies and translations into modern languages of each. Although the tables revealed that only eleven paragraphs had not been published somewhere in this form, it was noted that these translations of fragments of the *Primeros Memoriales* were somewhat uneven in quality and dispersed throughout widely scattered publications. Additional paleographies and translations of sections of the *Primeros Memoriales* that have appeared since the publication of Tables 5–8 in Nicholson 1973 are specified in Nicholson 1988d: 17–19 and in the footnotes in this volume.

In a 1964 monograph by Manuel Ballesteros-Gaibrois and a group of his students in the Seminario de Estudios Americanistas of the Facultad de Filosofía y Letras of the University of Madrid devoted to a study of the *Códices Matritenses,* the approximately 445 individual illustrations contained in the *Primeros Memoriales* manuscript were listed, with their later *Florentine Codex* equivalents indicated (1964, I: 304–326). In volume 2 of this work, color photographs of the illustrated pages of the *Primeros Memoriales,* much reduced in scale from the originals, were systematically published for the first time.

THE *PRIMEROS MEMORIALES* MANUSCRIPT

The physical description of the *Primeros Memoriales* manuscript, including consideration of its watermarks and gatherings, is undertaken by Eloise Quiñones Keber in the article that follows this introduction. Other relevant topics, such as indigenous sources, artists, possible European models for its overall structure, and the relationship between images and texts, are also discussed there.

THE *PRIMEROS MEMORIALES:* CONTENTS

A concise specification, chapter by chapter and paragraph by paragraph, of the contents of the *Primeros Memoriales* was included in Nicholson 1973. In the four tables in that article, I used Paso y Troncoso's Spanish titles, derived, where available, from Sahagún's own Nahuatl headings. In the next article, Eloise Quiñones Keber, in Tables 1–4, also systematically lists the paragraphs of the *Primeros Memoriales,* labeled with descriptive titles in English.

Chapter I

Owing to the loss of its first paragraph, Chapter I lacks its original title, but "Rituals and Gods," following Paso y Troncoso's "Ritos, Dioses," seems apt. Its thirteen paragraphs cover a wide range of aspects of the indigenous ritual-religious system, including the major ceremonies geared to the eighteen *veintenas* (twenty-day periods), plus five, of the 365-day vague tropical year, together with an important ceremony held only every eight years; a large number of basic ritual practices; types of priests; the insignia and costumes of the principal deities and some data concerning their supernatural jurisdictions; temple structures; supplications and oaths; and twenty of the sacred chants sung in honor of the gods.

As Eduard Seler was the first major Mexicanist scholar to recognize, the contents of Chapter I of the *Primeros Memoriales* convey some of the most valuable information extant on the religion of Central Mexico at the time of the Conquest. Seler took particular advantage of Paragraph 5A, featuring forty-one illustrations of deities or deity impersonators, each of which is identified by name(s) and is accompanied by a detailed specification of the Nahuatl terms for items of the figure's costume and insignia. These data provided the pioneer German scholar with invaluable keys to deity and insignia identifications in his commentaries on various of the pre-Hispanic and early colonial ritual-divinatory pictorials, particularly members of the *Codex Borgia* group (see Nicholson 1988b).

Also of great value for the Nahuatl nomenclature for a wide range of ritual acts, paraphernalia, and structures are Paragraphs 3(A–E), 6, 11, and 12. Paragraph 7, which features a diagram of a temple precinct, along with the Nahuatl terms for the structures and images within it, is one of most frequently illustrated scenes in the *Primeros Memoriales.* Its community location is not indicated, but it is usually identified with the Templo Mayor of Mexico Tenochtitlan, perhaps only the "inner precinct" of the Huitzilopochtli-Tlaloc temple and associated structures. Since it is included in a manuscript compiled in Tepepolco, however, the possibility that it represents all or a portion of the temple precinct of this community must also be entertained.

Paragraph 2A, illustrating and describing the principal rituals and the deities propitiated during the eighteen annual *veintena* ceremonies, provides one of the most valuable accounts of this most important of all Mesoamerican ritual cycles as it was performed in Central Mexico at contact. A much more detailed account of these eighteen ceremonies was subsequently collected by Sahagún in Tlatelolco; it was included, with scattered, more Europeanized illustrations, in Book 2 of the *Florentine Codex.* The briefer Tepepolco version, however, is of special value because it is the most comprehensive one extant deriving from a provincial center. The account and illustration of the Atamalcualiztli ceremony, celebrated only every eight years, in Paragraph 2B is unique to the *Primeros Memoriales.*

Paragraphs 4 and 9 provide significant lists of priestly titles and, in Paragraph 4, specifications of their duties that are the most detailed extant accounts of this type. Although these data have been utilized by some students of the native priesthood (e.g., Acosta Saignes 1946), they clearly require additional analysis if we are to understand more satisfactorily how these religious functionaries were organized and operated within the overall sacerdotal structure.

Paragraph 10's itemization of "things attributed to the gods" is of considerable interest in relation to the pantheonic system. Most of the "things" listed appear to be congruent with the generally accepted natures and supernatural jurisdictions of the deities that are included. Paragraph 13 describes the "eating of earth" to confirm the truth of an oath or as a means of supplicating divine aid, a well-known ritual pattern also described in other sources.

The twenty sacred chants contained in Paragraph 14 constitute a small but virtually unique surviving remnant of a rich, lost corpus of pre-Hispanic Nahuatl religious songs. Composed in a difficult and often archaic idiom, they have posed a formidable challenge to Nahuatlatos since Daniel Brinton (1890) somewhat prematurely attempted an English translation. Seler, writing in German (1902–1923, II: 961–1107), and Garibay, writing in Spanish (1958), were considerably more successful in extracting the basic meanings of the strophes. The English translations of Thelma Sullivan in this volume and of Anderson and Dibble both in their *Florentine Codex* (Sahagún 1981: 221–247) version and here were heavily influenced by their work. Thelma Sullivan was actively studying the dialectology of these songs, leaning toward the view that some seemed to reflect certain linguistic features of the northeast Nahua dialects, in the direction of the Huaxteca. Her promising research in this area was unfortunately cut short by her early death.

Chapter II

This chapter, "The Heavens and the Underworld," covers, in seven paragraphs, the celestial bodies, meteorological phenomena, the 365-day vague year, the 260-day divinatory cycle, auguries, dreams, and aspects of the underworld. Paragraph 1 is best known for its five diagrams of constellations, labeled in Nahuatl, which have given rise to modern investigators' differing identifications of the constellations with commonly recognized asterisms. An unusual feature of the 260-day divinatory cycle, or *tonalpohualli,* presented in its entirety both pictorially and textually in Paragraph 4, is that it commences not with 1 Cipactli (Crocodilian Monster), its normal beginning, but with 1 Itzcuintli (Dog). Quite important are the concise texts that accompany each *trecena* (thirteen-day period) of the *tonalpohualli,* summarizing the divinatory significance—favorable, unfavorable, or indifferent—of each. They can be compared with the considerably longer equivalent texts collected later by Sahagún in Tlatelolco, which were included in Book 4 of the *Florentine Codex,* and with others contained in the *Codex Borbonicus,* in the *Codices Telleriano-Remensis/Vaticanus A,* and in the book dedicated to the indigenous calendar, finished in 1579, that constitutes the second part of the *Historia de las Indias de Nueva España e Islas de la Tierra Firme* of Sahagún's contemporary missionary-ethnographer, the Dominican Fray Diego Durán (1967, 1994).

The only two dates in the Christian calendar found in the *Primeros Memoriales,* which are highly relevant to the date of the composition of the manuscript, are contained in Paragraphs 3 and 4 of Chapter II. The first, in a Spanish annotation to the year 2 Acatl, identifies it with "este año de 1560." The second, in a Nahuatl annotation, identifies the day 9 Ehecatl with September 25, 1560, which differs considerably from what it would be in the widely accepted Caso correlation of the Christian and Mexica calendars (day 4 Calli; Caso 1967: 41–73).

The listing of auguries in Paragraph 5A is of considerable interest and can be compared to a similar but somewhat longer itemization gathered by Sahagún in Tlatelolco, to which Book 5 of the *Florentine Codex* is devoted. The list of dream interpretations in Paragraph 5B is unique to the *Primeros Memoriales.* According to the final statement, these interpretations were made by the same diviners, the *tonalpouhque,* who interpreted the auguries of the 260-day cycle, consulting the same source, the "book of the day signs," or *tonalamatl.* Some of the scenes in these books, particularly certain members of the *Codex Borgia* group, therefore, could relate to dream interpretation—and students interested in these pre-Hispanic ritual-divinatory pictorials might well be advised to further investigate this possibility.

The last two numbered paragraphs of Chapter II, 6 and 7, provide a vivid picture of the horrors of the afterworld, Mictlan, the last resting place of the majority of mankind. And in a final, unnumbered paragraph, unfortunately incomplete, a poetic, haunting vision of the special afterworld, Tlalocan, presided over by the Rain God, is conveyed in the course of a narrative about the visit to this place by the spirit of Quetzalpetlatl, a royal lady of Tlatelolco who died ten or twelve years before the arrival of the Spaniards.

Chapter III

This chapter, "Rulership," the longest in the *Primeros Memoriales,* includes, in seventeen paragraphs, the dynasties of Mexico Tenochtitlan, Tetzcoco, and Huexotla; considerable information concerning the lives of the native rulers and the nobility, including their duties, adornments, amusements, food and drink, residences, their admonishments to their subjects, and reasons for their anger and compassion; names and techniques of sorcerers and evil men and women; the education of youths of both sexes; and a short account of the origin of certain of the principal Central Mexican groups from Chicomoztoc, the "Seven Caves."

The pictorial and textual dynastic listings of Paragraph 1 (A–C) generally agree in name and sequence with listings from other sources, but there are some discrepancies. The reign lengths, particularly for the earlier rulers, are often quite divergent (no dates in the native calendar are provided). Sahagún included these dynastic lists, slightly modified, adding that of Tlatelolco and new versions of the illustrations, in Book 8 of the *Florentine Codex.* Paragraphs 2–10 provide valuable information concerning the lifestyles and responsibilities of the rulers, noblemen, and noblewomen. Many of these topics are also covered from Tlatelolcan data, often in greater detail, in Book 8 of the *Florentine Codex.*

Paragraphs 11 and 12 provide some of the most valuable data extant on indigenous shamanism and sorcery, which have been much tapped by modern students. These paragraphs also contain lists of vituperative terms for both sexes, reflecting a rich Nahuatl vocabulary in this area. Useful information concerning the education of both sexes is covered in Paragraph 13, but characteristically, Sahagún preferred his Tlatelolcan data for the *Florentine Codex* (Book 3, Appendix, Chapters 4–8).

Paragraph 14 provides the only significant historical data in the *Primeros Memoriales,* apart from the dynastic lists of Paragraph 1(A–C). It is rather stylized, however, beginning with the creation by Topiltzin Quetzalcoatl and the departure from their legendary homeland, Chicomoztoc, of seven major groups, the Acolhuaque, Colhuaque, Otomi, Mexica, Cuexteca (Huaxtec), "Tenime Chichimeca," and Totonaca. Interesting is the omission of the Tepaneca, although the later portion of the paragraph is largely concerned with the glory, power, and wealth, gained through conquest and tribute (itemized in great detail), of the final political order of Central Mexico, the Triple Alliance of the Mexica (Mexico Tenochtitlan), Acolhuaque (Tetzcoco), and Tepaneca (Tlacopan). This paragraph constitutes one of the most eloquent expressions in any primary source of the rationale and justification for the privileges of the Triple Alliance ruling class.

Paragraph 15 is dedicated to a long series of admonishments by the judges to the assembled people, lecturing them on correct behavior, describing punishments and rewards, respectively, for improper conduct and virtuous living, and specifying the appropriate times for judging to be undertaken. There are many resemblances here to the well-known *huehuetlatolli,* "discourses of the elders," to which Book 6 of the *Florentine Codex* was largely dedicated—discourses that Dibble has suggested might have been collected earlier in Tepepolco itself. This paragraph constitutes one of the most important extant statements of the indigenous moral and ethical codes. The final two paragraphs, 16 and 17, express, also in a style resembling that of the *huehuetlatolli,* aspects of the responsibilities of rulership, describing the reasons for the ruler's anger and displeasure, his compassion for his people, and his dejection during troubled times.

Chapter IV

"Things Relative to Man," with eleven paragraphs, is concerned with kinship terms, male and female personal names, human physiological terminology, nomenclature of the nobility, warrior costumes and insignia, diseases and cures, and terms of address among both nobles and commoners. Some of these topics, but not all, were also covered, utilizing Tlatelolcan data, in the *Florentine Codex,* mostly in Book 10. Sociocultural anthropologists interested in late pre-Hispanic Central Mexican civilization will encounter considerable relevant data in this chapter, particularly in Paragraphs 1–4, 7, and 10–11. Those interested in medicine and physiology have tapped Paragraphs 5–6 and 9 to good advantage. Paragraphs 10 and 11 provide words and phrases of courteous and disputatious speech for nobles and commoners, respectively, that relate them, as in the cases of Paragraphs 15–17 of Chapter III, to the more elegant idiom of the *huehuetlatolli.*

Probably the best-known section of *Primeros Memoriales* Chapter IV is constituted by Paragraphs 8A and 8B, listing the military insignia and accouterments of rulers, captains, and warriors—along with folios 72r–80v of the Academy manuscript, inserted by Paso y Troncoso after folio 68v because of their similarity of subject matter, which contain illustrations of these insignia and accouterments, with Nahuatl captions.

CONCLUDING OBSERVATIONS

From this concise review, it is evident that the *Primeros Memoriales* provides much valuable data on contact-period indigenous culture in one large Central Mexican community, Tepepolco, while apparently incorporating some data derived from the imperial capital, Mexico Tenochtitlan. Religion and ritual receive substantial attention, but it is noteworthy that a wide range of "secular" aspects of the culture is also covered. This clearly indicates that, although Sahagún directed much of his inquiry to the religious-ritual sector—congruent with his announced desire to convey this type of information to his fellow missionaries to aid them in discovering and extirpating all traces of pagan survivals—his ethnographic investigations, from the outset of his project, went far beyond that goal. It has even been suggested that the *Primeros Memoriales* might originally have included a fifth chapter devoted to "natural history."[5] In any case, Sahagún's interest in this topic is well illustrated by the copious data he later compiled concerning it in Tlatelolco, consigning it to Book 11 of the final *Historia*.

Some major absences in Sahagún's coverage in the *Primeros Memoriales* are also worth mentioning. Apart from the dynastic sequences in Chapter III, Paragraph 1(A–C), and the very brief Chicomoztoc narrative in Paragraph 14, genuine history, the recording of which was of considerable importance in the indigenous culture, is absent in the *Primeros Memoriales.* As has often been noted, pre-Hispanic history is generally slighted throughout the entire *Historia* (Book 12 concerns the Conquest). The *Primeros Memoriales* also contains no material on crafts and craftsmen, although later, in Tlatelolco, Sahagún did gather valuable data on the native metallurgists, feather workers, and jewelry makers (*Florentine Codex,* Book 9). Agricultural techniques, economic patterns (including the role of merchants and markets), the legal system, and mythology (unless this was treated in the lost Chapter I, Paragraph 1), among other major topics, receive no attention in the *Primeros Memoriales*—although some of these themes were covered to some extent (above all, the mercantile activities and ritual practices of the Tlatelolca merchants) in Sahagún's subsequent investigations in Tlatelolco and Tenochtitlan.

In spite of these significant gaps in its coverage, the invaluable ethnographic and linguistic information contained in the *Primeros Memoriales,* now available for the first time in a unitary edition that contains a complete transcription of the Nahuatl text and its translation into a single modern language, constitutes one of the prime sources for our knowledge of indigenous Central Mexican culture at European contact. And knowledge of this culture, fully functioning when overrun by the Spaniards in the sixteenth century, provides the touchstone for our knowledge and understanding of pre-Hispanic Mesoamerican civilization as a whole. Significant studies of portions of the *Primeros Memoriales* have been cited here, but it deserves much more investigation and analysis. One of the principal aims of this unitary edition is precisely to facilitate fresh studies of the *Primeros Memoriales,* many of which, it is hoped, will be undertaken in the years to come.

5. See Nicholson 1973: 208–34.

LINGUISTIC AND LITERARY ASPECTS OF THE *PRIMEROS MEMORIALES*

The style of the Nahuatl of the *Primeros Memoriales* is quite close to that of the texts collected by Sahagún in Tlatelolco and Tenochtitlan. His informants in Tepepolco were local, and this community belonged to the province of Acolhuacan, of which the capital from 1431 onward was Tetzcoco. The Tepepolcan speech patterns, therefore, could have reflected dialectical features that might have characterized the reputedly elegant Nahuatl of Tetzcoco. If so, these characteristics are not particularly evident in the *Primeros Memoriales*. It must also be kept in mind that the manuscript available to us was copied by Sahagún's native scribes, usually considered to have been his four trilinguals, who hailed from other communities in the Basin of Mexico (Tlatelolco, Cuauhtitlan, Azcapotzalco). If so, the text would have passed through the screen of their own speech patterns, which might have filtered out the putative idiosyncratic aspects of the Tepepolco (= Tetzcoco?) dialect. In any case, further research on the language and style of the *Primeros Memoriales* would be desirable and might reveal localisms not immediately apparent to the students who have worked with it up to this point.

As to the literary values of the Nahuatl text of the *Primeros Memoriales*, it is noteworthy that much of it consists of word lists and abbreviated captions and labels. Some portions, however, such as the aforementioned Paragraphs 15–17 of Chapter III, Paragraphs 10–11 of Chapter IV, and the tale of the visit to Tlalocan of the spirit of the noble lady of Tlatelolco added to paragraph 7 of Chapter II, do display certain literary qualities that link them to the *huehuetlatolli*. Thelma Sullivan was always interested in conveying as fully as possible in her translations what she considered the literary excellence of Classical Nahuatl at its best. She was obviously very much guided by this approach throughout her *Primeros Memoriales* translation. Arthur Anderson and Charles Dibble have tried to preserve as much of her style as possible, commensurate with basic accuracy of meaning and expression.

THE RELATION OF THE *PRIMEROS MEMORIALES* TO THE LATER STAGES OF THE *HISTORIA* PROJECT

As I emphasized in my 1973 article concerning the *Primeros Memoriales*, remarkably little of the ethnographic information collected by Sahagún and his trilingual assistants in Tepepolco passed into the twelve books of the final *Historia:* only five full paragraphs and parts of two others.[6] And only twenty of the deity representations (Book 1) and the ruler images of the Huexotla and Tetzcoco dynasties (Book 8) in the *Florentine Codex* were directly derived from illustrations in the *Primeros Memoriales*.[7] After he had gathered much more copious ethnographic data from informants in Tlatelolco and Tenochtitlan, Sahagún consistently preferred them to the information he had earlier obtained from his Tepepolco informants. The *Primeros Memoriales*, therefore, generally stands apart from the later *Historia* as a fundamentally separate document. It describes the cultural patterns of a major community of Acolhuaque, rather than Mexica, affiliation.

It was this fact, together with the highly scattered and uneven quality of the previous paleographies and translations of sections of the *Primeros Memoriales*, that led me to state in my 1973 article: "Certainly the publication of paleographies of all its texts and

6. Specification in Nicholson 1973: Tables 5, 7.

7. See Quiñones Keber 1988b for a discussion of the relationship between the illustrations of the *Primeros Memoriales* and those of the *Florentine Codex*.

their translation into a current major language, as a unit, with all other normal apparatus of modern critical scholarship, would seem to be one of the most obvious needs of Sahaguntine studies. . . . It is hoped that this task will be taken up by Sahagún scholars in the not too distant future."

Thelma Sullivan did take up this task and nearly finished it before her untimely death. Now that her labors have been completed by two of her good friends and colleagues, the current leading Sahagún scholars, Arthur J. O. Anderson and Charles E. Dibble, we present this volume, dedicated to her memory, hoping it will be received as another significant contribution to the publication of the remarkable research of the "father of modern ethnography."[8]

8. See Anderson 1994 for a concise, useful comparison of the data contained in the extant numbered paragraphs of the *Primeros Memoriales* with those included in the twelve books and appendices of the *Florentine Codex* version of the final *Historia*.

An Introduction to the Images, Artists, and Physical Features of the *Primeros Memoriales*

ELOISE QUIÑONES KEBER

What the ancients said most vividly they expressed not with words but by signs; they did not tell, they showed.
J.J. ROUSSEAU,
Essai sur l'origine des langues

In 1993 the University of Oklahoma Press published the first color facsimile of the *Primeros Memoriales*, a sixteenth-century Mexican manuscript (Sahagún 1993). The present volume, which presents the late Thelma Sullivan's paleography and English translation of its Nahuatl texts, as well as contributions by other Sahagún scholars, was envisioned as the companion volume for this facsimile edition. Its publication now completes the translation project begun by Thelma Sullivan and brought to completion, in an expanded form, by H. B. Nicholson.

Publication of the color facsimile of a manuscript as rare and visually striking as the *Primeros Memoriales* would be a major event in any case. But the importance of this edition was enhanced by the fact that it was the great missionary-ethnographer Bernardino de Sahagún and his indigenous collaborators who compiled the manuscript, that it represents the "first stage" or "primeros memoriales" of his monumental *Historia* project, that it contains an invaluable ethnographic, linguistic, and pictorial record of late pre-Hispanic Central Mexico, and that together with the appearance in 1979 of the color facsimile of the *Florentine Codex* it made available the surviving treasury of Sahaguntine images. Moreover, since the manuscript is now divided between two repositories located in different sections of Madrid, the facsimile has once again made it possible for a reader to view the manuscript as an integrated whole.

The Significance of the Images of the *Primeros Memoriales*

Despite Paso y Troncoso's astute recognition of the critical chronological position of the *Primeros Memoriales* in Sahagún's *Historia* project, study of the manuscript's images and texts has not been commensurate with its importance.[1] As the first stage (ca. 1559–

1. I first undertook research on Mexican manuscripts in Madrid repositories in 1981 with the support of a fellowship from the Kress Foundation. In 1986, grants from the American Philosophical Society and the National Endowment for the Humanities enabled me to focus on the *Primeros Memoriales* in the libraries of the Real Palacio and Real Academia de la Historia.

1561) of this vast enterprise, carried out in the town of Tepepolco in what is now the state of Hidalgo, it has often been considered an early "version" of the larger project. As such, it has been eclipsed by the final manuscript of the *Historia*, produced two decades later (ca. 1578–1580), the textually more extensive and profusely illustrated work now known as the *Florentine Codex.*

Only in more recent years has the special character of the *Primeros Memoriales* been recognized. In 1973, H. B. Nicholson demonstrated that relatively little of the Tepepolco data survived in the Florentine manuscript, which consisted primarily of material subsequently gathered in the neighboring cities of Tlatelolco and Mexico Tenochtitlan (present-day Mexico City). In a later article (1974) he concluded that the *Primeros Memoriales* should be regarded less as a preparatory "draft" than as a separate document worthy of independent consideration. And as I have shown more recently (Quiñones Keber 1988b), only a fraction of the images in the *Primeros Memoriales* were redrawn in the *Florentine Codex,* and then in a more Europeanized manner.

As Nicholson noted in his introduction to this book, Sahagún's methodical interviewing of indigenous elders in Tepepolco represented an innovative technique for the gathering of ethnographic data in the mid-sixteenth century. Just as remarkable was the friar's utilization of pictorial materials. Indeed, the double-column format generally adopted throughout the *Primeros Memoriales* for presentation of the pictorial and textual data suggests that image and text were conceived integrally; each column was intended to be read in conjunction with the other. The manuscript thus offers both a visual and a verbal record of Aztec culture as it was known and recalled four decades after the Spanish conquest of Mexico in 1521.

Like the texts, the images too must have been designed as evangelical aids for Sahagún's fellow Franciscan missionaries. Because of this intent, Sahagún and his collaborators must have approached very carefully their task of selecting the pictorial material to be copied, and their concern is apparent. Viewed collectively, the numerous images of the *Primeros Memoriales* are notable for their range and representativeness. Drawn with a didactic clarity by several Indian artists, the 546 paintings depict an array of subjects central to Aztec (Nahua) culture: religion, the natural world, the calendar, rulership, and military insignia.

Inclusion of images also coincided with Sahagún's aim that the *Historia* provide a contextual linguistic resource for the Nahuatl language. Like a verbal phrase, a pictorial statement also informs beyond the capacity of an isolated word. For example, the paintings of military array in Chapter IV greatly amplify the information conveyed by the accompanying written inventory. With their designs, sizes, shapes, colors, decorative details, and associated items or insignia clearly made manifest, the images effectively demonstrate the manner in which costume elements were assembled and worn.

To a later viewer, the images of the *Primeros Memoriales* are significant not only for what they reveal about indigenous culture but also for what they disclose about the process of cultural interaction in post-Conquest Central Mexico. For example, although Sahagún indicates that the intended audience of the *Historia* was Spanish, the paintings he included embody an indigenous mode of communication. Most European books of the period were predominantly textual, whereas pre-Hispanic books consisted of literal or symbolic images rather than alphabetic texts. The incorporation of pictorial material in the *Primeros Memoriales* thus acknowledged the manner in which information had been communicated and preserved during the pre-Hispanic period, as well as the means by which it could be most faithfully reproduced for the interested outsider in the colonial period. The reciprocity between image and text, Nahua and European features, and indigenous and foreign interests is one of the hallmarks of this exceptional bicultural document.

EUROPEAN ASPECTS OF THE *PRIMEROS MEMORIALES*

As a collaborative effort between a Spanish missionary, his indigenous but acculturated assistants, who stemmed from different centers in the Basin of Mexico, and indigenous residents of the town of Tepepolco, the *Primeros Memoriales* is a hybrid work that displays both native and European features. The features of the manuscript provide evidence of its having been a cooperative undertaking, for the distinctive hands of several scribes and artists are clearly recognizable. Although its contents focus on pre-Hispanic culture as it existed in Central Mexico at about the time of European contact, the overall appearance of the *Primeros Memoriales* reveals a colonial document produced in the manner of European manuscripts and early printed books.

Rather than the traditional extended panel of native bark paper or treated animal skin, the *Primeros Memoriales* consists of folded sheets of European paper that produce bifolios approximately 32 centimeters long by 22 centimeters wide. Following European practice, ruling lines drawn lightly in pale brown ink or impressed with a stylus delimited the working area of the folios, usually double columns. The Indian artists and scribes used European inks and pens to copy the texts and outline the images. The combining of an alphabetic text with visual images represented a departure from the practice of using solely pictorial constituents in native painted manuscripts in Central Mexico. The Nahuatl text was arranged in chapters and paragraphs and employed the Latin alphabet and Gothic and cursive European scripts to transcribe what had formerly been preserved in pictorial form or oral tradition. Finally, the completed folios were gathered and bound on one side as a codex, a manuscript form unknown in pre-Conquest Mexico but standard in Europe.

European models also offered a convenient scheme for systematically organizing the abundant data gathered by Sahagún and his team of indigenous aides. The hierarchical arrangement of subjects in the *Primeros Memoriales* and later stages of the *Historia*, proceeding from divine to human to inanimate, has suggested to several scholars that Sahagún structured it after well-known classical and medieval encyclopedias. Angel M. Garibay (1971, II: 68–71), for example, proposed Pliny's *Historia Naturalis* as a prototype, while Donald Robertson (1959: 169–172; 1966) suggested the thirteenth-century *De Proprietatibus Rerum* of Bartholomaeus Anglicus, "modified by both Renaissance learning and native culture."

Whether the medieval encyclopedia provided an immediate or merely a remote organizational model for Sahagún is problematical. The encyclopedia plan, with its disciplined partition of reality into subjects and chapters, might have supplied Sahagún with an overall framework for organizing his data; on the other hand, his use of these divisions may merely indicate the adoption of traditional taxonomies common to educated people of his time. It seems significant that many categories included by Bartholomaeus Anglicus do not appear in the *Primeros Memoriales*, although some that relate to the natural world were later incorporated into the *Florentine Codex*.[2] Furthermore, certain subjects included in the *Historia* fell outside the scope of the proposed European prototypes, some of them because of their novelty as exotic topics (e.g., gods and rituals), but others for other reasons. Bartholomaeus Anglicus, for example, did not treat social or political organization, whereas the subject of rulership is one of the four chapters of the *Primeros Memoriales*. The departures of the *Primeros Memoriales* (and later stages of the *Historia*) from the encyclopedia model underscore Sahagún's selective use of its plan.

2. Robertson's chart (1959: 170–12) comparing the two works accentuates their resemblances because it does not list the numerous categories included by Bartholomaeus Anglicus but omitted by Sahagún.

The necessity of ordering a mass of data, including abundant pictorial material that did not fall within the usual parameters of the medieval encyclopedia, highlights the originality of Sahagún's structure for the *Primeros Memoriales.* Very likely he was aided in this task by his indigenous collaborators, the trilingual ex-students variously called collegians, grammarians, and Latinists, whom he credits in the prologue to Book 2 of the *Florentine Codex* with helping him to gather the information and then explicate, amend, and copy it (Sahagún 1950–1982, introductory volume: 54–55). A more immediate influence may have been the extensive ethnographic work compiled earlier by Sahagún's Franciscan colleague Andrés de Olmos, which another Franciscan friar, Gerónimo de Mendieta (1971: 75–76), reports was similarly based on indigenous paintings (i.e., painted manuscripts) and interviews with Nahua elders.[3] Unfortunately, since the work of Olmos survives only in fragments incorporated in other sources, a direct comparison between the Olmos and Sahaguntine materials cannot be made.

INDIGENOUS ASPECTS OF THE *PRIMEROS MEMORIALES*

In the prologue to Book 2 of the *Florentine Codex,* Sahagún relates that during his two years in Tepepolco the elders gave him "all the matters we discussed in pictures," which the grammarians then explained directly by adding Nahuatl annotations (Sahagún 1950–1982, introductory volume: 54; also Book 10: 583). This frequently quoted statement offers a rare insight into Sahagún's innovative methodology in compiling the *Primeros Memoriales.* It highlights, however, only one procedure that must have been exploited for gathering data, that derived from the conventionalized figures and symbols (commonly if incorrectly called "glyphs") painted in pre-Hispanic manuscripts. To be fully understood, these manuscript images were intended to be accompanied by verbal commentaries provided by trained interpreters. Painted chronicles, for example, would have served as a kind of pictorial outline for fuller oral recitations of a community's past events and achievements. Presumably, the explanations given by the grammarians drew upon this collective oral tradition, although how much specialized lore was still available to them or was contributed by the Tepepolco elders is hard to determine.

Aside from these reciprocal sources, other more discursive statements and set pieces, not necessarily tied to visual images, were also utilized. These included orations, narratives, sayings, songs, and poetry that existed in an independent verbal form that was committed to memory and recited on appropriate occasions. A visual stimulus for some of the discursive sections of the *Primeros Memoriales* is not precluded, but related pictorial material did not exist for many such sections.

It thus would not have been possible to amass by pictorial means alone information on all the subjects that appear in the *Primeros Memoriales,* contrary to the implication of Sahagún's reference to the annotated paintings. In fact, the contents of the *Primeros Memoriales* belong to different categories: some dominated by images, some by words, and others by various combinations of images and texts (see Tables 1–4 at the end of this chapter).

COMBINING IMAGES AND TEXTS

As reconstructed by Paso y Troncoso from the voluminous Sahaguntine materials in Madrid—the so-called *Códices Matritenses*—the *Primeros Memoriales* consists of four chapters, the first two in the library of the Royal Palace and the last two in the library

3. See López Austin 1974 and Baudot 1983: 129–245 for a discussion of the relationship between the works of Olmos and Sahagún.

of the Royal Academy of History. These are further subdivided into 49 paragraphs. Of its 176 "pages" (88 folios), 99 display illustrations.

The contents of the folios are not disposed in a single format. When both images and texts occupy a folio, the figures generally appear in the right-hand column, with the related texts (words, phrases, or longer statements) in the left-hand column. In paragraphs without images, texts are variously disposed. In some cases words or phrases appear at the far left with their explanations or descriptions extending across one or both columns. In other sections blocks of text occupy one or both columns. The arrangement of image and text thus depends mostly on the content of the chapter or paragraph, that is, on the kind of information that was being recorded.

The relationship of the images and texts to their native sources also varies. For example, in Chapter I, Paragraph 5A, "How Each of the Gods Was Arrayed," the deity figures were adapted from traditional figural types like those found in a few surviving pre-Conquest (non-Aztec) manuscripts and in Aztec colonial copies. The *Primeros Memoriales* representations, however, differ from the native models. In the native *tonalamatl* (book of days), a painted handbook consulted by diviners, deities do not appear as isolated figures, as they do in Paragraph 5A, but as components of more intricate pictorial arrangements. Indeed, in the *Primeros Memoriales* the focus of attention is not on the deities themselves but on their attire and insignia, which the accompanying text itemizes like an extended gloss. In this case, as Sahagún related in his prologue, the methodical listing of insignia probably derived directly from the image at hand.

The way some word lists may have derived directly from images may actually be seen in the first three paragraphs of Chapter III, "Rulership." There, Nahuatl glosses identify items of apparel worn by the rulers depicted. The accompanying text, however, which provides additional information about the ruler's reign, derives not from the images but from oral tradition.

Chapter II, Paragraph 4, "The Day Count," exemplifies another type of relationship between pictorial and oral sources. There, the names of the days that made up the 260-day cycle, or *tonalpohualli* (count of days), were excerpted, as were the deity images of Chapter I, from a *tonalamatl.* In the *Primeros Memoriales* the right-hand column of the folio displays the day signs while the text to the left names the days, giving a verbal equivalent of the visual representation. But the auguries provided for the 13-day periods into which the 260-day cycle was divided were not recorded in the *tonalamatl.* Instead, they derived from oral lore, in this case from the calculations and interpretations made by the diviner during the augural ritual.

In a few paragraphs, an intimate connection between the image and accompanying text is lacking. For example, the seated male and female figures in Paragraph 15 of Chapter III, "How They Admonished the People," do not provide the source for the text, nor do they explicate it. Although adapted from traditional images, they are used here in a European manner to adorn and enliven the text.

The most direct method for eliciting information for nonpictorial sections must have been oral communication (see Dibble 1982: 12–13), but the information obtained was recorded in different ways in different sections of the manuscript. Some sections consist of a series of words or phrases forming what is essentially a vocabulary list. This is seen, for example, in the lineage terms of Chapter IV, Paragraph 1, and in the itemization of ceremonial objects in Chapter I, Paragraph 6. In other paragraphs, such as 3C, 3D, and 3E of Chapter I, which discuss rituals, a description or statement accompanies the word or phrase. Possibly the skeletal word lists represent a preliminary step in the information gathering process, when the terms pertinent to a subject were first collected, whereas the annotated lists exemplify a second, more advanced stage. In any case, the verbal rather than pictorial origin of these lists demonstrates another method used to gather information, one that underscores Sahagún's linguistic concerns in compiling the *Historia.*

Other sections of the *Primeros Memoriales* contain neither images nor lists of words but rather discursive texts in paragraph form. These passages do not appear to have derived from either pictorial material or anterior word lists. Some of these extended texts, such as Chapter III, Paragraph 15, "How They Admonished the People," Paragraph 16, "How the Ruler Became Angry," and Paragraph 17, "How the Ruler Felt Compassion for the People," also include narrative features and patterned phrases. Another, the unfinished story of the journey of Moquihuixtzin's daughter-in-law in the afterworld (Tlalocan) in Chapter II, Paragraph 6, is an oral narrative that would have been recited or possibly enacted in pre-Hispanic times. Like the "Songs of the Gods" in Paragraph 14 of Chapter I, as well as the *huehuetlatolli* (sayings of the ancients; see Sullivan 1974), these set pieces undoubtedly existed as coherent units in Nahua oral tradition. Independent of any pictorial reference, they would also have been elicited through oral interviews with knowledgeable Nahua elders.

THE MAKING OF THE MANUSCRIPT

Despite Sahagún's comments regarding his activity in Tepepolco, many questions surround the way in which the *Primeros Memoriales* was actually produced. Both parts of the now divided manuscript are today in fair condition, although spotted folios, frayed edges, and an occasional effaced word are signs of unavoidable age and wear. The manuscript also reveals signs of alteration at the time of composition, such as glued-in leaves, cut sheets, words deleted by white overpainting, marginal and intertextual notations, and inserted Spanish chapter titles in Sahagún's own handwriting. Despite some fading, the colors of the inks and pigments still appear remarkably vivid.

The watermarks of sixteenth-century European paper provide clues not only to the general dating of a manuscript but also to the correct ordering of folios and aspects of the manuscript's planning and execution. Since the *Primeros Memoriales* watermarks corroborate a dating that is already rather well determined, their most useful contribution lies in helping to reconstruct the manuscript's original form. The paper of the Palace manuscript displays six types of watermarks, three of which are repeated in the Academy manuscript (Figures 1 and 2). The six are variants of two designs widely dispersed in Europe and New Spain during the sixteenth century: the pilgrim in a circle, and the open hand (or glove) with a flower at its fingertip.[4]

When watermarks are considered in conjunction with the gatherings (the sequential groups of folios that constitute the manuscript), further information may be gleaned about the manuscript's original structure. Unfortunately, identifying the gatherings of the *Primeros Memoriales* is hampered by tight modern bindings, incorrectly bound folios, the addition of some leaves, and the loss of others. On the other hand, some of the strings used to bind each gathering at the center can still be located, and both halves of many folded sheets can still be discerned. Some tentative observations can therefore be offered regarding the original organization of the manuscript.

Chapters I and II of the Palace manuscript contain four gatherings with an uneven number of sheets (Figure 3). Chapter I has two

4. See Briquet 1985, II:7584–7607, III:10731–10772; Mena 1926; and Vals i Subirà 1980 for general information on the watermarks of sixteenth-century manuscripts. See Ballesteros-Gaibrois 1964, I: 329–342 and Dibble 1982 for information specifically on watermarks in Sahaguntine manuscripts; Ballesteros, however, identifies only four watermarks in the *Primeros Memoriales.*

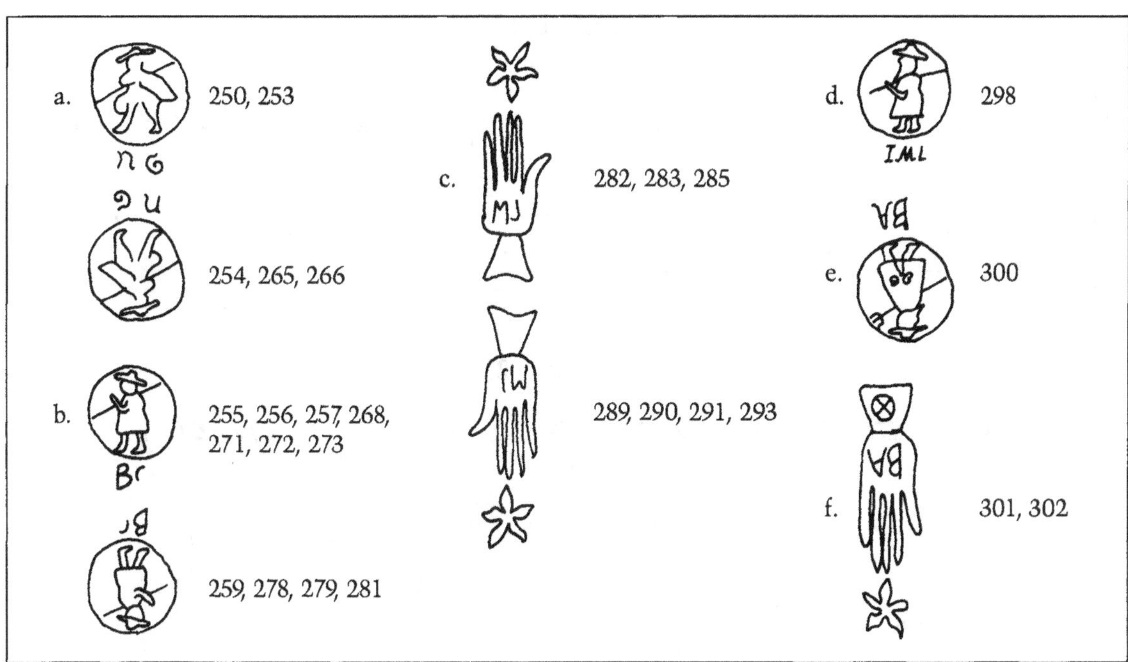

Figure 1. Watermarks in the Palace manuscript. Numbers indicate the folios on which the watermarks appear.

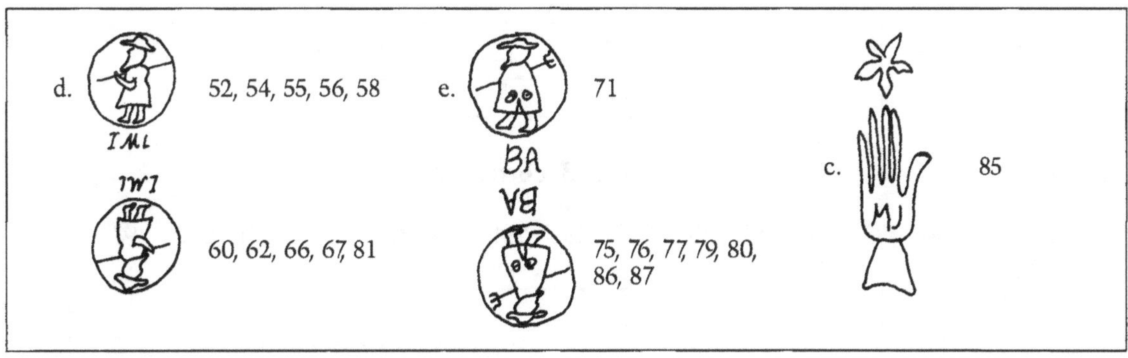

Figure 2. Watermarks in the Academy manuscript. Numbers indicate the folios on which the watermarks appear.

gatherings: gathering 1 with nine folded sheets (fols. 250–267) and gathering 2 with seven sheets (fols. 268–281), one of them cut, plus a single glued-in leaf (fol. 281) at the end. Chapter II has two gatherings, both misbound. The present gathering 3 includes six folded sheets (fols. 282–294), with a single glued-in leaf (fol. 282) at the beginning. The present gathering 4 has four sheets (fols. 295–303), with an added leaf (fol. 303) at the end. Its two binding errors can be recognized by examining the contents of this section, which consist of sequential date glyphs. Two sheets (fols. 297–300) at the center of gathering 4 should be bound at the center of gathering 3 between folios 288v and 289r. In addition, the sheet with folios 84 and 85 of the Academy manuscript should have been bound at the end of gathering 4, with folio 85 preceding folio 84.

Chapters III and IV of the Academy manuscript contain two main gatherings, both with binding errors (Figure 4). Gathering 5 includes nine folded sheets (fols. 51–67), with

Chapter I
Gathering 1

* 250 251 252 *253 *254 *255 *256 *257 258–*259 260 261 262 263 264 *265 *266 267

Gathering 2

*268 269 270 X *271 *272 *273–274 275 276 277 *278 *279 280 *281

X = cut folio

-/- = glued

Chapter II
Gathering 3, present manuscript

*282 *283 284 *285 286 287 288–*289 *290 *291 292 *293 294

Gathering 3, corrected

*282 *283 284 *285 286 287 288 297 *298–299 *300 *289 *290 *291 292 *293 294

Gathering 4, present manuscript

295 296 297 *298–299 *300 *301 *302 303

Gathering 4, corrected

295 *296–301 *302 303 *85 84

* Watermark

Figure 3. Gatherings in the Palace manuscript.

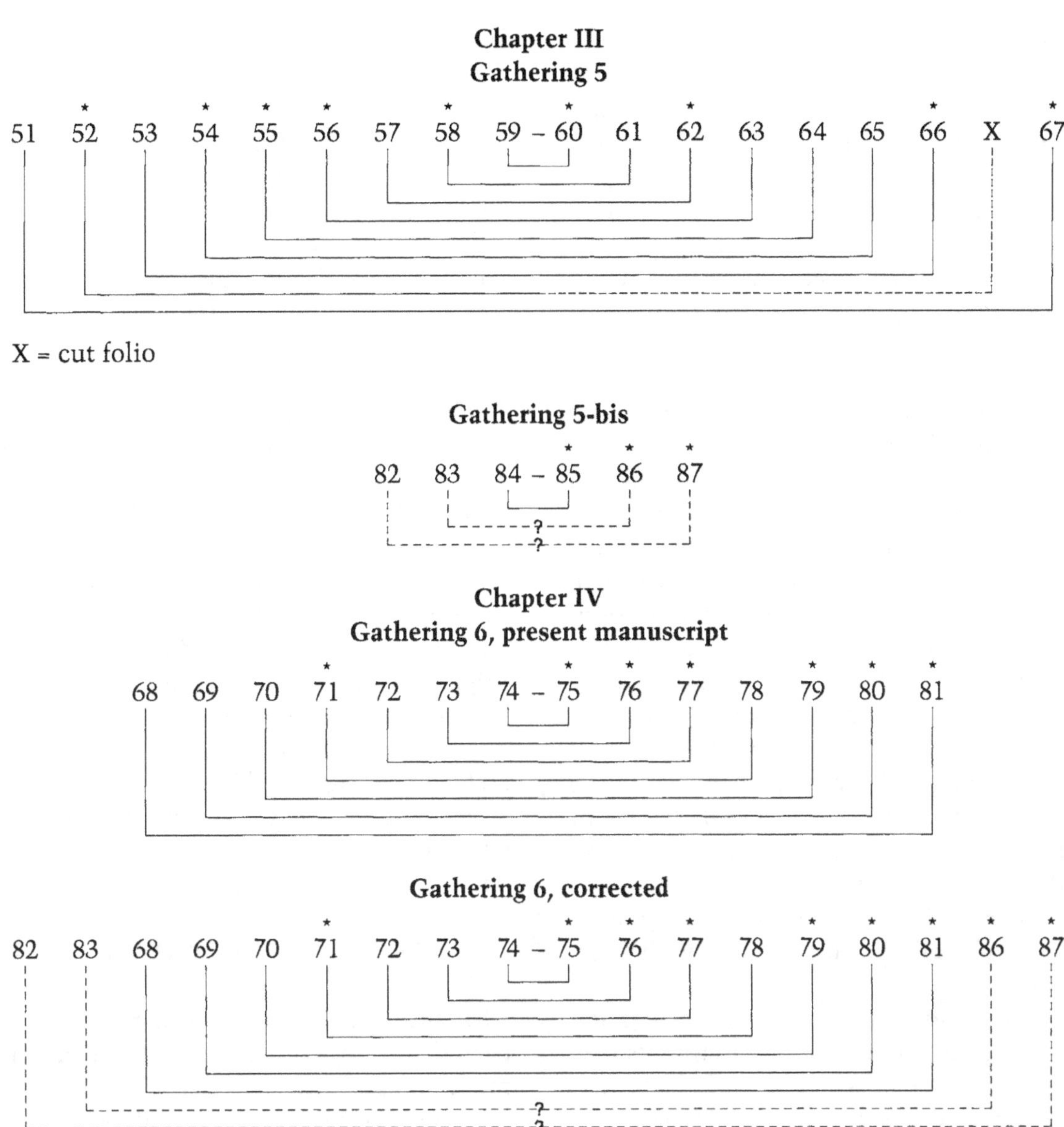

Figure 4. Gatherings in the Academy manuscript.

folio 52 cut. Gathering 6 has seven folded sheets (fols. 68–81). Inserted incorrectly between gatherings 5 and 6 (here called 5-bis) are folios 82–87, bound so tightly that it is difficult to ascertain whether folios 82 and 87 and 83 and 86 are, respectively, parts of one sheet. Again, folios 84–85 should be bound (as 85–84) in the Palace manuscript. The two sheets with folios 82–87 and 83–86 belong in gathering 6, 82–83 preceding it and 86–87 (blank) at the end. Paso y Troncoso's insertion of folios 72–80 (illustrating military insignia) after the text relating to this subject on folio 68 produced a rupture in the text, which continues briefly on folio 69r. The insignia illustrations should follow folio 71, as they are now bound.

Despite its present binding irregularities, it appears that the *Primeros Memoriales* manuscript originally comprised six gatherings, with nine sheets favored for each gathering. Additional sheets in Chapters I and II, the longest chapters, formed smaller, separate gatherings. Chapter I thus consisted of two gatherings of nine and seven sheets, respectively, the latter with an added leaf; Chapter II, two gatherings, one of nine and the other of three sheets, the latter with an added leaf; Chapter III, one gathering of nine sheets; and Chapter IV, one gathering of nine sheets.

Watermarks appear to correlate with chapters. Only Chapter I has paper with the first two watermarks, the pilgrim in a circle with "N G" below and the pilgrim in a circle with "B C" below. The second watermark appears only on paper in the second gathering of Chapter I. Paper in Chapter II shows examples of the four remaining watermarks. The watermark on folio 84–85, misbound in the Academy manuscript, appears only in Chapter II of the Palace manuscript, where that folio belongs. All paper in Chapter III bears the pilgrim in the circle watermark with "I M L" below, which is found on only two other folios, one in Chapter II and one in Chapter IV. The other folios in Chapter IV display the pilgrim in the circle with "BA" below.

Taking into account the six gatherings and the distribution of the six watermarks, the following inferences can be made about the planning and execution of the *Primeros Memoriales.* That the watermarks roughly coincide with different chapters and gatherings indicates that chapters—or, for Chapters I and II, even individual gatherings—were prepared as a group by the artists and scribes. It also suggests that the work progressed sequentially from the first to the fourth chapter. Charles Dibble (1982:25) notes that in the sixteenth century, all paper was imported into New Spain, and it was often in short supply, making prolonged storage of any one stock unlikely. If paper for each manuscript project depended on the supply of a single religious house, it can be surmised that manuscripts (or sections of them) with paper bearing only one or two watermarks were produced during a shorter period of time than those with paper bearing several kinds of watermarks. It thus seems likely that a certain interval separated the execution of the four chapters of the *Primeros Memoriales.* Chapter I, which uses paper with watermarks that do not appear again in the manuscript, apparently took the longest time to execute, probably because it was the longest chapter and because it contained the most complex illustrations.

John Glass (1975: 365n7) questioned whether folio 81 had been correctly inserted as part of the manuscript. Although the careless handwriting on this folio differentiates it from the neat scripts of the manuscript as a whole, its watermark and position in the gathering (apparently forming one sheet with folio 68) support its inclusion in the original manuscript. The intrusive hand, however, and the location of folio 81 at the end of the Academy manuscript, immediately preceding two blank folios (and not after folio 69, where Paso y Troncoso inserted it), suggest that the writing on this folio may have been added at a later time.

INCORPORATING THE IMAGES

After the organization of the manuscript had been determined and material gathered, the preparation of the manuscript itself began with the laying out of individual folios. This task was executed by the artists; the idiosyncrasies of the ruling lines that apportion the contents of the folio correspond to their hands rather than to those of the scribes. The images were drawn before the text was copied; the glosses for figures such as the rulers in Chapter III and the warriors in Chapter IV presuppose the presence of the images, as do the phrases or lines of script that extend above or around some figures, such as the gods and ministers in Chapter I. This procedure contrasted with the usual preparation of European manuscripts, in which scribes generally copied the text first and left spaces reserved for illuminations that would be added by the artists.

Aside from several figures outlined only in black in the Academy manuscript (fols. 61v, 65r, 65v) and two sketches in the Palace manuscript (fol. 267v), all the images were painted. Since color in pre-Hispanic painting frequently had symbolic import, its use in this manuscript added yet another dimension of information for the reader. The attentiveness to the image in the *Primeros Memoriales* underscores the fact that the paintings served not as mere decorations but, as in the pre-Hispanic period, as conveyers of meaning.

Fifteen of the 49 paragraphs of the *Primeros Memoriales* display a total of 546 images: 81 in Chapter I, 334 in Chapter II, 64 in Chapter III, and 67 in Chapter IV.[5] This is a remarkable number of drawings for such a manuscript, and the prodigious investment of time, materials, and effort accentuates the importance of the Tepepolco project. Aside from a few colonial manuscripts that replicate pre-Hispanic pictorial manuscripts, the *Primeros Memoriales* contains the greatest number of native-style images that had been gathered and duplicated under Spanish patronage up to that time. This total would be exceeded only by that of a later Sahaguntine production, the *Florentine Codex.* Although a few other sixteenth-century ethnographic works, such as Durán's *Historia,* also feature illustrations, most, like the Franciscan Motolinia's sizable *Memoriales,* do not.

In addition to preserving, to a certain extent, native reliance on the visual image, the considerable use of images in the *Primeros Memoriales* may also relate to a didactic use of pictorial material in European works. Remarks by Sahagún elucidating his linguistic aims in compiling the *Historia* indicate that he regarded it as a kind of living Nahuatl dictionary (Sahagún 1950–1982, introductory volume: 47). And just as words presented in context convey a more accurate sense of their meaning than would the more stringent format of a "vocabulario," so might images further clarify the meaning of words by literally picturing them. When discussing the relationship between texts and images in medieval manuscripts and early printed blockbooks produced in Europe, Sandra Hindman (in Hindman and Farquhar 1977: 167) reports that in translated texts, illustrations were sometimes used as didactic devices to teach the meanings of new words and concepts. She cites research showing that in one translation of Aristotle's *Politics* and *Ethics* from Latin to French, certain neologisms were not only listed in a glossary but also illustrated in accompanying miniatures. Possibly a variation of this European practice was incorporated in the *Primeros Memoriales.*

When attempting to assess the extent to which the images of the *Primeros Memoriales* adhere to or depart from pictorial models painted in pre-Hispanic native books, comparisons cannot be made with pre-Conquest manuscripts from Tepepolco or other Basin of Mexico communities because no manuscripts of undisputed pre-Conquest date have survived from these areas. The documents closest to the *Primeros Memoriales* geographically and culturally are early colonial pictorial manuscripts from the Basin of Mexico or closely neighboring areas that duplicate each other in some sections. These were painted by indigenous artists using pre-Hispanic stylistic and iconographic conventions, and some sections appear to be faithful copies of lost originals. Among this group, the most useful for comparison are the *Codex Borbonicus,* the partially related *Codex Mendoza* and *Matrícula de Tributos,* the partially related *Codex Telleriano-Remensis* and *Codex Vaticanus A,* and the partially related *Codex Magliabechiano* and *Codex Tudela.* Especially valuable for understanding the conventions of indigenous painting style and manuscript production are extant pre-Conquest (non-Aztec) manuscripts from other areas of Mexico, in particular the religious-ritual screenfolds of the *Codex Borgia* group,[6]

5. Tallies of the images may vary, however, depending on how multifigural groups are counted.

6. Major members of the *Codex Borgia* group include the codices *Borgia, Vaticanus B, Laud, Fejérváry Mayer,* and *Cospi.*

probably from southern Puebla, western Oaxaca, and the Gulf Coast, and, to a lesser extent, historical and genealogical Mixtec screenfolds from the Oaxaca area, such as the *Codex Zouche-Nuttall* and *Codex Vindobonnensis.*

The range of images depicted in the *Primeros Memoriales* is broad. The major categories encompass religious rituals and deities in Chapter I, celestial bodies, meteorological phenomena, and standardized signs for the days and years in Chapter II, pre-Hispanic and colonial rulers in Chapter III, and warrior costumes and insignia in Chapter IV.

In pre-Hispanic manuscripts or manuscript sections, deity figures or their impersonators appear chiefly in the divinatory handbook, or *tonalamatl,* and in depictions of the annual ceremonies *(veintenas).* The *tonalamatl* is also the primary source for symbols of the individual days that made up the 260-day calendric and ritual count, as well as for illustrations of priests who appear as secondary figures performing ritual activities.

Ruler representations and consecutive year signs are a major feature of pictorial annals. This type of manuscript also includes representations of celestial and atmospheric phenomena. Many figures in these historical manuscripts also wear military costumes; this type of attire occurs as well in tribute lists that illustrate commodities requisitioned by rulers from various subject areas.

In the *Primeros Memoriales,* the images copied from these various types of native books were reoriented from the generally horizontal sequence of painted panels to the vertical format of discrete leaves of European paper. In addition to being rearranged, the images were sometimes used in new ways, and they occasionally show assimilated European stylistic features.[7]

Images based on major pictorial types such as deity figures appear with few changes, indicating that in this case the *Primeros Memoriales* artists were largely guided by traditional models. Images representing minor figures were handled more freely. For example, although priests appear as subsidiary figures in pre-Hispanic manuscripts, no extant manuscript or manuscript section focuses on ministers performing private rituals like those depicted in Chapter I, Paragraphs 3A, 3B, and 3C. Lacking a repertory of standardized sacerdotal prototypes, the artists of the *Primeros Memoriales* repeated one basic figural type throughout, differentiating it only minimally by the garb worn and ritual items held. The most Europeanized figures of the manuscript, the seated male and female figures of Chapter III, Paragraph 15, similarly derive from minor figural types, the anonymous dignitaries and ordinary folk who appear intermittently in historical chronicles or genealogies.

Some assembled images of the *Primeros Memoriales,* such as the astronomical and meteorological items of Chapter II, provide pictorial catalogues that are unique among surviving Central Mexican manuscripts. In the case of these phenomena, which were occasionally depicted in religious-ritual manuscripts and in pictorial chronicles as one of several kinds of celestial events that were recorded, available native models were sometimes bypassed altogether. Instead, the artist based several images in this section on European examples. These models were accessible in book illustrations or prints imported into or produced in New Spain after the Conquest.

THE IMAGES OF THE PALACE MANUSCRIPT[8]

Chapter I

The 81 images of Chapter I of the Palace manuscript (fols. 250r–281v) deal with rituals and

7. On the incorporation of European elements in the *Primeros Memoriales,* see especially Robertson 1959:169 and Baird 1979, 1983, 1988b, 1993.

8. For more detailed discussions of individual images in the *Primeros Memoriales,* see Durand-Forest 1977; Baird 1979, 1983, 1988b, and especially 1993; Quiñones Keber 1988b, 1988c; Nicholson 1988b.

gods (see Table 5). They are among the most frequently reproduced and discussed of the *Primeros Memoriales* images because they and their accompanying texts provide enlightening, sometimes unique, information about this vital aspect of native culture.[9] As can be seen in the facsimile (Sahagún 1993), Paragraph 2A, the opening section of the manuscript, features illustrations of eighteen feasts corresponding to the eighteen twenty-day periods *(veintenas),* plus five extra days, into which the vague solar year was divided. The descriptive texts to the left provide useful summaries of these elaborate public ceremonies, which propitiated different deities in order to gain religious, social, and agricultural benefits.

In contrast to the majority of the manuscript's images, which display single figures, these *veintena* representations teem with people and activities. Arranged vertically, two or three scenes occupy each folio. Within a red-framed rectangular field, most scenes depict multiple episodes of the type George Kubler and Charles Gibson (1951:39) called "simultaneous illustration." Included in these busy scenes are idols, deity impersonators, costumed participants, ritual paraphernalia and activities (especially processions, offerings, and human sacrifices), sacred images, and temples and other religious structures.

The first image, which depicts the feast of Cuahuitl ehua (fol. 250r), in honor of the rain gods (Tlalocs), is typical of the kinds of visual and verbal data recorded in Paragraph 2A. The illustration shows a temple in profile (upper left); a second structure (lower left) with a banner conspicuously displayed in front of it; a procession, indicated by footprints, led by two priests clad in blue mantles and bearing incense bags, followed by two others who wear white mantles and bear similar large banners; and a culminating mountaintop sacrificial scene showing a victim and three small images of the Tlalocs (upper right). The closely related text describes the sacrifice of children on mountaintops, the display of paper banners on houses, and the conveying of "sacrificial papers" by commoners, noblemen, and lords, led by Tlaloc's priests, to the "temple of the devil" on the summit.

Although competently drawn in general accord with indigenous stylistic and iconographic conventions and exhibiting only minor deviations, the figures nevertheless lack the linear dexterity typical of the most accomplished pre-Hispanic painting. Clarity and "readability," rather than realistic representation, were the artist's priority. With images and space characteristically conceived in two rather than three dimensions, pictorial components were distributed somewhat evenly about the picture plane without attention to ground lines or the illusionistic creation of depth.[10] There was correspondingly little volumetric development in the depiction of the human body or architectural elements, which the artist preferred to define with strong, dark outlines and flattened forms. Rather than being individualized, human figures were rendered as standardized types. Usually shown in profile, these simplified figures assumed conventionalized poses and gestures, imparting a formal, somewhat static quality to the scenes.

As the most detailed pictorial group in the manuscript, these *veintena* scenes are nearly comparable in complexity, although not in artistic sophistication, to the *Codex Borbonicus* series. They are also more informative than the sparely depicted *veintenas* of the *Codex Telleriano-Remensis/Codex Vaticanus A* and *Codex Magliabechiano/Codex Tudela.*

That no pre-Conquest *veintena* series now

9. The *veintenas* have been widely studied; see especially Seler 1899a; Kubler and Gibson 1951; Jiménez Moreno 1974; Brown 1978; Couch 1985; Quiñones Keber 1988a and 1995. For a more extended discussion of the *veintena* section of the *Primeros Memoriales,* see Baird 1993: 104–117.

10. Robertson (1959:172) refers to this type of representation as "scattered attribute," although the components are rarely "attributes." See Quiñones Keber 1987 for a different explanation of these items.

exists has raised the question of whether these feasts were actually depicted in pre-Hispanic manuscripts or instead represent a colonial invention.[11] Although no argument has yet proved conclusive, the existence of several independently executed post-Conquest *veintena* series suggests that they may have been a pre-Hispanic form of which no examples have survived. It is uncertain whether the images in such manuscripts were consulted for performing specific rituals as the *tonalamatl* was consulted for divinatory rites. Nevertheless, the *veintena* images may have served as guides for assembling the requisite components for the ceremonies from year to year, such as the costumes to be worn by participants, the ritual exercises to be performed, the items to be used, and the offerings to be made.

Atamalcualiztli, the great feast held every eight years, is the subject of Paragraph 2B (fol. 254v). One of only two full-page illustrations in the manuscript, the representation of this ceremony is unique among Central Mexican images. Its numerous lively figures capture something of the spirit of this colorful festival, in which participants impersonated the gods, donned animal disguises, consumed vast numbers of tamales, and engaged in dancing, processions, offerings, and other activities. Its composition is similar to that of the *veintena* series, although, because of its large size, it incorporates even more events. Its pictorial detail is matched by the extensive description of the feast on the facing page. Eight year signs at the upper right refer to its occurrence every eight years. Footprints around the outer edge signify not only movement but also, in this case, the dancing that was part of the celebration.

In contrast to the cyclical, communal *veintena* feasts of Paragraph 2A, Paragraphs 3A, 3B, and 3C (fols. 254v–255v) depict eighteen types of private offerings performed by individuals in honor of the gods. Among these presentations were food, drink, incense, birds, and human blood. Except for one pair of figures and one group, the images in this section show single, unframed, male and female celebrants in profile. Most hold ceremonial items but lack associated figures or contextual settings. Like the *veintena* scenes, these images relate closely to the adjacent text, which describes the offering being enacted. As usual, the figures are drawn in a vertical column with the name of the ritual written opposite at the far left. At a later time, another hand added the descriptions of the actions; the writing extended into the right-hand pictorial column, moving around and past the figures. On folio 254v, where the descriptions exceeded their prescribed zones, lines had to be drawn to connect the headings with the proper texts.

Analogous sacerdotal figures appear in religious-ritual manuscripts and in ethnographic sections of some manuscripts, such as the *Codex Mendoza,* and it seems likely that the celebrants in this section were adapted and redrawn from such types of related images. No extant manuscript, however, presents the range of private devotions depicted in the *Primeros Memoriales.*

The images of Paragraph 5A, the accouterments of the gods, are another important and frequently studied section of the *Primeros Memoriales* (fols. 261r–267r).[12] The attention they receive is owing to the fact that these folios depict an extensive group of deities, in full regalia, with their Nahuatl names glossed above their heads. In native manuscripts, deities appeared without name signs, because their costumes and insignia served to identify them. Over the centuries, as this knowledge was lost, identifying the Central Mexican pantheon became increasingly difficult. It was only in the nineteenth century, when glossed colonial manuscripts like the *Primeros Memoriales, Codex Telleriano-Remensis,* and *Codex Magliabechiano* once again became known, that the correct Na-

11. See Kubler and Gibson 1951 and Brown 1978, who favor a colonial origin for *veintena* representations.

12. For recent studies of this section see Quiñones Keber 1988b; Nicholson 1988b; and Baird 1993.

huatl names could confidently be assigned to these deities.

With a few exceptions, the forty-one male and female figures, in profile, are arranged vertically in the right-hand column, with their costumes and insignia itemized to the left. The array, distinctive for each deity, includes headdresses, face painting, accessories (chiefly ear plugs, with an occasional nose or chest ornament), costumes (mantles and hip cloths for the males, shifts or skirts for the females), sandals, and shields and standards held in each hand.

Depictions of the gods or their impersonators appear in several pre-Hispanic and colonial pictorial manuscripts, although not in sections specifically devoted to them as a group, as they appear in the *Primeros Memoriales.* Rather, these deities dominate the *tonalamatl* as divinatory patrons of the thirteen-day periods *(trecenas)* and of the day and night. Among the best examples of this kind of image are the deities of the *Codex Borbonicus, Tonalamatl Aubin,* and *Codex Telleriano-Remensis/Codex Vaticanus A,* along with those in various members of the *Codex Borgia* group. In the *Primeros Memoriales* the isolated deity figures give no clue to their original manuscript context.[13] They may have derived from a single source or may have been culled from different manuscripts.

Unpainted outlines of two priests appear on the last folio of Paragraph 5B without heading or text or even a paragraph designation (fol. 267v). Since they follow the section on the array of the gods, Paso y Troncoso surmised that these sketches were intended to be part of a section dealing with the attire of priests, but this remains conjectural.

The temple precinct depicted in Paragraph 7 is the second full-page illustration of the *Primeros Memoriales* (fol. 269r). It presents a walled enclosure with several religious structures and items placed around a courtyard: at the top, a single temple dedicated to the solar god of war, Huitzilopochtli; below it, paired pyramid temples dedicated to the rain god, Tlaloc (left), and Huitzilopochtli (right); other smaller shrines; an I-shaped ball court; a priest's house *(calmecac);* a circular gladiatorial stone mounted on a pyramid base; and a rack for displaying the skulls of sacrificial victims. A costumed priest holds a censer and incense pouch, and two seated standard bearers hold shields and banners, with the calendric names 5 Cuetzpallin (Lizard) and 5 Calli (House) alongside. At the far right is a standing figure of an impersonator, or possibly an idol, of the war and fertility deity Xipe Totec, holding his characteristic rattle staff before him.

The text on the facing page merely lists the structures shown but does not describe them. A "snake wall," that is, an enclosure with projecting snake heads, and an "eagle vessel" for containing blood offerings are also listed but do not appear. The reason the central double pyramid is called the "Colhuacan Temple" is unclear. The roof markings indicate that the two shrines were dedicated to Tlaloc and Huitzilopochtli, as were the main temples of Mexico Tenochtitlan, Tlatelolco, and Tetzcoco,[14] and possibly other centers in the Basin of Mexico as well.

Structures are depicted frontally, and figures in profile preserving the essentially planar visual effect of pre-Hispanic painting. Although individual temples and religious structures appear in several religious-ritual and historical manuscripts, no other manuscript portrays an entire ritual precinct in such detail as the *Primeros Memoriales.*

Another distinctive feature of this painting is that it appears to represent an actual, if schematic, architectural layout rather than the generic type more common in pre-Hispanic depictions. A correspondence be-

13. See Van Zantwijk 1963; Barthel 1964: 79–100; Baird 1979:179–222; and Nicholson 1988b for speculations on this issue.

14. See *Codex Telleriano-Remensis* 1995: fol. 39r for Mexico Tenochtitlan and fol. 36v for Tlatelolco, and *Codex Ixtlilxochitl* 1976: fol. 112v for Tetzcoco, with the illustration derived from Pomar's *Relación de Texcoco.*

tween the types and placement of structures in this illustration and archaeologically known features of the central shrine of Mexico Tenochtitlan has led some scholars to identify the temple precinct in this painting as the Main Temple of that city or—to allow for the fact that the capital's Main Temple was far larger and contained more structures—as its central section. Since the drawing was made in Tepepolco, however, and information was provided by Tepepolco elders with the help of the grammarians, none of whom was from the capital, I would argue that it more likely represents the chief temple compound of Tepepolco itself, a not insignificant religious center.[15]

Chapter II

In addition to the heavens and the underworld, which the title of Chapter II specifies, this section also encompasses two major indigenous calendric constructs. Its 334 images depict not only celestial bodies and meteorological phenomena but also the 52-year count and the 260-day ritual count.

The images of Paragraph 1 (fols. 282r–282v part) show twelve celestial phenomena, including the sun and moon, solar and lunar eclipses, several constellations, the morning star, a comet, and a shooting star. Only some of these images appear in other pictorial manuscripts, and then not in a special section of their own but as secondary elements of religious-ritual or historical sections. It is interesting to note that although symbolic representations of the sun, moon, and eclipses were still available in pre-Hispanic manuscripts, the artist of this section rejected these potential models and chose to base some of these images on European prototypes. The sun essentially imitates a pre-Hispanic model, albeit with the face of the sun god shown in profile rather than frontally, whereas the moon follows European convention.

The five constellations can be identified by the groupings of native-style circular stars connected by red lines. Apparently, however, constellations were not portrayed in Central Mexican manuscripts, or at least no examples of them have survived, and the depictions of constellations may have been newly created for the *Primeros Memoriales*. In the Maya *Codex Dresden*, planets are depicted in the form of gods connected with them, a pictorial convention followed to some extent in Central Mexican manuscripts. The planet Venus may be represented symbolically, for example, by a conventionalized emblem or occasionally by a fierce, spear-hurling deity. Here it is shown simply as one circle inside another.

The adjoining text does not deal with astronomy as such; instead, it offers a miscellany of information regarding rituals connected with the celestial bodies and popular beliefs about them. Information on native astronomy was not extensively recorded in the sixteenth century, creating gaps in our understanding of this branch of indigenous knowledge and making this unique group of images in the *Primeros Memoriales* particularly valuable.

The eight meteorological phenomena depicted in Paragraph 2 (fols. 282v part–283r part) are wind, lightning, rain, a rainbow, frost, clouds, snow, and hail. These images are represented in the following ways: wind, by an image of the deity Ehecatl (Wind), wearing his characteristic mouth mask and conical hat and surrounded by raindrops; lightning, by a zigzag shape topped by a paper decoration; rain, by the combined image of the head of the rain god Tlaloc atop a native-style mountain; the rainbow, by a multicolored arch; and frost, by a black-and-white image of the god of frost, Itztlacoliuhqui (Curved Obsidian Knife), wearing his bent, knife-edged hat. Except for the rainbow, of which no example exists in the extant pre-Hispanic manuscripts, the images were

15. Compare the extensive discussion of Paragraph 7 in the notes to it in this volume.

adapted from indigenous prototypes. Unique to this manuscript, the rainbow depiction undoubtedly derived from a European model. Like the celestial bodies, the indigenous images in this paragraph appear in a schematized fashion in pre-Hispanic chronicles but were not the focus of independent sections. Their inclusion is yet another distinctive feature of the *Primeros Memoriales.* The descriptive texts to the left recount beliefs about these phenomena, as well as their causes and effects, but in this case say nothing about related rituals.

The symbols of the fifty-two-year count (with the first year of the next fifty-two-year count added at the end) comprise the images of Paragraph 3 (fols. 283r part–286r part). The names of the years were formed by combining a number from one to thirteen with one of the four day signs that also functioned successively as year names: Tochtli (Rabbit), Acatl (Reed), Tecpatl (Flint Knife), and Calli (House). Shown vertically in the right column, the year signs are depicted with double-outlined blue dots, representing the numbers, beside or above them. Only the name of the year is given at the left. Although sequential year signs provided the temporal framework for chronicling events in several historical manuscripts, no Central Mexican manuscript consisted only of the repeating year signs of the fifty-two-year cycle. These reduced schemes occur only in colonial manuscripts, often structured as calendric charts.

Fifty-two years formed a complete calendric period analogous to our century. Although the first year shown in the *Primeros Memoriales* is 1 Tochtli, in Central Mexico 2 Acatl launched the new cycle, inaugurated by the New Fire ceremony. This dramatic, world-renewal ritual celebrated the completion of one fifty-two-year cycle (at which time the world would one day be destroyed) and the beginning of another. Although the four thirteen-year groups of the cycle are provided with written auguries, the text makes no mention of this crucial ritual or the ideological implications of the fifty-two-year cycle and the threat of cosmic annihilation.

The 260-day ritual count, or *tonalpohualli* (with the first day of the next series added at the end), is the subject of Paragraph 4 (fols. 286r–303r). The largest single pictorial group in the *Primeros Memoriales,* the 260 symbols of this count constitute almost half of the manuscript's total paintings. Formed by combining numbers from one to thirteen with each of twenty signs, each image represents the name of a day. The day names appear as double-framed red squares enclosing the outlined signs, with dots standing for numerals. It is curious that the cycle begins with the day 1 Itzcuintli (Dog) rather than the standard 1 Cipactli (Crocodilian Monster).

The text merely lists the day name, along with an augury for each thirteen-day grouping and the fate of one born during this period. The prognostications provide but a vestige of the function of the *tonalamatl* as a guide during pre-Hispanic times for conducting divinatory rituals.

Several pre-Hispanic and early colonial *tonalamatls* feature the 260-day count, accompanied by illustrations of deity patrons of various kinds, all representing mantic forces weighed by the diviner in determining his prognostications. In the *Primeros Memoriales,* however, the extracted day signs function more in the manner of a European calendar of days. Like the preceding fifty-two-year cycle, this count represents a pre-Hispanic calendric construct that has been rearranged in a columnar format. In this new, sanitized format, the *tonalamatl* has been divested of its suspect role as a divinatory device.

THE IMAGES OF THE ACADEMY MANUSCRIPT

Chapter III

The sixty-nine images of Chapter III relate to selected aspects of rulership. Paragraphs 1A, 1B, and 1C show sixteen pre- and post-Conquest rulers from the Mexica (Aztec) capital, Mexico Tenochtitlan (fols. 51r–52r part), thirteen from the Acolhuaque capital, Tetzcoco, to which Tepepolco was subject (fols.

52r part–53r part), and thirteen from the neighboring Acolhuaque city of Huexotla (53r part–53v part). Why the *Primeros Memoriales* includes the rulers of Huexotla but not those of Tepepolco is curious. Following native convention, rulers are shown wearing the royal mantle and seated on the royal woven reed seat, with identifying name signs drawn above their heads. The first three rulers from Tetzcoco and the first five from Huexotla are dressed in rustic animal-skin cloaks and sit on reed bundles to signify their Chichimec origins.

Several glosses accompany each figure. The first provides the ruler's name in written form in red ink; the others, in keeping with the linguistic aims of the manuscript, list the items of apparel. The format is thus similar to that of Chapter I, Paragraph 5A, which depicts a deity with adjoining text itemizing his array. In the ruler section, however, the costume glosses remain in the right-hand column. The text in the left-hand column gives the length of each ruler's reign and significant details about his career.

Since the chronological framework of many Central Mexican histories was built around the years of the sovereign's reign, models for this section were readily available. The addition of the colonial-period Indian governors indicates that even after the Conquest, native rulers continued in administrative positions under Spanish aegis. The figures of these rulers were probably drawn expressly for the manuscript, although, as is evident, they were based on the conventionalized forms of the pre-Conquest rulers who had preceded them. The additional pictorial material that was included in pre-Hispanic chronicles but not copied in the *Primeros Memoriales* may yet have been utilized for the information about each ruler's reign that appears in the related text. Thus, even within one section, some indigenous features could be transformed or replaced, while others, such as the pictorial formula that was retained for colonial-period governors, endured.

Paragraph 2 depicts several of the ruler's aides (fols. 53v part–54r part). Two groups resemble the seated ruler types of the preceding section, while two standing pairs are closer to the generic figural types from the offerings section of Chapter I. The first group shows four dignitaries seated on the woven mats reserved for royalty and other high-ranking individuals. Speech volutes emerging from their mouths convey their role as counselors. The second group presents a lord surrounded by four attendants, illustrating the ruler "who heard all" described in the text. These figures do not constitute the source of the text, however, which consists chiefly of titles; instead, they illustrate it in a European manner.

In Paragraph 5, two large, richly dressed male and female figures in profile display, respectively, the adornments of rulers and noblewomen (fols. 55v–56r). In contrast to the section on deity attire, where the texts read as glosses on the images, the text here consists of an extended inventory of elite male and female attire, without specific reference to the figures that are represented. Two mantles near the male figure serve as examples of listed items.

No section of a pre-Hispanic manuscript is devoted to apparel, again making these images an unusual inclusion. The closest earlier examples of this type are the garments and mantles pictured as tribute items in the *Codex Mendoza* and *Matrícula de Tributos* and the section on mantles in the *Codex Magliabechiano* and the *Codex Tudela*. Ethnographic sections of the *Codex Vaticanus A* and *Codex Tudela* also feature several standing figures in native costume, probably reflecting Spanish interest in this everyday aspect of indigenous life.

Among the most interesting images in the manuscript are the seven seated male and female figures in Paragraphs 15, 16, and 17, which deal with how the people were admonished, how the ruler became angry, and how the ruler felt compassion for the people. Unlike the previous sections, where images were placed on the right, these are set at the heads of their respective paragraphs. On folio 61v, twelve figures occupy both columns in the upper section of the page, and two others head columns on folios 65r and 65v. The extended text, in paragraph form, derives from oral tradition rather than from the generic images, which here serve a subsidiary role by illustrating the text in a European manner.

Like the rulers and advisors in Chapter III, these figures were based on pre-Hispanic figural types, and four of them in the top row on folio 61v likewise sit on woven mat seats with speech volutes coming from their mouths. But evident in their rounded bodily contours and more volumetric human forms is a pronounced European stylistic influence. Abandoning the traditional, detached profile view, the head of one seated figure even turns to face the viewer. These finely drawn, unpainted figures display a harmonious integration of pre-Hispanic and European graphic techniques.

Chapter IV

Only one section of Chapter IV, which deals with human concerns, features illustrations: the sixty-seven military costumes and insignia of rulers, nobles, and warriors of Paragraph 8 (fols. 72r–80r).[16] This section, distinctive to the *Primeros Memoriales*, opens with fully accoutered figures, two per folio, with the related texts to the left itemizing their garments and emblems. These lists again function in a manner similar to the glosses on the attire of the rulers in Chapter III and the deities in Chapter I, and likewise demonstrate their derivation from the images. The remaining drawings depict the various components of military gear: body costumes, headgear, feather banners, battle standards, shields, and other types of accessories. The names of these items, listed at the left—in effect glosses—collectively form yet another vocabulary list.

In Central Mexican manuscripts, warriors in battle garb are featured throughout the pictorial chronicles, which devote much attention to the conquests of rulers and the increasingly elaborate costumes worn by successful combatants. Warrior costumes and insignia also appear significantly as tribute items in the *Codex Mendoza* and *Matrícula de Tributos*. No other manuscript, however, devotes a special section to this aspect of military life, a major aspect of an expansionist Aztec society. Some warrior standards in the *Primeros Memoriales* appear to be closer to those shown in the *Lienzo de Tlaxcala* than to those in the *Codex Mendoza* and *Matrícula de Tributos*, which were both from Mexico Tenochtitlan. This similarity may reflect contact between Tepepolco and Mexico Tenochtitlan's Tlaxcallan adversaries in the "flowery wars"; Tlaxcallan territory bordered Acolhuaque territory on the southeast.

THE ARTISTS OF THE *PRIMEROS MEMORIALES*

In a prologue to the *Florentine Codex*, Sahagún identifies the ex-students who assisted him in compiling the *Historia* (Sahagún 1950–1982, introductory volume: 54–55). He names four grammarians, Antonio Valeriano from Azcapotzalco, Alonso Vegerano and Pedro de San Buenaventura from Cuauhtitlan, and Martín Jacobita from Tlatelolco, as well as three scribes, Diego de Grado and Bonifacio Maximiliano from Tlatelolco, and Mateo Severino from Xochimilco. He does not, however, credit them with the paintings, nor does he name the several artists who painted *Primeros Memoriales* images. The artists have been identified both with the Tepepolco elders and with the grammarians. Ellen T. Baird's (1988a, 1993:157–158) arguments in favor of the grammarian hypothesis have been the most extensively developed.

That six artists, however, apparently drew the images of the manuscripts argues against

16. For discussions of pre-Hispanic warrior costumes see Seler 1902–1923, II: 509–619 and Anawalt 1981, 1992.

equating the artists with the four grammarians. Moreover, because the artists' hands do not match those of the scribes on given folios, it seems unlikely that the scribes functioned simultaneously as artists. Although the distinctive drawing styles of several artists can be recognized, one can only speculate about who they might have been. Given the somewhat provincial character of the paintings, it is not unlikely that they were local Tepepolco artists who learned and practiced their craft at some remove from the imperial capital or major regional centers. The paintings may, therefore, express the provincial style of Tepepolco or the use of local pictorial models, as well as the possible decline by the mid-sixteenth century of the high standards of pre-Hispanic manuscript painting.

Clearly, however, the artists of the *Primeros Memoriales* were still knowledgeable about pre-Hispanic manuscript conventions and still had access to painted native books. And since it was the artists who prepared the manuscript according to European specifications and who occasionally used European models or stylistic features, we can surmise that they were also familiar with printed European books and their illustrations. But the nature and extent of the contributions made by the artists, as well as by the grammarians and informants and possibly others, in selecting images to reproduce is uncertain. Like questions regarding the artists' identities and the specific models they used, this one remains unresolved.

Except for figural groups in Chapters I and III and black-and-white drawings in Chapter III, the majority of the *Primeros Memoriales* images are single figures. The images were first sketched in a diluted gray or brown ink, which is still visible beneath the black or sometimes brown outlines painted over them. Departures from the underdrawings were frequent. The black outlining does not always follow the preliminary sketch exactly, nor does it completely cover it. Occasionally the sketch is better drawn than the outline over it, suggesting that the painter may have differed from the artist who drew the initial sketch. Sometimes the artist painted additional details; at other times he ignored details already sketched. For example, on folio 250r, in the depiction of the first *veintena* feast of Cuahuitl ehua, some footprints sketched at the top are not painted; in the feast of Tlacaxipehualiztli beneath it, the sketched feet of the figure at the top right are drawn more correctly than the black outlining that covers it, and the painted legs of the musician in the center are shorter than those sketched.

The black outlines vary in intensity and width depending on the artist, but overall they differ from the firm, precise outline characteristic of pre-Hispanic painting, which Robertson (1959:65–66) termed the "frame line." Color washes used to fill in the outlined areas are still well preserved, with blue, rose, green, gold, orange-red, black, gray, and shades of brown the most prominent. Thin or splotchy patches of color in some areas contrast with the more opaque, even application of paint in pre-Hispanic manuscripts. All these features—adherence to the sketches, the width and intensity of the frame line, and the manner of applying color—vary according to the artist involved and help to characterize the individual style of each artist.

The personal traits of the *Primeros Memoriales* artists are also revealed in other ways, particularly the manner in which details of the human form are drawn. Because the individual deity figures of Chapter I, Paragraph 5A, are larger and more carefully drawn than the small-scale figures of the rest of the manuscript, each artist's idiosyncrasies are more conspicuous in this section. Here one can more easily discern the distinctive ways in which each artist delineated facial profiles, eyes, noses, and mouths, as well as the size and shape of limbs, hands, and feet. For this reason, the letter designations I use to identify the six anonymous artists reflect the order in which they appear in this paragraph. Stylistic variations are evident, however, in an artist's work in different sections, and these modifications may be partially owing to the features of the pictorial model that was being copied.

My identifications of artists in Chapter I for the most part agree with those made by Baird (1993:139–158), with differences occurring chiefly in later sections of the manuscript. Our characterizations of the artists' individual styles vary somewhat, however, as do the letters we assign to their names (my artists A, B, C, D, E, and F correspond to her E, A, B, D, C, and F). Our observations about the artists and their work in the various chapters of the *Primeros Memoriales* also lead us to differing conclusions regarding the way in which the manuscript may have been produced.

In the Palace manuscript, Artist A is responsible for the deities Painal and Huitzilopochtli on folio 261r, Atlahua Chachalmeca, Ixcozauhqui, and Ixtlilton on folio 262v, the Atamalcualiztli feast on folio 254r, offerings on folio 255, and the temple precinct on folio 269r. The frame line of Artist A is weak and uneven. His deity figures have an ungainly, tentative look about them, and their legs and downcurved feet appear to dangle from their bodies. Their eyes are generally large and downturned, and their pointed chins are small and recessive. Although long-limbed, the torsos of the figures are often rather small, with narrow shoulders. Despite some shortcomings, Artist A worked on most of the chapters, which may indicate that he was an especially productive worker.

Artist B is responsible for the deities Tezcatlipoca on folio 261r, Quetzalcoatl, Totochtin, and Tlaloc on folio 261v, Chicomecoatl, Otontecuhtli, and Yacatecuhtli on folio 262r, the Tepictoton on folio 267r, *veintenas* on folio 250, and offerings on folio 254v. Artist B displays a fairly firm black outline, but he frequently departs from the preparatory sketches and leaves some areas uncolored. Generally, noses on his faces are short and pointed and chins small and rounded. The eye, often shown without an eyebrow, may be a strong oval shape or just a curved top line with a dark eye attached. Bodies of his deity figures have a compact, chunky look, with arms and legs slightly rounded. Hands are large, with prominent thumbs. Knees are slightly bent, and the short, squared-off feet angle downward. While the artists tended to paint both sides of a given illustrated folio, Artist B frequently worked in tandem with Artist A.

Artist C is responsible for Xipe Totec, Teteoinnan, and Opochtli on folio 263r, Yauhqueme, Chalchiuhtlicue, and Xilonen on folio 263v, Tlacochcalco Yaotl, Cihuapipiltin, and Xochipilli on folio 266r, Chantico, Chalmecacihuatl, and Omacatl on folio 266v, *veintenas* on folio 251, and day signs on folios 286v to 303r. The frame line of Artist C, done in either brown or black ink, is weak and somewhat irregular. His drawings have a sketchy look, and his colors are correspondingly pale and watery looking. The pupils of the oval eyes are filled in; the prominent noses are often pointed and the chins recessive. His deity figures tend to lean forward, giving them an awkward, unbalanced look. The straight legs of his rather long-limbed figures also appear to dangle, with the large, squared-off feet pointing downward. Hands are often disproportionally small and poorly drawn, although the outstretched hands of one female deity display long, curved fingers.

Artist D is responsible for Zapotlantenan, Cihuacoatl, and Huixtocihuatl on folio 264r, Coatlicue, Amimitl, and Tomiyauhtecuhtli on folio 264v, and *veintenas* on folio 253r. The frame line of Artist D is strong, dark, and even. His deity figures appear upright and sturdy, if somewhat static, an effect conveyed not only by the erectness of the figure but also by the generally flat-footed placement of the feet, as if on an imaginary ground line. Occasionally, however, the feet turn slightly downward. The eye is a strong oval, sometimes with no eyebrow indicated. The chin is small and rounded, and the small nose sometimes turns slightly upward. Legs are rather short and straight, with the toes of the short feet very even. Despite his skill, Artist D apparently worked only on the first gathering of Chapter I.

Artist E is responsible for Atlahua, Nappatecuhtli, and Totoltecatl on folio 265r, Macuiltochtli, Macuilxochitl, and Tezcacoac Ayopechtli on folio 265v, *veintenas* on folio 252, astronomical and meteorological images on folios 282r to 283r, and year signs on folios 283r to 286r. The frame line of Artist E is thin, confident, and fluid. His deity figures convey an impression of movement and appear to be striding forward. This adept artist frequently disregards the underdrawings, and his figures have a sketchy, unfilled-in look. The head is sometimes slightly large in proportion to the body, and occasionally the contours of the body are gently rounded, with knees somewhat flexed. Feet are rather large, and hands are sometimes poorly drawn. Distinctive facial features include a rounded eye with pupils sometimes left unfilled and an "overbite," with the upper lip protruding beyond the lower one. A major contributor to Chapters I and II, Artist E does not appear in later sections of the manuscript.

In the Academy manuscript, apparently only artists A, B, and C continued to work, often in collaboration, on the ruler figures of Chapter III. In this section the small size and more cursory execution of most figures make firm identification of the artists somewhat problematical. Artist A can be credited with rulers on folios 51r and 53r (lower six), ruler advisors on folio 54r, and the two elegant figures on folios 55v and 56r. Artist B painted rulers on folios 51v (upper five) and 53v (upper seven). Artist C contributed ruler figures on folios 51v (lower three), 52, and 53r (upper four) and advisors on folio 53v (lower four). The male and female figures of folios 61v and 65 are probably the work of Artist B painting in a Europeanized mode that incorporates such novel features as a cursive line and contour shading to lend three-dimensional volume to the two-dimensional depiction of the human form standard in pre-Hispanic painting.

The images of warrior attire in Chapter IV also vary in style and execution from the other drawings. Notable differences include outlining in brown rather than the usual black ink and the use of more opaque, thickly applied colors. Torsos of the six costumed warriors are robust, although the arms are short and thin and the fingers and toes small and poorly defined. Characteristic facial features include strongly outlined oval eyes and a heavy, rounded jaw. While the firm outlining of the figures most closely resembles that of Artist D, these images more likely represent the work of a new artist, Artist F.

Altogether it appears that six artists drew the images of the *Primeros Memoriales.* Five of them participated in creating Chapter I, the most pictorially ambitious section of the manuscript. Only Artists C and E undertook the numerous, if somewhat repetitive, drawings of Chapter II. In the Academy manuscript, Artists A, B, and C rendered the images of Chapter III without the help of Artist D or E. To compensate for the absence of two of the original group of artists, the new Artist F may have been added to work on the warrior array of Chapter IV.

The execution of this section by a different hand further distinguishes this chapter from the rest of the manuscript, a problem faced by Paso y Troncoso when he extracted the *Primeros Memoriales* folios from the *Códices Matritenses.* His attempt to insert it into the manuscript at what he felt was the appropriate place resulted in an interruption in the text into which he placed it.

Whereas Sahagún's remarks on the production of the *Historia,* cited earlier, emphasize the cohesiveness of his production team, changes in personnel evident in the drawings of the *Primeros Memoriales* manuscript indicate that the initial group in Tepepolco may have been more loosely knit. In my opinion, the grouping of artists in certain chapters supports the conclusion, based on watermarks, that chapters were worked on sequentially and as units with intervals separating the artistic campaigns. My proposed identification of the artists as a group separate from the scribes or informants also implies that a greater number of indigenous workers contributed to the making of the

Primeros Memoriales than has previously been recognized. The hypothesis that local Tepepolco artists painted the images of the *Primeros Memoriales* also directs new attention to the contributions that may have been made by the inhabitants of this town, who have hitherto been cited only as informants. Although the six artists who painted the *Primeros Memoriales* varied in ability and did not attain the achievements of pre-Conquest painting masters, they nevertheless fulfilled their tasks admirably. Working over a period of years under the direction of Sahagún and in collaboration with the manuscript's scribes and other contributors to the project, these capable and diligent artists created an invaluable pictorial record of a rich and still vividly remembered pre-Hispanic past.

TABLE 1
Contents of the *Primeros Memoriales*
Chapter I: Rituals and Gods

Paragraph	Folios	Subject	Image/Text Format
Palace Manuscript			
[1]	Missing		
2A	250r–253r	Festivities of the Gods (18 *Veintenas*)	18 scenes Image related description
2B	253v–254r	Atamalcualiztli Feast	Full-page image Image-related description
3A	254v	How the Gods Were Served: Offerings	6 single figures Heading/description
3B	255r–255v (part)	Blood Offerings	8 single figures Heading/description
3C	255v (part)–256r (part)	Other Offerings	4 single figures; 1 group Heading/description
3D	256r (part)–256v (part)	Ritual Practices	No images Heading/description
3E	256v (part)–257v	Other Practices	No images Heading/description
	258r blank		
4	258v–260v	Those Who Served in the Temples	No images Heading/description
5A	261r–267r	How Each of the Gods Was Arrayed	41 single figures Image-related description
5B	267v	[Array of Priests]	2 sketches No text
6	268r	Ritual Items	No images Word list
7	268v–269r	Temple Structures	Full-page image Word list
8	269v	Of Some of the Gods' Wrath	No images Paragraph heading only
9	270r	Names of the God-keepers	No images Word list
10	270v–271r	Things Attributed to the Gods	No images Word list
11	271v–272r	How the Sun Was Served	No images Paragraph form
12	272v	Tasks Performed in Temples	No images Heading/description
13	273r	Supplications and Oaths	No images Paragraph form
14	273v–281v	Songs of the Gods	No images Song/statement

Note: See Nicholson 1973 for related Tables 5–8 with correlations of folios and Paso y Troncoso's pagination, the relationship of paragraphs to Books in the *Florentine Codex*, and major translations to circa 1970. Paragraphs are as determined by Paso y Troncoso (Sahagún 1905–1907, VI: 1–176)

TABLE 2
Contents of the *Primeros Memoriales*
Chapter II: The Heavens and the Underworld

Paragraph	Folios	Subject	Image/Text Format
Palace Manuscript			
1	282r–282v (part)	Celestial Bodies	12 single figures Image-related statements
2	282v (part)–283r (part)	Meteorological Phenomena	8 single figures Image-related descriptions
3	283r (part)–286r (part)	The Year Count (52-Year Cycle)	53 single figures Image-related names
4	286r (part)–303r	The Day Count (260-Day Cycle)	261 single figures Image-related names/statement
5A	303v	Auguries	No images Statement
Academy Manuscript			
5A	85r	Auguries (cont.)	No images Statement
5B	85v	Dreams	No images
6	84r–84v (part)	What Was Consumed in Mictlan	No images Statement
7	84v (part)	Offerings Dedicated to Mictlantecuhtli and Mictecacihuatl	No images Statement

TABLE 3
Contents of the *Primeros Memoriales*
Chapter III: Rulership

Paragraph	Folios	Subject	Image/Text Format
Academy Manuscript			
1A	51r–52r (part)	Those Who Ruled Mexico Tenochtitlan	16 single figures Glosses/image-related text
1B	52r (part)–53r (part)	The Rulers of Tetzcoco	13 single figures Glosses/image-related text
1C	53r (part)–53v (part)	The Rulers of Huexotla	13 single figures Glosses/image-related text
2	53v (part)–54r (part)	Names of Rulers' Aides and Keepers of the Gods	2 groups, 2 pairs Image-related names
3	54r (part)–54v (part)	Duties of the Ruler	Word list/paragraph form
4	54v (part)–55r	Food and Drink of Rulers and Noblewomen	No images Word list
5	55v–56r (part)	Adornments of Rulers and Noblewomen	4 single figures Word list
6	56r (part)–56v (part)	Adornments of Rulers When They Danced	No images Word list
7	56v (part)	Amusements of Rulers	No images Word list
8	56v (part)–57r (part)	Articles the Noblewomen Worked with	No images Word list
9	57r (part)–57v (part)	The Rulers' Houses	No images Word list
10	57v (part)	Articles for the Rulers' Houses	No images Word list
11	58r–58v	Names of Evil Men	No images Word list/paragraph form
12	59r	Names of Evil Women	No images Word list/paragraph form
13	59v	How Youths and Maidens Were Reared	No images Paragraph form
14	60r–61r	How the Chichimeca Came Forth from Seven Caves	No images Paragraph form
15	61v–64v	How They Admonished the People	12 single figures Paragraph form
16	65r–65v (part)	How the Ruler Became Angry	1 figure Paragraph form
17	65v (part)–66r	How the Ruler Felt Compassion for the People	1 figure Paragraph form
	66v blank		
	67 blank		

TABLE 4
Contents of the *Primeros Memoriales*
Chapter IV: Things Relative to Man

Paragraph	Folios	Subject	Image/Text Format
Academy Manuscript			
1	82r (part)	Lineage Terms	No images Word list/paragraph form
2	82r (part)	Male and Female Terms	No images Word list/brief description
3	82r (part)–82v (part)	Names Appropriate Only to Males	No images Word list
4	82v (part)	Names Appropriate Only to Females	No images Word list
5	82v (part)–83r	Exterior Parts of the Body	No images Word list/statement
6	83v (part)	Interior Parts of the Body	No images Word list/statement
7	83v (part)–68r (part)	Designations for Illustrious People	No images Word list/statement
8A	68r (part)	Military Insignia and Accouterments of Rulers and Captains	No images Word list/description
8B	68v–69r (part)	Military Insignia and Accouterments of Warriors	No images Word list/description
9	69r (part)–69v	Diseases and Cures	No images
10	70r	Words with Which Nobles Greet and Quarrel with One Another	No images Paragraph form
11	70v–71r	How Commoners Greet and Quarrel with One Another	No images Paragraph form
	71v	Blank	
(8)	72r–80r[1]	Military Insignia and Accouterments (Illustrations)	67 single figures Image-related word list/ description
	80v	Blank	
(9)	81r–81v[2]	Diseases and Cures	Word list (disease)/ Statement (cure)
	86r–87v	Blank	

1. Arranging the folios by content, Paso y Troncoso placed folios 72–80 after folio 68, followed by folio 69.
2. Paso y Troncoso placed folio 81 after folio 69, followed by folios 70–71.

TABLE 5
Images of the *Primeros Memoriales*

Paragraph	Folio	Image
Chapter I: Rituals and Gods Palace Ms.		
2A Festivities of the Gods (Veintena Feasts)	250r	Cuahuitl ehua[1] (the Tlalocs honored; children sacrificed) Tlacaxipehualiztli (captives and slaves flayed) Tozoztontli (offering of flowers and roasted snakes)
	250v	Hueytozoztli (maize plant honored) Toxcatl (Tezcatlipoca, Yacatecuhtli, Huitzilopochtli honored) Etzalcualiztli (Tlaloc honored; impersonator sacrificed)
	251r	Tecuilhuitontli (Huixtocihuatl impersonator sacrificed) Hueytecuilhuitl (Xilonen and Cihuacoatl impersonators sacrificed) Miccailhuitontli (procuring and setting up *xocotl* pole)
	251v	Hueymiccailhuitl (*xocotl* pole ceremonies) Ochpaniztli (Teteoinnan impersonator sacrificed)
	252r	Teteoeco (arrival of the gods; offerings of first fruits) Tepeilhuitl (mountain gods honored) Quecholli (Mixcoatl honored)
	252v	Panquetzaliztli (Huitzilopochtli honored) Atemoztli (Tepictoton dough mountain deity images honored and sacrificed)
	253r	Tititl (dancing ceremony of deity impersonators) Izcalli (Ixcozauhqui impersonator sacrificed; ceremonies for children)
2B Atamalcualiztli	254r	Atamalcualiztli
3A How the Gods Were Served	254v	Offerings (of food, capes, animals) Offering of Fire The Throwing of Incense Eating Earth Casting [of Food] Libation
3B Blood Offerings	255r	Human Sacrifice The Passing of Twigs The Passing of Straws Offering of Thorns The Drawing of Blood The Cutting of the Ear [Lobes] Decapitating [Birds]
	255v (part)	Feeding [the Gods]
3C Other Offerings	255v (part)	Payment [to the Gods] The Laying of Fir Branches The Ritual Making of Bundles of Wood Sweeping
5A How Each of the Gods Was Arrayed	261r	The Array of Huitzilopochtli The Array of Painal The Array of Tezcatlipoca
	261v	The Array of Quetzalcoatl The Array of the Totochtin The Array of Tlaloc
	262r	The Array of Chicomecoatl The Array of Otontecuhtli The Array of Yacatecuhtli

TABLE 5 *(continued)*

Paragraph	Folio	Image
	262v	The Array of (Atlahua) Chachalmeca[2]
		The Array of Ixcozauhqui
		The Array of Ixtlilton
	263r	The Array of Xipe
		The Array of Teteoinnan
		The Array of Opochtli
	263v	The Array of Yauhqueme
		The Array of Chalchiuhtlicue
		The Array of Xilonen
	264r	The Array of Zapotlantenan
		The Array of Cihuacoatl
		The Array of Huixtocihuatl
	264v	The Array of Coatlicue
		The Array of Amimitl
		The Array of Tomiyauhtecuhtli
	265r	The Array of Atlahua
		The Array of Nappatecuhtli
		The Array of Totoltecatl
	265v	The Array of Macuiltochtli
		The Array of Macuilxochitl
		The Array of Tezcacoac Ayopechtli
	266r	The Array Tlacochcalco Yaotl
		The Array of Cihuapipiltin
		The Array of Xochipilli
	266v	The Array of Chantico
		The Array of Chalmecacihuatl
		The Array of Omacatl
	267r	The Array of the Tepictoton:
		Popocatepetl (Tlaloc)
		Iztactepetl
		Matlalcueye
		Chalchiuhtlicue
		Quetzalcoatl
5B	267v	Unidentified Priest
[Array of Priests]		Unidentified Priest
7	269r	Temple Precinct with Structures
Temple Structures		
Chapter II: The Heavens and the Underworld		
1	282r	The Sun
Celestial Bodies		The Moon
		Eclipse of the Sun
		Eclipse of the Moon
		The Fire Sticks (constellation)
		The Many (constellation)
		The Market (constellation)
		The Morning Star (Venus)
		The Comet
		The Shooting Star
	282v (part)	S-Shaped Constellation
		Scorpion
2	282v (part)	The Winds
Meteorological		Lightning
Phenomena		Rain
		Rainbow
		Frost

TABLE 5 *(continued)*

Paragraph	Folio	Image
	283r (part)	Clouds
		Snow
		Hail
3	283r (part)	1 Tochtli (1 Rabbit)
The Year Count		2 Acatl (2 Reed)
(52-Year Cycle)		3 Tecpatl (3 Flint Knife)
		4 Calli (4 House)
		5 Tochtli (5 Rabbit)
		6 Acatl (6 Reed)
		7 Tecpatl (7 Flint Knife)
	283v	8 Calli (8 House)
		9 Tochtli (9 Rabbit)
		10 Acatl (10 Reed)
		11 Tecpatl (11 Flint Knife)
		12 Calli (12 House)
		13 Tochtli (13 Rabbit)
		1 Acatl (1 Reed)
		2 Tecpatl (2 Flint Knife)
		3 Calli (3 House)
		4 Tochtli (4 Rabbit)
	284r	5 Acatl (5 Reed)
		6 Tecpatl (6 Flint Knife)
		7 Calli (7 House)
		8 Tochtli (8 Rabbit)
		9 Acatl (9 Reed)
		10 Tecpatl (10 Flint Knife)
		11 Calli (11 House)
		12 Tochtli (12 Rabbit)
		13 Acatl (13 Reed)
	284v	1 Tecpatl (1 Flint Knife)
		2 Calli (2 House)
		3 Tochtli (3 Rabbit)
		4 Acatl (4 Reed)
		5 Tecpatl (5 Flint Knife)
		6 Calli (6 House)
		7 Tochtli (7 Rabbit)
		8 Acatl (8 Reed)
	285r	9 Tecpatl (9 Flint Knife)
		10 Calli (10 House)
		11 Tochtli (11 Rabbit)
		12 Acatl (12 Reed)
		13 Tecpatl (13 Flint Knife)
		1 Calli (1 House)
		2 Tochtli (2 Rabbit)
	285v	3 Acatl (3 Reed)
		4 Tecpatl (4 Flint Knife)
		5 Calli (5 House)
		6 Tochtli (6 Rabbit)
		7 Acatl (7 Reed)
		8 Tecpatl (8 Flint Knife)
		9 Calli (9 House)
		10 Tochtli (10 Rabbit)
	286r (part)	11 Acatl (11 Reed)
		12 Tecpatl (12 Flint Knife)
		13 Calli (13 House)
		1 Tochtli (1 Rabbit)

TABLE 5 *(continued)*

Paragraph	Folio	Image
4	286v	1 Itzcuintli (1 Dog)
The Day Count		2 Ozomatli (2 Monkey)
(260-Day Cycle)		3 Malinalli (3 Grass)
		4 Acatl (4 Reed)
		5 Ocelotl (5 Jaguar)
		6 Cuauhtli (6 Eagle)
		7 Cozcacuauhtli (7 Vulture)
		8 Ollin (8 Movement)
		9 Tecpatl (9 Flint Knife)
	287r	10 Quiahuitl (10 Rain)
		11 Xochitl (11 Flower)
		12 Cipactli (12 Crocodilian Monster)
		13 Ehecatl (13 Wind)
		1 Calli (1 House)
		2 Cuetzpallin (2 Lizard)
		3 Coatl (3 Snake)
	287v	4 Miquiztli (4 Death)
		5 Mazatl (5 Deer)
		6 Tochtli (6 Rabbit)
		7 Atl (7 Water)
		8 Itzcuintli (8 Dog)
		9 Ozomatli (9 Monkey)
		10 Malinalli (10 Grass)
		11 Acatl (11 Reed)
		12 Ocelotl (12 Jaguar)
		13 Cuauhtli (13 Eagle)
	288r	1 Cozcacuauhtli (1 Vulture)
		2 Calli (2 House)[3] [2 Ollin]
		3 Tecpatl (3 Flint Knife)
		4 Quiahuitl (4 Rain)
		5 Xochitl (5 Flower)
		6 Cipactli (6 Crocodilian Monster)
		7 Ehecatl (7 Wind)
		8 Calli (8 House)
		9 Cuetzpallin (9 Lizard)
	288v	10 Coatl (10 Snake)
		11 Miquiztli (11 Death)
		12 Macatl (12 Deer)
		13 Tochtli (13 Rabbit)
		1 Atl (1 Water)
		2 Itzcuintli (2 Dog)
		3 Ozomatli (3 Monkey)
	297r[4]	4 Malinalli (4 Grass)
		5 Acatl (5 Reed)
		6 Ocelotl (6 Jaguar)
		7 Cuauhtli (7 Eagle)
		8 Cozcacuauhtli (8 Vulture)
		9 Ollin (9 Movement)
		10 Tecpatl (10 Flint Knife)
		11 Quiahuitl (11 Rain)
		12 Xochitl (12 Flower)
	297v	13 Cipactli (12 Crocodilian Monster)
		1 Ehecatl (1 Wind)
		2 Calli (2 House)
		3 Cuetzpallin (3 Lizard)
		4 Coatl (4 Snake)

TABLE 5 *(continued)*

Paragraph	Folio	Image
		5 Miquiztli (5 Death)
		6 Mazatl (6 Deer)
	298r	7 Tochtli (7 Rabbit)
		8 Atl (8 Water)
		9 Itzcuintli (9 Dog)
		10 Ozomatli (10 Monkey)
		11 Malinalli (11 Grass)
		12 Acatl (12 Reed)
		13 Ocelotl (13 Jaguar)
	298v	1 Cuauhtli (1 Eagle)
		2 Cozcacuauhtli (2 Vulture)
		3 Ollin (3 Movement)
		4 Tecpatl (4 Flint Knife)
		5 Quiahuitl (5 Rain)
		6 Xochitl (6 Flower)
		7 Cipactli (7 Crocodilian Monster)
		8 Ehecatl (8 Wind)
		9 Calli (9 House)
		10 Cuetzpallin (10 Lizard)
	299r	11 Coatl (11 Snake)
		12 Miquiztli (12 Death)
		13 Mazatl (13 Deer)
		1 Tochtli (1 Rabbit)
		2 Atl (2 Water)
		3 Itzcuintli (3 Dog)
		4 Ozomatli (4 Monkey)
	299v	5 Malinalli (5 Grass)
		6 Acatl (6 Reed)
		7 Ocelotl (7 Jaguar)
		8 Cuauhtli (8 Eagle)
		9 Cozcacuauhtli (9 Vulture)
		10 Ollin (11 Movement)
		11 Tecpatl (11 Flint Knife)
		12 Quiahuitl (12 Rain)
		13 Xochitl (13 Flower)
	300r	1 Cipactl (1 Crocodilian Monster)
		2 Ehecatl (2 Wind)
		3 Calli (3 House)
		4 Cuetzallin (4 Lizard)
		5 Coatl (5 Snake)
		6 Miquiztli (6 Death)
		7 Mazatl (7 Deer)
	300v	8 Tochtli (8 Rabbit)
		9 Atl (9 Water)
		10 Itzcuintli (10 Dog)
		11 Ozomatli (11 Monkey)
		12 Malinalli (12 Grass)
		13 Acatl (13 Reed)
	289r	1 Ocelotl (1 Jaguar)
		2 Cuauhtli (2 Eagle)
		3 Cozcacuauhtli (3 Vulture)
		4 Ollin (4 Ollin)
		5 Tecpatl (5 Flint Knife)
		6 Quiahuitl (6 Rain)
		7 Xochitl (7 Flower)
		8 Cipactli (8 Crocodilian Monster)

TABLE 5 *(continued)*

Paragraph	Folio	Image
		9 Ehecatl (9 Wind)
		10 Calli (10 House)
	289v	11 Cuetzpallin (11 Lizard)
		12 Coatl (12 Snake)
		13 Miquiztli (13 Death)
		1 Mazatl (1 Deer)
		2 Tochtli (2 Rabbit)
		3 Atl (3 Water)
		4 Itzcuintli (4 Dog)
	290r	5 Ozomatli (5 Monkey)
		6 Malinalli (6 Grass)
		7 Acatl (7 Reed)
		8 Ocelotl (8 Jaguar)
		9 Cuauhtli (9 Eagle)
		10 Cozcacuauhtli (10 Vulture)
		11 Ollin (11 Ollin)
		12 Tecpatl (12 Flint Knife)
		13 Quiahuitl (13 Rain)
	290v	1 Xochitl (1 Flower)
		2 Cipactli (2 Crocodilian Monster)
		3 Ehecatl (3 Wind)
		4 Calli (4 House)
		5 Cuetzpallin (5 Lizard)
		6 Coatl (6 Snake)
		7 Miquiztli (7 Death)
	291r	8 Mazatl (8 Deer)
		9 Tochtli (9 Rabbit)
		10 Atl (10 Water)
		11 Itzcuintli (11 Dog)
		12 Ozomatli (12 Monkey)
		13 Malinalli (13 Grass)
	291v	1 Acatl (1 Reed)
		2 Ocelotl (2 Jaguar)
		3 Cuauhtli (3 Eagle)
		4 Cozcacuauhtli (4 Vulture)
		5 Ollin (5 Movement)
		6 Tecpatl (6 Flint Knife)
		7 Quiahuitl (7 Rain)
		8 Xochitl (8 Flower)
		9 Cipactli (9 Crocodilian Monster)
		10 Ehecatl (10 Wind)
	292r	11 Calli (11 House)
		12 Cuetzpallin (12 Lizard)
		13 Coatl (13 Snake)
		1 Miquiztli (1 Death)
		2 Mazatl (2 Deer)
		3 Tochtli (3 Rabbit)
		4 Atl (4 Water)
	292v	5 Itzcuintli (5 Dog)
		6 Ozomatli (6 Monkey)
		7 Malinalli (7 Grass)
		8 Acatl (8 Reed)
		9 Ocelotl (9 Jaguar)
		10 Cuauhtli (10 Eagle)
		11 Cozcacuauhtli (11 Vulture)
		12 Ollin (12 Movement)

TABLE 5 *(continued)*

Paragraph	Folio	Image
		13 Tecpatl (13 Flint Knife)
	293r	1 Quiahuitl (1 Rain)
		2 Xochitl (2 Flower)
		3 Cipactli (3 Crocodilian Monster)
		4 Ehecatl (4 Wind)
		5 Calli (5 House)
		6 Cuetzpallin (6 Lizard)
		7 Coatl (7 Snake)
	293v	8 Miquiztli (8 Death)
		9 Mazatl (9 Deer)
		10 Tochtli (10 Rabbit)
		11 Atl (11 Water)
		12 Itzcuintli (12 Dog)
		13 Ozomatli (13 Monkey)
	294r	1 Malinalli (1 Grass)
		2 Acatl (2 Reed)
		3 Ocelotl (3 Jaguar)
		4 Cuauhtli (4 Eagle)
		5 Cozcacuauhtli (5 Vulture)
		6 Ollin (6 Movement)
		7 Tecpatl (7 Flint Knife)
		8 Quiahuitl (8 Rain)
		9 Xochitl (9 Flower)
	294v	10 Cipactli (10 Crocodilian Monster)
		11 Ehecatl (11 Wind)
		12 Calli (12 House)
		13 Cuetzpallin (13 Lizard)
		1 Coatl (1 Snake)
		2 Miquiztli (2 Death)
	295r	3 Mazatl (3 Deer)
		4 Tochtli (4 Rabbit)
		5 Atl (5 Water)
		6 Itzcuintli (6 Dog)
		7 Ozomatli (7 Monkey)
		8 Malinalli (8 Grass)
		9 Acatl (9 Reed)
		10 Ocelotl (10 Jaguar)
		11 Cuauhtli (11 Eagle)
		12 Cozcacuauhtli (12 Vulture)
		13 Ollin (13 Movement)
	295v	1 Tecpatl (1 Flint Knife)
		2 Quiahuitl (2 Rain)
		3 Xochitl (3 Flower)
		4 Cipactli (4 Crocodilian Monster)
		5 Ehecatl (5 Wind)
		6 Calli (6 House)
		7 Cuetzpallin (7 Lizard)
	296r	8 Coatl (8 Snake)
		9 Miquiztli (9 Death)
		10 Mazatl (10 Deer)
		11 Tochtli (11 Rabbit)
		12 Atl (12 Water)
		13 Itzcuintli (13 Dog)
	296v	1 Ozomatli (1 Monkey)
		2 Malinalli (2 Grass)
		3 Acatl (3 Reed)

TABLE 5 *(continued)*

Paragraph	Folio	Image
		4 Ocelotl (4 Jaguar)
		5 Cuauhtli (5 Eagle)
		6 Cozcacuauhtli (6 Vulture)
		7 Ollin (7 Movement)
		8 Tecpatl (8 Flint Knife)
	301r	9 Quiahuitl (9 Rain)
		10 Xochitl (10 Flower)
		11 Cipactli (11 Crocodilian Monster)
		12 Ehecatl (12 Wind)
		13 Calli (13 House)
	301v	1 Cuetzpallin (1 Lizard)
		2 Coatl (2 Snake)
		3 Miquiztli (3 Death)
		4 Mazatl (4 Deer)
		5 Tochtli (5 Rabbit)
		6 Atl (6 Water)
		7 Itzcuintli (7 Dog)
		8 Ozomatli (8 Monkey)
	302r	9 Malinalli (9 Grass)
		10 Acatl (10 Reed)
		11 Ocelotl (11 Jaguar)
		12 Cuauhtli (12 Eagle)
		13 Cozcacuauhtli (13 Vulture)
	302v	1 Ollin (1 Movement)
		2 Tecpatl (2 Flint Knife)
		3 Quiahuitl (3 Rain)
		4 Xochitl (4 Flower)
		5 Cipactli (5 Crocodilian Monster)
		6 Ehecatl (6 Wind)
		7 Calli (7 House)
		8 Cuetzpallin (8 Lizard)
	303r	9 Coatl (9 Snake)
		10 Miquiztli (10 Death)
		11 Mazatl (11 Deer)
		12 Tochtli (12 Rabbit)
		13 Atl (13 Water)
		1 Itzcuintli (1 Dog)
Chapter III: Rulership		
Academy Ms.		
1A	51r	Acamapichtli
Those Who Ruled		Huitzilihiutl
Mexico Tenochtitlan		Chimalpopoca
		Itzcoatl
		Motecuhzoma Ilhuicamina
		Axayacatl
	51v	Tizoc
		Ahuitzotl
		Motecuhzoma II
		Cuitlahuac
		Cuauhtemoc
		Motelchiuhtzin
		Xochiquentzin
		Huanitzin
	52r (part)	Don Diego Tehuetzquititzin
		Don Cristóbal

TABLE 5 *(continued)*

Paragraph	Folio	Image
1B	52r (part)	Tlaltecatzin
The Rulers of		Techotlalatzin
Tetzcoco		Ixtlilxochitl
		Nezahualcoyotl
		Nezahualpilli
	52v	Cacamatzin
		Coanacochtli (Coanacochtzin)
		Tecocoltli
		Ixtlilxochitl
	53r (part)	Yoyontzin
		Tetlauhehuetzquititzin
		Don Antonio Tlahuitoltzin
		Don Hernando Pimentel
1C	53r (part)	Mazatzin
The Rulers of		Tochintecuhtli
Huexotla		Ayotzintecuhtli
		Cuatlahuice
		Totomotzin
		Yaotzintecuhtli
	53v (part)	Xilotzin
		Itlacauhtzin
		Tlazolyaotzin
		Tzontemoctzin
		Cuitlahuatzin
		Tzapocuetzin
		Cuitlahuatzin
2	53v (part)	Group of 4 Ruler Aides
Names of Rulers'	54r (part)	Unidentified Pair
Aides and the		Unidentified Pair
Keepers of the Gods		Ruler and 4 Aides
5	55v	Nobleman
Adornment of Rulers		2 Mantles
and Noblewomen		
	56r	Noblewoman
15	61v	Group of 12 Males and Females
How They Admonished		
the People		
16	65r	Male Figure
17	65v	Male Figure
Chapter IV: Things Relative to Man		
8	72r	[Battle] Accouterments of Ruler/Nobleman
Military Insignia		[Battle] Accouterments of Ruler/Nobleman
and Accouterments		
	72v	[Battle] Accouterments of Nobleman
		Warrior's Insignia
	73r	Warrior's Insignia
		Warrior's Insignia
	73v	Quetzal [Feather] Banner
		Troupial [Feather] Banner
		Quetzal [Feather] Horns
		Quetzal [Feather Headdress]
		Quetzal [Feather Headdress]
	74r	Quetzal Bird [Insignia]
		[Feather] Butterfly [Insignia]
		Troupial [Feather] Sun [Insignia]
		Two-Rabbit Insignia
	74v	Warping Frame [Insignia]

TABLE 5 *(continued)*

Paragraph	Folio	Image
		Troupial [Feather] Butterfly [Insignia]
		Gold Drum [Insignia]
		Red Coyote [Insignia]
	75r	Turquoise Coyote Insignia
		Quetzal [Feather] Conical Headpiece
		White Coyote [Insignia]
		Water Ears [Insignia]
	75v	Eagle's Foot Shield
		Jaguar Foot Shield
		Silver Stones Shield
		Cleft Quetzal [Feather] Shield
		Golden Beetle Necklace
		Gold Palm Ear Plug
	76r	Red Parrot [Feather] Tunic
		Red Xolotl Head [Insignia]
		White Xolotl Head [Insignia]
		Compressed Dart [Insignia]
	76v	Compressed Macaw [Feather Insignia]
		Compressed Crow [Feather Insignia]
		Crackling Fire [Insignia]
		Red Feather Ball
	77r	White Feather Ball
		Five Flag [Insignia]
		Heron [Feather] Hair [Insignia]
		Heron [Feather] Conical Headpiece
	77v	Yellow Parrot [Feather] Serpentine [Insignia]
		Colored Arrowhead [Insignia]
		Black Butterfly [Insignia]
		Straw Hut [Insignia]
	78r	Masonry House [Insignia]
		Grass Hut [Insignia]
		Fretful Child [Insignia]
		Bundle [Insignia]
	78v	Thigh-skin Mask Insignia
		Obsidian Butterfly [Insignia]
		Maguey Fiber Pulling Board [Insignia]
		Turkey Cock [Insignia]
	79r	Transverse Banner [Insignia]
		Red Coyote [Insignia]
		Fire Coyote [Insignia]
		Shield Insignia
	79v	Star-studded Coyote [Insignia]
		Black Coyote [Insignia]
		Curved Eye Shield
		Star-studded Shield
	80r	Shield with Curved Lip Ornament
		Blue Disk Shield
		Hand Shield
		Shield with Feather Border
		Shield with Open Feather Border
		Whitened Shield

1. See Nicholson 1971: Table 9 for the meaning of the names of the *veintena* feasts.

2. The "Atlahua" heading of the deity array is a scribal error. The deity described and depicted is Chachalmeca; his image is correctly glossed.

3. Incorrectly drawn day sign. Two Calli (House) should be 2 Ollin (Movement).

4. Folios 297–300 are out of order. Corrected by Paso y Troncoso.

Primeros Memoriales

PALEOGRAPHY OF NAHUATL TEXT AND ENGLISH TRANSLATION

CHAPTER I
RITUALS AND GODS

PARAGRAPH 2A
[fol. 250r]

[Prefatory note: It has been generally agreed that the information contained in this paragraph concerning the major rituals conducted during the eighteen annual *veintena* ceremonies was provided by Sahagún's Tepepolco informants. He later collected more detailed accounts of the *veintena* ceremonies in Tlatelolco—which, although basically similar, differed significantly in some features from those gathered in this northern Acolhuaque community. The Tlatelolco versions appear in Book 2 of Sahagún's final product, the *Historia* (Sahagún 1975: 70–183; 1981; 1988, I: 77–199). For a comprehensive, annotated listing of most of both the textual and pictorial versions of the Central Mexican annual *veintena* ceremonies, see Kubler and Gibson 1951. For a concise summary of the principal rituals conducted in each *veintena*, see Nicholson 1971: Table 4.

Seler (1899a: passim) was the first to publish a paleography of the Nahuatl text of this paragraph, with German translation and uncolored line drawings of the illustrations—but only of the first five *veintenas*—which were interpreted and discussed. After his death, his widow published his Nahuatl transcription and German translation of the entire paragraph, with line drawings of the illustrations of all of the *veintenas* (Seler 1927: 54–251, passim). In 1948, Garibay published another paleography of the Nahuatl text, Spanish translation, and re-publication of the Seler drawings. Jiménez Moreno in 1974 published, with extensive notes, a new paleography of the Nahuatl text and a Spanish translation (except for Atamalcualiztli, for which he reprinted Garibay's translation), with colored versions of the illustrations, which he described and interpreted.—HBN]

Jnic ij. ipan mitoa ym inilhuiuh, in teteu.

Quavitl eoa, yn ipan i, ilhuiquixtililoya, in tlalloque: ioã nextlavaloya, ỹ noviã tepeticpac mochi tlacatl in maçeoalli:

ipan vmpevaya ỹ cecempoallapualli yn ce xivitl, auh macuililhuitl y ça nen vntemj.

Second [paragraph], in which are told the festivities of the gods.

In Cuahuitl ehua, "The Raising of the Pole," a festival was celebrated in honor of the Tlalocs,[1] and the debt[2] was paid [to them], everyone, all the commoners, [paid it] everywhere on the mountaintops.

At this time, the count of the twenty-day periods of the year and the five extra days began.

1. Tlaloque (pl. of Tlaloc): These deities, believed to dwell on hills and mountaintops, were the preeminent rain deities. See note 19, Paragraph 5A.

2. Propitiatory sacrifice was conceived of as payment of a "debt" to the gods.

Yn. y. ilhuitl qujçaya ipan ic cemjlhvitl hebrero: in ipan ilhuitl i miquia in pipiltzitzinti motenevaya tlacateteuhme ỹ vmpa tepeticpac: ioã in calpã novian moq̃quetzaya in matlaquauhpitzaoac, itech mopipiloaya in amatl, holtica, tlacuiloli, motenevaya amatetehvitl.

This festival fell on the first day of February.[3] In this festival little children, called "human sacrificial papers," died there on the mountaintops, and in the homes everywhere thin net poles were erected on which were hung papers with designs painted with liquid rubber, called *amatetehuitl.*

Auh in iquac ye onaquiz tonatiuh. auh in iqc teteuhxallaquilo, vncã mochi quivalcuja, ycalpã mochivaya tetevitl. vncã onevaya in tepeticpac ic omoxtlavaya macevalli in vncã diablo jtoalco, muchintin q'valcuia in macevalti, in pipilti, in tetecuhti, ipãpa ỹ motenevaya teteuhxalaquilloya: ioã tlayavaloloya, auh in tlalloca vevetqz teyacanaya valtenanamictivia ynic tlayavaloloya: quiqueq̃chpanotihvi ỹ inteteuh.

Just before sundown[4] the sacrificial papers were put in the sand.[5] They took all the sacrificial papers they had prepared in their homes [and] went there to the tops of mountains.[6] In the courtyard of the temple of the devil, there the people paid their debt [to the gods]. All the commoners, noblemen, [and] lords took [the papers] there: for this reason it was called "Putting the Sacrificial Papers in the Sand." Also there was a procession. And the old [priests] of the Temple of Tlaloc led the people; they arranged the people in order; they went in procession carrying the sacrificial papers on their shoulders.

Ynic ontetl tlacaxipevaliztli iquac in miquia mamalti ioã tlatlacuti, quixipevaya, ioã iquac nemja, in xixipeme, in quimaquitinenca in imevayo ỹ oq̃xipeuhqz: ioã oncã qualoya yn vilocpalli, i. necutlaxcalli, ioã olchicalli, quiquaya ỹteteuatzitzin.

The second [festival] was Tlacaxipehualiztli, "Flaying of Men."[7] At that time captives and slaves died, [and] they flayed them. It was also when the "flayed ones" went about: those who went about wearing the skins of the flayed.[8] Also at that time cakes of uncooked maize, honey tortillas, and *olchicalli*[9] were eaten; their priests ate them.

Yn i, ilhuitl quiçaya, ypan ic cempoalli vnchiquace hebrero, yn ipan j iquac miquia ioã quĩxipevaya, mamalti, ioã tlatlacvti. Auh yn imoztlayoc: no izquintin temallacac, quinquetzaya, oncã quivavanaya quixipevaya

This festival fell on the twenty-sixth of February. At this time captives and slaves died, and they flayed them. And the following day also they stood them all on the round stone of gladiatorial sacrifice.[10] There they

3. See Prem 1988 for a recent discussion of Sahagún's differing correlations of the indigenous and Christian calendars.

4. Following *tonatiuh,* there appears to be an erasure of the words *auh in iqc.* Possibly this was intentional, as the meaning of the sentence is clear.

5. *Xalaquia,* "to put in the sand," appears to have been a metaphorical expression for a type of ceremony performed on the eve of a sacrifice; see discussion in Dibble 1980.

6. *Vncã onevaya in tepeticpac ic omoxtlavaya macevalli* is inserted in the left margin.

7. Although he is not mentioned by name here, Tlacaxipehualiztli was dedicated to the propitiation of the major martial/fertility deity, Xipe Totec. See note 48, Paragraph 5A.

8. *Oq̃xipeuhqz:* read *oquinxipeuhque.* Nasalizations were sometimes ignored; the abbreviation for *-ue* is like *z* in the manuscript.

9. *Olchicalli* is listed among the foods of the rulers in the *Florentine Codex* (Sahagún 1950–1982, Part IX [Book 8]: 138); the etymology is uncertain.

10. The *temalacatl* was a round stone with a circular perforation in the center, to which a rope was attached and tied to the victim, who, equipped with dummy weapons, attempted to defend himself against fully armed warriors. The ritual was called *tlahuahuanaliztli,* "striping." See Beyer 1920, Nicholson 1956.

Auh in imevayo oquixipeuhq̃ cequĩnti tlaca conmaquiaya, campoalilhuitl ipã mitotitinenca: ipan tequiquixtiloya in evatl, q. n. mochintin valquiçaya in macevalti vallalataya:

"striped" them, they flayed them. And some people dressed themselves in the skins of those whom they had flayed, [and] for twenty days went about in them dancing. At that time they were relieved of their skins; this means that all the commoners came out [and] saw.

ioã in iviptlayoc çacapã valnemanalo. Jn. y. iquac yancuicã neaquiloya yn imevayo tlaca, ynic mitoa çacapã, ca motzetzeloaya ỹ çacatl, in ipã quivalmanaya xixipeme, ioã moteneva ayacachpixollo auh ynic mochivaya ca vncã vmpevaya inetotiloya in jchã diablo ça no quezqui tlacatl mochi tlacatl yyayacach in ipã mitotiaya in pipilti in maçevalti auh in vmpa tianquizco vmpa onechicavia in ixq'ch macevali mochi tlacatl yyayacach yn ipã mitotiaya

And on the following day was the "Placing upon Straw." This was when for the first time the skins of the [flayed] men were donned. It was called "upon straw" for this reason: straw was strewn about; upon it they exhibited the "flayed ones," And also what was called "The Sowing of the Rattles" was done in this manner: there began the dancing in the temple of the devil. Everyone, all the noblemen and commoners, danced with their rattles; and in the market all the commoners, everyone who gathered there, danced with their rattles.

Yn ipã ilhuitl i icempoalilhuitl mochi tlacatl valcujcatequitia yn iyoyolloco altepetl, mochi tlacatl ic mochichivaya yn ica, çeçeyaca, ynechichiuh.

On the twentieth day of this festival everyone paid tribute with song in the center of the city. Everyone, each one, was arrayed in his adornments.

Jnic etetl moteneca toçoztontli, iquac xochimanaloya: ioã covaixcalmanaloya. Ynic mitoaya xochimanaloya, yehica in ixquich yancuicã cueponja, nepapa xochitl ic tlamanaloya. Auh inic moteneva covaixcalmanaloya: yehica in cocoa, tleco, moxcaya inic tlamanaloya ipan motecaya in ventli ynic vntlamanaloya yn ichã diablo, In ilhui. Auh intla aca caçiz covatl ayamo quiquaya, quin iquac in ocovaixcalmanaloc iquac vel quiquaya. Ça no iuhqui xuchitl ayayac vel quitequia, achtopa ic tlamanaloya

The third [festival] was called Tozoztontli, "The Small Vigil." At this time flowers were offered and roasted snakes were offered. It was called "The Offering of the Flowers" because all the diverse flowers first bloomed; this is why they were offered. And it was called "The Offering of the Roasted Snakes" because snakes were roasted in the fire. They were offered thus: The offerings were set down, the offerings were made in the temple of the devil.[11] And if someone were to catch a snake, he would not yet eat it. Later, after the offering of the roasted snakes was made, he could then eat it. It was the same with the flowers. No one could cut them [without] first making an offering of them.

Jnjn ilhuitl quiçaya ipã ic caxtoli omey março. Yoã mitoaya hevatlatillo inic mitoaya hevatlatilo, iquac in çempoalilhuitl oneaquiloc yn imevayo, tlaca, çatepã contlatiaya,

This festival fell on the eighteenth of March. And it was also called "The Hiding of the Skins." It was called "The Hiding of the Skins" because when the skins of the Paragraph
[flayed] men had been worn for twenty days, 2A

11. After *diablo*, the words *Jn ilhui* appear.

in vztoc contocaya, contlalpachoaya vncã palanja.

they afterwards hid them. They buried them in a cave; they covered them with earth; there they rotted.

[fol. 250v]

Vey toçoztli, iquac in motenevaya, Centeuanaloya, inic mochioaya ilhuiquixtililoya in toctli: in çeçeyaca, tlacatl, yn quezquican tocyotoc ymil, yn iuh cecentacapã, y. çeçen canaya ỹ itoc, in quezquicã ymilpã novian, çeçen canaya: auh quivalcuja yn inchã, vncan quitlamaniliaya ỹ toctli: ioan vncã Cemilhuitiaya y çeçeyaca tlacatl yn inchan pipilti, anoço maçevalti: yuh mochioaya. y. y noviã Calpan.

Huey tozoztli, "The Great Vigil," was the time called "The Taking of the God of Maize." It was performed, it was celebrated in honor of the maize plant in this manner: Wherever there were maize plants in one's fields, in every place that there were plants, each person, everyone, took a stalk of his maize. From all the maize fields everywhere, everyone took one; they took them to their homes. Then they made offerings to the maize stalks. There, nobleman or commoner spent the day; this was done everywhere in their houses.

Auh in ocemilhuiti yn inchã, ioan oquitlamaniliqz, niman yc quinmamaltiaya y çeçeme ychpupuchti concaoaya in iteupã chicomecovatl: ynic moteneva Çenteupan.

And after celebrating one day in their homes and after making the offerings, then they had each of the maidens carry [the ears of maize] on their backs. They left them in the Temple of Chicomecoatl.[12] For this reason it is called the Place of Centeotl.

Auh ynin, ilhvitl quiçaya: ypan ic chicome Abril yn metztli.

And this festival fell on the seventh of April.

Toxcatl moteneoa, iquac tlacatia ỹ tezcatlipuca: ioan yyacatecutli, Auh in ipã ilhuitl. y. amo tlacamictiloya, çan tlamanaloya, tlacutonaloya. Auh ỹ ye tevtlac, teteuhaquiaya ỹ civa, quitoznequi: in civa çeçeyaca quitquitivia ỹ imamauh tlacuiloli, holtica, quitotitivia: ioan qujtlayavalochtitivia, quiyavaloaya yn iteucal tezcatlipvca, Çan ceppa, Auh ioã ỹ amatl vncan concavaya.

[The festival] called Toxcatl[13] was when [the figures of] Tezcatlipoca[14] and Yiacatecuhtli[15] were fashioned, and in this festival no people were sacrificed. Only offerings were made, only birds were decapitated, and at sundown the women planted sacrificial papers. This means that the women, each one of them, went along dancing, carrying their papers painted in designs with liquid rubber. And they went along, winding in and

12. Chicomecoatl, "Seven Snake," a calendric name, was the fundamental maize/fertility goddess. Centeotl, "Maize Cob Deity," was sometimes employed as another designation for her but more frequently referred to the male aspect of the maize deity (cf. Nicholson 1971: 416–418). See note 25, Paragraph 5A.

13. The etymology of the word *Toxcatl* has long been a problem. The verb *toxcauia* is a verbalized noun derived from Toxcatl. Such verbs, ending in *-uia* or *-huia*, signify action executed by, with, from, or on the noun from which the verb is derived (Sullivan 1976a: 205). If the noun Toxcatl is, as Jiménez Moreno (1974: 31) suggests, a form of *tozcatl*, throat, then *titotoxcauia*, the reflexive form of the verb, could mean "we are dry in the throat" or "our throats are dry." *Tozcatl*, throat, might by extension in this context mean "parched throat." Jiménez Moreno also raised the possibility that *tozcatl* might be an archaic form of *tezcatl*, mirror, thus relating the name of the ceremony to the name of the deity, Tezcatlipoca, "Mirror's Smoke," to whom it was dedicated.

14. Tezcatlipoca was the supreme deity, the omnipotent, capricious master of human fate, in the Central Mexican pantheon at the time of the Conquest. See note 11, Paragraph 5A.

15. Yiacatecuhtli, or Yacatecuhtli, was the patron deity of the merchants. See note 32, Paragraph 5A.

out; they went in procession around the Temple of Tezcatlipoca only once and they also left the papers there.

Auh ỹ ye yovac mitoaya toxcachocholoya, in ixquichtin novian tlamacazque: ioan telpuchachcacauhti, ioã in intecuhyovã. Ceyoal, in mitotiaya, in moteneva toxcachocholoaya. Auh in ichã vitzilopuchtli, cuicoyanoloya, mitoa, necocololo: auh in civa tlanavaya mitotiaya, ipã ỹmumuchicozquj.

And at night all the priests everywhere and the young constables and their lords [danced] what was called the "Toxcatl Leap." The whole night they danced what was called the "Toxcatl Leap." And at Huitzilopochtli's[16] abode, they sang[17] and danced holding hands. It was called "Winding In and Out," and the women danced in their popcorn necklaces, their arms around each other.

Auh in ilhuitl quiçaya, ipã inic cempoali vnchicome metztli Abril.

And the festival fell on the twenty-seventh of April.

Etzalqualiztli vncã ilhuiquixtililoya ỹ tlalloc, ioan miquia. Auh inic muchivaya ilhuitl, cempoalilhuitl ỹ ciuapã cuicoya. Auh ỹ oc iuh muztla, miquiz, tlalloc; motenevaya tenanamico ioã tlayavaloloya, ioã totopatlanaitiloya: quauhtitech quimiylpiaya in totome, quitquitivia in iquac tlayaloloya, yc mitotitivia in telpupuchti. Ynin muchivaya ye teutlac, auh ceyoal in quitotiaya tlalloc. Auh in iquac ye tlatlalchipava iquac miquia in tlalloc: auh in omjc, oc cepa moyavaloaya ỹ teucallj: yc mitoaya mocalnavatia in tlalloc: auh çatepã contlaliaya ỹ oztoc, auh ioã tolpã onovaya macujlilhuitl, ynic neçaviliiloya.

Etzalcualiztli, "The Eating of Etzalli,"[18] was when the festival was celebrated in honor of Tlaloc, and [his impersonator] died. And when the festival was celebrated, it was the time when, for twenty days, there was singing by the women.[19] And the day before [the impersonator of] Tlaloc was to die was called "People Are Met"[20] and there was a procession. And also birds were made to fly. They tied birds to poles; when the youths carried them in procession, they went dancing along with them. This was done at sundown, and they had [the impersonator of] Tlaloc dance all night. At dawn [the impersonator of] Tlaloc died, and when he had died, once again there was a procession around the temple. Hence it was said, "Tlaloc was dispatched to the house." And afterwards they placed him in a cave. And also, for five days, they lay on rushes when they fasted.

Auh in ilhuitl quiçaya. y. ipã inic caxtolli omome metztli mayo.

And the festival fell on the seventeenth of May.

16. Huitzilopochtli was the particular patron deity of the Mexica. His cult was also active in Tepepolco and elsewhere as a result of the political dominance of Mexico Tenochtitlan. See note 1, Paragraph 5A.

17. *Cuicoyanoloya* is the imperfect impersonal form of the intransitive verb *cuicoyanoua*, which is derived from the noun *cuicoyanotl*, "in the style of the *cuicoyan*." The Cuicoyan is described by Alvarado Tezozomoc (1987: 279) as the "casa de canto de mujeres que cantaban y bailaban." Probably these were the women who were described as the *amigas*, or concubines, of the warriors.

18. *Etzalli*, according to Sahagún (1975: 116; 1988, I: 126), was "hecho de maiz cocido a manera de arroz, y era muy amarillo."

19. *Cihuapan* can mean "on the woman," "on behalf of the women," "about the women," or "in the time of the women." This last connotation, a temporal construction, might be acceptable because of the mention of the twenty days to which it is related. Jiménez Moreno (1974: 34), on the other hand, took the term to mean "priestess's house."

20. *Tenenamico:* alternatively, "are favored" (cf. Jiménez Moreno 1974: 35).

[fol. 251r]

Tecuilhuitontlj moteneva iquac miquia in vixtoçyvatl. Auh in vixtocivatl motenevaya, ỹteuh catca yn iztatlatiqz. Auh miquia ce çiuatl, yn ixiptla muchivaya, in vixtoçiuatl, Auh no cenpoalilhvitl ỹ ciuapan cuicoya, auh inic muchichiuaya Cyuapan cuicaya, ymiyztauhyaxochiuh catca.

[The festival] called Tecuilhuitontli, "The Small Festival of the Lords," was when [the impersonator of] Huixtocihuatl[21] died. Huixtocihuatl was the name of the goddess of the salt makers. And it was a woman who died; she was made the likeness of Huixtocihuatl. And also it was the time when there was singing by the women for twenty days. And at the time when the women sang, they were arrayed in garlands of wormwood flowers.

Auh in ilhuitl quiçaya, y. ypan ynic chiquacen metztli junjo.

And this festival fell on the sixth of June.

Vei tecuilhuitl, iquac miquia in motenevaya xillone auh vitznavac yn miquia: no cempoalilhuitl y cioapan cuicaya. Auh inic vntlamantli no miquia yn civacovatl: ioã mitoaya xillotlaxcalqualloya ytlacotyã ỹ Vei tecuilhuitl: in iquac quimictiaya Çiuatl. Auh in iquac mitotiaya Çiua, yancuic ỹ incue, ymvipil, ỹ conmaquiaya ioã conmaquiaya inxochicozquj ioã ymicpacxochiuh. Auh in tlavizcalpa, tlayavaloloya ỹ ayamo miqui çiuatl. Auh çeyoval, in çiuapã cuicoya toçovaya i muchi tlacatl ixtoçoya: yca yn icuic mitotiaya.

Huey Tecuilhuitl, "The Great Festival of the Lords," was when [the impersonator of the goddess] called Xilonen[22] died, and she died in Huitznahuac.[23] It also was when the women sang for twenty days. And secondly, [the impersonator of] Cihuacoatl[24] also died. It was also called "The Eating of Fresh Maize Tortillas" at the time of the sacrifice[25] in Huey Tecuilhuitl. This was when they sacrificed the woman. And when the women danced, they were dressed in their new skirts and shifts, and they wore garlands of flowers around their necks and on their heads. And at dawn, before the woman died, they went in procession. At the time that there was singing by the women, they kept vigil the entire night. Everyone kept the vigil; they danced to her song.

Auh yn ilhuitl quiçaya. y. ypan ynjc cempoalli vnchiquace metztlj Junjo.

And the festival fell on the twenty-sixth of June.

Micaylhuitontli, iquac vallaçia yn xucutl, ynic muchiuaya, y. yquac ỹ quivallaxitiaya

Miccailhuitontli, "The Little Festival of the Dead," was when the *xocotl*[26] arrived. It

21. Huixtocihuatl, as here stated, was the supernatural patroness of the saltmakers. See note 70, Paragraph 5A.

22. Xilonen was a youthful aspect of the maize goddess. See note 61, Paragraph 5A.

23. Huitznahuac, "Next to the Spines," was a term for the south in general. It was the name of a temple in the central ceremonial precinct of Mexico Tenochtitlan and of a ward located in the southeastern quarter (Teopan) of the city—as well as wards in other Central Mexican communities. According to the commentator of the *Codex Magliabechiano* (1970: fol. 36v), some temples to Tezcatlipoca bore this designation. Here, it may refer to a particular temple (or ward?) of Tepepolco (cf. Seler 1927: 138).

24. Cihuacoatl was an important aspect of the fundamental terrestrial/maternal/fertility deity. See note 67, Paragraph 5A.

25. *Tlacoti* meant to be a slave and, by extension, to be sacrificed like a slave (cf. differing translations of Seler 1927: 138; Garibay 1948: 301; and Jiménez Moreno 1974: 37).

26. *Xocotl,* the term applied to the pole employed in this and in the *veintena* ceremony that follows, may have been a contraction of *xiuh-* or *xo-* from *xihuitl,* turquoise, metaphorically "precious," and *ocotl,* pine, thus "precious pine." The word *xocotl,* as such, means "fruit."

xucutl. ỹ conanaya quauhtla: ipanpa in motenevaya xucutl vallacia: yehica ca iquac yancuican quivallaxitiaya ỹ quauhtla omanato. Auh in iquac oacico xucutl, ỹ vncã moteneva xocutl itlaquaya: vncã muchi tlacatl conamiquia, contlamaniliaya, no vmpa via ỹ teteu ynan, yoã conxuchimacaya ỹ xucutl, ioã in ixquichtin tlavillanque muchintin muxochitiaya ỹ oquivillanato xocutl, ioã yn ciuapipilti ỹ contlamanjliaya xucutl, yc motenevaya xocunamicoya.

was done in this manner: When they brought in the *xocotl,* they took it from the forest. Therefore it was called "The Xocotl Arrives," because it was when it was first brought in after it was taken from the forest. And when the *xocotl* came to arrive at a place called "The Eating Place of the *Xocotl,*" everyone went out to receive it [and] made offerings to it. Teteoinnan[27] also went there and offered flowers to the *xocotl.* And everyone pulled it in. All those who went to pull in the *xocotl* were decked with flowers. And the noblewomen also made offerings to the *xocotl.* It was for this reason that they called it "Meeting the Xocotl." On the following day they stood the *xocotl* upright. It stood for just twenty days.

Auh yn jmoztlayoc queoatiquetzaya in xocutl, çan oc yuh ycacca cempoalilhuitl.

Yn ilhuiquixtililoya. y. ypan ic caxtolli oçe metztli Julio.

The festival was celebrated on the sixteenth of July.

[fol. 251v]

Vey micailhuitl, iquac in moteneuaya xocutl valuetzi. Jnic muchivaya. y. iquac in itech motlaliaya yn inacayo otontecutlj, tzovallj, yuhquima tototl yc tlachichiuhtli catca: icpac unmoq̃quetzaya yn xocutl.

Huey miccailhuitl, "The Great Festival of the Dead," was the time called "The Xocotl Falls." When this took place, the body of Otontecuhtli,[28] made of amaranth seed dough, was placed on it. It was made in the form of a bird; it stood on top of the *xocotl.*

iquac miquia ỹ moteneva yyacateçutli pochteca ỹteuh, iquac tealtiaya ỹ pochteca. Auh in iquac omicovac, çatepan tlayavaloloya: yc moteneva quauhtitlã tlanavaloya necocololoya, ye teutlac, quiyavalotinenca, in xocotl. Auh ỹ ye teotlac nimã ye quitlecavia ỹ xocutl, auh ỹ aquĩ achto pavetzia mitoaya ocaçic in xocutl. Auh in icpac catca ocatca xocutl in tzovallj vmpa, conquechcotonaya. Auh in oaltemoc quichixtimanj yn iveveyovã, njmã ic conanaya, quicallaquiaya in ichãn diablo vncã quinacaztecpamiviaya:

It was the time when [the impersonator of the] god of the merchants, called Yiacatecuhtli, died, when the merchants bathed people.[29] And when their death had occurred, then there was a procession. It was called the embracing and winding dance beside the pole [because] at sundown they circled the *xocotl* in procession. When the sun set then they climbed the *xocotl,* and the one who reached the top first, it was said, gained the *xocotl,* and he cut off the head of the amaranth seed dough figure that was on top.

27. Teteoinnan, impersonated here, was another major aspect of the basic terrestrial/maternal/fertility deity. See note 54, Paragraph 5A.

28. Otontecuhtli, an igneous/mortuary deity, was the principal deity of the Otomi-speakers of Central Mexico. See note 29, Paragraph 5A.

29. The *tlaaltilti,* "bathed ones," were purchased by the merchants for sacrifice in lieu of war captives (see Anderson 1982b).

nimã yc quivica in quicavazq̃ yn jchã ỹ ocaçic xocutl vmpa ce xivitl quipiaz: no iquac quitlacatilititiuh ỹ oc ce xivitl in iquac ylhuiuh, quicavaquiuh.

When he came down his old men[30] were waiting for him. They then took him and put him in the temple of the devil [the god Xiuhtecutli] and drew blood from his ears with a flint knife. Then they went with the one who had gained the *xocotl* to deposit [a piece of the figure] in his home. There he was to keep it for one year; also the next year, when they again went to fashion the figure [of the god], when it was his feast day, he would surrender it.

Yn ilhuiquixtililoya ipã in agusto metztli yc macuililhuitl.

The festival was celebrated on the fifth of August.

Ochpaniztli, iquac miquia in teteu inan, moteneva tecomapiloloya, auh cempoalilhuitl ỹ çiuapã cuicuya: auh mochi tlacatl mitotiaya ỹ teteoatzitzin, ioã in tlatoq̃, in tetecuti in tequivaqz, in tlamacazq̃: ioan in çiua. Auh in tetecuhti in tlatoq̃ inic muchichivaya, conmaquiaya yn ixicol, ioã inpapalotilma yn imiyeteco. Auh in tequiuaqz ic muchichivaya yn jntlamecayouh, ioã in intlalpiaya: auh in çiua, çan ixquich yn incue, ỹ ỹuipil, inic muchichiuaya.

Ochpaniztli, "Sweeping," was when Teteoinnan died. It was called "The Hanging of the Gourds,"[31] and there was singing by the women for twenty days. And everyone danced—the god-keepers, and the rulers, the lords, the seasoned warriors, the offering priests, and the women. And the lords [and] rulers arrayed themselves thus: They wore their *xicolli*[32] and their butterfly capes,[33] and [they had] their tobacco gourds. And the seasoned warriors arrayed themselves in their hair tresses and their waist bands. And the women were arrayed only in their skirts and shifts.

Auh inic netotiloya in ipan j, çã nececenpantililoya: necuecuepaloya: auh in ixquich maçeuallj muchi tlacatl mitotiaya. Auh in iquac otaçiq̃ ilhuiuh y ye valyova miquiz moteneva itianquiz quicça, Auh in omic, in oquixipeuhq̃, ce tlacatl conmaquiaya yn iyeuayo, yc motenevaya çacapã valmoquetzaya, mitoaya, quinanavaya, yn vmpa iteupan:

In this [festival] the dance was in this manner: Rows were formed; there was going back and forth. All the commoners, every one, danced. And when we arrived at the day of the festival, when it became night and [the impersonator] was to die, it was called "She Tramples on Her Market Place." After she had died, they flayed her; a man dressed himself in her skin; it was called "Standing Forth on Straw." It was said: "They danced holding hands there in her temple."

nimã ye ic yauh yn itoalco vitzilopochtli, yc motenevaya yveveuh quicça, auh in iteut-

Then he went to the courtyard of [the Temple of] Huitzilopochtli; it was called

30. *Iveveyova (ihuehueyohuan),* "his old men," apparently refers to priests of the Fire God, one of whose appellations was Huehueteotl, "Old God."

31. *Tecomapiloloya,* "The Hanging of the Gourds," may refer to the fact, according to the account of the Ochpaniztli ceremony obtained by Sahagún in Tlatelolco (Sahagún 1981: 119), that the participants in the female mock battle, *iniietecon ic mocuicuitlalpia,* had gourds filled with tobacco tied to their backs.

32. *Xicolli:* the sleeveless ritual jacket worn, in certain ceremonial contexts, by the priests and lords (see Anawalt 1976).

33. *Papalotilmatli:* compare "manta de mariposa" in the *Codex Magliabechiano* (1970: fol. 8v).

lacyoc motenevaya macuexyecoaya: auh in yovaltica mitoaya moçacaicalia necalivaya, auh in otlatvic: yn ithvalco, vitzilopuchtli, netotiloya: ipan in ixq'ch tlaviztlj, yautlatquitl, ioan maquauhtica netotiloya. Auh y ye teutlac mitoaya payna, achto yauh in imexayac: auh nima ye oneva inic quitlalizq̃ quauhticpac, necalivaya, inic contlaliaya quauhticpac inic motenevaya yauçivatl.

"Trampling Her Drum." And at sundown it was called "The Battle of the Armlets." And at night it was called "Battling with Straws"; there was a skirmish. And at dawn in the courtyard of [the Temple of] Huitzilopochtli there was dancing; there was dancing with all the insignia and war array, and with their obsidian-studded clubs. And when the sun went down it was called "He Runs Swiftly." [The man] with his thigh-skin mask went first, and then [the others] went off [with him] to place [the mask] on top of a pole. There was a skirmish when they placed it on top of the pole. For this reason [Teteoinnan] was called "Woman Warrior."

In ilhuitl quiçaya ipã in augusto metztli ic cẽpoalli vnmacuillj:

The festival fell on the twenty-fifth of the month of August.

[fol. 252r]

Teteu, heco, auh inic mitoaya quilmach cãpa ỹ ovia teteu cempoalilhuitl: auh in jquac vallacia yc mitoaya ohecoq̃ i, oaçico, ovallaq̃ in teteu, Auh in ica uncat ỹmachiyouh yn iveveyoã, inic chialoya, tlaultextli cenca vellayectilli, ca iuhquj yn ivitl, cã tlamach quicopinaya iuhqui xamjtl auh ic mitoaya ymicxj, auh q'lmach in iquac vallacia teteu, xitinja in iuhquj xamitl tlaultextlj, ỹ quemã aço yoalnepantla in xitinia: anoço tlaca, anoço otlatvic. Auh in iquac yuh quitaya, y. yn iveveyoã, ic quimatia ca oaçico in teteu, njmã yc tlapitzaloya, tlenamacoya: ioã tlamanaloya, ixquich yc tlamanaloya in tlein yancujcã muchivaya tonacayutl: ioã necocololoya yvitica, necujloloya, ica tlapalilhuitl.

And Teteo eco, "The Gods Arrive," was so called because they said that for twenty days the gods had gone away somewhere. When they returned it was said: "The gods have arrived; they have come." And [Huehueteotl's] old men waited for [their footprints to appear] in maize flour that was very pure, that was like feather down. Carefully they had made it like an adobe brick. And so it was called "Their Feet," [for] they said that when the gods arrived, the maize dough in the form of a brick was shattered [by their feet]. Sometimes it was at midnight that it shattered, or during the day, or at dawn. And when they thus saw this, [Hueheuteotl's] old men knew that the gods had come to arrive. Then the trumpets were sounded, offerings of incense were made, and offerings were set down [before the idols]; all the first fruits of the earth were offered. And with feathers, the winding dance was danced; there was adornment with red feathers.

Auh in ilhuitl quiçaya ipã setiembre yc matlactli onavi.

And the festival fell on the fourteenth of September.

Tepeilhuitl, iquac quintlacatiliaya yn tetepe, tzovalli. Auh inic muchichivaya tzovalti tetepe, muchi tlacatl quintlacatiliaya yn inchacha y yoaltica in tlacatia in tetepe. Auh in iquac otlacatq̃ yc nimã quintlenamaquilia-

Tepeilhuitl, "The Festival of the Mountains," was the time when they fashioned [the figures of] the mountains from amaranth seed dough, and the amaranth seed dough figures of the mountains were arrayed

Paragraph 2A

ya: ioan quintlenamaquiliaya: no ioã quincuicatiaya quimeviliaya in tlein, incuic, çeçentetl tepetl. Cecentlamantli yc quincuicatiaya, ipãpa ỹ motenevaya tepeilhuitl nextlaoaloya quintlacotoniliaya ynic tlamanjliloya tamalli.

in this way: Everyone fashioned them in their homes. [The figures of] the mountains were fashioned at midnight, and after they had been fashioned, they made an offering of incense to them.[34] They also sang to them; they sang what were their songs, a song to each of the mountains. They sang a different song to each one; hence it was called "The Festival of the Mountains." Payment [to the gods] was made. They decapitated birds in their honor when they made offerings of tamales to them.

Auh in ilhvitl quiçaya. y. ipã in octobre metztli, yc navilhvitl.

And the festival fell on the fourth day of the month of October.

Qhecholli, iquac çacapã quixoaya. Auh in ipan j motenevaya temixcovatlatlavitecoya inic muchivaya, no micovaya, in miquia tlacutlj, anoço mallj. Auh inic motenevaya temixcovatlatlavitecoya inic muchivaya, tlalpã quitecaya in tenopallj, y netzollj, in teumetl, ixco quitzetzeloaya çacatl uncã muchivaya in mixcovateupã. Auh in malli anoço tlaaltili quinmailpiaya: ioã quimicxilpiaya, vncan quintlatlavitequia: çatepã quimeltequia: ỹ vncã tlacpac mixcoateupã ioan netotiloya çanioque: in oquichtĩ yoã quĩcuicatiaya inteteuatzitzĩ.

Quecholli, "Roseate Spoonbill *(Ajaja ajaja)*," was the time when there was going out on the straw. And at this time was performed what was called "The Striking of the People by the Lightning Rays of Mixcoatl."[35] There were deaths also; slaves or captives died. And when [the rite] called "The Striking of the People by the Lightning Rays of Mixcoatl" was performed, thus was it done: They placed prickly pears, thorny cactus, and the fine *octli* magueys on the earth [and] sprinkled straw over them; this was done in the Temple of Mixcoatl. And they bound the hands and feet of captives or bathed ones and there they beat them. After this they cut open their breasts on top of the Temple of Mixcoatl, and there was dancing of only the men; god-keepers sang to them.

Yn ilhuitl quiçaya y. ipã in metztli octobre: yc cempoallj onavi

The festival fell on the twenty-fourth of October.

[fol. 252r]

Panquetzaliztli, iquac tlacatia in vitzilopuchtli, yn ipan nenapoalçavaloya, yece amo tlaqualizcavaloya, çan tlaqualoya, ça ye ayac mamoviaya, ano ac motemaya, ayac çiuapan cochia.

Panquetzaliztli, "Raising of Banners," was when [the figure of] Huitzilopochtli was fashioned. At this time abstinence was practiced for eighty days, although there was not abstaining from eating. There was eating, but no one washed himself with soap or took a steam bath; no one slept with a woman.

34. In the text, *ioan quintlenamaquiliaya* is repeated.

35. Mixcoatl, "Cloud Serpent," was a stellar hunting deity particularly associated with the more barbaric, nomadic "Chichimec" lifestyle of the ancestors of many of the leading Central Mexican peoples at contact, including those of Tepepolco.

Auh in iquac tlamacuilti muchi tlacatl tlacatlaquaya ioã in pipiltotonti. Auh no iquac muchivaya in ixquich tlacpac omitto, in ipã tlacaxipeoaliztlj no micoaya in iuh mochivaya ipã paynal:

ioan cuicoyanoloya napoalilhuitl valcuicatequitia in ixquich altepemaitl ỹ vncã yyolloco altepetl. Auh in ixquich valmitotiaya in ichpochtlj, in telpochtlj i napoalilhuitl. Auh in ventlj ynic quitlamanjliaya yehvatl ỹ veyac tlacuelpachollj. Auh in iuhqui omito tlacpac: in iquac oxiti in ixiptla vitzilopuchtlj: oc ceppa tlecoaya, yn teucalticpac vmpa vnjvaya in moteneva matlalloctlj: ioã macuiloctlj, nimã ye caltemo yn itoca chunchayotl yxiptla in vitzilopuchtli, in iuh muchichiuhtiuh vitzilopuchtli, no iuh muchichiuhtihvia in chvnchayutl: ic mitoaya chunchayocacalioaya: yehica ca necalioaya: auh inic muchioaya ỹ aquĩ, otlica ipan oquiçato, nimã canaya, ixpan quihoalhvicaya in vitzilopuchtli: uncã quinacaztecpamiviaya, ioan quitzoncuj.

On the fifth day [of the festival] everyone, including the children, fasted. And also it was when was done everything that was described above in [the festival of] Tlacaxipehualiztli.[36] There were also deaths like those occurring in [the festival of] Painal.[37]

And there was singing and dancing holding hands during eighty days. All the surrounding villages had the task of singing in the heart of the city. And during eighty days, all the maidens and youths danced. And they made offerings to [Huitzilopochtli] of long, large tortillas. And as was told above, when [the figure of] Huitzilopochtli was broken up, once again they went to the top of the temple where was drunk what were called blue *octli* and fivefold *octli.* Then the impersonator of Huitzilopochtli, called Chonchayotl, descended. As Huitzilopochtli went arrayed, so Chonchayotl went arrayed. It was called, "The Battle of Chonchayotl" because they skirmished, and it was done in this manner: Anyone who went forth on the road they at once seized [and] brought before Huitzilopochtli. There they made cuts in his ear [lobes] and seized him by the hair.

Yn ilhvitl quiçaya ipan in metztli noviembre ic matlactli omey.

Atemoztli, yn ipan j atemoztli y nouiã tepeticpac, nextlaoaloya, ic mitoaya, yãcuicã, temoya, in tlalloq̃. Auh in mocuiltonoanj in inchacha motetepictiaya, yoalnepantla in tlacatia tepictoto: ioã quincuicatiaya, auh çã tlavizcalpã ỹ miquia in tepictoto: çan iquac ỹ onextlavaloya. Auh ỹ aca quintlacatiliaya itepicoã matlactetl: auh ỹ aca çã macuiltetl. quintlacatlachialtiaya quimaamacaltiaya, quimaamatlaquẽtiaya. Auh çatepã quĩquechcotonaya yca in intzotzopaz çiua ynic quĩmictiaya. Auh yn imaamatlaqz çã. ithvalco, tlatlaya, auh in inacayo tzovalli, quiquaya.

The festival fell on the thirteenth of November.

Atemoztli: "Descent of the Water," in [the festival of] Amemoztli there was debt-paying on the mountaintops everywhere because it was said that the Tlalocs were descending anew. The [figures of the] Tepictoton[38] were fashioned at midnight in the homes of the rich, and they sang for them. The [figures of the] Tepictoton died just at dawn; right then payment was made. And any who fashioned ten Tepictoton in human form, and who fashioned only five, dressed each in paper headdresses [and] paper garments. And later they cut off their heads

36. The statement that everything was repeated in this ceremony that had occurred in Tlacaxipehualiztli is probably not to be taken too literally, since no description of Panquetzaliztli mentions flaying and skin-wearing, the highlight of the former ceremony.

37. Painal was the deputy or representative of Huitzilopochtli (see note 7, Paragraph 5A); this reference to him (or his ceremony) is obscure.

38. Tepictoton: small amaranth-seed dough images of the fertility deities believed to dwell on mountaintops. See note 100, Paragraph 5A.

with women's battens; thus they killed them. And only in the courtyard the paper garments burned and they ate the bodies of amaranth seed dough.

Yn ilhujtl quiçaya ypã in metztli deciēmbre. yc eilhvitl.

The festival fell on the third day of December.

[fol. 253r]

Tititl, iquac in moteneva teu, itotiloya: ioan mitoaya ilamatecuhchololoya. Auh inic muchioaya y. in ixq'chtin, teteu, ayac mocavaya inic mitotiaya: muchintin ic muchichioaya y ceceme intlatquj, omilhuitl y netotiloya ynic cemilhuitl motenevaya yancuj temoa: ynjc homilvitl mitoaya centlamoa, iquac tlayaoaloloya: ioã mitoaya vetzi in chiquatl techichiquaviloya, oquichtin in techichiquaviaya auh ciua in quichichiquavia:

Tititl, "Stretching(?),"[39] was the time called "The Dancing of the Gods," and it was also called "Ilamatecuhtli's Leap."[40] And it was done in this manner: All the gods so danced; not one was left out. Each was arrayed in his vestments. For two days there was dancing. The first day it was called "There Is Descent Anew," and the second day it was called "It Is Entirely Finished." At this time there was a procession and also what they called "The Barn Owl Falls"; people were struck with "barn owl" [bags]. Men struck others with "barn owl" [bags], and they struck the women.

no yquac, illamatecuhchocholoya inpan moquixtiaya in civateteu, yn mitotiaya moxayacatiaya. Auh yn iomilviyoc tlayavaloloya moyaoaloaya in teucallj: in muchintin diablome tlacpac omoteneuhq̃. Auh in vntlayavaloloc njmã ic quivivica yn inteoã in inchacha: oc cepa vmpa, quimitotiaya, yc mitoaya mocxipacaya ỹ omoitotiq̃ teteu.

This was also the time of "Ilamatecuhtli's Leap," when [priests] assumed the likenesses of the Cihuateteo[41] [and] danced wearing masks. And two days later there was a procession; the temple was circled [by] all the devils mentioned above. After the temple was circled, they took their gods to their homes. Once again they made them dance there. It was said that when the gods danced, their feet were washed.

Yn ilhuitl quiçaya. y. ipan ỹ metztlj deciembre yc cempcallj omey.

The festival fell on the twenty-third of December.

Yzcalli quac mitoaya vauhquiltamalqualoya ioã yancuicã tocoya, ym mochivaya imatlacyoc ỹ izcallj. Auh in ipã metztlj ipã in henero ic matlactlj omome: auh ỹ oc no imatlacyoc in iquac moteneva yzcallamj iquac miquia ỹ ixcoçauhquj: iquac moz-

Izcalli, "Growth," was the time called "The Eating of the Tamales Made of Amaranth Greens" and also "The Sowing of the Seed Anew"; these were done on the tenth day of Izcalli. And on the twelfth of January, after another ten days, was the time called

39. Durán (1967, I: 289) translates Tititl as *estirar*. The word appears to be related to the verb *tititza*, which, according to Molina (1944, Part II: 113v), means *desperezarse* or *estirarse boceando*. Possibly it derived from the intransitive form *titica*, or *titina*, neither of which is recorded in Molina but which can be reconstructed on the basis of Classical Nahuatl grammar.

40. Ilamatecuhtli, "Old Lady," was another appellation of Cihuacoatl (see note 24, this paragraph).

41. Cihuateteo, "Goddesses," is the common term, along with Cihuapipiltin, "Noblewomen," for the deified women who died in childbirth with the child still in the womb. See note 90, Paragraph 5A.

callaanaya in pipiltonti: ioã in quavitl in metl, y nopallj, quizcallaanaya, yc mitoaya yçiuhca manaz

"Izcalli Ends." This was when [the impersonator of] Ixcozauhqui[42] died [and] when the children were stretched in order to grow. They also stretched the trees, the magueys, [and] the cacti to make them grow. They said that thus they would grow rapidly.

auh in aquĩ tealtiaya quimictiaya in ixcozauhq' ioã netotiloya. Auh inic mitoa tealtianj yehica yn itlacauh muchipa caltiaya atotonjltica in ixquichcauh cempoalilhuitl: ioã muchipa quimaca in quallj tlaquallj, ioã in itepixcauh aviani çiuatl muchipa in tlacuchia, in ixquichcauh cenpoalilhujtl. Auh in iquac miquia tlaaltili ỹ ciuatl avianj muchi quicuia in ixq'ch itlatqui tlaaltillj;

Anyone who bathed someone killed him as [the impersonator of] Ixcozauhqui, and a dance was performed. And one was called a bather of people because he constantly bathed his slave in hot water during the entire twenty days, and he always served him fine food. His guardian was a pleasure girl who always slept with him during the twenty days, and after the bathed one had died the pleasure girl took all the bathed one's possessions.

ioã nauhxiuhtica ỹ pilquixtiloya: ioã pillavanoya ioã motecuitotiaya in tlatoq̃. Auh inic mitoa pillavanoya yehica in ixquich piltontlj cocoltica onoc muchi vmpa vnmitotiaya in iteupã ixcoçauhqui, muchi tlacatl tlavanaya in pipiltotonti. Auh in omochiuh ilhuitl in çemilhuitl auh in ye teutl ac nimã ye tlayavalolo neneuhqui in muchivaya yn ipã atemoztli no iuhq' muchivaya.

And every four years there was "The Taking Out of the Children" and "The Drunkenness of the Children," and the rulers danced the dance of the lords. And it was called "The Drunkenness of the Children" because all the children still lying in the cradle danced in the Temple of Ixcozauhqui [and] everyone became intoxicated, [including] the children. And the celebration was done in one day, and at sundown a procession was held; exactly what was done in Atemoztli was likewise done [now].

Yn muchivaya. y. ipã ic cẽpoallj onmatlactlj oçe henero ynic moteneva yzcallamj.

It occurred on the thirty-first of January; hence it was called "The End of Izcalli."

PARAGRAPH 2B
[fol. 253v]

Auh ỹ atamalqualiztli chicuexiuhtica in mochiuhtivia: ỹ quẽmanjã ipan yn muchi-

Atamalcualiztli,[43] "The Eating of the Water Tamales," was celebrated every eight years.

42. Ixcozauhqui was one of the appellations of the Fire God, more commonly designated Xiuhtecuhtli or Huehueteotl. See note 39, Paragraph 5A.

43. The page on which the text describing Atamacualiztli appears displays at the top this annotation in Spanish: *Apendiz del segundo libro, en que se trata de las fiestas mobibles. Capitulo primero de la fiesta q̃ se hazia de quatro en quatro años. Capitulo 2, de la fiesta q̃ se hazia de ocho ẽ ocho años.* In the upper left margin is this note in Nahuatl: *Jn oc ceq̃ ilhujtl ỹ mjquanjtinemi ipan mitoa ỹ ic naui amoxtli,* "the rest of the festivals which go separate are told of in the Fourth Book." These Sahaguntine annotations relate to the organization of the final *Historia,* where Chapter 2 of the Appendix to Book 2 does indeed repeat the *Primeros Memoriales* account of the Atamalcualiztli ceremony.

Seler first published a paleography of the Nahuatl text of this sub-paragraph, with German and English versions, accompanied by a color version of the illustration, in an English language article (Fewkes 1893). Another version of his Nahuatl paleography and German translation, with an uncolored line drawing of the illustration, was posthumously

vaya quechollj. auh anoço quemanian ipã yn tepeilhuitl, muchioaya. Auh chicomilhvitl y neçaoaloya, çan tlapactli atamalli in qualoya, amono chilo amono, yztayo, amono chilo, amo tequixquiyo amono tenexyo: auh tlacatlaqualoya. Auh in aquin amo moçaoaya yn ipan j intla machoya: niman tzacuiltiloya. Auh cenca ymacaxoya. y. in atamalqualiztli: auh yn aquin amo quichioaya ỹtlacamo yttoya, anoço machoya quilmach xixiyotia.

Sometimes it occurred in Quecholli, sometimes it occurred in Tepeilhuitl. For seven days there was abstinence. Only cleansed water tamales were eaten; they had no chili, or salt, or chili, or saltpeter, or lime. And there was fasting. If anyone did not practice abstinence at this time, if it was discovered, he was at once punished. And this [festival of] Atamalcualiztli was held in great awe. And one who did not do [this], if not seen or known, they said, became covered with pustules.

Auh in iquac ilhvitl qujçaya, moteneoa, ixnextioaya: ioan atecocoltioaya, ioan in iquac cenca muchintin mitotiaya ỹ teteuh: ic mjtoaya teujtotiloya, ioan ixquich vncan valneçia in vitzitzilli, papalutl, in xicotli, in çayoli / in tototl, temollj / tecujtlaololo in ipan moquixtiaya, tlaca in ipã valmitotiaya. Auh no cequintin ipã moquixtiaya in cochiztli, in ixocotamalcozqui: ioã totolnacatl, in jcozquj: ioã ixpan icaca in tonacacuezcomatl tẽticac xocotamalli, auh no muchi, vncan valnecia in ipã moquixtlaya in motolinja in motequiquilmaquilia in motequaquamaquilia: no ioã vncã valneçia in teucucuxquj in ipã moquixtiaya: ioã in oc cequintin totome in tecolutl in chichtli ipan quiçaya ioã oc cequj in ipã moq'xtiaya.

And when it was the day of the festival, it was called "The Hoarding Up [of Good Fortune]" and "Becoming Conch Shells." And at that time all the gods danced; hence it was called "The Dancing of the Gods." And the people all appeared there in guises of hummingbirds, butterflies, bees, flies, birds, beetles, dung beetles; in these [guises] they danced. And there were also some who went as sleep. Some had necklaces of fruit tamales, [some] necklaces of turkey [tamales]. And before them stood a maize bin filled with fruit tamales, and also those in the guise of all the poor people who sold greens, who sold wood, appeared there, as well as those in the guise of the infirm. And there were others who went as birds, horned owls, barn owls, and other disguises.

Auh motlaliaya in tlalloc ixpã manca, ỹ atl, vncã temia in cocoa, ioã cueyame, ioã ỹ yeoantin motenevaya maçateca, vncã quin-

And before Tlaloc was placed [a pool of] water which was filled with snakes and frogs there, and those called Mazateca[44] each

published in 1927 (Seler 1927: 246–251). Seler (especially, 1902–1923, II: 1059–1070; 1963, I: 133, 157, fig. 386) discussed the significance of the ceremony, suggesting, because of its periodicity, a possible Venusian connection. He also interpreted its illustration and attempted a not entirely accurate identification of the deity impersonators depicted. Garibay in 1948 published another version of the paleography of the text, with Spanish translation and a reprint of the Seler drawing (Spanish version only republished in Jiménez Moreno 1974).

44. Mazateca: a gentilitial term meaning "Person of Mazatlan (Place of the Deer)." Mazatlan is a fairly common Mesoamerican toponym. The reference here is obscure, but it seems unlikely that there is any connection with the group known as Mazateca, speaking a language belonging to the Macro-Otomangue family and located in northern Oaxaca. Seler (1902–1923, II: 1063; 1963, I: 157), on the other hand, speculated that these "Mazateca" who swallowed the live frogs and snakes were priests of the particular region where the ceremony had originated, specifically the Mazatec-speaking Teotitlan del Camino district of Oaxaca. León-Portilla (1958: 63) believed that they were affiliated with a Mazatlan "barrio" in Mexico Tenochtitlan. However, in Caso's (1956) comprehensive reconstruction of the late pre-Hispanic and colonial barrios of that metropolis, no barrio of that name is listed. There was a Mazatlan, either an alternate name for (San Mateo) Tetecpilco or a place coterminous with it, located a substantial distance south of Mexico Tenochtitlan, just east of the Itztapallapan causeway (Sahagún 1988, I: 164; Torquemada 1975–1983, I: 144; González Aparicio 1973: 110, map), which might qualify. On the other hand, since this account of Atamalcualiztli was compiled by Sahagún in Tepepolco, Mazatlan might refer to a "barrio" of that community or some place in its vicinity.

toloaya in cocoa çã yoltivia çeçeyaca, ioã in cueyame çã incamatica yn quimonanaya, amo ynmatica: çã quimontlãquechiaya injc quimonanaya ỹ atlã in vncã ixpan tlalloc. Auh çã quinquaquativia, in cocoa inic ipã mitotitivia maçateca, Auh in aquin achto quitlamjaya y coatl in quitoloaya: nimã ic tzatzi, tlapapavia, quiyaoaloa in teucallj: auh quintlauhtiaya in quintoloaya coatl.

swallowed the snakes, which were alive, and the frogs. They seized the frogs with their mouths, not their hands; they just chewed them up. Thus they took them from the [pool of] water in front of Tlaloc. And while the Mazateca were eating the snakes they went dancing along. And whoever first consumed a snake, when he swallowed it, then he shouted; he cried out; he circled the temple. And they rewarded those who swallowed the snakes.

Auh omilhuitl i netotiloya. Auh injc omilhuitl netotiloya, ye teutlac in tlayavaloloya: nappa in moyaoaloaya teucallj. Auh in xocotamalli iquac qualoya in tonacacuezcomac temja, muchi tlacatl concuja in iquac tlamia ilhuitl. Auh y iehoantin in çiva illamatq̃, ioã vevetq̃ cenca chocaya quilnamjquia ỹ acaçocmo açizq̃ chicuexivitl quitoaya: ac oc ixpã in mochioaz y.

And for two days there was dancing. And on the second day of dancing, at sundown, there was a procession. Four times was the temple circled. And fruit tamales were eaten at that time; they filled the maize bin. Everyone took them when the festive day ended. And the old women and the old men wept much; they remembered that perhaps they would not attain another eight years. They said: "Before whom [of us] will this yet occur?"

Auh inic mochivaya. y. quilmach yc mocevitivia in tonacayutl in chicuexiuhtica ipãpa quilmach cenca tictlayhioviltia, inic tiqua, in ticchilhvia in tiquiztavia in tictequixqujvia, in motenexvia, yn iuhqujma ticatzonmjctia inic ticnemjtia quilmach ic mopilquixtitivia, in tonacayutl, iuhqui ỹ muchioaya.

And for this reason was this done. It was said that thus the maize was made to rest in the eighth year, because it was said that we tormented it greatly in order to eat it, when we used chili on it, when we salted it, when we treated it with saltpeter, when it was treated with lime. It was as if we had killed it; therefore we revived it. It was said that thus the maize was made young [again]. Thus was it done.

Auh in iquac otzõquiz ilhuitl, yn imoztlayoc motenevaya, molpalolo, yehica ca oneçavililoc, yn tonacayutl

And when the festival ended, the next day was called "Sauce Is Tasted," because the maize had been fasted for.

PARAGRAPH 3A
[fol. 254v]

Jnic. iij. parrapho ipan mitoa yn izquitlamantlj ynic tlayecoltiloya teteu.

Third paragraph, in which are told the various things with which the gods were served.[1]

1. Over the Nahuatl title, Sahagún wrote: *Capitulo tercero de las ofrendas que se ofreciá a los demonjos en el templo y fuera,* "Third chapter, concerning the offerings they made to the devils inside and outside the temple." As indicated, these Spanish annotations related to the organization of Sahagún's final *Historia,* where most of this paragraph constitutes the third section of the Appendix to Book 2. There (Sahagún 1981: 194), the first portion of this section is entitled *Nican moteneoa in quenin tlamanaia, yoan in tlein ic tlamanaia yn inteupan, in Mexica,* "Here is told in what manner the Mexica made offerings and what they made as offerings in their temples," which Sahagún (1975: 164; 1988,

Tlamanaliztlj

Jnic tlamanaloia tlaqualtica ioã tilmatica, tlamanaloya, ioã yca yn tlein yoyolli aço totolli, anoço tototl anoço tilmatlj, ano in tlein iancuican mochioa aço centli anoço chiã aço xochitl anoço in tlein,

auh inic tlamanaja civatzitzinti yovac in quimixitiaya ỹ tenavã in tetavã inic quimanativi ventlamapictlj in tlaxcaltzintlj tepitoton. ynic içiuhca quimanativi ixpã diablo, caxtica in quitquia vẽtlj ỹic conmanaia, çã inchã mochivaia in tlaxcalli ic tlamanaia civatzitzinti

Offerings

Thus were offerings made.[2] Offerings were made of food and capes, and also of all kinds of animals—such as turkey hens, or birds; or capes; or else with whatever grew earliest, perhaps maize, or *chía*, or flowers, or anything else.

And the young women made the offerings in this manner: The mothers and fathers awakened them before daybreak in order to go to make offerings of very small tortillas which they carried in their hands, to go quickly to set down the offerings before the devil.[3] They carried the offerings in bowls; in these they made the offerings. The tortillas which the young women thus offered were made in their homes.

Tlenamaquiliztlj

Auh inic mochivaya tlenamaquiliztlj, ỹ ica tlemaitl, çoquitl tlachioalli, cacalacho, vncã contemaịa in tlexochtlj in tlemaco yc conxopiloaya in tlexochtlj ỹ ocoxupiloq̃ tlexochtlj nimã yc contemã copallj yc valquiça in ixpã diablo anoço yn ithvalnepãtla ỹ vncã icac tlequaztlj çvquitl tlachichivallj auh ỹ omoquetzaco ixpã diablo nimã nauhcãpa quiyava in tlemaitl inic tlapopochvia auh in icoac onauhcãpa oconiyauh yc nimã õcontema in tlequazco vncã popucatica ỹ copalli

Offering of Fire

And thus the offering of fire was done. It was with an incense ladle[4] made of clay that had clay rattle-stones [in the hollow parts].[5] They put the burning coals there in the incense ladle; with it they scooped up the burning coals. When they had scooped up the burning coals, then they threw in the copal[6] and went forth before the devil, perhaps in the center of the courtyard, where there was a brazier made of clay. And when they came to stand before the devil, then

I: 189) rendered in Spanish as "Relacion de los Mexicanos de las cosas que se ofrecian en el templo." Sahagún normally employed Mexica and Mexicano for Tenochca. Consequently, although collected in Tepepolco, the information in this paragraph may pertain—but perhaps not exclusively—to Mexico Tenochtitlan. This view receives further support from the later mention in the paragraph of the springs, Tlilapan and Coaapan, that were included in Sahagún's itemization, in the third section of the Appendix to Book 2 of the *Historia*, of the structures contained within the sacred enclosure of Tenochtitlan's Templo Mayor. See note 34, this paragraph.

2. In the Spanish versions (Sahagún 1975: 164; 1988, I: 189) these offerings are specified to have been made in the "casas que llaman calpulli, que eran como iglesias de los barrios."

3. The Spanish *diablo*, devil, in the Nahuatl text is a consistent substitute for *teotl*, deity.

4. *Tlemaitl* (literally: "fire-hand/arm") was a ladle censer consisting of a shallow bowl, often perforated, in which the incense was burned, attached to a long handle, often in the form of a serpent (cf. depiction of Mexica priest holding one of these in *Codex Mendoza* [1992, III: fol. 63r]). A number of these have been found archaeologically, especially various polychromed examples discovered during the 1900 Calle de las Escalerillas excavation in a portion of the Templo Mayor precinct of Mexico Tenochtitlan (Batres 1902: 21; Seler 1902–1923, II: Abb. 57a–c, 60a–c).

5. Many of the ladle censers that have been found archaeologically (see note 4) contain these ceramic rattle-stones, which provided the utensil with a noisemaking capacity during religious rituals.

6. *Copalli:* the odoriferous resin of certain trees and shrubs of the Burseraceae family, genera *Icica* and *Elaphrium*, which was burned as incense and also used medicinally (Standley 1920–1926: 542; Hernández 1959–1984, I: 176–183).

they raised the incense ladle in the direction of the four cardinal points, thus offering the incense. When they had presented the incense to the four cardinal points, they threw the coals into the brazier, where the copal continued smoking.

Auh inic muchivaia no iovatzinco in quimixitia in tepilhoa in oquichtin ỹ anoço çiva, quimixitiaya in tenavã in tetaoã inic tlenamacazq̃ içiuhca quimixitiaya ynic amo tlatzihuizcuizq̃ techã ĩ mochivaya y

And it was also done in this manner: Before daybreak, also, they awakened the children—boys or girls. The mothers and fathers awakened them to make the offering of fire. They got them up quickly, so that they would not become lazy. This was done in people's homes.[7]

Copaltemaliztlj

The Throwing of Incense

Auh in copaltemaliztlj yc mochioaia in icoac in tlein tlatolli ie mitoz, aço tecuhtlatolli achto contemaia in copallj in tleco yn aquin ie tlatoz çã vncã mãca in copallj xicaltica: anoçv cuicanj in ie cuicaz, ie peoaz achto cõtema in copallj in tlequazco njmã ic peoa in cuicanj.

And the throwing of incense was done in this manner: When any kind of speech was to be made, perhaps a sentence to be passed, they first threw incense on the fire. Before a person spoke, there, in a bowl, was the copal. Or when a singer was to sing, when he was about to begin, first he threw the copal into a brazier. Then the singer began.

Tlalqualiztlj

Eating Earth

Jn tlalqualiztlj yc mochivaia: icuac in campa valhuiloaia, muchi tlacatl vntlalquaia yca in ce imapil aço ixpã diablo anoço tlecuilixcoac ioã yc tlaneltililoya yc neltia in tlatollj in icoac ỹ tlein amo cenca neltocoia tlatollj yc teilhuiloya, intla nellj in tiquitoa tla xontlalqua. yc nimã tlalquaia ỹ aquin ynic quineltiliaia itlatol.

Eating earth was done in this manner: Upon arriving somewhere, everyone ate earth with one finger either before the devil or before the hearth. Also in this manner they attested to things, they attested that words were true. When some statement was not much believed, the person [who made it] was told, "If what you say is true, eat earth." Then the person ate earth and thus attested that his words were true.

Tlatlaçaliztlj

Casting [of Food]

Auh ynic muchivaya tlatlatlaçaliztlj icoac in tlein qualoz ỹ aiamo quallo aço tlaquallj achtopa achiton tepiton mocotonaia tlecuilixcoac vnmotlaçaya ỹ vntlatlatlaçaloc nimã

And the casting [of food] was done in this manner: When something was to be eaten, before it was eaten, first a small amount, a tiny piece of the food, was cut off and cast before the hearth. When it had been cast there, Paragraph 3A

7. In the Spanish versions (Sahagún 1975: 164–165; 1988, I: 189) it is stated that the householders incensed the deity images in their oratories and patios twice daily, in the morning and in the evening.

ic peoa ynic tlaqualoz aiac achto tlaquaia vel achto tlatlatlaçaloya in tlecuilixcoac

then they began to eat. No one ate before [the food] had been cast before the hearth.

Tlatoyavaliztlj

Jnic muchivaia tlatoyavaliztlj icoac in tlavanaloya aço vitziecoloya, icoac in aca iancuicā quitlaliaya vctlj in icoac oquitlapivi y yoc, ic tenotzaya quivalmana apaztica, tlecuilixcoac yoā tetlavācaxtepito auh ỹ icoac ie tetlavantiz coxopiloa tetlavantica ỹ vctlj, nimā yc cōtoyava in tlecuilixcoac nauhcampa contoiavaia ỹ octlj auh in icoac ocōtoiauh octlj nimā ic muchi tlacatl quiya in vctlj, nimā ic peva in tetlavātiloya

Libation

Libation was done in this manner: When *octli* was drunk, for example when they tasted the new *octli,* when someone had just made *octli,* when he had made his *octli* strong, he summoned people. He set it out in a vessel before the hearth, along with small cups for drinking. Before having anyone drink, he took up *octli* with a cup [and] then poured it before the hearth; he poured the *octli* in the four directions. And when he had poured the *octli* then everyone drank it; then they began to serve the people *octli.*

PARAGRAPH 3B
[fol. 255r]

Tlamictiliztli

Jnic muchiuaja tlamictiliztli ynic miqz ỹ malli yoā tlacotlj ỹ mitoaia teomjcquj ynic contlecaviaja ixpā diablo ça caantivi ymatitech auh ỹ tevelteca motocajotiaya yevatl cōtecaja yn ipā techcatl. auh in icoac oipā contecac navi tlacatl ỹ quititilinia yn ima yn icxj auh ie imac onoc in tlenamacac tlamacazquj in tecpatl yni queltequiz tlaaltillj. auh nimā ic coneltequi conanilia achto in iyollo auh çā ioltoc yn queltequia auh in icoac oconaniliq̃ yyollo conjaviliaya in tonatiuh

Human Sacrifice[8]

In this manner they performed human sacrifice: When a captive or slave died, they called him *teomicqui* [one sacrificed to the gods]. Thus they led him up the temple steps before the devil: They just held him by the hand, and one called a placer laid him on the sacrificial stone. And when he had laid him upon it, four men held his hands and feet taut. And in the hand of the fire priest lay the flint knife with which he would cut open the breast of the ceremonially bathed sacrificial victim. And then he cut open his breast [and] first took out his heart. And he was still alive when he cut open his chest. And after he took out the heart, he presented it as an offering to the sun.

Tlacoquixtiliztli

Jn tlacoquixtiliztlj ic muchivaia ça no ipā in tleī tonallj in tlacoquixtiloya auh ca noviā

The Passing of Twigs

The passing of twigs was done in this manner: It was on certain days, also, that twigs were

8. Sahagún's title at the head of the page reads: *Capitulo 4. de la sangre que se derramava a honrra del demonjo en el templo y fuera,* "Of the blood they shed in honor of the devil inside and outside the temple." A similar title heads this section of the Appendix to Book 2 of the *Historia.* In the *Florentine Codex* (1979, 1: fol. 175v), the Spanish version of this first entry, *Tlamjctiliztli,* is highly abbreviated, but just below, occupying the rest of the space in the column, is a large, very graphic illustration of the heart extraction method of human sacrifice.

aço ynacazco, anoço in aquin quinequiz ynenepilco anoço ymetzpã auh ynic quicoyonjaya ynacajo, iehoatl in vitzauhquj in itztlj auh yc njmã vncã quiquixtiaya in tlacotl anoço çacatl auh inic quitiliniaya yn inacajo mecatica ynic oncã quiquixtiaja tlacotl. inic tlamaçevaloya auh in icoac otlacoquixtiloc yn imoztlajoc tlachpanoya mochpanaja in tlacotl ioã in çacatl cenca ezço auh in muchivaia y ichã diablo anoço otlica ỹ vncã manj diablome.

passed, and [they were passed] just everywhere, such as the ears, or if anyone so desired, through the tongue, or the thighs. And he made an opening in the flesh with a sharp-pointed obsidian knife, and then drew twigs or straws through there. And he stretched the flesh with a cord to pull the twigs through there. In this manner they gained merit.[9] And the day after the twigs had been passed there was sweeping up; the twigs and straws which were covered with blood were swept up. And this was done in the temple of the devil, or else along the road where there were devils.

Çacaquixtiliztlj
Nevitzmanaliztlj

Jn nevitzmanaliztlj yc muchivaja cõcuia in acxoiatl ioã contequia ỹ mevitztl auh quezviayaic quivalmanaja, yn ipã acxoiatl ome in vitztlj, noviã in aca aço vcã, anoço excã, in quimanaja vitztlj anoço macuilcã, çá teiollotlama

The Passing of Straws[10]
The Offering of Thorns[11]

The offering of thorns was done in this manner: They took a fir branch, and they cut maguey thorns and stained them with their blood. On the fir branch they laid two thorns in offering. People made offerings of the thorns everywhere—in two places, or three, or five, voluntarily.

Neçoliztlj

Jn miçoya inic quichivaya itztlj, ica in ontequia yn inacazco auh njmã yc quivalpipiloaya in eztlj in inacaztitlã

The Drawing of Blood[12]

The drawing of blood was done in this way: With an obsidian knife they made a cut in their ear [lobes], and then from their ear [lobes] they forced the blood.

Nenacaztequiliztlj

Ça ie no iehvatl yn neçoliztlj y nenacaztequiliztlj ỹ miçoya ỹ monacaztequia

The Cutting of the Ear [Lobes]

The cutting of the ear [lobes] was the same as the drawing of blood. They drew blood

9. *Tlamacehua* means "to acquire or merit something." Usually it is translated as "to do penance," a meaning possibly given to this term by the missionaries. It is interesting to note that the lexicon of the putatively Sahaguntine *Evangelarium, Epistolarium et Lectionarium Aztecum* (Biondelli 1869: 120) gives only the first meaning. Molina (1944, Part II: fol. 50v, 125r), in his 1571 dictionary, provides both meanings. Penance in atonement for sin is a Christian concept. Pre-Hispanic "penance" involved auto-sacrificial acts such as those described in this entry or, in some cases, the sacrifice of a slave by means of which the "penitent" would gain merit with the gods.

10. Apart from the illustration of a "penitent" thrusting a straw through his tongue, there is no text. The ritual appears to have been the same as that described in the preceding section.

11. The Spanish texts (Sahagún 1975: 166; 1988, I: 190) add that this ritual was performed by the priests at night on mountains and in caves.

12. The Spanish versions (Sahagún 1975: 166; 1988, I: 190–191) state that this drawing of blood from the ear lobes was performed five days before the celebration of a *veintena* ceremony and that with the blood the women traced a circle on their faces and the men a stripe from their eyebrows to their jaw lines. The women would perform this ritual over a period of eighty days, undertaking it every three or four days.

from themselves when they made a cut in their ear [lobes].

Tlaquechcotonaliztlj

Jn tlaquechcotonaliztlj yc muchivaia ca icoac intla tototzintlj ixpã quiquechcotonaja in diablo no coniaviliaya oncã contlaçaia yn ixpã diablo vncã tlapapatlatoc, in itlac in tototzintlj.

Decapitating [Birds][13]

The decapitation [of birds] was done in this manner: When they decapitated a bird before the devil, they also presented it as an offering: [then] they cast it there before the devil; there the body of the bird lay fluttering.

PARAGRAPH 3C
[fol. 255v]

Tlatlatlaqualiliztli

Jnic muchivaja tlatlatlaqualiliztlj in icoac oconeltecqz in tlacotlj, anoço mallj, nimã quicuja yn iezço caxtica, yoã aço amatl contlaçaia in caxic, quichichinaltiaya ỹ eztlj nimã ic quitquia caxtica, yn izquintin diablome intenco quintlatlaliliaya ỹ eztlj muchintin yn jezço teomjcquj

Feeding [the Gods]

The feeding [of the gods] was done in this manner: When they cut open the breast of a slave or a captive, they then collected the blood in a bowl and perhaps cast a paper into the bowl, which absorbed the blood. Then they carried [the blood] in the bowl and on the lips of all the devils they smeared the blood, all the blood, of the sacrificial victim.

Nextlavaliztli

Jn nextlavaliztli inic muchivaia in iquac aço aca in tlein ipã muchiva aço cocoliztlj in iquac opatic nimã aço copallj yoã amatl ynic muxtlava inic amo omic iuhquima ic tlaxtlava iehica ca omjquizquia.

Payment [to the Gods][14]

Payment was done in this manner: When, for example, something befell someone, such as an illness, after he recovered he then paid [the gods] with copal and papers because he had not died. He paid thus because he might have died.

Acxoyatemaliztlj

Jnic muchivaia acxoiatemaliztlj ca concuia quauhtla in acxoiatl xoxouhqui ynic ipã nevitzmanaloz. achto contemaja ỹ acxoiatl ipã comanaja ỹ vitztlj ome ezço,

The Laying of Fir Branches[15]

The laying of fir branches was done in this manner: They gathered green fir branches in the woods in order to place the offering of maguey thorns upon them. First they set down the fir branch; on it they laid two thorns [covered] with blood.

13. The birds decapitated in this ritual usually were quail, *zollin*. The Spanish versions (Sahagún 1975: 166; 1988, I: 191) state that this ritual was performed particularly before the Mexica patron deity, Huitzilopochtli.

14. Above this section, Sahagún's annotation reads: *Capitulo 5. de otros servicios que se hazian a los demonios en el tẽplo y fuera*, "Chapter 5, of the other rites performed for the devils inside and outside the temple." A similar title heads this section of Book 2's Appendix in the *Historia*.

15. Compare "The Offering of Thorns" in Paragraph 3B.

Teuquauhquetzaliztlj

Jn tequauhquetzaliztlj ic muchivaja ca concuja in xoxouhqui quavitl in quauhtla contequia, ỹic vncã tlatlaz ichã diablo quimaquetzaya iehoãti quichivaja in vncã nẽca ychã diablo in tlamaceva

The Ritual Making of Bundles of Wood

The ritual making of bundles of wood was done in this manner: They gathered green wood in the forest which they cut in order to burn there in the devil's home. They set it up by hand. Those who lived in the house of the devil and performed rites to gain merit with the gods did this.

Tlachpanaliztlj

Jn tlachpanaliztlj yc muchihuaja cenca cui tlaviltiloya in tepilhuã ỹ aço civa anoço oquichtin ỹ cã inchachã yn imitvalco inic tlachpanazq̃ auh in icoac yoatzinco ỹ oachto tlachpãq̃ nimã quichivaja in ventlamapictlj yn comanaja ixpã diablo auh in icoac otlamanato nimã yc concuja yn ĩtlema ynic tlenamacazq̃

Sweeping

Sweeping was done in this manner: Great care was taken to see that the children, girls or boys, swept the courtyards of their homes. And before daybreak, when first they had swept, then they made offerings which they carried in their hands [and] set down before the devil. And when they had gone to make the offering, they then took their incense ladles to make an offering of incense.

Toçoualiztli. i. ixtocoliztlj

Jnic muchivaja toçoliztlj icoac in yovaltica iehoantin yn vncã nenca ichã diablo in quipiaya yoallj cenca ixtoçotinenca ynic amo tlacochcavazq̃ ynic quipiaya yoalli in ixquichca tlatviz. ynic quipiaya iehica in tlein mochivaz in iquac yovalnepãtla anoço tlaquauhyovac anoço ye tlatvinavac ipampa in vel quipiaya yoallj yoã quipiaya in tletl

Vigils, or Staying Awake at Night

The vigils were kept in this manner: When it was night, those who lived in the home of the devil, who guarded it at night, remained very wide awake all night so that they would not neglect their duties by sleeping. Thus they kept watch all night until dawn. The reason they kept watch was because of the things that had to be done at midnight, or later at night, or at the approach of dawn. For this reason they kept strict watch at night and guarded the fires.

[fol. 256r]

Neçavaliztli

Jnic neçavaloya amo tlacatlaqualoya ça ye aiac mamoviaya aiac motemaia amono ac civa cochia çaniyo icoac in in pãquetzaliztlj tlacatlaqualoya chicomilhuitl.

Abstinence

When they practiced abstinence they did not fast, but no one washed with soap, no one took a steam bath, nor did anyone sleep with a woman. Only at the time of [the festival of] Panquetzaliztli did they fast for seven days. Paragraph 3C

PARAGRAPH 3D

Couatololiztli

Jnic muchivaja in covatl quitoloaya iquac in atamalqualoya quichivaya motenevaja maçateca çã yoltivia in quintoloaya çã in camatica ỹ quimonanaya quixaxamatztivia ynic quintoloaya auh in iquac oquintoloq̃ çatepã motlauhtiaya yn iuhqui ipã omito atamalqualoya chicuexiuhtica

The Swallowing of Snakes[16]

It was done in this way: They swallowed snakes when [the festival of] Atamalcualiztli was celebrated. The people called Mazateca[17] did this; [the snakes] were quite alive when they took them up with their mouths, when they swallowed them. And after they had swallowed them, they received gifts, as has been told in [the festival of] Atamalcualiztli, which was every eight years.[18]

Cueyatololiztlj

Auh in cuecueya quĩtoloaya ça no yoltivia ça no iquac muchivaja ça no ievantin ỹ maçateca quichivaja.

The Swallowing of Frogs

And they swallowed frogs which were also alive. It was done at this same time also; it was also the Mazateca who did this.

Totopatlanaltiliztli

Jnic muchivaja totopatlanaltiloya iquac in etzalqualiztlj in telpupuchti quauhtitech quimilpiaya in totome ic mitotitivia in iquac tlayavaloloya

Making Birds Fly

Making birds fly was done in this manner: At the time of [the festival of] Etzalcualiztli[19] the youths tied birds to poles. They danced along with these while going in procession.

Tlayavaloliztli

Jn tlayavaloliztlj inic muchivaia iquac in tlein ilhuitl motlalitivia iquac mochivaia mochi tlacatl tlaiavaloaya aço yoatzinco anoço ye teotlac ic tlaxinia

Processions

Processions were held in this way: When certain festivals took place this was then done. Everyone went in a procession, either before daybreak or at sundown; then they broke ranks.

Cyuapãcuiquiztli

Auh in civapãcui[qui]ztlj ic muchivaia iquac in aço tlacatia diablo in tlein icuac muchintin mitotiaya yn civa noviã yoã oquichti iquac in ilhuiuh tlalloc

The Time of the Singing of the Women

The time of the singing of the women was done in this manner: When, for example, a devil was fashioned, all the women danced with the men everywhere; it was at the time of the festival of Tlaloc.[20]

16. Sahagún's title for this section reads: *Capitulo 6. de ciertas cerimonjas q̃ se haziã a honrra del demonjo*, "Chapter 6, of certain ceremonies that were performed in honor of the devil." Equivalent titles head this section of Book 2's Appendix to the Spanish versions of the *Historia*.

17. See note 44, Paragraph 2B.

18. See description of Atamacualiztli in Paragraph 2B.

19. See description of Etzalcualiztli in Paragraph 2A.

20. The referent for the "festival of Tlaloc" here must be Etzalcualiztli, which was dedicated to the propitiation of this deity and included in its ritual program the singing of women.

[fol. 256v]

Tiçapaloliztli

Jnic muchivaja tiçapaloliztlj in icuac concuitiquiça in tiçatl. nimã ic motlaloa in tiçapaloanj yc necia ỹ cenca tlacça ioã cequintin quitocaja quitepachotivia auh in aquĩ amo tlacçaia içiuhca tetica vetzia

The Tasting of the Chalk

The tasting of the chalk was done in this manner: When the chalk-taster grabbed the chalk, then he ran. He could be seen running swiftly, and the others chased him throwing stones at him. Anyone who did not run with great swiftness fell [under] the stones.[21]

Teizcalaanaliztli

Jnic muchivaja teizallaanaliztlj no ipã in tlein tonallj muchintin yn pipiltotonti quimizcallaanaia otlica yoã in ixquich tlalticpac onoc in nopallj ioã aço metl. ic mitoaya ynic iciuhca mozcaltiz.

The Stretching of People for Them to Grow

The stretching of people for them to grow was done in this manner: On a certain day also, on the roads they stretched all the little children, so that they would grow, as well as everything that was on the earth—the cacti and, perhaps, the magueys. It was said that thus they would grow quickly.[22]

PARAGRAPH 3E

Neelpiliztli

Jnic muchivaia yc neelpiloya yca icpatl in quimiylpiaya pipiltotontin yn imaquechtlan yoã in inquechtlã yoã ymitac ellotlaxcaltotontli ỹ vncã conmanaja vacaltonco yoã tecontontlj vacalnacazco conquetzaja tentiuh yn atl, yn imajtac

auh in iquac oacico ipã cempoalilhuitl yn iquac moteneva teteu ecco iquac quintomiliaya yn icpatl potonqui ynic omovlpique pipiltotonti

Tying[23]

Tying was done in this manner: They bound small children about their wrists and necks with thread. And they placed their provisions of small tortillas of fresh maize in a little wooden carrier. And they stood a small jar in the corner of the carrier; it went filled with water; it was their provision of water.

And when the twenty days when it was called Teteo eco arrived, then they undid the foul-smelling thread with which the children had been tied.[24]

21. According to Sahagún's Tlatelolco informants (Sahagún 1975: 134–135; 1981: 125; 1988, I: 151–152), a somewhat similar ceremony took place during Ochpaniztli, when warriors grabbed handfuls of chalk and feathers and ran off, pursued by the priest, who wore the skin of the woman sacrificed to Toci. They threw the feathers and chalk at him.

22. This was done during Izcalli (Paragraph 2A).

23. Sahagún's title for this section reads: *Capitulo 7. de otras ceremonjas que tambiẽ se haziã a honrra del demonjo,* "Chapter 7, of other ceremonies that were also performed in honor of the devil." Similar headings commence this section of the Appendix to Book 2 of the Spanish version of the *Historia.*

24. The Spanish versions of this passage (Sahagún 1975: 168; 1988, I: 193–192) vary considerably from the Nahuatl. They state that a ball of copal incense was hung from the thread which, in addition to the neck and wrists, was also tied around the ankles. These were tied on by an "astrologo" on a particular day sign, and, after the child had worn them the number of days specified by him, he removed and burned them. This was done as a health measure four times a year.

Necocololiztli

Auh y necocololiztlj ic muchivaya ipã ilhuiuh acolmiztlj mivicuicuiloaya in pipiltotonti tlapallivitica noviã yn itech yn inacayo Auh ỹ veveitlaca, çanjo yn imelpã yn iyollopã yoã yn icuitlapã quinamictiaya yn ivitl ini quipotoniaya quilmach ipampa ynic amo teyolloquaz acolmiztlj

Making Detours[25]

Making detours was done in this manner: On the festival of Acolmiztli the little children were decorated all over their bodies with colored feathers. And the adults only applied the feathers, they only pasted the feathers, to their abdomens, chests, and backs. It was said that thus Acolmiztli would not bewitch people.

Pilquixtiliztli

Jnic muchivaya pilquixtiliztlj vmpa muchintin quivicaya in iteopã in diablo in pipiltotonti vel muchinti vmpa quimitotiaya yoã quĩtlavantiaya ynic moteneva pilquixtilo ca muchintin quivalquixtia in pipiltotonti in diablo ychã

Taking Out the Children[26]

Taking out the children was done in this manner: They took all the small children there to the temple of the devil [and] they had indeed all of them dance and drink *octli.* It was called "taking out the children" because they took all the little children out to the home of the devil.

Tlavavanaliztlj

Jnic muchioaja in moteneva tlavavanaliztlj in icoac mali moyaochichioaja ichimal ymaquauh, ymac onoc aocmo itzo yn imaquau[h] auh in tlavavanque ỹchimal ỹmaquauh ynic tlavavanaja iuhqui quicallj in mallj anoço tlacotlj

Striping[27]

What was called striping was done in this way: When a captive was arrayed for battle [and] his shield and his obsidian-studded club lay in his hand, the club did not have obsidian blades. And the stripers with their shields and obsidian-studded clubs made the stripes as they fought the captive or slave.

[fol. 257r]

Tolpã onoliztlj

Macuililhuitl in tolpã netecoya ynic neçaviliiloya tlalloc in iquac vztoc tlaliloya omocalnavati

Lying on Rushes[28]

For five days there was lying on rushes. In this way they practiced abstinence in honor of Tlaloc, when he was placed in a cave, when he was dispatched to the house.

25. The Spanish versions (Sahagún 1975: 168; 1988, I: 193), which supply a few additional details, specify that this prophylactic ritual took place during Teotleco. Acolmiztli, literally, "Shoulder-Mountain Lion," seems to have been an aspect of the Death God, Mictlantecuhtli. See note 78, Paragraph 4.

26. The Spanish versions of the *Historia* (Sahagún 1975: 168; 1988, I: 193) do not translate this passage but do specify that this ritual occurred every four years in Izcalli.

27. The *Manuscrito de Tolosa* and the printed versions of the *Historia* derived from it omit this and the two following rituals. In the *Florentine Codex* it is not translated, but it is specified that the ritual took place in Tlacaxipehualiztli (Sahagún 1988, I: 193).

28. This passage is untranslated in the *Florentine Codex,* where it is specified only that this ritual, which is designated there, by error, "Teupan onoliztli," took place during Etzalcualiztli (Sahagún 1988, I: 193).

Çacapa nemanaliztlj

J çacapã nemanaliztlj iehoantin in quixipevaja tlaca yn imevajo cequintin comaquiaya yn evatl, ỹ motenevaja xixipeme auh motzetzeloaja in çacatl ipã quĩvalmanaja in xixipeme ipãpa in motenevaja çacapã valnemanalo

Placing on Straw[29]

Placing on straw: Of those who flayed people of their skins some put on the skins. They were called *xixipeme* [flayed ones]. And straw was strewn about; they placed the flayed ones on it. For this reason it was called placing on straw.

Tlazcaltiliztlj

Jn tlazcaltiliztlj yc muchivaya icoac ỹ monacaztequia acopa contzetzeloaya yn eztlj anoço tleco contzitzicuinjaya ynic mitoaya quizcaltia yn tletl yoã yn tonatiuh.

Nourishing[30]

Nourishing was done in this way: When they cut their ear [lobes], they flicked the blood upward or they spattered it on the fire. They said that in this way they nourished the fire and the sun.

Tlatzmolintemaliztlj

Jn tlatzmollintemaliztlj inic mochivaja in iquac omocuito quauhtla tlatzmolljn niman ic motetema in noviian momozco acan mocava iehoatl in mitoaia tlamacuiltetemaliztli.

Laying Down Shoots[31]

Laying down shoots was done in this way: After the shoots that had sprouted were gathered in the forest, they were then laid on the altars everywhere; no place was neglected. This was called the laying down of things gathered by hand.[32]

Neçacapechtemaliztlj

J neçacapechtemaliztlj ic muchivaya ça no iuhqui ỹ tlalqualiztlj ipan poia yn iquac campa quixoaya yn canin icac ixiptla diablo inic ixpã quixoaya conpia yn çacatl ixpã contzeteloa yn diablo in icoac tlaixpã quiçaya

oc cequĩtin ỹ otlj quitocaya yoã in iquac yaoc iuhquima ic nenetoltiloya in icoac aca yauh yaoc intla itla yc motolinitinemi quitoaya amo njcã yn nimiquiz yauc y nimiquitiuh

Laying Down a Bed of Straw

Laying down a bed of straw was done in this way: Like eating earth, it was proper when somewhere there was passing by a place where there was an image of a devil, when they passed before it. They pulled up straw [and] strewed it before the devil when they passed before it.

For others who were journeying along the road and when there was war, this was the same as making a vow. When anyone went off to war, if he went in anguish, he said, "I shall not die here; I go to die in battle."

29. This passage also is not translated in the *Florentine Codex*, but it is stated that this ceremony occurred during Tlacaxipehualiztli (Sahagún 1988, I: 193).

30. The Spanish versions (Sahagún 1975: 168; 1988, I: 193) add interesting details, including the statement that this ritual was performed when someone completed a new house or when the special sign of the sun reigned (i.e., the day 4 Ollin).

Paragraph 3E

31. This passage was not translated in the Spanish versions (Sahagún 1975: 168; 1988, I: 193), but it is stated that this ritual was the same as Acxoyatemaliztli.

32. Read *tlamacuitemaliztli*, as in the *Florentine Codex* (Sahagún 1981: 204).

auh ỹ iquac ye mochivaz yauyutl achto quipia in çacatl quitzetzeloaya yn ivicpa in tonatiuh quitoaya vnnipopoliviz y. intla miquiz anoço tlamaz. iuhqui ic monetoltiaya ivic tonatiuh.

And when a battle was about to start, first they pulled up straw [and] they tossed it in the direction of the sun. They said: "There I shall perish!" If he was to die or be captured, he had thus made his vow to the sun.

[fol. 257v]

Tlatlapitzaliztlj

Jnic muchivaya in tlatlapitzaliztlj iquac in ye tlaquauhyoyac y ye onacitiuh yovalnepantla iquac tlapitzaloya yc neçovaya yn ichã diablo ic teixitiloya

The Blowing of Trumpets[33]

The blowing of trumpets was done in this manner: When it was well into the night, when it was drawing close to midnight, then the trumpets were blown [and] then they drew blood from themselves in the home of the devil. They were awakened for this purpose.

Tlaticatlaviliztli

Jnic muchivaja tlaticatlaviliztlj yn icoac ye ticatla ỹ yovalnepantla oaçic no tlapitzalo. ic teixitillo yc pevaya in tlapializ motenevaja tlavitequini.

auh in aqujn amo vel iça atl ipa quinoquiaia anoço tletl ipã quitzetzeloaia anoço atlan contlaçaia. caantiquiça vnpa cõtlaçaia in tlillapa anoço coapã

The Midnight Rite

The midnight rite was done in this manner: When it was midnight, when midnight had arrived, trumpets were also sounded so that people were awakened [and] so that those who were called beaters began to keep watch.

And they poured water or shook coals of fire over anyone who could not awake. Or else they threw him into the water; they seized him and threw him into the spring of Tlilapan, or Coaapan.[34]

Nenacazxapotlaliztlj

J nenacazxapotlaliztlj no ic tlaieiecalhuiloya in diablo ynic nenacazcoyoniloya

Piercing the Ear [Lobes]

By piercing the ear [lobes] they also served the devil; for this reason they made perforations in the ear [lobes].

Netexapotlaliztlj

Ça no iuhqui y netexapotlaliztlj ça no ic tlaieiecalhuiloya ỹ diablo.

Perforating the Lips

In the same way, by perforating the lips they also served the devil.

33. These trumpets were made from conch shells.

34. According to Sahagún's itemization of the principal ceremonial structures and features of the Templo Mayor precinct of Mexico Tenochtitlan (Sahagún 1981: 181, 187; 1975: 159–162; 1988, I: 186, 188), these were two sacred springs where priests undertook ritual bathing.

PARAGRAPH 4
[fol. 258v]

Jnic. iijj. parapho ypan moteneva yn izquinti tlatequipanovaya yn ĩchan çeçeyaca teteu.

Fourth paragraph, in which are told all those who serve in the temples of each of the gods.[1]

Mexicatl teovatzin.

The Priest of Mexico

Jnic muchichivaya mexicalteovatzĩ yxicol, ytlema, yxiquipil ynic quimaviztiliaya diablo yoã yc tlapiaya ca iuhqui in tetta muchiuhticatca ỹ calmecac, iuhqui in ma intlatocauh catca in teteuvatzĩtzĩ ynic noviã

yoã ixquich in tepilhoã intech vncavaloya ynic quimizcaltiz ynic quivapavaz tlatoltica ynic vel nemizque ioã in aço tlatocatizq̃ anoço mocuiltonozq̃ anoço teyacanazque tlapachozq̃ muchi yevatl itequiuh catca ỹ mexicalteuvatzĩ

yoã no iehoatl tlanavatiaya y noviã teteupã quimilhuiaya in tlein quichivazq̃ teteuvatzitzĩ auh in anoço aca tlatlacoa muchi yevatl quimatia ỹ mexico teuvatzĩ

The priest of Mexico was arrayed with his sleeveless shirt, his incense ladle, [and] his [incense] pouch, with which he venerated the devil. And he watched over things, for he was like the father of those in the *calmecac*;[2] he was like the ruler of the priests everywhere.[3]

And all their noble children were entrusted to him,[4] so that, with words, he would rear them, he would educate them to live properly and also to be rulers, or to be rich men, or[5] to be leaders, to be governors. All these were the duties of the priest of Mexico.

And also he issued orders in the temples everywhere; he told the priests what they were to do, and if, by chance, anyone did something wrong, the priest of Mexico knew all.

Vitznavac teuvatzin. Omacatl idẽ.

The Priest of Huitznahuac, Same as Omacatl[6]

Jn vitznauac teuvatzĩ ça no iuhqui ynic tlamanitiaya yn iuhqui ic tlamanitiaya mexico

The priest of Huitznahuac in the same way enforced the same traditions that the priest

1. Below this heading is written, in Sahagún's hand: *Capitulo. 8. de las diferẽtias de mjnjstros que servian a los dioses,* "Chapter 8, of the different [kinds?] of ministers who served the gods." As mentioned, these interpolated Sahaguntine chapter headings relate to the final organization of the *Historia,* where this paragraph, with modifications, appears in the Appendix to Book 2.

2. The *calmecac* was a structure located adjacent to the temples that functioned both as a dormitory for the priests and as a school mainly for the education of the sons of the nobility.

3. The Spanish versions (Sahagún 1975: 168–169; 1988, I: 193–194) state that this functionary was appointed by the two high priests and was in charge of all of the other priests and all matters relating to the divine cult "en todas las provincias subjetas a Mexico." This statement would seem to support the common assumption that the titles listed in this paragraph belonged to priests of Mexico Tenochtitlan—in spite of the fact that there is nothing in the Nahuatl text, aside perhaps from the appellation itself, that indicates this. The use of the name Atlcahualo rather than Cuahuitlehua for the *veintena* during which a priest designated Ome Tochtli prepared the *octli* points in this same direction, for Sahagún (1981: 1) states that the former term was employed by "los Mexicanos," while "en otras partes" the latter label was preferred. Also, the mention twice of Motecuhzoma, later in this paragraph, as well as various structures included in Sahagún's list of those in the Templo Mayor precinct of Mexico Tenochtitlan, seems to provide further support for the assignment of these priests to the Mexica capital.

4. *Intech:* read *itech.*

5. *Anoco:* read *anoço.*

6. Omacatl: a contraction of Ome Acatl, "Two Reed," a calendric name of Tezcatlipoca in his aspect as deity of banquets and festivities; he is pictured in the next paragraph 5A. For Huitznahuac, see note 23, Paragraph 2A.

teovatzĩ no iuhqui ynic tlapiaya in calmecac in quenj vel tlacavapavaja tenonotzaja.

of Mexico enforced. In the same way he watched in the *calmecac* how they properly educated people, [how] they were counseled.

Tepan teuvatzin.

The Priest Over the People

Jn tepã teuvatzĩ ça no iuhqui yn itlapializ catca yn iuhqui yn iuhqui yc tlapiaya in mexico teuvatzĩ iehica ca muchi iehoatl quinavatiaya in quenj tlapiazq̃ calmecac, in quenj tlacazcaltiaya tlacavapavaia çã muchiuhqui in quichivaia ynic noviã teteuvatzitzĩ

The responsibility of the priest over the people was the same as what the priest of Mexico watched over, because he gave orders to all on how they should watch in the *calmecac* how they reared, how they educated people, and all that the priests in all places did.

Ometochtzin.

[The Priest of] Ometochtzin[7]

Jn ometochtzin itequiuh catca in quinnechicoaia centzontotochti in ie mochintin aiac molcaoaia, vncan tepan icaca in patecatl iuhquin tachcauh mochioaia. nimã ie quiq̃tza in tochtecomatl ṽcan cõteca in macuilloctli in quilviaia tevoctli,

The duties of [the priest of] Ometochtzin were to gather together [the priests of] all the Centzontotochtin.[8] No one was overlooked. Pahtecatl[9] was over the others; he became as a constable. Then he set up the *octli* jars[10] [and] there poured the fivefold *octli*,[11] which they called sacred *octli*.

nimã ie quioalquistia in pãtecatl ỹ piaztli acatl vncã cõmana in teuoctli ipã ça matlacpoalli omej çaz çe in coiõq̃ auh in õcõma nimã ie ic netotilo tlaiaoaloa in cẽtzõtotochtj. niman ie ic vi in ivicpa in teuoctli, cẽca moquequeça in ac iehoatl quittaz coionqui, auh in oquittaq̃ in aq'n oquicuic coionqui nimã ipan mochintin quitlalcavia ça icel quiticac in tevvctlj auh in otevtlavanoc nimã ye ic viviloa.

The [priest of] Pahtecatl took out tubes of reeds and set them there in the sacred *octli*. There were two hundred and [sixty] of them,[12] only one of which was hollow. And after they were put in, then there was dancing; [the priests of] the Centzontotochtin went in procession. Then they went to the sacred *octli*; they pushed and shoved each other a great deal [to be] the one to see the hollow [reed], and when they saw who got

7. Ometochtzin = Ome Tochtli, "Two Rabbit," the calendric name for the numerous deities, in the aggregate, of the standard alcoholic beverage of pre-Hispanic Central Mexico, the fermented saccharine exudate of the maguey. It was called *octli* in Nahuatl; the Spaniards introduced the term *pulque*, of uncertain origin, for it, which has replaced the indigenous word. The Spanish versions (Sahagún 1975: 169; 1988, 1: 194) characterize this functionary as "maestro de todos los canteros que tenían cargo de cantar en los *cues*."

8. Centzontotochtin = "Four Hundred Rabbits," another designation for the *octli* deities. The number four hundred stood for "innumerable," expressing the notion of the countless types of drunkenness, symbolized by the rabbit (cf. Sahagún 1950–1982, Parts V and VI [Book 4]: 11–17). See Nicholson 1991.

9. Pahtecatl, "He of the Medicine," was one of the most important of the *octli* deities, the patron of the eleventh *trecena* of the *tonalpohualli* commencing with 1 Ozomatli (Monkey); see discussion in Seler 1900–1901: 87–90. He is pictured in *Codex Magliabechiano* (1970: 53r) and its cognate *Códice Tudela* (1980: 35r).

10. *Tochtecomatl:* "rabbit vessel," a common designation for containers of *octli*. On the significance of the rabbit in relation to this drink, see notes 7 and 8, this paragraph.

11. Macuilloctli = "five *octli*." In Nahuatl, five was the number signifying "excess" and implied the overindulgence that caused inebriation (cf. Sahagún 1950–1982, Part XI [Book 10]: 193). It may have been an extra-strong variety of the drink or a symbolic name for it when it was imbibed during certain rituals.

12. Although Sahagún (e.g., 1988, I: 194) translated *matlacpohualli omei* as 203, it should be read *matlacpohualli omeipohualli*, 260, in this and similar contexts (cf. Sahagún 1981: 207).

the hollow [reed], they all made way for him [and] he alone stood drinking the sacred *octli.* And when he became ritually drunk, then they all left.

Epcovacuacuiltzin

Jn epcohoacuacuiltzin izca in itequiuh catca, in icoac ilvitl quiçaz in aço xiuhtzitzquilo in ie mochi ilhvitl mochi ipã tlatoaia inic tletemaloz, in ie mochi mochioaz mochi iehoatl ic tlanavatiaja ipã tlatoaia.

Epcoacuacuiltzin[13]

Here were the duties of the Epcoacuacuiltzin.[14] When there was to be a festival or when there was a binding of the years, for all festivals he saw to it that all the fires were laid, that everything was done.[15] He ordered, he saw to everything.

Molonco teuva

Jn molonco teuhoa, çan no iehoatl itequiuh catca, ipã tlatoaia, in copalli, in olli, in amatl, in tlilli inic moçaia in iehoatl chicvnavecatl, yoan ipã tlatoaia in tlemaitl ỹ çollin, yoã ihvitl tliltic ic mopotoniaia in chicunavecatl.

The Priest of Molonco

The duties of the priest of Molonco were the same. He saw to the copal, the rubber, the papers, and the black paint with which Chiconauhecatl[16] was painted, and he also saw to the incense ladle, the quail, and the black feathers with which Chiconauhecatl was covered.

[fol. 259r]

Cinteutzin xilonen idẽ cinteutl

Jn itequiuh catca in cinteutzin çan isquich in ipã tlatoaia ic tlanaoatiaia inic monechicoaia in amatl in copalli in olli yoan i iauhtli in itech monequia xilonen in jcoac ilhuiuh quiça yoã mochi ipã tlatoaia in tleytl yn vnca

[The Priest of] Centeotl;[17]
Xilonen Is the Same as Centeotl

The duties of [the priest of] Centeotl were to see to, to order that there be gathered together the papers, copal,[18] rubber, and powdered sweet-scented marigold[19] that were required at the time of the festival to Xilonen.

13. Epcoacuacuiltzin: "Tonsured Priest of the Mother-of-Pearl Serpent." The Spanish versions (Sahagún 1975: 169; 1988, I: 194) designate this functionary as "maestro de cerimonias." The old priests designated *cuacuacuiltin* shaved the crowns of their heads but otherwise wore their hair long. According to Sahagún's (1975: 158; 1981: 179–180; 1988, I: 181–182) itemization of the seventy-eight principal structures of the Templo Mayor of Mexico Tenochtitlan, Epcoatl was the name of the temple of Tlaloc, the major rain/fertility deity, where the ceremonies of the *veintena* of Etzalcualiztli, dedicated to this god, were performed.

14. After *catca,* the following is crossed out: *in tlatemaliztli, in teteuchioaliztli in ye mochi tlalocã tequitl,* "the laying of fires, the preparing of the sacrificial papers (to be burned), all the duties in the Temple of Tlaloc."

15. After *mochi, tlamanaliztli,* "the making of offerings," is crossed out.

16. Chiconauhecatl: a contraction of Chiconahui Ehecatl, "Nine Wind," a calendric name of Quetzalcoatl.

17. Centeotl: "Maize Cob Deity," as indicated in note 12, Paragraph 2A, was a generic term applied, in different contexts, to both the female and male maize deities. Xilonen, an aspect of the fundamental maize deity, was pictured in the next paragraph 5A.

18. After *copalli,* the following is crossed out: *in itech monequi xilonen,* "which Xilonen required."

19. *Yauhtli:* Powdered sweet-scented marigold, *Tagetes lucida* (Hernández 1959–1984, II: 324–325, VII: 356), especially used in rituals propitiating the rain/fertility deities.

monequia ococalli yn icoac miquia xilonē.

He also saw to the incense ladle[20] required there in the Ococalli[21] when [the impersonator of] Xilonen died.

Atenpã teuvatzin

The Priest of Atempan[22]

Jn atenpã teuhoatzin izca in itequiuh catca iehoatl ipã tlatoaia ic tlanaoatiaia inic monechicoaia ihuitl in quauhtlachcaiotl yoã quauhtevitztli inic mopotoniaia toçi in icoac miquia, yoan iehoatl quintzatziliaia in cuecuesteca in telpopochti inic moçaoazque in vncã atempa

Here are the duties of the priest of Atempan. He saw to, he gave orders that the feathers—the eagle down and the eagle's pointed bill[23]—with which [the impersonator of] Toci was covered when she died, be gathered together, and he summoned the Huaxtec youths[24] to fast in Atempan.

Tlapixcatzin

The Custodian

Jn tlapiscatzin quimocuitlaviaia yn incuic diablo ynic mochi yn teucuicatl ynic aiac tlatlacoz vel quimocuitlaviaia ynic quitemachtiaia in teucuicatl quintzatziliaia ynic monechicozq̃ in maçeualti ynic vel q'matizque yn cuicatl.

The custodian was in charge of the songs of the devils[25]—all the sacred songs. He took great care to see that no one made a mistake when he taught the sacred songs.[26] He summoned the commoners to gather together so that they would know the songs well.

Tzapotla teuva

The Priest of Zapotlan

Jn tzapotla teuhoa. çan no iuhqui in itequiuh catca in iuhqui itequiuh catca atenpan teuhoatzin, iehica ça no mochi ipan tlatoaia ic tlanaoatiaia inic monechicoaia Amatl in copalli yn olli yoan in iiauhtli in itech monequia in tzapotla tenan in icoac miquia

The priest of Zapotlan's duties were the same as the duties of the priest of Atempan, because he also saw to, he ordered that the papers, copal, rubber, and powdered sweet-scented marigold be gathered, which were required for [the impersonator of] Zapotlantenan[27] when she died.

20. Read *tlemaitl in itech,* as in the *Florentine Codex* (Sahagún 1981: 208).

21. Ococalli, "Pine House," apparently was a temple or shrine dedicated to Xilonen.

22. Atempan: "On the Shore." In the Spanish versions (Sahagún 1975: 169; 1988, 1: 194), Atempan is designated a "barrio" (cf. Caso 1956: 45). In Sahagún's (1981: 122) account of the rituals in Ochpaniztli, the priest who wore the skin of the female victim who had impersonated the goddess Teoteoinnan/Toci, to whom this *veintena* was primarily dedicated, "went to her home there at Atempan." A structure of this name was also included in Sahagún's (1981: 192) itemization of those located within the ceremonial precinct of the Templo Mayor of Mexico Tenochtitlan. However, it is associated here not with Teteoinnan/Toci but with the assembling of the children who were to be sacrificed to Tlaloc (during the *veintena* of Cuahuitlehua/Atlcahualo).

23. Read *quauhtenuitztli;* compare Sahagún 1950–1982, Part XII (Book 11): 55.

24. "The Huaxtec youths" were ritual performers in the *veintena* of Ochpaniztli (see Sahagún 1981: 120), which was dedicated to Teteoinnan/Toci. This earth/fertility goddess was connected with the Huaxteca of the northern Gulf Coast area.

25. After *diablo,* the following is crossed out: *iehoatl quimocuitlaviaia in ie mochi teucuitlatl,* "he cared for all the sacred songs."

26. After *quitemachtia,* the following is crossed out: *yn noviia cacalpulco,* "everywhere in the *calpulcos.*"

27. Zapotlantenan, a fertility goddess, is pictured in the next paragraph 5A.

Tecanmã teuva

Jn tecanmã teuhoa iehoatl ipã tlatoaia in ocotl in tlepilli iez yoan iehoatl itequiuh catca quinechicoaia in tlavitl in tlilli yoan poçolcactlj yn xicolli yn tzitzilli in itech monequia xiuhtecutlj veueteotl in icoac miquia.

Tezcatzoncatl ometochtlj

Jn tezcatzõcatl ometochtlj çan no iehoatl ipan tlatoaia in xicolli, in tzitzilli in poçolcactli in amatl yn aztatzõtli in ocoxochitl ic tlanaoatiaia inic mochi monechicoz ynic oalcenquiçaz yn ventli yn itech monequia in tezcatzõcatl in icoac miquia. ipan in tepeilvitl mochioaia.

Ometochtlj yyauhqueme

Jn ometochtli iiauhqueme çan ie nohoatl ipã tlatoaia in amatl in copalli in olli, yoã in poçolcactlj yn tzitzilli in xicolli in aztatzõtli yn ocoxochitli ic tlanaoatiaia ynic monechicoz yn isquich omito, icoac monequia yn icoac miqz ometochtli yiauhqueme. çan no icoac in tepeilvitl.

The Priest of Tecanman[28]

The priest of Tecanman saw to the pine wood to be used as torches, and his duties also were to gather together the red and black paint, and also the foam sandals, the sleeveless shirt, the bells that were needed for [the impersonator of] Xiuhtecuhtli Huehueteotl when he died.

[The Priest of] Tezcatzoncatl[29] Ometochtli

[The priest of] Tezcatzoncatl Ometochtli saw to the sleeveless shirt, the bells, the foam sandals, the papers, the headdress of heron feathers [and] the clover. He ordered that all the offerings be brought together, be gathered, that were required for [the impersonator of] Tezcatzoncatl when he died. This was done in Tepeilhuitl.[30]

[Priest of] Ometochtli Yauhqueme[31]

[The priest of] Ometochtli Yauhqueme: He also saw[32] to the papers, the copal, the rubber, as well as the foam sandals, the bells, the sleeveless shirt, the heron feather headdress, and the clover. He ordered that all the above-mentioned objects be brought together when they were required when [the impersonator of] Ometochtli Yauhqueme died. This was also when it was Tepeilhuitl.

28. Tecanman: "In the Stone Mouth"? Sahagún (1975: 108; 1988, 1: 117), in the Spanish versions of his account of the final days of the impersonator of Tezcatlipoca during the *veintena* of Toxcatl, refers to a ritual that took place in the "barrio" of Tecanman. Tecanman is also mentioned in his accounts of the ceremonies performed in the *veintenas* of Tlacaxipehualiztli and Ochpaniztli (Sahagún 1981: 49, 70). In any case, here it seems to have been the name of a temple or other type of sacred structure devoted to the cult of the Fire God, Xiuhtecuhtli/Huehueteotl.

29. Tezcatzoncatl, "He of Tezcatzonco (Place of Mirror-Hair)," was one of the most important of the *octli* deities. He heads the extensive series of pictures of these deities in *Codex Magliabechiano* (1970: 54r) and *Códice Tudela* (1980: 36r). He is also described and illustrated by Sahagún (1970: 51; 1979, I: fol. 12), who in one place (Sahagún 1970: 74) credits him with the invention of *octli*. The seventeenth Sahaguntine hymn of Paragraph 14, this chapter, is dedicated to him.

30. Although principally dedicated to the cult of the mountain/rain deities, Tepictoton, Tepeilhuitl was also the *veintena* most involved with the propitiation of the closely related *octli* deities. See Nicholson 1991: 163–164.

31. Yauhqueme was illustrated in the next paragraph 5A. Clearly a rain/mountain deity, he is not directly connected with the *octli* cult in any other context, Sahaguntine or otherwise. Yauhqueme was also the name of a hill near Atlacuihuayan (modern Tacubaya), west of Mexico Tenochtitlan, where a child who ritually bore the name of this eminence was sacrificed during the *veintena* of Cuahuitlehua/Atlcahualo, dedicated to Tlaloc (Sahagún 1975: 99; 1981: 43–44; 1988, I: 105).

32. Read *çan no iehoatl.*

Ometochtlj, tomiyauh

Jn ometochtli tomiiauh iehoatl itequiuh catca ipã tlatoaia in isquich in monequia in icoac miquia ometochtli tomiiauh, in amatl in copallj in olli yn tzitzillj in xicolli yn ie mochi omito. çã no tepeilvitl.

[The Priest of] Ometochtli Tomiyauh[33]

The duties of [the priest of] Ometochtli Tomiyauh were to see to all the things that were needed when Ometochtli Tomiyauh's [impersonator] died—the papers, the copal, the rubber, the bells, the sleeveless shirt—all the things mentioned above. This was also in [the festival of] Tepeilhuitl.

Acalhoa ometochtlj

Jn acalhoa ometochtli, çan no iehoatl itequiuh catca ypã tlatoaia yn isquich itequiuh catca ometochtli tomiiauh.

[The Priest of] Acalhua[34] Ometochtli

The duties of [the priest of] Acalhua Ometochtli were to see to all of the same things that were the duties of the priest of Ometochtli Tomiyauh.

Quatlapãqui ometochtlj,

Yn quatlapanqui, in itequiuh catca iehoatl ipã tlatoaia in amatl in copalli in xicolli in tzitzilli in itzcactli in itech monequia quatlapanqui in icoac miquia ipã panquetzaliztli.

[The Priest of] Cuatlapanqui[35] Ometochtli

[The priest of] Cuatlapanqui: His duties were that he saw to the papers, the copal, the sleeveless jacket, the bells, the black sandals that were needed for [the impersonator of] Cuatlapanqui when he died, when it was [the festival of] Panquetzaliztli.

Tlilhoa ometochtlj

In tlilhoa ometochtli çã no iehoatl ipã tlatoaia in amatl in copalli in xicolli in tzitzilli, yn isquich omjto çã no iehoatl itech monequia in tlilhoa ometochtli ipan tepeilvitl

[The Priest of] Tlilhua[36] Ometochtli

[The priest of] Tlilhua Ometochtli also saw to[37] the papers, copal, sleeveless shirt, bells, [and] all the objects mentioned above that were required for Tlilhua Ometochtli in [the festival of] Tepeilhuitl.

[fol. 259v]

Ometochtlj patecatl,

Jn ometochtli pãtecatl iehoatl quiiollitiaia in macuiloctli imac concaoaia in toltecatl iehoatl

[The Priest of] Ometochtli Pahtecatl[38]

[The priest of] Ometochtli Pahtecatl enlivened the fivefold *octli*. He turned it over to

33. Tomiyauh = Tomiyauhtecuhtli, another rain/mountain deity, pictured in the next paragraph 5A. This god, as in the case of Yauhqueme, is not otherwise directly connected with the *octli* cult.

34. Acalhua, "Possessor of Canoe(s)," is not mentioned elsewhere as an *octli* deity, although Sahagún (1970: 51) includes an Acolhua in a list of these gods.

35. Cuatlapanqui, "Head Breaker," was one of the recognized *octli* deities; cf. Sahagún 1950–1982, Part XI (Book 10): 193.

36. Tlilhua, "Possessor of Black," was an *octli* god; he is pictured in *Codex Magliabechiano* (1970: fol. 59r) and *Códice Tudela* (1980: fol. 41r).

37. After *tlatoaia*, the following is crossed out: *itiquiuh catca*, "it was his duty."

38. Pahtecatl: see note 9, this paragraph.

quichioaia in tevoctli ipan panquetzaliztli popolivia in macuilloctli.

[the priest of] Toltecatl[39] [Ometochtli], who prepared the sacred *octli.* The fivefold *octli* was consumed in [the festival of] Panquetzaliztli.[40]

Ometochtli napatecutli,

[The Priest of] Ometochtli Nappatecuhtli[41]

Jn ometochtli nappatecutli ipã tlatoaia in copalli in amatl in olli yn ie isquich monequia in icoac miquia nappatecutli ipã tepeilvitl

[The priest of] Ometochtli Nappatecuhtli saw to the copal, papers, rubber, [and] everything that was needed when [the impersonator of] Nappatecuhtli died in [the festival of] Tepeilhuitl.

Ometochtlj papaztac,

[The Priest of] Ometochtli Papaztac[42]

Jn ometochtli papaztac, çan no iehoatl quichioaia in octli in mitoaia tiçavctli iehoatl cõmacaia in motecuçoma auh icoac tlanaoaia in ie isquich pipiltzitzinti in aço oquichtli anoço çihoatl ipã toçoztlj.

[The priest of] Ometochtli Papaztac also prepared *octli* called white *octli,* which he gave to Motecuhzoma and [which was drunk] when all the children—boys or girls—danced with their arms around each other in [the festival of] Tozoztli.

Ometochtlj idẽ.

The Same [Priest of] Ometochtli

Jn ometochtli ipã tlatoaia in tlaqualli in ietl in xochitl, yoã in amatl in copalli yn ie isquich omito auh itech moneqz in ometochtli in icoac motonaltiaia ipan atl caoallo.

[This priest of] Ometochtli saw to the food, the tobacco, the flowers, as well as the paper, copal, and all the things that were mentioned above and which were required for Ometochtli when sacrifices were performed in [the festival of] Atlcahualo.

Çyuaquacuily.

The Cihuacuacuilli [Priestess][43]

Jn cihoaqualli itequiuh catca in is vẽtli ĩ vncã moneqz atẽchicalcã in suchitl yn ietl ynic quitlamaniliaia in toci, vel isquich in vntla-

The duties of the Cihuacuacuilli[44] [priestess] were[45] [to provide] all[46] the offerings of flowers and tobacco needed in Atenchical-

39. Toltecatl, "He of Tollan," was another of the *octli* deities; he is pictured in *Codex Magliabechiano* (1970: 51v) and *Códice Tudela* (1980: 34r). However, Toltecatl was also a generic term for "expert craftsman, artisan," which is an alternative translation here (preferred by Anderson and Dibble in Sahagún 1981: 210).

40. The final words in this entry, *in macuiloctli,* as is rarely the case, extend into the left margin of the page.

41. Nappatecuhtli, included among the deities pictured in the next paragraph 5A, was one of the Tlaloque, the preeminent rain/fertility deities (Sahagún 1970: 45). Like Yauhqueme and Tomiyauh (tecuhtli), Nappatecuhtli is only here connected with the *octli* gods.

42. Papaztac, "White Locks of Hair," was another well-known *octli* god (Sahagún 1970: 51; 1950–1982, Part XI [Book 10]: 193; 1981: 187); he is pictured in *Codex Magliabechiano* (1970: 50r) and *Códice Tudela* (1980: 32r).

43. Cihuacuacuilli: "Female Tonsured Priest"; see note 13, this paragraph.

44. Read *cihoaquacuilli.*

45. After *catca, iehoatl* is crossed out.

46. Read *ixquich.*

manaia in cihoa, yn icoac naoaloa iehoatl mochi itequiuh catca in cioaquacuilli.

can[47] when they made offerings to Toci, and all the offerings the women made when they danced with their arms about each other. All these were the duties of the Cihuacuacuilli [priestess].

Çyuaquacuilj, iztac çiuatl.

Jn cioaquacuilli iztac civatl çã no ṽpa tlapiaia vnpa tlamocuitlaviaia in atenchicalcã, yoan ipã tlatoaia in tlachpanaliztli in tletlaliliztli, yoã in aquin õpa monetoltiaia iehoatl conilviaia in cioacoacuilli iztac cioatl iehoatl mochi quitzõtequia in tlein vncã mochioaia atẽchicalcã

The Cihuacuacuilli [Priestess of] Iztac Cihuatl

The Cihuacuacuilli [priestess of] Iztac Cihuatl watched over [and] cared for things in Atenchicalcan. And she saw to the sweeping, the laying of fires. Also, anyone who there made a vow told it to the Cihuacuacuilli [priestess of] Iztac Cihuatl; she determined all that was done there in Atenchicalcan.

Yxcoçauhquj tzomolco teuva

Jn iscoçauhqui tzõmolco tevhoa itequiuh catca in xiuhtecuquavitl quitzatziliaia, inic mocuitiuh quauhtla, auh in cõcuia çan iehoantin in telpopochti intequiuh catca, auh yn oquicuito xiuhtecuquavitl vnpa onquetzaia yn tzonmolco calmecac.

The Priest of Ixcozauhqui[48] in Tzonmolco[49]

The duties of the priest of Ixcozauhqui in Tzonmolco were that he called for the Fire God's wood which was taken from the forest. And it was the duty of the youths to get it. And after they had collected the Fire God's wood, they made it into bundles in the Tzonmolco Calmecac.

Tlaçolquacuillj

Jn tlaçolquacuilli itequiuh catca vncã tlapiaia vncan tlamocuitlaviaia in mecatlã in quimaquiaia ixicol iieteconton ietinemj
cẽca tlamaviçotiaia in teupan yn vncã

The Tlazolcuacuilli [Priest][50]

The duties of the Tlazolcuacuilli [priest] were to watch over, to take care of [the Temple of] Mecatlan.[51] He wore his sleeveless shirt and carried his tobacco gourd.

47. Atenchicalcan: "On the Shore of the Shrimp"? A place of this name in Mexico Tenochtitlan played a role in the rituals that involved the sacrifice of a female victim who impersonated the goddess Xilonen during the *veintena* Hueytecuilhuitl (Sahagún 1981: 103). A canal called Atenchicalco crossed the causeway to Tlacopan, the third from the western gate of the Templo Mayor precinct (Sahagún 1975: 67). In any case, the Atenchicalcan mentioned here appears to have been connected with the cult of Teteoinnan/Toci and related earth/fertility goddesses such as Coatlicue/Iztac Cihuatl (see next entry).

48. Ixcozauhqui, "Yellow Face," was one of the names of the Fire God, Xiuhtecuhtli/Huehueteotl; he is pictured in the next paragraph 5A.

49. A Tzonmolco, "Place of the Fluffed Hair,"? and a Tzonmolco Calmecac, both dedicated to the cult of the Fire God, are included in Sahagún's (1981: 190) enumeration of the structures in the Tenochtitlan Templo Mayor precinct.

50. Tlazolcuacuilli: literally, "Filth-Tonsured Priest." León-Portilla (1958: 101) interprets this title as connoting a priest of Tlazolteotl, "Filth-Goddess," an earth/fertility deity apparently of Huaxtec origin who was merged with Teteoinnan/Toci.

51. Mecatlan, "Place of Cords," is listed by Sahagún (1981: 186) among the structures of the Tenochtitlan Templo Mayor precinct and specified as a place for the teaching of conch shell trumpet blowing.

mecatlã, aiac vncã mexixaia, auh in aquin vnca omaxis nimã quitzitzquiaia quicalaquiaia ỹ mecatlã vnpa quiçoçoia.

They had great respect for the temple there at Mecatlan. No one urinated there,[52] but anyone who did urinate there they at once apprehended; they locked him up in Mecatlan, and there they drew blood from him.[53]

Tecpantzinco teuva.

The Priest of Tecpantzinco[54]

Jn tecpantzinco teuhoa vncan tlapiana tlamocuitlavjaia in tecpantzinco yoan itequiuh catca in vẽtli ipan tlatoaia quitzatziliaia inic tlamanaloz oncan tecpantzinco.

The priest of Tecpantzinco watched over, took care of [the Temple of] Tecpantzinco, and his duties were also to see to, to call for the offerings that were to be set down there in [the Temple of] Tecpantzinco.

[fol. 260r]

Epcouaquacujllj tepictoton.

The Epcoacuacuilli[55] [Priest of the] Tepictoton

Jn epcoaquacuilli tepictotõ ipã tlatoaia in cuicatl, icoac in aquin tepiquiz iehoatl conilhuiaia inic quimisquetzaz quinnaoatiz in cuicanime ynic cuicativi ichã in aquin tepiquiz vel iehoatl quitzontequia

The Epcoacuacuilli [priest of the] Tepictoton saw to[56] the songs. When anyone was to fashion a figure [of a mountain] he told [the priest] so that he could assign, he could order the singers. When they were going to sing at the home of someone who was to make a figure, it was he who passed judgment [on the singing].

Yxtlilco, teuva,

The Priest of Ixtlilco[57]

Jn istlilco teuhoa ipã icaca, ipã tlatoaia quitzatziliaia in ventlj inic motenmanalia in pipiltzitzinti in aço oquichti anoço cihoa quitquitivi in inven in aço xochitla anoço copalli in ie isquich vẽtli mochioaia cecentlamãtli in quitquia.

The priest of Ixtlilco was responsible for, saw to, called for the offerings when the children—boys and girls—spoke their first words. They went carrying their offerings of flowers or copal. All the different kinds of offerings were prepared, which they carried.

52. Read *maxixa*.

53. After *quicocoia*, *quimictiaia*, "they killed him," is crossed out.

54. Tecpantzinco, "Place of the Little Palace," was the name of the West Gate of the Templo Mayor precinct of Mexico Tenochtitlan and of the first canal crossing the causeway to Tlacopan. It also seems to have been a "barrio" in this vicinity (see Caso 1956: 16–17, 44–45).

55. Epcoacuacuilli: see note 13, this paragraph. The Tepictoton, the rain/mountain deities who overlapped with the Tlaloque, are pictured in the next paragraph 5A.

56. After *tlatoaia*, *iehoatl* is crossed out.

57. Ixtlilco, "Place of Ixtlilton," was, according to Sahagún (1975: 170; 1988, I: 196) the temple of Ixtlilton, a deity pictured in the next paragraph 5A.

Aticpac teuvatzĩ, xochipillj,

Jn aticpac teuhoatzin ipan tlatoaia in aticpac calquj cihoatl. quinechocoaia in amatl, in copalli, in olli, yn itech moneqz aticpac calqui cihoatl. yn icoac miquia auh quixipeoaia in iehuaio cõmaquiaia in tlenamacac, yoan quintlancoaltivia çollin icamac pilcatiuh quitlãquatiuh.

The Priest of Xochipilli[58] in Aticpac[59]

The priest of Aticpac saw to the [goddess inhabiting] Aticpac. He gathered together the papers, copal, and rubber[60] that the [impersonator of the goddess] inhabiting Aticpac required when she died, and they flayed her. A fire priest wore her skin and went about with a quail which he went holding in his teeth;[61] it went hanging from his mouth; he went holding it in his teeth.[62]

Atlixelivhqui teuva, opochtlj,

Jn atlixeliuhqui teuhoan, opochtlj, ipã tlatoaia, quinechicoaia in inechichioal in amatl, in copalli, in olli, yoan in poçolcactli in xicolli, in tzitzilli in iiauhtli, in tlilli, in tiçatl in iappalli yoã aztatzontli papatli in itech monequia obuchtli in icoac miquia ypan tepeilhuitl.

The Priest of Atlixeliuhqui Opochtli[63]

The priest of Atlixeliuhqui Opochtli saw to [and] gathered together [the god's] accouterments: the papers, copal, rubber, and foam sandals, the sleeveless shirt, the bells, the powdered sweet-scented marigold, the black paint, the chalk, the black stain, and the heron feather headdress, and the locks which [the impersonator of] Opochtli required when he died in [the festival of] Tepeilhuitl.

Xipe, yopico teuva,

Jn xippe iopico teuhoa, quimocuitlaviaia in ipan miquia in iehoatl tequitzin, in amatl, in

The Priest of Xipe[64] in Yopico[65]

The priest of Xipe in [the Temple of] Yopico, at the time Tequitzin[66] died, cared for the pa-

58. Xochipilli: this deity is pictured in the next paragraph 5A.

59. Aticpac, "On the Water," was the name of a "barrio" of Mexico Tenochtitlan (Caso 1956: 46). Sahagún, who, in the Spanish versions (1975: 170; 1988, I: 196), called it a "cu" (temple), also (1981: 189) listed it among the structures of the Tenochtitlan Templo Mayor precinct where rituals were performed on the day 7 Coatl (Snake), the calendric name of the principal aspect of the maize goddess, Chicomecoatl.

60. After *olli, yoã in çolin,* "and the quail," is crossed out.

61. Read *quitlanquativia.*

62. The ritual described here, with the priest wearing the skin of the sacrificed female victim who impersonated the earth goddess, Teteoinnan/Toci (merged with the maize goddess Chicomecoatl), and holding a sacrificed quail in his teeth, is depicted in the *Codex Borbonicus* (1974: 7, 29, 30, 31), especially in the pictorialization of the ritual program of Ochpaniztli (discussion in Paso y Troncoso 1898: 24, 71, 137–143).

63. Atlixeliuhqui: "Water Divider." Opochtli, an aquatic deity, is pictured in the next paragraph 5A.

64. Xipe, a major fertility deity, is pictured in the next paragraph 5A.

65. Yopico, "Place of the Yopi," was the name of the temple of the deity Xipe Totec in the Templo Mayor precinct of Mexico Tenochtitlan (Sahagún 1981: 188), as well as that of one of the primitive "barrios" of the city, located in the southwest quarter, (San Juan) Moyotlan (Caso 1956: 13). The pyramid temple of Xipe in the diagram of the ceremonial center of Paragraph 7 also bears this appellation. For its significance, see note 48, Paragraph 5A.

66. Tequitzin: in the Spanish versions (Sahagún 1975: 170; 1988, I: 196) this word is translated as *imagen,* i.e., a deity impersonator sacrificial victim. This interpretation—which is favored here and by Anderson and Dibble (Sahagún 1981: 213)—seems to be confirmed by the entry under Yopico in Sahagún's (1981: 188) enumeration of the structures of the Templo Mayor, where Tequitzin is characterized as a captive who was sacrificed during Tlacaxipehualiztli. However, León-Portilla (1958: 105), focusing on its literal meaning, *oficio,* translated it with this word and suggested that it referred to the duty of the priest to provide the items listed.

copalli, yoã poçolcactli in tlavitl auh inic mopotoniaia iehoatl in iztac totolihuitl, yoa in tollectilmatli tultecaiotl in ipã vetzia

pers, the copal, and the foam sandals, the red ochre paint, and the white turkey hen feathers[67] with which he was covered, and the Toltec cape[68] in the Toltec style which sat on him.

Pochtlã teuva, yyacatecutlj

The Priest of Yacatecuhtli[69] in Pochtlan[70]

Jn pochtlã teuhoa quinechicoaia, inic mochichioaia in iiacatecutli in nepapan ihvitl in tocihvitl, yoã in tlaçotilmatli, yoã xicolli tzitzilli tlatlapalcactli.

The priest of [the Temple of] Pochtlan gathered together the various feathers, the yellow parrot feathers, the fine cape, and the sleeveless shirt, the bells, the multicolored sandals with which [the impersonator of] Yacatecuhtli was adorned.

Chicõquiyavitl pochtlã idẽ.

[The Priest of] Chiconquiahuitl[71] in Pochtlan, the Same

Jn chiconquiiavitl çan no iehoatl ipã tlatoaia in isquich omito, in ipan tlatoaia pochtlan tevhoa.

[The priest of] Chiconquiahuitl saw to all the same things that the priest of Pochtlan saw to.

[fol. 260v]

Yzquitlan teuvatzĩ

The Priest of Izquitlan[72]

Jn izquitlan teuhoatzin, ipã tlatoaia in xicolli in tzitzilli yoã in poçolcactli yoan tevoctli cõcuicuia in necutli iehoatl in quin omotlapã in aioiac qui.

The priest of Izquitlan saw to the sleeveless shirt, the bells, the foam sandals. He also collected the juice of the maguey for making the sacred *octli.* Afterwards, this, which no

67. After *totolihuitl,* the following is crossed out: *auh inic moçaia tlauitl,* "and with which he painted himself ochre-red."

68. Written *tolectilmatli* in the *Florentine Codex* version (Sahagún 1981: 213) and translated by Anderson and Dibble as "*totec* cape." León-Portillà (1958: 104–105) transcribed it as *toltectilmatli* and translated it as "manto artístico."

69. Yacatecuhtli: this deity is pictured in the next paragraph 5a.

70. Pochtlan, "Place of the Ceiba Tree," the usual name of the "barrio" of the professional merchants in Central Mexican communities, from which their designation, Pochteca, was derived. Accounding to Sahagún (1950–1982, Part X [Book 9]: 13, 37; 1981: 187–188), one was located in the Mexica capital, and there was a structure of this name in the Tenochtitlan Templo Mayor precinct, in which lived the priests who daily offered incense on the summit of the temple of the merchant god, Yacatecuhtli.

71. Chiconquiahuitl: "7 Quiahuitl (Rain)," a calendric name for a deity that Sahagún (1975: 47; 1988, I: 58) lists, along with four others and a sister, as a "hermano" of Yacatecuhtli. In the Mixteca pictorials, *Vindobonensis* and *Zouche-Nuttall,* this calendric name is assigned to the Mixtec equivalents of both Tlaloc and Xipe Totec (Caso 1977–1979, II: 415, 423; on *Zouche-Nuttall* 33 the two deities are fused).

72. Izquitlan, "Place of Toasted Maize Kernels," was one of the original "barrios" of Mexico Tenochtitlan (Caso 1956: 44, 45). According to Sahagún (1975: 145; 1981: 145; 1988, I: 164–165), it was also the name of a river and a temple near Chapultepec. Izquitecatl, "He of Izquitlan," is named in one place by Sahagún (1950–1982, Parts V and VI [Books 4 and 5]: 17) as the principal *octli* deity, and in another (1981: 36), as the second in importance. The functionary described in this section was clearly in the service of this god.

one [else] drank, was broken up.[73]

Tzapotla teuvatzī, chachalmeca,

The Priest of the People of Chalma at Zapotlan[74]

In tzapotla teuhoatzin ypã tlatoaia inic mochichioaia yn ipã miquia tzapotlacatl, in amatl in copalli yoã in tlemaytl in ie isquich ytech monequiz tzapotlacatl yn icoac miquia ypã tepeilvitl.

The priest of Zapotlan saw to [the adornments] in which [the impersonator of] the Lord of Zapotlan was arrayed when he died—the papers, the copal, and the incense ladle—everything that was required when [the impersonator of] the Lord of Zapotlan died in [the festival of] Tepeilhuitl.

Chalchiuhtlicue acatonal cuacuillj

The Tonsured Acatonal[75] [Priest of] Chalchiuhtlicue[76]

In chalchiuhtli ycue acatonal cuacuilli ypan tlatoaia in ventli, quitzatzilia in isquich ytech monequia yn iehoatl chalchiuhtli ycue yn ipã miquia in ococalcueitl acueytl yoã in isquich ỹ amatl in copalli in olli.

The Acatonal [priest of] Chalchiuhtlicue saw to the offerings, called for everything that was required at the time [the impersonator of] Chalchiuhtlicue died—the *ococal* skirt,[77] the skirt the color of water, and all the papers, copal, [and] rubber.

Acolnahoacatl, acolmiztlj,

[The Priest of] Acolnahuacatl,[78] Acolmiztli

Jn acolnahoacatl acolmiztli ypã tlatoaia yn ie isquich nechichioalli ynic mochichioaia motecuçoma yn ipã moçavaia yn tilmatli xicolli yoã poçolcactli.

[The priest of] Acolnahuacatl, Acolmiztli saw to all the array with which Motecuhzoma adorned himself at the time he fasted[79]—the cape, the sleeveless shirt, and the foam sandals.

73. The end of this passage is difficult to understand. León-Portilla (1958: 104–105) read the last few words as in *aio ac qui,* "que todavía a nadie lo ha bebido." In the *Florentine Codex* (Sahagún 1981: 214), it reads: *in aiaiac qui, in aiaic concui,* "so that no one might drink it, so that no one might take it." It might be read *in aia ac qui,* "which one no longer drinks"—as approximated in the present translation (cf. quite different Spanish versions in Sahagún 1975: 171; 1988, I: 196).

74. Zapotlan, "Place of Zapotes (*Achras sapota*)," was a common Nahuatl toponym. A "barrio" of this name was located in the southwest quarter of Mexico Tenochtitlan, (San Juan) Moyotlan (Caso 1956: 10). The addition in the title here of Chachalmeca appears to indicate that the deity served by this priest was connected with the province of Chalman, or Chalco, in the southeast Basin of Mexico (cf. Seler 1902–1923, II: 457; León-Portilla 1958: 107).

75. Acatonal, "Acatl (Reed) Day Sign," refers to a calendric name, by implication that of Chalchiuhtlicue. Acatonal is also mentioned later in Chapter I, in the third hymn in Paragraph 14, dedicated to Tlaloc, but here the referent seems to be male.

76. Chalchiuhtlicue: the water goddess, pictured in the next paragraph 5A.

77. *Ococalcueitl:* translated "pine-nut skirt" in Sahagún 1981: 214.

78. Acolnahuacatl, "He of Acolnahuac (Next to the Shoulder?)," was another name for the Death God, Mictlantecuhtli (Sahagún 1950–1982, Part IV [Book 3]: 41). For Acolmiztli, see note 25, Paragraph 3.

79. The parallel entry in the *Florentine Codex* (Sahagún 1981: 214) contains this addition: *çan ipan in veuey ilhujtl mocaoaia, ipan in netlalocacaoaloia, yoan in netonatiuhcaoaloia, yoan in nequecholcaoaloia: ipan tlatoaia,* "only at the time of the great feasts did he fast: at the time when there was fasting for Tlaloc, and when there was fasting for the sun, and when there was fasting for (the feast of) Quecholli, he saw to. . . ."

Totollã teuva totoltecatl.

The Priest of Totoltecatl[80] at Totollan

Jn totollan teuhoa Jehoatl ypã tlatoaia in itech monequia in totoltecatl, in amatl in copalli in olli, yoã in itzcactli, yoã aztatzontli, yoã in tevxochitl yn isquich ytech monequia totoltecatl yn icoac miquia in quecholli tlamj auh in quẽmã tepeilhuitl ypã.

The priest of Totollan saw to everything that [the impersonator of] Totoltecatl required—the papers, the copal, rubber, as well as the obsidian sandals, and the heron feather headdress, and the sacred flowers,[81] which [the impersonator of] Totoltecatl required when he died[82] at the end of Quecholli and sometimes in Tepeilhuitl.

PARAGRAPH 5A
[fol. 261r]

[Prefatory note: This paragraph is the best known section of the *Primeros Memoriales.* It illustrates thirty-seven deities or deity impersonators (including one set of five), with a detailed specification of the Nahuatl terms for items of their costumes and insignia. First published in 1890 by Eduard Seler (for later publications, see Nicholson 1973, 1988d), with line drawings of the illustrations and German translations of the Nahuatl text, it was used to great advantage by the Berlin scholar in all of his subsequent writings on pre-Hispanic Central Mexican religion, ritual, and iconography, particularly his classic commentaries on most members of the ritual-divinatory pictorials of the *Codex Borgia* group. To explain the criteria of choice of these particular deities and their ordering in the paragraph, some rather speculative hypotheses have been suggested (briefly discussed in Nicholson 1988b: 229–231), none of them very convincing. Whatever the specific reasons for their selection, this paragraph provides the most valuable single source for the iconographic terminology of the religious-ritual system functioning in Late Postclassic Central Mexico.—HBN]

Jnic. v. parapho ypan mitoa in quenin mochichivaya y çeçeyaca teteu.

Fifth paragraph, in which it is told how each of the gods was arrayed.

Vitzilopuchtlj. ynechichiuh

The Array of Huitzilopochtli[1]

ytozpulol quetzaltzoyo, icpac manj,

On his head is a headdress of yellow parrot feathers with a quetzal feather crest.

80. Totoltecatl, "He of Totollan (Place of Turkeys)," was one of the *octli* deities. He is pictured in the next paragraph 5A and in *Codex Magliabechiano* (1970: 57r) and *Códice Tudela* (1980: 39r). In the *Florentine Codex* (Sahagún 1981: 214–215; 1988, I: 196) there is confusion between Tollan and Totollan: although the name of the deity is correctly written "Totoltecatl," the former rather than the latter gentilitial toponym is incorrectly given in both the Nahuatl and Spanish versions.

81. Instead of *tevxochitl,* the *Florentine Codex* version (Sahagún 1981: 215) has *tecusuchitl,* "lordly flower."

82. After *miquia, totoltecatl ypan* is crossed out.

1. *Vitzilobuchtli* (Huitzilopochtli): "The Left-Hand Side of the Hummingbird" or "The Hummingbird's Left," rather than "Hummingbird on the Left" or "Hummingbird from the Left," as it is often translated. There is no prepositional suffix in the name. The left was associated with the cardinal direction south (see Seler 1902–1923, II: 973). Huitzilopochtli, whose militaristic role was preeminent, was the particular patron deity of the Mexica. Sahagún (1975: 31;

yezpitzal, ixquac, icac,	His blood bird[2] is on his forehead.
y ixtlan tlanticac in ipã ixayac,	There are stripes on his face, on his countenance.
xiuhtototl, in inacuch	Ear plugs of lovely cotinga feathers.
yxiuhcoanaval, y yanecuyouh, in quimamaticac,	On his back he bears his fire-serpent disguise,[3] his *anecuyotl.*[4]
yquetzalmapãca, in imac	On his arm is an armlet with a spray of quetzal feathers.
xiuhtlalpilli, inic motzinilpiticac	The knotted turquoise cloth is bound around his loins.
motexovava, in icxic,	His legs are painted with blue stripes.
tzitzilli, oyoalli, in icxic catquj,	On his legs are small bells, pear-shaped bells.
ytecpilcac,	His lordly sandals.
tevevelli in ichimal	His shield is the *tehuehuelli.*[5]
tlaoaçomalli in ipã temi chimallj	Across the shield lie stripped [arrows].[6]
ycoatopil, yn imac, icac, çentlapal	His serpent staff is in his other hand.
paynal inechichiuh	The Array of Painal[7]
Ytozpolol, icpac manj,	On his head is a headdress of yellow parrot feathers.

1988, I: 37), who describes him as a deified man, calls him "otro Hercules, el cual fue robustisimo, de grandes fuerzas y muy belicoso, gran destruidor de pueblos y matador de gentes." His iconography, for the terminology of which this *Primeros Memoriales* itemization is the major source, was recently discussed in Nicholson 1988b (cf. Boone 1989: 5–9).

2. *Yezpitzal (ezpitzalli)* is apparently derived from *eztli,* blood, and *pitza,* to blow, to play a flute or similar instrument, and to cast gold or silver, in which process blowpipes were used. There is a verb, *tototlapitza,* which means to fashion a decoy. The same term is included in the itemization of the costume and insignia of the next deity, Painal, where what appears to be a marginal annotation identifies it as *ihuitzitzilnahual,* "his hummingbird disguise." This led Seler (1902–1923, II: 424) to conclude that *ezpitzalli* probably refers to this element in Huitzilopochtli's costume, often depicted as a helmet mask. However, it is also possible that it refers to the vestigial bird motif worn on the god's forehead.

3. *Yxiuhcoanaval (Xiuhcoanahualli),* "turquoise ("fire") serpent disguise," featured here as a back device, is only included in the Huitzilopochtli iconography in the Sahaguntine corpus. Elsewhere, this device is confined to Tezcatlipoca and Xiuhtecuhtli. Nahualli was the sorcerer who possessed the power to transform himself into another form, usually that of an animal, and, by extension, also connoted the form or "disguise" itself (see Seler 1899b; 1902–1923, II: 460). As indicated in note 2, this paragraph, the hummingbird was Huitzilopochtli's standard *nahualli* (cf. Nicholson 1988b: 241–244).

4. *Yanecuyouh (anecuyotl),* of uncertain meaning (Garibay, in Sahagún 1975: 917, suggests "ceñidero"), seems to be designated here as a back device (= *Xiuhcoanahualli*?). Elsewhere (Sahagún 1981: 72; 1950–1982, Part IV [Book 3]: 3, 5; 1975: 109; 1988, I: 118), however, it is described as a basketlike headdress composed of bark paper and feathers, originally an insigne of the Centzonhuitznahua, Huitzilopochtli's half brothers, slaughtered by him as an incident in the myth of his birth.

5. *Tevevelli (tehuehuelli),* possibly "people-destroyer" (from *huehueloa,* "disperse, destroy, vanquish"), was the designation for Huitzilopochtli's shield, which was usually decorated with down balls arranged in a quincunx pattern (see Seler 1902–1923, II: 428).

6. *Tlaoaçomalli (tlahuazomalli):* This term, apparently for arrows without points such as those used in the gladiatorial sacrifice, *tlahuahuanaliztli,* was probably derived from the verb *huazoma,* "to skin, to strip off bark" (cf. Seler 1902–1923, II: 428–429). León-Portilla (1958: 115) preferred "flechas de rastrillo."

7. Paynal (Painal), "Swift Runner," was the "delegate," the "substitute," the "deputy" of Huitzilopochtli, his "sota capitan" and "vicario" (Sahagún 1970: 3; 1975: 31; 1988, I: 37–38). His image, carried by a priest, headed the lengthy, swiftly moving procession that was a highlight of the Panquetzaliztli ceremony dedicated to Huitzilopochtli (Sahagún 1981: 141–150).

mixquauhcalichiuhticac in ipã ixayac	A cagelike design is painted across his face.
mixçitlalhviticac, moteneva tlayoallj	His face is painted with the star design called darkness.
yxiuhyacamjuh, yyacac, icac,	In his nose is his turquoise nose arrow adornment.
yezpitzal, contlalitica, yuitzitzilnaual.	His blood bird[8] he places [on his forehead]. (His hummingbird disguise is on his back.[9])
yteucuitlaanaoauh yelpã manj, yeltezcatl,	On his chest is his gold ring[10] (his breast mirror).
yxiuhchimal, xiuhtica tlatzaqualli chimalli jmac manj,	His turquoise shield, the shield covered with a mosaic of turquoise, is in his hand.
xiuhtlalpilli, yni quimiliuhticac	He wears the turquoise knotted cape.
mamallitli, tecuitlapanitl, yn imac, icac.	The fire sticks, the golden banner are in his hands.

Tezcatlipuca, inechichiuh,	The Array of Tezcatlipoca[11]
Tecpatzontli, in icpac, contlaliticac,	The flint knife headdress [of feathers] he places on his head.
yxtlan tlaanticac	Stripes are painted across his face.
tzicoliuhqui in inacuch teucuitlatl,	His ear plugs are gold in the form of a hook.
quetzalcomitl, in quimamaticac,	On his back he bears a quetzal feather vessel.
tecpatl yn imapan caca,	His armlet has a flint knife.
motlitlilicxipuztec	Half of his leg is painted black.
tzitzilli, oyoalli, in icxic caca, coyolj,	There are small bells on his legs—pear-shaped [and] round bells.
yhitzcac	His obsidian [serpent] sandals.
ychimal yviteteyo amapãyo, ymac manj,	In [one] hand is his shield with the feather balls and paper flags [at the bottom].
tlachialonj yn imac icac çentlapal, coyunqui, ic teitta.	In his other hand is the viewer (*tlachialoni*);[12] it has a hole through which he watches people.

8. See note 2, this paragraph.

9. See note 2, this paragraph.

10. *Yteucuitlaanaoauh (teocuitlaanahuatl):* The *anahuatl* was a shell ring pectoral held in place by red bowlike fastenings; it was particularly diagnostic of Tezcatlipoca and his avatars. In the cognate representation of Painal in the *Florentine Codex* (Sahagún 1979, I [Libro I]: fol. 10r) it is depicted with its usual white color and designated only by the term *eltezcatl,* "breast mirror," while it is added here as a marginal gloss.

11. Tezcatlipuca (Tezcatlipoca): "The Mirror's Smoke," from *tezcatl,* mirror, and *pocatl,* smoke. This deity was the omnipotent, omnipresent, protean "supreme god" of the late Pre-Hispanic Central Mexican pantheon. Sahagún (1975: 31; 1988, I: 38) calls him "otro Jupiter," who was "invisible, el cual andaba en todo lugar, en el Cielo, en la tierra y el Infierno."

12. *Tlachialoni:* This object is described by Sahagún (1975: 40; 1988, I: 49) as "una manera de cetro que era una chapa de oro redonda agujerada por el medio, y sobre ella un remate de dos globos, otro mayor y otro menor, con una punta sobre el menor. Llamaban a este cetro tlachialoni que quiere decir 'miradero' o 'mirador,' porque con el ocultaba la cara y miraba por el agujero de medio de la chapa de oro."

[fol. 261v]

quetzalcoatl inechichiuh,	The Array of Quetzalcoatl[13]
y iocelocupil in icpac contlaliticac	On his head he has set his conical jaguar-skin headpiece.
mixtlilmacaticac, muchi yn inacayo,	His face, his entire body are painted black.
mecaichiuhticac, motlatlacuetlanili	His face is painted with the wind design,[14] it is twisted.
tzicoliuhqui teucuitlatl in inacuch	His gold ear plugs are in the form of a hook.
yteucuitlaacuechcuzquj	His necklace of gold shells.
Cueçalvitonquj ỹ quimamaticac,	On his back he bears the adornment of flaring red macaw feathers.
ytentlapal inic motzinilpiticac,	[His cloth] with red border is bound around his loins.
ocelotzitzili yn icxic contlaliticac,	He has placed bands of jaguar skin with bells on his legs.
yiztaccac,	His white sandals.
yn ichimal hecaillacatzcuzcayo	His shield has the wind spiral jewel design.
ychicuacul, içentlapal ymac icac,	In his other hand is his curved staff.
totochtin ynechichiuh,	The Array of the Totochtin[15]
mixchictlapanticac	His face is painted in two colors.[16]
y yaztatzon	His heron feather headdress.
yyacametz	His nose ornament in the form of a crescent.
y yamanacuch	His paper ear plugs.

13. Quetzalcoatl: "Quetzal Feather Serpent." This major deity, like Tezcatlipoca, with whom he was sometimes paired in opposition, exercised multiple functions—above all, creativity and fertility, particularly in his aspect as Ehecatl, Wind. He was also merged with a semilegendary Toltec ruler, the dynastic ancestor of the royal lineage of Mexico Tenochtitlan, whose future return to reclaim his throne was expected (Nicholson 1957, 1979; Carrasco 1982). Sahagún (1975: 32; 1988, I: 39) calls him "dios de los vientos" and states that "aunque fue hombre, tenianle por dios y decian que barria el camino a los dioses del agua." At contact, the focus of the Quetzalcoatl cult in Central Mexico was the great pilgrimage and mercantile center of Cholollan (Cholula, Puebla).

14. *Mecaichiuhticac:* A verb derived from *e (he) catl,* "wind," *i (x) chihua,* "to paint the face," and *icac,* an auxiliary verb that refers to vertical objects. Seler (1902–1923, II: 434–436) and León-Portilla (1958: 117) assign this "wind design," to the god's body and clothing, respectively, rather than to the face. However, this entry precedes the description of the ear ornaments and, since the itemizations of deity insignia and costume in this paragraph follow a strict order, beginning at the head and ending at the feet, it appears more likely that the reference is to the vertical line on the face.

15. Totochtin: "Rabbits." Also known as the Centzontotochtin. "The Four Hundred Rabbits," they were the gods of *octli* (see note 7, Paragraph 4). A considerable ritual revolved around these important fertility deities. All were known by the generic calendric name Ome Tochtli, "Two Rabbit," but many also bore individual names, often gentilitial (for a concise discussion of their cult and iconography, see Nicholson 1991). See also the entries for Totoltecatl and Macuiltochtli later in this paragraph.

16. *Mixchictlapanticac:* This bicolored facial painting, the central field red, flanked by two fields of black or dark green (occasionally vice versa), sometimes decorated with yellow lozenge-shaped elements, was one of the prime iconographic diagnostics of the *octli* deities.

ycueçalvitoncauh quimamaticac.	On his back he bears his adornment of flaring red macaw feathers.
ytlachayaoalcuzqui	His necklace of radiating pendants.[17]
culotlalpili, ic motzinapanticac.	Around his loins is bound a cloth with a scorpion design.
tzitzili, oyoalli, in icxic contlaliticac	On his legs he has placed small bells, pear-shaped bells.
y yometochcac	His Two Rabbit sandals.
ometochchimallj, ymac manj,	The Two Rabbit shield[18] is in his hand.
ytztopollj ymac, ycac.	In the [other] hand is his obsidian ax.
Tlalloc, inechichiuh	The Array of Tlaloc[19]
mixtlilmacaticac	His face is painted black.
moçaticac tliltica in inacayo,	His body is covered with black paint.
mixchiaviticac,	His face has a [white] patch with spots like chia seeds.[20]
y yavachxicol,	His sleeveless dew jacket.
y yaztatzon icpac contlaliticac	He has set his heron feather headdress on his head.
ychalchiuhcuzquj,	His green stone necklace.
temimiliuhqui yc motzinilpiticac, itilma	Around his loins is bound his cape of vertical bands.[21]
ytzitzil, ycxic, contlaliticac	He has placed his small bells on his legs.
ypuçulcac	His sandals with ties covered with white down.[22]
atlacueçonãchimallj in imac manj, auh y	In his hand is the shield with the water lily

17. *Itlachayaoalcuzqui (tlachayahualcozqui):* The somewhat unclear drawing may have been intended to represent the long, loose neckpiece apparently composed of *malinalli* grass (*Muhlenbergia emersleyi* Vasey and other subspecies), usually bound with a red leather strap and a bark paper device. It often depends from a wide greenstone collar edged with gold bells or shells from which hangs a circular gold pectoral. This whole ensemble was apparently called the *chayahuac cozcatl,* translated by Seler (1902–1923, II: 438) as "Flockenhalsband." It constituted another prime iconographic diagnostic of the *octli* gods.

18. *Ometochchimalli:* The design layout on the shield replicates the facial painting and the nasal ornament of the deity.

19. Tlalloc (Tlaloc): "He Who Has Earth," "He Who Is Made of Earth," by extension, "Lord of the Earth" (see Sullivan 1972b: 213–219). Sahagún (1975: 32; 1988, I: 38) calls him "el dios de las lluvias," who "da a los hombres los mantenimientos necesarios para la vida corporal." He is usually shown with "goggle eyes" and a thick labial band with tusklike teeth, but here he displays human features. His ancient cult was of paramount importance in late pre-Hispanic Central Mexico.

20. *Mixchiaviticac (mixchiauhticac):* This patch, or plaster, was composed of the crushed seeds of chia plants, *Salvia chia,* prized for their fine oil-bearing seeds.

21. *Temimiliuhqui yc motzinilpiticac itilma:* Literally, "a cloth like stone pillars."

22. *Ypuculcac (pozolcactli):* Literally, "foam sandals." Compare Sahagún (1950–1982, Part X (Book 9): 80), who, in his account of the array of Centeotl, specified here as one of the deities especially propitiated by the lapidaries, described this footgear as "ipolcucac, can iztac, potonqui inic tlatlapilli," "his white foam sandals; with down feather laces were they tied." Sahagún (1975: 516; 1988, II: 578) renders this in Spanish as "unas cotaras blancas, las ataduras de ellas de algodon flojo." These sandals were also assigned by Sahagún to the attire of Quetzalcoatl and the two allied fertility goddesses, Chalchiuhtlicue and Huixtocihuatl.

yoztopil in imac icac i centlapal

design,[23] and in his other hand is his rush staff.[24]

[fol. 262r]

Chicomecoatl, inechichiuh

Mixtlaviticac
y yamacal yn icpac manj
ychalchiuhcuzquj
y yaxochiauipil. in conmaquiticac y yaxochiacue,
tzitzilli oyoallj, in icxic,
ytecpilcac
yn ichimal tonalochimallj
yçenma ycentlapal imac icac.

The Array of Chicomecoatl[25]

Her face is painted ochre red.
Her paper crown is on her head.
Her green stone necklace.
She is wearing her shift with the evening primrose design, [and] her skirt with the evening primose design.[26]
On her legs are small bells, pear-shaped bells.
Her lordly sandals.
Her shield is the shield with the sun symbol design.[27]
Her double maize ears[28] are in her other hand.

Otontecuhtlj inechichiuh,

yxtlã tlaanticac

The Array of Otontecuhtli[29]

Stripes are painted across his face.

23. *Atlacueconanchimalli (atlacuezonan):* the white water lily (Nymphaea). This shield device is also assigned by Sahagún in this paragraph to Yauhqueme, Tomiauhtecuhtli, Nappatecuhtli, Chalchiuhtlicue, and Huixtocihuatl, all intimately interrelated rain/water deities. Although an appropriate symbol of fertility, it appears in no other source.

24. *Yoztopil (oztopilin):* Seler (1902–1923, II: 445) believed that this term was probably synonymous with *aztapilin,* which Sahagún (1975: 112; 1988, I: 122), in his account of the *veintena* of Etzalcualiztli, described as "muy grandes y muy gruesas juncias . . . muy largas y todo lo que esta dentro del agua es muy blanco." The *oztopilin,* which Sahagún also assigns to Tomiauhtecuhtli, Nappatecuhtli, and Huixtocihuatl, is depicted here and in other sources as a white plaited staff to which are attached cuplike devices of bark paper spotted with liquid rubber. They contain plants that are tipped with paper streamers, also spotted with liquid rubber.

25. *Chicomecoatl:* "Seven Snake," a calendric name. She was the preeminent goddess of maize, the most important Mesoamerican cultigen. Sahagún (1975: 33; 1988, I: 40) describes her as "la diosa de las mantenimientos, asi de lo que come y de lo que bebe," calling her "otra diosa Ceres."

26. *Yaxochiauipil (axochiahuipilli): Axochiatl* (literally, "water flower"), also called *tonalxihuitl* and other names, has been variously identified (Hernández 1959–1984, VII: 23) as *Oenothera laciniata* Hill or *Senecio vernus.* Appropriately, in view of its association with a fundamental fertility goddess, Hernández (1959–1984, II: 19) describes it as a flower—with many medicinal properties—that appeared at the commencement of the rainy season and lasted until its termination.

27. *Tonalochimallj:* Because the shield device is a floral blossom, Seler (1902–1923, II: 447) preferred the translation "der Sommerblumenschild oder Sonnenblumenschild." This finds support in the *Florentine Codex* version (Sahagún 1970: 13) of the array of this deity, where *tonatiuhchimalli* (literally, "sun shield") is given as an additional designation for the shield, whose emblem is Spanished by Sahagún (1975: 33; 1988, I: 40) as "una flor grande."

28. *Ycenma (= cenmaitl):* Literally, "maize *(centli)* hand *(maitl)*." This typical attribute of the maize goddess consists of double maize ears with ritual bark paper *(tetehuitl)* attachments; they are frequently featured on the numerous stone images of this deity (e.g., Nicholson and Quiñones Keber 1983: 76).

29. *Otontecuhtlj* (Otontecuhtli): "Otomi Lord," the patron deity of the Central Mexican Otomian peoples, including the Tepaneca, masters of the imperium that just preceded that of the Triple Alliance (Mexico Tenochtitlan-Tetzcoco-Tlacopan), among whom the Otomi element was particularly important. A deity of fire and of the dead war-

y yamatzon, ioã itzpapalutl, itech ca

His paper crown, and on it obsidian butterflies.[30]

y yamaneapanal, imapãca,

His paper stole; he has his armlet.

y yamamaxtli,

His paper breechcloth.

tzitzilli oyoalli in icxic ca

On his legs are small bells, pear-shaped bells.

yyztaccac

His white sandals.

ychimal yviteteyo in ipã temi tzioactlacuchtlj

His shield is edged with feather balls on which are small cactus spears.

tzivacmitl, yn imac, ycac.

In his [other] hand is a cactus arrow.[31]

yyacatecuhtli ynechichiuh.

The Array of Yacatecuhtli[32]

motlatlatlalili in ixayac,

His face is painted in several places.[33]

ytemillo id est. ixquatzon.

His frontal hair, that is, his hair is arranged in the form of a column.[34]

yquetzalalpiaya

[It is bound with] his quetzal feather ties.

iteocuitlanacuch

His gold ear plugs.

xiuhtlalpillj, yn itilma,

His cape is the knotted turquoise one.

ytlaçomaxtlj

His precious breechcloth.

tzitzilli oyovalli. idẽ. contlaliticac, icxic

He has placed bells, the same as pear-shaped bells, on his legs.

ytec[pil]cac i[n] cactlj

His sandals are the lordly sandals.

xicalcoliuhqui, yn ichimal

His shield with the stepped fret design.

ytlacçaya. id est itopil yn imac ycac.

His foot, that is, his staff, is in his [other] hand.[35]

---

riors (Seler 1902–1923, II: 448–449; Carrasco Pizana 1950: 138–146), who was also known as Ocotecuhtli, Xocotl, and Cuecuex, Otontecuhtli was especially propitiated during the *veintena* of Xocotlhuetzi/Hueymiccailhuitl that featured a spectacular pole ceremony and fire sacrifices (see Paragraph 2A; Sahagún 1981: 111–117).

30. *Itzpapalutl (itzpapalotl):* This is the name of an important "Chichimec" earth/fertility goddess. Here, however, it appears to refer to the notched plates attached to the headband, a particular diagnostic of the array of Otontecuhtli/Xocotl (discussion in Seler 1902–1923, II: 449–452).

31. *Zioactlacuchtlj (tzihuactlacochtli), tziuacmitl (tzihuacmitl):* Two designations for spears/arrows made from a species of cactus, probably a *Cereus (Nyctocereus?*; Hernández 1959–1984, VII: 155–156; Sahagún 1950–1982, Part XII [Book 11]: 218), a typical "Chichimec" weapon (see Seler 1902–1923, II: 452–453).

32. Yiacatecuhtli (Yacatecuhtli): Literally, "Nose Lord"; perhaps, more metaphorically, "Lord Guide." The former translation may relate this deity to "God M," the "Pinocchio Nosed God," the merchant god of the Lowland Maya (see Thompson 1966). Concerning Yacatecuhtli, Sahagún (1975: 45; 1988, I: 56) states: "Hay conjectura que comenzo los tratos y mercaderias entre esta gente, y ansi los mercaderes le tomaron por dios y le honraban de diversas maneras."

33. *Motlatlatlalili in ixayac:* As Seler (1902–1923, II: 454) noted, this phrase described the facial painting appropriate for warriors who performed as dancers. It consisted of black stripes broken by the application of powdered pyrites. The same facial decorative scheme was displayed by Tlacochcalco Yaotl and Omacatl, described later in this paragraph.

34. *Ytemillotl (temillotl):* This term, meaning "stone column," was applied to the distinctive coiffure that was worn, along with another, *tzotzocolli* (see note 89, this paragraph), by the champion warriors, the *tequihuaque.*

35. *Ytalccaya (tlaccayatl):* The sole of the foot and, by extension, the foot itself. Since the staff was an indispensable aid to the merchant on his long and arduous journeys, it probably was regarded, in a sense, as another foot.

[fol. 262v]

Atlava inechichiuh / chachalmeca /.	The Array of Atlahua[36] [God of the] Chalmeca
mixquauhcalichiuhticac,	A cagelike design is painted on his face.
motenchichillo,	His lips are painted red.
ychalmecatlatqui ỹ contlaliticac	He has put on his Chalmeca dress.
yixqua, techimal	His forehead rosettes.
ycuexcuchtechimal.	His occipital rosette.
ypantoyaoal, in icpac icac,	On his head is his drooping flag.
y yamaneapanal	His paper stole.
ymapanca	He has his armlet.
ytzitzil icxic caca,	On his legs are his small bells.
ycac,	His sandals.
ychimal eztlapanquj,	Half of his shield is [painted] the color of blood.[37]
ytlavitimeuh, ymac ycac.	His red *timetl* [staff][38] is in his [other] hand.
Yxcoçauhquj inechichiuh	The Array of Ixcozauhqui[39]
motenhvlcopinticac	His lips are painted with rubber.
ychalchiuhtetel yn icpac contlaliticac y yamacal quetzalmicoayo	On his head he has placed his paper crown with a band of green stone discs; it has a quetzal feather crest.[40]
ytlacuchtzon	His spear shaft head adornment.
yxiuhcoanaval yn quimamaticac,	On his back he bears his fire serpent device.[41]
y yamaneapanal	His paper stole.
tzitzilli oyoallj, yn icxic contlaliticac,	On his legs he has placed small bells, pear-shaped bells.

36. The figure is labeled Chachalmeca, "They (Deities?) of Chalman," while the list of costume items and insignia is headed *Atlava inechichiuh*, "the array of Atlahua." Seler (1902–1923, II: 456–458) apparently assumed that the Atlava heading was an error and that the text referred only to Chachalmeca, since Atlahua, so labeled, was illustrated and his costume and insignia itemized separately later in the paragraph. León-Portilla (1958: 124–125) combined the heading and the label of the illustration and translated them together as "Atavios de Atlahua y los dioses de Chalman." The latter toponym, as Seler noted, was, according to Tovar (*Codex Ramírez*, 1987: 18), derived from *challi*, "cleft, fissure, opening." It was applied to the southeast sector of the Basin of Mexico, the sector adjacent to the great volcanos Iztaccihuatl and Popocatepetl, and was more commonly designated as the province of Chalco. According to Durán (1967, I: 30–31), the priests who performed human sacrifices were called *chachalmeca*. The insignia worn here by the figure are diagnostic of deities with macabre, underworld, and mortuary associations.

37. *Ychimal eztlapanquj:* In the depiction, the other half is green.

38. See note 76, this paragraph.

39. Yxcocauhquj (Ixcozauhqui): "Yellow Face," the Fire God, more commonly called Xiuhtecuhtli, "Turquoise Lord," and Huehueteotl, "Old God." An important deity, propitiated particularly during the *veintena* of Izcalli, he was considered to be the patriarch of the pantheon and the archetype of the rulers in their paternalistic role.

40. Read *quetzalmiaoayo (quetzalmiahuayo)*, a plumed head ornament that imitated the male efflorescence of the maize plant, *miahuatl*, with the long, green feathers of the quetzal bird. It was particularly diagnostic of the fertility deities. See discussion in Seler 1902–1923, II: 459; Nicholson 1963: 19–21.

41. See note 3, this paragraph.

Ycac,
chalchiuhtepachiuhquj
tlachialonj y centlapal imac ycac.

His sandals.
[His shield] is set with green stones.
In his other hand is the viewer.[42]

Yxtlilton

mixtlilmacaticac
ytecpaquachichiquil
yxopilcuzquj
vitonquj yn quimamaticac, itonalopã, ipã icac,

ytonalloamaneapã.
ymapãca
tzitzillj oyoallj in icxic caca

ytonalocac,
ytonalochimal in imac manj,
yiollotopil ynic ma icac cẽtlapal.

Ixtlilton[43]

His face is painted black.
His flint knife crest [on his head].
His toe-shaped necklace.[44]
On his back he bears a flaring [feather] device on which is his flag with the sun symbol.[45]
His stole with the sun symbol.
His armlet.
On his legs are small bells, pear-shaped bells.[46]
His sandals with the sun symbol.
In his hand is his shield with sun symbol.
In his other hand is his heart staff.[47]

42. See note 12, this paragraph.

43. Yxtlilton (Ixtlilton): "Little Black Face," also called Tlaltecuin, "Earth-stamper." This deity has been included in the "Centeotl-Xochipilli Complex" of contact-period Central Mexican deities (Nicholson 1971: 416–419). More specifically, he belonged with the Macuiltonaleque, the young solar deities who presided over flowers, feasting, singing, dancing, gaming, and painting and who bore the names of the five *tonalpohualli* days assigned to the south, with numerical coefficients of five (the number signifying "excess"). Their most prominent member was Macuilxochitl, "Five Flower," described later in this paragraph (see also Macuiltochtli). According to Sahagún (1970: 35–36), Ixtlilton's temple, Tlacuilocan, "Painted Place" or "Place of the Painter/Scribe," all of wood, contained tubs of "black water" that possessed the power to cure children. He also described ceremonies featuring an impersonator of the deity and concerned with the consecration of new *octli* as well as divination involving the "black water."

44. *Yxopilcuzquj (xopilcozqui, xopilcozcatl):* A more literal translation would be "toe-jewel." Seler (1902–1923, II: 461), influenced by what he regarded as a depiction of this or an allied deity in the *Codex Fejérváry-Mayer,* translated *xopilcozqui* as "Halsband aus (Thier-) Klauen." No ornament that seems to fit either label is visible on the figure of Ixtlilton here, but a collar ornament, similarly designated, on the figure of Macuiltochtli, a deity blending the features of the Macuiltonaleque and the *octli* gods, is shown as a large, hollow oval ornament. Seler (e.g., 1900–1901: 54), citing an illustration of a mantle decorated with this ornament in the *Codex Magliabechiano* (1970: 8r) labeled "oyoyl," believed that the name for this ornament, a prime iconographic diagnostic of the Macuiltonaleque and related deities (cf. Beyer 1921), was *oyohualli*—and this view has been widely accepted. However, some years ago Nicholson questioned the accuracy of this label, and this doubt was confirmed by José Luis Franco (1969), who discussed the question at some length. León-Portilla (1958: 127), who derived *xopilcozqui* from *chopilotl,* rock crystal, translated it as "un collar de cristal fino," but, as Franco noted, this appears to be unacceptable since it is clear that the material of this ornament was shell.

45. *Itonalopan (tonallopantli):* "*Tonallo* banner." The *tonallo* symbol, with clear solar connotations, consisted of four circles in a quadrangular arrangement. It was one of the most diagnostic symbols of the Macuiltonaleque and related deities. See Seler (1902–1923, II: 493), who suggested a possible connection with 4 Ollin, the calendric name of the sun, and/or with the beans used as "dice" in the *patolli* game presided over by Macuilxochitl.

46. *Tzitzillj oyoallj (tzitzilli oyohualli):* On these two types of bells, see discussion in Franco 1969; concerning the latter, specifically, see note 44, this paragraph.

47. *Yiollotopil (yollotopilli):* See note 86, this paragraph.

[fol. 263r]

Xippe inechichiuh	The Array of Xipe[48]
mixçolichiuhticac	His face is painted with the quail design.[49]
motenmaxaloticac	His lips are parted.
yyopitzon contlaliticac, icpac, maxaliuhquj.	He has placed his Yopi headdress[50] on his head; it is bifurcated.[51]
comaquitica ỹ evatl y yevayo tlacatl	He has put on a skin; it is a human skin.
ytzonchayaval	His loose-hanging locks.
iteocuitlanacuch	His gold ear plugs.
ytzapucue	His sapote leaf skirt.[52]
ytzitzil, icxic contlaliticac	He has placed his small bells on his legs.
ycac	His sandals.
ychimal tlauhtevilacachiuhquj	His shield has red circles.
ychicavaz yn imac icac.	His rattle staff[53] is in his hand.

Teteu ynã / inechichiuh,	The Array of Teteoinnan[54]
motenholcupinticac	Her lips are painted with rubber.
tlaxapochtli in contlaliticac, ycamapã	She has placed a round patch [of rubber] on her face.

48. Xippe (Xipe): "Flayed One," probably a truncated form of *xipeuh.* In addition to this name, the figure is also labeled *anavatl itec,* "Lord of the Coastland." Xipe was particularly associated with the Yopi/Tlappanec of the Guerrero-Oaxaca border region and the neighboring Zapotec of the Oaxacan Pacific littoral. In the *Florentine Codex* (Sahagún 1970: 39), Xipe is called *Anaoatl iteouh: tzapoteca in vel inteuh catca:* "The god of the Coastland, the proper god of the Zapoteca." An ancient, widely venerated fertility deity with strong militaristic overtones, his cult was distinguished by its macabre flaying ritual. See, especially, Seler 1899a: 76–100; 1963, I: 126–135; Nicholson 1972; Heyden 1986.

49. *Mixcolichiuhticac:* This reference to his face being painted with the quail motif may refer to the broad stripe that runs through the eye, which features a featherlike pattern. A narrow line through the eye is a frequent feature of depictions of Xipe. The quail, *zollin,* a prolific breeder that was sacrificed in large numbers in rituals, was associated with the earth and with both male and female fertility deities. In the *Tonalamatl Aubin* (1900–1901), the face of Xipe peers out of the open bill of the fourth of the Thirteen Sacred Birds, the quail, which Seler (1900–1901: 32, 102–103) suggested was considered to be the *nahualli,* the "disguise," of this deity.

50. *Yyopitzon (yopitzontli):* This conical headpiece is one of the most diagnostic and characteristic elements in the Xipe iconography. Its name ascribes it to the Yopi/Tlappanec (see note 48, this paragraph), but, as Seler (1902–1923, II: 466–467) recognized, the royal headpiece of their Zapotec neighbors was also similar in form.

51. *Maxaliuhquj (maxaliuhqui):* This reference to bifurcation must refer to the strips with "swallow-tail" ends that depend from the *yopitzontli.* Swallow-tail adornments were another prime iconographic diagnostic of Xipe.

52. *Ytzaocucue (zapocueitl):* The sapote leaf skirt is another typical element of Xipe's costume. The tree called *zapotl* (see Sahagún 1950–1982, Part XII [Book 11]: 116; *sapodilla [Lucuma mammosa, achras sapota]*) yielded a tasty, sweet fruit. A possible reference to the Zapoteca (those of Zapotlan, "Place of Sapotes") might also be involved here.

53. *Ychicavaz (chicahuaztli):* This ritual instrument, assigned to many fertility deities (here, also to Opochtli, Yauhqueme, Chalchiuhtlicue, Xilonen, and Zapotlantenan), is described by Sahagún (1975: 515; 1988, 2: 576) as "un baculo que estaba hueco de dentro, y tenia sonajas, el cual, en moviendole para andar, luego las sonajas hacian sus son." Seler (1902–1923, II: 467) translated *chicahuaztli* as "womit etwas kraftig gemacht wird," apparently connoting the fecundating power of the instrument and the rituals in which it was employed. On its "shamanic" aspect, see Neumann 1976.

54. Teteu yna (Teteoinnan): "Mother of the Gods." This was perhaps the commonest appellation for the Late Postclassic Central Mexican version of the great earth mother, a major Mesoamerican deity from the earliest times onward. She also bore other names, including Toci, "Our Grandmother," and Tlalli iyollo, "Heart of the Earth" (Sahagún 1970: 15)—and, as Seler (1900–1901: 93–100) recognized, she was identified iconographically and conceptually with Tlazolteotl, "Filth-Goddess," of ultimate Huaxtec origin. See Nicholson 1971: 420–422.

ychcaxochiuh contlaliticac.

yxiuhtotonacuch.
yçoyatemal
cuechtli, in icue, in i mitoa, çitlallicue.

yn ivipil, i piloyo,
yztaccue.
ycac
ychimal teucuitlaxapo
yzquiz.

She has placed her headdress of unspun cotton [on her head].
Her ear plugs of lovely cotinga feathers.
Her palm leaf tuft [is on her head].[55]
Her skirt of snail shells is called the skirt of stars.[56]
Her shift has fringes.
Her white skirt.
Her sandals.
Her shield with the gold disc.
Her broom.

Opuchtli inechichiuh.

The Array of Opochtli[57]

moçaticac
mixchiaviticac.

y iamacal. icpac ca
y yaztatzon quetzalmiavayo.

y iamaneapanal.
y yamamaxtlj
yztaccac.
ytonalochimal
ychicavaz imac icac.

He is painted [black].
On his face is [a white, round patch with black dots, like] chia seeds.
On his head is his paper crown.
His heron feather crest with a quetzal feather crest.
His paper stole.
His paper breechcloth.
His white sandals.
His shield with the sun symbol.
In his [other] hand is his rattle staff.

[fol. 263v]

yyauhqueme ynechichiuh

The Array of Yauhqueme[58]

y yauhpalli yn iamacal

y yaztatzon quetzalmiavayo

y yamaneapanal.

His paper crown is the color of the sweet-scented marigold.
His heron feather crest has a quetzal feather crest.
His paper stole.

55. *Ycoyatemal (zoyatemalli):* The *temalli (timalli)* was a spherical head ornament into which feathers were most commonly inserted, but here either strips of a fan palm, *zoyatl* (*Brahae dulcis* HBK), or, as Seler (1902–1923, II: 470) suggested, perhaps feathers resembling these palm strips.

56. *Citlallicue:* "stars-her-skirt." This term for an important element in Teteoinnan's costume was also employed as another name for her and related mother goddesses (e.g., Sahagún 1950–1982, Part VII [Book 6]: 203). Molina (1944, Part II: 22v) defines the word as "camino de Santiago en el cielo" (= Milky Way).

57. Opuchtli (Opochtli), "The Left," was one of the Tlaloque, who were aspects of Tlaloc, the preeminent rain/fertility deity. Opochtli was the patron deity of the Atlaca, those specializing in fishing and other aquatic subsistence activities, and was credited with the invention of the fishing net, the *atlatl* (spear-thrower), the *minacachalli,* the three-pronged fishing harpoon, the pole for propelling canoes, and the snare for catching aquatic birds (Sahagún 1970: 37).

58. Yyauhqueme (Yauhqueme), literally, "Owner of the Sweet-scented Marigold Vestment," was another one of the Tlaloque. *Yauhtli,* as was stated in note 19, Paragraph 4, is the sweet-scented marigold, *Tagetes lucida.* The *quemitl* was a biblike ritual vestment worn on the chest. As was also indicated, a hill west of Mexico Tenochtitlan, near Atlacuihuayan (Tacubaya), bore the name Yauhqueme.

y yamamaxtlj,	His paper breechcloth.
icac	His sandals.
ychimal atlacueçonayo.	His shield has the water lily design.
ychicavaz yn imac ycac.	In his [other] hand is his rattle staff.
Chalchiuhtlicue inechichiuh.	The Array of Chalchiuhtlicue[59]
yxaval	Her [yellow ochre] face paint.[60]
ychalchiuhcozquj	Her green stone necklace.
y yamacal quetzalmiavayo	Her paper crown has a queztal feather crest.
atlacuiloli yn ivipil.	Her shift has the water design [of horizontal, blue, wavy lines].
yn icue, atlacuiloli.	Her skirt has the water design.
ytzitzil.	Her little bells.
ycac.	Her sandals.
ychimal atlacueçonāchimallj	Her shield is the water lily shield.
ychicaoaz, imac, icac.	In her [other] hand is her rattle staff.
Xillone, inechichiuh.	The Array of Xilonen[61]
yxaoal, centlacul chichiltic, centlacul, cuztic.	Her facial paint is half red, half yellow.[62]
Y yamacal quetzalmiavayo	Her paper crown has a quetzal feather crest.
ychalchiuhcozquj	Her green stone necklace.
y yaxochiavipil	Her shift with the evening primrose design.
y yaxochiacue	Her skirt with the evening primrose design.[63]
ytzitzil	Her small bells.
ycac	Her sandals.
ychimal	Her shield.
ychicavaz imac icac chichiltic.	In her [other] hand is her red rattle stick.

59. Chalchiuhtlicue, literally, "Precious Green Stone-Her-Skirt," was an important fertility goddess—characteristically blending with others of this numerous group—who was considered to be the elder sister of the rain gods, the Tlaloque (Sahagún 1970: 21). She had jurisdiction over all bodies of water. Concerning her iconography, see Nicholson 1988b.

60. *Yxaval (xahualli):* Facial paint, a noun derived from the verb *xahua,* to ripen (fruit), i.e., to redden or to yellow. By extension, it came to mean to paint the face a reddish or yellowish color (with yellow ochre, *tecozahuitl*), particularly the latter, with *xahualli* connoting facial paint in general. Molina (1944, Part II: 158v) defines the verb as "afeitarse la yndia a su modo antiguo o pintar la fruta."

61. Xillone (Xilonen): Literally, "Tender Maize Ear-Doll." She seems to have been essentially just a younger aspect of Chicomecoatl.

62. In the depiction, the upper half is red, the lower half, yellow.

63. See note 26, this paragraph.

[fol. 264r]

Tzaputlatena inechichiuh.	The Array of Zapotlantenan[64]
yxaval omequipillo	Her [yellow ochre] facial paint has two [black] pendants.[65]
y yamacal holtica tlacuiloli q̃tzalmiavayo.	Her paper crown is painted with liquid rubber; it has a quetzal feather crest.
ychalchiuhcuzquj.	Her green stone necklace.
yvipil.	Her shift.
ycue.	Her skirt.
ytzitzil	Her bells.
ycac.	Her sandals.
ychimalquapachiuhquj	Her shield is covered with eagle feathers.[66]
ychicavaz imac ycac.	In her hand is her rattle staff.
Çiuacoatl inechichiuh.	The Array of Cihuacoatl[67]
yxaval motenolcopi, centlacul chichiltic, centlacol tliltic.	Her facial paint; the lips are painted with rubber; [her face] is half red, half black.
yquauhtzon.	Her headdress of eagle feathers.
teucuitlatl in inacuch.	Her gold ear plugs.
y yaxochiavipil ypan j.	On her is her evening primrose shift.[68]
jn tlanj ipiloyo in ivipil.	Her undershift has her fringes.
iztaccue.	Her white skirt.

64. Tzaputlatena (Zapotlantenan): "Mother of Zapotlan." A fertility goddess who was credited (Sahagún 1975: 34; 1988, I: 41) with the invention of *oxitl*, a turpentine unguent that was employed medicinally to cure many ailments, particularly certain skin diseases. The problem of the location of Zapotlan, from which this deity apparently originally derived, is still unresolved. Zapotlan, "Place of the Zapotes," is a relatively common toponym. Seler (1902–1923, II: 475–476) preferred Zapotitlan, a small community located on the north shore of Lake Xochimilco in the southern Basin of Mexico. León-Portilla (1958: 93, citing Caso 1956: 10), suggested that it might be identified with a "barrio" of that name in the Moyotlan (southwest) quarter of Tenochtitlan.

65. *Omequipillo:* These "pendants," which constitute dark stripes on both cheeks of the goddess, probably correspond to the stripes, singly or in pairs, that are a common feature of depictions of Chalchiuhtlicue (Nicholson 1963: 12–15). Seler (1902–1923, II: 476) suggested that those on Zapotlantenan were composed of the turpentine unguent with which the goddess was particularly associated.

66. *Ychimalquapachiuhquj:* Seler (1902–1923, II: 476–477) believed that the second element should be read *quappachiuhqui*, i.e., *cuauh-pachiuhqui*, "in welchem Adler (federn) eingesetzt sind," and he compared it with the shield with the eagle's claw motif called *cuauhtetepoyo*, i.e., *tetepoyyo*, assimilated from *teteponyo*, "having the knee (= leg) of an eagle" (see Nicholson 1994). The shield carried here by Zapotlantenan is also carried by Cihuacoatl, Chantico, and Coatlicue as depicted in this paragraph, all closely interrelated earth/fertility goddesses.

67. Ciuacoatl (Cihuacoatl): "Woman Serpent," also known by various other names (Quilaztli, "Plant Generator"?, Tonan[tzin], "Our Mother," Cuauhcihuatl, "Eagle Woman," Yaocihuatl, "Warrior Woman," etc.). She was an important earth/fertility goddess who was especially propitiated in Colhuacan, capital of a city-state that formed a key dynastic link between the rulers of imperial Tollan and those of Mexico Tenochtitlan. Her name was borne as a title by the high priests of Azcapotzalco and Tetzcoco and by the Mexica "vice ruler." She exercised a significant martial role as the sister of Huitzilopochtli and the patroness of parturient women, who were likened to warriors waging a battle (discussion in Seler 1902–1923, II: 478–479).

68. Although the upper garment that is worn here over the standard shift, the *huipilli*, is also called a *huipilli*, from the illustration it is obviously a different, poncholike item of apparel with a triangular point hanging down in front and back, the *quechquemitl* (see Seler 1902–1923, II: 479). Apparently, it was not commonly worn by the women of Central Mexico at the time of the Conquest but was assigned to various goddesses in the ritual-divinatory pictorials (cf. Tezcacoac Ayopechtli, Chantico, and Chalmecacihuatl later in this paragraph).

ytzitzil.	Her small bells.
ycac.	Her sandals.
ychimal quapachiuhquj.	Her shield is covered with eagle feathers.
ytzotzopaz.	Her batten.[69]

Vixtociuatl, inechichiuh.	The Array of Huixtocihuatl[70]
yxaval cuztic.	Her facial paint is yellow.
Y yamacal quetzalmiavayo	Her paper crown has a quetzal feather crest.
yteucuitlanacuch.	Her gold ear plugs.
yvipil atlacuiloli,	Her shift has the water design.
yn icue atlacuiloli	Her skirt has the water design.
ytzitzil	Her small bells.
ycac	Her sandals.
ychimal atlacueçonayo.	Her shield has the water lily design.
y yoztopil imac icac.	In her hand is her reed staff.

[fol. 264v]

Coatlicue ynechichiuh.	The Array of Coatlicue[71]
Yxaval tiçatl,	Her facial paint is chalk.
quauhtzontli yn contlaliticac	On her head is the eagle feather headdress.
yvipil yztac,	Her shift is white.
yn icue coatl.	Her skirt is of serpents.
ytzitzil.	Her small bells.
ycac yztac	Her sandals are white.
yn ichimal quapachiuhquj	Her shield is covered with eagle feathers.
ycoatopil	Her serpent staff.

69. *Ytzotzopaz* : The *tzotzopaztli* was the batten or weaving stick. It was the instrument of women par excellence, not only in their role as ordinary weavers but also in their role as procreators, the weavers of the tissue of life. See Sullivan 1982.

70. Vixtociuatl (Huixtocihuatl): "Woman (Goddess) of the Huixtotin." Sahagún (1950–1982, Part XI [Book 10]: 187–188) designated the people of the southern Gulf Coast as the Olmeca Huixtotin Mixteca. Besides some Nahuatl, at the time of the Conquest they spoke a Mixe-Zoquean language called Popoloca. In Sahagún's (1981: 93–94) account of the rituals performed in the *veintena* of Tecuilhuitontli in Tenochtitlan/Tlatelolco, dedicated to Huixtocihuatl, the sacrificial victims are called Huixtotin; they wore headpieces featuring upright eagle claws (see Caso 1927: 21–23). As Seler (1902–1923, II: 480) noted, in the *Codex Vaticanus A* the fifth of the thirteen celestial tiers is labeled *ylhuicatl huixtutla* (Ilhuicatl Huixtotlan). In the 1566 Latin letter to Philip II of Pablo Nazareo (Zimmermann 1970: 23–31), colonial cacique of Xaltocan, the "vixtocanorum" (Sp. "vixtocanos" [Huixtocanos]) are included in a listing of sequent peoples who ruled the area in pre-Toltec times. It is possible that Huixtocihuatl was connected with this closer-to-home lacustrine group in the northern Basin of Mexico rather than with the much more distant Gulf Coast people with a similar name. In any case, as the elder sister of the rain deities, the Tlaloque, she overlapped in function with the water goddess, Chalchiuhtlicue, and was the special patroness of those who prepared and traded in salt, the Iztachiuhque (Sahagún 1970: 91–95).

71. Coatlicue: "Snake(s)-Her-Skirt." The illustration also labels her *yztac ciuatl* (Iztac Cihuatl), "White Woman." A significant member of the important complex of earth/fertility goddesses, Coatlicue was also the name borne by the mother of Huitzilopochtli in the myth of his birth (Sahagún 1950–1982, Part IV [Book 3]: 1–5). According to Sahagún (1981: 57; 1975: 104; 1988: 112), as the patroness of the "barrio" of Coatlan, she was also known as Coatlantonan, "Our Mother of Coatlan (Place of the Serpent)," and was propitiated by "estos maestros de hacer flores" during the *veintena* of Tozoztontli. Two "barrios" of Coatlan are documented, one in the Aztacoalco (northeast) quarter of Tenochtitlan, the other in Tlatelolco (Caso 1956: 26, 39–40, Plano 2).

amimitl inechichiuh,	The Array of Amimitl[72]
yxaval tiçatl,	His facial paint is chalk.
y yamanacoch	His paper ear plugs.
ytzoncuetlax.	His headdress of leather thongs.
yquetzaltemal.	His queztal feather tuft.
motiçavavanticac.	He is painted with [vertical] stripes of chalk.
y yamaneapanal.	His paper stole.
ytzitzil	His small bells.
ycac	His sandals.
ymatlavacal	His net carrier.
ytzivactlacuch yn imac icac.	In his hand is his cactus spear.
Tomjauhtecuhtlj inechichiuh.	The Array of Tomiyauhtecuhtli[73]
moçaticac mixchiaviticac.	He is painted [black]. On his face is [a round patch with black spots like] chia seeds.
y yamacal	His paper crown.
y yaztatzon quetzalmiavayo.	His heron feather crest has a quetzal feather crest.
y yamaneapanal.	His paper stole.
y yamamaxtlj,	His paper breechcloth.
ytzitzil.	His small bells.
ycac iztac.	His sandals are white.
y yatlacueçonāchimal.	His shield with the water lily design.
y yoztopil yn imac icac.	In his hand is his reed staff.

[fol. 265r]

atlava inechichiuh.	The Array of Atlahua[74]
motenchichillo	His lips are painted red.

72. Amimitl: "Hunting Arrow." As Seler (1902–1923, II: 483) noted, this deity displays various insignia (white striping on arms and legs) and accouterments (netted pouch, *matlahuacalli*, and cactus-spine spear, *tzihuac tlacochtli*) that relate him to the major hunting/stellar "Chichimec" deity, Mixcoatl/Camaxtli, and to Otontecuhtli, the special patron of the Otomi, who, in some contexts, were considered to be Chichimeca. Amimitl, together with Atlahua (see note 74, this paragraph), was a god of special importance in Cuitlahuac and in general among the Chinampaneca of the freshwater lacustrine zone of the southern Basin of Mexico (e.g., Sahagún 1970: 79; *Historia de los Mexicanos por Sus Pinturas* 1891: 239). Sahagún (1950–1982, Part XI [Book 10]: 195) also assigns the name Amimitl to the ancestral ruler of the Tarascans (Purepecha) of Michoacan.

73. Tomjauhtecuhtlj (Tomiyauhtecuhtli): "Our Maize Tassel Lord." As is evident from his insignia and apparel, this deity was another of the rain/fertility gods, the Tlaloque. Seler (1902–1923, II: 483) speculated that, as in the case of others of the Tlaloque (cf. Yauhqueme, note 58, this paragraph), a mountain also bore the name of this deity, most likely—judging from its position here between two Chinampaneca deities—in the neighborhood of lakes Chalco and Xochimilco. In the previous paragraph, the inclusion of the priestly title "Ometochtli Tomiyauh" indicates, as pointed out in Note 33 to that paragraph, that Tomiyauhtecuhtli and other rain/mountain deities were merged with the *octli* gods (cf. Nicholson 1991).

74. Atlava (Atlahua): "Lord (Possessor) of the Spear-thrower *(atlatl)*." Seler (1902–1923, II: 485, 1090) provided this etymology but also suggested another possibility, "Lord of the Water's Edge." Garibay (1958: 213) preferred the first version but also recognized the possibility of "dueño del agua," in which he was followed by León-Portilla (1958: 141). As indicated in note 72, this paragraph, Sahagún specified that this god, together with Amimitl, was a particular deity of

mixtetlilcomolo	A black domino covers his eyes.[75]
mixçitlalviticac.	The star design is painted across his face.
yxquatechimal	His forehead rosette.
ypantoyaval	His flag that hangs forward [on his head].
motexovavãticac	He is painted with [vertical] blue stripes.
y yamaneapanal	His paper stole.
y yamamaxtlj	His paper breechcloth.
ytzitzil.	His small bells.
ycac iztac.	His sandals are white.
ychimal eztlapãqui yviteteyo.	His shield is half red [and half white]; it has feather balls.
ytlavitimeuh imac icac.	In his hand is his *timetl* staff.[76]

Napatecuhtli inechichiuh.	The Array of Nappatecuhtli[77]
moçaticac.	He is painted [black].
mixtlilmacaticac.	His face is painted black.
mixchiaviticac.	He has [a round white patch] on his face [with spots like] chia seeds.
y yamacal	His paper crown.
y yamacuexpal.	His paper locks on the nape of his neck.[78]
Yamamaxtlj	His paper breechcloth.
ytzitzil.	His small bells.
ycac yztac.	His sandals are white.
y yatlacueçonãchimal.	His shield with the water lily design.
y yoztopil yn imac icac.	In his hand is his reed staff.

Totoltecatl inechichiuh.	The Array of Totoltecatl[79]
y yacametz.	His nose ornament in the form of a crescent.
y yamacal	His paper crown.
y yaztatzon	His heron feather crest.
ytentlapal ynic motzinilpiticac	His cloth with a red border is bound around his loins.

---

the Chinampaneca, the dwellers in the region of the freshwater lakes Chalco and Xochimilco. Atlahua (i.e., his ritual impersonator) is pictured three times in the depictions of the eighteen *veintena* ceremonies in the *Codex Borbonicus* (1974: 26, 28, 36), which may derive from the Chinampaneca zone (Nicholson 1988c).

75. *Mixtetlilcomolo:* Literally, "black holes are made on his eyes." This facial painting (cf. Painal, note 7, this paragraph) is particularly diagnostic of the Chichimec stellar/hunting god, Mixcoatl/Camaxtli, and allied deities, including Tlahuizcalpantecuhtli, the Venus god (discussion in Seler [1902–1923, II: 430]).

76. *Itlavitimeuh: Timetl* was the designation for the somewhat enigmatic bicolored (red/white or green/white), bilobed object held in the figure's left hand (cf. Chachalmeca). Seler [1902–1923, II: 485, 1094], on the basis of certain strophes in the song dedicated to Atlahua in Paragraph 14, suggested that the *timetl* was a cleft reed.

77. Napatecuhtli (Nappatecuhtli): "Fourfold Lord." Sahagún (1970: 45) included him among the rain/fertility gods, the Tlaloque, and states that he was the special patron—and inventor of their craft—of the mat makers, the Petlachiuhque.

78. *Yyamacuexpal:* The *cuexpalli* was a long lock of hair left at the nape of the neck of young boys when their hair was trimmed (Molina 1944, Part II: 26v). The *amacuexpalli* was a fanlike, pleated, bark paper ornament attached to the nape of the neck, and it is a prominent feature on many stone sculptures of the fertility deities (e.g., Nicholson and Quiñones Keber 1983: figs. 17b, 18). Although Seler (1902–1923, II: 487) correctly identified this ornament here, when it occurred on the stone images he always referred to it, erroneously, as the *tlaquechpanyotl.*

79. Totoltecatl: "He of Totollan (Place of the Turkey)." This deity was another of the many *octli* deities and is arrayed in the fashion typical of these gods.

ytzitzil. ycac.
yn ichimal, y yacalchimal
yytztopol centlapal quitquiticac.

His small bells; his sandals.
His shield; his quadrangular shield.[80]
In his other [hand] he holds his obsidian ax.

Macuiltochtli yn inechichiuh.

The Array of Macuiltochtli[81]

motemacpalhuiticac
yhuitzoncal eticac
yquachichiquil
yxopilcozqui
ytentlapal ic motzinilpiticac

ytzitzil yyztacac
ychimalxupil
yytztopol.

A hand is painted on his mouth.[82]
His is a feathered headdress.
His feather crest.
His necklace in the shape of a toe.[83]
His cloth with a red border is bound around his loins.
His small bells; his white sandals.
His shield with the toe design.
His obsidian ax.

Macuilxuchitl, yn inechichiuh.

The Array of Macuilxochitl[84]

motẽmacpalhuiticac.
mixtlapalvatzalhuiticac.
yyhuitzoncal eticac.
iquachichiquil
ihuitocauh, quimamaticac.

ipan, icac, itonalopan, quetzaltzoio.

I motzinilpiticac, itentlapal.

itzitzil, ytonalocac.

motlauiticac ytonalochimal

A hand is painted on his mouth.
His face is painted bright red.
His is a feathered headdress.
His crest of feathers.
On his back he bears his flaring feather adornment.
On it stands his flag with the sun symbol;[85] it has a quetzal feather crest.
His red-bordered cloth is bound around his loins.
His small bells; his sandals with the sun symbol.
His shield with the sun symbol is painted with red ochre.

80. *Yyacalchimal (acalchimalli):* Literally, "boat shield." As Seler (1902–1923, II: 488; cf. León-Portilla 1958: 143) recognized, this designation for the quadrangular shield frequently carried by the *octli* gods probably indicates that it was being compared to the quadrangular form of the native boats, dugout canoes.

81. Macuiltochtli: "Five Rabbit," a calendric name. He exhibits iconographic features of both the *octli* deities and the Macuiltonaleque (see note 43, this paragraph), whose quintet included a deity of this name. Sahagún (1950–1982, Part X [Book 9]: 84) also listed Macuiltochtli as one of the special tutelary deities of the Amanteca, the featherworkers of Tenochtitlan/Tlatelolco, propitiated by them along with six others (four male, two female) headed by Coyotlinahual. This supernatural ensemble incorporated elements of the *octli* cult, the Macuiltonaleque, and the fertility deities in general.

82. *Mote(n)macpalhuiticac:* The white hand covering the mouth area, sometimes simplified to a lobed motif (as in the case of the drawing of the next deity, Macuilxochitl), is one of the prime iconographic diagnostics of the Macuiltonaleque. As Seler (1902–1923, II: 492) noted, this motif probably expressed the element *macuilli,* "five," in the composition of their names.

83. See note 44, this paragraph.

84. Macuilxuchitl (Macuilxochitl): "Five Flower," the calendric name for the preeminent member of the Macuiltonaleque (see note 43, this paragraph).

85. *Itonalapan:* The *tonallo* symbol (see note 45, this paragraph) here is pictured on both the banner and the shield borne by the deity.

yyollotopil, quetzaltzoio. centlapal, quitquiticac.

In his other [hand] he carries his heart staff[86] with the quetzal feather crest.

Tezcacoac aiopechtli

yn inechichiuh eticac
motenolcopinticac texuctica

tlaxapoch, contlaliticac

y yamacal, contlaliticac.

ychalchiuhcozqui
y yaxochiauipil
yyztaccue
ytzitzil, yyztacac.
tlaauitectli in ichimal
yn itopil i centlapal quitquiticac tlaitzcopintli in itlaque.

Tezcacoac Ayopechtli[87]

Her array is:
Her mouth is painted with rubber, with the color blue.
She has placed a patch [not visible] on her face.
She has placed her paper crown [on her head].
Her green stone necklace.
Her shift with the evening primrose design.
Her white skirt.
Her small bells; her white sandals.
Her shield is whitewashed.
In her other [hand] she carries a staff; its covering has a design of obsidian points.

[fol. 266r]

Tlacochcalco yautl, yn inechichiuh.

yn ixaiac motlatlatlaliliticac

motlitlilicxipuztecticac.
ytenzacauh eticac
yteucuitlanacoch.
ytzotzocol veiacauh

The Array of Tlacochcalco Yaotl[88]

His face is painted with designs in various places.
His legs are painted half black.
His is a labret.
His gold ear plugs.
His water-jug hair arrangement[89] of the great warriors.

86. *Yyollotopil:* The *yollotopilli* was another of the leading iconographic features of the Macuiltonaleque (discussion in Seler 1902–1923, II: 492–493).

87. Tezcacoac Ayopechtli: "Mirror-Snake Tortoise-Bench." This was another designation for Mayahuel, or an avatar, the goddess of the maguey plant, the source of *octli.* A prominent member of the intimately interrelated complex of maternal fertility goddesses (Nicholson 1963), she was conceived as a woman with four hundred (i.e., innumerable) breasts. In the Mixteca-Puebla-style divinatory-ritual screenfold, *Codex Laud* (1966: 9), a version of Mayahuel is pictured naked and seated on a tortoise, which correlates with the appellation Ayopechtli. See discussion of the iconography and nature of Mayahuel/Tezcacoac Ayopechtli in Seler 1902–1923, II: 493–495, 1045–1047; 1963, I: 191–192; Thompson 1966; Quiñones Keber 1989b; Nicholson 1991.

88. Tlacochcalco yautl (Tlacochcalco Yaotl): "Spear-House Enemy." As Seler (1902–1923, II: 496–497) recognized, this deity was only an aspect of Tezcatlipoca (see note 11, this paragraph), who bore as one of his many appellations the name Yaotl, "Enemy," explicitly expressing his militaristic dimension. According to the *Codex Magliabechiano* (1970: 36v), Tlacochcalco, which was also one of the designations for the cardinal direction north, was, along with Huitznahuac, denoting the south, a name borne by temples dedicated to Tezcatlipoca—including the small shrine in the province of Chalco where the *ixiptla,* the annual impersonator of Tezcatlipoca, was sacrificed in the *veintena* of Toxcatl. Although Tlacochcalco Yaotl's costume and insignia differ substantially from those displayed by Tezcatlipoca "proper," as he is arrayed here as a warrior in gala dance attire, he does hold one of the most characteristic objects associated with this great god: his circular, perforated "viewer," here called *tlachiaya* rather than *tlachialoni* (see note 12, this paragraph).

89. *Yzotzocol (tzotzocolli):* This coiffure, with the hair pulled up high on one side, was another style, complementary to the *temillotl* (see note 34, this paragraph), worn by the champion warriors, the *tequihuaque.*

y yaztaxexel, quetzalmiavaio.
His double heron feather headdress has a quetzal feather crest.

ymecaayauh, tenchilnavaio.
His thin, net maguey cape has a red border of rings.

ychipulcozqui
His necklace of snail shells.

ytzitzil yyztaccac.
His small bells; his white sandals.

yn ichimal amapaio.
His shield has paper flags [along the bottom].

y centlapal imaquicac, itlachiaya.
In his other hand is his viewer.

Vtlamaxac manca civapipilti motenevaia, yn inechichiuh

The Array of Those Called Cihuapipiltin,[90] Who Hover Over the Crossroads

mixticauitimanca
Their faces are painted with chalk.[91]

inteteucuitlanacoch
Their gold ear plugs.

ypiloio in iuipil
Their shifts have fringes.

tlalpipitzauac in incue
Their skirts have thin black lines.

ipan i quimocuetiaia tlaitzcopintli in amatl
On these were [banks of] paper painted with obsidian points.[92]

ym iyztaccac.
Their white sandals.

Xuchipilli, in inechichiuh.

The Array of Xochipilli[93]

motlauiticac
[His face] is painted with red ochre.

ychoquizxaual eticac
His is the teardrop facial paint.

ytlauhquecholtzoncal eticac
His is the headdress of roseate spoonbill feathers.

ychalchiuhtenteuh eticac
His is the green stone labret.

ychalchiuhcozqui eticac
His is the green stone necklace.

y yamaneapanal ymapanca
His paper stole; his armlet.

ytentlapal ic motzinilpiticac
His red-bordered cloth is bound around his loins.

ytzitzil, yxuchicac,
His small bells; his sandals with a flower design.

90. *Civapipilti* (Cihuapipiltin): "Noblewomen." These were the souls of the deified women, also known as Cihuateteo, "Goddesses," and Mocihuaquetzque, "Those Who Arose as Women," who died in first childbirth (Sahagún 1950–1982, Part V [Book 4]: 41–42, Part VII [Book 6]: 161–165; 1970: 19; 1988, I: 42, 247–248, 409–413). They were the female counterparts of the warriors who had died in battle or on the stone of sacrifice. They daily transported the sun from the zenith—to where it had been carried by the souls of the slain warriors who dwelled in the east—to its setting in the west, their abode (Cihuatlampa, "The Place of Women"). They were much feared, for on the days that initiated the five *trecenas* of the 260-day divinatory cycle, the *tonalpohualli,* assigned to the west (1 Mazatl, 1 Quiahuitl, 1 Ozomatli, 1 Calli, 1 Cuauhtli), they hovered over the crossroads and inflicted diseases and deformities on children.

91. Read *mixticauitimanca.*

92. *Tlaitzcopintli:* These V-shaped black markings, compared to obsidian points, commonly decorate bark paper attachments to items of costume and accouterments of the earth/fertility deities (discussion in Seler 1900–1901: 69; Nicholson 1967a: 87).

93. Xuchipilli (Xochipilli): "Flower-Prince (= Nobleman)." This deity overlapped with and complemented Macuilxochitl and other members of the Macuiltonaleque (see note 43, this paragraph). Although other items of Xochipilli's costume and insignia are somewhat distinct from those characteristic of Macuilxochitl, both deities carry the diagnostic *yolotopilli,* the heart-staff.

ytonalochimal xiuhtica tlatzaqualli	His shield with the sun symbol is covered with a mosaic of turquoise.
centlapal quitquiticac yyollotopil quetzaltzoio.	In his other [hand] he carries his heart staff with the quetzal feather crest.

[fol. 266v]

Chantico yn inechichiuh.	The Array of Chantico[94]
motenolcopiticac	Her lips are painted with rubber.
centlacol mixtlapalhuiticac	Half of her face is painted red.
yn contlaliticac itlaçolxochiuh	She has placed her headdress of rags on her head.[95]
yteucuitlanacoch	Her gold ear plugs.
y quimamaticac meiotli	On her back she carries the sun ray symbol.[96]
y yaxochiauipil	Her shift with the evening primrose design.
yn ichimal quauhpachiuhqui	Her shield is covered with eagle feathers.
y centlapal ymaquicac yvitopil, yn itlaque tlaitzcopintli	In her other hand is her feather staff; its covering has a design of obsidian points.
yyztac, cue	Her white skirt.
ytzitzil	Her small bells.
yyztaccac.	Her white sandals.

Chalmecaçivatl, yn inechichiuh.	The Array of Chalmecacihuatl[97]
motenolcopiticac	Her mouth is painted with rubber.
mixtecoçauiticac	[The upper half of] her face is painted yellow.
y yamatzon	Her paper crown.

94. Chantico: The name of this deity is usually translated "In the House." However, "in the house," strictly speaking, would be *chanco.* The *ti* could be a nonsemantic "ligature," or the word could be an archaic form of the locative—or even, conceivably, a borrowing from another language. Chantico, also called Cuaxolotl ("Xolotl-Head"—possibly also connoting "Double" or "Split-Head"), was a fertility deity with igneous associations. She overlapped with Xochiquetzal, Cihuacoatl, and other fertility goddesses and was merged with the malevolent sorceress-half sister of Huitzilopochtli, Coyolxauhqui (discussions in Seler 1900–1901: 114–118; 1963, II: 224–228; Nicholson 1985). The discovery of the colossal relief sculpture representing the decapitated and dismembered Coyolxauhqui/Chantico (perpetrated by Huitzilopochtli as an incident in the myth of his birth) in Mexico City in 1978 sparked the Proyecto Templo Mayor, 1978–1982, that resulted in the complete clearing and excavation of Mexico Tenochtitlan's Templo Mayor of Huitzilopochtli and Tlaloc.

95. *Yn contlaliticac itlaçolxochiuh:* The translation offered here agrees basically with that of Seler (1902–1923, II: 501): "Ihre Stirnbinde aus Lumpen (aus zerzupftem Stoff, aus Werg) hat sie um den Kopf gebunden." León-Portilla (1958: 149) renders it very differently: "Tiene un ramillete de yerbas secas." Based on the sculptured images of this deity and representations of her in the native tradition pictorials (Nicholson 1985: figs. 1, 6–8, 10–12, 14), what is depicted here appears to be a headcloth decorated with down balls.

96. *Meiotli (meyotli):* For the problems connected with the identification and connotation of this symbol, see Seler 1902–1923, II: 501–502. It is difficult to discern anything on the figure that could be identified with this element.

97. Chalmecacivatl (Chalmecacihuatl): "Woman of the Chalmeca." The Chalmeca were the inhabitants of Chalman (discussed in note 36, this paragraph). Seler (1902–1923, II: 503) believed that she was the female counterpart, the "wife," of the Chachalmeca (also discussed in note 36). Sahagún (1950–1982, Part X [Book 9]: 43; 1975: 47; 1988, I: 58) names her as the "sister" of Yacatecuhtli, the merchant god. Durán (1967, I: 121) includes her in a list of five deities, including Yacatecuhtli, impersonated by slaves offered by the merchants as sacrificial victims during the *veintena* of

ycuexcochtechimal
y yaxochiauipil
yyztac, cue
ytzitzil
yztaccac
yn ichimal, tlaieçicuilolli
yyollotopil, centlapal quitquiticac quetalmiavaio.

Her occipital rosette.
Her shift with the evening primrose design.
Her white skirt.
Her small bells.
Her white sandals.
Her shield with the blood design.
In her other [hand] she carries her heart staff with quetzal plumes.[98]

Omacatl yn inechichiuh

The Array of Omacatl[99]

motlatlatlalili.
yvitzoncal
tlacochtzontli contlaliticac
ymecaaiauh tenchilnauaio
yn ichimal amapaio
centlapal quitquiticac ytlachiaya.
ytolicpal

[His face] is painted in various places.
His feather locks.
He has placed a spear-shaft headdress on his head.
His net maguey fiber cape has a red border of rings.
His shield has paper flags [along the bottom].
In his other [hand] he carries his viewer.
His rush seat.

[fol. 267r]

Tepictoton, yn inechichiuh.

The Array of the Tepictoton[100]

yn aquin tepiquia ynic monetoltiaia quimixiptlatiaia yn tetepe yn quezquitetl, quinequiz quimixiptlatiz yn tetepe,

yn iuhquima quiyacatiaia tetepe pupuca tlaloc ipan quiquixtiaia inic quichichiuaia tzoalli moçaticatca y yamacal y yamacuexpal

Anyone who fashioned a figure because he had made a vow, fashioned images of the mountains. He fashioned images of as many mountains as he wished.

Thus, if Popocatepetl was first, it was made in the likeness and arrayed in the adornments of Tlaloc. It was covered with

Xocotlhuetzi/Hueymiccailhuitl. Whatever her specific function as a deity, her insignia and costume items present an interesting mix of attributes. They include those associated with the earth/fertility goddesses (the black lower face), mortuary symbols (the *cuexcochtechimalli*), and the Macuiltonaleque (the *yolotopilli*).

98. *Quetalmiavaio:* Read *quetzalmiahuayo.*

99. *Omacatl,* i.e., Ome Acatl, "Two Reed," the chief calendric name of Tezcatlipoca, derived from the date of his mythical birth from the Heart of the Earth (Nicholson 1954). This aspect of the Late Postclassic Central Mexican supreme deity is arrayed in a ceremonial dance costume similar to those of Yacatecuhtli and Tlacochcalco Yaotl. The figure wears a distinctive headdress, the "stellar crown," called here *huitzoncalli,* which is also sometimes displayed by Tezcatlipoca (e.g., *Codex Borbonicus* 1974: 22; Tezcatlipoca relief on giant jaguar *cuauhxicalli* [Nicholson and Quiñones Keber 1983: 31]). According to Sahagún (1970: 33–34), Omacatl was the particular god of feasts and banquets, whose image was brought to these festivities. In his own special ceremony, celebrants ate portions of a large bone molded from amaranth-seed dough, which represented the god (cf. eating of Huitzilopochtli images molded from the same kind of dough during the *veintenas* of Toxcatl and Panquetzaliztli). See also note 6, Paragraph 4.

100. *Tepictoton:* "Small Molded Ones." These were diminutive images molded from amaranth *(huauhtli)* seed dough, *tzoalli,* which represented various Central Mexican hills and mountains believed to be the abodes of the dwarfish rain deities, the Tlaloque. There, the clouds were brewed that furnished the rain on which the fortune of the crops depended. The manufacture and eating of these images played prominent roles in the *veintenas* of Tepeilhuitl/Hueypachtli and Atemoztli (Sahagún 1981: 131–133, 152–154).

quetzalmiavaio y yamatlaque y yoztopil ymac ycac:

amaranth seed dough; it had its paper crown, its paper locks on the nape of the neck, the quetzal feather plumes [on top of the crown], its paper vestments, [and], in its hand, its reed staff.

Çan no iuhqui yn iztac tepetl yn inechichiuh ym oltica tlacuiloli yn itlanque iniquim omexti.

The array of Iztac Tepetl was the same. The vestments of both were painted with rubber.

Jnic etetl matlalqueie texutica tlacuiloli in itlaque yn iamacal.

The third [figure] was Matlalcueye. Her vestments[101] and her paper crown were painted blue.

Jnic naui chalchiuhtli icue ça no iuhq' in itlaque yn i yamacal yn texuctica tlacuiloli yn itlatlatqui yn vmenti

The fourth was Chalchiuhtli Icue. Her vestments and paper crown [were painted] the same [color]; the vestments of both were painted blue.

Auh inic quintlaliaia y. tlalchipa itztoca: auh teixnamictoca inic macuiltetl, quitocaiotiaia quetacoatl yn inechichiuh mecaichiuhtica y yecaxochiuh contlalitica yn imacal tliltic quetzalmiyava yn itlaque yn itlaque oltica tlacuiloli tlayavaliuhcatectli ça no iuhq' yn imac icac quitoaia ichiquacol.

They were placed on the ground, the one following the other in a row, and they were facing the fifth [figure] which they called Quetzalcoatl.[102] His array; his face was painted with the wind design. [On his head] he had placed his wind flowers [and] his black paper crown with the quetzal feather crest. His vestments were painted with rubber. [The base of the figure] was cut round, as was [the base of] what they called his crook, which was in his hand.

O ca iuhquin i ynic quinchichivaia ypampa mitoaia tlaloque intech tlamiloya yehoan quichiva in quiavitl.

In this manner they were fashioned. They were called Tlalocs [gods of rain] because of them it was supposed that they made rain.

[fol. 267v]

[2 sketches, no text]

PARAGRAPH 5B: ILLUSTRATIONS

[fol. 261r]

vitzilopuchtli.	Huitzilopochtli
Paynal.	Painal
Tezcatlipuca.	Tezcatlipoca

[fol. 261v]

quetzalcoatl.	Quetzalcoatl
totochtin.	Totochtin
Tlalloc.	Tlaloc

101. *Itlaque:* Read *itlaquen.*
102. *Queţalcoatl:* Read Quetzalcoatl.

[fol. 262r]

chicomecoatl	Chicomecoatl
otontecuhtlj	Otontecuhtli
yacatecutli	Yacatecuhtli

[fol. 262v]

atlaua chachalmeca	Atlahua Chalchalmeca
yxcoçauhqui	Ixcozauhqui
ixtlilto	Ixtlilton

[fol. 263r]

xippe anavatlitec	Xipe Anahuatlitec
teteujnã.	Teteoinnan
opuchtli.	Opochtli

[fol. 263v]

yyauhqueme.	Yauhqueme
chalchiuhtlicue.	Chalchiuhtlicue
xillone.	Xilonen

[fol. 264r]

tzaputlatena	Zapotlantenan
çiuacoatl, quilaztli	Cihuacoatl, Quilaztli
vixtoçiuatl	Huixtocihuatl

[fol. 264v]

vztac çinatl coatlicue	Iztac Cihuatl Coatlicue
amimitl.	Amimitl
tomiauhtecutli	Tomiyauhtecuhtli

[fol. 265r]

atlava	Atlahua
.napatecutlj	Nappatecuhtli
totoltecatl	Totoltecatl

[fol. 265v]

macuiltochtli	Macuiltochtli	Paragraph
macuilxochitl	Macuilxochitl	5B
tezcacoac aiopechtli	Tezcacoac Ayopechtli	

[fol. 266r]

tlacochcalco yautl
vtlamaxac çivapiplti manca
xuchipilli

Tlacochcalco Yaotl
The Cihuapipiltin who gathered at crossroads
Xochipilli

[fol. 266v]

chantico
chalmecaçiuatl
omacatl

Chantico
Chalmecacihuatl
Omacatl

[fol. 267r]

Tepictotõ.

Tepictoton

PARAGRAPH 6
[fol. 268r]

Jnic. vi. parrapho. ipan mitoa in quezqui tlamantlj tlatquitl, yn vncã monenequia tlacatecolocalco.

Techcatl
Tecpatl
Tlemaytl.
Amatl.
Copalli.
Mumuztli.
Vitztli.
ytztli.
tlequa.vitl
Teuquavitl.
Acxuyatl.
Tzitzicaztli
Vmitl.
Holli
yyaqualli

Sixth paragraph,[1] in which are named some of the properties that were required in the devils' houses.[2]

Sacrificial stone.
Flint knives.
Incense ladles.
[Ritual] papers.
Copal (incense).
Platform altars.
Thorns.
Obsidian knives.
Firewood.
Ritual firewood.
Fir branches (*Abies religiosa*).
Nettles (*Japtropha urens*).
Bones.
Rubber.
Tobacco pellets.[3]

1. Over the Nahuatl title, Sahagún wrote: *Capitulo. 9. de los ornamētos o atavios de los dioses*, "Chapter 9, of the ornaments or array of the gods." Although this annotation obviously related to the organization of Sahagún's final *Historia*, this paragraph is not included in any extant version of it.

2. According to Sahagún (1975: 234; 1988, II: 247), in the Spanish versions of Book 4 of the *Historia*, *tlacatecolotl* "propiamente quiere decir nigromantico o brujo. Impropiamente se usa por diablo." In the Nahuatl version (Sahagún 1950–1982, Part V [Book 4]: 41), the word is also translated by the Spanish word *diablo*. *Tlacatecolotl*, "man-owl," was frequently employed in colonial sources for both the Christian devil and the native deities.

3. Sahagún (1975: 114; 1988, I: 124–125), in the Spanish version of Book 2 of the *Historia*, described this item, which was carried by the priests in "*talegas*" *(yiequachtli)*, as "una manera de harina, hecha a la manera de estiercol de

Tecciztli	Conch shells.
Copalxicalli	Incense gourds.
Puçolcactli	Foam sandals.[4]
yyequachtli.	Tobacco pouches.[5]
Xiculli.	Sleeveless tunics.[6]
yyetecumatl.	Tobacco vessels.
Papalotilmatli	Capes with the butterfly design.[7]
tleçaoallayatl	Maguey fiber capes with the fire spider web design.[8]
Tlamecayutl	Cords.

PARAGRAPH 7

[fol. 268v]

Jnic vij. parrapho ipan moteneoa in tlein itotoca catca, y çeçecni tlacatecvlocalco.

Seventh paragraph, in which are told what were the names of the diverse houses of the devil.[1]

---

ratones, que ellos llaman *yiaqualli,* que era conficionada con tinta y con polvos de una yerba que ellos llaman *yietl,* que es como belenos de Castilla." *Yietl (yetl)* was tobacco.

4. *Puçolcactli:* See note 22, Paragraph 5A.

5. *Yequachtli:* See note 3, this paragraph.

6. *Xiculli:* See note 32, Paragraph 2A.

7. *Papalotilmatli:* See note 33, Paragraph 2A.

8. The translation is problematic.

1. Over the Nahuatl title, Sahagún wrote: *Capitulo. 10. de los edificios de los templos,* "Chapter 10, of the edifices of the temples." This paragraph does not appear in any extant version of the later *Historia.*

This well-known diagram of a ceremonial precinct and its "legend" were first published (as an uncolored line drawing) and interpreted by Eduard Seler (1900: 114–126; slightly modified version, 1902–1923, II: 770–782; English translation: Seler 1990–1993, III: 115–117). He assumed that the diagram constituted a simplified plan of the ceremonial center of Mexico Tenochtitlan and interpreted it with the aid of various primary ethnohistorical sources—especially those of Sahagún, Durán, and Alvarado Tezozomoc—that contain descriptions of the structures of this sacred precinct. He attempted to connect each Nahuatl term of the legend with an appropriate feature on the plan.

It must be recognized, however, that the *Primeros Memoriales* were compiled in Tepepolco. The diagram is not labeled as to place. It seems possible that Sahagún's Tepepolco informants supplied him with a plan of the main ceremonial center of their community, copying it from—or at least basing it on—an earlier plan, conceivably even pre-Hispanic. Alternatively, it might have been a reconstruction from memory.

Virtually all later students have agreed with Seler's assignment of the plan to the Mexica imperial capital. Sahagún was aided in Tepepolco by his four trilingual assistants, who stemmed from communities in the vicinity of Tenochtitlan, including Tlatelolco. Because of the preeminence of Tenochtitlan's ceremonial center, one or more of the assistants, even if they were not specifically Tenochca, could conceivably have reconstructed some version of it from memory for the Franciscan friar. As indicated, the information contained in Paragraphs 3 and 4 of this chapter, or at least substantial portions of it, seems to relate to the Mexica capital.

The problem is further complicated by Sahagún's itemization of no less than seventy-eight structures and other features that clearly were located within the principal ceremonial center of Tenochtitlan. It is known from a statement of Sahagún's quoted by Torquemada (1975–1983, I: 219) that a pictorialization of Tenochtitlan's sacred enclosure was prepared for him and later sent to Spain. The list of seventy-eight structures added to Book 2 of the *Historia* as an appendix (Sahagún 1975: 158–164; 1981: 175–193; 1988, I: 181–189) was almost certainly the legend of this plan. It indicates—and this is also clear from other sources—that Tenochtitlan's ceremonial center contained far more structures than those featured in the *Primeros Memoriales* diagram.

Although the key account (Durán 1967, I: 21) is somewhat ambiguous, there may have been an inner walled precinct enclosing the Templo Mayor of Huitzilopochtli and Tlaloc and adjacent lesser structures. It has been suggested (Nicholson 1971: 438; 1987: 439) that the *Primeros Memoriales* plan possibly depicts this *patio particular,* as Durán called it, of Tenochtitlan's main pyramid temple rather than constituting a simplified version of the entire sacred enclosure. Various of the structures pictured in the *Primeros Memoriales* diagram do correlate with those listed in the Historia's appendix to Book 2. And some are located in the correct positions relative to each other as known from accounts, particularly those of Sahagún and Durán, of certain of the major rituals performed in Tenochtitlan. That in the diagram the enclosing wall displays only three entrances might favor this interpretation, since it is well established that the wall surrounding the entire Tenochtitlan Templo Mayor precinct was pierced by four openings (see Caso 1956: 44).

On fol. 42r of the *Codex Aubin* (1981: 256), a colonial pictorial Mexica history with Nahuatl text, there is a depiction of the Tenochtitlan Templo Mayor illustrating Pedro de Alvarado's massacre of the Mexica nobility during the Toxcatl ceremony in late May, 1520. It shows only the four-staged pyramid temple with the twin shrines of Huitzilopochtli and Tlaloc, fronted by a walled patio similar in configuration to that in Durán's (1967, I: Lám. 4) illustration of this temple. Aside from a musician beating an upright drum and a Mexica warrior combating an armed Spaniard, nothing else is included within the sacred enclosure, which is surrounded by a massive wall with four gates. This *Codex Aubin* diagram might provide additional support for the existence of a walled *patio particular* for the main Tenochtitlan temple. However, it has usually been interpreted as another representation of the entire Templo Mayor enclosure of Tenochtitlan, much more simplified than even the *Primeros Memoriales* diagram.

Unfortunately, the archaeological evidence now available from the 1968–1969 Mexico City Metro and the 1975–1976 Catedral Metropolitano/Sagrario salvage projects (Vega Sosa 1979) and the 1978–1982 Proyecto Templo Mayor (Matos Moctezuma 1982, 1988) is of little aid in relation to this problem. The excavated structures surrounding the Templo Mayor proper (see Vega Sosa 1979: 50; Matos Moctezuma 1988: 66) do not correlate well with those pictured in the *Primeros Memoriales* diagram. However, those closest to the pyramid temple appear to belong to a construction stage (VI) earlier than those of the stage (VII) encountered by Cortés (and destroyed in the wake of the Conquest). Thus, they may not be relevant to the problem.

The Templos Mayores of at least two other major communities in the Basin of Mexico—Tlatelolco, Tenochtitlan's twin city, and Tetzcoco, her chief partner in imperialism—also featured pyramid temples with twin shrines dedicated to Huitzilopochtli and Tlaloc (see Nicholson 1987: 477–479). Little is known otherwise of their ceremonial precincts. It is conceivable that the *Primeros Memoriales* diagram represents the main sacred enclosure of one of these communities. Martín Jacobita, one of Sahagún's trilingual assistants, was from Tlatelolco, while Tepepolco had close political and cultural ties with Tetzcoco, capital of the province of Acolhuacan, to which Tepepolco belonged. However, neither seems very likely. Regarding Tlatelolco, apart from its principal pyramid temple, the ethnohistorical sources provide almost no information concerning the other structures in its ceremonial precinct—and the archaeological evidence (e.g., plan of the excavated structures in González Rul 1964; Dennis 1988: fig. 4; Matos Moctezuma 1989: fig. 112), appears to provide no support for this assignment. No archaeological data are available for Tetzcoco's main ceremonial center, now buried under the modern community of Texcoco.

Returning to the Tepepolco hypothesis, it would appear that it can be seriously entertained, but various problems with it must be recognized. That its Templo Mayor should be dedicated to the particular patron god of the Mexica, Huitzilopochtli (along with the preeminent, fertility deity, Tlaloc), might not be considered so anomalous, since the chief temple of Tetzcoco, the capital of Acolhuacan, was also dedicated to these two deities. Tepepolco possibly rendered at least part of its tribute to Mexico Tenochtitlan, and the Huitzilopochtli cult had spread widely in the wake of the Triple Alliance conquests, led by the Mexica. In any case, Mexica cultural influence appears to have been quite strong in Tepepolco, particularly in the religious-ritual sphere (see Nicholson 1974).

The absence of pyramid temples dedicated to other deities, with the exception of Xipe Totec and probably Cihuacoatl, within the enclosure of the *Primeros Memoriales* diagram might also appear to militate against its acceptance as an illustration of Tepepolco's ceremonial center. This relatively large community must have possessed numerous other temples to different deities. Perhaps the diagram, instead of representing the *patio particular* of the Huitzilopochtli/Tlaloc pyramid temple of Tenochtitlan, represented instead an equivalent compound in Tepepolco (at least partly modeled on that of Tenochtitlan?). Tepepolco's other temples might have occupied other locations within the larger overall ceremonial center, or they might have been dispersed throughout the community, or both. Of course, the possibility that the diagram represents just a substantially simplified version of Tepepolco's main ceremonial center must also be considered.

Another possible point in favor of the Tepepolco hypothesis is the lack of stages on the main pyramid temple of the *Primeros Memoriales* diagram. It is well established that the Tenochtitlan Templo Mayor (and its replications in Tlatelolco and Tetzcoco) rose in four stages, and most of the native-style representations of the structure display this feature. However, none of the other pyramid temples included in the *Primeros Memoriales* plan is portrayed with stages, so probably not too much should be made of this. The artist may just have preferred a more streamlined and less literal mode of depicting all of these structures.

Finally, it must also be recognized that this diagram could be interpreted as merely a confection, an idealized and

Teucalli.	Pyramid temple.[2]
Quauhxicalli	Eagle vessel (for sacrificed hearts and blood).
Calmecatl.	Priestly dormitory/school.[3]
yxmomoztl.	Front platform altar.[4]
Quauhcalli.	Eagle house.[5]
Teutlachtli	Sacred ball court.
Tzunpantlj.	Skull rack.
yopico teucalli	Yopico temple (of Xipe Totec).[6]
Temallacatl.	Gladiatorial stone.[7]
Colhvacan teucalli.	Colhuacan temple.[8]

---

typical contact-period Central Mexican ceremonial center, rather than as a depiction of a center belonging to a particular community. The specificity of various of the identifications of the features of the plan—particularly the "Colhuacan teocalli"—would appear to favor the view that the sacred enclosure pictured was indeed an actual one. If so, its particular locus should be determinable—but, with the data at hand, perhaps no conclusive identification can be made. In any case, it does seem clear that the almost universally accepted assignment of this famous diagram to Mexico Tenochtitlan, although it may be correct, cannot be accepted unreservedly.

2. *Teucalli:* All students, from Seler on, who have assumed that the plan depicts the Templo Mayor precinct of Mexico Tenochtitlan have naturally held, as a corollary, that the twin shrines atop the pyramid temple in the center of the diagram were dedicated to Huitzilopochtli (right) and Tlaloc (left). These affiliations are not specified in the legend, but—even if the Tepepolco assignment is preferred—the manner in which their roofs are adorned appears to provide support for this view. Nearly all of the more authentically native-style representations of the Templos Mayores of Tenochtitlan, Tlatelolco, and Tetzcoco, which are known to have been dedicated to these gods, display the same decorative layouts on their shrine roofs as those of the *Primeros Memoriales* diagram: the "starry sky" on Huitzilopchtli's shrine, and the four vertical blue stripes on that of Tlaloc.

3. Seler, undoubtedly correctly, identified the *calmecatl* as the two-doored structure to the lower left of the principal temple—from which sacerdotal footsteps lead out from the right-hand doorway to the *cuauhxicalli.* On the function of the *calmecac* in general, see note 2, Paragraph 4.

4. *Yxmomoztli:* The *momoztli* was a raised platform altar normally with steps on all four sides. Seler failed to indicate the location of this feature on the diagram, but he located the *cuauhxicalli* on the small platform, clearly a *momoztli,* that is depicted in front of the main *teocalli,* on which stands a priest, in typical attire, holding a copal incense bag and a handled *incensario.*

5. *Quauhcalli:* Seler, citing the solar connotation of the eagle and Durán's placement of the Temple of the Sun at the southwestern corner of the sacred enclosure, the site of the cathedral, identified as the *cuauhcalli* the structure in the lower left corner of the *Primeros Memoriales* diagram, which he accepted as dedicated to the solar cult. However, the head shown in the doorway of the shrine, with its blackened lower face, a diagnostic of the earth/fertility goddesses, must connote one of these deities, probably Cihuacoatl or one of her avatars. The eagle was closely associated with Cihuacoatl, and one of her names was Cuauhcihuatl, "Eagle Woman." Alcocer (1935: 58–59), noting these facts and citing Durán's (1967, I: 131) placement of the Cihuacoatl temple of Tenochtitlan in this general location, identified it as this structure. Whether Alcocer's assignment of this plan to Tenochtitlan is accepted or not, this temple of Cihuacoatl identification is probably correct (see discussion in Nicholson 1988c: 80–81). Seler's misidentification seems to have stemmed in part from his rotating the *Primeros Memoriales* plan by 90 degrees, making the Templo Mayor face south rather than west.

6. *Yopico teucalli:* As indicated earlier (see note 48, Paragraph 5A), because of the association of the deity Xipe Totec with the Yopi/Tlappaneca of the Guerrero-Oaxaca border region, his temples characteristically bore this appellation.

7. *Temallacatl:* Concerning the function of this stone, see note 10, Paragraph 2A. The deity Xipe Totec (or a ritual impersonator arrayed in his typical costume and insignia), to whom the gladiatorial sacrifice, *tlahuahuanaliztli,* was dedicated, is pictured, holding the *chicahuaztli,* the "rattle staff," next to the *temalacatl,* which is shown on a stepped platform, another *momoztli.*

8. *Colhvuacan teucalli:* Seler, who identified this structure, located behind the main temple in the diagram, as a replica of the Huitzilopochtli temple in the legendary Colhuacan in the Azteca-Mexica homeland, equated it with the pre-Motecuhzoma I Templo Mayor. A fairly typical image of Huitzilopochtli (see Nicholson 1988b: fig. 2) is pictured in the doorway of the shrine, which displays the same "starry sky" roof facade as the right-hand shrine on the main pyramid temple. However, no temple of this name is mentioned in any other source. Aside from the question of whether Seler was correct in his identification, the Tepepolco hypothesis seems to require some other explanation for

Macuilcuetzpalli
Macuilcalli.
ytvalli
covatenamitl.
Teuquiyaoatl. yc excã callacovaya

Five Lizard.[9]
Five House.
Courtyard.
Wall of snakes.[10]
Sacred portals; entryways in three places.

PARAGRAPH 8
[fol. 269v]

Jnic. vijj. parrapho, in quezqui tlamantli in intetlavelil, in tetev.

Eighth paragraph: of some of the god's wrath [directed at] people.[1]

PARAGRAPH 9
[fol. 270r]

Jnic ix. parrapho ipã moteneva in intotoca teteuatzitzĩ.
Mexical teuatzin,
Mexjco teveltzin.
Mexico totecquacuiltzin.
Mexico, tlamazvevetzin.
Totec tlamacazquj mexjco,

Ninth paragraph, in which are noted the names of the god-keepers.[1]
Mexica god-keeper.[2]
Elder sister in Mexico.
Our lord the tonsured one in Mexico.
Old offering priest in Mexico.
Our lord offering priest in Mexico.

---

the presence of this structure within the sacred enclosure—an explanation that might invoke Colhuaque migratory movements into Acolhuacan, as documented in various ethnohistorical sources (Nicholson 1974: 174–175).

9. *Macuilcuetzpalli* (5 Cuetzpallin [Lizard]), *Macuilcalli* (5 Calli [House]): These were two of the Macuiltonaleque, the youthful solar deities of sensual and esthetic pursuits headed by Macuilxochitl/Xochipilli (see notes 43 and 84, Paragraph 5A). Each holds aloft the *yolotopilli,* the "heart-staff," a prime diagnostic of these deities. Seler interpreted these figures as representing the two stone images that, according to Durán (1967, I: 21, Lám. 4), were positioned at the heads of the ramps flanking the stairways of the Tenochtitlan Templo Mayor and served as "standard bearers" supporting wood poles tipped with banners connoting different ceremonies. He cited the well-known "*Indio Triste*" image in the collection of the Mexican National Museum (Seler 1902–1923, II: 813 [Abb. 14]) as possibly one of these figures (similar, better-carved but less well-preserved images have since been discovered in Mexico City). The seemingly exaggerated emphasis given to these figures in the diagram is somewhat puzzling, but Seler's interpretation—which appears to apply as well to the Tepepolco Templo Mayor—has been generally accepted.

10. Durán (1967, I: 21, Lám. 4) designated the wall of the *patio particular* of the Tenochtitlan Huitzilopochtli/Tlaloc pyramid temple as the *coatepantli,* "que toda ella era de piedras grandes, labradas como culebras, asidas las unas de las otras." His illustration depicts it as a wall, not enclosing the temple but surrounding a patio fronting it, composed of a connected series of snake heads. That the legend for the *Primeros Memoriales* diagram designates its enclosure wall with virtually the same term as that given by Durán for the wall surrounding the patio of the Tenochtitlan Templo Mayor has undoubtedly reinforced the traditional view that this diagram should be assigned to the Mexica capital.

1. There is only the heading for this paragraph. No text was added.

1. Below the heading, Sahagún wrote "ojo." This brief paragraph does not appear in any extant version of the later *Historia.*

2. All of these priestly titles contain the word Mexico (or, in one case, a variant form, Mexical). The most obvious interpretation is that these titles designated priests of the Mexica twin cities, Tenochtitlan and/or Tlatelolco. As mentioned earlier, there are various indications that the priestly titles of Paragraph 4 pertain to the Mexica. The only Mexicatl known to have been assisting Sahagún during this period, Martín Jacobita, from Tlatelolco, might have been responsible for this paragraph. However, in view of the Tepepolco origin of the *Primeros Memoriales,* these titles conceivably could have been borne by priests of this Acolhuaque community who were particularly involved with the religious-ritual system most as-

PARAGRAPH 10
[fol. 270v]

Jnic. x. parrapho ypan moteneoa in tlein intech tlamjloya teteo.

Tenth paragraph, in which are named what were attributed to the gods.[1]

Vitzilopochtlj

Tenemjtia.
Tetlamachtia.
Tecuiltonoa.
Tetlatocatilja.
Tetlauelia.
Temjctia.

Huitzilopochtli

He nourishes people.
He makes people rich.
He makes people wealthy.
He makes people rulers.
He is wrathful with people.
He kills people.

Tezcatlipoca

Tlayocuya. i. Teyocuya.
Teyavchjoa.

Tezcatlipoca[2]

He creates things; that [is], he creates people.
He makes war on people.

Tlalloc.

Qujavy.
Tlatlatzinja.
Tlavitequj

Tlaloc

He rains.
He thunders.
He strikes [with lightning].

Quetzalcoatl.

Ehecca
hecamalacutl quichiva
Tlapitza
Tlamamally.

Quetzalcoatl

He blows the[winds].
He makes whirlwinds.
[As if they were gold] he casts things.
[As if they were green stones] he perforates things.

/chicomecoatl.

Tlaixvaltia

Chicomecoatl

She makes things sprout.

---

sociated with the Mexica. The latter obviously enjoyed great power and influence in this region and might have imposed the cult of their particular patron god, Huitzilopochtli, and other deities, such as Painal, closely associated with him.

1. Below this heading, Sahagún wrote: *Capitulo. 11. de los effectos q̃ atribuyã a cada vno de los dioses,* "Chapter 11, of the effects that (they) attribute to each one of the gods." This paragraph does not appear in any extant version of the later *Historia.* This listing of single-term attributes of twenty-three named deities and/or their aspects (all included in Paragraph 5A) is unique in the ethnohistorical corpus of late pre-Hispanic Central Mexico. Most of them appear to be appropriate to what is known about the deities' basic functions and jurisdictions.

2. The contrastive dualistic nature of Tezcatlipoca, the Shiva-like creator and destroyer, is forcibly conveyed by the terms applied to him here. They clearly express the opposing thrusts of the supernatural personality of this omnipotent supreme god of the late pre-Hispanic Central Mexican pantheon. This same contrastive dualism, as the terms applied to him in the preceding entry indicate, was also inherent in the supernatural personality of Huitzilopochtli, the special patron deity of the Mexica, who was merged conceptually and iconographically with Tezcatlipoca.

Tlatzmolinaltia.	She makes things green.
Tlapia.	She preserves things.
tzapotlatena.	Zapotlantenan[3]
Oxitl.	Turpentine.
Atlava	Atlahua
/ eztlj /	Blood.[4]

[fol. 271r]

Cyvateteo	Cihuateteo[5]
/tetlaximaliztlj /	Adultery.
ixcoçauhqui, xiuhtecutlj	Ixcozauhqui, Xiuhtecuhtli
Tletl.	Fire.
Xillone	Xilonen
/ xilotl.	Young, green ear of corn
painaltzī	Painaltzin
iteyacācauh vitzilopochtlj	Huitzilopochtli's administrator.
tezcatzoncatl.	Tezcatzoncatl
Octlj /	Pulque.
yyauhtencatl	Yauhtecatl
idē	The same.
yyauhqueme	Yauhqueme
Octlj	Pulque.

3. In the entry on this goddess in Paragraph 5A, she is explicitly credited with the invention of *oxitl,* turpentine.

4. The precise significance of this attribute of Atlahua, a deity of the Chinampaneca area of the southern Basin of Mexico, above all, Cuitlahuac (see note 74, Paragraph 5A), is somewhat obscure. Seler (1902–1923, II: 486) first suggested that it indicated that Atlahua was considered to be a "Kriegsgott," comparable to Huitzilopochtli. Later, Seler (1902–1923, II: 1090) advanced the notion that it might refer to the diseases ascribed to this deity (Sahagún 1970: 79)—along with Amimitl—which included the voiding of blood and bloody excrement.

5. The Cihuateteo (Cihuapipiltin; see Paragraph 5A), the malevolent spirits of women who died in childbirth, besides posing a great danger to children instigated sinful, lascivious behavior, including adultery (discussion in Seler 1963, II: 973).

Nahuatl	English
tomjyauhtecutlj	Tomiyauhtecuhtli
Octlj	Pulque.
acalhva.	Acalhua
Octlj	Pulque.
quatlapanquj	Cuatlapanqui
Octlj	Pulque.
tlilhoa	Tlilhua
Octlj	Pulque.
ome tochtlj.	Ome Tochtli
Octlj.	Pulque.
Cyvacovatl	Cihuacoatl
ynãtzĩ teteu	Mother of the gods.
teteu ynã	Teteoinnan
idẽ	The same.
yztac civatl.	Iztaccihuatl
idẽ	The same.
Otontecutli	Otontecuhtli[6]
tlatequjliztlj, teocujtlapitzaliztlj	Gemstone cutting. Goldcasting.

PARAGRAPH 11
[fol. 271v]

Jnic. xj. parrapho ipan moteneoa in quenjn tlayecoltiloya tonatiuh ioã quezquipa in tlapitzaloya in cemjlhuitl in ceyoual, ioã quezquipa in tlenamacoya ioã neçavaloya.

Eleventh paragraph, in which it is told how the sun was served, and how many times the trumpets were sounded during the day [and]

6. This ascription of the lapidary and goldcasting crafts to Otontecuhtli, the patron deity of the Otomian speakers (see Paragraph 5A), might be connected to the reputed role of Azcapotzalco, the capital of the Tepaneca, who had intimate Otomian ties, as a major metallurgical and lapidary center (Díaz del Castillo 1960: 157; cf. Seler 1902–1923, II: 451).

the night; also how many times incense was offered and fasting was observed.[1]

Yn momoztlae ynic valquiça tonatiuh tlacotonaloya ioã tlenamacoya, Auh inic tlacotonaloya, quiquechcotonaya ỹ çollj coniyaviliaya yn tonatiuh, ioã quitlapaloaya, quitoaya Oquiçaco in tonatiuh, yn totonametl, xiuhpiltontlj, ỹ quauhtleuanjtl; auh quẽ onotlatocaz, quẽ cemilhuitiz, cuix itla ipã mochivaz. ỹ ycuitlapil, yn iatlapal,

Each day when the sun came out, quail were sacrificed and incense was offered. And when the quail were sacrificed, they cut off their heads [and] held them up in offering to the sun. And they greeted him; they said: "The sun, the resplendent one, the precious child, the eagle ascendant, has risen! But how will he travel his course? How will the day be? Will something befall his common folk?"

Conilhuiaya ma ximotequitillj, ma ximotlacotillj totecujoe. Auh ynin momoztlae yn iquac valquiçaya tonatiuh mitoaya.

They said to him: "Our lord, may you labor, may you toil!" And this was said daily when the sun rose.

Auh inic tlenamacoya, nappa yn cemilhuitl, auh macuilpa yn yoaltica, Jnic ceppa yquac yn valmomana tonatiuh. Auh ynic oppa iquac yn tlaqualizpã: auh inic expa iquac ynepantla tonatiuh. auh inic napa iquac ỹ ye oncallaqui tonatiuh.

And thus was incense offered: It was four times during the day and five times during the night. The first time was when the sun appeared; and the second time was when it was time to eat; and the third time was at midday; and the fourth time was when the sun went in.

Auh yn yoaltica ynic tlenamacoya Jnic cepa tlapoyava ynjc oppa netetequizpã. Ynjc expa tlatlapitzalizpã, Auh injc nappa ticatla, Auh injc macuilpa tlatvinavac,

And during the night, incense was offered in this way: The first time was when it was becoming dark; the second was at bedtime; the third was at the sounding of the trumpets; and the fourth was at midnight; and the fifth was near daybreak.

Auh in iquac tlapoyava tlenamacoya, tlapaloloya yn yoallj mitoaya. Ovalçouh ỹ yoaltecutlj, y yacaviztlj, auh quẽ ovetziz yn jtequiuh

And when it became dark, incense was offered: The night was greeted. It was said: "The Lord of the Night,[2] the Sharp-nosed One, has unfolded himself. What will his work bring?"

Auh in ilhuiuh quicaya ipã cemilhuitonally navi olly, matlacpoallj omey yca, Auh yn iquac ye onaçi ilhuiuh neçavaloya, navi ilhuitl: tlacatlaqualoya.

And his festival fell[3] on the day Four Movement, every two hundred and [sixty] days.[4] When the day arrived, there was fasting; for four days there was abstention from eating.

1. Above this heading, Sahagún wrote: *Capitulo. 12. del tañer y quãtas vezes tanjã en el templo entre noche y dia: q̃ era como taner a las horas,* "Chapter 12, of the blowing (of trumpets) and how many times they blew (them) in the temple during the night and the day: how they blew (the trumpets) at (certain) hours." The paragraph was included, with a slightly truncated title, as the ninth section in the Appendix to Book 2 of the *Historia* (Sahagún 1975: 171; 1981: 216–217; 1988, I: 196–197).

2. In the Spanish versions, the ceremony is called "la fiesta deste Yoaltecutli," This was certainly incorrect; Yohualtecuhtli, "Night Lord," was identified by Sahagún (1950–1982, Part VIII [Book 7]: 60) with a star, apparently Castor. The *tonalpohualli*-geared ceremony of 4 Ollin (Movement), celebrated every 260 days, was the major ritual dedicated to the solar deity, Tonatiuh. See Nicholson 1993: 10.

3. Read *quiçaya.*

4. *Matlacpoallj omey yca* is read *matlacpohualli omeipohualtica,* to conform to the requisite 260-day length of the divinatory cycle, the *tonalpohualli.*

Auh yn ipã cemilhuitonallj ỹ oacic ylhuiuh, ynepãtla tonatiuh tlapitzaloya, tlacoquixtiloya: auh yn pipiltzitzinti coçolco onoq̃, quinacaztequia: auh mochi tlacatl miçoya. Auh atle ic tlapaloloya, Çan jxquich ỹ neçoçovaya, tlacoquixtiloya, tlena-

And at the time of the day [Four Movement], when the day of [the festival] arrived, at midday, the shell trumpets were sounded. Twigs were passed through the flesh, and they made cuts on the ear [lobes] of the infants in the cradle, and everyone drew blood from himself. And they said nothing to each other in greeting. On the part of everyone, of everybody, there was drawing of blood from oneself, the passing of twigs through one's flesh,

[fol. 272r]

macoya mochi tlacatl ayac ixcauhticatca,

and the offering of incense; no one was remiss.

Auh in vncan catca yxiptla, yeuatl yn motenevaya quauhxicallj: vncã moquetzaya yn ixiptla, ynic miCuiloaya ỹ yxiptla yuhquin tlacaxayaq̃ ytonameyo ytech quiztoya, itonatiuhtlatquj, yavaltic, vey, yvitica tlatzaquallj, tlauhquechol injc tlatzaquallj. oncã ixpã mochivaya neçoliztlj, in tlacoquixtiliztlj: yn tlamanaliztlj; in tlacotonaliztlj.

And the image of [the sun] was there at the place called Quauhxicalli;[5] there his image stood. His image was painted in this manner: It had what was like a human face; his rays emanated from it. His sun-adornment was round, large; he was covered with feathers, covered with roseate spoonbill feathers. There, before him, were performed the drawing of blood, the passing of twigs through the flesh, the setting down of offerings, and the decapitation of birds.

Auh yn ilhuiuh ipã no miequientĩ miquia mamalti, auh no mitoaya yn oyaomjc. tonatiuh ychã via, ytla nemj in tonatiuh.

And at the time of his festival, also, many captives died. And also it was said that he who died in battle went to the home of the sun, that he lived near the sun.

PARAGRAPH 12
[fol. 272v]

Jnic xij. parrapho. ipan mjtoa yn quezqui tlamantlj, yn vncan mochivaya tlatlatequipanoliztlj ỹ vncã tlacatecolocalco.

Twelfth paragraph, in which are told some of the tasks performed in the devils' houses.[1]

Tlacazcaltiliztlj

The Rearing of People

Jn teiztaltiaia tlenamacac inmac cõcaoaia in tlamacazque ỹ tlavitequini in tlapiani.

Fire priests instructed [young] people; [then] they put them in the hands of offering priests, those who punished, those who guarded.

5. The Spanish versions position the image of the sun "en un *cu* que se llamaba Quauhxicalco." Into, or on, the *cuauhxicalli*, "eagle vessel," were deposited the hearts of sacrificed victims. See Seler 1902–1923, II: 704–716.

1. Below this heading, Sahagún wrote: *Capitulo 13 de los exercicios o trabajos q̃ avia en el templo.* "Chapter 13, of the exercises or works that there were (i.e., took place) in the temple." This paragraph was included, with a somewhat distinct title, in the later *Historia* as the tenth section of the Appendix to Book 2 (Sahagún 1975: 172; 1981: 218–219; 1988: 198–199).

Tenonotzaliztlj

quinnonotzaia inic vel nemizque ỹ amo maviltizque ỹ amo tlatziuhtinemizque.

Admonitions

They admonished them so that they would live properly, so that they would not spend their time amusing themselves, so that they would not be lazy.

Tlachpanaliztlj

Inic tlachpanazque in teuitvalco quitzatzilia in isquich in tlamacazcatepitzin ynic tlachpanaz.

Sweeping

So that they would sweep the temple courtyard, they shouted at all the young offering priests to sweep.

Tletlaliliztlj

yoan quincuitlaviltiaia ynic tletlalizque inic tlapialo, vncã neteteco in tletitlã. auh çã noviian in tletlaliloia yn teuitvalco, in tlequazco in õcã tlatlaia aço matlactecpãtli cenca miec

Lighting the Fires

And they saw to it that they lit the fires. There was lying down by the fire; thus there was guarding. And in all parts of the temple courtyard fires were lit in the braziers; there rows of ten or many more burned.

Ioallapializtli

Jn ioallapializtli iehoantin quimocuitlaviaia in tlamaceuhq̃ in istlamatque intequiuh catca.

Keeping Watch at Night

Those who were performing acts of devotion took charge of keeping watch at night. It was the duty of the experienced [priests].

Quauhçaquiliztli

Jn quauhçaquiliztli inic tlapiaya in tlatlaia calmecac iehoãtin cõcuia in tlamacazcatepitzitzĩ in ayamo cẽca istlamati.

Hauling Wood

The hauling of the wood to store [and] burn in the *calmecac;* the young offering priests who were not very experienced gathered it.

Vitztequiliztli

Jn vitztequiliztli iehoãtin conteqz in tlamacazq̃ yn aiamo cẽca istlamati in quinontlacuisque.

Cutting Thorns

Cutting thorns: The offering priests who were not yet very experienced cut them. It was they who gathered them.

acxoiaçaquiliztli

Jn acxoiaçaquiliztli iehoãtin cõcuia in tlamacazq̃ in ie istlamati.

Hauling Fir Branches

Hauling fir branches: The offering priests who were already experienced gathered them.

tlatlapitzaliztlj

In tlatlapitzaliztli, iehoãtin intequiuh catca in tlamacazcatepitzitzin yoan in ie istlamati neneliuhtivia.

Sounding the Trumpets

The sounding of the trumpets was the task of the young offering priests as well as the already experienced ones; they went mixed.

tlilpatlaliztlj

The Preparation of the Black Stain

Jn tlilpatlaliztli, iehoantin intequiuh catca in tlamacazcatepitzitzin in quipatlaia mochi tlacatl ic moçaia, vel moçemaquiaia inic moçaia acan mocaoaia

The preparation of the black stain was the task of the young offering priests; they dissolved it in water. Everyone painted himself with it; they covered themselves completely; when they painted themselves, no part was overlooked.

aun in quipatlaja vncan in tlillacalco, auh in tlilpatlaloia çan ioaltica, auh in neoçaloia ycoac in tlavizcalli ehoa

And when they prepared the stain, it was there in the black canoe;[2] and when the black stain was prepared, it was only at night, and when there was painting of oneself, it was at daybreak.

PARAGRAPH 13
[fol. 273r]

Jnic xjji. parrapho ipan moteneva in quenin tlatlauhtiloya diablome ivã juramẽto.

Thirteenth paragraph, in which it is told how the devils were supplicated and oaths [were made].[1]

Jn iquac mochioaya juramẽto ỹ iquac aca quinetoltia yconeuh ivicpa Diablome: aço vcã, anoço excã, quinetoltia in tlein quinchiviliz diablome

When an oath was made, when someone made a vow for his child to the devils, he vowed what he would do for the devils in two or three places.

aço motlavitequi piltontlj: anoço tlein ypã mochioa; yquac quinetoltiaya, iniquivicpa tlamacevaz,

[If] perhaps the child stumbled and fell, or something [else] happened to him, he made a vow to [the god] that he would perform a penance.

Auh no ioã iquac mochioaya in juramento yn jquac aca, tlein quiteilhuiaya ynic quineltiliaya, ilhuiloya, Ynic neltiz motlatol ỹyc amo tiztlacatiz tla xontlalqua?

And also when an oath was made, when someone stated something to someone, he confirmed it in this way. He was told, "So that your words will be confirmed, so that you will not lie, [will you] please eat earth?"

iquac njmã tlalquaya ỹ aquĩ, tlein quiteilhujaya yc quineltiliaya yn itlatol, ỹyc amo yztlacamachoya

Then when the person ate earth, he confirmed his words, what he said to one. Thus he was not thought to lie.

quitoa vel quimati ĩ tonatiuh ĩ tlaltecutli

He said: "The Sun, the Lord of the Earth[2]

2. *Tlillacalco:* The black stain with which the priests daily painted their bodies was apparently mixed and prepared in the type of dugout canoe that plied Lake Texcoco—or, possibly, in large wood containers that resembled the canoes in form.

1. Below this heading, Sahagún wrote: *Capitulo. 14. de los votos y jurametos:* "Chapter 14, of the vows and oaths." This paragraph was included, with a slightly enhanced title, as the eleventh section in the Appendix to Book 2 of the *Historia* (Sahagún 1975: 172; 1981: 220; 1988, I: 198).

2. In the Spanish versions, Sahagún translated Tlaltecuhtli, usually rendered in English as "Earth Lord," as "nuestra señora la tierra," focusing on the feminine aspect of this essentially androgynous terrestrial deity. Thus conceived, the deity formed, in juxtaposition to the male sun, the appropriate female member of a contrastive dualistic pair, so typical of Mesoamerican ideology (discussion in Nicholson 1967a: 85–87).

ye nõtlalqua yuhqui ynic mochioaya juramẽto.

Auh in tlatlatlauhtiliztlj yc mochioaya ça yeoatl in tlenamaquiliztlj ioã nextlavaliztlj, ioã tlalqualiztlj. nextlaoaliztlj.

will know that I have now eaten earth."[3] In this way oaths were made.

And supplications were made in this way; by offering incense, and offering blood, and eating earth, by paying the debt [to the gods].

PARAGRAPH 14
[fol. 273v]

[Prefatory note: This paragraph contains the texts of twenty sacred hymns and constitutes a uniquely valuable section of the *Primeros Memoriales.* However, there are challenging problems in accurately translating them and in comprehending their meaning. As Anderson and Dibble (in Sahagún 1981: 221) pertinently expressed it: "Whether because of surviving archaisms; or of distortions due to their poetic expression, their presentation sung and danced, their having been constantly and unthinkingly repeated; or of mistakes in copying the text, their Nahuatl is very difficult."

Sahagún included them, with slight alterations and without the clarificatory glosses that accompany most of them in these *Primeros Memoriales* versions, in the twelfth section of the Appendix to Book 2 of the *Florentine Codex* version of the *Historia* (Sahagún 1979, I: fols. 191–198; 1981: 221–245). He did not, however, include even a paraphrastic Spanish version of the hymns but only a statement ascribing their obscurities to the diabolic machinations of the Evil One.

The proveniences of these hymns present a certain problem. Although ostensibly collected by Sahagún during his Tepepolco project, they may have originally derived from different places (cf. Garibay 1958: 9–14). Most of the deities specified in the hymns' titles are those listed in Paragraph 5A, including two (Atlahua, Amimitl) who were especially propitiated in Cuitlahuac and among other Chinampaneca of the freshwater lake district of the southern Basin of Mexico (see note 72, Paragraph 5A). Various places are mentioned in the songs. Some, as Seler and Garibay noted, can putatively be identified with known Central Mexican communities or sites within these communities, or both. Others cannot be so identified—and there is the further problem of distinguishing between real and mythical places. Mexico is mentioned only once, at the beginning of the third hymn, to Tlaloc; the Mexica appear to be mentioned in the eleventh hymn, to Otontecuhtli. Huitzilopochtli is featured in the first and fifth songs; these two chants probably stemmed ultimately from Tenochtitlan/Tlatelolco, but because Huitzilopochtli's cult had been widely adopted elsewhere—including, it would seem, Tepepolco—they may not necessarily have been the versions of the Mexica capital itself. In any case, whatever the precise origins of these hymns, their archaic idioms provide useful clues concerning earlier stages in the evolution of the Nahuatl language.

Various modern scholars have attempted translations and interpretations of these sacred songs. The first to publish paleographies of these *Primeros Memoriales* versions, including the explanatory glosses and noting any variations in the

3. The passage *quitoa vel quimati ĩ tonatiuh ĩ tlaltecutli ye nõtlalqua* is inserted at this point.

Florentine Codex versions, was Daniel Brinton in 1890. His attempts at English translations and his interpretaions were not very successful. Eduard Seler, in 1904 (Seler 1902–1923, II: 958–1107), published more accurate transcriptions of the *Primeros Memoriales* texts, also noting the slight divergences of the *Florentine Codex* versions. He translated them into German and included extensive notes devoted both to resolving linguistic problems and to clarifying the meaning of each hymn. Although he left many questions unanswered and frequently propounded rather speculative explanatory hypotheses, Seler's effort constituted a landmark in the scholarly treatment of the songs and has been used as a point of departure by all subsequent students. A Spanish translation of Seler's German translations of the hymns, together with his notes, was published in Mexico in 1938 (Sahagún 1938, V: 7–192). The following year, mimeographed English translations of them were made available to scholars and libraries by the Carnegie Institution of Washington (Seler 1939, Vol. 2, Part 4: 1–93), and these were republished in 1992 in the third volume of the *Labyrinthos* reprint of Seler's *Collected Works* (Seler 1990–1993, Vol. III: 231–301).

In 1951, Anderson and Dibble published, with a minimum of notes, English translations of the hymns in the third volume (Book 2) of their edition of the *Florentine Codex.* They acknowledged heavy dependence on the Selerian translations. In 1958, Angel María Garibay K., who in 1940 had published Spanish versions of thirteen of the hymns, closely following Seler, published paleographies and fresh translations of the *Primeros Memoriales* versions of the hymns, with extensive notes, both linguistic and exegetical. He took full cognizance of Seler's work with the songs but was frequently critical of his predecessor's translations and interpretations. In 1981, Dibble and Anderson published a second, revised edition of *Florentine Codex* Book 2, with new English versions of the hymns. They acknowledged heavy dependence on the translations of Garibay as well as those of Seler, and they included many more notes than in their first version. Anderson also published these revised English translations of eight of the hymns, with slight modifications, in 1982, along with a general discussion of Aztec religious ideology and a detailed exegesis of each translated hymn. Other versions and interpretations of certain of the hymns have been published (e.g., Gingerich 1988), but those cited stand out in importance.

Thelma Sullivan was still working on her translations and her notes to the hymns at the time of her death and left this paragraph quite unfinished. Arthur Anderson thoroughly revised and corrected the translations of the hymns for which Sullivan had completed preliminary versions, and also filled out her unfinished notes. Although there were differences in detail between her versions and his, he felt that on the whole they were much the same even without his revisions of some parts of her translations and that he had succeeded in preserving her style without much change. In any case, it must be understood that this paragraph is very much the result of a collaborative effort by Thelma Sullivan and Arthur Anderson—although the actual wordings of the latter's revised translations, with Charles Dibble, of the *Florentine Codex* versions of the hymns often differ from those employed here.

Concerning the notes, the difficult decision was made to keep them to a minimum. To have done justice to all of the difficult linguistic and exegetical questions inherent in these often obscure sacred chants would have required a much more extensive series of notes than would have been appropriate for this edition of the *Primeros Memoriales.* The versions and studies already cited have, with varying degrees of success, dealt with the most challenging problems these hymns present, and readers with special interest in this unique remnant of the rich religious poetic corpus of the contact-period Central Mexican Nahua speakers is referred to them. Only the most relevant information necessary to comprehend the basic content of the hymns is included in these notes, for the final versions of which I assumed responsibility.—HBN]

Jnic matlactli onahvi parrapho ipã ipan mitoa in icuic catca vitzilopochtli

Fourteenth paragraph, in which is told the Song of Huitzilopochtli.[1]

Vitzilopuchi, yaquetl *a ya.*
yyac onay, y nohvihvi *hvia*
ane nicuic, toçiquemitl *a, yya, ayya, yya yyo via.*
que*ya*noca, o*ya*tonaqui *yyaya, yya yyo.*

Huitzilopochtli,[2] wayfaring warrior.
None is my equal.
Not for nothing did I take the yellow parrot feather garb.
Because of me the sun has shone.

q.n. J nivitzilopochtli ayac no vivi, i. ayac nechnenevilia, ayac iuhqui, i niuhqui.

This means, *j nivitzilopochtli ayac novivi,* i. [e.], I am Huitzilopochtli; no one is my equal, no one is like what I am like.

ane nicujc. i. amo ça nẽ nonicujc. ỹ quetzallj in chalchivitl in ixquich y notlatquj, toçiquemitl/

ane nicuic: i. [e.], not in vain did I take the quetzal feathers, the green stones; all are my possessions [as well as] the yellow parrot feather vestment.

queyanoca oyatonaquj. id est. onoca tonac onoca tlatvic.

queyanoca oyatonaqui: i.e., because of me the sun has shone, the day has dawned.

Tetzaviztli
ya mixtecatl, ce ymocxi pichavaztecatl *a*
poma ya, *ovayyeo, ayyayye.*

He is terror!
Now the Mixtec, the Pichahuaztec have one foot.
There he's gone!

q. n. Tetzaviztlj. id est oquintetzavito. in mixteca inic oquiyaochiuhque: oquimanjlito in imicxi no pichavazteca, ioã in mixteca.

This means: Tetzahuiztli: i.e., he went terrifying the Mixteca when they warred with him. He removed the feet also of the Pichahuazteca and the Mixteca.

Ay tlaxotla tenamitl
yvitli macoc
mupupuxotiuh,
yautlatoa *ya, ayya yyo*
noteuh *aya,*
tepan quizqui mitoa *ya*

Oh, the walls of Tlaxotlan!
Feathers have been given out.
Churning up the earth he goes.
He gives the call to war.
He is my god,
One known as Tepanquizqui.

Ay tlaxotla tenamitl. q. n. quitopeoa in intena in aquiq̃ yauchivallo.

Ay tlaxotla tenamitl means, he stirs up fire on the walls of those on whom war is made.

1. Below the Nahuatl heading, in Sahagún's hand, appears the following: *Capitulo 15. de los cantares que deziã a hõrra de los dioses en los templos y fuera dellos,* "Chapter 15, of the songs that they said (i.e., sang) in honor of the gods in the temples and outside of them." Sahagún included the texts of all of the hymns, without the explanatory glosses, in the Appendix to Book 2 of the *Florentine Codex* version of the *Historia,* omitting Spanish translations of them.

2. *Vitzilopuchi:* Probably an archaic form of the name of the Mexica tutelary god, with the absolutive suffix *-i(n)* instead of the standard *-tli.* On Huitzilopochtli, to whom this hymn is dedicated, see note 1, Paragraph 5(A). For detailed discussions of this hymn, including the putative places mentioned in it, see Seler 1902–1923, II: 964–970, Garibay 1958: 19–39.

ivitli macoc. q. n. oncã quitema in tiçatl in ihvitl.

ivitli macoc means, there he places the chalk, the feathers.

mopopuxotiuh yautlatoa ya. q. n. inic mopupuxoticalaquj yauc, ioã q. n. yevatl quitemaca ỹ yauyutl quitemacevaltia.

mopupuxotiuh yautlatoa ya means, thus he goes into battle churning up the earth, and it means he offers the people war; he makes them meritorious.

tepan quizqui mitoa ya q. n. yehuatl quichioa yauyutl.

tepan quizqui mitoa ya means, it is he who makes war.

oya yeva vel mamavia, y tlaxotecatl
teuhtla, teuhtla millacatzoa *ya.*
i tlaxotecatl
teuhtla, teuhtla milacatzoa *ya.*

The Tlaxotec is fearful.
The dust, the dust is whirling.
The Tlaxotec . . .
The dust, the dust is whirling.

Oya yeva huel mamavia. q. n. çan oc momamauhtiaya in ayamo mochiva yauyutl

Oya yeye yeva huel mamavia means, first he became frightened before the battle was fought.

teuhtla milacatzoa ya. q. n. ỹ olin in opeuh yauyutl. aocac momamauhtia in iquac ye teuhtli moquetza ỹ oteuhtica tlayoac.

teuhtla milacatzoa ya means, war has stirred; it has commenced. No one was fearful any longer when the dust rose, when with the dust [day] became night.

Amanteca toyavã
xinechoncentlalizqui *via.*
ycalipã yautiva,
xinechoncentlalizquj

The Amanteca are our foes.
Join yourself to me!
The foe is battled in his house.
Join yourself to me!

Amanteca toyavã. q. n. yn iyaoã yn aquique in canj omocentlaliq̃ ca icalipã ỹ yautioa ca tlatlaz yn incal.

Amanteca toyavan means, his enemies are those who are gathered in their houses, where there is fighting; their houses will burn.

Pipiteca toyavan
xinechoncentlalizquj *via;*
ycalipan yautiva,
xinechoncentlalizquj.

The Pipitecas are our foes.
Join yourself to me!
The foe is battled in his house.
Join yourself to me!

Pipiteca toyaoã xinechõcentlalizq̃. q. n. yn pipiteca yyaoã mochiuhq̃ ỹ calla in mochioa yauyutl incalipã.

Pipiteca toyaoan xinechoncentlalizqui means, the Pipiteca became his enemies; in the town there is fighting in the houses.

[fol. 274r]

Paragraph 14

¶ Vitznaoac yautl icujc.

¶ Song of Yaotl[3] of Huitznahuac[4]

Ahvia tlacochcalco notequioa *aya*
yvinoc aqu *ia* tlacatl *ya* nechyapinavia, *aya*

My seasoned warrior of the house of spears.[5]
Decked with feathers is the man who maligns me;

3. Yautl: Yaotl, "Enemy," was an appellation of Tezcatlipoca, as was Yaotl Necoc, "Enemy on Both Sides" (e.g., Sahagún 1970: 67). On this supreme deity of the Central Mexican Nahua speakers, to whom this hymn appears to be dedicated, see note 11, Paragraph 5A.

4. *Vitznaoac:* On Huitznahuac, "Next to the Spines," the south, and its relation to Tezcatlipoca, see note 23, Paragraph 2A.

5. *Tlacochcalco:* "Place of the House of Spears," an appellation for north, which also bore a special relation to Tezcatlipoca (see note 88, Paragraph 5A).

ca nomati nitetzavitli, *avia*,
aya ca nomati ni*ya*, yautla,
aqu itoloc tlacochcalco notequioa,
i vexcatlatoa *ay* nopilchã.
Jhiyaquetl tocuilechcatl quaviquemitl
nepapanoc vitzetla
Hvia oholopa telipuchtla,
yviyoc ỹ nomalli,
ye nimavia, ye nimavia,
yviyoc ỹ nomalli.
Hvia vitznavac telipochtla,
yviyoc ỹ nomalli,
ye nimavia, ye nimavia
yviyoc ỹ nomallj.
Hvia ytzicotla telipochtla,
yviyoc, ỹ nomallj,
ye nimavia, ye nimavia
yviyoc ỹ nomalli.
Vitznavac teuaqui
machiyotla tetemo *ya*.
ahvia oy*a*tonac *yahuia*, oyatonac
ya machiyotla tetemo *ya*.
Tocuilitla teuaquj,
machiyotla tetemo *ya*,
ahvia oy*a*tonac *yahvia* oy*a*tonac
via machiyotla tetemo *ya*.

For I know I'm Tetzahuitl.
I know I'm Yaotl.
Of whom has it been said, "My seasoned warrior of the house of spears"?
They revile my noble house.
Wayfaring warrior, man of Tocuillan in eagle-feather garb.
With thorns diversely placed.
The youth of Olopan.
Decked with feathers is my captive.
I am afraid, I am afraid.
Decked with feathers is my captive.
The youth of Huitznahuac.
Decked with feathers is my captive.
I am afraid, I am afraid.
Decked with feathers is my captive.
The youth of Itzcotlan.
Decked with feathers is my captive.
I am afraid, I am afraid.
Decked with feathers is my captive.
The priest of Huitznahuac.
The model descends.
Daylight has dawned, daylight has dawned.
The model descends.
The priest of Tocuillan.
The model descends.
Daylight has dawned, daylight has dawned.
The model descends.

[fol. 274v]

¶ Tlalloc ycujc

Ahvia mexico teutlaneviloc
amapanitla, *ã* nauhcanpa, ye moquetzquetl,
ao yequena ychocaya.

Avia mexico teutlaneviloc: q. n. ỹ mexico onetleneviloc in tlaloc /.

Amapanitl ã nauhcanpa ye moquetzquetl. q. n. amapanitl nauhcampa omoquequetz/.

ao yequena ichocaya id est itlaocuyaya.

Ahvia an neva *ya* niyocoloc
an noteva eztlamiyaval

¶ Song of Tlaloc[6]

In Mexico the god has been on loan.
The paper flags have stood in four locations.
At last it was his time to weep.

Avia mexico teutlaneviloc means, in Mexico Tlaloc had been borrowed.

Amapanitl ã nauhcanpa ye moquetzquetl means, paper flags were raised in four places.

Ac yequena ichocaya: that is, his time of sadness.

I have been formed.
My god is stained with blood.

6. Tlalloc: On Tlaloc, the preeminent rain/fertility deity, to whom this hymn is dedicated, see note 19, Paragraph 5A. The chant contains various references to places and rituals connected with his cult; most of them were specified and discussed in Seler 1902–1923, II: 982–993, and Garibay 1958: 54–64.

a ylhuiçolla
nic*ya*vica*ya* teuitvalco *ya*.
Avia an neva ya niyocoloc. q. n. y nehuatl nitlalloc oniyoculoc/
An noteua eztlamiyaval. q. n. noteu eztlamiyavaltitiuh.
A ylhuiçolla. q. n. ỹ ompa ilhuiçololo/

nicyavica ya teuitvalco ya. q. n. in teuitvalco.
Ahvia an notequiva navalpilli
aqu i tlanella motonacayouh tic*ya*chiuhqui

tla ca tlachtoquetl, çã mitzi*ya*pinavia.

Ahvia an notequiva navalpillj. q. n. in tinoteuh navalpillj id est tlalloc.
aqu i tlanella motonacayouh. q. n. ca nellj tevatl ticmochivilia in motonacayuh.
ca tlachtoquetl. q. n. tevatl ticmochivilia auh in aquĩ mitzpinavia
Ahuia canacatella nech*ya*pinavia a nech *ya* yca vel matia,
a notata, y noquacuillo ocelocoatl *aya*.

Ahuia canacatella nech*ya*pinavia. q. n. ca tel nechpinavia camo nechvelmati.

an notata y noquacuillo ocelocoatl *aya*. q. n. yn notava ioã y noquacuiloa ỹ oceloquacuilj.
Ahuia tlallocan *a*, xivacalco *aya*
quizquj aqua motta acatonal *aya*.

Ahuia tllallocan *a* xivacalco. q. n. in tlalocã xiuhcalco id est acxoyacalco.
aya quizqui. q. n. vmpa valquizq̃.

The festive day is long.
I bring water to the temple court.
Avia an neva ya niyocoloc means, I, Tlaloc, have been fashioned.
An noteua eztlamiyaval means, my god goes stained with blood.
A ylhuiçolla means, the festival lasts the day through.
Nicyavica ya teuitvalco ya means, in the courtyard of the temple.
My *tequihua*, Nahualpilli,[7]
For in truth you've bred your sustenance

The first fruit [gifts] of which just offer you offense.
Ahvia an notequiva navalpillj means, you are my god, noble sorcerer, that is, Tlaloc.
Aqu i tlanella motonacayouh means, in truth you make your sustenance.
Ca tlachtoquetl means, you produce it and someone offends you.
But they offend me, give me no pleasure.

My fathers, my shorn-heads, my jaguar-serpents.[8]
Ahuia canacatella nechyapinavia means, but they offend me, they do not give me pleasure.
An notata y noquacuillo ocelocoatl aya means, my fathers, my old priests, my old jaguar priests.
From Tlalocan, from the turquoise house.
Your forefathers, Acatonal, have come forth, have seeped forth.
Ahuia tlallocan a xivacalco means, Tlalocan, house of turquoise, that is, house of fir.
Aya quizqui means, from there he came forth.

7. Navalpilli (Nahualpilli), "Sorcerer-prince," has usually been interpreted as an additional epithet of Tlaloc, an identification supported by the explanatory gloss. Sahagún (1950–1982, Part X [Book 9]: 79), however, gives a detailed itemization of the attire of a deity with the same name who was one of four described as the "grandfathers and fathers" of the *tlatecque,* the lapidaries of Tenochtitlan/Tlatelolco who stemmed from Xochimilco. His adornment is described as that of a Huaxtec (who were considered great sorcerers) and does not contain any elements characteristic of Tlaloc (see discussion in Seler 1902–1923, II: 985).

8. *Ocelocoatl:* "Jaguar-serpent." Although the explanatory gloss interprets this term as *oceloquacuilli,* "jaguar priest," the combination of feline and reptile has suggested to some the jaguaroid visage, sometimes incorporating ophidian features (e.g., the bifid tongue) that was the hallmark of the archaelogical Olmec stylistic-iconographic tradition. Seler (1902–1923, II: 987–988) also noted the addition of a jaguar's ear to the serpent helmet mask of the water goddess depicted in the Mixteca-Puebla-style *Codex Fejérváry-Mayer,* which explicitly fused the two creatures.

aqua motta acatonal *aya*. q. n. y notavã y noquacuiloã acatonal.

Ahvia xiy*a*novia, *nahuia* xiy*a*moteca *ya ay* poyauhtla,

ayauhchicavaztica, *ay* avicalo tlallocan *aya*

Ahvia xiyanovia navia xiyamoteca ya q. n. xiviã ximotecati.

ay poyauhtlan. q. n. in vmpa poyauhtlã tepeticpac,

ayauhchicavaztica ayavicalo tlalocan a. q. n. ayauhchicavaztica in avicalo tlallocã.

Ava nach *a* tozcuecuexi

niyayalizqui *aya*

ychocaya

Ava nach tozcuecuexi niyayalizqui. q. n. y nach tozcuecuex y ye niauh nimã ye choca

Ahviya queyamica xinechiva *ya,*

temoquetl *a* itlatol

a niquiy*a*ilhuiquetl. tetzauhpilla niyayalizquj *aya*

ychocaya.

Ahuia queyamica xinechivaya. q. n. Quenamicã y ye niauh aço anechtemozque.

a niquiyailhuiquetl tetzapilla niyayalizqui aya ichocaya. q. n. oniquilhuj ỹ tetzapillj ye niyauh nimã ye choca.

Aqua motta acatonal aya means, my fathers, my shorn-heads, Acatonal.

Go forth, gather in Poyauhtlan.

With mist-rattles water is brought from Tlalocan.

Ahvia xiyanovia navia xiyamoteca ya means, go, settle.

Ay poyauhtlan means, there is Poyauhtlan, on the mountaintop.

Ayauhchicavaztica ayavicalo tlalocan a means, with the mist-rattle water is brought from Tlalocan.

My older brother is Tozcuecuexi.

I shall go.

It is his time to weep.

Ava nach a tozcuecuexi niyayalizqui means, my brother Tozcuecuexi. When I go, then he weeps.

Send me to Unknown Beyond.

His words come down.

I told Tetzauhpilli I'd go.

It is his time to weep.

Ahvia queyamica xinechivaya means, now I go to the Unknown Beyond; perhaps they will not look for me.

Aniquiyailhuiquetl tetzapilla niyayalizqui aya ichocaya means, I have told Tetzauhpilli, "Now I go." Then he weeps.

[fol. 275r]

Ahuia nauhxiuhtica *ya* i topan ecaviloc

ayoc ynomatia, *ay* motlapoallj,

aya ximovaya ye quetzalcalla nepanavia

ay yaxcan *a* teizcaltiquetl.

Ahuia nauhxiuhtica ya a i topan ecaviloc. q. n. nauhxiuhtica in topan ecaviloz. id est in topan mochivaz.

Ayoc i nomatia ay motlapoallj. q.n. aocmo nomatia in iquĩ motlapoalpã

ca oximoac ye quetzalcalla nepanavia. q. n. ye qualcã ye netlamachtiloyã y nemoa

Ay yaxcan a teizcaltiquetl. q. n. in iaxca inic oteizcalti.

For four years it has fallen to our lot.

No more in my time has been [what was told] in your tale,

The place where all go, the quetzal plume house, the place shared by all,

Which is owned by the rearer of men.

Ahuia nauhxiuhtica ya a i topan ecaviloc means, for four years suffering will befall us; that is, it will happen to us.

Ayoc i nomatia ay motlapoalli means, not in my time was the time of your account.

Ca oximoac ye quetzalcalla nepanavia means, it is a fine place, a place where one is rich; all live [there].

Ay yaxcana teizcaltiquetl means, his property, with which he rears people.

Ahvia xiyanovia: *ahvia* xiyamoteca *ya ay* poyauhtla,
ayauhchicavaztica a*ya*vicallo tlalloca.

Go, gather in Poyauhtlan.

With mist-rattles water is brought from Tlalocan.

Ahvia xiyanovia. q. n. xivia.
Avia xiyamoteca ya ay poyauhtlã. q. n. ximotecati ỹ vmpa poyauhtla.
Ayauhchicavaztica avicallo tlalocã q. n. ayauhchicavaztica in avicallo in vmpa tlallocã.

Ahvia xiyanovia means, go.
Avia xiyamoteca ya poyauhtlã means, go and settle in Poyauhtlan.
Ayauhchicavaztica avicallo tlalocã means, with mist-rattles water is brought from Tlalocan.

¶ Teteu ynã ycujc.

¶ Song of Teteoinnan[9]

Ahuiya coçavic xochitl *a oya*cueponca
yeva tonan *a* teumechave

moquiçicã tamoanchã,
avayye, avayya, yyao, yya yyeo, aye aye, ayy ayyaa.

The yellow flower bursts into bloom.
She our mother with the godly thigh-skin face paint
Comes forth from Tamoanchan.

q. n. Jn tonã ocueponja vmpa oalquiz yn tamoanchã.
Coçavic xochitl *a oya*moxocha
yeva tonan *a*, teumechave,

moquicicã tamoanchã,
ovayye, avayya, yyao, yya yyeo, aye aye, ayya ayyaa.

This means, our mother burst into bloom; she came forth from Tamoanchan.
The yellow flower has opened up.
She our mother with the godly thigh-skin face paint
Comes forth from Tamoanchan.

q. n. J namona ca izca y noxochiuh ca vmpa onjquiz ỹ tamoãchã

Ahvia iztac xochitl *a*, *oya*cueponca
yeva tonan *a* teumechave

moquiçicã

This means, I am your mother; behold, I have opened up; I have come forth from Tamoanchan.
The salt-white flower bursts into bloom.
She our mother with the godly thigh-skin face paint.
Comes forth from Tamoanchan.

[fol. 275v]

tamoanchã,
ovayye, ayayya, yyao, yya yyeo, aye aye, ayya, ayyaa.

9. Teteu yna (Teteoinnan), "Mother of the Gods," to whom this hymn was dedicated, was the fundamental earth/fertility goddess, with numerous aspects (see note 54, Paragraph 5[A]). Various passages in the song clearly relate to the propitiation of the earth mother under various guises (discussions in Seler 1902–1923, II: 996–1003; Garibay 1958: 70–76; Gingerich 1988: 206–226). Tamoanchan, the mythical "terrestrial paradise," home of the gods (see Davies 1977:99–106), is prominently featured in this hymn. It concludes with references to Itzpapalotl, "Obsidian Butterfly," another aspect of the mother goddess, and to two "Chichimec" (Mimixcoa) demigods, Xiuhnel and Mimich, who were prominently involved with her in a mythic episode that was incorporated into the Azteca/Mexica, Tlaxcalteca, and probably other Postclassic Central Mexican migration narratives.

q. n. Jn tonã ocuepo in vmpa oquiz tamoanchan.

This means, our mother burst into bloom; she came forth from Tamoanchan.

Ahuiya iztac xochitl *a*, *oya*moxoch *a*
yeva tonan *a* teumechave
moquicican tamoanchã
ovayye, avayya, yyao, yya yyeo, aye aye; ayya, ayyaa

The salt-white flower has opened up.
She our mother with the godly thigh-skin face paint
Comes forth from Tamoanchan.

q. n. J namona yztac y noxochiuh. yn vmpa onjquiz tamoãchã.

This means, I am your mother. White are the blossoms I put forth. I came forth from Tamoanchan.

Ahuija ohoya teutl ca teucontlj pac *a*
tona *aya* itzpapalotlj
ayayye, avayya yyao yya yyeo ayyaa.

Oh, the goddess is atop the barrel cactus.
She's our mother Itzpapalotl.

q. n. Jn tonan ca teucumjtl ycpac ỹ quiz yn itzpapalotl.

This means, our mother Itzpapalotl is on the barrel cactus; from it she came forth.

Ao, ava ticy*a*itaca chicunavixtlavatl *a*
maçatl yyollo, yca mozcaltizquj
tonã tlaltecutlj.
ayao, ayyao, ayyaa.

Oh, you've seen her [on] the ninefold plains.
On deer hearts she's been fed—
Our mother Tlaltecuhtli.

q. n. jn tonã ixtlavacã in mozcaltito auh injc mozcalti macatl yyollo y yeva tonã tlaltecutlj.

This means, our mother went out on the plains to be fed and she, our mother Tlaltecuhtli, was fed on deer hearts.

Aho, ye yancuic tiçatl *a*
ye yancujc yvitl *a oya*potoniloc
yn avicacopa acatl xamantoc *a*

Oh, new is the chalk,
New are the feathers in which she is clad.
In every quarter broken lie the darts.

q. n. Auh inic potonjloc, tonan, yancujc tiçatl ioã yancujc yn ivitl, auh nauhcampa quitz yn acatl

This means, our mother was covered with new chalk and with new feathers; and arrows went off in four directions.

Aho maçatl mochiuhca
teutlalipã mitz *iya* no ittac *o*. yeva xiuhnell *o* yeva mimjch *a*.

Oh, she's been changed to a deer.
There on the plains Xiuhnel and Mimich have had mercy on you.

q. n. In macatl yevan canjliaya ỹ ixtlavacã yuhqui injc quicnoitaya y yevatl mimjch ioã in xiuhnel.

This means, Xiuhnel and Mimich caught the deer on the plain; they had mercy on it.

¶ Chimalpanecatl icujc ioã tlaltecava. nanotl,

¶ Song of Chimalpanecatl[10] and
Tlaltecahua, the mother

[fol. 276r]

Jchimal ipã chipuchica veya,
mixiviloc yautlatoa *ya*

On her shield the virgin girl grows large.
At the call to the fray he is given birth.

10. Although their versions differ considerably in wording, all of the major translators of, and commentators on, this brief hymn have agreed that it refers to the birth of the Mexica patron deity, Huitzilopochtli—notwithstanding that he is not named, nor is his mother, Coatlicue—in the well-known account of his miraculous parthenogenesis (Sahagún 1978: 1–5). This interpretation is ostensibly supported by the song's mention of Coatepec, Huitzilopochtli's birthplace, and his special shield, *tehuehuelli,* and by Sahagún's naming him in the first explanatory gloss. The song's titles have presented some problems. Chimalpanecatl, literally, "Person of Chimalpan (Place of the Shield)," could be considered

ichimal ipan chipuchica veya,
mixiviloc yautlatoa.
q. n. yautlatollj ipã omjxiuh y nanotl chimalpã in omjxiuh id est ipã oquitlacatillj y nanotl in vitzilopochtlj ỹ yauyutl,

On her shield the virgin girl grows large.
At the call to the fray he is given birth.
This means, at the time the battle was joined, the mother gave birth; she gave birth on the shield; that is, on [the shield] the mother brought forth Huitzilopochtli, war.

Coatepec tequiva. tepetitla
moxayaval tevevel

On Coatepetl, among the hills,
The seasoned warrior put on face paint, [took up] shield.

ayaqui nellj moquichtivivi
tlalli cuecuechivia aqui moxayaval tevevella.
Q. n. Coatepec otepeuh tepetitlã yc moxauh ioã ytevevel id est ichimal ic otepeuh. aocac omoquichquetz. in iquac pevaloq̃ Coatepeca yn iquac otlallj cuecuechiuh. id est iquac opopoliuhq̃

None dared rise against him
The earth was quaking as he put on face paint, [took up] shield.
This means, on Coatepetl, among the hills, with his face painted and his *tehuehuelli* he vanquished the others; that is, with his shield he vanquished the others; no one rose up against him. When the Coatepeca were vanquished, then the earth shook; that is, then they were annihilated.

¶ Yxcoçauhquj icujc.

¶ Song of Ixcozauhqui[11]

Huiya tzonimolco notavane ye namech*maya*pinauhtiz.

In Tzonmolco, O my fathers, I'll offend you;

tetemoca ye namech*maya*pinauhtiz.
q. n. J nitzonmolcatl notavane ye nemechpinauhtiz nachcã nochã tetemocã, ye nemechpinauhtiz.

In Tetemocan, I'll affront you.
This means, I, the man from Tzonmolco, shall affront you, my fathers. I whose home is over there, in Tetemocan, shall affront you.

A uncã mecatla notecvã ycçotl mimilcatoc

In Mecatlan, my lords, the [drumbeat] throbs.

chicueyocã navalcallj navali temoquetl *aya*

In the eightfold place, the sorcerer from the house of sorcery descends.

q. n. Jn mecatla anotecuhvã in vncã iccotl mjmjlcatoc veya quixtoc icçotl vncã njtemoc yn chicueyocã

This means, in Mecatlan, you who are my lords, [the beat of] the yucca [drum] throbs; the yucca grows; it shoots up. From the eightfold place I descended.

Huiya tzonimolco cuico tipeuhque
aya tzonimolco cuico tipeuhq̃,

In Tzonmolco we began to sing,
In Tzonmolco we began to sing.

a toponym but has been interpreted by the hymn's modern translators as a reference to the miraculous nativity of the god, with or on his shield. Tlaltecahua, literally, "Earth Person (Tlaltecatl)," with the possessive suffix *-hua*, perhaps refers to the earth mother, which would seem to be reinforced by the added term *nanotl* (= *nanyotl*), "motherhood."

11. Yxcoçauhquj (Ixcozauhqui), "Yellow Face," to whom this hymn is dedicated, was the Fire God, more commonly known as Xiuhtecuhtli and/or Huehueteotl (see note 39, Paragraph 5A). Most of the references in the song—with the possible exception of the final stanza—seem to relate appropriately to the cult of the fire deity and have been so interpreted by its principal translators and analysts (Seler 1902–1923, II: 1010–1016; Garibay 1958: 87–92). Tzonmolco, the name of the principal temple of the Fire God in the Templo Mayor precinct of Mexico Tenochtitlan (Sahagún 1981: 190–191) and perhaps elsewhere, is prominently featured (see note 49, Paragraph 4). Another Templo Mayor structure, Mecatlan, where instruction in flute playing was given (Sahagún 1981: 186), is also mentioned; its connection with the Fire God, if any, is not very obvious (see note 51, Paragraph 4).

aya yz tleic anavalmoquizca *via*,
iz tleic anavalmoquizca
q. n. jn tzonmolco otipeuhq̃ ma cuico yn tzonmolco ma cujco otipeuhq̃ tleica in amo anvalquiça tleica ỹ ayavalquiça
Hvia tzonimolco. macevallj ma *ya* temaco *via*.
o*ya*tonaquj,
o*ya*tonaquj
macevallj ma *ya* temoco *viya*
q. n. Jn tzonmolco otonac auh i nomaçevalhoã xinechmacaquj notech povizq̃ iquac y nenetoltiloya

Why have you not appeared?
Why have you not appeared?
This means, in Tzonmolco we began the singing, in Tzonmolco we began the singing. Why do you not appear? Why do not appear?
In Tzonmolco let men be offered up.

The sun has shone,
The sun has shone.
Let men be offered up.
This means, in Tzonmolco the sun has shone, and give me my people, those who will be meant for me when the vow is made.

[fol. 276v]

Hviya tzonimolco xoxolcuicatl cacavantoc
ya ayovica mocuiltono acitontecuitl
moteicnelil, maviztlj
q. n. Jn cuicatl tzomolco ca yecavanj ma ic necuiltonollo netotilo in tetecuti yehica in teicnelil ca maviztic

In Tzonmolco the *xoxol* song is ending.
With little care the lord is rich, attains [his wealth].
Wondrous is your grace.
This means, the song in Tzonmolco is ending. May the lords become rich by virtue of the dancing because [the god's] beneficence is awesome.

Hviya civatontla xatenonotza,
ayyauhcalcatl
quiyavatla xatenonotza
q. n. Jn tiCivatontlj xitenonotza in quiavac ayauhcalcatl. id est. in ticivatontlj xitenonotza.

Little lady, pray the gods.
Lady of the house of mist,
In the entryway pray the gods.
This means, you, little lady, pray to the gods in the entryway. That is, lady of the house of mist, pray to the gods.

¶ Mimixcoa ỹcujc.

¶ Song of the Mimixcoa[12]

Chicomoztoc quinevaquj,
cani aveponj
çani, çanj, teyomj.
q. n. chicomoztoc onivallevac çani ave-

From the seven caves has he set forth.
Çani aueponi.
Çani çani teyomi.
This means, he set forth from the seven

12. The Mimixcoa, "Cloud Serpents," were the martial hunting/stellar deities assigned to the north and headed by Mixcoatl/Camaxtli. They exemplified the rustic Chichimec lifestyle, based largely on hunting and gathering. They were especially connected with what has been called the "Chichimec Interregnum," between the fall of the Toltec imperium, headquartered at Tollan, and the rise of the Tepanec empire of Tezozomoc, ruled from Azcapotzalco. This era was particularly characterized by a series of migratory movements, predominantly from north to south, of the ancestors, collectively known as Chichimeca, of the leading Nahua-speaking groups who dominated Central Mexico in late pre-Hispanic times. These migrants, emerging from Chicomoztoc, the "Seven Caves," had traversed the cactus-studded deserts of the north on their way south. This hymn celebrates these northern steppes, Mimixcoa Tlalpan, "Land of the Cloud Serpents," and the Chichimec way of life so closely associated with this region. Although there are some difficult translation problems (discussed by Seler [1902–1923, II: 1018–1024] and Garibay [1958: 95–97]), most of the references are clearly appropriate to the overall theme of the hymn.

poni, ichichimecatlatol. çani aveponj çanj çanj teyomj.
Tzivactitla quinevaquj
çani a aveponj
çani, çani teyomi.
q. n. tzivactlj in itlan onivallevac çani aveponj çani çani teyomj
Oyanitemoc, o*ya*nitemoc
aya ica nitemoc notzivaquimiuh
aya ica nitemoc notzivaquimjuh
Oyanitemoc. q. n. onitemoc onitlacat ipã y notziacmiuh; onitemoc ipã y notzivacmjuh ça nimã ipã nitlacat y notlavitol y nomjuh

O*ya*nitemoc o*ya*nitemoc
aya yca nitemoc nomatlavacal
q. n. Onitemoc onitlacat in ipã nomatlavacal ça nimã ipã nitlacat.
Niquimacuj, niquimacuj, *yvaya*

niquimacuj, niquimacuj

yvan *ja ayo* macujvj
y yãcatlatol, yca amja in chichimeca. in chichimecatlatol.

caves. *Çani aueponi* are Chichimec words; *Çani aueponi, çani çani teyomi.*
From among the *tzihuactli*[13] he's set forth.
Çani aueponi,
Çani çani teyomi.
This means, I set forth from among the *tzihuactli, çani aueponi, çani çani teyomi.*
I descended, I descended,
With my *tzihuactli* dart have I descended,
With my *tzihuactli* dart have I descended.
Oyanitemoc means, I descended, I was born with my *tzihuactli* dart. I descended with my *tzihuactli* dart; then I was born with my bow, my dart.
I descended, I descended,
I descended in my netted carrying frame.[14]
This means, I descended, I was born in my netted carrying frame; then I was born in it.
With my hand I catch it, with my hand I catch it,
With my hand I catch it, with my hand I catch it,
And with my hand it's caught.
They are a hunter's words. With them the Chichimecs went off to hunt; they are Chichimec words.

[fol. 277r]

Tlachtli icpac *aya,* vel in cuica *ya,* quetzalcuxcox *aya,*
quinanquilia Çinteutl *a, oay.*
q. n. Jntla taçica tictecazque totlach vncan ticuicazque no yehoatl in quetzalcocox.

Above the ball court the *quetzalcoxcoxtli* sings out.
Centeotl replies.
This means, if we arrive, we shall build our ball court. There shall we sing, as well as the *quetzalcoxcoxtli.*

¶ Xochipilli ycuic.

¶ Song of Xochipilli[15]

Ye cuica *ya* tocniva *ya ovaya yeo,*
ye cuica *ya* ye quetzalcoxcux *a* yoaltica

Now do our friends sing.
Now through the night the *quetzalcoxcoxtli* sings out.

13. *Tzivactitla:* On *tzihuactli,* see note 31, Paragraph 5A.

14. *Nomatlavacal:* The netted pouch, the *matlalhuacalli,* was a basic item in the hunting gear of the Chichimeca (see note 72, Paragraph 5A).

15. Xochipilli, "Flower-Prince," the young solar deity of flowers, music, dancing, singing, gaming, and all aesthetic pursuits to whom this hymn was dedicated, was merged with Macuilxochitl, "Five Flower," the preeminent member of the Macuiltonaleque (to whom the final hymn was dedicated). He also overlapped with Centeotl, "Maize Cob Deity," the young god of maize (see notes 43, 84, and 93, Paragraph 5[A]; Nicholson 1971: 416–419). As Seler noted, the last

tlao çinteutl *a oay,*

He's the red Centeotl.

q. n. Ca otonac ca otlatvic ca ye cuico ca ye cuica centeutl in quetzalcocox.

This means, the sun has shone, the day has dawned. Now there is singing; now Centeotl, the *quetzalcoxcoxtli,* sings.

Çan quicaquiz nocuic ocoyoalle teumechave

o quicaquiz nocuic *a* yn cipactonalla *atilili ovayya.*

Just the lord of the bells with the thigh-skin face paint will yet hear my song.

Cipactonal will yet hear my song.

q. n. Ma caco in tocuic y nican ma quicaquican ỹ nican tlaca.

This means, let our song be heard here; let the people who are here hear it.

Ayao, ayao, ayao, ayao, nitlanavati *ay* tlalocã tlamacazq̃ *ayyao, ayao, ayao.*

I bid my farewell to Tlalocan's providers.

q.[n.] In tlaloque tlamacazque niquinnavatia ye niauh in nochã

This means, I take my leave of the *tlaloque tlamacazque.* Now I go to my home.

Ayao, ayao, ayao, tlallocã tlamacazq̃ nitlanavati *ay, ayyao, ayyao.*

I bid my farewell to Tlalocan's providers.

q. n. Jn tlaloqz tlamacazqz niquinnavatia ye niauh in nochã.

This means, I take my leave of the *tlaloque tlamacazque.* Now I go to my home.

Ao ça in vallaçic, otli nepanivi *a,*
ça niçinteutl *a*
campa ye noyaz.
campa otli nic*ya*tocaç *a oay.*

I've reached where the roads join,
I, Centeotl.
Where shall I go?
Which road shall I take?

q. n. Ca onitlanavati in tlaloca catli ye nitocaz vtli.

This means, I took my leave of Tlalocan. Which road shall I follow?

Ayyao, aya, ayao, tlalocã tlamacazq̃ quiavi teteu *ayyao, aya, ayao.*

Tlalocan's providers, gods of the rain.

q. n. Jn ãtlaloqz yn antlamacazqz catli nictocaz yn ãteteuh

This means, Tlalocs, providers, gods, whom shall I follow?

¶ Xochiquetzal icujc.

¶ Song of Xochiquetzal[16]

[fol. 277v]

Atlayavicã nixochiquetzalli tlac *ya* nivitz *aya* motencal ivã tamoanchã *oay.*

From the place of watery mists come I, Xochiquetzal, from near my dwelling near the shore, and from Tamoanchan.

---

stanza of the preceding hymn appears actually to be the first stanza of this hymn, and it is so considered here. In spite of the hymn's title, Xochipilli is not named in any of the stanzas, but his virtual conceptual equivalent, Centeotl, is prominently featured. The ballcourt, *tlachtli,* where the game over which Xochipilli presided was played, is mentioned, and so is the *quetzalcocoxtli,* the crested bird that seems to have constituted his *nahualli,* his "disguise," and served as his helmet-mask. Besides Centeotl, the rain gods, Tlaloque Tlamacazque, are also featured, and there is mention of another putative deity, Cipactonal, seemingly related to both Xochipilli and Centeotl (discussion in Seler 1902–1923, II: 1029–1030).

16. This brief hymn was dedicated to Xochiquetzal, "Flower-Quetzal Feather," who was, *au fond,* the feminine counterpart of Xochipilli/Macuilxochitl. She was also an important member of the interrelated complex of maternal earth/fertility goddesses and was merged with the female half—Tonacacihuatl, "Lady of Our Sustenance"—of the androgynous primordial creative deity, Ometeotl. She was not included in the extensive list of deities of Paragraph 5A, but she is pictured in the complex scene of the Atamalcualiztli ceremony in Paragraph 2B. There, she is identified by the two bunches of quetzal feathers she wears as a headdress as she weaves at a backstrap loom. The "terrestrial par-

q. n. Vmpa nivitz y nixochiquetzal tamoanchã

Ye qui tichoca *ya* tlamacazecatl *a* piltzintecutl *o*
quiyatemoa *ya* ye *o* xochinquetzall *a*,
xoyavia *ay* topa niaz, *oay*.

q. n. Choca piltzintecutli. quitemoa in xochique[tza]l xoyavia no vmpa niaz.

This means, I, Xochiquetzal, come from Tamoanchan.

Now and afterwards you weep, Piltzintecuhtli of Tlamacazecan.
He is seeking Xochiquetzal.
To the place of moldy maize, to what extends overhead us shall I go.

This means, Piltzinintecutli weeps. He is seeking Xochiquetzal. To the place of moldy maize, there shall I go.

¶ Amimitl icuic.

¶ Song of Amimitl[17]

Cotivana cotivana
cali totochmãca *huiya*
yya limanjco o quixa
nimanjco tlacochcalico, *ovayya*
yya, ma tonica *ya*, ma tonicatico, *ovayya ya*.
çana, çana, *ayo* veca nivia, çana cana *yo*, veca nivia *yya, yya, yyevaya*, çana, çana *ye* veca nivia.

Cotihuana, cotihuana,
It's the house where rabbits are.[18]
You are at the exit way;
I am at the house of spears.
There you stay, there you stay;
I alone go far, I alone go far, I alone go far.

Jn amimitl icuic yuh mitoa in veli chichimecacuic amo vel caquizti in tlein quitoa in tonavatlatol ypa.
Ye necuiliva *ya*
niva *ya*, niva *ya*, niva *ya*, *a* ycanauh
niva *huaya*, niva *ya*, niva *ya*, *a* ycanauh.

The song of Amimitl is said to be a Chichimec song. It is impossible to make what it says understandable in our Nahuatl tongue.
I am grasped
I am sent, I am sent, I am sent unto his duck.
I am sent, I am sent, I am sent unto his duck.

---

adise," Tamoanchan, so closely associated with the fertility deities, is featured in this song as the dwelling place of the goddess. Piltzintecuhtli, "Prince-Lord," another member of the Centeotl-Xochipilli complex and the consort of Xochiquetzal, appears in a context that Seler, followed by Garibay, suggested might have been connected with a myth possibly analogous to the Classical Greco-Roman myth of Proserpina. Considering the many difficult translation problems of this hymn, however, which are discussed at length by Seler (1902–1923, II: 1032–1035) and Garibay (1958: 110–112), this notion must be considered quite speculative.

17. On Amimitl, "Hunting Arrow," the deity to whom this hymn is dedicated, see note 72, Paragraph 5A. This is linguistically one of the most obscure of the hymns, so much so that the native annotator professed not to understand it since it was in the "Chichimeca" language rather than in his own Nahuatl. Brinton (1890: 43–44) attempted, unsuccessfully, to translate it into English, while Seler (1902–1923, II: 1036–1037) suggested possible German versions of only four of the strophes. Garibay (1958: 113–116), on the other hand, recognizing—as Seler also implied—that the song appears to be in a very archaic, essentially Nahuatl dialect, attempted a somewhat speculative but substantially fuller Spanish translation. Anderson and Dibble, in their second English translation of the *Florentine Codex* version (Sahagún 1981: 233), largely depended on Garibay's effort. Thelma Sullivan left no translation of this hymn. Anderson, accordingly, composed a slightly modified version of his and Dibble's translation, which is presented here.

18. This possible reference to rabbits and, later in the hymn, references more certainly to ducks seem congruent with the apparent role of Amimitl as a deity connected with the hunting activities—especially the aquatic ones—of the Chinampaneca of Cuitlahuac in the southern Basin of Mexico. Seler, in fact, argued that the repeated phrases (which seemingly refer to obsidian) in the final strophe of the hymn constitute part of a hunting charm employed by those who pursued aquatic birds.

Tla ixtotoca ye canauhtzin j,
tla ixtotoca ye canauhtzin j *ayoaya, yoayã.*
ye canauhtzin j
Aveya itzipan *a* nomavilia,
aveya itzipan *a* nomavilia,
aveya itzipan *a* nomavilia

Let him chase this little duck;
Let him chase this little duck, this little duck.
In obsidian I delight,
In obsidian I delight,
In obsidian I delight.

¶ Otontecutli ycujc.

Onoalico, onoalico poma ya *yyaya ayyo ayyo aya, aya, aya ayyo.*
Chimalocutitlan *a* motlaquevia,
avetzinj
nonovalico
quavinochitla;
cacavatla motlaquevia,
avetzinj.
Nitepanecatlj *aya* cuecuexi
niquetzallj coatlj *aya* cuecuexi,

¶ Song of Otontecuhtli[19]

In Nonoalco, Nonoalco, there he's gone.

With pinewood shield he goes arrayed.[20]
This does not fall.
In Nonoalco
Among eagle-prickly pears,
Among cacao pods he goes arrayed.
This does not fall.
I'm the Tepaneca man Cuecuextzin;
Quetzalcoatl am I—Cuecuextzin.

[fol. 278r]

Ca ne, ca *ya* ytziveponj,
ca neca *ya* itziveponj
Otomico
noyoco, navaco,
mexicame *ya* y avilili
noyoco navaco
mexicame *ya*
A chimalljca *ya,* xa, xavinoquj y avilili
noyoco navaco mexicame *ya.*

For I'm the wind that drags obsidian.
For I'm the wind that drags obsidian.
In the land of Otomis,
In nearby neighbors' lands
The Mexica delight.
In nearby neighbors' lands
The Mexica with shields now feel delight
In nearby neighbors' lands

¶ Ayopechtli ycuic.

Cane cana ichã ayopechcatl

¶ Song of Ayopechtli[21]

There in the home of the one on the turtle shell bed,

19. On Otontecuhtli, to whom this hymn, which lacks the usual explanatory glosses, was dedicated, see note 29, Paragraph 5A. The many difficult translational and referential problems in this song have been discussed at length by both Seler (1902–1923, II: 1039–1044) and Garibay (1958: 119–127), who often differ substantially in their views. Thelma Sullivan did not leave a translation of this hymn; the version presented here was composed by Arthur Anderson, generally following, but with some significant modifications, his and Charles Dibble's second translation of the hymn in their revised edition of Book 2 of the *Florentine Codex* (Sahagún 1981: 234).

20. Among the various putative places and personages mentioned in this hymn, the "pinewood shield" was interpreted by Seler, followed by Garibay, as the shield placed atop the Xocotl pole that was the highlight of the *veintena* of Xocotlhuetzi, dedicated to Otontecuhtli (see Paragraph 2A). Other pertinent references in this hymn are those to Tepanecatl(i), Otomi, and Cuecuextzin, the last another name for the deity as well as the spirit of the slain warrior that he symbolized. The reference to Nonoalco, a widely distributed toponym of doubtful etymology, is somewhat puzzling. Both Seler and Garibay preferred an identification with a "barrio" of that name that was situated on an islet off the northwestern tip of Tlatelolco (Caso 1956: 41), bisected by the causeway to Tlacopan, capital of contact-period Tepanecapan.

21. On Ayopechtli, "Tortoise-Bench [Turtle Shell Bed]," to whom this hymn was dedicated, see note 87, Paragraph

cozcapãtica mixiuhtoc

With necklace adorned she lies giving birth.

q. n. ỹ oncã ichã ayopechtlj oncã mixivi qujtlacatilia in cuzcatl quetzallj

This means, there in her home the one on the turtle shell bed gave birth; she begot the necklace, the quetzal [feather].

Cane cana ichã ayopechcatl

There in the home of the one on the turtle shell bed,

cozcapãtica mixiuhtoc

With necklace adorned she lies giving birth.

cane ichã chacayoliva *ya*

There in her home one is given life.

Cane cana ichã. q. n. in vncã ichã ayopechcatl vncã quitlacatilia in cozcatl quetzallj, oncã yoliva. tlacativa.

Cane cana ichan means, there in her home the one on the turtle shell bed begets the necklace, the quetzal [feather]. There, there is being born, there is begetting.

Xivalmeva *ya via* xiva, xivalmeva *ya*
aviaya yancuipilla xivalmeva *ya*

Arise, arise,
Newborn child, arise!

Q. n. ximeva, ximeva in tipiltzintlj xivalmeva in quin otitlacat tipiltzintlj

This means, get up, get up, child. You, child, you who now were to have been born.

Aviya xivalmeva *ya*. *viya* xiva xivalmeva *ya*
cozcapilla xivalmeva *ya*

Arise, arise,
Jewel-child, arise!

Q. n. xivalmeva xivalmeva in tipiltzintlj yn ticuzcatl in tiquetzallj

This means, get up, get up, you who are a necklace, a quetzal [feather].

[fol. 278v]

¶ CiuaCoatl ycujc

¶ Song of Cihuacoatl[22]

Quavi quavi, quilaztla
coaeztica xa*ya*valoc

The eagle, the eagle Quilaztli,
Her face has been painted with the blood of a snake.

viviya quavivitl vitz alochpã

In eagle plumes dressed she comes sweeping the road.

5A, where the deity bears the additional name Tezcacoac ("Mirror-Snake"). As explained in that note, she appears to have been an avatar of Mayahuel, the goddess of *metl,* the maguey plant, whose saccharine exudate, fermented, produced *octli.* She was a significant member of the interrelated complex of fertility goddesses, overlapping particularly with Chalchiuhtlicue and Teoteoinnan/Tlazolteotl (see Nicholson 1991: 170, 176–177). This hymn, which presents fewer translation difficulties (discussed in Seler 1902–1923, II: 1046–1047; Garibay 1958: 130–133) than many of the others, is largely concerned with human birth, expressed in the metaphoric mode typical of Classical Nahuatl. Seler interpreted the hymn as a whole as a "Zauberlied" to ease the labor of giving birth, and Garibay agreed that the second part of the hymn constituted a conjuration chanted by the midwife to facilitate the birth of the child.

22. On Cihuacoatl, "Woman-Serpent," a major maternal earth/fertility goddess, to whom this hymn is dedicated, see note 67, Paragraph 5A. Some of her other names and/or aspects (e.g., Quilaztli, "Plant Generator(?)," Cuauhcihuatl, "Eagle-Woman," Yaocihuatl, "Warrior-Woman," Tonan, "Our Mother") are alluded to in the hymn, as are two places particularly associated with her, Chalman and Colhuacan—above all, the latter, of which she was the tutelary deity. Also pertinent are references to two ritual objects significant in her cult, the "rattle staff," *chicahuaztli,* and the *malinalli,* broom. The dualism of her being, combining the contrastive roles of provider-nurturer and voracious destroyer, is also clearly emphasized in the imagery of the hymn, which is interpreted in detail by Seler (1902–1923, II: 1051–1058) and Garibay (1958: 138–149). Since Thelma Sullivan did not leave a translation of this hymn, this version is that of Arthur Anderson, similar but not identical to his and Charles Dibble's revised translation of the *Florentine Codex* version in the second edition of Book 2 (Sahagún 1981: 236–237).

chalima avevetl ye colhoa.	Bald cypress of Chalma, now Colhuacanian.
q. n. Jn quauhcivatl, yc oxavaloc in coaeztlj, ioã in quauhtlj yhyvio in moteneva iquauhtzon. ipan valvicoc ỹ vmpa colhoacã	This means, Eagle-woman. Her face has been painted with serpent blood, and of eagle feathers is what is called her eagle headdress, which is on her [head]. She has been brought there to Colhuacan.
Huiya tonacaacxolma centla teumilco chicavaztica motlaquechizca.	Fir branches of our sustenance, Maize ear in the godly field, With rattle sticks she is supported.
q. n. Jnic motocaya Çentlj, in mochivaya teumilpã, ichicavaztica ynic tlatatacaya. ynic tocaya	This means, when the maize was planted, it was done in the divine field. With rattle sticks they dug; thus they planted.
Vitztla, vitztla nomac temi vitztla, vitztla nomac temj *a* çã teumilco chicavaztica motlaquechizca	The thorn, the thorn lies in my hand. The thorn, the thorn lies in my hand. With rattle sticks in the godly field She is supported.
Vitztla, q. n. nomac temj nochicavaztica ynic nitocaya ynic nitlatatacaya.	*Vitztla* means, in my hand lie my rattle sticks with which I sow, with which I dig.
Malinalla nomac temj, *a* çã teumilco chicavaztica motlaquechizca.	The broom lies in my hand. With rattle sticks in the godly field She is supported.
malinalla, victlj. q. n. victica in tlachpanaya. id est. ic elimiquia, ỹ vncã teumilpã auh ychicavaztica inic nitlatatacaya injc nitocaya.	*Malinalla, victli* means, with the digging stick she sweeps; that is, with it she works in the divine field and with her rattle stick she has dug, she has planted.
A vmey quauhtlj, ye tonan *aya* chalmecatecutlj	Thirteen Eagle is our mother, Chalman lady.
a ytzivac ymaviztla nech*ya*tetemillj,	He fills me with the glory of his cactus dart,
yeva nopiltzin *aya* mixcoatla.	He who is my lord Mixcoatl.
q. n. Matlactli vmei quauhtli ỹ notonal in namonã auh yn ãnopilhoã anchalmeca xicuiti in tzivactli xinechtemilica.	This means, Thirteen Eagle is my sign. I am your mother and you people of Chalma are my children. Take the cactus dart; fill me with it.
Ya tonan j yauCivatzī. *aya* tonã yauÇivatzī *aya* ymaça colivaca y yvitla ypotocaya.	Our mother, warrior-woman, Our mother, warrior-woman, Deer of Colhuacan who is covered with feathers.
q. n. J niyaucivatzin y namona vmpa nochan in colvaca auh in quavivitl nictemaca ynic oquauhtivac.	This means, I am your mother, the warrior-woman. My home is there in Colhuacan, and I give someone an eagle feather with which she becomes an eagle.
Ahuiya ye tonaquetlj yautlatocaya, *ahuia* ye tonaquetlj yautlatocaya ma nevilano tlaca cenpoliviz	The sun has shone, war goes on. The sun has shone, war goes on. Let men be dragged up; they will come to an end.
aya ymaca colivacã y yvitla ypotocaya	The deer of Colhuacan is covered with plumes.
q. n. Ca otonac ca otlatvic ma mochiva	This means, the sun has shone, the day has

yauyutl ma tlamalo tlalpiliviz nictemaca in quavivitl.

dawned. Let there be war, let captives be taken, let the land be decimated. I give people eagle feathers.

[fol. 279r]

Ahuia quavivitl amoxa*ya*vallj
onaviya yecoyametl amoxa*ya*vallj
q. n. *Aahuia* yn otlamaloc in quavivitl yc moxava.

Eagle feathers are your facial paint,
Of the fighter is your facial paint.
This means, captives have been taken. His face is painted with eagle feathers.

¶ Jzcatqui ỹ Cuicatl chicuexiuhtica mevaya in iq̃c atamalqualoya.

¶ Here Is the Song Sung Every Eight Years when Water Tamales Were Eaten[23]

Xochitl noyollo cuepontimanja:
ye tlacoyoalle, *oaya, oovayaye.*
Yecoc ye tonã
yecoc, ye teutl tlacolteutla *oaya oovayaye.*
Otlacatqui çenteutl tamiyoanchãnj
xochitlicacanj,
çe y xochitlj *yantala, yantata, ayyao, ayyave tililiyao ayiave oayyave.*
Otlacatqui çenteutl, atl, yayavicanj

tlacapillachivaloya chalchimichvacã. *yyao, yantala, yantanta ayyao, ayyave, tililiyao, ayyave oayyave.*

My heart is a flower that bursts into bloom.
He is the lord of the midnight hour.
Our mother has come.
The goddess has come—Tlazolteotl.
Centeotl was born in Tamoanchan,
Where flowers stand erect;
He is One Flower.

In the region of water, of mist, was Centeotl born.
In the place of the lord of the fish made of jade are the offspring of lords given being.

[fol. 279v]

O*ya*tlatonazqui tlavizcallevaya

inan tlachichinaya nepapã quechol,

xochitlacaca *yyãtala, yantata, ayyao, ayyave, tililiyao, ayyave oayyave*
Tlalpã timoquetzca,
tianquiznavaquj *a*

The sun has come forth, the morning has dawned,
And sundry red spoonbills sip nectar from flowers
Where flowers stand erect.

On earth you are standing
By the marketing place.

23. This long hymn (without explanatory glosses) was apparently sung at the ceremony of Atamalcualiztli, "Eating of Water Tamales," that was performed every eight years in the *veintenas* of either Quecholli or Tepeilhuitl (see account in Paragraph 2B). Featuring a complicated ritual program that involved dancing and extensive impersonations of deities and a variety of insects, birds, and other creatures, plus snake swallowing, the ceremony was ostensibly performed to rest and rejuvenate the staple cultigen, maize. Because of its eight-year periodicity, Seler speculated that it was connected with the Venus calendar (eight solar years = five Venus years), and this view—in spite of the absence of elements in the ceremony that exhibit clear-cut Venusian associations—has been widely accepted. The hymn is rich in allusions to fertility deities (Tlazolteotl, Tonan, Xochiquetzal, Centeotl, Piltzintecuhtli, Quetzalcoatl) and mythical places that featured the fertility aspect (Tamoanchan, Xochitlicacan, Atlyahuican, Chalchimichhuacan), as well as some actual places (Chalollan, Oztoman, Chacallan). Of considerable interest is the reference to a magic ball court, Nahua(t)lachco, in relation to a deity, Xolotl, closely associated with the ritual ball game. For detailed interpretations of this rich hymn, see Seler (1902–1923, II: 1061–1070) and Garibay (1958: 154–172).

nitlacatla niquetzalcoatla *yyantala yãtanta, ayyao, ayyave, tililiyao, ayyave, oayyave.*	I am the lord Quetzalcoatl.
Ma *ya* aviallo xochinquavitl itlanj nepapã quechollj	Let sundry red spoonbills rejoice among flowering trees.
ma *ya* in quechollj xicaqui *ya* tlatoa *ya* y toteuh	Give ear to our god, the red spoonbill; he sings.
xicaq̃ *ya* tlatoa *ya* y quechol	Hear the red spoonbill; he sings.
amach yeva tomjcauh tlapitza amach yevã tlacalvaz. *ovao.*	May our death not be blown; may he not use the blowgun.
aye oho. yya yya ça niquiyecavizca noxocha	I'll bring only my flowers,
tonacaxochitlj	The flower of our sustenance,
ye izquixochitla,	The flower like popped corn,
xochitlicaca. *yyaa.*	From where flowers stand erect.
Ollama, ollama vive xolutl navalachco,	On the magical ball court old Xolotl plays with the ball; he plays with the ball.
ollama *ya* xolutl chalchivecatl	Xolotl, lord of the land of green stones, is playing with the ball.
xiquitta mach. *oya* moteca piltzĩtecutlj yoãchã, yoanchã	Look! Does Piltzintecuhtli recline in the House of the Night, in the House of the Night?
Piltzintle, Piltzintle,	Piltzintli, Piltzintli,
toçivitica timopotonja	You paste on yourself yellow parrot plumes.
tlachco timotlallj	On the ball court you sit.
yoanchã yoanchã	In the House of Night, in the House of Night.

[fol. 280r]

Oztomecatla *yyave* oztomecatla	Merchant, merchant.
xochiquetzal quimama	Xochiquetzal packs him on her back.
ontlatoa chollola	In Cholula she rules.
ayye ayyo oye mavi noyol, *oye* mavi noyol,	My heart is contented, my heart is contented.
aoya yecoc centeutl.	Centeotl has arrived;
ma tivia obispo,	Let us go to the bishop.
oztomecatl chacalhoa xiuhnacochtla y teamjc ximaquiztla y teamjco *ayye ayyo*	The wares of the merchant, the wares of the man from Chacallan
Cochina cochina cocochi	Are ear plugs of turquoise, are arm bands of turquoise,
ye nicmaololo nican j ye çivatl	The sleeper, the sleeper is dozing.
nicochina *yyeo ovayeo, yho, yya, yya,*	I turn the woman here over.
	The sleeper am I.

¶ Xippe ycujc, totec, yoallavana/	¶ Song of Our Flayed Lord, the Night Drinker[24]
Yoalli tlavana, yz tleicã timonenequi *a*	Drinker by night, why are you difficult?
xiyaqui mitlatia	Go in what covers you;

24. On the deity Xipe Totec, "Flayed One/Our Lord," to whom this hymn was dedicated, see note 48, Paragraph 5A.

teucuitlaquemitl ximoquētiquetl *ovia*
Q. n. Jn tiyoallavana, tixipe, totec, tleica in timonenequj, in timoçuma in timotlatia, id est. tleica in amo quiavi.

Apparel yourself in the garments of gold.
This means, you, Night Drinker, our Flayed Lord, why are you difficult? Are you angry? Do you hide? That is, why does it not rain?

teocuitlaquemitl xicmoquenti. q. n. ma quiavi.ma valauh yn atl,
Noteu achalchimama
tlacoapan aytemoya, *oy*

Teocuitlaquemitl xicmoquenti means, may it rain, may the water come.
My god carries waters of jade on his back.
The waterway's midpoint is not its way down.

quetzallavevetl, *ay* quetzalxivicoatl nech*i*-*ya*yquinocauhquetl, *oviya*.
Q. n. Jn tinoteuh, otemoc in mauh ovalla ỹ mauh. ay quetzalavevetl id est. ye tlaquetzalpatia ye tlaxoxovia, ye xopantla, ay quetzalxiuhcoatl nechiaiquinocauhquetl. id est. ca ye otechcauh ỹ mayanaliztlj

The quetzal-plume cypress, the quetzal-plume fire snake have left me bereft.
This means, you are my god; your water has descended, your water has come.
Ay quetzalavevetl: That is, now it becomes the color of the quetzal feather, now it is greening, now it is spring.
Ay quetzalxiuhcoatl nechiaiquinocauhquetl: That is, now famine has left us.

Ma niya *via*, ma niapoliviz
niyoatzin
a chalchiuhtla noyollo,
a teucuitlatl nocoy*a*itaz
noyolcevizquj
tlacatl achtoquetl tlaquava *ya*
otlacatqui yautlatoaquetl *oviya*.
Q. n. ma niauh, ma nipolivi, ỹ niyoatzī. id est ovatl, iuhquī chalchivitl noyollo. Ateocuitlatl nocoyaitaz. q. n. in catlevatl achto mochivaz ninoyolceviz.

Let me go, let me perish.
I am the green stalk of maize;
My heart is a precious green stone.
I shall look at the gold:
My heart will repose.
The leader is hardened.
The war lord's been born.
This means, let me go, let me perish, I who am Yoatzin, that is, the green maize stalk; my heart is like a jade.
Ateocuitlatl nocoyaitaz means, whatever is first to form, I shall be tranquil.

[fol. 280v]

Noteua ceintla co xaya
iliviz çonoa
y yoatzin
motepeyocpa mitzvalitta moteua,
vizquin
tlacatl achtoquetl tlaquava *ya,*

otlacatqui yautlatoaquetl, *oviya,*
Q. n. J noteuh cequi tlatlacotyā in mochiva

My lord the maize, face up!
He fears in vain.
He is the tender maize.
Your god observes you from your hills.
My heart will be at rest.
The leader is hardened, The war lord's been born.
This means, he is my god. Some of his sustenance is growing where there is labor, and

---

Yohuallana, "Night Drinker," was a title applied to the priest who presided over the gladiatorial sacrifice, *tlahuahuanaliztli,* the highlight of the *veintena* of Tlacaxipehualiztli, Xipe's particular ceremony (Sahagún 1981: 51–53). The hymn was interpreted in detail by Seler (1902–1923, II: 1073–1078) and Garibay (1958: 177–185); they often differed significantly in their translations and their exegetical analyses. In spite of many obscurities, the fertilization and growth of maize appears to constitute a basic theme of the hymn, which appropriately fits Xipe's role as a major fertility deity.

Paragraph 14

in itonacayuh, auh in tlein tlatlacotyã achto mochiva muchi tlacatl achto mitzvalmaca. auh in iquac ye omuchi mochiuh oc cepa no mochi tlacatl mitzvalmaca ỹ motonacayuh.

what comes up first where there is labor, everyone gives to you first; and when everything has now come up, once again everyone gives you your sustenance.

¶ Chicomecoatl icujc.

Chicomollotzin xa*ya*meva, ximiçotia,
a ca tona titechicnocavazqui
ti*ya*via muchi tlallocan *ovia*
q. n. Jn tichicomolutl. id est in ticentlj. ximeva, xiça, xixva, ca otonmovicaya yn mochan tlallocã

Xa*ya*meva, ximiçotia
a ca tonã titechicnocavazquj
ti*ya*viã mochã tlallocã *noviya.*
q. n. Xayameva id est ximeva, xixva, xiça ca otimovicaya yn mochãtzinco in tlalocã ca iuhquĩ titonãtzĩ.

¶ Song of Chicomecoatl[25]

Arise, wake up, Seven Ears of Maize,
You, our mother, will leave us bereft;
You have gone to your home in Tlalocan.
This means, you who are Seven Ears of Maize, that is, you who are the maize, arise, wake up, sprout up, for you have taken yourself off to your home in Tlalocan.

Arise, wake up;
You, our mother, will leave us bereft;
You have gone to your home in Tlalocan.
This means, *Xayameva,* that is, arise, sprout up, wake up, for you have taken yourself off to your home in Tlalocan; you are like our mother.

¶ Totochtin incujc tezcatzoncatl

Yyaha, yya yya, yya ayya, ayyo oviya, ayya yya, ayya yya yyo viya, ayya yya ayya yya yyo viya.

¶ Song of the Rabbits; Tezcatzoncatl[26]

Yah aha
Yah yah yah yah yoh
O yah
Yah yah yah yah yoh
O yah
Yah yah yah yah yoh
O yah[27]

25. On the subject of this short hymn, Chicomecoatl, "Seven Coatl (Snake)," the fundamental maize deity—merged here, as Tonan, "Our Mother," with the Earth Goddess—see note 25, Paragraph 5A. Chicomollotzin, "Seven Maize Cobs," the epithet by which she is addressed in the hymn, was linked by Seler (1902–1923, II: 1081) with the ritual carrying of the seed maize, in bunches of seven cobs (called here *chichicoomollotl*), by a procession of young girls to Centeopan, the temple of Chicomecoatl, a highlight of the *veintena* of Hueytozoztli dedicated to this goddess (Sahagún 1981: 63–64). The hymn, which also mentions Tlalocan, the paradise of the Rain God, consists of only two strophes, virtually repeated; it could be interpreted as a kind of conjuration to promote the growth of the maize crop.

26. Totochtin, "The Rabbits," were the *octli* gods in the aggregate (see note 15, Paragraph 5A). Tezcatzoncatl, "He of Tezcatzonco (Place of Mirror-Hair)," was one of the most important of these gods and was named by Sahagún (1970: 74) in one passage as the inventor of this intoxicating beverage. He was not included among the deities pictured in Paragraph 5(A), although two gods, Totoltecatl and Macuiltochtli, and a goddess, Tezcacoac Ayopechtli (= Mayahuel), that were pictured can be assigned to the *octli* cult (see notes 79, 81, and 87, Paragraph 5A). Tezcatzoncatl was described in Chapter 22 of Book 1 of the *Florentine Codex* (Sakagún 1970: 51, Pl. 21) and illustrated on fol. 12 of the manuscript (Sahagún 1979, I).

27. The initial passage of this hymn is composed of a series of meaningless utterances featuring the ubiquitous *ya,* widely employed for rhythmic effect throughout the hymns. It constituted what Garibay called an "apoyo a la música preludial del canto." Garibay (1958: 196–197) also presented a cogent argument that fol. 281 of the Real Palacio manuscript had been inadvertently turned around, probably when the manuscript was bound, so that its original verso side became the recto page immediately following fol. 280 verso. This resulted in the two final strophes of the Tezcatzon-

ytlauelcujc, tlauelcujca,
Colivacã mavizpã *a* tlacatl jchan *a, yyo, ayya yya, yyo.*
Colivacã mavizpã tlacatl jchan a: q. n. in tlacatl id est vctlj vmpa ichã nicolhoacã / mavizpã. q. n. temamauhtican.

His angry song; he sings angrily.
Colhuacan is a place of fear; it's the dwelling of the lord.
Colivacan mavizpan tlacatl ichan a means, the lord, that is, *octli,* has his home in Colhuacan.
Mavizpan means, place where they frighten people.

Tezcatzonco tecpan teutl. macoc
ye choca *ya, avia*
maca ivi maca yvi teutl. macoc
y ye choca *ya*
Tezcatzonco tecpan teutl. q. n. ye choca in omacoc teutl tezcatzonco tecpã id est uctlj, quimonacayotia in teutl. / maca ivi teutl, q. n. macamo omaconj in teutl. id est uctlj ye choca cayamo ynemac.

In Tezcatzonco, in his lordly house, the god's been given gifts.
Now he weeps.
Let not, let not thus the god be given gifts.
Now he weeps.
Tezcatzonco tecpan teutl means, now he weeps; the god in the palace of Tezcatzonco was given gifts, that is, *octli,* which the god personified.
Maca ivi teutl means, the god—that is, *octli*—is one who was not given gifts. Now he weeps; he has no gifts.

Huia axalaco tecpa teutl macoc
y ye choca *ya*
maca yvi maca yvi teutl, macoc
y ye choca *ya*
Avia axalaco tecpã teutl. q. n. axala in tecpã teutl, ye choca ỹ omacoc id est uctlj axala tecpã ye choca in omacoc macamo omaconi ye choca cayamo ynemac.

Ah!
In Axalaco, in his lordly house, the god's been given gifts.
Now he weeps.
Let not, let not thus the god be given gifts.
Now he weeps.
Avia axalaco tecpan teutl means, the god in the Axala palace now weeps; he was given gifts. That is, the *octli* in the Axala palace now weeps; it was given gifts. He is one who is not given gifts. Now he weeps; he has no gifts.

[fol. 281v]

Tezcatzonco moyolcã
ay yaquetl *yya* tochi quiyocuxqui *a* noteuh,
niqui*ya*tlaçaz niqui*ya*mamaliz. mixcoatepetl colhoacã.
Tezcatzonco moyolcã. q. n. tezcatzonco, oyul, in tochtlj ynic yaz. oquiyocux, oquipic,

Tezcatzonco is your place of birth.
A warrior, a rabbit, my god has created.
I've cast forth, I've drilled [fire] on Mixcoatl's mountain in Colhuacan.
Tezcatzonco moyolcan means, in Tezcatzonco the rabbit was born in order to go off.

catl hymn being wrongly positioned so that they concluded the hymn to Macuilxochitl, and they were copied accordingly into the *Florentine Codex* version. Accepting Garibay's hypothesis—and Anderson and Dibble do accept it in their revised version of the hymn in their second edition of Book 2 (Sahagún 1981: 242)—these final two strophes are here restored to their proper position in this hymn to the *octli* god. Although this expansion of the hymn's length has perhaps slightly enhanced its intelligibility, most of it is still quite difficult to understand on a specific level, as is evidenced by the considerable differences between the exegeses of Seler (1902–1923, II: 1084–1087) and Garibay (1958: 196–199).

Paragraph 14

y noteuh, oquito nictlaçaz nicmamaliz in mixcoatepetl colhoacã, id est, nictopevaz.

My god created, he invented [fire]. He said, "I'll cast it forth, I'll drill it on Mixcoatl's mountain in Colhuacan"; that is, "I'll kindle the fire."

Tozquiva *ya,* nictzotzon *iyao,* y tezcatzintli
tezcatzintli tezcaxoco yeva
tzoniztapalatiati
tla oc xoconoctli *a. ho. a.*

Tozquiva ya nictzotzon iao, q. n. nictzotzona in tezcatzintlj oncãn eva in tezcatzonco, oncã oyol. tzoniztapalatiati oc xconj in uctlj.

Lord of song, I've struck the little mirror,
Tezcatzonco's little mirror.
[Octli's] white top has cleared.
Drink up the *octli!*

Tozquiva ya nictzotzon iyao means, I heat the little mirror. It rises there in Tezcatzonco; there it lives. White top has cleared; now drink the *octli.*

¶ Yyacatecutlj ycujc.

¶ Song of Yacatecuhtli[28]

Anomatia *a* ytoloc,
anomatia *a* ytoloc tzocotzontla

a ytoloc tzocotzontla
anomatia *a* ytoloc

Anomatia. q. n. amo nixpã in omito yauyutl inic otepevaloc tzocotzontla, amo nomatia in omito yauyutl.

Not with my knowing was [the war] declared.
Not with my knowing was [the war] declared on Tzocotzontla.
Was it declared on Tzocotzontla?
Not with my knowing was it declared.

Anomatia means, not in my presence was war declared by which Tzocotzontla was conquered. Not with my knowing was war declared.

Pipitla *a* ytoloc,
pipitla anomatia *a* ytoloc,

cholotla *a* ytoloc
pipitla anomatia *a* ytoloc.

Pipitla a ytoloc. q. n. ynic tepevaloc pipitla, amo nicmati inic omito yauyotl, in cholotla ic toepevalloc amo nixpã ynic oyautlatolloc.

It was declared on Pipitla.
Not with my knowing was it declared on Pipitla.
On Cholotla it was declared.
Not with my knowing was it declared on Pipitla.

Pipitla y ytoloc means, when Pipitla was vanquished, I did not know that war had been declared. When Cholotla was vanquished, not in my presence was war declared.

Tonacayutl nicmaceuh
açan axcã noquacuillo
atl iyollo, nechval*ya*vicatiaque
xalli itepeuhya

Tonacayutl nicmaceuh. q. n. yn tonacayutl inic onjcmaceuh ayaxcã, onechvalhuicaqz i

I have obtained the sustenance of life.
With trouble have my shorn-head priests
Brought me the water's heart
From where the sand is strewn.

Tonacayutl nicmaceuh means, I obtained the sustenance of life because my shorn-

28. On Yacatecuhtli, probably "Nose Lord," the merchant god, see note 32, Paragraph 5A. Although the hymn is ostensibly dedicated to this deity, there is little in it that appears, in any obvious way, to relate to him or to the commercial or ritual activities of the group called *pochteca oztomeca,* well documented in Book 9 of the *Florentine Codex* (Sahagún 1950–1982, Part X), of which he was the patron deity. Much of the hymn is obscure, even though the explanatory glosses are more extensive than usual. The first portion appears to refer to a series of military actions (interpreted by the native annotator as conquests) against three places: Tzocotzontla(n), Pipitla(n) (= same place mentioned in hymn to Huitzilopochtli?), and Cholotla(n) (Seler: Xolotlan?). None can be surely located geographically. The second portion conveys a very different series of images involving sustenance, aqueous fertility, Tlalocan, and the priesthood. For more detailed analyses, see Seler (1902–1923, II: 1104–1107) and Garibay (1958: 204–208).

noquacuiloã in xochayutl, in çoquiayutl in tevelteca, quimilhuj in iquĩ tonaz tlatviz anoquacuiloã ayezq̃, xalli tepeuhya id est tlalocã / quilmach chalchiuhpetlacallj in quitopeuh inic tepeuh.

head priests with difficulty brought me the flower turtle, the mud turtle, the people of Tehuellan. He said to them, "When the sun shines, when the day dawns, you, my shorn-head priests, are to be in the place where the sand is strewn," that is, Tlalocan. They say that he set fire to the green stone coffer; thus they were strewn about.

Chalchiuhpetlacalco ninaxca
açan axcã noquacuillo,
atl iyollo nechval*ia*vicatiaque
xalli itepeuhya

Chalchiuhpetlacalco ninaxcã. q. n. oncã ninotlati in chalchiuhpetlacalco. ayaxcã y nechalhvicatiaqz y noquacuiloã atl iyoloa in vmpa tlallocã

In the jade coffer I burn myself up.
With trouble have my shorn-head priests
Brought me the water's heart
From where the sand is strewn.

Chalchiuhpetlacalco ninaxcan means, there in the green stone coffer I burned myself up. With difficulty my shorn-head priests brought me the heart of the water from Tlalocan.

[fol. 281r]

¶ Atlava ycuic.

Hvia nichalmecatl,
nichalmecatl
neçavalcactla, neçavalcactla,
olya quatonalla
olya

Q. n. J nichalmecatl, y nineçavalcac oquicauhtevac yn ioholli, yn ioya, ixquatechimal iquatonal.

Veya, veya, macxoyauh quilazteutl yllapani
macxoyauh.

Q. n. maxiyauh tiquilazteutl. nomac temj yn macxoyauh.

Nimitzacatecunotza *ya*
chimalticpac moneço *ya*

nimitzacatecunotza *ya*

Q. n. in iquac onimitznotz, mochimalticpac timiçoya.

¶ Song of Atlahua[29]

I am the man from Chalma,
I am the man from Chalma,
Nezahualcactli, Nezahualcactli.
The forehead insignia is swaying;
It sways.

This means, I am the man from Chalma, I am Nezahualcac. He left behind the rubber, the jewel, his frontal rosette, his head adornment.

Your fir branch, the broom of Quilaztli,
Your fir branch.

This means, your fir branch, Quilazteotl, your fir branch lies in my hand.

I call you, lord reed.
On top of the shield he draws blood from himself.
I call you, lord reed.

This means, when I call you, you draw blood from yourself on top of the shield.

29. On Atlahua, probably "Possessor of Spear-thrower," see note 74, Paragraph 5A. He was a hunting deity especially venerated, along with Amimitl, in Cuitlahuac in the Chinampaneca freshwater lacustrine district of the southern Basin of Mexico. Various of the references in the hymn seem appropriate to the cult of this deity, who overlaps—but in a more aquatic aspect—with the Chichimec hunting deity par excellence, Mixcoatl/Camaxtli. These references include Chalma(n) (see note 36, Paragraph 5A), Acatecuhtli, "Reed-Lord," and the split reed, *acaxelihui*, as arrow (= *timetl!*; see note 76, Paragraph 5A). Two other deities important in this zone, Quilaztli (= Cihuacoatl; see note 67, Paragraph 5A) and Opochtli (see note 57, Paragraph 5A), are also mentioned, along with an apparent toponym, Tetoman, otherwise unknown.

Ayac nomiuh timalla
a ytolloca acatl nomiuh
acaxelivi timalla,
Q. n. atle nomjuh yc notimaloa, ca vel itoloc in acatl nomjuh. yn acatl xelivi yn ninotimaloa.

No arrow is mine; it is [my] pride.
It was said that the reed is my arrow.
The split reed is [my] pride.
This means, no arrow is mine; thus I am filled with pride, for it is said that the reed is my arrow, the split reed; I am filled with pride.

Tetomã *a* moyolcan *a* tlamacazquin tetometl.
açan axcã ye quetzaltototl nic*ya*izcaltiquetl *a*.
Q. n. oncã evac in tetomã, nitlacochtetometl. auh in axcã ye quetzaltototl ynic nitlazcaltia
Y yopuchi noteuh atlavaquetl,
açan axcã ye quetzaltototl nic*ya*izcaltiquetl *a*.
Q. n. tiacauh i noteuh in atlava: auh in axcã iuhquĩ quetzaltototl ic nitlazcaltia.

Tetoman was your place of birth, Priest Tetometl.
Laboriously I feed the quetzal bird.
This means, there in Tetoman he rose; I am Tlacochtetometl. And now he is a quetzal bird; therefore I feed him.
Opochtli, my god, is Atlahua.
Laboriously I feed the quetzal bird.
This means, the war chief is my god, Atlahua, and now he is like a quetzal bird; therefore I feed him.

¶ Macuilxochitl icuic.

¶ Song of Macuilxochitl[30]

Ayya yao, xochitl icaca vmpa nivitz *a*
tlamacazecatl *a* tlamocoyoale *a*.
Q. n. vmpa nocha in xochitl icaca ỹ nitlamacazqui nimacuilxvchitl.

From where flowers stand erect, thence come I,
The priest, lord of red dusk.
This means, my home is there where flowers stand erect. I am the priest, I am Macuilxochitl.

Ayya yyao. a yvin tinozic *aya* teumechave *oya, yao*
tlavicoyacalle *a* tlamacazecatl *o* tlamocoyovale *a*.
Q. n. Ma tihuia in tinoçi in vmpa titlaecoltilozque vmpa tochã ez
tetzauhteutl *a* notecujo tezcatlipuca
quinanquilicã çinteutl *a oay*.
Q. n. Jn tetzavitl in tezcatlipvca ca oyaque auh ynic tivi vmpa titlananquilizque in centeutl

So also you, grandmother mine with the thigh-skin face paint,
Rosy dawn's lady [and] priest[ess], red gloaming lady.
This means, you, my grandmother, go. We shall be served where our home is to be.
God of ill omen, my lord Tezcatlipoca,
Answer Centeotl.
This means, he of ill omen [and] Tezcatlipoca went off, and therefore we must go there to answer Centeotl.

30. This final hymn was dedicated to Macuilxochitl, the preeminent member of the Macuiltonaleque (see notes 43 and 84, Paragraph 5A). Even in its truncated and possibly incomplete form—after the transfer of its ostensible concluding strophes to the earlier hymn dedicated to Tezcatzoncatl—the hymn contains references that are appropriate to the cult of the Macuiltonaleque, including Xochitlicaca, a well-recognized synonym for Tamoanchan, and Centeotl, the young maize god who overlaps with Macuilxochitl/Xochipilli. There also appears to be a reference to the maternal earth/fertility goddess Toci, "Our Grandmother," an aspect of Teteoinnan/Tlazolteotl, who wears the thigh-skin face paint featured in the rituals of the *veintena* of Ochpaniztli (compare the foregoing hymn to Teteoinnan). Also mentioned is the head of the pantheon, Tezcatlipoca, apparently designated by the appellation Tetzahuitl, "Omen," which was more commonly applied to Huitzilopochtli.

CHAPTER II
THE HEAVENS AND THE UNDERWORLD

PARAGRAPH 1
[fol. 282r]

Jnic vme Cap. ytech tlatoa in ilhuicacaiutl: yoã ỹ mictlancaiutl

Second chapter, which tells of the things pertaining to the heavens and the things pertaining to the underworld.

Inic ce parrapho ipan mitoa in intoca ỹtech tlanextilia.

First paragraph, in which are told the names of [the bodies] that shine [in the heavens].

In iquac valmomana tonatiuh tlenamaco tlaquechcotonalo neçoyoa mitoaya ovalquiz in tonatiuh ca ye tequitiz ca ye tlacotiz que vetziz in cemilhuitl.

When the sun appeared, offerings of incense were made, [quail] were decapitated, blood was drawn. It was said, "The sun has come out. Now it will work; now it will perform its labors. How will the day turn out?"

Jnic opa tlenamaco icuac in tlacualizpa

The second time offerings of incense were made was at eating time.

inic. 3. iquac in nepantla tonatiuh

The third [time] was when the sun reached its zenith.

ic. na 4. iquac ỹ mopiloa tonatiuh.

The fourth [time] was when the sun was going down.

Jnic. v. iquac in õcalaqui tonatiuh mitoaya otequit otlacotic in tonatiuh.

The fifth [time] was when the sun had set. It was said, "The sun has done its work; it has performed its labors."

The Moon

metztli. quimoteotiaya in xaltocameca.

The people of Xaltocan[1] worshiped it.

Eclipse of the Sun[2]

tonatiuh qualloya. cenca nemauhtiloya mitoaya intla quitlamiz in quiqua tonatiuh quilmach çentlaiovaz valtemozque in ţiţimime techquazque: auh in iquac cenca miec miquia im mamalti yoã mochi tlacatl mizo-

There was great fear. It was said that if [the moon] finished eating the sun, so it was said, all would be in darkness; the *tzitzimime*[3] would descend here; they would devour us. And at that time very many captives died,

1. Xaltocameca: Xaltocan was a major Otomi-speaking center in the northern Basin of Mexico. On the importance of lunar cults among the Otomi, see Carrasco Pizana 1950: 137.

2. *Tonatiuh qualloya:* literally, "the sun is eaten," the standard Nahuatl expression for a solar eclipse.

3. *Ţ iţimime:* Read *tzitzimime.* These were stellar death demons, most feared during eclipses; they were also connected with certain deities (see Seler 1900–1901: 52–53).

ya in noviã momuzco yoã in çacacalco yoã tlacoquixtiloya ỹ novia teteupã mochi tlacatl monacaztequia oyvin i ỹ mochivaya.

and everyone drew blood from himself everywhere—at the crossroads shrines[4] and in the Zacacalco [House of Grass][5]—and twigs were passed [through various parts of the body] in the temples everywhere, [and] everyone cut his ear [lobes]. Thus was it done.

Eclipse of the Moon[6]

metztli cuallo. yn otztiti catca çenca momauhtiaya quitoaya quilmach quimichti mocuepazque auh im pipiltotonti tlacatia in ipan qualoya metztli in aca yacaquatic anoço tenquatic. auh impipiltoton moximaya in ipa çeçentetl metztli intlacamo moximaz i cocolizcui oyvin i im mitoaya.

The pregnant women were very fearful. They said, it was said that they would turn into mice and the children born during an eclipse of the moon would be noseless or lipless. And the heads of the babies were shaved each month; if they were not shaved, they took sick. Thus was it said.

The Fire Sticks[7]

mamalhuaztli. Jn iquac oya tonatiuh y ye tlayacavi iquac çeppa tlenamaco ic mitoaya ovalvetz y iovaltecutli yacavitztli ye tequitiz ye tlacotiz.

When the sun departed,[8] when it was now dark, was the first time an offering of incense was made. It was said, "Yohualtecuhtli Yacahuitztli has appeared. Now he will do his work; now he will perform his labors."

Auh inic opa tlenamaco iquac yn tlaquauh tlapoyava.

And the second time an incense offering was made was when it was completely dark.

Jnic. 3. tlenamacoc iquac ỹ netetequizpa.

The third [time] an incense offering was made was at bedtime.

jnic. 4. tlenamaco iquac in tlatlapitzalizpa. Auh ỹ machiyotl ỹ mamalvaztli yoã miec yoan tiyanquiztli yquac nepãtla omomanaco nima ye ic tlatlapiçallo ic mitoaya tlatla-

The fourth [time] an incense offering was made was when the flutes were sounded. And when the sign of the Fire Sticks, and also those of the Many and the Market[9] reached

4. *Momuzco:* On the *momoztli,* see note 4, Paragraph 7, Chapter I.

5. *Çacacalco:* Read *zacacalco.* These were structures where autosacrificial and other ritual activities took place.

6. *Metztli cuallo:* literally, "the moon is eaten," signifying a lunar eclipse, a phrase parallel to that for a solar eclipse (see note 2, this paragraph).

7. Mamalhuaztli: This asterism, which is diagramed and labeled, is here and elsewhere (Sahagún 1950–1982, Part VIII [Book 7]: 11) designated by two other names, Yohualtecuhtli, "Lord of Night," and Yacahuiztli, "Nose-Thorn." An apparent alternative for the first name was Yohualitqui, "Night Bringer" (Alvarado Tezozomoc 1987: 574). It has been variously identified by modern scholars; the most frequent suggestions have been: the belt and sword of Orion (Orozco y Berra 1960, I: 27; Coe 1975: 26; Aveni 1980: 35–36), Hyades in Taurus (Gallo 1955: 19; Aveni 1980: 35), Aldebaran (Orozco y Berra 1960, I: 27; Gallo 1955: 18), and Castor and Pollux in Gemini (Anderson and Dibble in Sahagún 1950–1982, Part VIII [Book 7]: 60).

8. *Tlayacavi:* Possibly this should be read *tlayoac.* Otherwise the term might be translated as "it nosed (or pointed) something"—a possible reference to Yacahuiztli.

9. *Miec yoan tiyanquiztli:* It has been generally agreed that these terms referred to the Pleiades, which played an important role in the mythology and ritual of many Mesoamerican and other native New World groups (see Aveni 1980: 30–34). Observation of this asterism determined the timing of the initiation of the great New Fire ceremony, *toxiuhmolpia,* of 1507 (Sahagún 1950–1982, Part V [Book 4]: 143). Although not specifically labeled as such, one of the stellar diagrams clearly represents the Pleiades (e.g., Seler 1904: 357).

piçalizpa.

their zenith, then the flutes were sounded. Thus it was called the time of the sounding of the flutes.[10]

Inic. v. tlenamaco yquac ỹ mitoaya ticatla iquac nezovaya vitztli mocui nevitzmanalo. Auh ỹ machiyotl ỹ mamalvaztli yoã miec yoã tiyanquiztli omopiloto.

The fifth [time] an offering of incense was made was at what was called midnight, when there was bleeding of oneself; maguey thorns were taken; there was the offering of thorns. And the signs of the Fire Sticks, and the Many, and the Market were going to set.

Jnic. vi. tlenamaco yquac y valcholoa çitlali.

The sixth [time] an offering of incense was made was when the [morning] star appeared.

Auh inic. 7. tlenamaco yquac yn tlatlalchipava auh ỹ machiyotl quipatla in çitlali ỹ miec. - /

And the seventh [time] an offering of incense was made was when it began to dawn and the [morning] star took the place of the sign, the Many.

The Morning Star[11]

çitlalpul. tlanextia.

It shines brightly.

The Comet

çitlalin popuca. ipã mitoaya cana ye valmotzacuaz yauyutl mochivaz anoço aca vey tlaçopilli miquiz.

About it, it is said that wherever it is, there will soon be a rebellion [against the ruler], war will be made, or some esteemed nobleman will die.

The Shooting Star

çitlalin tlamina. amo nẽquiça aço tochtli anoço chichi in quimina ytic moteca ocuili amo qualo mochi iuh mochiva yn oc çequi ocuilti ytic calaqui.

It does not appear without purpose. When it strikes a rabbit or a dog, a worm is extended inside it. [The animal] is not eaten. All of it becomes like this; other worms find their way inside it.

[fol. 282v]

The S-Shaped Constellation[12]

xonecuilli. tlanextia

It shines brightly.

10. *Tlatlapicallo, tlatlapicaliztli:* read *tlatlapitzalo* and *tlatlapitzaliztli.*

11. *Citlalpul:* literally, "great star," the standard Nahuatl appellation for the planet Venus, recognized as both the morning and evening star. This planet played a major role in Mesoamerican calendrics, ritual, and divination (see Seler 1904; Coe 1975: 19–20; Aveni 1980: 23–26).

12. *Xonecuilli:* This asterism, which is diagramed and labeled, has been identified with different constellations: Ursa Minor (Anderson and Dibble in Sahagún 1950–1982, Part VIII [Book 7]: 66; Aveni 1980: 37), Ursa Major (Aveni 1980: 37), the Southern Cross (Seler 1904: 358; Aveni 1980: 36), and a stellar configuration in Hercules and Draco (Seler 1904–1909, I: 261–262). Sahagún (1950–1982, Part VIII [Book 7]: 13; 1988, II: 483–484) states that this constellation took its name from its resemblance to an S-shaped maize or amaranth seed cake ritually eaten on the days named Xochitl (Flower) in the 260-day divinatory cycle, *tonalpohualli.* See discussion of the *xonecuilli* in Seler 1904–1909, I: 259–263.

Paragraph 1

Scorpion[13]

colutl. çan onoc tlanextia.

It is only there; it shines brightly.

PARAGRAPH 2

Jnic ome parrapho ypã mitoa in jntoca yn tlacpac eecaticpac muchiva.

Second paragraph, in which are told the names of what are found on high, on the winds.

eecatl.

The Winds[1]

Jnic çentlamãtli y eecatl çiuatlãpa itztiviz. auh inic ontlamãtli eecatl chalcopa itzivitz iquac motzineva quauitl anoço calli xitini. Jnic. 3. eecatl mictlãpa itztivitz. Jnic. 4. eecatl tiquitoa chichimecapa itztivitz çenca ic micova. auh yn eecatl mitoaya quetzalcoatl tiquitoa quintlachpania in tlaloque.

The first wind comes from the west, and the second wind comes from the direction of Chalco. At that time trees are uprooted or houses crumble. The third wind comes from the north. The fourth wind we say comes from the region of the Chichimeca; with it there is much death. And the wind that is called Quetzalcoatl, we say, sweeps the road for the Tlalocs.

tlapetlanilutl.

Lightning

tlatlatziniliztli. tiquitoa quichiva in tlaloque quitquitiviçe in tlapetlanilutl ic tlauitequi in iquac cana tlauiteco.

The Bolt of Lightning. We say that the Tlalocs produce it. They go bearing[2] the lightning bolts with which they strike things when something is struck [by lightning] somewhere.

quiyavitl.

Rain

tiquitoa quichiua in tlaloque.

We say that the Tlalocs make it.

13. *Colotl:* Again, modern students differ concerning the identification of this constellation (called *colotl ixayac,* "scorpion face," by Alvarado Tezozomoc [1987: 574]), which is diagramed and labeled. Suggestions have included Arcturus (Seler 1904: 357), Ursa Major (Anderson and Dibble in Sahagún 1950–1982, Part VIII [Book 7]: 66; Gallo 1955: 19–20), and the Old World Scorpio (Orozco y Berra 1960, I: 28; Coe 1975: 26; Aveni 1980: 37). On the symbolic ideological connotations of the scorpion in pre-Hispanic Mesoamerica, see Seler 1902–1923, IV: 740–750.

1. The Tepepolco provenience of this scheme of the winds seems to be evidenced by the designation of the southern wind as that from the direction of Chalco, which lies almost directly south of the Tepepolco zone. Comparing this scheme with that obtained later by Sahagún in Tlatelolco and included in the *Historia* (Sahagún 1950–1982, Part VIII [Book 7]: 14; 1988, II: 484), some interesting differences are apparent. The latter presents the formally structured scheme that assigns the winds to the four cardinal directions, listed following the standard counterclockwise ritual circuit: east-north-west-south. Here, the description of the winds commences with that from the west, followed by that from the south. Two winds are assigned to the north (Mictlampa, Chichimecapan), and although it is not explicitly stated, the "Quetzalcoatl wind" must have been considered to have come from the east, in keeping with the usual directional assignment of this deity.

2. *Quitquitivice:* read *quitquitivitze.*

ayauhcoça]malvtl.

Yn omoqueçaco tiquitoa ye quiçaz yn quiavitl ye quiçazque in tlaloque. auh in ipã moqueça metl ayauhcoçamalutl macueçaliçivi.

Rainbow

When it comes rising[3] we say the rain will cease, that now the Tlalocs will stop [raining]. And when the rainbow rises[4] over a maguey, the leaves become reddened.

Çetl.

tiquitoa itztlacoliuhqui çexiuhtica y vallauh in çevetzi ypã çempovallapoalli ochpaniztli. Auh chicuaçempovaliluitl i çevetzi ipã quiça çempovallapovalli tiquitoa tititl tiquitoa oquiz in çetl ye toquizpa. ye tlatotonia. ye qualca.

Frost

We say that the frost is Itztlacoliuhqui.[5] During the year the frost comes in the twenty-day period of Ochpaniztli.[6] And for one hundred and twenty days there is cold. It ceases in the twenty-day period we call Tititl.[7] We say, "The cold has ceased. Now it is the time of the green leaves of maize; now it is warm; now the weather is good."

[fol. 283r]

mixtli.

yn iquac tepeticpac omotlatlalli tiquitoa ca ye quiaviz ye viçe in tlaloque omotlatlalli ỹ mextli.

Clouds

When they have settled on the tops of the mountains we say that now it will rain, that now the Tlalocs are coming;[8] the clouds have settled.

çepayavitl.

çan itlauical yn çetl iuhquin quiyauitl ypã povi in iquac çepayavi tiquitoa pixcoz.

Snow

It is the companion of the frost. It is prized like the rain. When it snows we say there will be a harvest.

teçivitl.

ic muchiva in iquac motlatlalia mextli tepeticpac cenca iztac mitoa ca ye tetiviz. Auh nimã quitaya in teçiuhtlazque quitoaya ca ye teţiviz. auh quitlacoa in tonacaiotl.

Hail

It occurs when the clouds that settle on the mountaintops are very white. It is said that now it will hail. And then when the hail-ejectors[9] had seen it, they said, "Now it will hail." And it damages the fruits of the earth.

3. *Omoquequecaco:* read *omoquequetzaco.*

4. *Moqueca:* read *moquetza.*

5. Itztlacoliuhqui: "Curved Obsidian Blade." This name was applied to the male maize deity, Centeotl, in the context of the role of his ritual impersonator during the Ochpaniztli ceremony. It was also the name of a strange, enigmatic deity that served as the regent of the twelfth *trecena* of the *tonalpohualli* commencing with 1 Cuetzpallin (Lizard). See the analyses and interpretations in Seler 1900–1901: 90–93; 1904–1909, II: 246–252; Sullivan 1976a.

6. Ochpaniztli: The duration of this *veintena* at the time of the Conquest was from September 2 to September 21 (Caso correlation of the Mexica calendar [Caso 1939]). Paragraph 2

7. Tititl: According to the Caso correlation of the Mexica calendar (Caso 1939), at the time of the Conquest this *veintena* ran from December 31 to January 19.

8. *Vice:* read *vitze.*

9. *Teciuhtlazque:* These "hail-ejectors" or "hail-throwers" used their supernatural powers to protect the fields from

PARAGRAPH 3

Ynic yei parrapho ypan mitoa yn xiuhpovalli.

Nican mitoa yn cecexiuhtlapohualli Compevaltica yn itoca
.1. tochtli. [illus.]
.2. acatl. Jn ipan omacatl [illus.] xiuhtonali mochipa ipan molpilia in toxiuh vmpoalxiuhtica omatlactli vmome. Este año de 1560 se
.3. tecpatl. [illus.] cũplierõ los cincuẽta y dos años con este caracter q̃ se llama vmacatl y comjença el primero para otros 52 sobre este caracter que se llama ey tecpatl
.4. calli. [illus.]
.v. tochtli [illus.]
.6. acatl. [illus.]
.vii. tecpatl. [illus.]

Third paragraph, in which the year count is told.[1]

Here is told the count of the years, which commences with [the year] called:
One Rabbit
Two Reed At the time of the year-sign Two Reed there was always the binding of the fifty-two-year period.
Three Flint Knife This year, 1560, ended the fifty-two years with this sign called Two Reed and the next fifty-two years begin with the sign called Three Flint Knife.
Four House
Five Rabbit
Six Reed
Seven Flint Knife

[fol. 283v]

.8. calli. [illus.]
.9. tochtli. [illus.]
.x. acatl. [illus.]
.xi. tecpatl. [illus.]
.x2. calli. [illus.]
.x3. tochtli [illus.]
Auh nima ye moqueça yn itoca
.1. acatl. [illus.]
.2. tecpatl. [illus.]
.3. calli. [illus.]
.4. tochtli. [illus.]

Eight House
Nine Rabbit
Ten Reed
Eleven Flint Knife
Twelve House
Thirteen Rabbit
And then there set in[2] [the year] named:
One Reed
Two Flint Knife
Three House
Four Rabbit

[fol. 284r]

.v. acatl. [illus.]
.vi. tecpatl. [illus.]

Five Reed
Six Flint Knife

---

damaging hail storms (e.g., Sahagún 1950–1982, Part VIII [Book 7]: 20; 1988, II: 486). They are included in the list of magicians in Chapter III, Paragraph 11. See Seler 1899b: 41–42; López Austin 1967: 100; Nicholson 1971: 439.

1. This paragraph comprises a complete fifty-two-year cycle, *xiuhmolpilli*, itemized year by year, both textually and pictorially (the four "year bearers," Tochtli [Rabbit], Acatl [Reed], Tecpatl [Stone Knife], and Calli [House], with their numerical coefficients, in order, from 1 Tochtli to 13 Calli). Of special interest is the specification of "este año de 1560" as the year during which the termination of one cycle and the commencement of another occurred. The paragraph also contains a concise description of the "New Fire Ceremony," the Toxiuhmolpillia, "Binding of the Years," observed on this occasion, a ceremony narrated at somewhat greater length in the *Historia* (Sahagún 1950–1982, Part VIII [Book 7]: 25–32; 1988, II: 488–492).

2. *Moqueca:* read *moquetza.*

.7. calli. [illus.]
.8. tochtli. [illus.]
.9. acatl. [illus.]
.10. tecpatl. [illus.]
.xi. calli. [illus.]
.x2. tochtli. [illus.]
.x3. acatl. [illus.]

Seven House
Eight Rabbit
Nine Reed
Ten Flint Knife
Eleven House
Twelve Rabbit
Thirteen Reed

[fol. 284v]

ce tecpatl [illus.]
vme calli. [illus.]
yei tochtli [illus.]
navi acatl. [illus.]
macuilli tecpatl. [illus.]
chicuacen calli [illus.]
chicome tochtli [illus.]
chicuey acatl. [illus.]

One Flint Knife
Two House
Three Rabbit
Four Reed
Five Flint Knife
Six House
Seven Rabbit
Eight Reed

[fol. 285r]

chicunavi tecpatl. [illus.]
matlactli calli. [illus.]
matlactli oçe tochtli. [illus.]
matlactli omome acatl [illus.]
matlactli omey tecpatl. [illus.]
Ce calli [illus.]
vme tochtli [illus.]

Nine Flint Knife
Ten House
Eleven Rabbit
Twelve Reed
Thirteen Flint Knife
One House
Two Rabbit

[fol. 285v]

yei acatl. [illus.]
navi tecpatl. [illus.]
macuilli calli [illus.]
chicuacen tochtli [illus.]
chicume acatl. [illus.]
chicue tecpatl [illus.]
chicunavi calli. [illus.]
matlactli tochtli. [illus.]

Three Reed
Four Flint Knife
Five House
Six Rabbit
Seven Reed
Eight Flint Knife
Nine House
Ten Rabbit

[fol. 286r]

matlactli oçe acatl. [illus.]
matlactli vmome tecpatl. [illus.]
matlactli vmey calli. [illus.]

Oc cepa ompevaltia yn ce tochtli ynic tlayavalotiuh cexiuitl

Auh inic tlamanca motenevaya toxiuh molpillia vmpovalxiuhtica vmmatlactica

Eleven Reed
Twelve Flint Knife
Thirteen House

Paragraph 3

Once again One Rabbit begins. Thus the year goes making its round.

And then was customary what was called the binding of our years, every fifty-two

yoan vxiuitl. Auh inin iuh mochiuaya mitouaya otlaiavallo yn xiuhpovalli omonamiquito: auh in iquac cenca momauhtiaya yn tlatoque quitoa quilmach vncã ticempollivizque ayac tlalpã motlaliaya mitoaya ic tlapanco tlecovaya. Auh ynic nenavatiloya Cenca mochi tlacatl quimocuitlaviz yn ilhuicatl yn çiçitlalti in itoca miec ỹ mamalvaztli. Auh yn oaçico nepantla yn aocmo vtlatoca ie ixquich ye ic ticempolivizque; auh ynic mochivaya y vmpovalxiuhtica ṽmatlactli yoan vxiuitl novian Çevia ỹ tletl vmpa vetzia in itocaiocan vexachtla culhuaca in tepetl moteneva vixachtecatl mochi tlacatl vmpa Concuiya in tletl ça çeioval ỹ mochivaya y.

years. And [when] this so occurred, it was said that the year count had made a round; they went meeting each other. And at this time the rulers were very frightened. They say that it was said that here we should all perish. No one remained on the ground. They said that for this reason they climbed up to the rooftops. And for this reason it was ordered that everyone fix his attention on the sky, on the stars called the Many, the Fire Sticks.[3] And when [the constellation] arrived at the zenith, if it no longer followed its path, this was all; with this we would all perish. And thus it was done every fifty-two years. Everywhere the fires were extinguished. [The new fire] was drawn at a place called Huixachtitlan, a hill in Colhuacan known as Huixactecatl.[4] Everyone took the fire from there. This was done only on one night.

Jnin xiuhpovalli ỹ çevevetiliztli vppa tlayavaloa macuilpovalxiuitl yoã nauhxiuitl.

In this year count an old age was one hundred and four years, when they made the round twice.

PARAGRAPH 4

Jnic navi pararapho ypã mitoa in tonalpovalli.

Jzcatqui in cecemilhuitlapovalli Compevaltiaya yn itoca Ce itzcuintli, ynin matlaquilhuitl omey yzquilhuitl qualli tonalli yn tlatoque ipã motecutlaliaya yoã ipã motecualtiaya navacatl Jn cemilhuitonalli yoã ipan tlacatiuaya vncan tlacatia ym pipilti tla-

Fourth paragraph, in which is told the day count.[1]

Here are the counts of the days. They begin [on the day] named One Dog. These thirteen days were all good day signs. At this time [One Dog] the rulers were installed and also on Four Reed a feast was given. And when there were births on the [first] day sign, noblemen who

3. Concerning the constellations called Miec and Mamalhuatzi, see notes 7 and 9, Paragraph 1. In the *Historia* account of the New Fire Ceremony, only the former is specified as indicating the moment of producing the New Fire when this asterism reached the zenith at midnight.

4. Vixachtlan/Vixachtecatl (Huixachtitlan/Huixachtecatl): This prominent hill east of Colhuacan and south of Itztapallapan in the freshwater lacustrine zone of the southern Basin of Mexico, today called Cerro de la Estrella, was the locus of the great Central Mexican New Fire Ceremony celebrated every fifty-two years, probably at least since the fourteenth century.

1. In this paragraph, the descriptive texts precede each thirteen-day period *(trecena),* whose day signs, in square cartouches, are depicted in vertical columns in the original manuscript. The paragraph covers a complete 260-day divinatory cycle *(tonalpohualli)* divided into twenty *trecenas,* the most common format in the ritual-divinatory pictorials, the *tonalamatl.* Unusually, the series commences with the *trecena* initiated by 1 Itzcuintli (Dog), rather than that beginning with 1 Cipactli (Crocodilian Monster), as is standard. The favorable, unfavorable, or mixed fortunes of the different *trecenas* are presented in an essentially formulistic, repetitive mode, generically, with scant attention to the individual day signs. In Book 4 of the *Historia,* Sahagún (1950–1982, Part V; 1988, I: 231–284) provides a considerably more detailed account, derived from his Tlatelolco informants, of the fortunes of the twenty *trecenas* of the *tonalpohualli,* which do not always agree with those in this paragraph of the *Primeros Memoriales* (see Dibble 1984).

toque mochiuaya. Auh ỹ macevalli ipan tlacatia motlamachtiz tecouaz tealtiz nanacacuaz yoã ipã necaltiloya yoã tecutlato yez yoã ipã tlamaloia. Auh intla çiuapilli vncan tlacatia iuhquin tlatoani mochiva Auh intla macevalli çihuatl çenca tlamachiuani ez yoã motlamachtiz.

were then born became rulers. And a commoner born on it would become rich. He would invite people to feasts,[2] he would sacrifice slaves,[3] he would eat mushrooms.[4] And also on [this sign] houses were built and one would be a judge, and at that time captives were taken. And if a noblewoman was born then, she became like a ruler. And if the woman was a commoner, she would be[5] a good embroiderer and she would become rich.

[fol. 286v]

Çe itzcuintli. [illus.]
vme vçomatli. [illus.]
yei malinalli. [illus.]
navi acatl. [illus.]
macuilli vcelutl. [illus.]
chicuacen quauhtli. [illus.]
chicome cuzcaquauhtli. [illus.]
chicuey olli. [illus.]
Chicunavi tecpatl. [illus.]

One Dog
Two Monkey
Three Grass
Four Reed
Five Jaguar
Six Eagle
Seven Vulture
Eight Movement
Nine Flint Knife

[fol. 287r]

matlactli quiavitl. [illus.]
matlactli oçe xuchitl [illus.]
matlactli omome çipactli. [illus.]
matlactli vmey. yecatl. [illus.]

Jnin matlactetl omey tonalpovalli amo qualli tonalli mitoaya tequãtonalli. Jn aquin pilli ipan tlacatia aço yaomiquiz anoço tetlaximaz anoço monamacaz. Auh çã no ivi ỹ macevalli in aquin ipan tlacatia aço yaumiquiz aço tetlaximaz anoço monamacaz aço ichtequiz quiçacutiyez. in itlatlacul Auh yn aquin ipan tlamaya mitouaya ça netoliniliztli yn oaçic maçivin tequiva monamacaz atle quiquani ez acan ichan yez teumiquiz.

Ten Rain
Eleven Flower
Twelve Crocodilian Monster
Thirteen Wind

This thirteen-day period was of bad fortune. It was called a beastly day sign. When the person born on it was a nobleman, he would either die in battle or commit adultery or sell himself into bondage. It was the same when the person born on it was a commoner. Either he would die in war or commit adultery, or sell himself into bondage, or steal, [and] they would jail him[6] for his transgressions. And he who took captives at this time, it was said, attained poverty. Even though he was a seasoned warrior, he would sell himself into bondage. He would become one who had nothing to eat; his house would be nowhere; he would be sacrificed.

Paragraph 4

2. *Motlamachtiz:* literally, to bring people together.
3. *Tecouaz tealtiz:* literally, to bathe people. Prisoners were frequently ritually bathed before they were sacrificed.
4. *Nanacacuaz:* Hallucinogenic mushrooms, *teonanacatl,* were often served to guests at banquets.
5. *Ez:* read *yez.*
6. *Quicacutiyez:* read *quitzacutiyez.*

Jn ipan i Çan vey quiçaya in aquin motlamachtiaya mitouaya amo quicochcavaz çenca moçavaz mizoz yntla utlama mitouaya ic quizcaltiaya in tonalli ic patia.

At the time of this [day sign], he who was rich was successful, it was said, [when] he did not neglect things by sleeping, he practiced abstinence diligently, he drew blood from himself. If he played the rubber ball game,[7] it was said that he thus nourished the day sign, that thus it improved.

Çe calli. [illus.]	One House
vme cuetzpalli. [illus.]	Two Lizard
yei couatl. [illus.]	Three Serpent

[fol. 287v]

navi miquiztli. [illus.]	Four Death
macuilli maçatl. [illus.]	Five Deer
chicuaçen tochtli. [illus.]	Six Rabbit
chicome atl. [illus.]	Seven Water
chicuey itzcuintli. [illus.]	Eight Dog
chicunavi vçomatli. [illus.]	Nine Monkey
matlactli malinalli. [illus.]	Ten Grass
matlactli ozçe acatl. [illus.]	Eleven Reed
matlactli omome vcelutl. [illus.]	Twelve Jaguar
matlactli vmey quauhtli. [illus.]	Thirteen Eagle

[fol. 288r]

Jnin matlactetl vmey tonalpovalli. Çenca no qualli in itoca. Ce cozcaquauhtli mitouaya veve tonalli in aquin vncan tlacatia pilli vevetiz. Auh çã no iuhqui in tlacpac omito yn intech povi pipilti yoã in macevalti motlamachtiz. &c.

This thirteen-day period was also very good. It was named One Vulture. It was said to be the day sign of the aged. The person who was born then who was a nobleman would have a long life. By the same token, as mentioned above, it was the lot of noblemen and commoners to be rich. Etc.

Çe cuzcaquauhtli. [illus.]	One Vulture
vme calli. [illus.]	Two House
yei tecpatl. [illus.]	Three Flint Knife
navi quiauitl. [illus.]	Four Rain
macuilli xvchitl [illus.]	Five Flower
chicuaçen çipactli. [illus.]	Six Crocodilian Monster
chicome ecatl. [illus.]	Seven Wind
chicuey calli [illus.]	Eight House
chicunavi cuetzpalli. [illus.]	Nine Lizard

[fol. 288v]

matlactli couatl [illus.]	Ten Serpent
matlactli oçe miquiztli [illus.]	Eleven Death

7. *Utlama:* read *ollama.*

matlactli omome maçatl. [illus.]
matlactli vmey tochtli. [illus.]

Jnin matlactetl omey tonalpovalli çan no amo qualli yn iuhqui tlacpac omito tequantonalli in aquin pilli ipan tlacatia aço yaumiquiz anoço tetlaximaz monamacaz çã no iuhqui ỹ maçevalli tetlaximaz monamacaz. Çan aca yn oncan vei quiçaya: auh anoço atocoz atlã vetziz auh intla pochtecatl mitoaya tlaatoctiz yehica ca iuhqui in tonalli in ipan otlacat amo quallj.

Twelve Reed
Thirteen Rabbit

This thirteen-day period was also adverse like the beastly day sign mentioned above [One House]. The person who was born in it who was a nobleman either would die in battle or commit adultery [or] sell himself into bondage. Similarly, the commoner would commit adultery [or] sell himself into bondage. Anyone who then was successful would perhaps be carried off by the water; he would fall into the water. And if he was a merchant, it was said that he would cast his things into the water. It was because such was the nature of the day sign in which he was born; it was adverse.

Çe atl [illus.]
vme itzcuintli [illus.]
yei vçomatli. [illus.]

One Water
Two Dog
Three Monkey

[fol. 297r]

navi malinalli. [illus.]
macuilli acatl. [illus.]
chicuaçe vçelutl. [illus.]
chicome quauhtli. [illus.]
chicuey cozcaquauhtli [illus.]
chicunavi olli. [illus.]
matlactli tecpatl. [illus.]
matlactli oçe quiavitl. [illus.]
matlactli vmome xvchitl. [illus.]

Four Grass
Five Reed
Six Jaguar
Seven Eagle
Eight Vulture
Nine Movement
Ten Flint Knife
Eleven Rain
Twelve Flower

[fol. 297v]

matlactli omey çipactli.

Jnin matlactetl omey tonalpovalli mitoaya amo qualli tonalli in aquin oncã tlacatia pilli iehoatl in quitoaya navalli amo tlacatl. Auh in macevalli iehoatl in quitoaya tlacateculutl tetlepanqueça tetlatlacatecoluvia acan ichan atle quicuanj petlauhtinemi. Çã no iuhquin im pilli motolinitinemia çan no iuhqui in çihoapilli motolinia nyma ye no iuhqui im maçevalli iehoatl mitoaya ca iuhqui itonal. ipan tlacat.

Thirteen Crocodilian Monster

This thirteen-day period was said to be [under] an adverse day sign. He who was born then who was a nobleman was what they called a sorcerer, an evil man. And a commoner was what they called a devilish one; he cast spells;[8] he bedeviled people. His home was nowhere; he was one who had nothing to eat; he went about naked. Likewise a nobleman lived in misery; likewise a noblewoman was miserable, just like a commoner. Of this it was said that so was his day sign in which he was born. Paragraph 4

8. *Tetlapanqueca:* read *telapanquetza.*

Çe ecatl. [illus.]
vme calli. [illus.]
yei cutzpalli. [illus.]
navi couatl. [illus.]
macuilli miquiztli. [illus.]
chicuaçe maçatl. [illus.]

One Wind
Two House
Three Lizard
Four Serpent
Five Death
Six Deer

[fol. 298r]

chicome tochtli. [illus.]
chicuey atl. [illus.]
chicunavi itzcuintli. [illus.]
matlactli vçomatli. [illus.]
matlactli oçe malinalli. [illus.]
matlactli omome acatl. [illus.]
matlactli omey vcelutl. [illus.]

Jnin matlactetl omey tonalpoalli catca çan no iuhqui amo qualli tonalli in aquin ipan tlacatia tetlaximaz anoço monamacaz yaumiquiz intla çihoatl ahavilnemiz atle vellaiz çan no iuhqui ỹ maçehoalli monamacaz tetlaximaz in iuhqui tlacpac omito.

Seven Rabbit
Eight Water
Nine Dog
Ten Monkey
Eleven Grass
Twelve Reed
Thirteen Jaguar

This thirteen-day period was similarly an adverse day sign. He who was born in it would commit adultery, or he would sell himself into bondage, [or] he would die in battle. If she was a woman, she would lead a licentious life, she would do nothing well. By the same token, a commoner would sell himself into bondage [or] commit adultery, as mentioned above.

[fol. 298v]

Çe quauhtli. [illus.]
vme cuzcaquauhtli. [illus.]
yei olli. [illus.]
navi tecpatl. [illus.]
macuilli quiauitl. [illus.]
chicuaçẽ xvchitl. [illus.]
chicome çipactli. [illus.]
chicuey ecatl. [illus.]
chicunavi calli. [illus.]
matlactli cuetzpalli. [illus.]

One Eagle
Two Vulture
Three Movement
Four Flint Knife
Five Rain
Six Flower
Seven Crocodilian Monster
Eight Wind
Nine House
Ten Lizard

[fol. 299r]

matlactli oçe couatl. [illus.]
matlactli omome miquiztli[illus.]
matlactli omey maçatl. [illus.]

Jnin matlactetl omey tonalpoalli moteneuaya qualli tonalli yn aquin oncan tlacatia. Çenca yiel catca motlamachtiaya çacamouani çenca vnca quicuani Çan no iuhqui intla çihoatl yn oncã tlacatia çenca yiel tla-

Eleven Serpent
Twelve Death
Thirteen Deer

This thirteen-day period was said to be a good day sign. He who was born at that time was very diligent; he was rich; he was a tiller of the soil; there was a great deal for him to eat. In the same way, if a woman was born

machiuani yoã mochi quipiaya in tonacaiutl yn izquican icac ỹ centli. yn etl. in vauhtli yn chia yoã vncate ytlacava motlamachtia. quipia quachtli.

then, she was a very diligent embroiderer and she had all the sustenances of life, the maize, the beans, the amaranth, the chia that grew everywhere; and [where] her people were, they were rich; they had large mantles.

Çe tochtli. [illus.] — One Rabbit
vme atl. [illus.] — Two Water
yei itzcuintli. [illus.] — Three Dog
navi vçomatli. [illus.] — Four Monkey

[fol. 299v]

macuilli malinalli. [illus.] — Five Grass
chicuaçẽ acatl. [illus.] — Six Reed
chicome vcelutl. [illus.] — Seven Jaguar
chicuey quauhtli. [illus.] — Eight Eagle
chicunavi cuzcaquauhtli. [illus.] — Nine Vulture
matlactli olli. [illus.] — Ten Movement
matlactli oçe tecpatl. [illus.] — Eleven Flint Knife
matlactli omome quiauitl. [illus.] — Twelve Rain
matlactli omey xuchitl. [illus.] — Thirteen Flower

[fol. 300r]

Paragraph 4

Jnin matlactetl omey tonalpoalli ỹ çeçemilhuitonalli yn çe çipactli mitoaya yectli tonalli. Jn aquin ipã tlacatia pilli tlatoani mochiuaya yoã motlamachtiaya. Çan no iuhqui intla çihoatl ipã tlacatia iuhquin tlatoani mochiuaya motlamachtiaya. Auh intla çan maçevalli ipã tlacatia no motlamachtiaya. yoan mitoaya maçivin qualli ipan tonalli otlacat y. Çequintin çan quicochcauaya quitlatziuhcauaya ic motolinia atle ỹtlatqui mochiuaya, çã motolinitinemj.

Each day sign [in] this thirteen-day period, One Crocodilian Monster, was said to be a good sign. He who was a nobleman who was born in it became a ruler and was rich. Similarly, if a woman was born in it she became like a ruler; she was rich. And if just a commoner was born in [this sign], he also was rich. And it was also said that although they had been born[9] under a good day sign, some neglected their tasks by sleeping, they neglected their duties out of laziness; hence they were miserable; nothing became their possessions; they just lived in misery.

Çe çipactli. [illus.] — One Crocodilian Monster
vme ecatl. [illus.] — Two Wind
yei calli. [illus.] — Three House
navi cuetzpalli. [illus.] — Four Lizard
macuilli couatl [illus.] — Five Serpent
chicuaçen miquiztli. [illus.] — Six Death
chicome maçatl. [illus.] — Seven Deer

9. *Octacat:* This verb is in the third person singular.

[fol. 300v]

chicuey tochtli. [illus.]	Eight Rabbit
chicunavi atl. [illus.]	Nine Water
matlactli itzcuintli [illus.]	Ten Dog
matlactli oçe vçomatli. [illus.]	Eleven Monkey
matlactli omome malinalli. [illus.]	Twelve Grass
matlactli omey acatl. [illus.]	Thirteen Reed

Jnin matlactetl omey tonalpoalli mitoaya amo qualli tecuantonalli. Yn aquin pilli ipã tlacatia yaumiquia yoã tetlaximaia motenevaya teuhtli tlaçolli quichihuaya. Ça no iuhqui intla çihoapilli tetlaximaya mitoaya iuhqui ipan tlacat. Auh intla çan maçevalli no iuhqui ipã mochiuaya auh intlanel aca tiyacauh muchiuaya vel monamacaya tlacotli mochiuaya iuh mitoaya ca iuhqui itonal. Auh ça vei quiçaya in tiyacauh in amo monamacaya iehoatl in amo tlacochcauaya moçavaya miçoya.

This thirteen-day period was said to be adverse; it was a beastly day sign. He who was a nobleman, who was born in it, died in battle and also committed adultery; it was said that he made filth, dirt. Similarly, if it was a noblewoman, she committed adultery; it was said that thus it was at the time she was born. And if it was just a commoner, the same happened to him. And even though someone became a brave warrior, he sold himself into bondage, he became a slave. So it was said that such was his lot. And the brave warrior who was successful, who did not sell himself into bondage, did not neglect his duties because of sleeping. He fasted, he drew blood from himself.

[fol. 289r]

Çe vçelutl [illus.]	One Jaguar
vme quauhtli. [illus.]	Two Eagle
yei cuzcaquauhtli [illus.]	Three Vulture
navi olli [illus.]	Four Movement
macuilli tecpatl [illus.]	Five Flint Knife
chicuaçen quiauitl. [illus.]	Six Rain
chicome xvchitl [illus.]	Seven Flower
chicuey çipactli. [illus.]	Eight Crocodilian Monster
chicunavi ecatl. [illus.]	Nine Wind[10]
matlactli calli. [illus.]	Ten House

[fol. 289v]

matlactli oçe cuetzpalli. [illus.]	Eleven Lizard
matlactli vmome couatl. [illus.]	Twelve Serpent
matlactli vmey miquiztli. [illus.]	Thirteen Death

10. A Spanish/Nahuatl gloss beside Nine Wind reads: *Setiembre xxv. de 1560 a^{o}s.: Jn axcã cemilhuitl chiucnauj ecatl/ypã miercoles cẽpoali õmacuillia ypã Seti^{e} de 1560 a^{o}s.*—"Today, Nine Wind, is on the 25th of September, 1560." This statement clearly indicates that at least this portion of the *Primeros Memoriales* was composed during the period of Sahagún's Tepepolco residence, 1559–1561. The assignment of September 25, 1560, to the *tonalpohualli* day 9 Ehecatl does not agree with the currently most favored correlation of the contact-period Central Mexican calendar with the European calendar, the Caso correlation (Caso 1939).

Jnin tonalpoalli matlactetl vmey motenevaya Çe maçatl iuh mitoaya qualli tonalli. Jn aquin ipã tlacatia pilli tlatoani mochiuaya yoã motlamachtiaya çan no iuhqui intla çihoapilli ipã tlacatia no iuhquin tlatoanj mochivaya motlamachtiaya. Auh intla maçevalli ipã tlacatia no motlamachtiani mochiuaya mocuiltonoanj. mochiuaya. yehica ca iuhqui ipã tlacat.
Çe maçatl. [illus.]
vme tochtli [illus.]
yei atl. [illus.]
navi itzcuintli [illus.]

This thirteen-day period was called One Deer. Thus was it said: It was a good day sign. He who was born in it who was a nobleman became a ruler and was rich. It was the same if a noblewoman was born in it. She also became like a ruler [and] she was rich. And if a commoner was born in it, he also became a rich man, he became a wealthy man, because such [was the day sign] in which he was born.
One Deer
Two Rabbit
Three Water
Four Dog

[fol. 290r]

macuilli vçomatli. [illus.]
chicuaçe malinalli. [illus.]
chicome acatl. [illus.]
chicuey vcelotl [illus.]
chicunavi quauhtli [illus.]
matlactli cuzcaquauhtli. [illus.]
matlactli oçe olli. [illus.]
matlactli vmome tecpatl. [illus.]
matlactli vmey quiauitl. [illus.]

Five Monkey
Six Grass
Seven Reed
Eight Jaguar
Nine Eagle
Ten Vulture
Eleven Movement
Twelve Flint Knife
Thirteen Rain

[fol. 290v]

Jnin tonalpoali matlactetl omey motenevaya. Ce xvchitl amo qualli yoã mitoaya achi qualli yn aquin ipã tlacatia pilli cuicani mochiuaya papaquini. Auh in aquin pilli ipã mimatia in icuac cuica pactinemi. Auh in aquin amo ipã mimatia in atle ipã quitaya quitlaveliaya in tonalli aço teucocoliztli itech motlaliaya aço ixpopoiutia anoço quexilivia çã no iuh ipã mochiuaya intla macevalli no cuicani mochiuaya. Auh intla çihoapilli ipã tlacatia vey tlamachiuhqui mochiuaya auh intlacatle ipã quitta no iuhqui ipã mochiuaya quitlaveliaya in tonalli Çan no iuhqui ipã mochiuaya in iuhqui tlacpac omopouh yn izquitlamãtli coculiztli yoã aviani mochiuaya iuh mitoaya ca iuhqui itonal ipã tlacat.

This thirteen-day period was called One Flower. It was an adverse [day sign], but it was said to be somewhat good. He who was born in it who was a nobleman became a singer; he was happy. And he who was a nobleman, who was devoted to [his day sign], lived happily when he sang. But for him who was not devoted to it, who misprized it, the day sign was angry with him. Either leprosy settled on him, or he went blind, or the groin was disordered. The same happened to one if he was a commoner; he also became a singer. And if a noblewoman was born in [this sign], she became a great embroiderer, but if she disdained it, the same would befall her. The day sign was
angry with her. The same befell her as is re- Paragraph
counted above. [She would be stricken by] 4
all kinds of maladies, and she would become a pleasure girl. So was it said. Such was the day sign in which she was born.

Çe xvchitl. [illus.]
vme çipactli. [illus.]
yei ecatl. [illus.]
navi calli. [illus.]
macuilli cuetzpalli. [illus.]
chicuaçẽ couatl. [illus.]
chicome miquiztli [illus.]

One Flower
Two Crocodilian Monster
Three Wind
Four House
Five Lizard
Six Serpent
Seven Death

[fol. 291r]

chicuey maçatl. [illus.]
chicunavi tochtli. [illus.]
matlactli atl. [illus.]
matlactli oçe itzcuintlj. [illus.]
matlactli vmome vçomatli. [illus.]
matlactli omey malinalli. [illus.]

Jnin tonalpoualli matlactetl omey mitoaya qualli tonalli yn aquin pilli ipã tlacatia tlatoani mochiuaya yoã mocuiltonouaya çan no iuhqui intla çihoatl ipã tlacatia no iuhquin tlatoani mochiuaya no mocuiltonouaya. Auh intla çã maçevalli ipã tlacatia no mocuiltonouaya motlamachtiaya motenevaya qualli tonalli in ipã tlacat iuhqui itonal.

Eight Deer
Nine Rabbit
Ten Water
Eleven Dog
Twelve Monkey
Thirteen Grass

This thirteen-day period was said to be of a good day sign. He who was a nobleman born in it became a ruler and became rich. Similarly, if a [noble]woman was born in it, she also became like a ruler; she also was rich. And if he was only a commoner who was born in it, he also became rich, he became wealthy. It was said that he was born in a good day sign; it was the nature of his sign.

[fol. 291v]

Çe acatl. [illus.]
vme vçelotl. [illus.]
yei quauhtli. [illus.]
navi cuzcaquauhtli. [illus.]
macuilli, olli. [illus.]
chicuaçen tecpatl. [illus.]
chicome quiavitl. [illus.]
chicuey xvchitl. [illus.]
chicunavi çipactli. [illus.]
matlactli, ecatl. [illus.]

One Reed
Two Jaguar
Three Eagle
Four Vulture
Five Movement
Six Flint Knife
Seven Rain
Eight Flower
Nine Crocodilian Monster
Ten Wind

[fol. 292r]

matlactli oçe calli. [illus.]
matlactli omome cuetzpalli. [illus.]
matlactli vmey couatl. [illus.]

Jnin tonalpoalli ỹ mitoaya Çe miquiztli amo qualli yoã mitouaya achi qualli in aquin ipã tlacatia pilli ipã mimatia tlamacevaya quimacaçia in tonalli. Yn aquin ipã mimatia hy. motlamachtiaya tecutia: auh intlacamo

Eleven House
Twelve Lizard
Thirteen Serpent

This day count was called One Death. It was adverse; and it was [also] said that it was somewhat good. He who was a nobleman born at this time revered, propitiated, venerated the day sign. He who revered it became

ipã mimatinemj iuh mitoaya ca ça no quicochcauh amo motlamachtiaya çan netoliniliztli ipã mochiuaya aço teucocoliztli anoço ixpopoiutia. Çan no iuhqui intla maçevalli çã no iuh ipã mochiuaya in izquitlamantli cocoliztli ça vey quiçaya yn amo iuhqui ipã mochiuaya.

rich, became a lord. But if he did not live revering it, so was it said, [if] he only neglected [his duties] by sleeping, he did not become rich but misery befell him, or leprosy, or he became blind. It was the same if he was a commoner. All kinds of maladies also befell him. Only if he turned out well, it did not thus befall him.

Çe miquiztli [illus.]
vme maçatl [illus.]
yei tochtli. [illus.]
navi atl [illus.]

One Death
Two Deer
Three Rabbit
Four Water

[fol. 292v]

macuilli itzcuintli. [illus.]
chicuaçẽ vçomatli. [illus.]
chicome malinalli. [illus.]
chicuey acatl. [illus.]
chicunavi vcelotl. [illus.]
matlactli quauhtli. [illus.]
matlactli oçe cuzcaquauhtli. [illus.]
matlactli omome olli. [illus.]
matlactli vmey tecpatl. [illus.]

Five Dog
Six Monkey
Seven Grass
Eight Reed
Nine jaguar
Ten Eagle
Eleven Vulture
Twelve Movement
Thirteen Flint Knife

[fol. 293r]

Jnin tonalpoalli matlactetl omey in motenevaya Çe quiaujtl amo qualli tonalli in aquin ipan tlacatia pilli navalli mochiuaya çan tlaveliloc. Auh in macevalli ipan tlacatia tlacateculotl mochiuaya tetlatlanonochilia iuh mitoaya amo qualli in itequiuh. Çan no iuhqui intla çihoapilli no iuhqui itequiuh mochiuaya çenca motoliniaya acan inchã immanel pilli anoço çiuapilli moch iuhqui impã mochiuaya mitoaya ca iuhqui itonal in ipã tlacat.

This thirteen-day period was called One Rain. It was not a good day sign. He who was born in it who was a nobleman became a sorcerer; he was a wicked man. And the commoner born in it became a devilish one; he was a magician. Thus was it said: His work was evil. Similarly, if she was a noblewoman, her work was the same. She was very miserable. She was homeless. Even though he was a nobleman or she a noblewoman, all this befell them. It was said that such was the day sign at the time that one was born.

— Çe quiauitl. — [illus.]
— vme xvchitl. — [illus.]
—. yei çipactli. — [illus.]
—. navi ecatl. — [illus.]
—. macuilli calli. — [illus.]
—. chicuaçẽ cuetzpalli — [illus.]
—. chicome couatl. — [illus.]

One Rain
Two Flower
Three Crocodilian Monster
Four Wind
Five House
Six Lizard Paragraph
Seven Serpent 4

[fol. 293v]

chicuey miquiztli. [illus.]
chicunavi maçatl. [illus.]
matlactli tochtli [illus.]
matlactli oçe atl. [illus.]
matlactli omome itzcuintli. [illus.]
matlactli vmey vçomatli. [illus.]

Jnin tonalpoalli matlactetl omey in motenehuaya Çe malinalli mitoaya tequantonalli amo quali in aquin ipan tlacatia im pilli iuh mitoaya amo qualli itequiuh yez aço navalli mochiuaz. Auh intla maçevalli ipan tlacatia mitoaya tlacateculotl muchiuaya. Çan no iuhqui intla çihoapilli ipã tlacatia amono qualli itequiuh catca: yn ipã tlacatia. y. intla pilli anoço çihuapilli anoço maçevalli çenca motoliniaya acan inchã atle quicuaya ic mitoaya ca iuhqui ipan tlacat, iuhqui ytonal,

Eight Death
Nine Deer
Ten Rabbit
Eleven Water
Twelve Dog
Thirteen Monkey

This thirteen-day period was called One Grass. It was said to be a beastly day sign, adverse. As to a person then born who was a nobleman, so was it said, his work would be evil; perhaps he would become a sorcerer. And if a commoner was born then, it was said that he became a devilish one. Similarly, if a noblewoman was then born, her work was also evil. If a nobleman or a noblewoman or a commoner was then born, he was very miserable; he had no home; he had nothing to eat. For it was said that thus was he born, thus was his day sign.

[fol. 294r]

Çe malinalli. [illus.]
vme acatl. [illus.]
yei vçelotl. [illus.]
navi quauhtli. [illus.]
macuilli cuzcaquauhtli. [illus.]
chicuaçen olli. [illus.]
chicome tecpatl [illus.]
chicuey quiauitl. [illus.]
chicunavi xuchitl. [illus.]

One Grass
Two Reed
Three Jaguar
Four Eagle
Five Vulture
Six Movement
Seven Flint Knife
Eight Rain
Nine Flower

[fol. 294v]

matlactli çipactli. [illus.]
matlactli oçe ecatl. [illus.]
matlactli vmome calli. [illus.]
matlactli vmey cuetzpalli. [illus.]

Jnin tonalli mitoaya Çe couatl yectli tonalli in aquin pilli ipã tlacatia tlatoani muchivaya mocuiltonoani catca çan no iuhqui intla çihuapilli ipã tlacatia mocuiltonoani catca miec quipiaya in tonacaiotl. Çan no iuhqui intla maçevalli ipã tlacatia no mocuiltonoani muchivaya. Auh maçivi in qualli tonalli ipã tlacatia Çequintin çan quitlatziuhcavaya quicochcavaya motoliniaya

Ten Crocodilian Monster
Eleven Wind
Twelve House
Thirteen Lizard

This day sign was called One Serpent. It was a good day sign. He who was born at that time who was a nobleman became a ruler; he was a rich man. Similarly, if a noblewoman was born at that time, she was rich, she had an abundance of foodstuffs. By the same token, if a commoner was born at that time, he also became a rich man. But although it was a good sign at the time that they were born, some

atle quiquanime catca.

Çe couatl. [illus.]
vme miquiztli. [illus.]

only neglected things out of laziness, they neglected them by sleep. They were miserable; they were those who had nothing to eat.
One Serpent
Two Death

[fol. 295r]

yei maçatl. [illus.]
navi tochtli. [illus.]
macuilli atl. [illus.]
chicuaçen itzcuintli. [illus.]
chicome vçomatli. [illus.]
chicuey malinalli. [illus.]
chicunavi acatl. [illus.]
matlactli vçelotl [illus.]
matlactli oçe quauhtli. [illus.]
matlactli omome cuzcaquauhtli. [illus.]
matlactli vmey olli. [illus.]

Three Deer
Four Rabbit
Five Water
Six Dog
Seven Monkey
Eight Grass
Nine Reed
Ten Jaguar
Eleven Eagle
Twelve Vulture
Thirteen Movement

[fol. 295v]

Jnin tonalpoalli matlactetl omey compevaltiaya in itoca Çe tecpatl mitoaya yectli tonalli in aquin pilli ipan tlacatia tlatoani mochiuaya motlamachtiani catca. Çan no iuhqui intla çihuapilli ipã tlacatia no mocuiltonovani catca. auh intla maçevalli ipan tlacatia no motlamachtiaya anoço çihuatl maçevalli ipã tlacatia no mocuiltonoani catca: auh in çequintin çan quitlatziuhcavaya maçivi in qualli tonalli ipã tlacatia motolinitinẽca.

This thirteen-day period began on [the day sign] called One Flint Knife. It was said to be a good day sign. He who was a nobleman who was born at that time became a ruler; he was a rich man. Similarly, if a noblewoman was born at that time, she also was rich. And if a commoner was born at that time, he, too, was rich. Or if a woman who was a commoner was born at that time, she also was rich. But even though it was a good day sign at the time they were born, some who neglected things out of laziness lived in misery.

Çe tecpatl. [illus.]
vme quiavitl. [illus.]
yei xvchitl. [illus.]
navi çipactli [illus.]
macuilli ecatl. [illus.]
chicuaçen calli. [illus.]
chicome cuetzpalli. [illus.]

One Flint Knife
Two Rain
Three Flower
Four Crocodilian Monster
Five Wind
Six House
Seven Lizard

[fol. 296r]

chicuey couatl [illus.]
chicunavi miquiztli. [illus.]
matlactli maçatl. [illus.]
matlactli oçe tochtli [illus.]

Eight Serpent Paragraph 4
Nine Death
Ten Deer
Eleven Rabbit

matlactli omome atl [illus.]
matlactli omey itzcuintli. [illus.]

Inin tonalli mitoaya çe vçomatli amo qualli yoã mitoaya achi cualli yn aquin pilli ipã tlacatia cuicani mochiuaya anoço tlacuilo mochivaya aço amantecatl muchivaz. Auh intlacamo tle ipã quittaz quitlaveliaya nimã itech motlaliaya teucocoliztli aço quexilivia anoço ixpopoiutia atle quiquani motolinitinemi. Auh intla ipã mauhcanemi motlamachtiaya: auh çan no iuhqui intla çivapilli no iuhqui ipã muchivaya ahavilnemia amo mochanittaya motolinitinẽca.

Twelve Water
Thirteen Dog

This day sign was called One Monkey. It was adverse and it was also said to be somewhat good. He who was a nobleman who was born at that time became a singer or he became a painter, or he would become a featherwork artist. But if he did not hold [the day sign] in esteem, it became angry with him. Then leprosy settled upon him, or a disorder of the groin, or he became blind. He was one who had nothing to eat; he lived in misery. But if he lived in fear he became rich. And in like manner, if she was a noblewoman, the same befell her. She lived licentiously. She was homeless; she lived in misery.

[fol. 296v]

Çe, vçomatli. [illus.]
vme, malinalli. [illus.]
yei acatl. [illus.]
navi vcelotl. [illus.]
macuilli quauhtli. [illus.]
chicuaçẽ cuzcaquauhtli. [illus.]
chicome olli. [illus.]
chicuey, tecpatl. [illus.]

One Monkey
Two Grass
Three Reed
Four Jaguar
Five Eagle
Six Vulture
Seven Movement
Eight Flint Knife

[fol. 301r]

chicunavi quiavitl. [illus.]
matlactli xvchitl. [illus.]
matlactli oçe çipactli. [illus.]
matlactli omome ecatl. [illus.]
matlactli omey calli. [illus.]

Jnin tonalli matlactetl omey in itoca çe cuetzpalli no mitoaya amo qualli tequantonalli in aquin ipan tlacatia pilli navalli muchivaya amo tlacatl çan no iuhqui intla çihoapilli ipã tlacatia no iuhqui ipã muchivaya. Auh in maçevalli ipã tlacatia amono qualli itequiuh muchivaya tetlatlacateculoviaya tetletlepãqueçaya tetlatlanonochiliaya yehica ca iuhqui ipã tlacat iuhqui ytonal. çã vey quiçaya yn aca motlamachtiaya.

Nine Rain
Ten Flower
Eleven Crocodilian Monster
Twelve Wind
Thirteen House

This day sign was called One Lizard. It was also said to be adverse, a beastly day sign. He who was a nobleman who was born at that time became a sorcerer, an evil man. Similarly, if a noblewoman was born at that time, it also so befell her. And when a commoner was born at that time, his work became evil; he bedeviled people, he enchanted people,[11] he was a magician; because thus was the nature of the day sign at the time that he was born. Only when it turned out favorably, a person became rich.

11. *Tetletlepãqueçay:* read *tetletlepanquetzaya.*

[fol. 301v]

Çe cuetzpalli. [illus.]
vme coatl. [illus.]
yei miquiztli. [illus.]
navi maçatl [illus.]
macuilli tochtli. [illus.]
chicuaçen atl. [illus.]
chicome itzcuintli. [illus.]
chicuey vçomatli. [illus.]

One Lizard
Two Serpent
Three Death
Four Deer
Five Rabbit
Six Water
Seven Dog
Eight Monkey

[fol. 302r]

chicunavi malinalli. [illus.]
matlactli acatl. [illus.]
matlactli oçe vçelotl. [illus.]
matlactli omome quauhtli. [illus.]
matlactli omey cuzcaquauhtli. [illus.]

Jnin tonalli yn itoca çe olli iuh mitoaya amo qualli tonalli yoã mitoaya achi qualli yn aquin pilli ipã tlacatia vey tiyacauh muchivaya: yoã motlamachtiaya mocuiltonoani catca. Çan no iuhqui intla çihoapilli ipan tlacatia no iuhqui ipã muchivaya, anoço maçevalli ipã tlacatia, no iuhqui ipã muchivaya. Auh in aquin ipã mimatia. y. tonalli yehoatl motlamachtiaya yn amo tlatzivia. Auh in aquin amo ipã mimatia maçihvin pilli yn ivan tiyacauh anoço cihoapilli ça monamacaya çan netoliniliztli in ipã nemia amo paquia çan no iuhqui yntla maçehvali no iuhqui ipã muchivaya acan chane atle quiquani motolinitinemia mitoaya ca iuhqui itonal ipã tlacat ỹ netoliniliztli.

Nine Grass
Ten Reed
Eleven Jaguar
Twelve Eagle
Thirteen Vulture

This day sign is called One Movement. Thus was it said: It was an adverse day sign and it was also said to be somewhat good. He who was a nobleman born at that time became a brave warrior, and he also was rich, he was a wealthy man. Similarly, if a noblewoman was born at that time, the same happened to her; or when a commoner was born at that time, the same also happened to him. And one [born] at that time who paid devotion to [this day sign] became rich if he was not slothful. But one [born] at that time who paid [his day sign] no devotion, even though one was a nobleman and a brave warrior, or a noblewoman, was sold into bondage, lived in dire misery; he was unhappy. It was the same if he was a commoner; the same also befell him; he had no home anywhere; he was one who had nothing to eat; he lived in misery. For it was said that thus was his day sign; he was born to misery.

[fol. 302v]

Ce olli. [illus.]
vme tecpatl. [illus.]
yei quiavitl. [illus.]
navi xvchitl. [illus.]
macuilli çipactli. [illus.]
chicuaçen ecatl [illus.]
chicome, calli. [illus.]
chicuey, cuetzpalli. [illus.]

One Movement
Two Flint Knife
Three Rain
Four Flower Paragraph
Five Crocodilian Monster 4
Six Wind
Seven House
Eight Lizard

[fol. 303r]

chicunavi, coatl. [illus.]
matlactli, miquiztli. [illus.]
matlactli oçe. maçatl. [illus.]
matlactli omome, tochtli. [illus.]
matlactli vmey atl. [illus.]

Oc ceppa compevaltia yn itoca Çe itzcuintli ynic tlayavalotiuh Çe xivitl.

Nine Serpent
Ten Death
Eleven Deer
Twelve Rabbit
Thirteen Water

Once again [the count] began with [the day sign] called One Dog. Thus it went making a round of one year.

PARAGRAPH 5A
[fol. 303v]

Jnic macuilli parrapho ypã mitoa in tetzavitl ỹ temictli.

Jnic centlamantli tetzauitl yehoatl yn aca quicaquia tequani choca, mitoaya ye yaumiquiz, anoço monamacaz.

Jnic vntlamantli tetzauitl yehoatl yn vactli vevetzca mitoaya ye yaumiquiz

Jnic etlamantli yehoatl yiovalteputztli iuhquin aca tlaxeloa quauhtequi iuh mitoaya aço ytla ipã muchivaz.

Jnic nauhtlamantli in teculotl choca y tlapãtenco mitoaya aço yaumiquiz anoço ipiltzin miquiz.

Jnic macuillamantli yehoatl in chicuatli in calixquatl quivitequi mitoaya ye miquiz ỹ chane.

Jnic chicuaçentlamantli yehoatl yn chichtli, yn aca ychan calaquia mitoaya ye tetlaximaz.

Fifth paragraph, in which are told the auguries, the dreams.

The first augury[1] is this: When someone heard a wild beast cry out it was said that he would soon die in battle or sell himself [as a slave].

The second augury is this: When a black-crowned heron[2] laughed, it was said that he would die in battle.

The third augury is this: The night-ax, as if someone were splitting, were cutting wood. Thus it was said that perhaps something would happen to one.

The fourth augury: When a horned owl[3] cried at the edge of the roof it was said that either one would die in battle or his child would die.

The fifth augury is this: When a barn owl[4] struck the façade of a house it was said that the owner of the house would soon die.

The sixth augury is this: When a barn owl[5] entered someone's house it was said that soon he would commit adultery.

1. *Tetzauitl (tetzahuitl):* Molina (1944, Part II: 111r) defines this term as "cosa escandolosa, o espantosa, o cosa de aguero." It is usually translated into English as "augury" or "omen." Sahagún (1950–1982, Part VI [Book 5]: 151–196; 1988, I: 286–306) also devoted Book 5 of the *Historia* to omens, the majority of them similar to those in this paragraph but usually described in somewhat greater detail.

2. *Vactli (huactli): Nycticorax nycticorax* (Linnaeus) (Friedmann et al. 1950–1957, Part II: 31). According to Sahagún's (1950–1982, Part XII [Book 11]: 39; 1988, II: 704) informants' statement in the *Historia*, this heron's name was derived from the sound, *huac, huac,* of its song.

3. *Tecolotl:* probably *Buho virginianus* (Linnaeus) (Garibay 1944–1947: 309).

4. *Chicuatli: Tyto alba pratincola* (Bonaparte) (Friedmann et al. 1950–1957, Part II: 137).

5. *Chichtli:* According to Sahagún (1950–1982, Part XII [Book 11]: 47) in the *Historia,* this was another name for the *chicuatli,* the barn or screech owl.

Jnic chicontlamantli, yehoatl yn coçatli coçamatl mitoaya yn aca quiyacaviltequi amo vel yaz in campa yaznequi mictiloz temac vetztitiuh otlica.

The seventh augury is this: [About] the weasel, it was said that when a weasel crossed in front of someone, he would not go where he wished to go. He would be killed; he would fall into someone's hands on the road.

Jnic chicuetlamantli tetzavitl catca yehoatl yn tochtli yn aca ychan calaquia mitoaya ye tlalpoliviz in ichan anoço ye choloz.

The eighth augury is this: When a rabbit entered someone's house it was said that his house would be destroyed, or he would flee.

Jnic matlactlamantli tetzavitl catca yehoatl ỹ pinaviztli yn otlica oquinamic anoço calli oquittac mitoaya aço cana teixpã ayoz pinauhtiloz.

The tenth augury[6] is this: [When someone] encountered a beetle on the road or saw it [in] the house, it was said that perhaps somewhere he would be reprehended[7] before people, he would be shamed.

[fol. 85r]

Jnic matlactlamantli oçe yehoatl yn epatl yn aca ychan callaquia anoço vncan mopilhoatia motenevaya ye miquiz yn chane.

The eleventh augury is this: When a skunk entered someone's home or gave birth to its young there, it was said that soon the owner of the house would die.

Jnic matlactlamantli omome tetzauitl catca yehoatl yn azcame yn aca ychã molonia mitoaya ie miqui ỹ chane.

The twelfth augury is this: When ants scurried through someone's house it was said that soon the owner of the house would die.

Jnic matlactlamantli vmey tetzavitl catca yehoatl yn tlacaveyac yn aca quittaya iuh motenevaya ye yaumiquiz.

The thirteenth augury is this: When someone saw a giant, thus was it said: Soon he would die in battle.

Jnic matlactlamantli vnnavi tetzauitl catca, yehoatl in tlacanexquimilli yn aca quittaya mitoaya ye miquiz.

The fourteenth augury is this: When someone saw a ghost[8] it was said that soon he would die.

Jnic caxtollamantli tetzavitl catca, yehoatl yn centlapachto, yn aca quittaya mitoaya ye miquiz.

The fifteenth augury is this: When someone saw a female phantom dwarf,[9] it was said that soon he would die.

Jnic caxtollamantli oçe tetzavitl catca yehoatl in coiutl yn aca quinamiquia anoço quiyacaviltequia mitoaya ye miquiz.

The sixteenth augury is this: When someone encountered a coyote or it crossed his path it was said that he would die soon.

Auh yn altepetl ytetzauh catca ynic muchivaya yehoatl in texcalli xitinia anoço tepetl xitinia: yoã oc cequi yn amo vel ticmati

And what was the augury of the city occurred when a cliff sundered, or when a mountain sundered. And there are others that we do not know.

6. There is no ninth augury. Either the scribe erred in the numbering or the ninth omen was omitted.

7. *Ayoz:* probably the passive voice of *ahau*.

8. *Tlacanexquimilli:* In the much longer account of this apparition in the *Historia* (Sahagún 1950–1982, Part VI [Book 5]: 77–78; 1988, I: 295–296), it is identified as a disguise of Tezcatlipoca.

9. *Centlapachto:* literally, "little squashed one." In the much longer *Historia* version (Sahagún 1950–1982, Part VI [Book 5]: 179–180; 1988, I: 296), this apparition is described as a long-haired female dwarf. Interestingly, two other names are given for it, and it is stated that it was called *centlapachto* in Acolhuacan—which appears to indicate that Sahagún's Tlatelolco informants recognized that it was an Acolhuaque regionalism that would well fit its Tepepolco origin.

Nimã yeevatl in tequanime choca no itetzauh catca yn altepetl. Auh oc no cequi yn amo ticmati.

Then there is this: When wild beasts cried out, it was also an augury for the city. And there were others that we do not know.

PARAGRAPH 5B
[fol. 85v]

Temictli.

Dreams

Jn aquin quitemiquia diablo quinoça ivic monetoltiaya.

He who dreamed that the devil[10] called[11] to him, made a vow to him.

Yn aquin quitemiquia, yn ical tlatla mitoaya ye miquiz, yoã in atoco quitemiquia, ye miquiz.

He who dreamed that his house was burning, it was said, would soon die. And also when he dreamed he was carried off by the water, he would soon die.

Jn aquin quitemiquia, yn quicochittaya, cuico yn ichã motenevaya ye miquiz.

He who dreamed, who saw in his dreams, that there was singing in his home, it was said, would soon die.

Auh yn aquin quitemiquia in tepetl xitini ipã no mitoaya ye miquiz.

He who dreamed that a mountain crashed on him, it was also said, would soon die.

Jn aquin quitemiquia, quavitl ipã puztequi mitoaya ye miquiz.

He who dreamed that a tree broke over him, it was said, would soon die.

Jn aquin quitemiquia mocaltia no mitoaya ye miquiz.

He who dreamed that he was building himself a house, it was also said, would soon die.

Jn aquin quitemiquia, tonatiuh quąlo no mitoaya ie ixpopoiutiz, anoço monamacaz.

He who dreamed of an eclipse of the sun, it was also said, would soon go blind, or else he would sell himself [into slavery].

Jn aquin quitemiquia, tequani quicua, motenevaya ye miquiz.

He who dreamed that a wild beast was devouring him, it was said, would soon die.

Jn aquin quitemiquia, coatl, quitlecavia no mitoaya covaçiviztli ic miquiz.

He who dreamed that a snake[12] climbed up him, it was also said, would soon die of gout.

Jn aquin quitemiquia, patlani, mitoaya ye yaumiquiz.

He who dreamed that he was flying, it was said, would soon die in battle.[13]

Auh oc no çequi yn amo vel ticmati yn temictli, Ca miec tlamantli.

And there are other dreams that we do not know about, for there are many different kinds [of dreams].

Jn tonalpouhque quitemelaviliaya in temictli ypã quitttaya in tonallamatl: yoã tlanavatiaya ynic nextlavaloz: yoan quitlatiaya,

The soothsayers interpreted the dreams to one. They read [the meanings] in the books of divination and ordered that payment be

10. *Diablo:* that is, a deity.

11. *Quinoça:* read *quinotza.*

12. *Coatl:* The snake had aquatic associations, as did the disease of gout. Its Nahuatl name, *coacihuiliztli,* could be translated "snakification."

13. The flying aspect of this dream might have been connected with the belief that the souls of slain warriors were eventually transformed into birds (Sahagún 1978, Part IV [Book 3]: 49).

in nextlavalli, auh in nextlavalli catca, amatl, copalli, olli.

made [to the gods]. And they burned the payment [to the gods]; and the payments were papers, incense, [and] rubber.

PARAGRAPH 6
[fol. 84r col. A]

Jnic chicuaçe parrapho ypã mitoa yn izquitlamantli yn ompa tlamiloia yn mictlan.

Sixth paragraph, in which are told all the different things that were consumed there in Mictlan.

Mictlantecutli, mictecaçivatl, in ompa quiqua mictlan xocpalli, macpalli: auh yn imul, pinacatl, in iatol temalli, ynic atli, cuaxicalli

In Mictlan,[1] Mictlantecuhtli and Mictecaciuhatl[2] eat feet, hands, and a fetid beetle stew. Their gruel is pus; they drink it from skulls.

in aqui çenca quicuaya tamalli yexixilqui, yn ompa quicua mictlan pinacatl ynic yexixilqui in tamalli.

One who used to eat tamales a great deal, eats what is full of a foul smell there in Mictlan; the tamales are full of a foul smell of fetid beetles.[3]

Jn aquin nican tlalticpac quiquaya. aiocomolli, yollotli yn ompa quiqua mictlan.

He who on earth ate a stew of black beans eats hearts in Mictlan.

Aun çan moch yehoatl in tequani xivitl yn ompa cuallo: yoã in ixquichtin yn ompa vi mictlan mochintin quicua chicalotl; yn ixquich nican tlalticpac amo quallo yn ompa mictlan cuallo. yoã mitoaya, aoc tle quallo çenca netolinillo yn ompa mictlan.

And all the poisonous herbs are eaten there, and everyone who goes to Mictlan, everyone eats prickly poppies.[4] Everything that is not eaten here on earth is eaten there in Mictlan, and it is said that nothing else is eaten, that there is great want in Mictlan.

itztli ecatoco.

The obsidian knives are carried off by the wind.

xalli ecatoco.

The sand is carried off by the wind.

quavitl ecatoco.

The trees are carried off by the wind.[5]

tzivactli.

[There are] *Cereus garambullo* cacti.[6]

tecpatl ecatoco.

The flintstone knives are carried off by the wind.

nequametl.

[There are] Mexican agaves.[7]

1. Mictlan: the region of the dead; literally, among the dead. This paragraph constitutes the most detailed description in any Central Mexican primary source of the horrors of the afterworld, the ultimate destination of the great majority of mankind, and especially of what was eaten there. In Chapter 1 of the Appendix to Book 3 of the *Historia*, Sahagún (1978: 41–46; 1988, I: 219–222) provided a longer account of Mictlan but one that concentrated much more on the funerary rituals preparing the soul of the deceased for its journey to Mictlan than on the nature of the place itself.

2. Mictlantecutli, Mictecaçivatl: The preeminent death deities, "Lord of the Region of the Dead" and "Woman (i.e., Goddess) of Those of the Region of the Dead," respectively.

3. *Pinacatl:* Called *pinacate* in Mexico today, this is a species of wingless beetle of the genus *Eleodes.*

4. *Chicalotl: Argemone mexicana* or *Argemone ochroleuca* Sweet (Martínez 1936: 142 ff.).

5. *Itztli ecatoco, xalli ecatoco, quauitl ecatoco:* These lines probably constitute a reference to the Itzehecayan, "Place of the Obsidian-bladed Wind," one of the hazard stations that had to be traversed by the soul of the deceased on its journey to Mictlan (Sahagún 1978: 43; *Codex Vaticanus A* 1979: fol. 1v).

6. *Tzivactli (tzihuactli):* See note 31, Chapter I, Paragraph 5A.

7. *Nequametl: Agave mexicana* (Sahagún 1975: 938; cf. Hernández 1959–1984, VII: 174–175).

netzolli.
çenca çeva.
teucomitl.
yoã çenca tlatequipanollo.

[There are] brambles.
It is very cold.
[There are] ferrocacti.[8]
And there is much work.

Auh yn aquin nican tlalticpac quinemitiaya, chichi, yn iquac miquia quinanavatiaya: quilhuia tinechvalmochialia in chicunavatenco. Auh quilmach quipanaviaya yn õcan chicunavatenco ic mitoaya chicunavizcuintli.

And he who bred a dog on earth, when he died gave him commands; he said to him: "Wait for me at the edge of the water in the ninth underworld." And it is said that he carried him on his back there to the shore of the ninth underworld. For this reason he was called Nine Dog.[9]

Auh in canin ic viloaya quilmach tepetl ymonamicyan intla oypã monamic tepetl vncan popolivi aocan itto yn õpa mictlan.

And the place to which there was going, it was said, was where the mountains met.[10] If the mountains met on one, he perished there; he was no more seen in Mictlan.

[fol. 84v col. A]

Auh in aquin miquia y ie achi telpochtontli yoan yn oc vel conetontli coçolco onoc mitoaya amo vmpa via ỹ mictlan çan ompa via yn xochatlapã. Quilmach ṽpa icac in chichivalcuavitl quichichi ỹ pipilçitzintli ytzintlã mocacamachalviticate ỹ pipilçitzinti in camac valixicaticac yn chichivalaiotl,

And he who died when he was a rather young child, and indeed still a babe in the cradle, it was said, did not go to Mictlan but only went to Xochatlalpan.[11] It was said that a tree of udders stood there [at which] the babies suckled.[12] Underneath it the babies[13] were opening and closing their mouths; the milk dripped into their mouths.

yoã in aquin nican tlalticpac, quiçeçẽmana tlaolli yn atle ipã quitta yn ompa mictlan quixtelolococopina, ỹ mictlantecutli, ỹ mictecaçihoatl.

And as for him who scattered maize grains on the ground, who despised them here on earth, in Mictlan Mictlantecuhtli and Mictecacihuatl plucked out his eyeballs.

PARAGRAPH 7

Jnic chicome parrapho ypan mitoa yn izquitlamantli in ventli yn itech povia in mictlãtecutli ỹ mictecaçihoatl.

Seventh paragraph, in which are told the various offferings dedicated to Mictlantecuhtli and Mictecacihuatl.[1]

8. *Teucomitl (teocomitl):* probably a species of *Echinocactus* (Hernández 1959–1984, VII: 157; cf. Sahagún 1950–1982, Part XII [Book 11]: 218).

9. Chicunavizcuintli (Chiconahui Itzcuintli): This was also the calendric name of Chantico, "In the House," a fertility goddess with igneous connotations (see discussions in Seler 1900–1901:114–118; Nicholson 1985: 84–86).

10. *Tepetl imonanicyan:* This corresponds to Tepetl Imonamiquiyan, "Where the Hills Clash Together," another of the hazard stations that had to be surmounted by the soul of the deceased on its trip to Mictlan (Sahagún 1978: 43; *Codex Vaticanus A* 1979: fol. 1r).

11. Xochatlalpan: "Place of the Abundance of the Water of Flowers."

12. *Chichivalcuavitl (chichihualcuahuitl):* This "udder tree" that nourished the dead infants is illustrated and also described in the *Codex Vaticanus A* (1979: fol. 3r).

13. *Pipilçitzintli, pipilcitzinti:* for both, read *pipiltzitzintin.*

1. As indicated in note 1, Paragraph 6, Chapter 1 of the Appendix to Book 3 of the *Historia* contains a somewhat more extensive account, derived from Sahagún's Tlatelolca informants, of the standard funerary rituals that extended over a period of four years. This paragraph does supply some interesting complementary details.

Jn iquac omic in tlatoani nimã tlatiloya yn inacayo. Auh navilhuitl tlamanililoya in mictlantecutli yn oncan otlatiloc miqui cõmanaya in tlaqualli, xochitl, yietl, tilmatli cactli.

Auh inic macuililhuitl icuac tetech pachivia no contlamaniliaya icuac tlacualoya oc cepa quichichiva in ixiptla ocotzontectli oc ceppa vmpa contlatiaya in ompa tlatlac in ixpã vitzilopuchtli tlacualoya netlauhtiloya.

Auh cempovalilhuitl in chocovaya yoan pialoya in tlatoani mitoaya ocempoalti.

Auh in icuac. y. oc ceppa mochichivaya in ixiptla oc no ceppa vmpa ontlatlaya in ixpã vitzilopuchtli. Auh in iquac xinia in çempoaltica oquineçavilique.

Auh in iquac cexiuhtiz oc no iuh mochichivaz. Jnic oxiuhtiz no iuh mochichivaz Ynic exivitl çan no ivi. Auh ynic nauhxivitl vmpa ontzonquiçaya inic molnamiquia ỹ tlatoque. Çan no iuhqui ỹpã muchivaya in çihuapipilti ỹ nauhxivitl tzunquiçaya in tlamanililoya mictlantecutli.

When a ruler died his body was cremated. For four days offerings were made to Mictlantecuhtli at the place where the deceased was cremated. They made offerings of food, flowers, tobacco, capes, sandals.

And on the fifth day, at that time they drew close to him. They also made offerings to him. At that time there was feasting. Once again they arrayed the image hewn of pine wood. Once again they cremated him where he had burned before Huitzilopochtli. There was feasting, there was speech-making.

And for twenty days the ruler was wept and guarded. It was said: "He has been twentied."

And at this time a figure of [the deceased] was arrayed once again. Once more it burned before Huitzilopochtli.[2] And when it collapsed, they performed acts of abstinence in his honor for twenty days.

And when a year would pass, [a figure] would again be arrayed in the same manner. When two years would pass, [a figure] would also be arrayed in the same way. The third year, it was the same. And on the fourth year, the remembrance of rulers stopped. The same was done for the noblewomen; in four years offerings to Mictlantecuhtli stopped.

UNNUMBERED PARAGRAPH
[fol. 84r col. B]

Esta historia mjlagrosa o pfecia acõtecio en mexico reynãdo mutectzuma vltimo deste nõbre diez o doze años antes q̃ venjesẽ los españoles a esta tierra.

Jn iehoatl in mochiv i moquivitzin yçi-

This miraculous story or prophecy[1] happened in Mexico in the reign of Motecuhzoma, last of that name, ten or twelve years before the Spaniards came to this land.[2]

This befell Moquihuixtzin's[3] daughter-in-

2. This emphasis on Huitzilopochtli might seem to imply a Mexica origin for the information in this paragraph. However, the abundant evidence that the Huitzilopochtli cult had been deeply implanted throughout Acolhuacan, beginning with the reign of the half-Mexica Nezahualcoyotl (1431–1472), appears to provide sufficient explanation for the role played here by the Mexica patron deity.

1. *Pfecia:* read *profecia.*

2. This heading is written in Sahagún's own hand. Not included within the paragraph structure of the chapter, the passage was clearly a later addition to it, perhaps added after Sahagún's move from the Franciscan monastery of Tepepolco to that of Tlatelolco in 1561. This version should be compared with the slightly differing versions of Arthur Anderson (1988a, 1988b) contained in two articles on the concept of Tlalocan, which include other relevant Nahuatl passages that describe this afterworld of the rain deity, with analysis and interpretation.

3. Moquihuix was the ruler of Tlatelolco, Tenochtitlan's twin city, from 1467 to 1473. Married to a sister of Axaya-

vamo, acaço ye q'mictia ceca ytla ic qualla, amo, ma, imac mic, ca vel q'tlacamicti vel quicoco, ic nimã ie mamina quinoqui, Auh y yehoatl, yn ioq'chvi chalco pixcato amo, ma ixpã ỹ mic can icãpa auh in omic nima ie quitoa yn itava ca vmic in tomatzin, ma tictlatican auh nima ie cequiti quitoa macamo tlatla ma çan tictocaca auh in ocetiac in tlatolli in q'tocazque. Auh nima ie ic quilpia, çan cototzcatca, miec in tilmatli inic cenca vel quiquimiloqz, auh miec in amatl inic quichichiuhque ca iuh mochivaia y ye vecauh ynic micoaia: Niman quitlatataquique ce nequetzali ynic vecatla, auh inic quitocaqz cenca vel quiquequezque, auh cenca vei tetl cenca cenca patlavac, auh cenca tillavac in ipan quimanque quiquilqz in inavac in itenco, Auh nauhyoal nauilhuitl, yn uncã catca y vel mic:

law. He may have killed her. Her uncle was very angry because of it. She did not die at his hands, [but] indeed he half-killed her,[4] indeed injured her, so that at once she had a flux, diarrhea. And her husband had gone to gather a harvest in Chalco; she died in his absence; he was away. And when she died, her elders then said: "Our niece[5] has died: let us cremate her." But then some said: "She must not be cremated; we must just bury her." And the decision was unanimous that they should bury her. And then they bound her up. She was flexed; in many capes they wrapped her very well and in many papers they adorned[6] her as was done of old when there was a death. Then they dug a grave as deep as a man's height. And when they had buried her they stamped [the earth] down very well, and they laid over it, at its edge they set up by it,[7] very large, very wide,[8] and very thick stones. And for four nights [and] four days she was there; she had indeed died.

Auh izcatqui in iuh tlachix, in quimonextili iuhquima telpuchtli cocoxcatzintli tlavelilocatzĩtli, iuhquima teachcauh inic moxima tlamanale, nimã q'notz, quilhui, auh teacapane, quetzalpetlae, otiquihiyovi, tla oque xocuica nimã ie cuica, yvi, in queuh in tlacatecvlutl icuic. Cozcatla chimalico ieva noca ia: cozcatla chimalico ieva noca ia ma ça cemilhuitl toiamiquica ma toiamiquica.

But behold what she saw. There appeared before her one like a sickly, deformed youth, his hair cut like that of a master of youths. He had gifts. Then he called to her; he said: "And you, first-born, Quetzalpetlatl, you have suffered. Come on! Sing!" Then she sang; it was as if she intoned a devil's song: "The jewel on the shield is with me: the jewel on the shield is with me. Let us die for only a day. Let us die."

Jehoa i in quevi in quetzalpetla in oconeuh nimã ie ic quivica iuhquima quilpitztia, mictlãpa, quitztiltitia ça vei in quitocti ixtlavatl çacatla atle calli yn vnca quiquixti: Nima ie quimitta cuecuetzpalti, necoc omac

This was what Quetzalpetlatl asked him.[9] When she had intoned [the song], then [the youth] took her away. It was as if he blew upon her. He went guiding her to the land of the dead; he made her follow the great plains, the

catl, the Tenochca ruler, his alleged mistreatment of her, along with other, more substantial political problems, including probably economic rivalry with Tenochtitlan, led to the Mexica "civil war" in 1473 that resulted in the killing of Moquihuix, perhaps by Axayacatl himself, and the defeat and subjugation of Tlatelolco (see Davies 1982: 128–139). If Moquihuix was at least partly responsible for Quetzalpetlatl's death, therefore, this would conflict seriously with the statement in the heading that her death occurred ten or twelve years before the Conquest (1509–1511). Perhaps another, otherwise unknown Moquihuix is the referent here, but this seems unlikely.

4. *Q'tlacamicti* read *tlacomicti.*

5. *Tomatzi:* read *tomachtzin.*

6. *Nequetzali:* derived from *quetza,* meaning, inter alia, to stop?

7. Compare *iquiltia,* rev. of *icac.*

8. *Cenca* is repeated in the text.

9. Compare *euia.*

in tetemi in quimopanavi, auh no cuel çecni quimopanavi necoc omac in cacate çiva iquiti conilhui ma tiquinotz auh nima ie ic q'vica in tlaloca niman quimopanavi tamaçolti in iuhqui xopantla motlatlalia tlaltzotzontli ipan cacate tamaçolme vnteme, itech, aantoc tetevitl ic viltectoc in otli ic nimã vncalac inic tlachia, yn ṽca ca iuhquima aiavhtimani, cecni yavaliuhtoque i cana, in ipan tlatlatzini y vitecoque inic micque,

Nimã ye conilhuia in telpuchtli ayac tiq'ximati

houseless grasslands.[10] When he took her from there, they then saw the lizards;[11] on both sides one entered where it was filled with stones, which they traversed. And again, farther on, they traversed [where] on both sides one entered where women were weaving. [The youth] said: "Do not call to them." And then he took her to Tlalocan. Then they traversed where there were frogs, as in the springtime. They were seated on a wall; on it were two frogs. From it lay extended rubber-spotted streamers with which the road ended. Then they entered where they saw that, farther on, a mist seemed to lie surrounding those who, struck by lightning when it thundered somewhere, had thus died.

Then the youth said to her: "Do you not know anyone who was struck by lightning

[fol. 84v col. B]

Ma vitecoc in anoço atla micque; conilhui ca quemaca ca nopilotzin in atlami. Nima' ie conilhuia ca ie qualli ca mitznotzaz ma ticnotz, auh in oitech açito niman ie vallatoa in omic, niman ic q'valilhuia nican timovicatz: auh amo ma conotz, ca ipãpa ca ie inavatil in oiuh quilhui in telpuchtli

or died in the water?" She said to him: "Yes, my nephew met his end in the water." Then he said to her: "It is well. He will call to you. Do not call to him." And when they reached him, he who had died then spoke forth; he then said to her: "Here you come." But she did not call out to him, because those were her orders, as the youth had told her.

auh nimã ie õpa quivica in ompa vnoc tlalocatectli, quilhui tla tiq'ttali in totechiuhcauh ie no vel mitznavatiz; auh niman itech açito in q'tac ie veve otlãcocoto cenca miec in olli in ixco vnoc ic mixtlilhuitoc in quenami, inezca in inechichival catca tp̃c in tlaloc vel iuhqui in quitac.

And then he took her there where the lord of Tlalocan was. He said: "Let us see our chief. He also will command you." And then they arrived where they saw one already old, toothless. Much [liquid] rubber was on his face; his face was blackened with it. What they saw was just what Tlaloc's features [and] adornment were like on earth.[12]

Auh niman ie quinotza, in telpuchtli in

And then the youth called out to the lord

Unnumbered Paragraph

10. *Ixatlvatl çacatla atle calli:* This specification of great plains and houseless grasslands in the area of Mictlampa well fits its assignment to the north in late pre-Hispanic Central Mexican cosmology, for this direction was known to be characterized by extensive plains and open deserts. Tlalocan itself was assigned to the east (Sahagún 1950–1982, Part VIII [Book 7]: 14).

11. *Cuecuetzpalti:* This mention of lizards at this location may be connected with a hazard station that had to be surmounted by the soul of the deceased on its way to Mictlan—one called *xoxouhqui cuetzpalin in xochitonal,* "the blue-green lizard, the Xochitl (Flower) *tonalli* (day sign)" (Sahagún 1978: 43).

12. The attribution here of toothless old age to Tlaloc is interesting and unusual. He was normally depicted with a thick labial band from which issued prominent tusks. It is known from archaeological evidence that he was one of the most ancient deities of Central Mexico. His blackened face was a standard feature of his iconography (see Chapter I, Paragraph 5A).

tlalocatectli, conilhuia moceloquichtle, ma ximeviltitie

of Tlalocan; he said to him: "Greetings, O unique man."[13]

quivalilhui, auh xole quen otivalla quivalilhui aq'n no tiqualhuicac,

[This one] said to him: "And how have you come, young man?" He said to him: "Also, whom have you brought here?"

quilhui, ca maceoalli,

[The youth] said to him: "She is a native."[14]

q'lhui, Cuix ocẽvalla

[The other] said to him: "Does she come forever?"

quilhui ca amo, ca çan tlachiaco, auh ça ca mitzmotilico,

"No," he replied, "she has come only to observe, and she has come only to see you."

auh niman quivalnotz, Jn tlalocatecutli, q'valilhui tla xioalauh çioatontle, in axcã mopal mitotia in tlaloque in tp̃c o tla xiquimitta, ca iç onoque,

And then the lord of Tlalocan spoke forth; he said to her: "Come, little woman. Now the Tlalocs are dancing for you on earth. Look at them, for they live here."[15]

auh in quimitta ceq' vevei cequinti quiqualtoton in tlamacazqz,

And she saw a number of great [and] a number of ordinary[16] offering priests.

auh niman ie conittitia in õpa, cecni caltentoqz in pipiltin in ipilhoan in oc pipiltotonti miqui, ca much quimiliuhtoque, cenca conixnamic conixima, in ichavaconeuh oc tepiton ỹ mic, aocmo ma quinotz, ça conitac,

And then he showed her that over there, apart, the sons of noblemen, who had died while still young children, lay crowded. All of them lay wrapped. She came close to [and] recognized her stepson, who had died while still small. She did not call to him; she only looked at him.

auh nimã ie quinaoatia, Jn tlalocatecutli, q'lhuia tla xivalauh macevalle oc onyaz in vitzitli oc ontlacazcaltitiuh, oc ontlacavapavatiuh in vitzitl in tp̃c,

And then the lord of Tlalocan commanded her; he said to her: "Come here, native woman; the hummingbird[17] will yet go there; one will yet rear, one will yet educate the hummingbird on earth."

Niman niman ie conilhuia, in telpuchtli, ma noço itla xicmotlavcolili, ĩ maceoalli

Then[18] the youth said [to the lord of Tlalocan]: "Show the native some favor."

niman çem iztetontli im petlacaltontli yelpa conaquili, auh nima centetl xoxuhqui i xicalli in q'macaqz

Then [Tlaloc] placed a small coffer of a small span's length on her breast, and then they gave her a blue-green gourd vessel.

nimã quilhuique o ca iehoatl i, in tiquaz in tiquiz inic titepatiz in tp̃c acan ticpinauhtiz in tlalocatecutli amo ça ie yo in unca in iaxca

Then they said to her: "This is what you are to eat, what you are to drink. With it you are to remedy [the lot of] people on earth. Nowhere

13. *Moceloquichtle:* Anderson, in his English translation of this passage in his 1988a article on Tlalocan, rendered this word as "my jaguar man," but in his 1988b article on Tlalocan he translated it as "O unique man." If the first translation is preferred, it may be significant that Tlaloc does seem to have had some jaguaroid associations (discussion in Seler 1902–1923, II: 987–988).

14. *Maceoalli (macehualli):* This word is usually translated, as it is here, as "commoner," contrasted with "noble," *pilli.* Anderson agreed in his 1988a article, but in his 1988b article opted for "native," which might be more appropriate in this context. Quetzalpetlatl, as the daughter-in-law of a paramount ruler, a *tlatoani* (Moquihuix), was certainly a member of the native nobility, a *cihuapilli.*

15. *Ic:* read *iz.*

16. *Quiqualtoton:* read *cualtoton.*

17. *Vitzilli (huitzilin):* The hummingbird here appears to stand for the soul of Quetzalpetlatl's stepson, yet to be born again (cf. Anderson 1988b: 159–160).

18. *Niman* is repeated in the text.

in itlatqui i motlamachtia im mocuiltonoa mochi tlacatl ĩ motolinia in ticpatiz iehoatl i: Jnic quinavati,

are you to offend the lord of Tlalocan. It is not only property, the goods of all the people who prosper, who live in abundance; [with it] you are to remedy [the lot of] all who are in misery." Thus he commanded her.

niman no cuel çecni, quivicac quilhui o tla xiquimittaqui ca niman vnoque in tlatoqz in tlachia atle calli çacatla in oncã onoqz ixtlavacã cenca eeca in oncã cate nimã no intech onaçic iehoatl in teacantica y Veve Moteçvmatzin auh nimã iehoatl,

Then also he took her farther on. He said to her: "Look at them. Here live the rulers." She saw that they had no houses. They lived in the grasslands, in the plains. A great wind blew where they were. She also approached those who had been leaders of the people, Motecuhzoma the Elder,[19] and then . . .[20]

19. Veve Omtecomatzin (Huehue Motecuhzoma): The great grandfather of the second Motecuhzoma, he reigned from 1440 to 1469 and was considered the greatest of the rulers of Tenochtitlan.

20. The narrative continued on the following page, but, due to the unfortunate loss of this page, it remains incomplete. Anderson (1988a: 156) suggested that the passage in Chapter 1 of Book 8 of Sahagún's *Historia* (1950–1982, Part IX: 3; 1988, II: 498) that describes the death and resurrection of a Tenochca noblewoman who returned from the dead to prophesy to Motecuhzoma II the coming fall of Mexico might have constituted the finale of the story (cf. Anderson 1988b: 159–160). In any case, Quetzalpetlatl must have returned to life and uttered some kind of ominous prophecy.

CHAPTER III
Rulership

PARAGRAPH 1A
[fol. 51r col. A]

Jnic ey capitulo ytech tlatoa in tlatocayutl

Jnic i. parrapho ypan mitoa yn otlatocatque yn mexico yn tenochtitlan yoã yn acolhuacan.

Mexico tlatoque

in quipeualti tlatocayutl, veve acamapichtli: auh inic tlatocatl epoalxiuitl yoan matlacxiuitl, amo tle ipan mochiuh: yehica ca yancuican motecutlali, yn toltzalã yn acatzalã, yc mitoaya.

Auh in quivaltoquili inic ome tlatoani mochiuh, in iquac omic acamapichtli; ytoca vitziliuitl, in tlatocat cempoalxiuitl oce: amo tle ipan mochiuh in iq̃c tlatocat.

Auh inic ei tlatoani mochiuh mexico, in iquac omicque in vmenti yn acamapichtli

Third chapter, which tells of rulership.[1]

First paragraph, in which are told those who ruled Mexico Tenochtitlan and Acolhuacan.

The Rulers of Mexico

Acamapichtli the elder began the rulership, and while he ruled[2] for seventy years, nothing happened[3] because lords were installed for the first time in Toltzalan Acatzalan,[4] as it was called.

And the second ruler, who followed when Acamapichtli died, was named Huitzilihuitl. He ruled twenty-one years. Nothing happened when he ruled.

And the third to become ruler in Mexico after both Acamapichtli and Huitzilihuitl

1. This paragraph and Paragraph 14 of this chapter provide the only significant amount of genuinely historical information in the *Primeros Memoriales.* It is interesting that the ruling dynasty of Tepepolco itself is not included, although it can be largely reconstructed from other sources (Nicholson 1974). Instead, in addition to the rulers of the leading member of the Triple Alliance, Mexico Tenochtitlan, the paragraph lists those of the second most important member, Tetzcoco, capital of the province of Acolhuacan, and of Huexotla, the large center just to the south.

These dynastic lists provide no dates in the native calendar, but only the putative regnal years of each ruler (sometimes confused with life spans). They can be compared with a wealth of dynastic data, both pictorial and textual, contained in other primary ethnohistorical sources concerning these centers. Agreement with most of the names of the rulers in these other sources is evident, especially in the case of the Tenochtitlan and Tetzcoco lists, but there are many serious discrepancies in the chronologies. Most of the dynastic lists for Mexico Tenochtitlan are included in Boone 1992. Offner 1983 summarizes much of the available dynastic information for Tetzcoco and its orbit, utilizing both primary sources and modern studies. The leading versions of the dynasty of Huexotla are summarized in García Granados 1952–1953, III: 422. The chronological aspects of the dynasties of these three centers are discussed in Nicholson 1978:305–307.

2. *Tlatocatl:* read *tlatocat* or *tlatocati.*

3. *Amo tle ipan mochiuh:* This phrase for "nothing happened" was obviously not intended to be taken literally but only to indicate that, for the annalist, no conquests or major political or natural events occurred during the reigns of these rulers.

4. *Yn totzala yn acatzala:* "among the rushes, among the reeds," a poetic metaphoric couplet sometimes applied to the site of Mexico Tenochtitlan.

ioã vitziliuitl: quiualtoquili teeca mochiuh, in itoca chimalpvpucatzin: auh in tlatocat çã matlacxiuitl, auh ipan vmpeui y yavyutl, y ye intech nexicolo tenochca:

had died, who became [ruler] following them in third place, was named Chimalpopocatzin. And he ruled only ten years. And in his time wars began. There was anger toward the Tenochca.[5]

Auh in omomiquili chimalpvpucatzin niman ic ualmotlatocatlali yn itzcoatzĩ. tenauhca mochiuh: yn ipan tlatocayutl: auh yehoatl ypan mochiuh yn yavyutl yehoatl quinpeuh in tepaneca: auh in tlatocat itzcoatzin castolxiuitl yc ipan tzinpeuh yn yavyutl inic nouian tepeuhque.

And when Chimalpopocatzin died, Itzcoatzin[6] was installed as ruler; he became fourth in the rulership. And in his time war was made; he conquered the Tepaneca. And Itzcoatzin ruled fifteen years. In his time was the beginning of wars; they made conquests everywhere.

Auh in omic itzcoatzin niman valmotlali in Motecuçomatzin veue iluicaminatzin: auh in tlatocat cempoalxiuitli vncastolli: in ipan mochiuh yehoatl in mitoa necetochhuiloc. i. ypan mochiuh mayanaliztli in cexiuhtonali ce tochtli.

And when Itzcoatzin died, Motechuzomatzin the elder, Ilhuicamina, was installed, and he ruled thirty-five years. In his time occurred what was called being one-rabbited; that is, in his time there was a famine in the one year sign One Rabbit.[7]

Auh in omic veue Motecuçomatzin niman ic ualmotlali y Aaxayacatzin in ipan tlatocayutl: auh inic tlatocat matlacxiuitl, ioan nauhxiuitl: auh

And when Motechuzomatzin the elder died, then Axayacatzin was installed in the rulership, and he ruled fourteen years.

[fol. 51v col. A]

yehoatl ipan mochiuh, ynic peualoque tlatilulca.

And in his time it happened that the Tlatelolca were conquered.[8]

Auh in iquac omic Axayacatzin niman ye oalmotlalia in Tizozicatzi in tlatocat Tiçozi-

And when Axayacatzin died, then Tizozicatzin was installed. Tizozicatzin ruled five

5. *Ye intech nexicolo tenochca:* This is a reference to the troubles between the Mexica and their Tepanec overlords of Azcapotzalco that resulted in the murder, at the hands of the Tepaneca, of Chimalpopoca, or else his suicide (see Davies 1982: 60–61). This was one of the incidents that led to the "Tepanec War" in which Azcapotzalco was conquered (1428) by a coalition of tributary city-states led by Itzcoatl of Tenochtitlan and Nezahualcoyotl of Tetzcoco. This overthrow eventuated in the formation of a new political order, the Triple Alliance of Mexico Tenochtitlan, Tetzcoco, and Tlacopan, which went on to forge, by conquest, the empire that ruled much of western Mesoamerica at the time of the Conquest.

6. Itzcoatzin (Itzcoatl): This fourth official ruler of Mexico Tenochtitlan is the first to be pictured wearing the turquoise mosaic diadem, the *xiuhtzontli (xiuhuitzolli),* the standard headgear of the lords in late pre-Hispanic Central Mexico. His three predecessors, in contrast, wear the headpiece of the more rustic Chichimeca lords, the *cozoyahualolli,* the circular fan device of yellow parrot feathers. Interestingly, this is the only source that assigns this badge of Chichimec status to the earlier Tenochca rulers, while they were tributaries of Azcapotzalco. Itzcoatl is also the first to be shown reclining on the backed mat throne, the *tepotzoicpalli;* his three predecessors sit on the cylindrical bundle of reeds, the *tolicpalli,* a seat of lesser dignity. The assignment of the *xiuhtzontli* and the *tepotzoicpalli* to Itzcoatl signaled his status as a paramount, independent ruler. See Nicholson 1967b: 71–73.

7. *I. ypan mochiuh mayanaliztli in cexiuhtonalli ce tochtli:* See Davies 1982: 92–94 for a summary account, based on primary sources, of the devastating famine of the mid-fifteenth century that culminated in the year 1 Tochtli, 1454.

8. *Peualoque tlatilulca:* Tlatelolco, Tenochtitlan's twin city, was politically autonomous, under its Azcapotzalco-derived dynasty (vs. the Colhuacan-derived dynasty of Tenochtitlan), until 1473, when it was conquered by the Tenochca under Axayacatl, the brother-in-law of Tlatelolco's ruler, Moquihuix. See Davies 1982: 128–132.

catzin macuilxiuitl yehoatl quiuauan in teucalli tenochtitlan.

Auh in omic Tiçozicatzin niman oalmotlatocatlali y Aauitzotzi: in tlatocat castolxiuitl, ypan exiuitl: yehoatl quitzonq'xtin quieco in teucalli tenochtitlan: iehoatl tlamamalcalchali: auh in ica tlamamaliuac: yehoantin tziuhcoaca, peualoque: auh yehoatl quiquetz yn acuecuexatl, yn ica pachiuhque mexica.

Auh in omic Avitzotzin niman ic ualmotlali in Motecuçumatzin in ipan oaçico castillan tlaca españoles: auh in tlatocat castolxiuitl ipan vnxiuitl no ipan mochiuh in mayanaliztli moteneua netlauluiloc.

Auh in omic Motecuçumatzin niman oalmotlali in ipan tlatocayutl Cuitlauatzin napoaliluitl in tlatocat ye ipan in castillan tlaca.

Auh in omic Cuitlauatzin niman oalmotlatocali in Quauhtemoctzin iehoatl ipan mochiuh yn yauyutl ineuanti Couanacochtli Acolhuacã ynic poliuhque mexica auh in tlatocat Quauhtemoctzin chiquacexiuitl

Auh in omic Quauhtemoctzin niman ic oalmotlatocatlali yn Motelchiuhtzin yn colhoacã miquito quiuicaca in guzmani in tlatocat çan chicoxiuitl.

Auh in omic Motelchiuhtzin niman oal-

years. He designed the temple in Tenochtitlan.[9]

And when Tizozicatzin died, Ahuitzotzin was installed as ruler. He ruled eighteen years. He finished, he completed, the temple in Tenochtitlan.[10] He ignited the fire [with the fire drill] to dedicate the building, and for this fire-drilling, the Tziuhcoaca were conquered. And he confined the waters of Acuecuexco, with which the Mexica were inundated.[11]

And when Ahuitzotzin died, Motecuhzomatzin was installed. In his time the people of Castile, the Spaniards, came to arrive. And he ruled seventeen years. In his time also there was famine,[12] which was called being maize-grained.

And when Motecuhzomatzin died, then Cuitlahuatzin was installed in the rulership. He ruled eighty days. It was at the time the people of Castile [were there].

And when Cuitlahuatzin died, then Cuauhtemoctzin was installed[13] as ruler. In his time, together with that of Coanacochtli of Acolhuacan, the war was fought in which the Mexica were destroyed. And Cuauhtemoc ruled six years.

And when Cuauhtemoctzin died, Motelchiuhtzin[14] was installed as ruler. He went away and died in Colhuacan; Guzmán had taken him away. He ruled only seven years.

And when Motelchiuhtzin died, then

9. *In teucalli tenuchtitlan:* The final major renovation of the Tenochtitlan Templo Mayor of Huitzilopochtli and Tlaloc was commenced by Tizoc, probably in 1482, and completed five years later, in 1487, by his younger brother and successor, Ahuitzotl.

10. *Quitzonq̃'xtin quizco in teucalli tenochtitlan:* The dedicatory rituals—including, as was standard, the drilling of New Fire—for the final major enlargement of the Tenochtitlan Templo Mayor in the year 8 Acatl, 1487, are described in numerous primary sources (see Davies 1982: 164–168). The conquest of Tziuhcoac (Tziccoac) on the southern border of the Huaxteca in northern Veracruz was ninety-fifth in the "official list" of Tenochca conquests (see Barlow 1990: 1–7).

11. *Quiquetz yn acuecuexatl, yn ica pachiuque mexica:* Ahuitzotl's construction of the aqueduct of Acuecuexatl in the year 7 Acatl, 1499, which tapped springs in the vicinity of Coyoacan and Huitzilopochco, south of Tenochtitlan, and which allegedly caused a disastrous flood, is described in numerous primary sources (see Davies 1982: 192–197).

12. *In mayanaliztli moteneua netlauluiloc:* This refers to another famine in the years 13 Calli, 1505, through 1 Tochtli, 1506, which in the native view was linked to the great famine fifty-two years earlier in another year 1 Tochtli.

13. *Oalmotlatocali:* read *ualmotlacotlali.*

14. *Motelchiuhtzin* (Andrés de Tapia Motelchiuh): This noble Tenochca warrior *(cuauhpilli)*, not a member of the royal family, was installed in 1526 by the Spanish administration as native ruler of Tenochtitlan. He accompanied the Nuño de Guzmán expedition to western and northwestern Mexico ("Colhuacan"), where he was killed in 1530. See Gibson 1964: 168–169 for the chronology and affiliations of the colonial native rulers of Tenochtitlan through Cristóbal (de Guzmán Cecepatic), who died in 1562.

motlali in Xochiquentzin exiuitl in tlatocat.

Xochiquentzin was installed. He ruled three years.

Auh in omic Xochiq̃ntzin niman oalmotlatocatlali in Vanitzin in tlatocat macuilxiuitl.

And when Xochiquentzin died, then Huanitzin[15] was installed as ruler. He ruled five years.

Auh in omic in Vanitzin niman ic

And when Huanitzin died, then

[fol. 52r col. A]

oalmotlatacatlali in teTeuetzquititzin, in tlatocat matlacxiuitl omei.

Tehuetzquititzin was installed as ruler. He ruled thirteen years.

Auh in omic Teuetzquititzin auh oxiuitl ça cactimãca vncã catca Juez.

And Tehuetzquititzin died, and for two years [rulership] just remained vacant; a judge was there.

Auh niman oalmotlali yn axcã tlatoani Don xp̃oal ye exiuitl in tlatocati.

And then the present ruler, don Cristóbal, was installed. He has ruled three years.

Auh ye ic mocẽpoa ynic otlatocatiuac mexico tenochtitlan yn ixquichica axcan yn ipan i xiuitl ticate in motenevaya ome acatl.

And with this is the complete account of when there was rulership in Mexico Tenochtitlan until now, the year in which we are, which was called Two Reed.[16]

PARAGRAPH 1B

Jzcate in tetzcoco tlatoque iniçizqui xiuitl tlatocatque

Here are the rulers of Tetzcoco; here are[17] all the years they ruled.

Quipeoalti in tlatocayutl in tetzcoco yehoatl in tlaltecatzin ça napoaliluitl in tlatocat atle ipan mochiuh chichimeca tlatoque y.

Tlaltecatzin[18] started the rulership in Tetzcoco. He ruled only eighty days. Nothing happened in his time. They were Chichimec rulers.

Aun ynic ome tlatoani mochiuh in quioaltoquili in Tlaltecatzin yehoatl yn Techotlalatzin chichimecatl auh in tlatocat yepoalxiuitl yoan matlacxiuitl amo tle ipã mochiuh.

And the second who became ruler, who followed Tlaltecatzin, was Techotlalatzin, the Chichimec. And he ruled seventy years. In his time nothing happened.

Auh inic ei tlatoani mochiuh acolhoacã yehoatl in veve yxtlilxochitl in tlatocat

And the third to become ruler was Ixtlilxochitl the elder. He ruled sixty-five years.

15. *Vanitzin:* After the demise in 1536 of (Pablo) Xochiquen, who had been only a noble administrator *(calpixcapilli)* in the pre-Hispanic government, Diego Huanitzin, grandson of Axayacatl and nephew of Motecuhzoma II—then ruling Ehecatepec, north of Mexico City—was appointed native *tlatoani* of Tenochtitlan, thus restoring the leadership of the former Mexica imperial capital to its legitimate royal dynasty.

16. *Ome acatl:* This correlates with 1559 in the indigenous year count and clearly dates the preparation of this paragraph of the *Primeros Memoriales* to the period when Sahagún was residing in Tepepolco. Later, probably just after he moved to Tlatelolco, Sahagún collected another, more detailed account of the ruling dynasty of Mexico Tenochtitlan, dated 1560, which he included as Chapter 1 of Book VIII of the *Historia* (Sahagún 1950–1982, Part IX [Book 8]: 1–5; 1988, II: 494–497), with somewhat different illustrations of the rulers and their name signs and with reign lengths that often differ from those of the *Primeros Memoriales* version (see Castillo Farreras 1974: chart, p. 166).

17. *Iniçizqui:* read *in izqui* or *in iz izqui.*

18. Tlaltecatzin: His other name, Quinatzin, is the one usually employed for this ruler. No other source gives anything like such a limited reign for him.

epoalxiuitl yoan macuilxiuitl amo tle ipan mochiuh.

Auh inic naui tlatoani mochiuh tetzcoco yehoatl y Neçavalcoyutzin in tlatocat epoalxiuitl yoan matlacxiuitl yoan ce xiuitl auh y yehoatl i y neçaoalcoyutzin ypan peuh yn yauyutl ym omextin yn tenochtitlan tlatoani Itzcoatzin ynic q'peuhque tepaneca auh i novian tepeuhque quiehoatl quipeualti y Neçaoalcoyutzin yn quitecac in petlatl in icpali ȳn acolhoacan tetzcoco.

Auh inic macuili mochiuh tlatoani yehoatl in Neçaoalpilli auh in

In his time nothing happened.

And the fourth to become ruler in Tetzcoco was Nezahualcoyotzin.[19] He ruled seventy-one years. And in the time of Nezahualcoyotzin, wars began when the two, [he and] Itzcoatzin of Tenochtitlan, conquered the Tepaneca, and they conquered all places; it was he, Nezahualcoyotzin, who began it, who set down the mat, the seat, in Acolhuacan Tetzcoco.

And the fifth to become ruler was Nezahualpilli, and

[fol. 52v col. A]

tlatocat vmpoalxiuitl vmatlactli yoã exiuitl in ipan mochiuh in yavyutl, y nouian ic tepeualoya auh y yeoãtin ym omextin y neçaoalcoyutzin yoan Neçaoalpili yn iquac tlatocatq̃ tzacuticatca in tlaxcalla ioan vexotzinco auh in Neçaoalpilli ipan peuh yn tlein oalmoquequetzaya ylhuicatitech in iuhqui tlanextli in iuhqui tlemiaoatl y ceyoal tlanextiticaca auh nauhxiuitl yn ipã mochiuh ypan xiuhtonalli chicome tecpatl yn yancuican neçico auh in poliuh ipan xiuhtonali mactlactloce tecpatli auh inic tlamanca nauhxiuitl miecca xitin tepetl in texcali auh in iquac poliuh in tlein oalmoquequetzaya vc iuh nauhxiuitl açiquiui in españolesme auh q̃c mic in Necaoalpili aucmo ixpan.

he ruled fifty-three years. In his time wars were made; people were conquered everywhere. And it was when these two, Nezahualcoyotl and Nezahualpilli, ruled that Tlaxcallan and Huexotzinco[20] were contained. And in Nezahualpilli's time commenced what kept rising up in the sky, which was like a light,[21] like a flame of fire, that shone each night. And it occurred for four years. It was in the year sign Seven Flintstone that it appeared for the first time, and it vanished in the year sign Eleven Flintstone, and thus it lasted four years. In many places the mountains, the crags sundered. And it was four years before the Spaniards arrived that what had kept rising up in the sky vanished. It was then that Nezahualpilli died;[22] he was no more.

Auh inic. vi. tlatoani mochiuh tetzcoco yehoatl in Cacamatzin in tlatocat nauhxiuitl

And the sixth to become ruler in Tetzcoco was Cacamatzin. He ruled four years. In his

19. Neçaualcoyutzin (Nezahualcoyotl): This outstanding ruler, who, in partnership with Itzcoatl of Mexico Tenochtitlan, established the independence and power of Tetzcoco (1431), is the first of the dynasty to be shown seated on the *tepotzoicpalli* and wearing the royal diadem, the *xiuhtzontli.* The metaphoric couplet, *in petlatl in icpalli* was the standard expression for royal authority. His reign length has obviously been confused with the duration of his life (1402–1472).

20. *Tzacuticatca in tlaxcalla ioan vexotzinco:* The powerful city-states of Tlaxcallan and its almost equally powerful ally, Huexotzinco, east of the Basin of Mexico, were never conquered by the Triple Alliance but were surrounded and besieged until the time of the Conquest. See Davies 1982: 225–232.

21. *Tlanextli:* This column of light seen in the east, which, according to the statement here, lasted from 1512 to 1516, was considered to have been one of the principal omens of the Conquest. It is described elsewhere in the *Historia* as well (Sahagún 1950–1982, Part IX [Book 8]: 3–4, 17–19; 1975: 1–3; 1988, II: 496, 501, 817–818). It is also mentioned in other primary sources, although it is usually dated somewhat earlier.

22. *Mic in Necaoalpili:* Most of the primary sources give 10 Acatl, 1515, as the year of Nezahualpilli's death, but a few agree with the statement here that it was in 11 Tecpatl, 1516. As in the case of his father, Nezahualcoyotl, the reign length given here was confused with his life span, 1464–1515/16.

yehoatl ipan mochiuh inic açico nican castillan tlaca.

Inic. vii. tlatoani mochiuh yehoatl in Coanacotzin in tlatocat macuilxiuitl yehoatl ipan mochiuh inic peoaloque mexica neoantin quauhtemoctzin tenochtitlan.

Inic viij tlatoani mochiuh yehoatl in tTecocoltzin in tlatocat ce xiuitl ye imixpan in castillan tlaca ye iquac in tetzcuco catca marques vncan moyauhchichiuh in i quinpeuh mexica.

Inic. ix. tlatoani mochiuh yehoatl iN ixtlilxuchitzin in tlatocat chicuexiuitl auh in iquac peoaloque mexica quivicatiuia in marques ytlan omoquetz ivan quivicaya in vei molan yehoantin ymixpã mochiuh ynic vel motlatlali altepetl inic tlavelalali marques neoan coanacuchtli.

time the people from Castile came to arrive.

The seventh to become ruler was Coanacochtzin.[23] He ruled five years. In his time it came to pass that the Mexica were conquered; both he and Cuauhtemoctzin of Tenochtitlan [were rulers].

The eighth to become ruler was Tecocoltzin. He ruled one year in the presence of the Castilian people when the marquis was in Tetzcoco, where he readied himself for war [and whence] he conquered the Mexica.

The ninth to become ruler was Ixtlilxochitl. He ruled eight years. And when the Mexica were conquered, he went accompanying the marquis; he was one of his party, and he accompanied him to Huey Mollan.[24] In his time it happened that the city was well established. The marquis together with Coanacochtli put things in order.

[fol. 53r col. A]

Inic x. tlatoani mochiuh iehoatl in yuyontzin in tlatocat ce xiuitl.

Inic. xi. tlatoani mochiuh yehoatl ỹ tetlavevetzquititzin yn tlatocat macuilxiuitl.

Inic. xii. tlatoani mochiuh yehoatl in Don anto º tlavitoltzin in tlatocat chiquacexiuitl.

Inic. xiii. tlatoani mochiuh yehoatl in axcã tlatoani Don hernando pimentel in tlatocati ecastolxiuitl in axcan ipan ticate.

Auh ye ixquich cauitl quipia in tlatocayutl yn acolhoaque y ye ic mocempoa castolpoalxiuitl yoan napoalxiuitl yoan nauhxiuitl yn ixquichica axcã ipan ticate xiuhtonalli vmacatl.

The tenth to become ruler was Yoyontzin. He ruled one year.

The eleventh to become ruler was Tetlahuehuetzquititzin. He ruled five years.

The twelfth to become ruler was don Antonio Tlahuitoltzin. He ruled six years.

The thirteenth to become ruler is the present ruler, don Hernando Pimentel. He has been ruling eighteen years in our time.

And all the time that the Acolhuaque held the rulership was three hundred and eighty-four years until the present time in which we live, the year sign Two Reed.[25]

23. Coanacotzin: Coanacochtzin was a son of Nezahualpilli. He succeeded his half-brother, Cacama, to the throne of Tetzcoco after the latter's death in 1520 while a Spanish prisoner. He was executed in 1525 together with Cuauhtemoc in Campeche by Cortés during the latter's expedition to Honduras.

24. *Vei molan:* Huey Mollan referred to the north coast of Honduras, the goal of Cortés's expedition of 1524–1526, when he was accompanied by a large retinue of native leaders. It included Ixtlilxochitl, another son of Nezahualpilli, who was appointed native ruler of Tetzcoco after the death of his half-brother Coanacochtzin. On the other colonial native Tetzcocan rulers featured in the *Primeros Memoriales* list, including their dates and familial relationships, see Gibson 1964: 170–171.

25. *Ome acatl:* see note 16, this paragraph. Sahagún included a virtually verbatim version of this *Primeros Memoriales* account of the Tetzcoco dynasty in the *Historia* (Sahagún 1950–1982, Part IX [Book 8]: 9–11; 1988, II: 499–510), with copies of the *Primeros Memoriales* illustrations. However, all of the rulers are shown seated on the *tepotzoicpalli* and wearing the *xiuhtzontli,* differing from the *Primeros Memoriales* version, in which the first three rulers wear the *cozoyahualolli* and are seated on the *tolicpalli.*

PARAGRAPH 1C

Auh izcate in chimeca tlatoque catca vexutla in moteneva acolhoaque in vmpa achto açico acolhoachichimeca.

Jnic. i. tlatoani mochiuh Maçatzin tecutli in tlatocat epoalxiuitl ipan castolxiuitl ioan exiuitl.

Jnic. ii. tlatoani tochin tecutli in tlatocat cempoalxiuitl ipan castolxiuitl ioan exiuitl.

Jnic. iii. tlatoani ayotzin tecutli in tlatocat epoalxiuitl ipan matlacxiuitl ioan nauhxiuitl.

Jnic. iiii. tlatoani quatlavice tecutli in tlatocat vmpoalxiuitl ioan castolxiuitl.

Jnic. v. tlatoani itoca totomochtzin ī tlatocat vmpoalxiuitl ipan matlacxiuitl ioan vnxiuitl auh in imacuilixtin i chichimeca tlatoqz in vel quipiaya in itlatocayo in acampa tequitia castolpoalxiuitl ioan matlacxiuitl ioan exiuitl in vel quipixqz in itlatocayo.

Jnic. vi. tlatoani itoca yavtzin tecutli

And here are the Chichimec[26] rulers who were in Huexotla, who were called Acolhuaque.[27] They were the first Acolhuachichimeca to come to arrive there.

The first to become ruler was Mazatzin tecuhtli. He ruled seventy-eight years.

The second ruler was Tochin tecuhtli. He ruled thirty-eight years.

The third ruler was Ayotzin tecuhtli. He ruled seventy-four years.

The fourth ruler was Cuatlahuice tecuhtli. He ruled fifty-five years.

The fifth ruler was named Totomochtzin. He ruled fifty-two years. And all five Chichimec rulers held its rulership. Nowhere did they pay tribute during the three hundred and thirteen years they held its rulership.[28]

The sixth ruler was named Yaotzin tecuhtli.

[fol. 53v col. A]

in tlatocat vmpoalxiuitl ioan castolxiuitl ipan exiuitl iehoatl ipan peuh inic tequitque tepanoaya chichimeca acolhoaque.

Jnic. vii. tlatoani itoca Xilotzin tecutli in tlatocat cempoalxiuitl ipan chicuexiuitl.

Inic. viij. tlatoani in itoca yTlacauhtzin in tlatocat cempoalxiuitl ipan chicuexiuitl.

Jnic. ix. tlatoani itoca Tlaçolyautzin in tlatocat vmpoalxiuitl ioan castolxiuitl ioan ex-

He ruled fifty-eight years. In his time the Acolhuaque Chichimeca began to pay tribute to Tepanohuayan.[29]

The seventh ruler was named Xilotzin tecuhtli. He ruled twenty-eight years.

The eighth ruler was named Itlacauhtzin. He ruled twenty-eight years.

The ninth ruler was named Tlazolyaotzin.[30] He ruled fifty-eight years. In his time

26. Chimeca: read Chichimeca.

27. Acolhoaque: The Acolhuaque were the Chichimec ancestors of those who settled the eastern Basin of Mexico in the Late Postclassic, after whom the province of Acolhuacan, whose final capital was Tetzcoco, was named.

28. The reign lengths given for these five earliest rulers of Huexotla add up to 297 years rather than 313. Since the regnal durations are improbably long anyway, this apparent mathematical error is only peripherally relevant to their possible historicity.

29. *Ipan peuh inic tequitque tepanoaya:* This apparently refers to the conquest of Acolhuacan by the Tepanec ruler Tezozomoc of Azcapotzalco in the second decade of the fifteenth century. Yaotzintecuhtli is shown seated on the *tepotzoicpalli,* rather than the *tolicpalli* of his predecessors, indicating an elevation in status as a Tepanec tributary. See Offner 1983: 40–44.

30. Tlaçolyautzin (Tlazolyaotzin): This ruler is the first to be shown wearing the royal diadem, the *xiuhtzontli,* to which he was entitled as one of the fourteen "grandees" of Acolhuacan, in the political order established by Nezahualcoyotl. See Offner 1983: 99–100.

iuitl quieoatl ipan mochiuh inic motecac petlatl icpalli tetzcuco inic motecutlali neçaoalcuyutzin monamicque tlaçolyavtzin vexotla.

Jnic. x. tlatoani itoca tzontemoctzin ĩ tlatocat castolxiuitl.

Jnic. xi. tlatoani itoca Cuitlaoatzĩ tecutli in tlatocat vmpoalxiuitl ioan ce xiuitl.

Jnic. xii. tlatoani itoca Tzapocuetzĩ in tlatocat matlacxiuitl ioan exiuitl.

Jnic xiij tlatoani ça no itoca Cuitlaoatzin ça tetoca in tlatocat matlacxiuitl ioan exiuitl.

Auh ye ixquich cauitl axcã ipan i xiuitl ticate y ye ic mocempoa y mopia tlatocayotl vexotla ye centzonxiuitl ioan chicuepoali xiuitl ioan vnxiuitl in ixquichica axcã ipan xiuhtonalli vmacatl.

the mat, the seat were set down in Tetzcoco. When Nezahualcoyotzin was installed as lord, [he and] Tlazolyaotzin of Huexotla contended against each other.

The tenth ruler was named Tzontemoctzin. He ruled fifteen years.

The eleventh ruler was named Cuitlahuatzin tecuhtli. He ruled forty-one years.

The twelfth ruler was named Tzapocuetzin. He ruled thirteen years.

The thirteenth ruler was also named Cuitlahuatzin. It was a name [of noblemen]. He ruled thirteen years.

And in all the time until the present, in the year in which we live, the entire count [of years] in which the rulership was held in Huexotla is five hundred and sixty-two years, until now, in the year sign Two Reed.[31]

PARAGRAPH 1A ILLUSTRATIONS
[fol. 57r col. B]

acamapichtli	Acamapichtli
icuçuyavalol	his circular fan device of yellow parrot feathers
mitl	arrows
yyeoatilma	his leather cape
itolicpal	his reed seat
Vitziliui	Huitzilihuitl
ycoçoyaoalol	His circular fan device of yellow parrot feathers
yyeoatilma	his leather cape
ytolicpal	his reed seat
chimalpopoca	Chimalpopoca
ycoçoyaoalol	his circular fan device of yellow parrot feathers
yyeoatilma	his leather cape
ytolicpal	his reed seat
yzcoatzin	Itzcoatzin
ixiuhtzon	his turquoise [mosaic] headdress
ixiuhyacamiuh	his turquoise nose-rod
ixiuhtilma	his turquoise [blue] cape
tenechilnavayo	edged by a red border with circles
itepotzoicpal	his seat with back rest

31. *Ome acatl:* see note 16, this paragraph. As in the case of the account of the Tetzcoco dynasty, Sahagún included this version of the Huexotla dynasty in the *Historia* (Sahagún 1950–1982, Part IX [Book 8]: 13–14; 1988, II: 500), with copies of the illustrations.

motecuçoma ylhuicamina	Motecuhzoma Ilhuicamina
ixiuhtzon	his turquoise [mosaic] headdress
ixiuhyacamiuh	his turquoise nose-rod
ixiuhtilma	his turquoise [blue] cape
techilnavayo	edged by a red border with circles
ytepotzoicpal	his seat with back rest
axayacatzin	Axayacatzin
ixiuhtzon	his turquoise [mosaic] headdress
ixiuhyacamiuh	his turquoise nose-rod
ixiuhtilma	his turquoise [blue] cape
techilnavayo	edged by a red border with circles
ytepotzoicpal	his seat with back rest

[fol. 57v col. B]

tiçocicatzin	Tizocicatzin
ixiuhtzon	his turquoise [mosaic] headdress
ixiuhyacamiuh	his turquoise nose-rod
ixiuhtilma	his turquoise [blue] cape
techilnavay	edged by a red border with circles
ytepotzoicpal	his seat with back rest
avitzotzin	Ahuitzotzin
ixiuhtzon	his turquoise [mosaic] headdress
ixiuhyacamiuh	his turquoise nose-rod
ixiuhtilma	his turquoise [blue] cape
techilnavayo	edged by a red border with circles
ytepotzoicpal	his seat with back rest
motecuçomatzin	Motecuhzomatzin
ixiuhtzon	his turquoise [mosaic] headdress
ixiuhyacamiuh	his turquoise nose-rod
ixiuhtilma	his turquoise [blue] cape
techilnavayo	edged by a red border with circles
ytepotzoicpal	his seat with back rest
Cuitlaoatzin	Cuitlahuatzin
ixiuhtzon	his turquoise [mosaic] headdress
ixiuhyacamiuh	his turquoise nose-rod
ixiuhtilma	his turquoise [blue] cape
techilnaoayo	edged by a red border with circles
ytepotzoicpal	his seat with back rest
quauhtemoctzin	Cuauhtemoctzin
ixiuhtzon	his turquoise [mosaic] headdress
ixiuhyacamiuh	his turquoise nose-rod
ixiuhtilma	his turquoise [blue] cape
techilnavayo	edged by a red border with circles
ytepotzoicpal	his seat with back rest
motelchiuhtzin	Motelchiuhtzin
governador	governor
xuchiquentzin	Xochiquentzin
governador	governor

vanitzin	Huanitzin

[fol. 52r col. B]

don Diego tevetzquititzin	Don Diego Tehuetzquititzin
don xp̃oual	Don Cristóbal

PARAGRAPH 1B ILLUSTRATIONS

tlaltecatzin	Tlaltecatzin
icoçoyaoalol	his circular fan device of yellow parrot feathers
ytlauitol	his bow
ymaçayevatilma	his deerskin cape
yquauhxiuicpal	his seat of tree branches
techotlalatzin	Techotlalatzin
icoçoyaoalol	his circular fan device of yellow parrot feathers
itlauitol	his bow
ymaçayeoatilma	his deerskin cape
iquauhxiuicpal	his seat of tree branches
ixtlilxuchitl	Ixtlilxochitl
icoçoyoyavalol	his circular fan device of yellow parrot feathers
itlauitol	his bow
imaçayevatilma	his deerskin cape
ixiuicpal	his herbage seat
neçavalcoyotl	Nezhaualcoyotl
ixiuhtzon	his turquoise [mosaic] headdress
ixiuhyacamiuh	his turquoise nose-rod
ixiuhtilma	his turquoise [blue] cape
techilnavayo	edged by a red border with circles
ytepotzoicpal	his seat with back rest
neçavalpili	Nezahualpilli
ixiuhtzon	his turquoise [mosaic] headdress
ixiuhtilma	his turquoise [blue] cape
techilnavayo	edged by a red border with circles
itepotzoicpal	his seat with back rest

[fol. 52v col. B]

Cacamatzin	Cacamatzin
ixiuhtzon	his turquoise [mosaic] headdress
ixiuhtilma	his turquoise [blue] cape
tetlapal	red (or colored) border
itepotzoicpal	his seat with back rest
coanacochtli	Coanacochtli
ixiuhtzon	his turquoise [mosaic] headdress

ytlatlapaltilma	his varicolored cape
ytepotzoicpal	his seat with back rest
tecocoltzin	Tecocoltzin
ytlatlapaltilma	his varicolored cape
ytepotzoicpal	his seat with back rest
ixtlilxuchitl	Ixtlilxochitl
ytlatlapaltilma	his varicolored cape
ytepotzoicpal	his seat with back rest

[fol. 53r col. B]

yoyontzin	Yoyontzin
ytlatlapaltilma	his varicolored cape
itepotzoicpal	his seat with back rest
tetlavevetzquititzi	Tetlahuehuetzquititzin
itlatlapaltilma	his varicolored cape
itepotzoicpal	his seat with back rest
Don ant°. tlauitoltzin	Don Antonio Tlahuitoltzin
itlatlapaltilma	his varicolored cape
ytepotzoicpal	his seat with back rest
Don hernando pimentel. yuian	Don Hernando Pimentel the temperate
itlatlapaltilma	his varicolored cape
ytepotzoicpal	his seat with back rest

PARAGRAPH 1C ILLUSTRATIONS

maçatzin	Mazatzin
ycoçoyaoalol	his circular fan device of yellow parrot feathers
ytlauitol	his bow
ymaçayevatilma	his deerskin cape
yxiuicpal	his herbage seat
tochintecutli	Tochintecuhtli
ycoçoyavalol	his circular fan device of yellow parrot feathers
ytlauitol	his bow
ymaçayeoatilma	his deerskin cape
yçacaycpal	his grass seat
ayotzintecutli	Ayotzintecuhtli
ycoçoyavalol	his circular fan device of yellow parrot feathers
itlauitol	his bow
ymaçayeoatilma	his deerskin cape
ixiuicpal	his herbage seat
quatlauice	Cuatlahuice
ycoçoyaoalol	his circular fan device of yellow parrot feathers
ymaçayevatilma	his deerskin cape

içacaicpal	his grass seat
totomutzin	Totomochtzin
içocoyavalol	his circular fan device of yellow parrot feathers
imaçayevatilma	his deerskin cape
içacaicpal	his grass seat
yautzin	Yaotzin
itlatlapaltilma	his varicolored cape
ytepotzoicpal	his seat with back rest

[fol. 53v col. B]

xilotzin	Xilotzin
icoçoyaoalol	his circular fan device of yellow parrot feathers
ixiuhtilma	his turquoise [blue] cape
techilnavayo	edged by a red border with circles
itepotzoicpal	his seat with back rest
ytlacauhtzin	Itlacauhtzin
icoçoyaoalol	his circular fan device of yellow parrot feathers
ixiuhtilma	his turquoise [blue] cape
techilnavayo	edged by a red border with circles
itepotzoicpal	his seat with back rest
tlaçolyautzin	Tlazolyaotzin
ixiuhtzon	his turquoise [mosaic] headdress
ixiuhtilma	his turquoise [blue] cape
itepotzoicpal	his seat with back rest
tzontemoctzin	Tzontemoctzin
ixiuhtzon	his turquoise [mosaic] headdress
ixiuhtilma	his turquoise [blue] cape
techilnaoayo	edged by a red border with circles
itepotzoicpal	his seat with back rest
Cuitlavatzin	Cuitlahuatzin
ixiuhtzon	his turquoise [mosaic] headdress
ixiuhtilma	his turquoise [blue] cape
techilnavayo	edged by a red border with circles
itepotzoicpal	his seat with back rest
itzapocuetzin	Itzapocuetzin
itlatlapaltilma	his varicolored cape
itepotzoicpal	his seat with back rest
ça no cuitlaoatzin	[Another] also [named] Cuitlahuatzin
itlatlapaltilma	his varicolored cape
itepotzoicpal	his seat with back rest

PARAGRAPH 2

Jnic ome parrapho in itoca in ixq'chti in itepaleuicava, in tlatoque, ioan teupixque catca.

Mixcoatlailtzin tecutli
tolnaoaltecutzintli
mexicaltecutzintli
atlauhcatzintli

Second paragraph: the names of all the ruler's aides and the keepers of the gods.[1]

Lord Cloud Serpent Sower of Discord.
Lord Beside the Rushes.
Lord of the House of the Mexica.
Esteemed One of the Gorge.[2]

[fol. 54r col. A]

quauhnochtli
vecatzin achcauhtlj
tlacotzin achcauhtli
acolnaoacatl achcauhtzintli
tolnaoacatl achcauhtzintli
atzaqualtzin achcauhtzintli

Nica cate in vel iehoanti tlatoque in mochi quicaquia in ixquich mochioaya.

Jn ixiptla mochiuhticatca in vitzilopuchtli Tlacatecutzintli.

tlacochcalcatzintli.
çioacoatzintli
vitznaoac tlacatecutzintli.
vitznaoa tlailotlacatzintli.

Eagle Prickly Pear.
Constable Distant.
Constable Stick.
Constable Beside the Shoulder.
Constable Beside the Rushes.
Constable Dam.

Here are the rulers who heard all, everything that took place.

He whose concern it was to be Huitzilopochtli's representative was the Lord of Men.

Chief of the House of Arrows.
Serpent Woman.
Lord of Men Beside the Thorns.[3]
Sower of Discord Beside the Thorns.

PARAGRAPH 3

Jnic iii parrapho ipan mitoa in izquitlamantli in ipan tlatoaya in tlatoque.

Third paragraph, in which are told all the different things the ruler attended to.[1]

1. This paragraph constitutes a valuable listing of the titles of various secular and religious functionaries in the late pre-Hispanic Central Mexican sociopolitical system. This titulary was quite extensive and can be reconstructed from a wide variety of sources; the full list has never been thoroughly compiled or analyzed. The correct translations and connotations of various of these titles pose challenging problems. Some appear to refer to particular places, others to deities and ethnic groups. The illustrations portray (1) four functionaries on woven backed thrones, *tzotzoicpalli*, apparently conferring and/or giving commands; (2) the "constables," the *achcauhtin*, executing condemned criminals by strangulation and skull bashing; and (3) four other functionaries conferring with or assisting a lord who wears, as befits his rank, the turquoise mosaic diadem, the *xiuhuitzolli*. It is difficult to determine with precision the source of the information in this paragraph. The reference to the *ixiptla*, the "representative," of Huitzilopochtli, and one of the titles, *Mexicaltecuhtzintli*, might point to a Mexica provenience, at least in part, although it is clear that these titles were in widespread use throughout the Nahua-speaking area at the time of the Conquest.

2. Two illegible titles follow at the foot of the page (*Quauh-* and another totally illegible). However, they may have been deleted in order to begin the list on the following page.

3. Between this entry and the next, a line of text has been painted out; it is only partially legible.

1. This paragraph contains a summary, from the native point of view, of some of the chief duties and responsibilities of the Conquest-period Central Mexican ruling elite. The left column of the original manuscript lists single words or very brief phrases; the right column consists of a running text that deals with the topic more comprehensively. Of special interest are the descriptions of the ritual rubber ball game, *ollamaliztli*, and the most popular gambling game,

in poliuiz altepetl
yauyutl
miquiztli
cuicatl maçeoaliztli
tlapializtli
tlachtli vlli
tianquiztli
patolli
tetlatocatlaliliztli
tetecutlaliliztli
in aço mayanalo
in aço necvcvlo
nextlavaloz
copaltemaloz
altepepializtli
vtli tlacuiliztli
tlachpanaliztli
netequioacatecoz
yn aço teumicoaz in aço çe maçeuali miquiz yn ixpan diablo.

That cities be destroyed.
War.
Death.
Singing, dancing.
Guarding.
The ball court; the rubber [ball].
The market.
The *patolli* game.
The installing of a ruler.
The installing of lords.
If there is a famine.
If there is a plague.
That payment [to the gods] be made.[2]
That copal be offered.
The guarding of the city.
Removing [filth] from the roads.
Sweeping.
The assembling of the seasoned warriors.
If there was to be sacrificing of captives; if a commoner was to be sacrificed before the devil.

[fol. 54v col. A]

tlacazcaltiliztli tlacaoapavaliztli
tlenamaquiztli
tlatzmolintli
neçoliztli
tlacoquixtiliztli
neçoçoliztli

The education of people; the instruction of people.
Offerings of fire.
Offering of shoots.
Drawing of blood.
Passing of twigs.
Stringing together.[3]

[fol. 54r col. B]

Jntencopa in tlatoqz iehoan quitzontequi, auh in oq̃tzotecque, niman quioalnotza in tlatlacateca in tlatlacochcalca yautequioaqz, nima ie ic quinaoatia micqui polozque, ce, altepetl inic mochioaz yavyutl auh in oaçito yn ompa mochioaz yavyutl nimã oc cepa iehoati tlamama in tlatlacateca in iuh mo-

By order of the rulers, these made the decision [to wage war against a certain city], and when they had made the decision, they summoned the commanders of men, the chiefs of the house of arrows, the seasoned warriors. Then they ordered death—that the city be destroyed, that war be made. And

patolli. Sahagún later, in Tlatelolco, compiled more data covering much the same ground, and, as was his usual custom, preferring them to this *Primeros Memoriales* material, he incorporated them in Book 8 of the *Historia* (Sahagún 1950–1982, Part IX; 1988, II: 493–536).

2. *Nextlavaloz:* This "payment" connoted sacrificial rituals, particularly the offering of hearts and blood, the food and drink of the gods. See note 2, Chapter I, Paragraph 2A.

3. *Neçoçoliztli:* Possibly this means the stringing together of flowers, as in the *veintena* of Tlaxochimaco (see Sahagún 1981: 108; 1988, I: 141).

chioaz yn yavyutl, inic vel poliviz yn altepetl.

when they had gone to arrive at the place where war was to be made, then once again the commanders of men took captives.[4] Thus, they were to make war so that cities were indeed destroyed.

Jn aca mictiloz iehoanti quitlatzontequiliaya in tlatoqz, auh in otlatzonteque; niman ie quioalnotza in tecutlatoque quinavatia inic quelacuaoazqz, nimã q'choquilia q'ticavia quipotonia q'lpilia tilmatli in iquimiliuhca mochioa; auh in tecutlatoqz niman quioalnotza, in intemicticaoa in tlatoqz, inic comictia aço quimecania aço quiquavivitequi.

When someone was to be put to death, the rulers sentenced him. And when they had done the sentencing,[5] the judges then summoned [the culprit]. They sent for him in order to give him courage. They wept for him, they consoled him, they comforted him, they gave him solace.[6] And the judges summoned the rulers' executioners. They put him to death thus: they either hanged him or beat his head.

Jnic cuicoia in aço maçeoaloz in aço nanacaqualoia no iehoatl quimati in tlatoque in tlei cuicatl meoaz quinaoatia in cuicanime.

For there to be singing, when there was to be dancing or there was the eating of mushrooms,[7] the rulers also arranged which songs were to be sung. They gave orders to the singers.

Jn tlapializtli iehoanti quitoa in tlatoque inic novia tlatlapialoz in tlatoca, in calmecac, in tequioacacali, in achcauhcali, in telpuchcali auh in apetlac in otlica ioan y yauteco chaneque q'navatia inic yautlapialoz inic ça mochipa yoaltica tlacatica in tlapialoz.

Guarding: The rulers ordered that all places be constantly guarded: the palace, the *calmecac,* the house of the seasoned warriors, the house of the constables, the house of the youths, and at the *apetlac,*[8] on the roads. And the inhabitants were organized for war; [the rulers] ordered that sentinels were to be posted; that guard was to be kept constantly, by night, by day.

Inic mochioaya in tlavllamaloz intencopa in tlatoqz nemia yn imollacaoa, quipia, in olli, in ollamaloni, quipia in queceoatl maiehoatl, nelpiloni, auh intla iehoa vllamazque in tlatoque niman ie ic mononotza in tlei quimotlanilizque in aço chalchivitl aço teucuitlatl aço quetzalli anoço tlacotli anoço xomoivitilmatli; auh in omononotz-

Thus was it done when the ball game was played by order of the rulers.[9] There were their ball players, those who guarded the rubber [ball], the ball with which the game was played, those who guarded the leather hip-guards, the leather gloves, the belts.[10] And if the rulers were to play ball, then they decided what they were to wager, perhaps

4. *Tlamama:* read *tlama.*

5. *Otlatzonteque:* read *otlatzontecque.*

6. For *q'tiçavia,* read *quitiçauia.* Olmos (1875: 213) gives *teticauia* as a metaphor for "hacer misericordia la persona o el señor." It would appear that *quilpili, tilmatli in iquimiliuhca mochioa* (he ties a cape on him that becomes as his shroud) has similar meaning.

7. *Nanacaqualoia:* "The eating of mushrooms" refers to the ingesting of the hallucinogenic mushroom *teonanacatl,* a common feature of certain ceremonies and during banquets.

8. *Apetlac,* literally, "reed mat of water," was the flat area, the platform, in front of the Templo Mayor of Huitzilopochtli and Tlaloc (see Sahagún 1950–1982, Part X [Book 9]: 66; 1988, II: 574).

9. *Inic mochicaya in tlavllamaloz intencopa in tlatoqz nemia yn imollacaoa:* For the Conquest-period Central Mexican version of the Mesoamerican rubber ball game, *ollamaliztli,* see the collection of texts from the relevant primary sources in Taladoire 1981: 560–597.

10. *Queceoatl (quecehuatl), maiehoatl (maiehuatl), nelpiloni:* These were items of leather protective body equipment worn by the ball players, the *ollamani* or *ollamaloni.*

Paragraph 3

que yn oquinanamictiqz niman quitlatlalia tlachquac nenecoc. nima ie ic momana quimomaca in queceoatl i maiehoatl i nelpiloni nimã ie ic peoa vllamalo auh in teulalataque necoc tlachticpac vnoqz xeliuhtoqz moch eoanti in pipilti anoço tetecuti anoço tequioaqz auh i necoc tlachticpac vnoqz cecẽtlapal intech pui mollama in mixnamictimani auh necoc vnoc in tlachmaitl itech mamani mitoa tlachtemalacatl cocoyoqui; auh in ac iehoatl tlacalaquiz vtetla iehoatl quicuiz in ixquich tlatquitl Auh mitoaya neneuhqui y yavyutl in ollamaliztli vel vncã nemimictilo nequatzatzayanalo auh intla aca atlei quitlanitoa namacoya tlacotli mochioaz.

green stones, or gold, or quetzal feathers, or a slave,[11] or else duck feather capes. And when they had decided, when they were in accord, they placed them on both ends of the court. Then the leather hip-guards, the leather gloves, the belts were given out; [the players] took them up. Then the playing of the ball game began. And the spectators[12] sat above the ball court on both sides; all the noblemen, or lords, or seasoned warriors sat divided into two sections. And on each side above the ball court, each on his own side, sat the contenders to whom the ball game pertained. And to each side of the court[13] was attached a [circular stone] called *tlachtemalacatl,* which had a hole [in the center]. And he who put [the ball] through it, won the game. He took all the goods. And it was said that the ball game was like war: one indeed was frequently killed there; heads were constantly split open. And if someone who had nothing lost in the game, he was sold; he would become a slave.

Jnic quimocuitlaviaya in tlatoqz iehoan quimatia in iuh tlapatiyoaz in ixquich monamaca tianquizco quinaoatiaya in puchtecatlatoque in quenin tlapatioaz iehoanti quimati in puchtecatlatoqz in iuh tlamaniz tianquizco yn ayac texixicoz auh intla itla ytlacaviz iehoanti quitzacutiazque in puchtecatlatoqz.

The rulers saw to, they determined how all that was sold in the market was to be priced. The merchant-rulers ordered what the prices were to be; the merchant-rulers determined how the customs were to be established in the market. No one was to cheat another, and if anyone did anything wrong, the merchant-rulers were to punish him.

Auh in patolli ça vel neneuhqui in tlachco mochioaya yn ollamaniztli ça no vmpa mochioaya in patolli micuiloa in tlalpantli anoço petlatl in omicuilo vncã quipoa inic netlanivaya yn etl nauhtetl cecetlapal mixcoyouia y patoaya q'maxaqualoa anoço quicemana inic motlania yn iuh mochioaya in tlachco Ça vel no iuh mochivaya nemimictilo nequatzatzayanaloya.

And *patolli*[14] is much similar to the ball game played on the ball courts; *patolli* is also played there. [Widely spaced lines] were painted on the ground, or a reed mat was painted. There they counted [the score] by which [the game] was won. There were four beans; holes were bored on the surface of each side. When they played *patolli,* they rubbed them [from] between their hands or they cast them in order for the game to be won. Just as was done on the ball court, so also indeed was it done [here]; there was continual injuring; heads were constantly split open.

11. *Tlacotli:* possibly to be read *tlaçotli,* "precious things."

12. *Teulalataque:* read as *te-ollalla-ittaque.*

13. *Tlachmaitl: Maitl,* hand, and by extension arm, also meant side or flank. Compare Molina 1944, Part II: 1v, *acalmaitl, costado de navio.*

14. *Patolli:* On this most popular of the contact-period Central Mexican games of chance, see Caso 1924–1927.

[fol. 54v col. B]

Jquac intla çe vmic in tlatoani iehoati quimatia in pipilti in tequioaque in aqui quipepenazque in aqui quitlatocatlalizque.

If at some time a ruler died, the noblemen, the seasoned warriors determined whom they were to elect, whom they were to install as ruler.

Ça no iehanti quimati in tlatoqz in aquique motecutecazque inic tecutlatoqz iezqz imomoztlae quicaquizqz in tlei in innetequipachol y maceoalti

These rulers[15] also designated those who were to be elevated to [the rank of] lord, so that they would become judges to hear every day what were the afflictions of the commoners.

Jntla vxivitl intla iexivitl in atle pixcoz cēca momauhtiaya in tlatoque nimā quimelaquavaya quichoq'tiaya i maceoalti q'milviaya ma metecaca ma nopalacaca ma q'tocaca in çimatl y ma çacamoca.

If for two years, if for three years nothing was harvested, the rulers became very fearful. Then they gave the commoners courage, they made the commoners weep. They told them they must plant magueys, they must plant cactus, they must plant *cimatl,*[16] they must cultivate the land.

Jn omoma in cocoliztli y novia in quitzacutimani ca no quimelaquavaya in maceoalti.

When plague spread, when it covered all places, they also gave courage to the commoners.

Jn iquac intlacamo quiavi in tonalmani in titonalvaqui intecopa in tlatoque inic nextlaoaloya y novian tepeticpac ic mitoaya tlatlauhtilo in tlaloqz: No ioan ic tlanavatia in tlachpanaloz vtlica ioan in tepetl quitlecaviticac yn otli mitoaya teuchpatli imovi in tlaloque.

If at some time it did not rain, if there was constant sun, if we were perishing from drought, it was by order of the rulers that blood sacrifices were performed on all the mountaintops. Thus, it was said, the Tlalocs were supplicated. Moreover, they also ordered that on the roads there be sweeping. And the roads that went up the mountains were called sacred roads; they were the roads of the Tlalocs.

PARAGRAPH 4
[fol. 54v col. A]

Jnic. iiii. parrapho ipan mitoa in izquitlamantli in itlaqual in imauh in tlatoqz yoan in tlaçocioapipiltin.

Fourth paragraph. In it are told the kinds of food and drink of the rulers and esteemed noblewomen.[1]

Tlacuelpacholi tlaxcali chiltecpimoli inamic.

Large folded tortillas with hot chili[2] sauce.

15. *Iehanti:* read *yehuantin.*

16. *Cimatl:* Variously identified botanically as *Phaseolus coccineus* (Linn.), *Phaseolus multiflorus* (Wild.), *Canavalia villosa* (Benth.), or *Desmodium amplifolium.* See Dressler 1953: 143: Sahagún 1950–1982, Part XII (Book 11): 125. It was ingested as a purge and, when cooked, was also eaten.

1. This paragraph comprises a useful listing of some of the most important items of food and drink of the rulers and members of the aristocracy. Sahagún later, in Tlatelolco, collected a somewhat similar but more extensive list that he included as Chapter 13 of Book 8 of the *Historia* (Sahagún 1950–1982, Part IX [Book 8]: 37–40; 1988, II: 512–517). The richness and variety of the Central Mexican native cuisine at contact is readily apparent from these two listings.

2. *Chiltecpin: Capsicum microcarpum* D. C. (Santamaría 1959: 388).

tlamatzoali tlaxcali miltomamoli inamic.	Folded tortillas with wild tomato[3] sauce.
quatecuicuilli tamali patzcalmoli inamic.	Tamales with a shell represented on them, with a sauce of small chilis, and ground squash seeds.
tlaçiocuepalli tlaxcali totolcozchilmoli inamic.	Broken up tortillas with a sauce of turkey hen and yellow chilis.
tlaxcalpacholli chilchotlatzatzayã inamic.	Dark tortillas with sliced hot green chilis.
nacatamali tlaxcalmimili ayoachmoli inamic	Meat tamales [and] thick, long tortillas with a sauce of gourd seeds.[4]
xocotamali totolatonilli ynamic	Fruit tamales with stewed turkey hen.
tlapacholi tlaxcalçoyatl chiltotocuitlamoli ynamic. iztac michi mochilcozuia, in xuuili mochiltecpiuia in cueyatl mochilchouia atepucatl mochiltecpiuia atozneneme moztayo inaya.	Yucca tortillas[5] covered with a sauce of chili and turkey rump; yellow-chilied white fish; red-hot-chilied small freshwater fish;[6] hot-green-chilied frogs; red-hot-chilied tadpoles; "water parrot"[7] steeped in brine.
xuchiayo cacauatl in tiqui	We drink chocolate with ground up flowers.
quauhnecuyo cacaoatl in tiqui	We drink chocolate with wild honey.
vei ynacazyo cacaoatl in tiqui	We drink chocolate with big-ear spice.[8]
amo tle neliuhqui cacaoatl in tiqui	We drink chocolate with nothing beaten in.
vllo cacaoatl in tiqui	We drink chocolate with [liquid] rubber.
temecaxuchio cacaoatl in tiqui	We drink chocolate with vanilla.[9]
tlachichioalcacaoatl in tiqui	We drink imitation chocolate.
vcyo cacaoatl	Chocolate with *octli.*
vctli vino.	Octli; wine.
chilo cacaoatl.	Chocolate with chilis.
tlilxuchio cacaoatl	Chocolate with vanilla.[10]
yuluxuchio cacaoatl.	Chocolate with magnolia blossoms.[11]

[fol. 55r]

J ça motlamachtiani in quiqua	He who is only rich eats:
yaoaliuhqui tlaxcalli	Round tortillas.
tamalli cuechiuhqui	Ground up tamales.
michin cueyatl	Fish; frogs.
axulutl atepucatl	Salamander;[12] tadpole.

3. *Miltomamoli (miltoma(tl)-moli: miltomatl:* Compare Santamaría 1959: 385.

4. *Ayoachmoli (ayo[tli]-ach[tli]-moli:* seeds of the *ayotli, Cucurbita* sp. (Sahagún 1950–1982, Part XII [Book 11]: 288).

5. *Tlaxcalçoyatl:* see Alcocer 1938: 368. *Çoyatl* was also a term applied to palm species and to agaves.

6. *Xouili, xouilin:* Known today as *juil* or *juile,* it can be identified botanically as *Cyprinus americanus* (Santamaría 1959: 647).

7. *Atozneneme:* unidentified aquatic creatures.

8. *Vey nacaztli (huey nacaztli): Cymbopetalum penduliflorum,* a peppery spice (Santamaría 1959: 774).

9. *Temecaxuchio:* probably the same as *mecaxochitl, Vanilla planifolia, V. flagrans,* or *Piper* sp. (Sahagún 1950–1982, Part XII [Book 11]: 192).

10. *Tlilxuchio (tlilxochitl): Vanilla planifolia* (Sahagún 1950–1982, Part XII [Book 11]: 198).

11. *Yuluxuchio (yolloxochitl): Talauma mexicana* Don (Sahagún 1950–1982, Part XII [Book 11]: 201).

12. *Axulutl: Amblystoma tigrinum* L., *Proteus mexicanus, Sideron humboldti* (Sahagún 1950–1982, Part XII [Book 11]: 64).

acuçiltin atozneneme.
Jn maceoali quiqua
tlaxcalpapaya
amo chipaoac tlaxcali tomamoli inamic
metzalaxcali chilmoli inamic
pulocatlaxcali iztayotl inamic.
nopalveve
exotlaxcali
mexcali
tlaquauhyutl
çimatl
ichpuli
tziviquilitl.
izcauitl
cuculi
vcuiltamali
vcuilaçoli
michpiltamali
tecuitlatl

aoauhtli
axaxayacatl
vcuiliztac

Freshwater shrimps;[13] "water parrots."
The commoner eats:
Bits of tortillas.
Dingy tortillas with tomato sauce.
Maguey pith tortillas with chili sauce.
Tortillas of [amaranth] chaff[14] with brine.
Old nopal cactus [fruit?].
String bean tortillas.
Baked maguey.
Hardened things.
Cimatl [root].[15]
Sow-thistle.[16]
[Unidentified cooked] water plant.
Water worms.
Waterfly larva nests.
Worm tamales.
Worm excretions.
Fish roe tamales.
Cakes of dried waterfly eggs that adhere to rocks.[17]
Waterfly eggs.[18]
Waterflies.[19]
White worms.

PARAGRAPH 5
[fol. 55v]

Jnic v. parrapho. ipan mitoa in izquitlamantli in inechichioaya in tlatoque ioã in cioapipiltin.

Fifth paragraph, in which are told the kinds of ways of adornment of rulers and noblewomen.[1]

13. *Acoçiltin: Cambarus, Cambarellus montezumae* (Santamaría 1959: 26).

14. *Pulocatlaxcali: polocatl: tamo, paja menuda* (Molina 1944, Part II: 83v).

15. See note 16, Paragraph 3.

16. *Ichpuli:* defined in Molina (1944, Part II: 32v) as *cerraja, yerua.*

17. *Tecuitlatl:* so according to Santamaría 1959: 1020. In Sahagún 1950–1982, Part XII [Book 11]: 65, it is a congealed mass of lake scum roasted on ashes.

18. *Aoauhtli:* Santamaría 1959: 42; Alcocer 1938: 372–373; Hernández 1959–1984, II: 392.

19. *Axaxayacatl: Ephidra californica* Torrey or possibly *Coixca* sp. (Sahagún 1950–1982, Part XII [Book 11]: 64).

1. This paragraph lists the names of thirty-seven male capes, *tilmatli,* and eight female shifts, *huipilli,* along with various techniques of male and female adornment. The colorful, highly variegated designs on these capes and shifts, worn by members of the upper class, particularly on ritual occasions, connoted significant ideological concepts connected with the religious-ritual system. Later, in Tlatelolco, Sahagún collected a similar list of the names of fifty-seven *tilmatli*—adding thirteen loincloths, *maxtlatl*—that overlaps with this one putatively gathered in Tepepolco. It was included as Chapter 8 in Book 8 of the *Historia* (Sahagún 1950–1982, Part IX [Book 8]: 23–25; 1988, II: 505–506 [much truncated]). He also collected another list of the names of thirteen *huipilli*—adding nine skirts, *cueitl,* and five types of ear plugs, *nacochtli*—plus various female beautification methods, to which he devoted Chapter 15 of the *Historia* (Sahagún 1950–1982, Part IX [Book 8]: 47–48; 1988, II: 521–522 [truncated]). Only three of the *huipilli* and six of the *cueitl* were illustrated in the *Florentine Codex.* In the cognate colonial pictorials, *Codex Magliabechiano* (1903, 1904, 1970, 1983: fols. 2v–8v) and *Codex Tudela* (1980: 85v–88v), a number of decorated capes are illustrated, forty-five (named in Nahuatl and Spanish) in the former and

Axayacayo tilmatli.	Cape with water-face design.[2]
quauhpapatlacyo tilmatli	Cape with flying eagle design.
yuitemalacayo tilmatli	Cape with design of stone discs, worked in feathers.
axayacayo tilmatli	Cape with water-face design.[3]
avitzoyo tilmatli	Cape with *ahuitzotl* design.[4]
tlachquauhyo tilmatli	Cape with ball court eagle design.
tonatiuhyo tilmatli	Cape with sun design.
tenchilnavayo tilmatli	Cape edged by a red border with circles.
teuizquixuchio tilmatli	Cape edged with a border of *Bourreria* flowers.[5]
vacalxuchio tilmatl	Cape with philodendron flowers.[6]
tlapaltecuxuchio tilmatli	Cape with the lordly red flower design.
vitzitzilxuchio tilmatli	Cape with *Loeselia* flower design.[7]
tentlapalo tilmatli	Cape with red border.
quauhtzontecomayo tilmatli	Cape with eagle head design.
vceloevatilmatli	Jaguar skin cape.
cuetlachevatilmatli.	Wolf skin cape.[8]
miceoatilmatli	Mountain lion skin cape.
vcutocheoatilmatli	Bobcat skin cape.
cuyoeoatilmatli	Coyote skin cape.
acucuxuchio tilmatli	Cape with dahlia design.[9]
teucuyo tilmatli	Cape with melon cactus design.[10]

---

thirty-six (unnamed) in the latter, both sets derived from a common source (see Anders 1970: 47–50; Tudela de la Orden 1980: 152–162; Boone 1983: 168–174). A number of other *tilmatli,* rendered as annual tribute to Mexico Tenochtitlan, are depicted in the *Matrícula de Tributos* (1980) and its cognate, Part 3 of the *Codex Mendoza* (1992; see Anawalt in Vol. 1, pp. 129–145, Appendix I-J). The classic discussion of upper-class Central Nexican contact-period costume and adornment, focusing on the decorated *tilmatli*—including his German translations of the Nahuatl nomenclature of this paragraph and that of Chapter 8 of Book 8 of Sahagún's *Historia*—is that of Eduard Seler (1902–1923, II: 512–535).

Two large illustrations accompany this paragraph: a lord attired in a rich blue cloak, a variant of the *xiuhtlalpilli,* the "royal cloak" (Anawalt 1993b) with the distinctive "eyed" *(tenixyo)* border. He also wears the *quetzaltlalpiloni,* the hair binder with double quetzal feather tassels (see Seler 1902–1923, II: 536), gold ear plugs, an elaborate gold and greenstone necklace, and a multicolored loincloth. Fronting him are depictions of two capes with complex, multicolored designs, the upper one also displaying the *tenixyo* border. The other illustration is of a noble lady wearing a striped *huipilli,* a multicolored checkered skirt, and an elaborate gold necklace.

2. *Axayacayo:* or, possibly, waterfly. See note 18, Paragraph 4.

3. *Axayacayo:* This is a repeat of the designation of the first cloak in the list.

4. *Ahuitzotl:* a partly fantastic creature but possibly based principally on the water opossum, *Chironectes panamensis,* as Eric Thompson suggested (see Nicholson and Quiñones Keber 1983: 120). Compare Sahagún 1950–1982, Part XII [Book 11]: 68: *Lutra felina.*

5. *Teuixquixuchio (izquixochitl):* "popcorn flower," *Bourreria formosa, B. huanita, B. littoralis* (Sahagún 1950–1982, Part XII [Book 11]: 202).

6. *Vacalxuchio (huacalxochitl):* probably *Philodendron affine* Hemsl. or *Philodendron pseudoradiatum* Matuda (Sahagún 1950–1982, Part XII [Book 11]: 209; Nicholson 1988a: 126–129).

7. *Vizitzilxuchio (huitzitzilxochitl): Loeselia cocciniea* Don or *Toluifera pereirae* (Klotz) (Sahagún 1950–1982, Part XII [Book 11]: 192).

8. *Cuetlachevatilmatli (cuetlachtli):* This animal has been variously identified, but the strongest case can probably be made for the wolf, an animal now extinct in Central Mexico but once common there (see Nicholson and Quiñones Keber 1983: 149; Leopold 1959: 399–405).

9. *Acucuxucho (acocoxochitl): Dahlia coccinea Cav.* (Sahagún 1950–1982, Part XII [Book 11]: 199).

10. *Teucuyo (teocomitl): Mamillaria tetracancantha* Salm-Dyck; *Ferrocactus* sp. (Sahagún 1950–1982, Part XII [Book 11]: 218).

cacaloxuchio tilmatli	Cape with plumeria flower design.[11]
vmixuchio tilmatli	Cape with polianthes flower design.[12]
tlacuxuchio tilmatli	Cape with bouvardia flower design.[13]
hecauitequi tilmatli	Cape with wind-struck design.
xicalculiuhqui tilmatli	Cape with step meander design.
cuetlaxuchio tilmatli	Cape with poinsettia design.[14]
coatzontecomayo tilmatli	Cape with snake head design.
itznepaniuhqui tilmatli	Cape with crossed obsidian knives design.
quapacho tilmatli	Tawny cape.
xiuhtlatl pili tilmatl	Cape with blue knots.[15]
culutlatl pili tilmatli	Cape with scorpion knots.[16]
quapachtlaxuchyo tilmatli	Cape with tawny stripes.
xumoyuitetlapalo tilmatli	Cape with duck feathers and red border.
iztac xumoyuitl tilmatli	Cape with white duck feathers.
tlapaliuitemalacaio tilmatli	Cape with red feather circles.
iztac yuitilmatli tliltic iuitilmatli.	White feather cape; black feather cape.

[fol. 56r]

xumoiuiuipilli xicalculiuhqui cueitl quinamiqui.	Duck feather shift with step meander skirt.
acucuxuchio vipilli miavacueitl .q.	Shift of dahlia design with skirt of maize flower design.
aculamachyo vipili tenacazyo cueitl .q.	Shoulder-embroidered shift with corner stone design.
putocatlacunepaniuhq' vipili tlilpitzavac cueitl .q.	Shift of crossed feathered twig design with skirt designed with fine lines.
cacaluxuchio vipili cacamoliuhq' cueitl .q.	Shift of plumeria flower design with the skirt like a bed covering.
xuchiteyo vipili iztac cueitl .q.	Flower-bordered shift with white skirt.
quapachyo vipili vcelucueitl .q.	Tawny shift with jaguar skirt.
ypiluyo vipili quapachyo cueitl .q.	Shift with its pendants with tawny skirt.
vel moximaya	Well did they beautify themselves.
matzotzocultiaya	They arranged themselves with the long girl's lock of hair on one side.
motlateteçiluiaya	They cropped their hair.
mixquatecpiltiaya	They left a tuft of hair over the forehead.
motzotzoquaquauhtiaya	They made hornlike tufts of hair.
quiayacanepanoa in itzon	They cut their hair short to reach their noses.

11. *Cacaloxuchio (cacaloxochitl): Plumeria rubra, Tigridia pavonia* (Sahagún 1950–1982, Part XII [Book 11]: 205).

12. *Omixuchio (omixochitl): Polianthes tuberosa, P. mexicana* (Sahagún 1950–1982, Part XII [Book 11]: 198).

13. *Tlacuxuchio (tlacoxochitl): Bouvardia tormifolia* Schl. (Sahagún 1950–1982, Part XII [Book 11]: 208).

14. *Cuetlaxuchio (cuetlaxochitl): Euphorbia (Poinsettia) pulcherrima* Willd. (Sahagún 1950–1982, Part XII [Book 11]: 203).

15. *Xiuhtlatl pili tilmatl:* read *xiuhtlalpilli tilmatli.*

16. *Culutlatli pili:* read *colotlalpilli.*

mopalinemi, xiuhquiltica	They go about staining themselves with indigo.[17]
mixtecuçauia	They apply yellow ochre to their faces.
mixtlapaloatzaluia tecuiluaztica	With a stamp they apply red coloring to their faces.
motlatlamiaoa.	Teeth are darkened.
motlanochezvia.	They stain their teeth with cochineal.
tziquaquatinemi	They go about chewing chicle.

PARAGRAPH 6

Jnic. vi. parrapho ypan mitoa in izquitlamantli in inechichioaya tlatoque in iquac maçeva.	Sixth paragraph, in which are told the kinds of ways of adornment of the rulers when they danced.[1]
quetzalalpiloni	[Head] band with quetzal feather tassels.[2]
teucuitlamatlepitztli	Hand cast in gold.
teucuitlanacochtli	Golden ear plugs.
chalchiuhtẽtetl	Green stone lip plug.
teucuitlatepiloli	Golden lip pendant.
teucuitlayacaquaztli	Golden nose plate.
chalchiuhcozcatl	Necklace of green stones.
quetzalmacopili	Quetzal feather arm band.
teucuitlacotzevatl	Golden band for the calf of the leg.
xupepetlactli	Gleaming anklet.
quetzalmacpanitl	Quetzal feather banner held in the hand.
quetzalquaquauitl	Quetzal feather horns.
teucuitlachipulcozcatl.	Necklace of golden beads and small seashells.

[fol. 56v]

Tlepiazyo maxtlatl	Breechclout with torch-holder design.
yvitemalacayo maxtlatl	Breechclout with disc design in feathers.
nochpalli maxtlatl	Carmine colored breechclout.
puztequi maxtlatl	Bicolored breechclout.
tepuçuqui maxtlatl	Breechclout with filigree border.
yacatlamachyo maxtlatl	Breechclout with embroidered ends.

17. *Xiuhquiltica (xiuhquilitl):* indigo *(Indigofero añil)* (Santamaría 1959: 639 *[jiquilite]*).

1. This paragraph consists of a listing of thirteen luxurious items of adornment (including headdresses, ear, lip, and nose plugs, arm and leg bands, and a necklace) worn by the lords during ritual dances. They were crafted from prized feathers, gold, and precious green stones *(chalchihuitl).* Seler (1902–1923, II: 535–36) was the first to translate and discuss some of the designations for these adornment items in his classic article on pre-Hispanic attire and insignia of social and military rank. In addition, nine types of decorated breechclouts conclude the list. Typically, Sahagún later collected in Tlatelolco an overlapping but somewhat more extensive listing, which he included in the *Historia* as Chapter 9 of Book 8 (Sahagún 1950–1982, Part IX [Book 8]: 27–28; 1988, II: 506–508).

2. *Quetzalalpiloni:* As indicated in note 1 to the preceding paragraph, the sumptuously attired lord who illustrates Paragraph 5 wears this hair ornament, which features the delicate, shimmering feathers of the rare quetzal bird—feathers that symbolized, along with jade, the quintessence of preciousness in pre-Hispanic Mesoamerica.

vcelomaxtlatl
çalitli maxtlatl
iztac maxtlatl

Jaguar design breechclout.
Glued breechclout.
White breechclout.

PARAGRAPH 7

Jnic vii. parrapho ipan mitoa in izquitlamantli inic melelquixtia inic maviltia in tlatoque.

Cuica
vllamaya
patoa
tlatlamina
tlatlacaloazuia
tlatlapechmatlauia
moxuchimiltia
matzopetztli chalchiuhmacuextli

Seventh paragraph, in which are told the kinds of things with which the rulers took their pleasure, with which they amused themselves.[1]

They sing.
They played the rubber ball game.[2]
They play *patolli.*[3]
They shoot at things with bow and arrow.
They shoot at things with blowguns.[4]
They hunt birds with a bird-net.
Flower gardens are laid out.
[They have] wrist bands, green stone bracelets.

PARAGRAPH 8

Jnic. viij. parrapho ipan mitoa in izquitlamantli in itlatqui inic tlatequipanoa in çioapipiltin.

Vtlatl tzotzopaztli
tzotzopazpitzavac teçacatl

Eighth paragraph, in which are told the kinds of articles the noblewomen worked with.[1]

Cane stalks; battens.
The thin batten; thick straws.

1. This paragraph is one of the shortest in the *Primeros Memoriales,* listing merely eight items "with which the rulers took their pleasure." As usual, Sahagún later in Tlatelolco collected somewhat more extensive information concerning the same subject, which he included in the *Historia* as Chapter 10, Book 8 (Sahagún 1950–1982, Part IX [Book 8]: 29–30; 1988, II: 508–509). There, in addition to giving more details about the items and including many more, he often provided useful explanations of them. Particularly valuable are the descriptions of the two principal games indulged in by the lords: the rubber ball game, *ollamaliztli* (and its court, *tlachtli[co]*), and *patolli,* the popular gambling game, somewhat resembling pachisi, played with bean counters on a diagram laid out in compartments on a mat.

2. *Vllamaya:* See note 9, Paragraph 3.

3. *Patolli:* See note 14, Paragraph 3.

4. *Tlatlacaloazuia:* The blowgun, *tlacalhuaztli, tlacalhuazcuahuitl,* in Mesoamerica was used primarily to hunt birds, employing pellets as ammunition. (Hassig 1988: 90; Sahagún 1950–1982, Part IX [Book 8]: 30, Part XII [Book 11]: 111; 1975: 460; 1988, II: 509; cf. Molina 1944, Part II: 115r).

1. This paragraph is divided into two sections. The first is devoted to the types of weaving equipment and materials used by the noblewomen. The second covers much of the same ground for women of the commoner class. Since cotton clothing, often trimmed with rabbit hair and feathers, was essentially confined to the nobility, the weaving technology employed by the women of this privileged social stratum clearly reflected this. The clothing of the commoners was mostly of maguey fiber, and this is also evident from the equipment and materials employed in its production. Later in Tlatelolco Sahagún collected information on female weaving equipment without differentiating between those of the nobles and commoners; he included this material in the *Historia* in Chapter 16 of Book 8 (Sahagún 1950–1982, Part IX [Book 8]: 49; 1988, II: 522 [much truncated]). See Anawalt 1981: 11–14 for a compact discussion of pre-Hispanic Mesoamerican weaving techniques and technology, making full use of the relevant illustration of weaving equipment in the *Florentine Codex* (her fig. 3, p. 12).

quatzontli xiyotl	The skein; the heddle.
tanatli malacatl	The basket; the spindle whorl.
tzatzaztli to	The warping frame.[2]
tochomitl	Rabbit hair.
vmitzotzopaztli	The batten made of bone.
tlacuilolquauitl	Colored wood.
yuitl çiyomitl	Feathers; hare hair.
mecamaxali cacalaca	The divided cord which crackles.
matlalcaxitl	The bowl for blue dye.

[fol. 57r]

yuitecomatl ţaoalcaxitl	The earthen bowl for feathers; the spinning bowl.[3]
tlamatzotzomatli	Bandages.
tilmaamatl tiçatl	Paper for capes; chalk.
yvitanatli	The basket for feathers.
tochomitanatli	The basket for rabbit hair.
malacatanatli quauhchiculi	The basket for the spinning whorl; the wooden hook.
tochomimalacatl	The spindle whorl for rabbit hair.
yvimalacatl neanoni	The spindle whorl for feathers; the device by which [the loom] is held.
pitzavatzavaloni malacatl	The distaff for fine spinning; the spindle whorl.
Jn macevali çioatl inic tlatequipanoa	What the female commoner works with.
ymetl	Her maguey (fiber).
acucutli	The hollow gourd for extracting juice from the maguey.
tlachictetl	Stone used for scraping the maguey plant.
içutultanatli	Her palm leaf basket.
ichicpautlatl	Stout cane for maguey threads.
ichicpatzotzopaztli	Batten for maguey threads.
teutlatl yn inequal	A stout cane is her [instrument to work the maguey threads].[4]
tomavac in iquatzõ in ixiouh	Her skeins, her heddles are thick.
tlaçimalvapali	Board on which maguey leaves are prepared for combing and cleaning fibers.
yhitztapal	Her paving stone.
quequetzaztli	The instrument for beating.
tlaculoaztli	The instrument for folding things.
ymatlaquauh	Her long pole.
ytlatesyuco.	Her jar of a ground maize preparation for dressing textiles.

2. *To:* Evidently the next word started in error.
3. *Tacalcaxitl:* read *tzaualcaxitl.*
4. Identification is tentative.

PARAGRAPH 9

Jnic. ix. parrapho ipan mitoa in tecpancali tlatocacali.
Tlatocacali
tequioacacali
tecali
pilcali
achcauhcali
cuicaoacacali
tequitlatocacali
telpuchcali
malcali

Ninth paragraph, in which are told the palaces, the rulers' houses.[1]
Ruler's house.
War leaders' council house.
Palace court house.
Noblemen's house.
Constables' house.
Song-dance houses for young men.[2]
Tribute bosses' house.
Young men's house.[3]
House for war captives.[4]

[fol. 57v]

quauhcalli.
calmecac.

Jail.
House for training young men in higher education.[5]

PARAGRAPH 10

Jnic. x. parrapho ipan mitoa in izquitlamantli tlatquitl yn oncā moneneq'.
Cuitlacheoaicpali
vcelueoaicpali
cuicuiliuhqui icpali
cuitlacheoapetlatl
vcelueoapetlatl

Tenth paragraph, in which are told the kinds of articles required there.[1]
Wolf skin seat.
Jaguar skin seat.
Varicolored seat.
Wolf skin mat.
Jaguar skin mat.

1. This paragraph lists eleven terms for structures, "palaces," connected with community government and education. Later in Tlatelolco Sahagún collected a considerably more extensive body of information that partially overlapped with the subject of this paragraph, to which he devoted Chapter 14 of Book 8 of the *Historia* (Sahagún 1950–1982, Part IX [Book 8]: 41–45; 1988, II: 517–522).

2. *Cuicaoacacali:* For a recent discussion of the educational role and function of the *cuicacalli* and its relationship with the *telpochcalli* and the *calmecac,* both also listed in this paragraph, see Calnek 1992: 88–90.

3. *Telpuchcali:* These "bachelor houses"—good exemplars of a type of institution widespread in early societies and long recognized for their importance by social anthropologists—provided the most fundamental kind of education for the largest number of young men in the urban centers of Central Mexico, with emphasis on military training. According to Sahagún in the *Historia* (1950–1982, Part IX [Book 8]: 58), there was one in every "barrio" *(calpolli/tlaxilacalli).*

4. Following *malcali, teucali* (temple) has been crossed out.

5. *Calmecac:* literally "rope of houses." These institutions served as the residences of the professional priesthood and as "colleges" for the education—with emphasis on religion and preparation for leadership positions in their communities—of young men, largely confined to the nobility. Sometimes called "temple schools," they were connected with major religious establishments (cf. Calnek 1992: 88–89).

Paragraph 10

1. This paragraph, a follow-up to the previous one, is devoted to a listing of items that belonged in the establishments of the rulers, including various types of thrones and mats, especially those draped with animal skins. Sahagún later in Tlatelolco gathered similar data, which he included in the *Historia* as Chapter 11, Book 8 (Sahagún 1950–1982, Part IX [Book 8]: 31; 1988, II: 509).

cuicuiliuhqui petlatl	Varicolored mat.
chipaoac petlatl	Pretty mat.
chipaoac icpalli	Pretty seat.
cuyoyeoaicpali	Coyote skin seat.
cuyoyeoapetlatl	Coyote skin mat.
miçeoapetlatl	Mountain lion skin mat.
mitl tlacuchtli	Arrows; spears.
vevetl ayacachtli	Upright drums; gourd rattles.
tepunaztli tetzilacatl	Horizontal drums; small bells.
xuchitl yyetl	Flowers; tobacco.
tlaçotli tlaquali	Costly food.
cacavatl maviztic	Marvelous cacao.
apatlecaxitl	Large braziers.
tlequaztli	Braziers.
tlemaxupili	Incense ladle.
xicalli anavacayutl	Gourd vessels of Anahuac style.[2]
aquavitl ayotochtli	Stirring sticks; tortoise-shell cups (for chocolate).

PARAGRAPH 11
[fol. 58r col. A]

Jnic. xi. parrapho ipan mitoa in itlaveliloca-toca in oquichtlaveliloque.

Eleventh paragraph, in which are told the bad names of the bad men.[1]

Naoali	Sorcerer.
tlaçiuhqui	Diviner.
teciuhtlazqui	Caster of hail.
tecutzquani	Caster of spells.
teyoloquani	Bewitcher of people.
tetlepanquetzqui	He who stands someone in the fire.
tetlacatecolouia	He bedevils people.
teuquiquixti	He who takes out the gods.

2. Anavacayutl (Anahuacayotl): *Anahuac* literally meant "coastland" and referred to the coastal areas of both the Gulf of Mexico (Veracruz/Tabasco), or Anahuac Xicalanco, and the Pacific (Tehuantepec/Chiapas), or Anahuac Ayotlan. Because of the common use of gourd vessels as goblets for drinking cacao and the importance of this prized plant in the Chiapas coastal region (Soconusco), the reference here may be to this area.

1. This paragraph provides, in the left column of the original manuscript, the terms for the many types of *oquichtlahueliloque,* "bad men," a remarkably broad category that included sorcerers, diviners, magicians (including sleight-of-hand performers), prophets, and deranged and/or dissolute persons. In the right column is a running text that describes the activities of many of the kinds of sorcerers, diviners, and magicians included in the list. Various of these terms were also included in the 1571 Nahuatl-Spanish dictionary of Fray Alonso de Molina (1944). Sahagún employed some of them in appropriate contexts in the later *Historia,* but this paragraph was not included in it.

Eduard Seler, in his 1899 study of magic and magicians in ancient Mexico, translated into German and discussed many of the terms listed in this paragraph. The entire paragraph was paleographized and translated into German in Seler 1927: 356–364. Garibay (1944–1947: 167–174, 235–254) also paleographized the paragraph and translated it into Spanish, adding copious notes. In 1956, he included his Spanish translation, omitting the notes, of the running text as an appendix to his edition of Sahagún's *Historia* (Sahagún 1956, IV: 307–312; 1975: 904–907). Nicholson's (1971: 438–443) summary account of the religious-ritual system of late pre-Hispanic Central Mexico contained a section on magic and its practitioners that included many of the data in this paragraph (cf. López Austin 1967).

amamalacacho	Water-whirler.
motetequi	He dismembers himself.
itilmaco miçequia	He pops maize on his cape.
tecalatia cueçaltica	He burns someone's house with flames of fire.
quiauhtlaça iztauhyatica	He casts rain with wormwood.
teutlipan moquetzaya itech q'neoa,	He appeared as a god; [the god] possesses him.
yolopuliuhqui	Madman.
amo mozcalia	He is senseless.
amo tlachia	He does not see.
amo tlacaqui	He does not hear.
atlanonotzali	One who is uncounseled.
atlazcaltili	One who is unreared.
atlacaoapavali	One who is uneducated.
atimozcalia	You are senseless.
atitlachia	You do not look.
atitlacaqui	You are incorrigible.
atitlanonotzali	You are uncounseled.
atompapul	You are a fool.
tiyolotlaveliloc	You are crazy.
taaqui	You are deranged.
tichocholoqui	You are running wild.
otiquaivintic	You have become dizzy.
otiquaxucomic	You have become a complete drunkard.
timoquatlaztinemi	You go proudly shaking your head.
timoquaviuixutinemi	You go shaking your head.
titlapaltontli	You are a little man.
titlapaquatinemi.	You go about with a broken head.[2]
titlavacapul	You are a great lunatic.
iuhqui nanacatl tiquatinemi	It is as if you went about eating mushrooms.[3]
tixolopipul	You are a great imbecile.

[fol. 58v col. A]

tixulupitanapul	You are a great empty-head.
titopuxpul	You are an addlepate.
titenipul	You are a great boor.
tinacazcocoyocpul	You are one who has great ear holes.
tinacatzatzapul	You are one who has great stopped-up ears.[4]
timeltzotzontinemi	You go about beating your breast.
titlanquiquizcuicatinemi	You go about whistling and singing.
titecacaltitlauia	You wander about from house to house.
tiquauhtlaveliloc	You are a bad piece of wood. Paragraph 11

2. *Titlapaquatinemi:* read *titlapanquatenemi.*

3. *Nanacatl:* Obviously the hallucinogenic mushroom, usually designated *teonanacatl,* is meant.

4. *Tinacatzatzapul:* read *tinacatzatzacpul.*

titelpuchtlaveliloc	You are a bad youth.
timotlayeoa titlalilitinemi	You are a beggar; you go about in misery.
timoquaxeloltitinemi.	You go about with your head divided in two.
titetlanecapul	You are a great wind among people.
titlatolçaçaca	You are a word-carrier.
titeaachcui	You are a gossip.
tinenepilmaxalpul	You have a forked tongue.
tetlachiuia	He is an enchanter.
tetlanonochilia.	He is a magician.
titenecuilpul.	You are a great people-twister.
necoc titenecapul.	You are a wretched two-edged one.
cuexcochcoyocpul.	Miserable hole in the nape of the neck.

[fol. 58r col. B]

Mitoa inic tlacatia napa polivia in ite in inantzin in iuhqui avcmo vtztli inic neçia, Jn iquac omozcali y ie telpuchtli quin icuac vel neçia in tlein itequiuh mitoaia, mictlanmatini ilh'cmatini q'matia in iqui quiaviz acanoçomo, q'aviz, q'melaquavaia ĩ pipiltin in tlatoqz ioan in maçevalti, q'navatia q'milvia xicmocaquitica, ca vqualaqz in tlaloqz ma nextlavalo ma tictlatlauhtica, in tlalocatecutli: niman iciuhca, iuh mochivaia, in oiuh tlanavati nextlavalo tlacamictilo.

It is said that when [the sorcerer] was being born, four times he disappeared in his mother's womb. It was as if she no longer appeared to be pregnant. When he had grown, when he was now a youth, then his vocation became manifest. It was said that he was a knower of the land of the dead, a knower of the heavens. He knew when it would rain or would not rain. He gave courage to the noblemen, to the rulers, and to the commoners. He gave orders; he said to them: "Listen. The Tlalocs have become angry. Let the debt be paid [to the god]; let us importune the Lord of Tlalocan." Then promptly it was so done. As he ordered, the debt was paid [to the god]; people were sacrificed.

Yoan quitoaia. ie necocoloz ie vitz i cocoliztli, ma mochicavaca in cuitlapili in atlapali ma aca quixicauh in inacaio,

And he also said: "Now there will be a plague; a plague is coming now. Let the common folk fortify themselves. Let no one be neglectful of his body."

yoã ic tlanavatiaia intla maianaloz q'toaia. maianaloz tlacaquiaviz, miec tlacatl monamacaz i maceoali in o ca q'quani macamo macamo cavilotinemi in itlatq' maco mopepechilhui oxivitl i maianaloz aço exivitl anoço nauhxivitl in q'toaia.

And he also gave orders if there was to be famine. He said: "There will be famine; there will be little rain.[5] Many people [among] the commoners will sell themselves. Let him who has food to eat not be disgraced if his property is given away or has been sealed away. For two years, or for three years, or for four years there will be famine," he said.

No ioan caçia in tlacateculutl intla quico-

He also was equal to the devilish one[6] if he

5. *Tlacaquiaviz:* The root *tlaca-* here seems to convey a negative meaning, as it does in *tlacacua,* to fast, that is, to not eat.

6. *Tlacateculutl:* literally, "human owl." The missionaries adopted the term for the Christian devil (cf. Burkhart 1989: 40–42).

colia in altepetl, anoço tlatoani, in q'nequi ma polivi in altepetl, in tlatoani i ma miqui. Yoan ic tlanavatiaia in tlacevetziz ioan in aço teçiviz q'toaia in axcã cexivitl ça mocheoatl in tetl in topã vetziz, ic no tlanavatia in teçiuhtlazqz, ma mochicavaca ma q'xicauhti i maceoalli. Auh aiac icivauh catca ca no çan catca in teopa moçauhq̃ in itlã neca. ic mitoaia navali tlaçiuhq'.

Jn tecotzquani mitoa tetlaielevilia, ioan tecocolia, in iquac quelevia in tlatquitl, nimã quicotzqua in tlatq'va, auh in tlatquiva nima q'notza, inic quipatiz quimacaz in itlatqui. Auh ça no iuhqui in q'cocolia aço, ocavac, anoço oq̃micti ic nimã quicotzqua inic miquiz in q'cocolia.

Ça no iuhqui in teiolloquani im moteneva in iuh omoteneuh.

Jn tetlepanquetzqui mitoa temicaq̃tza q'chichiva in quavitl amatl ica ioan amapanitl yoaltica nauhyoal in quichiva, niman tlaqualli mochiva, inic quitlamanilia, ça no yoaltica in quĩtlatia in aq'qz cenca quiqualania i cenca quicocolia nimã quinotza in tlavizcalpa in otlatvic, niman iehoatl quimaca in ive in oquimanili yoaltica iehoatl quiqua, intech qualani intech moxicoa inic quitoa ma içiuhca miquica inic monetlamachtia.

Auh ça no iuhq' intla altepetl itech moxicoa. Vmpa iaz novian nemiz in teteupan ioan in ichan in tlatoqz ioan in maceoalti in ichan, cacalaquiz Jn quinequi ma polivi in altepetl intla yauyutl, momanaz quinequi i ma vpa mochtin miquica in tlatoque in pipilti ioan in maçeoalti inic poliviz inic xiniz in altepetl. Auh intla machoz intla ittoz intla

hated a city or a ruler, if he wished that a city be destroyed, that a ruler die. And for this he ordered that there be frost or that it should hail. He said: "Now for a year all that will fall down upon us will be stones." The caster of hailstones also ordered: "Let the commoners fortify themselves; let them not neglect it." And no one was his wife. He stayed only in the temple; he lived in it. For these reasons he was called a sorcerer, a diviner.

He who was a caster of spells, it was said, desired something from people and hated people. When he wanted [someone's] possessions, he cast a spell over the owner of the possessions. And the owner of the possessions then called him; in order that he cure him [he said] he would give him his possessions. In like manner, when someone hated him or quarreled with him or mistreated him, he then cast a spell over him so that the one who hated him would die.

Likewise what has been said of the bewitcher of people was what was stated [of the caster of spells].

It was said that he who stood someone in the fire set people up as corpses. He adorned pieces of wood with paper and with paper flags. At night, for four nights, he did this. Then food was prepared with which he made offerings to them. Also at night he burned them. Those with whom he was very angry, whom he hated greatly, he then called at dawn, when it was daybreak. Then he gave them his offerings, those he had offered [the figures] at night. Those with whom he was angry, those with whom he was vexed, ate them. As he said: "May they soon die," so were they afflicted.[7]

And in the same way, if he was vexed with a city he would go there. He would go about everywhere in the temples, and he would enter the rulers' homes, the commoners' homes. When he wished that a city be destroyed, if war prevailed, he wished that all the rulers, noblemen, and commoners would Paragraph 11
die there, so that the city would disappear, so

7. *Monetlamachtia:* read *monentlamachtia.*

axivaz Vmpa temac miquiz anoço ichan miquiz quitzacutiaz.

that it would fall. But if he were to be recognized, if he were to be seen, if he were to be caught, he would die there by someone's hands; or he would die in his house, he would be the last.

Jn tlacateculutl, in aqui quicocolia in quimiquitlani ipan miçoia ioan in tlatquitl in quinequi i ma polivi in quiolquixtia ipan miçotinemi, conitztiuh comatocatiuh, amo ma quicuia intla quicuiz avcmo vel yaz in ichan vncan ipan tlatviz miquiz. ça cenca motolinia. Jnic tetlacateculouia vel teçotlava iuh mitoa tlalli quimictia niman tlatlacuiloa incaltech anoço tepan miçoz inic monextiz inic quinequi ma miqui in chane auh intla itla quicuiz avcmo no vel yaz içiuhca miquiz.

When the devilish one hated someone, when he wished him dead, he bled himself on him. And when he wanted [someone's] possessions to be destroyed, he molested him, he went bleeding himself on him, he went gazing at him fixedly, he went touching him with his hands. He did not take anything. If he took something he would not be able to leave his [victim's] house; he would die at dawn. He was very poor. In order to bedevil people, he made them swoon. As was said, he brought about deep night. Then he painted designs on the walls of their houses. Or he bled himself over someone. Thus it would be shown that he wanted the owner of the house to die. But if he took something, he would not be able to leave; he would soon die.

Jn teuquiquixti mitoa iuhquima tlatlaxochtli vncã in tlatoca calaquia itvalco moquetzaia niman quitzetzeloa in ixiquipil quivivixoa quinotza in onca cate in xiquipilco nimã valquiquiça iuhquima pipiltototi cequinti çiva vel quali in inechichiuh in çiva in icue in ivipil ça no iuhqz in oquichtin vel mochichiva quali in imaxtli in itilma in icozqui mitotia cuica queua in tlei quineq' in iollo in iquac in ocochiuhqz niman oc cepa quivivixoa in ixiq'pil nimã cacalactivetzi motlatia in xiquipilco. auh ic motlauhtiaya in iehoatl ĩ moteneva teuquiquixti.

He who took out the gods was said to be like a sleight-of-hand performer. He entered the house of the ruler. He stopped in the courtyard. Then he shook his pouch, he fluttered it, he called to what was inside the pouch. Then there kept coming forth what appeared to be little children. Some were women; their women's adornments—their skirts, their shifts—were very fine. Likewise the men were well adorned: their breechcloths, their capes, their necklaces were fine. They danced, they raised their voices in song, whatever [the conjuror] desired. When they had done this, once again he fluttered his pouch. Then they entered quickly, they concealed themselves in the pouch. And for this he was given gifts, he who was called the one who takes out the gods.

Jn amamalacacho moteneva ça no vncã in tlatoca calaq' xicali pechtic quimecayotia vncan quiteca in atl quitemitia nima ie quimamalacachoa amo ma noquivi y manoço chichipica amo que mochiva ça no ic motlauhtiaya ym motenevaya amamalacacho.

He who was called the water-whirler also entered the house of the ruler. He tied cords to a broad vessel; he poured water into it, he filled it. Then he whirled it around. [The water] did not spill out nor did drops of water fall. It was undisturbed. Because of this he, too, was given gifts, he who was called the water-whirler.

Jn motequia mitoa ça no tlatoca in q'chi-

He who was said to dismember himself

vaia itvalco nimã ie motequi nonoqua quitlalia in ima in icxi in izquica in içaçaliuhya izquicã quiquixtia auh in omotetec nimã q'tlapachoa tlatlapaltilmatica ynic oc ceppa mozcalia motlaloteva moquetzteva

also did it at the ruler's house, in the courtyard. At once he dismembered himself; he placed his hands, his feet, in various places. He removed his joints to various places. And when he was dismembered, then he covered [the members] with a multicolored striped cape. With this, once again he came back to life, he dashed up, he sprang up.

[fol. 58v. col. B]

yuhqui macamo omotetec inic neçi Ca no ic tlatlaxochtiaia ic motlauhtiaya.

He looked as if he had never been dismembered. Since he also performed sleight-of-hand tricks, he therefore was given gifts.

Jn itilmaco micequia, mitoa quiçoa in itilma niman onca quitema in itilmaco in tlavlli nima cuecuepoca tlatlatzca momochitia i quitta iuhquima nele comalco micequi in izquitl ça no onca in tecpa in quichivaio ī moteneva in itilmaco micequia, ic motlauhtiaya.

He who popped maize on his cape, it was said, spread out his cape; then on his cape he placed kernels of maize. Immediately they popped, they sputtered, they snapped. One saw what was truly like popcorn roasting on the griddle. He also performed what was called popping maize on a cape there in the palace. For it he was given gifts.

Jn tecalatia inic motaia ca cuezali in itlan caaquia in cali. quiayavaloa iuhqui maçanele ye tlatla in calli inic neçia ynic tezazanilhuiaya inic tlatlaxochtiaia vncã in tecpan quichivaya ic motlauhtiaya anoço tlavlli in quimomacaya in quichivaya y.

When [another bad man] burned someone's house it looked as if flames penetrated the house, as if they surrounded it. It was as if the house were truly burning; so it appeared. When he performed this sleight-of-hand trick, he thus entertained people. He did it in the palace. He was given gifts for it; perhaps they gave maize to him who did this.

Jn teutlipan moquetza mitoa in ac iehoatl in ipan quiça in aço Vitzilopuchtli in iuhqui in inechichiuh in vitzilopuchtli ça no iuhqui inic mochichiuaya motexoavanaya in ixquich in inechichiuh no iuh mochichiuaya. Auh vel quitlacayttaya quitlacanotzaia, auh quimacaia in quiquaia in anoço quimololoz in queman. Auh avctle quimauhcaittaya. in natlauhtli in tepetl. anoço quiauitl anoço yeecatl in quita quiacatiuh in campa quivicaz mouicatinemi. cequinti ipan miquia cequinti patia.

It is said that he who appeared as a god was one who perhaps simulated Huitzilopochtli. As were the adornments of Huitzilopochtli, so was he also adorned. He was painted with blue stripes. All his adornments were the same as [what Huitzilopochtli] was arrayed in. And they indeed saw him as a person; they addressed him as a person; and they gave him food to eat or sometimes clothed him. And no longer did they regard the gorges, the mountains, the rain, the wind with fear. He went leading whoever saw him. They were taken wherever he went taking them. Some died, some were cured.

Jn coatl quiolitia inic titziti, iehoatl ipampa in ichtequiliztli, quinotzaia, auh iehoatl ī

He who made a serpent come alive in order to soothsay[8] they called in case of a robbery. Paragraph 11

8. *Titziti:* read *ticiti.* Compare Molina 1944, Part II: fol. 113r : *ser, o tener officio de medico, o de agorero.* The second meaning obviously pertains here.

motlapolviani, niman quinechicoa, in icalnavactlaca in itech mochicomati in aço iehoati oq'cuiqz in itlatqui, auh iehoatl in tiçitl niman quicenteca in macevalti in oq̃cencaltilli, nimã ie q'nonotza quimilvia nican amonoltitoqz nopilhoane y iehoa i, inic aca in amocotoca in amovilteca, inic motequipachoa in oq'polo in iaxca in itlatq' i nican acate at aca, oquicuilli in iaxca in itlatq' ma çan ivia, quimaca in amocneli, ca ie valq̃çaz in tiçitl iehoatl mitznextiz. auh in aiac tlatoa ca ic omoquixti, nimã ie contlapoa, in caxitl in oquitlapo, oyol, in coatl, caxteco valmoteca, avic, tlachia, q'mitta, in onoqz in maceoalti çeçeiaca q'mitta, nima ie hoalquiça, in coatl, nimã ie teixtlan q'ça, in iquac in oquitac in aq' in oichtec nimã quitlecavia ipã moteca nimã ic conana, quilpia, iquac quimocuitia in oichtec. Auh intlacaiac quitta çan õpa mocuepa çan opa motecatiuh in caxic amo neltia in tlatolli çan ic pachivi in iiollo i motlapolviani.

And then the one who missed something gathered together the neighbors he suspected, those who perhaps had taken his possessions. And then the soothsayer assembled the commoners together; he brought them into one house. Then he addressed them; he said: "Here you are seated, my children. One of your relatives, one of your kin, is afflicted because he has lost his property, his possessions. You are present here because perhaps someone has taken his property, his possessions. Give them to him calmly; do yourself a service, for the soothsayer will now appear; he will find you out." And if no one spoke, [if no one] followed his conscience, then he uncovered a vessel. When he had uncovered it, a serpent came alive. It stretched itself out on the rim of the vessel. It looked in all directions. It looked at the commoners seated [there]; it looked at each one. Then the serpent slithered off; then it passed in front of the people. When it saw the one who had committed the theft, it climbed up him, it stretched itself out upon him. Then it held him, it tied him up. Then [the culprit] confessed that he had committed the robbery. But if [the serpent] looked at no one, it just returned; it just went to lie down in the vessel. It did not confirm the [accuser's] words. With no more than this, the one who had lost something was satisfied.

PARAGRAPH 12
[fol. 59r col. A]

Jnic. xii. parrapho ipan mitoa in itotoca in çioatlaveliloque in auianime.

Twelfth paragraph, in which are told the names of the bad women [and] the pleasure girls.[1]

1. This paragraph of the original *Primeros Memoriales* manuscript is similar in format to the preceding one, containing two distinct sections. The first, in the left column, is an extensive listing of terms for women of ill repute. "Pleasure girls," prostitutes, head the list, but many of the labels apply to the kinds of female behavior that were considered generally shameless, lewd, and immoral. The second, a running text in the right column, consists of descriptions of various techniques of medical divinatory and curative techniques practiced by the *tepatiani,* the female healers, who, perhaps because of fear of their reputed supernatural powers, were grouped with these *cihuatlahueliloque,* "bad women." Although some of the individual terms occasionally appear, nothing in Sahagún's later *Historia* really corresponds to this paragraph.

Seler (1899b) discussed some of the divinatory and therapeutic techniques described in the running text. Seler 1927: 364–367 included a transcription and German translation of the entire paragraph. Garibay (1944–1947: 240–243) also paleographized it and translated it into Spanish, with useful notes (second section repeated in Sahagún 1956, IV: 312–314; 1975: 908–909, sans notes).

Tauiani	You are a pleasure girl.
auiani	Pleasure girl.
titequixoco	You are a great disdainer.
titequimoçel	You are a great loner.
tzicuecuetzoc	You are agitated.[2]
titziyoyomocpul	You are a great itching rump.
titeixnotztinemi	You go about motioning to people with your head.
titeixvetzquilitinemi	You go about smiling at people.
titenenepiluitinemi	You go about using your tongue on people.
titetlanquiquixilitinemi	You go about whistling at people.
titemaquiquixilitinemi	You go about whistling through your fingers at people.[3]
titemanotztinemi	You go about beckoning to people with your hand.
timotetzitzquilitinemi	You go about feeling people's pudenda.
titecuilonaoatinemi	You go about permitting sodomy.[4]
tiçioacuecuel	You are a base woman.[5]
tichpuchcuecuel	You are a base girl.
tiçioatlaveliloc	You are a wicked woman.
timotlatlamiauhtinemi	You go about excelling [in evil].
timotlanochezvitinemi	You go about painted with cochineal.
titlatlaxupeuhtinemi	You go about kicking things with your feet.
titlatlauilantinemi	You go about dragging things.
titziquaquatinemi	You go about chewing gum.
otli tictotocatinemi	You go about following the road.
taquetzqui	You are shameless.[6]
taquetztinemi	You go about shamelessly.
tanenqui	You are restless.
atimochanita	You do not see your home.
titexuchiuia	You are a seducer of people.
titeyolomalacachoa	You corrupt people.[7]
titenavalnotza.	You summon people secretly.
titevetzquilitinemi	You go about smiling at people.
titecamanaluitinemi.	You go about joking with people.
timoquequetza tianquizco.	You wander about the market.

[fol. 59r col. B]

Paragraph 12

Jn tlaolli q'tepevaia, intla aca iconeuh mococoa nimã q'nochilia quitlapovia ixpã qui-

She who cast kernels of maize: If some woman's child was sick, she then invoked [the

2. *Tzicuecuetztoc:* read *ticuecuetzoc.*

3. *Titemaquiquixilitinemi: chiflar o siluar, tlanquiquici; chiflar con los dedos, mapipichoa* (Molina 1944, Part I: fol. 35v). By analogy, since literally *tlanquiquici* is to whistle through one's teeth, *maquiquici* must be to whistle with one's hand (i.e., fingers).

4. *Tiçioacuecuel:* read *ticihuacuecuech* or *-cuecuetz,* as in Seler 1927: 367.

5. *Titlatlaxupeuhtinemi:* or, possibly, you go about sowing discord.

6. *Taquetzqui:* literally, you are one who holds her head high.

7. *Titeyolomalacachoa:* literally, you turn people's hearts.

tlalia in piltontli quinapaloticate, nimã ie cõtema in tapachcaxic in tlaolli nimã q'cemana in tlaolli, auh inic quicemana tlatlapativetzi in tlaolli, inic quiteilhuia miquiz in piltontli ipapa in tlatlapaca, tlaolli. Auh intla patiz moquequetzvetzi in tlaolli ioã motlapiviaya. in tlaolli.

gods], she cast a spell for him, she exhibited it before the little child whom they were holding in their arms. Then she placed kernels of maize in a shell vessel. Then she scattered the kernels, and when she scattered them [and] the kernels fell scattered about, then she told the people that the child would die, because the kernels of maize were scattered about. But if it was to get well, the kernels fell in rows and the kernels were piled up.

Auh in oc centlamantli quichivaya mitoaya in atla teittaya quiquaqua in tlaolli cotepeoa in atla xoxouhq' xicalco. nimã contzatzaqua, niman ie cõtlapoa in conitta ieuhqui in tlaolli avcmo tlatlapaqui auh inic quihuia in pilva amo tlanaviz patiz auh intla miquiz avcmo iuhqui in tlaolli mochioaz za atlixco moyavatimani q'toa tlanaviz miquiz.

And another thing that she did was called looking at people in the water. She chewed the kernels of maize [and] cast them into water that was in a green vessel. Then she covered it. Then she uncovered it. She saw that the kernels were not as if scattered about, and so she said[8] to the parents: "He will not be very sick; he will be well." But if he was to die, the kernels of maize were no longer like this; they were only scattered on the surface of the water. She said: "He will be very sick; he will die."

Jn mecatlapuhqui nimã quiylpia in imecauh iyxpã in quitlapvia, nima quitilinitivetzi in mecatl intla motontivetzi iehoatl in quitoaya patiz in mococoa / Auh intla ça mocacatzilpitivetzin iehoatl in tlanaviz in anoço miquiz inic q'toaya

She who practiced divination by cords at once knotted her cords when she worked her spell before one. Then she quickly pulled the cords. If they quickly came undone, she said: "The sick one will be cured." But if they quickly became only more tightly tied, what she said was that he would become very sick, or he would die.

Jn tetlacuicuiliqui in aqui mococoa in quinotza inic quitlacuicuiliz achto quiquaqua in iztauhyatl ic calpichia ic quixaxaqualoa nimã ie quimamatoca, in cani quimatoca in quicocoa uncã conana, in aço tecpatl, anoço itztli, anoço amatl anoço ocutl, anoço in tlein, Auh intla oquitlacuicuilli cequi ic patia ceq' amo ic patia.

She who removed something from someone: When someone who was sick summoned her in order to remove something from him, first she chewed wormwood. With it she sprinkled him; with it she rubbed him. Then she touched him with her hand. From the place where she had touched the sick person she picked off perhaps flint, or obsidian, or paper, or wood, or some other thing. And if she removed something, some were thus cured, some were not thus cured.

Jn techichinani iehoatl in ielchiquiuh mococoa in piltontli niman quichichina iztauhyatica aço eztli in quichichina anoço timalli in quichichina cequi ic patia cequi amo ic patia.

She who sucked someone: When a small child's chest ailed, she sucked [his chest] with wormwood. Either she sucked out blood or she sucked out pus. Some were thus cured, some were not thus cured.

8. *Quihuia:* read *quilhuia.*

Jn teapatiani inic quipatia in pipiltotonti quitzonicpiloa quivivixalvia in itzonteco ioan quivalpachilhuia inic opac / cequi / quiyyoana ça no quivalpachoa inic opac ioan ichcatica quitzacuilia cequi ic pati cequi amo ic pati / Auh ca neneuhqui inic motzoponia in pipiltotonti iniqu içiuhca miqui, auh iniqu içiuh quipapachoa iztatica anoço tomatl inic quipapachoa in pipiltotonti.

The healer cured children in this way: She held children upside down, she moved their heads, and she pressed them. Thus, they were cleansed. From some she drew things out with her breath. She also squeezed them. Thus they were cleansed. And she covered them with cotton. Some were thus cured, some were not thus cured. And [she did] the same when the children were pierced, as a result of which they soon died. And for this she massaged them; she massaged the children with salt or [with] tomato.

PARAGRAPH 13
[fol. 59v col. A]

Jnic xiij. ipan mitoa in itelpopochti ioan yn ichpopochtin ynic moapavaya.

Jn ichpopochtin, yn telpopochtin, cẽnenca q'ncuitlauitinenca: yn telpochtlato yehoatl quimatia, yn telpochtlato yn aquin, quimacaz, ynic quimomecatiz, yehoatl yn iel ỹ motlamachtia, yn mocuiltonoa; no iehoatl yn noquichtli, yn tequiua, y yauc nemi; auh ayac ma çan conanaya yn çiuatl ynic quimomecatiz, yntla machoz momecatia yn çiuatl: yn anoço oquichtli, quitzacutiaz, quachichinoloz, vivitecoz; ioan namoyallo poliui yn itlatqui yn ical; auh intla omopilhoati yn çivatl yn oq'chpochpan nemi: aucmo ichpochtli quixtilo: auh in imecauh, vcatca, yntlac cẽpa itech açiz tzacuiltiloya quachichinollo viviteco; moteneua omilamaui, auh yehoatl i, yn ichpochtli: yehoatl quimati yn ita yn aço cana cocchotiz: auh yn iconeuh yn çiuatl, amo, quiuicaya, çan conanaya, yn itta moteneuaya, ytelpochpiltzin.

Thirteenth [paragraph], in which it is told how youths and maidens were reared.[1]

Maidens and youths lived together. The master of youths, who knew them, lived taking charge of them. The master of youths was one to whom [the youth] who was careful, who was rich, who was wealthy, was to give gifts so that he could take a paramour. The manly [warrior and] the seasoned warrior who engaged in war also [did so]. But no one just took a woman as a paramour. If it were known that one took a woman as a paramour, or [a woman] a man, [the culprit] would be punished: his head would be passed through the fire, he would be beaten, and his possessions, his house would be taken; they would be destroyed. And if a woman had a child while she still lived as a maiden, no longer was she considered a maiden, and he who was her lover, if he were to have sexual relations with her, was punished; his head was passed through the fire, he was beaten. It was called being old-ladied. And as for the girl, when her father knew that perhaps

1. This paragraph is concerned with the education of both boys and girls. Sahagún later in Tlatelolco collected more extensive data on education, with the *telpochcalli* and the *calmecac* treated separately, which he included in the *Historia* as Chapters 4–8 in the Appendix to Book 3 (Sahagún 1950–1982, Part IV [Book 3]: 49–65; 1988, I: 223–229). Chapter 20 of Book 8 of the *Historia* is also ostensibly devoted to an account of how the sons of lords and noblemen were reared. However, it is much more concerned with the honors and rewards that accrued to the young princes and nobles, following their education in the *calmecac*, based on the number of enemy warriors they had captured on the battlefield.

somewhere she was to take a husband, and when her child was a girl, she did not take [the child] with her; rather, her father took [the child]. She was called her youth child.

Jn telpochcalli, ynic tlamanca, in telpochtlatoque vncan tlacazcaltiaia vncan tlacauapauaya yn telpochtlatoque, ioan in ichpochtlatoque iehoatl quimati in aquin mutelpochtlaliz, yn anoço ichpochtli im mochpochtlaliz, quachtli quitlaliaya: ioan intetlapalol, quimaca cem acachiquiuitl, in xocotamalli, ioan centetl totolli ypan onotiuh yoan quachtli, vntetl, ixpan contlalia ỹ telpochtlato.

In the house of the youths it was the custom that there the master of the youths educated people; they instructed people. The masters of the youths and the mistresses of the maidens knew which youth was to be released, or [if it was] a maiden, [which maiden] was to be released; [and] these set forth [gift] cloths and their greetings. They gave them a reed basket of fruit tamales and a turkey hen—they outdid themselves—and they placed two cloths before the master of youths.

Auh ça no iuhqui intla tecutli, quimoçiuauhtiz, in ichpochtli yehoatl quitlanilitiuh, in telpochtlato, ioan yn ichpochtlato, quimacatiuh yn itetlapalol, ioan, vntetl quachtli, quiquachyotia, inic quimoçiuauatia. Auh intlacamo, quimati, in telpochtlato, in vncan tecutli niman no yc, totoco in tecutli namoyallo. Auh in aquin amo quiquixtiaia yn ichpoch, no totoco, namoyalloia.

And it was the same if a lord was to marry. He asked the master of youths and the mistress of maidens for the girl. He gave his greeting and two [gift] cloths, endowed him with [gift] cloths, because he was marrying. But if the master of youths did not know about it, then the lord, too, was at once expelled from there because of it; the lord was stripped [of his possessions]. But he who did not give up the girl [to a suitor] was also expelled [and] stripped [of his possessions].

[fol. 59v col. B]

Auh in aiel telpochtli, no tzacuiltilloia namoyalloia, iehica ca quitemacaia in intelpochtlaol çeçentlacol; ioan in iuauh: can no iuhqui yn ichpochtli, no quitemacaia, ichpochtlaolli, no ioan yvauh, ycacauauh in telpochtli cẽ.xx. Auh in ie muchi y, in tlaolli, in vauhtli, in cacauatl, quipiaia: ỹ telpochtlato, vmpa monequia in ixpa diablo ic tlamanaia in quimanaia, ce ciacatl in tlaxcalli in tlamapictli, ioã yn coateq'pan: ioan y veca yauc vmpa quiquaya, in tequiuaqz.

And the negligent youth was also punished, was also stripped [of his possessions] because he gave people part of their youth maize and their amaranth seed. It was the same[2] when a girl gave people the maiden maize. And also [the same applied to] the youth's amaranth seed, [or] his twenty cacao beans.[3] And all of these—the maize, the amaranth seed, the cacao beans—the master of youths guarded. They were needed there[4] before the devil; with them they made offerings—they offered an arm's length[5] of tortillas, handfuls—as well as for communal

2. *Can:* read *can.*

3. Problematical translation. *Ce xx* probably is to be read *cempohualli* (= 20).

4. The passage *in ixpa diablo ic tlamanaia in quimanaia, ce ciacatl in tlaxcalli in tlamapictli, ioã* is inserted in the right margin at this point.

5. *Ce ciacatl (ce ciyacatl):* one armpit, the distance from the armpit to the tip of the fingers, a recognized unit of linear measurement, calculated to average 70 centimeters (see Castillo Farreras 1972: 216–217, 219).

Jn telpopochtin, ioan yn ichpopochtin, yntequiuh catca, in coatequitl quauhquetzaia, in inchan tlatoque; ioan in vmpa mexico, unquauhquetzaia, ioan in otli quichichiuaia; ioã in cana tetzaqualli, motecaya, ioan in cana ayauhcalli, motlaliaya: vel intequiuh catca, in cuicoyanolloia in telpopochti, in ioã yn ichpopochtin. Auh inic cuicoyanolloia mochichiuaya, moçaia: ça mecaaiatl in quimolloloaya, yc neçia, in quexquich veyac, maxtlatl macoya; ioan in teucuitlatl, in intepilol: ioan in inacoch, xiuhtica tlatzaqualli. Auh in tequiuaque, ic mochichiuaia, ym pilli, quetzalalpilloni, yn contlaliaya, yxiuayauh, coçauhq' in teçacatl conaquiaya: Auh in çan quauhtli, quauhtlalpilloni, in contlalia: Auh in ichpochtli mochichiuaia yancuic yn icue, ioan yn ivipil: mopotoniaya, tlapaliuitica, moxauaia, intzatzallan aactiuia in telpopochtin ynic mitotiaya, in iquac, cuicoyanolloia iquac; in panquetzaliztli, ioan, yn tlacaxipevaliz, ioan in tecuiluitl, ioan toxcatl, ioan xocotl vetzin, ioan vei toçoztli.

labor; and the seasoned warriors ate them when far away there in battle.

The work of the youths and maidens was communal labor. They made bundles of wood for the houses of the rulers and there in Mexico they made bundles of wood and they fixed up the roads as well as wherever stone enclosures were built and wherever mist houses were located. The real work of the youths and maidens was that they sang and danced holding hands. And when they sang and danced holding hands, they adorned themselves, they daubed themselves with paint, they covered themselves only with rope net capes. Thus they appeared. They were given rather long breechcloths and their gold lip pendants and their ear plugs covered with a turquoise [mosaic]. And the seasoned warriors were arrayed as noblemen; they set in place headbands with [two] quetzal feather tassels; they donned their turquoise-colored net capes [and] yellow labrets. And the mere eagle warriors donned headbands with eagle feather tassels. And the maidens arrayed themselves; their skirts and shifts were new. They pasted themselves with red feathers, they painted their faces, they trotted around among the youths. Thus they danced when they sang and danced holding hands at the time of [the celebration of] Panquetzaliztli and Tlacaxipehualiztli and Tecuilhuitl and Toxcatl and Xocotl Huetzi and Huey Tozoztli.

PARAGRAPH 14
[fol. 60r col. A]

Jnic xiiij parrapho ipan mitoa inic chicomuztoc valquizqz in chichimeca

Fourteenth paragraph, in which it is told how the Chichimeca came forth from the Seven Caves.[1]

1. Together with Paragraph 1(A–C) of this chapter, this is the only portion of the *Primeros Memoriales* that contains any significant amount of history, however brief and legendary. The "Chichimec" ancestry of the major Late Postclassic Central Mexican ethnic groups is highlighted, as well as their origin in the traditional "Seven Caves," Chicomoztoc. When, as here and in other relevant primary sources, emergence from this mythical homeland constituted the initiation of pre-Hispanic Central Mexican history, it often featured the structuring of the peoples of the region into a seven-part ethnic scheme. The groups assigned to these different schemes vary considerably within the shared seven-division pattern.

This particular scheme is unique. Its constituent ethnic units appear to reflect the historical experience and geopolitical position of Tepepolco, a Triple Alliance tributary located in the northern region of the superprovince of Acol-

Jzcatqui in quimatia in totava in toculhua. in quitoaya itech quitlamiaya: chicomuztoc valquizque inic quitoaia vncan quizque, vncan yolque: chicōtlamantli,

Here is what our fathers, our grandfathers knew. They said, they claimed that they came forth from the Seven Caves. Thus they said that from there seven groups came forth, that there they were born.

quiyacatia quitoaya tecpilchichimeca ioan aculvaca chichimeca,

They said that the Tecpilchichimeca and the Acolhuacan Chichimeca came first.[2]

auh inic vntlamanti yehoanti in colhoaca chichimeca, auh maço ivi in chichimeca, quivalvicaqz: in inteuh quitoaya tona, quillaztli,

And second were the Colhuacan Chichimeca, but nevertheless they were Chichimeca. They brought their goddess, whom they called Tonan Quilaztli.[3]

Auh inic etlamantli mitoa, chichimeca iehoanti in vtontlaca, auh no quivalvicaque in inteuh iehoatl in otontecutli. mitoaya,

And the third group called Chichimeca were the Otomi, and they brought their god with them; he was called Otontecuhtli.[4]

Auh inic nauhtlamātin, chichimeca iehoantin in mitoa, mexica chichimeca, maço iui in chichimeca: quivalhuicaque yn inteuh in mitoa: vitzilopuchtli,

And the fourth group of Chichimeca were those called the Mexica Chichimeca; nevertheless, they were Chichimeca. They brought their god, called Huitzilopochtli.[5]

Auh inic macuillamātin in mitoa cuexteca chichimeca,

And the fifth group were called Cuexteca Chichimeca.[6]

Auh inic chiquaçentlamanti iehoanti in mitoa tenime: chichimeca,

And those of the sixth group were called Tenime Chichimeca.[7]

---

huacan (see Nicholson 1974). Thus, the first group to emerge and arrive from Chicomoztoc is specified as the Acolhua, also designated Tecpilchichimeca, "noble Chichimecs." Two other groups not commonly included among the emigrés from Chicomoztoc are the Cuexteca (Huaxtecs) and the Totonaca. Speakers of these languages occupied territories to the north and east of Acolhuacan; the Tepepolca must have been particularly cognizant of them.

The "historical" portion of this paragraph is quite brief. The bulk of it is devoted to a detailed specification of the privileges and prerogatives of the rulers and the nobility that were considered to be their due as a result of their success as courageous conquerors. Nothing really comparable to this paragraph was included by Sahagún in the final *Historia.* It constitutes a vivid and eloquent expression of the fundamental rationale for the privileged status and great power wielded by the upper class of the Triple Alliance city-states (Mexico Tenochtitlan/Tetzcoco/Tlacopan) in the highly stratified, aristocratic society of Central Mexico at the time of the Conquest.

2. *Tecpilchichimeca, aculvaca chichimeca:* This group, with its earlier capital at Coatlinchan and its final capital at Tetzcoco, dominated the eastern Basin of Mexico.

3. *Colhoaca chichimeca:* Colhuacan, in the southern Basin of Mexico, played a major political and cultural role in Central Mexico between the fall of Tollan and the rise of Azcapotzalco (ca. 1250–1350?). During this period, and later, the Colhua heavily influenced both their former subjects, the Mexica of Mexico Tenochtitlan, and the Acolhua of the eastern basin. Various sources describe Colhua migratory movements into Acolhuacan (Nicholson 1974: 149) and throughout the basin after the loss of the political power of Colhuacan, probably around 1350. It is well established (Nicholson 1988c: 78, 88) that their particular patron deity was the paramount maternal fertility goddess known as Tonan Quilaztli, among other names (see Chapter I, Paragraph 5A). Although the Colhua were often contrasted with the less civilized Chichimeca, in certain sociopolitical contexts they were also assigned to this group.

4. *Chichimeca . . . Otontlaca:* The Otomi, often geographically interdigitated with the Nahua speakers, were concentrated in the northern Basin of Mexico and areas farther to the north. On Otontecuhtli, see Chapter I, Paragraph 5A.

5. *Mexica chichimeca:* The Mexica were frequently designated Chichimeca, especially during their migratory period. On Huitzilopochtli, see Chapter I, Paragraph 5A.

6. *Cuexteca chichimeca:* The Huaxtecs, who were concentrated in northern Veracruz and southern Tamaulipas, spoke a Mayance language, but their culture was quite distinct from the other members of this linguistic family, from whom they were separated by a considerable distance (see Stresser-Péan 1971).

7. *Tenime chichimeca: Tenitl* (singular of *tenime*) is defined by Molina (1944, Part II: fol. 99r) as "hombre de otra nacion o boçal." English "barbarian" seems to fit it fairly well. In any case, these Chichimecs may have belonged to one

Auh inic chicontlamanti iehoanti, in mitoa totonaca chichimeca;

o ca yvin i, in quitoaia. in totavan, in toculhoan:

Auh inic quitoaya techiuh, techyvcux, techima, titlayvcuyaloan: in topiltzin, in quetzalcoatl, Auh quiyvcux in ilhuicatl in tonatiuh, in tlaltecutli; o ca iuhquin i in quitoaya in quitoaya, inic quimatia, inic valaqz inic açico, inic quimaçevaco. in tlalli:

auh in oquimaçeuhque, yn omutecaqz y ye inchan inic quitoa; ye novian ymaxca intlatqui inic intlalmaçevalpã,

Auh y yehoatl inic peuh y yauyutl yn aquiqz aquintlacamati: nimã ye ic muchiva y yavyutl, niman ie pevallo. Auh in opevaloque ic veix in tlacallaq'lli yn aquin muxicoa yc veya yn itla

And those of the seventh group were called Totonaca Chichimeca.[8]

Thus our fathers, our grandfathers spoke.

And they spoke as follows: Topiltzin Quetzalcoatl[9] created us, formed us, fashioned us; we are his creations. And he created the heavens, the sun, the lord of the earth. Thus they spoke; they said[10] that they knew that thus they came forth; they thus came to arrive; thus they came to merit the land.

And when they had merited it, when they had assembled in their homes, they said thus: that everywhere they had their property, their possessions, since they were in their land, which they merited.

And this is the way wars began. War was at once waged against those who did not obey them; then they were conquered. And when they were conquered, the tribute was increased. Those who were angered when their tribute was thus increased

[fol. 60r col. B]

calaquil, in pevalacatl muchiva: o ca iuhq'n i, ynic otepevaya, in mexicatl, in acolhoa, in tepanecatl, inic oquitoaya yn çemanavacatl, ycentlatqui, in mexicatl, in acolhuã, in tepanecatl, inic onovian tepevaya çemanavac:

o ca iuhquin i, inic tlamanca, ynic vnoviã calaquia: in mexicatl, in acolhoa, in tepa-

became conquered men. Thus the Mexica, the Acolhua, the Tepaneca[11] conquered people. They said that the inhabitants of the whole world were the common property of the Mexica, Acolhua, the Tepaneca, for they had conquered people in all parts of the world.

Thus they established the custom that the Mexica, the Acolhua, the Tepaneca pene-

---

or more groups that, according to some sources, populated parts of the Basin of Mexico after the fall of Tollan and were considered to be distinct from the Acolhua, the Tepaneca, the Otomi, and other groups.

8. *Totonaca chichimeca:* The Totonaca occupied a fairly extensive area of northern Puebla and Veracruz, comprising both highland and lowland zones (see Kelly and Palerm 1952). Their main urban center was Cempohuallan, near the coast.

9. *In topiltzin, in quetzlcoatl:* On the deity Quetzalcoatl, see Chapter I, Paragraph 5A. The designation Topiltzin Quetzalcoatl was more commonly applied to the legendary ruler of Tollan than to the creator/wind god, Ehecatl Quetzalcoatl. At least by the time of the Conquest, however, their personas had intertwined to the extent that it is difficult to sharply differentiate them (Nicholson 1979). Here, the deity's fundamental role as creator of the universe and mankind is clearly expressed.

10. *In quitoaya* is repeated in the text.

11. *In mexicatl, in acolhoa, in tepanecatl:* The importance of the Triple Alliance of these three powerful Basin of Mexico city-states, which dominated much of western Mesoamerica at the time of the Conquest, is emphasized throughout the paragraph.

necatl: ca ça iehoatl, in vquitemutinenca yn aquin aquitlacamatiz, ca ye y yauh, ca ye compeva, auh yc veya, yn itlacalaquil,

in quitoaya in mexicatl: quilhuiaya yn vquipeuh, a ça nen quitac yn iyaxca in itlatqui, yn icocvcauh, in noteuh, in tetzavitl vitzilopuchtli, ychimal, ixco, yeva, y yatlauh, yyacac, yeva;

o ca yvin i in quiteilhuia: açoc ceppa ticnequi aço timuxicoa,

ça yuhquin i, yn vquiteilviaya, y nvvian, ynic vquivalcavaya yntlacalaquil çemanavacatl in mexico.

Auh y yehoatl inic vmitoaya mvchi, ỹtonal in tlatoqz in tlaçotli, in canin mvchiva yn anavac, in quetzalli, ītonal, in tlatoque, ioan in tlaçoivitl, in tlaçotli tototl, in xiuhtototl, in tlauhquechol, in çaqua in tevquechol, in tzinitzca, in chalchiuhtototl, in xihuitzilli muchi intonal yn tlatoque:

auh ça no iuhqui, in chalchivitl, in tevxiuitl, in quetzalchalchivitl, in iztac chalchiuitl, in tlapaltevilutl, in acatic quetzalchalchivitl, in tomatic chalchivitl in tevilacachiuhqui, in quetzalchalchivitl, in xitic, chalchivitl, y ye ixquich, y ye muchi ca muchi ītonal in tlatoque:

Auh çan no iuhqui, in ixquich, yn izquican icac in cacavatl ca intonal in tlatoqz in nvmpa mvchiva cacavatl, novian vmpa mani incacavamil, mitoa ytonal.

Auh çan no iuhqui; in izquican icac in tonacayvtl, no muchi intonal vmpa novian mani yn imil inic mitoa ytonal muchi vncan mvchiva

trated everywhere; they went seeking those who would not obey them. They went, they conquered them, and their tribute therefore increased.

Those they conquered told the Mexica, they said to them: "Perhaps not in vain has your god,[12] Tetzahuitl Huitzilopochtli, come upon his property, his possessions, his goods. They are on the face of his shield, on the tip of his spear-thrower."

[The conquerors] spoke to the people in this manner: "Perhaps you wish it once more? Perhaps you are angry?"

Thus they spoke to the people. From everywhere, people from all parts of the world thus brought their tribute to Mexico.

And it was said that all precious things, wherever they were produced in the places along the coast, were the rightful due of the rulers. The quetzal feathers were the rightful due[13] of the rulers, as well as the precious feathers, the precious birds: the lovely cotinga, the roseate spoonbill, the troupial, the roseate spoonbill, the Mexican trogon, the blue honey creeper, the costa hummingbird.[14] All were the rightful due of the rulers.

And similarly green stone, turquoise, fine green jade, the white form of jade, amethysts, reedlike fine green jade, round green stone, circular fine green jade, navel-like[15] green stone—all, everything, all was the rightful due of the rulers.

And similarly all the places where there was cacao were the rightful due of the rulers. Wherever cacao grew, their cacao fields everywhere were said to be their rightful due.

And similarly everywhere that there was the sustenance of life, all of it was also their rightful due. Their fields which were everywhere were said to be their rightful due. Everything that was produced there,

12. *In noteuh:* read *moteuh.*

13. *Itonal: Tonalli* meant heat, solar heat, and summertime. It also connoted the day sign on which one was born and, by extension, someone's lot, portion, or share, material or otherwise. In a broad sense, it also meant patrimony.

14. For the identification of these birds, see Sahagún 1950–1982, Part XII (Book 11): 19–21.

15. *Xitic:* read *xictic.*

yn ixquich in tonacayvtl, in chia, in etl, in vauhtli, inic mitoa intonal in tlatoque:

all the sustenance of life—chia, beans, amaranth—were said to be the rightful due of the rulers.

Auh ça no iuhqui in canin muchiva ichcatl no ytonal vmpa mani, in imichcamil vncã mvchiva: in izquican icac in ichcatl.

And similarly all the places where cotton was produced were also their rightful due—wherever their cotton fields were, where [cotton] grew, all the places where there was cotton.

auh ca no iuhqui, in izquican icac in tlaçotli tilmatli muchiva muchi intonal. Auh in izquican icac, yhuitilmatli muchi itonal: in izquican icac in tochvmio tilmatli, muchi ytonal, in quiacatia yehoatl: in tlachquauhyo, in xomuyvitilmatli, in iztac xomvyvitilmatl niman yehoatl, in tlapalivitilmatli, niman yevhatl in tlamvhuipalli ivitilmatli, niman iehoatl in tlaztalevalli ivitilmatl, niman yehoatl in matlaltic yvitilmatli: in tlapallivi teçacanecuilo ivitilmatli; niman iehoatl in tliltic yuitilmatli: Jnin ca mvchi intonal catca in tlatoque, ayac vel quicuia: ayac, vel, itech,açia;

And similarly,[16] in all places where there were precious capes, all of them became their rightful due. And in all the places where there were feather capes, all were their rightful due. In all the places where there were rabbit-hair capes, all were their rightful due. First were the ones with the ball court tree design,[17] the duck feather cape, the white duck feather cape. Then was the cape of red feathers; then the dark blue feather cape;[18] then the pink feather cape; then the blue feather cape, the cape of colored feathers with the twisted straw design on the border; then the black feather cape. All these were the rightful due of the rulers; no one [else] could take them, no one [else] could have them.

ça no iuhqui in tlaçotli xicalli muchi itonal catca yc atlia yn izquican icac, xicalli,

Similarly the precious drinking vessels. All the vessels from which they drank in all places were their rightful due.

ça no iuhqui in tlaçotli quavitl mvchi itonal: in veca vnoc, yehoatl in tepunaztli muchiva, yehoatl in vevetl in veyac vevetl, in veveyavalli: intonal in tlatoque,

Similarly the precious trees: all were their rightful due. Those which were in far-off places, from which the two-toned drum was made, the upright drum, the tall skin drum, the upright drum on a circular support[19] were the rightful due of the rulers.

ça no yuhqui, in cvztic tevcuitlatl intonal, incvzqui mvchiva, intẽteuh muchiva ynacuch mvchiva, in tlatoque: ça no iuhqui, in iztac tevcuitlatl, yn intonal in tlatoque:

Similarly gold was their rightful due: their necklaces that were fashioned, their lip plugs, their ear plugs that were fashioned were the rulers'. Similarly silver was the rightful due of the rulers.

ça no iuhqui in çivapipilti mvchi intonal: in intonal cueitl vipilli pepechtli vevei tilmatli, in matlacmatl, in chicuematl y ma-

In like manner, all was the rightful due of the noblewomen. The skirts were their rightful due, the shifts, the bed coverings,

Paragraph 14

16. *Ca:* read *ça.*

17. *In tlachquauhyo:* "Ball court eagle design" might be another possibility (cf. Seler 1902–1923, II: 515).

18. *Tlamvhuipalli:* read *tla-mohui (tic)-palli* (dark blue).

19. *Veveyavalli (huehueyahualli): Yahualli* literally means a jar rest, usually of grass.

cuilmatl y namatl mvchi intonal catca in çivapipiltin; yn içivava in tlatoque,

the great cloths that [measure] ten, eight, five, four fathoms; all were the rightful due of the noblewomen, the wives of the rulers.

ça no iuhqui, yn izquican icac, quavitl intonal in tlatoqz yehoatl in tlaquavac quauitl, y yamanqui quavitl, ca yveycal; vevey, vapalli vey elquauhyvtl mvteneva vevey, tlaquetzalli muteneva vevey tlaixquaitl moteneva, Ça

Similarly, the wood that was everywhere was the rightful due of the rulers: the hard wood, the soft wood, the great houses, the great beams, what are called the great pillars, what are called the great lintels;

[fol. 60v col. B]

no iuhqui quamimilcali muteneva vevey, quamimilli yn vntemi mvteneva tlaquetzalmimilli, ça no iuhqui mimiltic in tlaixquaitl, o ca iuhquin i in muchi yntonal catca in tlatoque:

similarly the log houses, what are called the great logs which are laid down, what are called cylindrical pillars; likewise cylindrical lintels. All these were the rightful due of the rulers.

ça no iuhqui yn tetl yn izquican icac tetl, tliltic teçontli, in chichiltic teçontli, yn iztac tetl yn mvteneva texamitl: Auh in mvteneva vevey tlaquetzaltetl in tliltic tetl yn vei yztac tetl, ca muchi intonal catca. y. yn tlatoque:

Similarly the stones, the stones that were everywhere: black pumice stone, red pumice stone, white stones called stone adobes, and what were called great stones for columns; black stones, large white stones—all were the rightful due of the rulers.

Auh ça no ivi y yehoatl tolli yn izquican icac ca no intonal in tlatoqz in tiquitoa petlatolli petlatl mochiva ypetlayo in vevey calli Auh in oztopilli teputzoicpalli petlaixtli mvchiva, auh in tolquiyutl tlacuexcalli muchiva tlacuextli muchiva, ioan in veca muchiva petlatl in cuicuiliuhqui petlatl in cuicuiliuhqui tanatli, in cuicuiliuhqui icpalli muchi ỹtonal catca, in tlatoqz:

And similarly the rushes that were in all places were the rightful due of the rulers: those that we call mat rushes, from which mats are made—the great houses' particular mats; and the *juncus,* the seats with backs, mats made from the nodes of the reeds; and boxes made from the thickly woven shoots of the rushes; [mats] made from thickly woven *juncus,* and the long mats that were made; mats with painted designs; panniers with painted designs; seats with painted designs; all were the rightful due of the rulers.

ça no iuhqui in tlaçotli xvchitl Jn izquitlamantli xvchitli yn nepapã xvchitl ca mvchi intonal catca. Auh ça no iuhqui in tlaçotli y yetl yn ṽcan mvtlaliaya, in intlatocayeya muchi imixpan mutemaya:o ca iuhquin i in muchi intonal catca in tlatoqz:

Similarly, the precious flowers, all the different kinds of flowers, the various flowers, all were their rightful due. And in the same way, the precious tobacco which was placed on the rulers' daises, all was set down before them. Similarly all was the rightful due of the rulers.

Auh ça no iuhqui in tlaçotli, tlaqualli ca intonal muchi, yn izquican icac tlaçotli mvlli intonal,

And similarly the precious foods, all of them, were their rightful due; the precious sauces that were everywhere were their rightful due.

auh y ye muchi in ixquich tlaçotli tlalticpac vnoc yn nepapan tlaçotli ca muchi yntonal catca in tlatoque:

And all the precious things on earth, the various precious things, all were the rightful due of the rulers.

Auh ça no iuhqui yn izquican icac eoatl in

And similarly, the skins that were in all

tequanevatl yn oceloevatl, in cuitlachevatl in miçevatl in iztac, oçeloevatl in tlatlauhqui oçeloevatl, yn ocotochevatl in coyoevatl, auh in ye muchi yn izquican icac yevatl, ca intonal catca, ca inicpal ca inpepech muchivaya

places, the skins of the wild animals: jaguar skins, wolf skins, mountain lion skins, white jaguar skins, red jaguar skins, bobcat skins, coyote skins, and all the skins everywhere were their rightful due. They were fashioned into their seats, their bed coverings.

auh ça no iuhqui in izquican icac,

And similarly

[fol. 61r col. A]

yn tlavitolli, tlacalvaztli, in telolomatlatl, ca muchi ytonal.

the bows, the blowguns, the slings that were everywhere: all were their rightful due.

Auh ca no iuhqui in cactly, in moteneva tecpilcactli in izquitlamantli cactli in cuetlaxcactli cuitlachcac cactly tlacuilolli cactli in cacamuliuhqui cactly yoan in cenca canavac cactli yvan in pupulcactli vecapa yoan i nacazminqui cactli yoan yn ocelocactli: ioan in tochomio cactli, yn izquican icac ye muchi, cactli tlaçotli muchi intonal catca.

And similarly[20] the sandals, those called noble sandals: all the different kinds of sandals—leather sandals, wolf skin[21] sandals, sandals with painted designs, thick sandals like bed coverings, and very thin sandals, and *popol*[22] sandals from afar, and sandals with punched sides,[23] and jaguar skin sandals, and rabbit fur sandals. All the precious sandals in all places were their rightful due.

Aun ça no iuhqui in moteneva vllamaloni vlli, in collamaya tlachco in quezevatl in mayevatl in nelpiloni ca muchi intonal catca in tlatoque,

And similarly what they called the ball of rubber, [with] which they played ball on the ball court, [and] the leather hip guards, the gloves, the belts, all were the rightful due of the rulers.

y ye vllamazque niman ye muchichiva, niman ye conteca yn inquezevauh niman ye mvlpia niman ye mumayevatia: niman ye vllama in tlachco, inic mvteneva ynic ynchan, ynic quipia yn imaltepeuh, ynic mitoa yn intonal y ye mvchi yn vncã quitlanitoaya in tlaçotli chalchivitl in tlaçotli tilmatli in tlaçotli evatl ioã in cacavatl oyehoatl i inic mitoaya yn intonal in tlachtli in vlli inic mitoa yn inchan in intianquiz:

When they were to play ball, they then arrayed themselves; they put on their leather hip guards, then they put on their belts, then they drew on their gloves. Then they played ball on the ball court, as was said, as they guarded their homes, as [they guarded] their cities. It was said that they [won or] lost all their rightful due there: the precious green stones, the precious capes, the precious skins, and the cacao. It was said that their rightful due was the ball game, the rubber [ball]; it was said that it was as their home, as their marketplace.

o ca iuhquin i, ynic otlamanca inic oquipixque çemanavatl inic mitoa ynic tzintic inic peuh in çemanavatl ynic oquipixqz yn chi-

Thus were the customs; thus they guarded the world. It was said that when the world began, when it originated, the Chichimeca

20. *Ca:* read *ça.*

21. *Cuitlachcac:* read *cuetlachcactli.*

22. *Pupulcactli:* possibly *Popoloca-cactli.*

23. *Nacazminqui cactli: Nacaztli* in some contexts connotes "side"; *mina* can be understood to mean "pierce." However, *nacazminqui* is more usually construed as "diagonally divided" (cf. Seler 1902–1923, II: 525; Sahagún 1950–1982, Part IX [Book 8]: 23).

chimeca in inchan, yn intlal. Auh inic oquipixque yn imaçeval, y novian: ynic otlapialoc, ynic otlapix yn mexicatl in acolhoa in tepanecatl, o ca ye ixquich ynic ontlamaca, inic onemoac,

guarded their homes, their lands, and thus they guarded their commoners everywhere. Thus things were guarded; the Mexica, the Acolhua, the Tepaneca thus guarded things. Everything was thus established by custom; thus was life lived.

Auh yn oiuh mito yn tlacpac yn intonal in tlatoque ayac vel ytech açia ỹ manel pilli yn amo oquichtli avel ytech açia çan iuhqui macevalli yc nemia, yn amv oquichtli ca ytonal in tlatoque.

As was stated above, no one could have the rightful due of the rulers even though he were a nobleman. He who was not a manly [warrior] could not have it; he who was not a manly [warrior] lived like a commoner. It was the rightful due of the rulers.

Auh inic tlamanca muteneva: tetectitica octacayutica machyotica, ynic mitoa tlilotoc tlapalotoc yn nemiliztli

And thus were the customs said to be established: as with a warp thread,[24] as with a measuring rod, as with a model. Thus was it said: "The way of life is [according to] the black, the red[25] [writings]."

in amo oquichtli pilly ça navatiloya in tlein quicuiz in tlein ynechichiuh yez in queni nemiz.

The nobleman who was not a manly [warrior] was precisely ordered what he was to take, what were to be his adornments.

[fol. 61r col. B]

Auh in quauhtli in çan tiacauh quicuy, yn iquauhtlatqui: auh yn ce caçi, yn ome caçi ça no machiyotililo,in iuh nemiz. auh yuh muchivaya yn aquin quicuitivetzi yn intonal in tlatoqz y ye mvchi y ye yxquich tlacpac omito, ayac vel ytech açia ayac vel quicuia, Auh intla vmachoc yntla vittoc yn oquicuic yn intonal in tlatoque yca, tlatolloq' mvtzacuiltitiuh, mecaniloya in iuh miquia in tlein vei quichivaya in aço tetlaxima, in aço ichtequia: no iuh miq'a in quicuitivetzin in intonal in tlatoque

And the eagle warrior who was only a brave warrior took his eagle vestments. And when he took one [captive], when he took two, this was also being an example of how one was to live. And thus it happened that he who seized the rightful due of the rulers, all, everything that was mentioned above (which no one [else] could have, which no one [else] could take), and if it were known, if it were seen that he took the rightful due of the rulers, they conferred about it; he was punished; he was strangled. Like those who committed great [crimes], such as those who committed adultery or who robbed, so also died those who seized the rightful due of the rulers.

o ca ye ixquich ynic otlamanca nicã.

This is all of how the customs were established here.

24. *Tetectitica:* may be derived from *tetectli,* warp thread (Molina 1944, Part II: fol. 106v, *estambre de tela*). If so, as a length of thread or a cord it would fit in with measuring rod.

25. *Tlillotoc tlapalotoc:* a metaphor meaning the traditions and way of life of the ancestors. *Tlilli tlapalli,* "the black, the red," connoted the pictorial books in which the traditions were recorded.

PARAGRAPH 15
[fol. 61v col. A]

Jnic xv parrapho ipan mitoa inic tenonotzaya, tecentecaya muchi tlacatl mucētlaliaya in çivatl yn oquichtli.

Fifteenth paragraph, in which it is told how they admonished people, [how] they grouped people together, [how] everyone, men [and] women, were gathered together.[1]

Jzcatqui inic onoca in tecutlatoque in mvteneva in petlapan in icpalpa in catca inic mutlaliaya ynic quincentlaliaya ỹ macevalli y ye muchi inic quincentecaya in çivatl, in illamatlacatl in ichpuchtli nonqua vnoc in çivatl: noqua vnoc yn oquichtli, y ye ixquich in tecutli in pilly yn achcauhtli in tequitlato in telpuchtly yn pillapalivi: in tequivaque, in telpuchtlatoque: o ca yvin i, yn netecoya in moteneva inic tecutlatoloya: centlacol yc onvc yn oquichtli centlacol yc vnoc in çivatl.

Here is how the judges were when it was said they were on the mat, on the seat. When they seated themselves, when they gathered together all the commoners; when they grouped the matrons, the old women, the maidens, the women sat apart. The men sat apart—all the lords, the noblemen, the constables, the tribute bosses, the youths, the noblemen of marriageable age, the valiant warriors, the rulers of the youths.[2] Thus they were grouped; thus was held what was called a judgment. One half who were there for it were men, one half were women.

Auh in ontecoc nemauhtillo, tlatvllivi in tlein mitoz in tlein cacoz, mvmauhtia in tecutli intla ixco quinteca yn aço ytla oytlacauh yn intecutequiuh, açoce tecu-

And when they were gathered together, all were frightened. There were discussions as to what would be said, what would be heard. The lords were afraid, if they assembled them before [a judge], that perhaps they had done something wrong in their duties as lords, that perhaps

1. This paragraph is devoted to a long series of admonitions delivered by four *tecuhtlatoque*, or judges, to an assembly of lords, nobles, and commoners, both men and women, chiding them for their derelictions from their duties and threatening and proscribing various punishments. Sullivan (1974: 90, 101) classified the text of this paragraph as a *huehuetlatolli*, "the words of the elders or ancients," of the type she designated "court orations." She defined the *huehuetlatolli* as "the rhetorical orations in general—the prayers, discourses, salutations, and congratulatory speeches—in which the traditional religious, moral, and social concepts handed down from generation to generation were expressed in traditional language." This language was "characterized by the extensive use of metaphor, complementary phrasing, synonyms, and redundancy. . . . In the majority of cases the words or phrases are paired and thus give a definite rhythmic pattern to the oration." She estimated that Sahagún collected no less than eighty-nine of these rhetorical orations, which are scattered throughout the Sahaguntine Nahuatl texts in Madrid and the *Florentine Codex* (sixty of them in Book 6, the earliest collected, probably in Tlatelolco in 1547). Although Sullivan cites seven other court orations in the *Florentine Codex*, they are different in subject matter and even in style from this *Primeros Memoriales* example—which lends it special value. It is particularly valuable for the light it casts on indigenous concepts, for both sexes and for both the noble and commoner classes, of societal duties and obligations.

The paragraph is illustrated. At the top, the four judges, wearing knotted cloaks and seated on backed mat seats, are shown with speech scrolls to indicate that they are admonishing those assembled before them. The latter are pictured as four men and four women, seated facing each other in two rows. All of the women and three of the men are crying.

2. Translations of titles and offices largely follow those employed in Sahagún 1950–1982, Parts IV (Book 3) and IX (Book 8). It should be noted that throughout this paragraph, singular is used for plural as a rhetorical device.

[fol. 61v col. B]

tlacalozque:

they were to be cast out of their posts.[3]

ça no iuhqui yn achcauhtli mvmauhtia, in aço ytla oytlacauh yn imachcauhtequiuh aço quatzontecoz, aço ynca tlatoloz:

In the same way, the constables were afraid that perhaps they had done something wrong in their duties as constables. Perhaps their forehead hair would be cut or they would be accused.

ca no iuhqui in tequivaque momauhtia yn aço ytla oytlacauh, yn intequivacatequiuh aço yavc yn tley oquitacoque, aço ynca tlatoloz aço yxquatzontecozque, ypampa in cēca nemauhtilo:

In the same way,[4] the valiant warriors were afraid that perhaps they had done something wrong in their duties as valiant warriors. Perhaps they had done something wrong in battle. Either they would be accused, or the columnar tuft on their heads would be cut. Therefore there was great fear.

ça no iuhqui in telpuchtlatoque mvmauhtia aço ytla oytlacauh yn intelpuchtlatocatequiuh.

In the same way the rulers of youths were afraid that perhaps they had done something wrong in their duties as rulers of youths.

ça no yuhqui, in tequitlato momauhtia, ano ytla oytlacauh yn intequitlatocatequiuh yn aço ycan tlatoloz.

In the same way the tribute bosses were afraid that perhaps they had done something wrong in their duties as tribute bosses; perhaps they would be accused.

ça no yuhqui yn pilli çenca momauhtia, yn aço yehoanti ynca tlatoloz, yn acaçomo quichiva yn ipiltequiuh. Auh ypampa cenca momauhtiaya yntla yxco quintecaya yn tenotza, yn inpiltequiuh: yn tecenquixtia yehoāti yn altepeachcacauhtli.

In the same way the noblemen were much afraid that they would be accused; perhaps they had not discharged their duties as noblemen and therefore they were much frightened if they assembled them before [the judges] when they addressed the people about their duties as noblemen, when the city constables brought them together.

o ca yuhquin i,

Behold, in the same way

[fol. 62r col. A]

ynic cenca nemauhtiloya ça no iuhqui in civatl, yn illamatlacatl yn aço ytlacavi in içivatequivh ym moteneva y malacatl ỹ tzotzopaztli, no yehoatl yc momauhtiaya yn aço yehoatl yn avel tlacazcaltia yn avel tlacavapava: yn aço ymichmuchva yn avel quipia yn avel quimizcaltia yn aço otlatlaco yn aço ye momecatia, yn ichpuchtly yn amo macho:

the matrons [and] the old women were all very much afraid that perhaps the womanly work, what is called the spindle whorl, the batten, was done badly. They were also afraid that perhaps they had reared the children badly, that they had educated the children badly, that they had not guarded their daughters well,[5] that they had not reared them well. Perhaps the daughter had done something bad; perhaps she was living in concubinage with a man [and] it was not known.

3. *Tecutlacalozque:* read *tecutlaçalozque.*

4. *Ca:* read *ça.*

5. *Ymichmuchva:* read *imichpochuan.*

o ca yuhq'n i ynic çenca nemauhtiloya in tetecuti yn pipilti yn içivava yoan in tequivaque inçivava, ioan in calpixque inçivava ioan in tequitlatoque inçivava ioan in pipiltin ymichpuchvã ioan tecutli ichpuch ioan in tequiva ichpuch in calpixqui ichpuch, in tequitlatoque ymichpuchvan oixquich i yntla ixco quintecaya, yn tenonotza yn tecenquixtia ypampa in cenca nemauhtilo yn muchi tlacatl quitoa yn itic yn aço nehvatl noca tlatoloz: yuhquin in muchivaya, ycan oc necenteco, yn tlei mitoz.

Likewise the wives of the lords, of the noblemen, and the wives of the valiant warriors and the wives of the majordomos and the wives of the tribute bosses and the daughters of the noblemen and the daughters of the lords and the valiant warriors' daughters, the majordomos' daughters, the daughters of the tribute bosses, if they assembled them all before [the judges], when they admonished the people, when they grouped the people, were therefore all very much afraid. Everyone said to himself: "Perhaps it is I who will be accused." Such was what took place at the time that all were being grouped for what was to be said.

Auh n ovel netecoc niman ye hui, quimunilhuizque yn õpa cate, tecutlatoque, Quimunilvia. nopiltzitzine, cuix quiçaz yn ihiyotzin yn petlatl, yn icpally ca omoçentecac, yn icuitlapil, yn iatlapal yn totecuio.

Auh niman ye hui, in tecutlatoque yn oncan vmotecac, yn maceoalli, auh in oyaque niman: ye vmotlalia yn petlapa in icpalpa ynnepantla. Auh y ye vmpevaz tlatolli, niman ye cocui yn copalli contema yn tleco: Auh y yehoatl yn achto tlatoz iehoatl in contema copalli, tleco, Auh in achto tlatoz: niman ye motlatlauhtia, yn einti quimilhuia,

And when these were all assembled, they went to address those of the judges there. They said to them: "My sons, by chance will the words of the mat, of the seat come forth? Our lord's common folk have been grouped."

Then the judges went to where the commoners were grouped. And when they had gone [there], they then seated themselves on the mat, on the seat, in their midst. And before the discourse was to begin, [one of the judges] took incense; he cast it in the fire. And the one who was to speak first, cast the incense in the fire. The one who was to speak first then addressed the [other] three. He said to them:

amevitititicate. nopiltzitzine: tlatoquee, nican vnoc yn icuitlapil yn iatlapal yn totecuio, ocenquiçaco y ye ixquich, y ye mochi yn itconi ỹ mamaloni yn amocuixantzinco yn omucuitlapantznico, yn vnactica yn anquetiçiui, yn anquiciamiqui ỹ mvteneva yn tlacaquimilli in tlacacacaxtli, yn ica vntlaactoc yn amocuixantzinco yn amocuitlapantzinco. Auh cuix cẽcamatzintli cuix cententzintli tlacno-

"Here you are seated, my sons, high lords. Here are our lord's common folk, all of them. All the common people have come forth together; they have placed themselves on your lap, upon your back. You are weighed down bearing the burden, you are wearied with what is called the cargo of people, the carrying-frame of people who are placed on your lap, on your back. Will they merit the words, the utterances

[fol. 62r col. B]

pilhuizque in itechpa vitz, in itechpa yeva in petlatl in icpalli, cuix tlapuz in toptly in petlacalli yn amoxillã in amotozcatlã in tzacutoc yn amechmupialtilli yn amechmumaquilli, in tlacatl yn totecuio.

Je ac coneviliz ac conitalviz, in itconi in

that issue, that emanate from the mat, from the seat? Will the master, our lord, open the reed box, the reed coffer, in your entrails, in your throat, which is locked, which he entrusted to you, which he gave you? Paragraph 15

"Who will lift his voice now, who will ad-

mamaloni, yn yacanaloni ca nel iehoatl, yn oamechmotequitilli in tlacatl in totecuio yn ipalnemoani.

Auh oyaque otequitque, vtlacotique in oquipiaco yn petlatl yn icpalli yn oquitzitzquico yn oquipachoco, in petlatl, yn icpalli, in pipilti in tlatoque in chaneque, vquiminax, oquintlati yn totecuio mach oc ovitze mach oc yehoanti conitoquivi, conevaquivi: in itzitziquiloca in ipacholoca ỹ cuitlapilli yn atlapalli, auh in axcan ma çencamatzintli, quiça yn ihiyotzin in petlatl yn icpalli, ma tlacava yn amoyollotzin nopiltzitzine: ca ye ixquich inic nictlatlauhtia yn amoyollotzin yn amonacayotzī.

Auh yn oiuh quito y, niman ye mumalacachoa, yvicpa: tlachia yn oncan vnoc in macevalli yn oquichtli ivicpa tlachia, auh ceppa ivicpa tlachia in çiva, niman ye tlatoa quimilhuia

nican n amonoltitoqz nopilhoane y ye tixquich y ye timuchi otiçenquiçaco in titecutli, in tachcauhtli in titequiva in ticalpixqui in titelpuchtli, auh in tipilli in titlapallivi yn titlamacazqui in titelpuchtli y nican tetlan tonoc in timuzcaltia in timoapava oticenquiçaco y ye timuchi.

Auh ca no ivi i nican tonoc in ticueye in tivipille in pilli tiçivauh in tecutli tiçivauh in tequiva tiçivauh in achcauhtli tiçivauh. Auh y ye timuchi in tichpuchnemi in ticueye, in tivipille in timozcaltia in timoapava, oticenquiçaco in tivevetlacatl in tillamatlacatl yn tipillachcauhtli in tipiltecutli çan no tiuhqui yn iyollo tiçivatl yn tichpuchtli

ca ye ixquich ca vticenquiz, ca ye timuchi y nican tonoc amonoltitoque ca nican ca yn ihiyotzin yn itlatoltzin in tlacatl yn amotla-

dress the common people, those who are led? In truth, the master, our lord, by virtue of whom one lives, has given you the task.[6]

"But the noblemen, the rulers, the inhabitants of the land who labored, who toiled; those who came to guard the mat, the seat; who came to hold, who came to govern the seat, the mat, have gone. Our lord has hidden them; he has concealed them. Will they come now? Will they come to speak? Will they lift their voices in the holding, in the governing of the common folk? But now may the words, the utterances issue from the mat, the seat. My sons, may your hearts grant this. This is all with which I beseech your hearts, your bodies."

And when he had also thus spoken, then he turned around. He looked toward where the commoners were. He looked toward the men and once looked toward the women. Then he spoke. He said to [the men]:

"Here you are,[7] my sons; all of you have come forth together, you the lords, you the constables, you the valiant warriors, you the majordomos, you the youths, and you the noblemen, you the marriageable youths, you the priests, you the youths. Here you are among people. You have been reared, you have been educated. All of you have come forth together.

"And in the same way[8] you, too, are here, you with the skirts, you with the shifts, you the wives of noblemen, you the wives of valiant warriors, you the wives of constables. All of you with the skirts, with the shifts, you who go about like maidens; you who are reared, you who are educated; you who are old men, you who are old women, you noble constables, you noble lords, as well as you mature women, you maidens who have come forth together.

"Enough! You have come forth together; all of you are here; you are present; for here are the utterances, the words of the master,

6. *In tlacatl in totecuio yn ipalnemoani:* These terms were applied to an all powerful godhead most frequently identified with Tezcatlipoca and often addressed in the *huehuetlatolli.*

7. *Amonoltitoqz:* read *anmonoltitoque.*

8. *Ca:* read *ça.*

tocauh ynic tictequipachoa ynic ticciamictia y ye quicaqui yn ye quitta ynic tinemi yn munemiliz:

Xiqualcaqui y ye timuchi yn avcmo,

your ruler, because you afflict him, you weary him. Now he hears, he sees how you live your lives.

"Hear this, all of you.

[fol. 62v col. A]

yuhqui, yn avcmo iehoatl inic piallo in atl yn tepetl, inic tzitzquillo inic pachollo, inic tinemi, inic titlapia ynic titlatzitzquia inic titlapachoa, in titecutli in tipilli in tachcauhtli in titequiva in titequitlato in titelpuchtlato ym mach teva in toquiça in totlami in ticyacana in tiquixitia in icuitlapil in iatlapal in totecuio yn avcmo yuhqui yn avcmo iehoatl in tlatzitzquiliztli in tlapacholiztli in teyacanaliztli in avcmo iuhquim avcmo iehoatl, in tlacazcaltiliztli in tlacavapavaliztli yn tiqueva in tiquitoa in titeyana y ye timuchi in titecutli avcmo iuhqui in tiquitoa.

It is as if the city is no longer guarded, no longer held, no longer governed. The way you lords, you noblemen, you constables, you valiant warriors, you tribute bosses, you rulers of youths live, guard things, hold things, govern things is such that it is said that you abandon, you end, you finish your leading, your arousing of our lord's common folk. It is no longer as if there were the holding of things, the ruling over things, the leading of people; it is no longer as if there were the rearing, the educating of people, for which you make utterances, for which you speak, for which you lead people.[9] All of you lords no longer speak thus.

Auh in tachcauhtli avcmo iuhq' in tiquitoa,

auh in titelpuchtlato avcmo yuhqui in tiquitoa:

in titequiva avcmo yuhqui in tiquitoa

in titequitlato avcmo yuhqui in tiquitoa,

in titlamacazqui avcmo iuhqui in tiquitoa

ye tlayviti ye tlaxvcomiqui avcmo tlachia avcmo tlacaqui avcmo quimati in mozcaltia in moapava, ye tictlapolultia avcmo iuhqui intiquilhuia, yehoatl y ye ic cocoya in tlacatl in tlatoani: inic titlacocolizcuitia, auh ynin ma titlaxamani ma titlapuztec in tocozqui in toquetzal ye cocoya.

"And you constables no longer speak thus.

"And you rulers of youths no longer speak thus.

"You valiant warriors no longer speak thus.

"You tribute bosses no longer speak thus.

"You priests no longer speak thus.

"Now there is drunkenness; there is inebriation. No longer do those being reared, those being educated see; no longer do they hear; no longer do they know. You now trouble them; no longer do you speak thus to them. Therefore the lord, the ruler, is afflicted. Thus you disorder things. And this: do not shatter, do not break our necklace, our quetzal [feather] who is now afflicted.

Auh ca izca in motequiuh in titecutli in ye tiquilcava y ye ticpoloa in ticcuitlaviltia in maceoalli, yn itolol in imalcoch inic nemiz in pilli in piltecutli, in pilachcauhtli in pillapaliui ynic nemiz in tlavcoyaz in elçiçiviz in nētlamatiz in ivicpa in totecuio y yeva quicui y yeva cana, inic nemoa in tololli in malcochtli in nepechtequiliztli in tlavcolli in nelçiçiviztli, in can yeyo in quinequi in

"And you lords, here are your duties, you who now forget, who destroy, who provoke the common people. The noblemen, the noble lords, the noble constables, the noblemen of marriageable age are to live with heads bowed, with necks bent. Thus are they to live. They are to be sad, to sigh; they are to be afflicted toward our lord. They receive Paragraph 15
[the command]; they accept that all live with

9. *Titeyana:* read *titeyacana.*

macauhcanemiliztli in mauhcayvtl in tetlacamachiliztli in nemi, in ca, in tlalticpac yehoatl in toloa in momalcochoa in mopechteca, in tlaimacaçi i ma itla quitlaco in tetlacamati in çan mauhcayoa in mauhcacemilhuitia in quimacazi in ma itla quitlaco quenen in yehica tlatollo y yehica nenechicollo,

heads bowed, with necks bent, bowing low, sad, sighing as a separated way of life exclusively[10] requires; the fear,[11] the obedience of those who live now on earth. Those who bow their heads, who hold their necks bent, who bow low, who are respectful; who have sinned in nothing; who obey one, who only spend the night in fear, who only spend the day in fear, who fear lest they may commit some sin; of what have they been accused, for what[12] have all been gathered together?

Auh y yeva y, yn iuh nemi yn iuh quichiva y, yehoatl quipia in petlatl in icpalli iehoa yc tlatzitzquillo yc tlapachollo yehoa yc onoc in petlatl in ic-

"And as for him who lives thus, who acts thus, who guards the mat, the seat, for him for whom it is held, for whom it is ruled; for him who rests on the mat,

[fol. 62v col. B.]

palli: in aquen tlata in aque momati in ayyel in atle tlacamati acã mitoa ma iehva tlapacho y, in aiyel: auh ca ihoa tlavica in tollolli in malcochtli in tetlacamatiliztli.

on the seat, if he is without shame, if he is negligent, if he is disobedient, nowhere is it said: `Let him not rule; he is negligent.' But also he carries the bowed head, the bent neck, [in] obedience.

O ca iehoa y in mutequiuh in titecutli in ticteilhuia in tictecuitlauiltia in tlacazcaltiliztli in tlacavapavaliztli,

"These are your duties, you who are lords; you impart, you see to the rearing, the educating of people.

Auh in avcmo tiquitoa y yn avcmo ipan tiza, in avcmo ipã tinemi yehoatl y ye ic ticcocolizcuitia in tlacatl in tlatoani, Auh in axcan çan oc moquixtia in movicpa y ye timotlapololtia in titecutli ma xiquito ma xiqueva yn ipan yauh in motequiuh: auh intlacamo xvconcui xvconana aço mitztecutlaçaz in tlatoani anoço mitztotocaz anoço mitzmictiz.

"But no longer do you talk, no longer do you awaken for it, no longer do you live for it. You sicken the master, the ruler. But now while he fulfills his obligations to you, you forget your duties. You who are lords, speak; exert yourselves in what become your duties. But if you do not take [the words, if] you do not accept them, the ruler will either cast you from your station as lord, or will exile you, or will kill you.

Auh ca no iuhqui in motequiuh in tachcauhtli ic moquixtia in movicpa in tlatoani intlacamo xicchiva in motequiuh tiquatzontecoz aço titotocoz aço mitzmictiz in tlatoani.

"And it is the same[13] for you constables [with respect to] your duties. The ruler has fulfilled his obligations to you. If you do not discharge your duties, your forehead hair will be cut, or you will be exiled, or the ruler will kill you.

Auh çan no iuhqui in motequiuh in titequiva in ticyacana in telpuchtzintli in quauh-

"And it is the same as to your task, you valiant warriors who lead the youths, the ea-

10. *Can:* read *çan.*

11. *Nacauhcanemiliztli:* read *nauhcanemiliztli.*

12. *Quenen:* read *quen.*

13. *Ca:* read *ça.*

tli yn oçelotl in yaoc in moteneva in teoatl in tlachinolli in avcmo chicava in avcmo vapava in avcmo ticuitlaviltia, in tlatzontectli, in tlamatzayantli in moteneva in calixatl in apetlatl in avcmo quimocuitlauia in avcmo tlachpana in avcmo quimocuitlavia in otli i ça xiuhpachiuhtoc yehoa y ye ic moçoma y ye ic monenequi in tlacatl in totecuio, yn avcac chicava in avcac vapava iehoa y ye ic quinaya y ye ic quitlatia yn itotonca yn iyamanca, auh ça no iuhqui in ipan yauh in motequiuh yc moquixtia in tlatoani. Xiquilhui in tiquizcaltia in ticvapava. Auh intlacamo xiquilhui aço mitztotocaz in tlatoani aço mitzquatzontequiz anonoço mitzquechtequiz,

gles, the jaguars in battle, in what is called the flood, the conflagration.[14] No longer are they forceful, no longer are they strong. No longer do you exhort. They no longer see to the sentenced, the separated; to what is called the gateway, the small temple stairway landing terrace. No longer do they sweep, no longer do they see to the roads; they are covered with weeds. For this reason the master, our lord, is angry, capricious. Now no one is forceful, no one is strong. Therefore he hides his warmth, he conceals his softness. And in the same way as what your duties become, the ruler has fulfilled his obligations. Speak to those whom you rear, whom you educate. But if you do not speak to them the ruler will either banish you, or cut off your forehead hair, or[15] cut off your head.

auh ça no iuhqui in titelpuchtlato çan no tiuhqui, in tlamacazqui in titevatzin in avcmo ticuitlaviltia in tiquizcaltia in ticvapava in tlamacazcatzintli in avcmo quicui in vitztli yn acxoyatl in avcmo quipia in yoalli in ye mocochtecatoc çan no iuhqui in

"And you rulers of youths are the same; also you priests, you god-keepers. No longer do you exhort, rear, educate the novice priests. No longer do they take the maguey thorns, the fir branches. No longer do they keep watch at night. They lie sleeping. It is the same [with respect to]

[fol. 63r col. A]

motequiuh, intlacamo xicchiva y, mitztotocaz anoço mitzquatzontequiz in tlatoani anoço mitzmictiz o izca: yn motequiuh yn ipan tiyoa in ipan tecemilhuitia yn titeyacana

o yeva y, in ticcaquico in tiquiximatico in ye tixquich y ye timuchi yn acaçoc mitzilhuia in monanti in motatin yn monezcaliliz in monevapavaliz in aço mitzilhuia yn naço mitzmaca in monãti yn motati yn avc tictlacamati ça no ivi, ca ticmotzacuiltitiaz yn ac teva in atitlatlacamati in atitlacaqui yn aticmocaccanenequi in tlein mitzilhuia in mitziacana in mitzpachoa:

your duties. If you do not discharge these the ruler will banish you or cut off your forehead hair or kill you. Here are your duties: by night, by day[16] you guide people.

"This is what you have come to hear, what you have come to learn, all of you, everyone. By chance do your mothers, your fathers not impart to you your rearing, your education? Perhaps your mothers, your fathers tell you, perhaps they give it to you [but] you no longer obey. Likewise will you be punished. It is you who do not obey anyone, you who are rebellious, you who do not wish to know what they tell you, [how] they guide you, [how] they rule you."

Paragraph 15

14. *In teoatl in tlachinolli:* This was the standard metaphoric couplet for war (see Seler 1902–1923, III: 221–304; Quiñones Keber 1989a).

15. *Anonoço:* read *anoço.*

16. *Tecemilhuitia:* read *ticemilhuitia.*

o ca ivin i in quilhuiaya y ye muchi in ixquich in oquichtli in quauhtli in oçelotl in tecutl in achcauhtli yn pilli yuhqui ytlatollo catca y, ynic otlamanca, auh niman ye mocuepa invicpa in çiva, Quimilhuia

In this manner he spoke to everyone, to all the men—the eagles, the jaguars, the lords, the constables, the noblemen. Thus was his accusation, as was the custom. And then he turned around toward the women. He said to them:

nican tonoc yn ticueye in tivipille in tiçivatzintli: çã no iuhqui yn avc vel titlacazcaltia in avc vel, titlacavapava, yn tiquizcaltia in ticvapava in muchpuch in tiçivapilli yn tecutli tiçivauh in tequiva tiçivauh in calpixqui tiçivauh in tequitlato tiçivauh, in tiquizcaltia in ticvapava in muchpuch yn avcmo ticuitlauiltia in tlacuicuiliztli in tlachpanaliztli in avc vel tzava yn avc vel iquiti in avc tle vel quichiva: Cuix amo itquiuh in xochio in tlapallo yn itonal yn tilmatli, yn itonal maxtlatl yn tlaçotilmatly, yn itech quitlalia yn pilli yn oquichtli. Auh in quauhtli yn oçelotl y yehoa q'matataca in moteneva in icnoquauhtli, in icnooçelotl yn no ytech azi in itonal tilmatli in itonal maxtlatl yn açannen, quitta yn açannen itech azi yn itzonteco yn ielchiquiuh yc quitta yn itlachival yn muchpuch y yehoatl, in quimatataca in quauhtli in oçelotl, in ye tiquilcava y ye ticpoloa yn avc ticccuitlaviltia yn muchpuch in tivevetlacatl in tillamatlacatl y ye titlaivintia y ye titlaxocomictia, y ye tictepololtia in motlacazcaltiliz in motlacavapa-

"Here you are, you with the skirts, you with the shifts, you who are women. In like manner, no longer do you properly rear, no longer do you properly instruct, when you rear, when you instruct your daughters, you noblewomen, you lords' wives, you valiant warriors' wives, you majordomos' wives, you tribute bosses' wives. When you rear your daughters, when you instruct them, no longer do you urge them to gather up rubbish, to sweep. No longer do they spin well, no longer do they weave well; they do nothing well. Is it not their duty [to make] the flowered, multicolored capes, the breechcloths, the precious capes that the noblemen, the warriors wear, that is their right, that the eagles, the jaguars covet? It is said that the poor eagles, the poor jaguars also attain their rightful capes, their rightful breechcloths. Not in vain do they acquire them; not in vain do they attain them. With their heads, with their breasts they acquire your daughters' handiwork. The eagles, the jaguars covet it. Now you neglect it; now you ruin it. You old men, you old women no longer exhort your daughters. You are drunk, you are inebriated. Now you are corrupting the people with your rearing,

[fol. 63r col. B]

valiz,

with your instruction."

O ca inin i in quitoaya in achto tlatoaya, Auh in otlamito yn itlatol nimã ye conilhuia inevan:

So said the first one who spoke; and when he had ended his discourse, then he said to both [judges]:

timevititica nopiltzitzine nican, niccauilia yn ihiyotzin, yn itlatoltzin in tocozqui in toquetzal yn inetequipachol, ixtlavi pupvi:

"You are seated here, my sons. I accept the words, the utterances of our necklace, our quetzal [feather]. His work tribute has been paid; it has been rendered."

niman conilhuia, otimotequitilli, otimotlacotilli nopiltzitzine:

Then he said: "You have labored, you have toiled, my sons."

Niman iehoa niman ie tlatoa: ynic nevã yn tecutlatoque çan quiçentlaça can quicemitoa quimilhuia

nican tonoc y ye tixquich y ye timvchi in tipilli in tecutli in tachcauhtli in titeq'va in titelpuchtlato yn titeva, in titlenamacac. Auh y ye timuchi yn timutlateputztoquilia in tetlan timaquiltitoc. Auh çan no iuhqui yn ticueye in tivipille y ye tixquich y ye timuchi in tiçivapilli, y ye tillamatlacatl, in tichpuchtli, nican, otomotlamachti otomocuiltono in ticcaqui in tiquiximati yn ihiyo in itlatol yn tocozqui in toquetzal in tlatoani inic mitzitqui inic mitzmama in tipilli in tachcauhtli y ye timuchi in ticcaqui, nican, yn itetlaçotlaliz inic mitzmalhuia ynic mitztlaçotla in itlamanitiliz yn ac tehoatl in anoço ticcaqui ca ticmotzacuiltitiaz yn oticcac yn otiquixima in itetlaçotlaliz in tocozqui in toquetzal

Then they at once spoke. Thus both[17] judges just[18] came to a decision, just acted in agreement. They said to [the people]:

"Here you are, everyone, all of you who are noblemen, lords, constables, valiant warriors, rulers of youths, god-keepers, fire priests, and all of you who follow behind, who support them. And similarly, you with the skirts, you with the shifts, everyone, all of you who are noblewomen, old women, maidens. Here you have become rich, you have become wealthy. You have heard, you have become acquainted with the utterances, the words of the ruler, of our necklace, our quetzal [feather], as he carries you, as he bears you on his back. You who are noblemen, you who are constables, all of you here, are hearing of his love; how he cares for you, how he loves you. It is his custom. Who are you? Perhaps you hear that you will be punished. You have heard, you have learned of the love of our necklace, our quetzal [feather]."

çan oc no yuhqui, ym ma, ic quintlatlauhtia y, Auh niman ye conana niman ye cocui in moteneva in chicavac, in vapavac, in tlatolli in mitoa in chichinauhtiuh, in pupucatiuh in nelhuillo in nemaco, Quimilhuia

Now again, in the same manner,[19] he addressed this to them, and then they took, they received what are called the strong, the harsh words, which, as is said, burned, gave off smoke; what was spoken, what was given. He said to them:

y nican tonoc in tipilli in titecutontli in tachcauhtontli in titequivacatontli yn titelpuchtlatocatontly, yn titlenamacacatontli in titlamacazcatontli. Auh nican tonoc in ticivapilli, in pilli tiçivauh, y ye tivinti, y ye tixocomiqui y ye timuchi y nican timocaqui nican timiximati yn avcmo iuhq' yn avcmo iehoatl in monemiliz yn iuh nentihui yn amonavã in amotavan, yn omomiquilique in vel quitlavcolnonotztivi in vel quitlavcoltemotivi, ynic nentivi yn oquincaquiliaya,

"Here you are, you noblemen, you little lords, you little constables, you little valiant warriors, you little rulers of youths, you little fire priests, you little offering priests. And here you are, you noblewomen, you wives of noblemen. You are drunk, you are inebriated. All of you here understand, you are here aware that your way of life no longer is like that which your mothers, your fathers went about living, they who have died; they who in sadness went about crying out to, who in sadness went about seeking the master, our lord, as they went living. He heard

17. In the passage starting *o ca inin in* and ending *inic neva*, peculiarities of spelling permit more than one interpretation. *Inevan* might be read *in yehuan* or *in nehuan* (the latter seems more likely). *Niman iehoa* is probably to be read *niman yehuan; inic neva* is probably to be read *inic nehuan*. It appears necessary to be guided by the context of the passage. It is logical to assume that *niccuilia* is meant rather than *niccauilia*, although it is not quite correct grammatically.

18. *Can:* read *çan*.

19. *Iuqui, ym ma:* read *yuhquinma*.

Paragraph 15

[fol. 63v col. A]

yn inchoquiz, in intlavcol, in imelçiçiuh in tlacatl in totecuio in oquimomaquiliaya yn itotonca yn iamanca yn oquipiaco yn izquican icac in tonacayutl yn no tealtique in no nanacaquaqz yn omotlamachtitiaque yn amo yc atlamati yn amo ic cuecuenoti yn çã nilhuiz toloa, momalcochoa mopechteca ynic nentivi ynic onotivi.

their weeping, their sadness, their sighs. He gave them his warmth, his softness. They came to watch over every place where there were their fruits of the earth. They also bathed [sacrificial victims]; they also ate mushrooms; they were rich. Not because of this did they become arrogant, not because of this did they become proud. They bowed their heads the more, they bent their necks, they bowed. Thus they lived, thus they were.

Auh in axcan otiquiçaco, otimoquetzaco in titecutontli in tiquacviltontli, in tachcauhtontli in tipilli y ye timochi in titelpuchtontli in titlamacazcatõtli y ye nican tixcuecuechotinemi y ye nican timoquatlaztinemi, Auh y yehoatl yn avcmo ticpinava in pilli in tlatoani, y nican chaneque quimacazi in atl in tepetl quimacazi in pilli in tlatoani in vevetzin in illamatzin quipinava quimaviztilia quitoa y nican channeque quẽ techitaz in tonan in totan.

"And now you have come forth, you have stood up, you little lords, you little tonsured ones,[20] you little constables, you noblemen, all you little youths, you little novice priests. Here you go about with your noses in the air, here you go about tossing your heads, and you are no longer modest in the presence of noblemen, of the ruler. Here the inhabitants respect, the city respects noblemen, the ruler, old men, old women. They are modest, they honor them. The inhabitants here say: 'How will our mother, our father regard us?'

Auh in axcan otiquiçaco otimoquetzaco in titlamauiltia in titlacuicuitivetzin, in amo monemac in motech tictlalia y ye mitztlapololtia ym maxca in motlatqui y ye ic tivinti y ye ic tixocomiqui in tiqui, in ticqua yn avcmo tictlamauiçalhuia in totecuio in otimotlapololti ypampa yn amo titlanonotzalli in tehoatl mopan, mitoa in ticnopillaveliloc yn amo titlatlaçocamatini:

"And now you have come forth, you have stood up. You amuse yourselves with something,[21] you snatch things. They are not your possessions that you set beside you. Your possessions, your property craze you. You are drunk because of them, you are inebriated because of them. You drink them, you eat them. You no longer venerate our lord. You have become crazed because you are not reprimanded. About you it is said that you are ingrates, that you are ungrateful.

çan no tiuhqui y nican, tonoc in tiçivatl yn titlatlavelilocacuitia yn çan no tiuhqui in avcmo yuh tinemi inic nentivi in amopihoã yn iuh tzava in iuh iquiti yn iuh motlamachtitivi yn iuh mocuiltonotivi yn iuh tlatlaçomativi yn iuh quitlapialitivi in totecuio: yn oanquipoloqz yn amonemiliz:

"You are also like this, you women who are here. You are a bad influence, you who are also like this. You no longer live as your elder sisters go living [and] thus spin, weave, go becoming rich, becoming wealthy, showing gratitude, watching over things for our lord, you who here have destroyed your way of life.

20. *Tiquaviltontli:* perhaps to be read *tiquacuiltontli; tiquauhtontli* is also possible, although the text would be expected to match the term with *tocelotontli.*

21. *Titlamauiltia:* It seems necessary to assume a verb *mauiltia.* Derivation from *auiltia* would mean interpreting the term as *qui-tla-m(o)-auiltia,* in which the sequence of prefixes is unusual.

auh in ac tehoatl yn amo ticmocaccanenequi in mitoa in tlatolli y. yn at a nican tinemiznequi xitechtlalcavi canapa xiauh xictlalcavi yn atl in tepetl xictlalcaui in petlatl in icpalli ticxolopicuitia

i nican ca iuh meva ca iuh mitoa ca iuhqui tlatolli, O ca yvin i in quitoa inic ome tecutlato. Auh yn otlamito yn itlatol nima ye q'mo-

"And who are you that you do not wish to listen to what is said, to these words? Perhaps you do not wish to live here. Leave us! Go away somewhere! Leave the city! Leave the mat, the seat! You make a fool of it."

Such were the words thus spoken, thus uttered here. Thus the second judge spoke. And when he had concluded his oration, then

[fol. 63v col. B]

tlatlauhtia yn oc cequinti quimilhuia, conilhuia otimotequitilli otimotlacotilli.

Auh inic ey, tecutlato niman ie tlatoa niman ie quitoa quimotlatlauhtia yn otlatoqz quimonilhuia oanmotequitilique oanmotlacotilique, oanquimonanamiquilique in tlacatl in totecuio: oquiz yn ihiyotzin in petlatl in icpalli.

Auh niman ye tlatoa niman ye quinonotza y ye ixquich y ye muchi çan no iuhqui, in quimilhuia

y nican tonoc y ye tixquich y ye timuchi nican ticcaq' yn ihiyo yn itlatol in petlatl in icpalli in cantica: Cuix ticcaqui cuix noço aticcaqui yc ixtlaui ic pupui yn itlatol in atl in tepetl in titconi, in timamaloni in aticmomachitia. in quenin titquiva in quenin timamalo in quenin tiyouiltillo in quenin ticemilhuitiltilo: auh nican tomotlamachtia nican tomocuiltonoa ic nequixtillo in movicpa in moztla in viptla in tlein no tiquittaco in tlei no timailli in tlein oticmochiuilli in titecutli in tachcauhtli in titequiva in titelpuchtlato yn titlamacazqui in titevatzin.

the others spoke. They said to him: "You have labored, you have toiled."

And the third judge then spoke; he then addressed the [other] high lords. He said to them: "You have labored, you have toiled; you have aided the master, our lord. The utterances of the mat, the seat have come forth."

And then he spoke; he admonished all, everyone, in the same fashion. He said to them:

"Here you are, all of you, everyone. Here you hear the utterances, the words of the mat, of the seat; you are receiving them. Perhaps you listen, perhaps you do not listen. The debt has been paid; the payment has been rendered with the words of the city. You common people do not inform yourselves as to how you are ruled, how you are governed, how you have been passed through the night, how you have been passed through the day. But here you become rich, you become wealthy. Thus the obligations for you have been discharged for tomorrow, for the day after, for what you have also acquired, for what you have also done for yourselves, for what you have also effected for yourselves, you lords, you constables, you valiant warriors, you rulers of youths, you offering priests, you god-keepers.

Auh y ye timuchi in tiçivatl in tiçivapilli y ye tixquich in nican tonoc in tlein no tax ca ticmotzacuiltitiaz ca timiquiz ca titotocoz in ac tehoatl yn atitlacanemi in tepan ticacalaqui, in ticmocuitlavitinemi in aqually, yn aiectli yn achivaloni in teiçollo, yn tecatzauh yn aticmauhcaitta in teçivauh yn

"And all of you women, you noblewomen, all of you who are here now: for what you do you will be punished, you will die, you will Paragraph
be banished. Who are you? You are dissolute, 15
you wander from house to house, you go about devoting yourselves to evil, to wickedness, to what should not be done, to what

cavalli yn mopan mitoa in titlacuicuitivetzin in ticcuitivetzin yn amo monemac yn amo molhuil yn amo momaçeval yn ipã titlayxami yn ipan tiquixami, yn teçivauh auh in cavalli, ynin, camo nemoaloni in moteneva in teuhtli in tlaçolli yntla ipan xano xitzitzquillo titetepacholoz ca vtlica tivetztoz in mitoa y yehoatl i in ticmotequititinemi intla ipan tinemihi,

soils people, to what defiles people. You do not regard others' wives [or] widows with respect. Of you it is said that you are snatchers of things, grabbers of what is not your property, what is not your possession, what is not rightfully yours. You deliberately attract women; you run after others' wives and widows. This is not the way one lives. It is called dirt, filth. If you are caught in it, if you are seized, you will be stoned, you will be cast forth on the road. This is what is said: that you go about burdening yourself with it if you persist.[22]

[fol. 64r col. A]

xiccava ça xitlamatinemi Auh intlanoço oticchiuh ximotlacavalti ximilochti ximocuitivetzin ca ic moquixtia in tecutlatoque in mitzitqui in mitzmama i nicã tiquintzontetconeva ca yeppa mitoa amo nemoaloni:

Stop; go calmly. And if, perhaps, you have done this, stop; draw back; turn back. With this the judges discharge their obligation. They carry you, they bear you on their backs. Here you give them headaches. It has been said before that this is not the way one lives.

auh ye izca inic nemoa in tlavcolli yn elçiçiuhtli nica mani in tevatl in tlachinolli at cana itla motech, quichivaz in tonatiuh in tlaltecutli, in tiçatl yn ihuitl, yehoa ic tiyoliz yehoa ic tinemiz yehoa yc timotlamachtiz

"And now here is the way one should live: it is in sadness, it is with sighs. Here there is the flood, the conflagration [of war]. Perhaps somewhere the sun, the lord of the earth, will make the chalk, the feathers [of sacrificial victims] of you.[23] With this you will be born again, with this you will live, with this you will be rich.

Auh acanocomo velli ma ye mel xiçacamo, xitlacuentoma, xitlacuentlapana ximeteca xictlaça in nopalli yehoa yc timotlamachtiz, ticpiaz in tonacayutl titecoaz titealtiz tinanacaquaz timocaltiz qualcã yez in mochan: o yeva y o yehoa i, yn nemoaloni, yehoa yn tilhuillo iehoa in ticaquitillo.

"But perhaps[24] this is not possible. Be diligent. Rework the soil; make ridges; break up the earth; plant the magueys; cultivate cacti. In this way you will become rich. You will take care of the sustenance of life. You will buy slaves; you will bathe [sacrificial victims]; you will eat mushrooms; you will build yourselves houses; your homes will be fine places. This, this is a life worthy of being lived. This is what you are told, this is what you are given to understand.

Jn axcan, amo, tayo, amo mitzaoa, in petlatl ynicpalli: titlachialtillo, titlacaquitillo,

"Now you are not corrected. The mat, the seat does not berate you. You are instructed,

22. *Tinemihi:* read *tinemini.*

23. *In tonatiuh in tlaltecutli, in tiçatl in ihuitl:* This phrase, following the metaphoric couplet for war, *in teoatl in tlachinolli* (see note 14, this paragraph), refers to the sacrificial death that was necessary to maintain the sun and the earth. Sacrificial victims were streaked with chalk and pasted with feathers.

24. *Acanacomo:* read *acanaçomo.*

in mitznonotza yn mitzilhuia; in petlatl yn icpalli yntla ye timotlamachtia: cuix timacaz yntla omitzmacac in totecuio yntla ye ticpialia yn iaxca yn itlatqui yn icococauh, yn totecuio:

o ca yxquich i, in quitoa in teeca in tecutlato. Auh in otlato yn otlan yn itlatol, niman ye quimotlatlauhtia, yn otlatoque, achto quimonilhuia:

Nopiltzitzine, oanmotequitilique oanmotlacotilique.

Auh niman, ye valmiquania, Jnic navi, in tecutlato niman ye quintlatlauhtia in tecutlatoque, eynti. Quimonilvia.

nopiltzitzine tlatoquee, oanmotequitilique oanmotlacotilique, o nicã omotlamachti, o nican, õmocuiltono: yn icuitlapil yn iatlapal in totecuio, o nican vncecẽma: o nican vnchachayavac, yn iuhqui chalchiuitl, yn iuhq' tevxivitl, in xictic yn olloliuhqui in tevilacachiuhqui, yn nacatic in tomatic yn nican, vncecetlalma yn ihiyo yn itlatol yn petlatl in icpalli yn atl in tepetl ca tel yehoatl ynic etiçivi ynic ziamiqui yn amoyollotzin, in amo-

you are informed; the mat, the seat exhorts you, tells you: If you are rich, perhaps you have been given [something]; if our lord has given you[25] [something], if you guard it for him, it is the property, the possession, the riches of our lord."

This is everything that the third judge said. And when he had spoken, when he had ended his oration, then they addressed those who had spoken. First they said to them:

"My sons, you have labored, you have toiled."

And then they left their places. Then the fourth judge addressed them. He said to the three judges:

"My sons, high lords, you have labored, you have toiled. Here the lord's common folk have become rich; they have become wealthy.[26] Here have been scattered, here have been strewn what are like green stones, like turquoises, green, round, circular, [long] as a reed, [plump] as a tomato. Here the utterances, the words of the mat, of the seat, of the city are strewn over the ground.[27] However, your hearts, your bodies are heavy with fatigue; they are dropping with fatigue. Rest your hearts,

[fol. 64r col. B]

nacayotzin, ma motlalli yn amoyollotzin, ma xicmoçevilican yn amonacayotzin, nopiltzitzine tlatoquee:

ca ye ixquich inic nictlatlauhtia yn amotecuyotzin yn amotlatocayotzin, can ca, yn cana, in quicui, ca yc ixtlaui ca ic pupui yn ihiyo yn itlatol yn petlatl ynicpalli: ma ximovetzitican.

niman ye mocuepa yn ivicpa, y ye ixq'ch y ye muchi, Quimilhuia

nican tonoc y ye tixquich y ye timochi: oticenquiçaco nicã otican, nican, oticcuic yn intlatol yn imihiyo in tlatoque yn motiçayo

refresh your bodies, my sons, high lords.

"This is all I have to address to your lordships, your high lordships. Where are those who take, who receive the utterances, the words of the mat, of the seat with which the debt is paid, the service is rendered? May you take your repose."

Then he turned around toward all of them, everyone. He said to them:

"Here you are, all of you, everyone who has gathered together. Here you have received, you have taken the words, the utter- Paragraph 15

25. *Timacaz:* read *timacoz.*

26. *Omocuiltono:* read *omocuiltono.*

27. *Vncecetlalma:* meaning is suggested by *vnceceme,* above.

yn mihuio yn tiquauhtli in toçelutl yn ye timuchi, Auh in tiçivatl in ticueye in tivipille çan no yhui, nican, ticcui yn motiçayo ỹ mihuiyo yn oticac yn ac tehoatl in titlacaqui: tla motech xocomopachilhuitiuh tla xicmomapiquilitiuh yn ihiyo, in petlatl in icpalli yn atl in tepetl: tla ic xõmauhcaye tla ic xomauhcanemi. Auh in ac tehoatl in atitlacaqui, a ye tonquiçaz, a ye ic tivetzca a ye ic timotepeva a ye ic tivetzcatiuh yn açiuhqui yn acacehoatl yn oticac yn oticuic: Auh in tiçivatl tlacuelle cana xocontlaztiquiçaz in tilhuilo in timaco, tlacuelle yca xivetzca yca xicamanalo ica ximotopeva: auh ca motiçayo ca mihuiyo y moztla y viptla, ỹ macuil ỹ matlac yn omopan muchiuh yn oticnamiquito yn otilhuiloc yn oticaquitiloc.

ances of the judges. [and] your chalk, your feathers, you eagles, you jaguars, all of you; and you women, you with the skirts, you with the shifts: likewise you receive your chalk, your feathers. You have heard them. Who are you that you should hear things? Clamp them to you; hold fast to the utterances of the mat, of the seat, of the city. Be in fear[28] of it; live in fear of it. And who are you that you should not listen? Will you come to naught? Are you not mocking, are you not laughing, are you not poking fun at what is perhaps like [or] perhaps not[29] what you have heard, what you have grasped? And you who are women, hurry and quickly cast away somewhere what you have been told, what you have been given. Hurry and laugh at it, make fun of it, mock it. But your chalk, your feathers will have come to you tomorrow, the day after, in five days, in ten; you will have met with them, as you have been told, as you have been informed.

Auh ca ça tequitl tonchochoquililoz ca ça tequitl tontlatlauhtiloz ca vc tle motlatollo yn omopan açic, yn vmopan muchiuh yn aticcaqui in çã ticvetzca yn otilhuiloc in tlatolli:

O nopilhoane y ye tixquich y ye timuchi y nican tonoc in tiçiuatl, o, ca vnequixtiloc, in movicpa omoquixtique in tecutlatoqz in tichoquililoni in ticuitlapill in tatlapalli manoço yhuian manoço yocoxca in ximonemiti y ye tixquich y ye timuchi, macamo xixtomavatinemi, macamo xiçicatinemi. o. yehoa y, ynic tiçentlalilo, y ye timuchi amo tiquitoz ỹ man ic caquini in intlatol in tonanti in totatin, o. ca yehoa y, in nelhuillo in nemaco onicã vnquaquauhtiticatca yn amoyollo yn amonacayo ma yhuian ximovicatihuia

"And you will only be wept for, you will only be supplicated, for now what you have been accused of has overtaken you, has befallen you. You do not listen; you only laugh at the words you are told.

"My daughters, everyone, all of you who are here, you women: the obligations have been discharged; the judges have discharged their duty to you. You common folk should be wept for. May all of you, everyone, live in peace, in tranquillity. Do not go about foolishly; do not go about madly. The reason you have been gathered together, all of you, is not so that you should speak [but] that the words of our mothers and fathers are to be heard. [With] what has been spoken, with what has been given, your hearts, your bodies have been made firm here. Go in peace.

[fol. 64v col. A]

ca oquiz ca vtlan in tlatolli.

o. ca yvin i in quitoaya, inic navi, in tecutlato ca chocaya in q'toaya. Auh in oquiz, yn

The oration is ended; it is concluded."

Thus the fourth judge spoke. He wept as he spoke. And when he had ended his dis-

28. *Xomauhcaye:* read *xonmauhcayez.*

29. *Aciuqui in acacehoatl:* read *aço yuhqui in acaço yehuatl;* cf. *acaçono.*

itlatol niman ye quimotlatlauhtia, in tecutlatoque yn eintin.o.yn muchivaya ynic tecutlatoloya. Auh in tlacpac vmito yn iuh nemauhtiloya yn ayamo quiça tlatolli y çan oc neteteco y yehoa ic nemauhtillo.

inic momauhtia tecutli
in pilli ic momauhtia
in tequiva ic momauhtia

in calpixqui ic momauhtia
in telpuchtlato ic mȯmauhtia

ca iuh mochivaia, yn aquin tlein quitlacoaya, ca yca, tlatolloya, ca teixpan yn aço totoco yn anoço quatzonteco yn anoço vey in tlein no quitlaco ca teixpan in miquia in mecaniloya in mitoa yca tlatolloya intla çan totocoz, ca teixpan in valquixtillo ca teixpan in valtopevalotiuh ca teixpan in valquiçaya in altepeachcauhti, ynic tlapialoz in inchan inic atle quiquixtiz intlatqui. o. ca iuhquin i, ynic mauhcamanca.

Auh cenca vel ic otetlacamachoc ynic onemauhtiloya in cenca nemauhtilo tlatoloz in necentlaliloz. Auh in iquac yn omochivi in oquiz in tecutlatolli in atle, omuchiuh ca iquac moyolalia yn ixq'chtin in tlatequipanoa in ixquichtin yn omoteneuhque yn tlatequipanoa, ca iuh mochivaya ca ic mauhcamãca ca çenca ic mavizmanca çenca muchi tlacatl ic muzcalitinenca çẽca ic nezcaliloya o ca iuhquin i inic muchivaia ynic amo çan nen quiçaya yn intecutlatol yn tecutlatoque.

Auh in tlein no mito tlapac, ca çan oc onequixtiloc intlatoltica.

auh inic oppa tecutlatoloz yuh muchivaz,

course, then the three judges there addressed him.[30] Thus the judging was done. And as it has been said above, since all were fearful, now no words came forth. Now they were only assembled. For this reason all were fearful.

For this reason the lords were afraid.
For this reason the noblemen were afraid.
For this reason the valiant warriors were afraid.
For this reason the majordomos were afraid.
For this reason the rulers of youths were afraid.

Thus was it done. If someone did something wrong, because of it there was accusation. In the presence of the people he was banished or his forehead hair was cut. Or if the crime he committed was something great, he died in the presence of the people; he was hanged, as was said, because of the accusation. If he was banished, in the presence of the people he was driven away; in the presence of the people he was banished, he was cast out. In the presence of the people the constables of the city came forth so that their homes would be guarded, so that none of their possessions would be removed. Thus fear was established.

And indeed the people were therefore very obedient. Therefore there was fear; there was great fear that there would be accusations, that there would be a gathering together. And when this happened, the sentences came forth. When nothing happened, at that time they rejoiced. All worked; all did what were called services. In this manner was it done. With this fear was established. With this great respect was established. Everyone lived thus reared; they were thus well reared. Thus it came about that the sentences of the judges were not issued in vain.

And as to what has also been mentioned above,[31] obligations were discharged through their discourses.

And the second time there was to be a Paragraph 15

30. *Quimotlatlauhtia:* read *quimotlatlauhtilia.*
31. *Tlapac:* read *tlacpac.*

in iuh omito, Auh in iquac tecutlatoloya matlacpoaltica omey, ipan cemilhuitonalli navacatl tlatocatonalli mitoaya ytonal in petlatl in icpalli, Auh inic oppa tecutlatoloia iquac in tlacaxipevaliztli in ayac mally yn ayac temalacac quetzaloz ic nonotzaloya pilli ic nonotzalloya in quauhtli,

judging, it would be as has been described; and the time that there was judging was every two hundred and [sixty] days,[32] on the day sign Four Reed, the ruler's day sign, called the day sign of the mat, of the seat. And [also a] second time that there was a judging was at the time of Tlacaxipehualiztli, if there were no captives, if no one were to stand on the stone of gladiatorial sacrifice. For this reason the noblemen were admonished, the eagle warriors were admonished.

auh inic expan tecutlatoloya iquac in acaço q'avi yn aço mayanallo iehoatl ic mitoaia yn avcmo vellamaçeva ỹ muzcaltia ỹ moapava in quauhtli in ocelutl in telputzintli in tlamacazcatzintli in çivatl in ichpuchtli yn avcmo quimocuitlavia in tlacuicuiliztli in tlachpanaliztli.

And the third time there was judging was when there was perhaps no rain, or there was famine. Therefore it was said that no longer did those being reared, those being educated, the eagle [and] jaguar warriors, the young warriors, the young priests, the women, the maidens perform their penances. No longer did they see to gathering up rubbish, to sweeping.

Auh inic

And

[fol. 64v col. B]

napa, tecutlatoloya yn tlacpac omito yuh mochiva in aquin tlein no quitlaco, ica, tlatollo, yca, nenechicollo, ica, maviztli moteca, teilhuillo in tlein quitzacutiuh teixpan ỹ miq' yn aço telpuchtzintli, omillamavi mitoaya xiqualcaquican yehoatl i yn quitzacutiuh yn omillamavi in telpuchtontli yehoatl, in mitoa, in tlacximimictia yn yavc, quicximimictia in quauhtli yn oçelutl. Auh ioan mitoaya tlacuecuechmictia quitlacoa in vevetl yn ayacachtli yn ipialoca in atl in tepetl.

the fourth time there was judging took place as mentioned above also when someone did something wrong. Because of him there was accusing; because of him there was assembling; because of him there was spreading of fear. The people were told for what [reason] they punished one. In the people's presence there died perhaps a youth who had become old-womanish.[33] It was said: "Hear this. That youth whom they punish is one who has become old-womanish." It was said that he impeded something in battle; he hindered the eagle [and] jaguar warriors. And it was also said that he ill used, he defiled the upright drum, the rattle, the watching of the city.

Auh y yehoatl mitoaia tlatlaçolmictia avc tle muchiva in qualli. avcac, tlama, in pilli in quauhtli yn oçelotl.

And it was said of him who was put to death for sexual excesses that no longer had anything good been done. None of the noblemen, the eagle [and] jaguar warriors took captives.

32. *Omey:* read *omeipoaltica.* On the day *navacatl (nahui Acatl),* Four Reed, as a day celebrating with feast and ceremony the installation of new lords, a day especially consecrated to them, see Sahagún 1950–1982, Parts V-VI (Books 4–5): 88–89.

33. *Omillamavi:* The term may be broken down to *o-in(o)-ilama-hui,* literally, he was old womaned or he old-womaned himself.

Auh ynin muchivaya yn ica, tlatolloya iquac in muchivaya tequantonalli cemilhuitonalli o ca iuhquin i in muchivaya ynic tlatolloya yn aquin ica, tecutlatolloya.

And this was done, there was accusation, because of these things, when there was a beastly day sign. This was what was done when there was accusation when someone was judged because of it.

PARAGRAPH 16
[fol. 65r col. A]

Jnic xvi parrapho in quenĩ qualania, in tlatoani yn ipan mitoa.

Jnic peva in quallantli inic quallani tlatoani yehoatl yn oquichotl yn yavyutl yn iuhcan tlamanca yn ivivi tlama yn ovican tlama ynic oquichtli: auh in yacuican tlama ayamo ixquich in quicui in pilatquitl, auh quin iquac yn omoxi y ye tequiva y ye navi, ocaçic iquac quicui in tlatocatlatquitl in quetzalalpiloni yn inacoch tevxivitl yn itenteuh qztzalchalchivitl: auh in icozqui tevcuitlatl chayavac cozcatl auh contlalia tevcuitlaievacozcatl ioan cõtlalia in matemecatl ioan tevcuitlacotzevatl, ioan quicui in tlatocatilmatli in tlaçotli, ioan tlaçomaxtlatl: o ca iuhquin i ynic quicuia, in tlatocatlatquitl

mitoaya açan nen quicui ytzonteco yelchiquiuh

ynic quicui yc pachivi yn iollo yn ixquich pilli in ixquich quauhtli yn oçelutl ioan ỹ maçeoalli ca amo çã nen oytech azic yn ixquich ytech quitlalia in tlatocatlatquitl ca imiquiz ypatiuh o ca iuhquin i, ynic ayac vel

Sixteenth paragraph, in which it is told how the ruler became angry.[1]

In this way the anger began; in this way the ruler became angry. For prowess, for war, thus was it customary: When with difficulty one took a captive, when in a dangerous place one took a captive, one thereby became a manly [warrior]. But when he took a captive the first time, he did not yet receive all the noble accouterments. But later, when his hair was cut, when he was now a valiant warrior, when he had now attained four [captives], he assumed vestments of the high nobility: the [head] band with [two] quetzal [feather] tassels, his turquoise ear plugs, his quetzal [feather] colored green stone lip adornment, and his necklace, which was the gold necklace with radiating pendants. And he set in place a leather [and] gold necklace. And he set in place a bracelet and a golden band for the calf of the leg, and he assumed a cape of high nobility which was precious, and a precious breechcloth. In this way he attained the vestments of high nobility.

It was said: "Not for nothing did he assume his head, his breast."

When he assumed [the adornments], his heart was thereby satisfied. Not for nothing did all the noblemen, all the eagle warriors, the jaguar warriors, and the commoners attain [and] set in place vestments of high no-

1. Sullivan also included this paragraph in the category of *huehuetlatolli* that she denominated "court orations." The topic dealt with is the anger of the ruler, instigated by various derelictions of his subjects, above all cowardice and/or failure to perform properly on the battlefield in time of war. The courageous warriors who captured enemy prisoners were rewarded, in a very structured system, with insignia and costume items that proclaimed their valor and miltary successes. Those who failed could be publicly disgraced or even put to death.

At the head of the paragraph is an illustration of a bearded lord seated on a backed mat throne, his arm extended and finger pointing, with speech scrolls indicating the giving of commands.

itech moxicoaya tlatoani. Auh in aquin ytech moxicoaya in can quauhtli yn oçelutl ca quimictiaya yc quallani.

bility, for their death was their price. For this the ruler was angered by no one. But [he was angered] by anyone who somewhere killed an eagle warrior, a jaguar warrior; because of this he became angry.

Auh in pilli yn amo çenca ovican tlama yn yavc, auh nixquich nipa tlacpac omito in itech quitlalia tlatoani niman no quicuitivetzin no ixquich ytech q'tlalia ic quallani in tlatoani amo quiça in itlatol çan niman ye moxixinia in iquac ilhuitl avcmo quicui in ixquich

But if a nobleman did not in very dangerous places take captives in war, and all those mentioned above whom the ruler placed by his side [also failed], he also turned against all those whom he had placed by his side; for this the ruler became angry. His word did not come forth. Then, at the time of a festival [the nobleman] was ruined. He no longer assumed all

[fol. 65r col. B]

yn itlatocatlatqui, çan concui, aço, ayatl, anoço tequitilmaçolli: auh ça iztac maxtlaçol, avcmo quicui in itlatocatlatqui auh niman ye itto tlachia in tlacatecatl intlacochcalcatl, auh in pipilti oquichti tlatoque ioan in tecutlatoque niman ye nemauhtillo yn oquitaque avctle ytech ca yn itlatocatlatqui yn tlatoani niman ye mitoa tlein ic cocoya tlatoanin avcmo quicui yn itlatocatlatquy niman ye tlachiallo niman ye conitta, yn pilli yn amo oquichtli yn amo çenca ovican otlama yavc.

his vestments of high nobility; rather, he assumed a maguey fiber cape or a worn cape of rough cloth, and only a worn white breechcloth. He no longer assumed his vestments of high nobility. And then he was seen; the commander of men, the chief of the arrow house[2] looked. And then the noblemen, the manly [warriors], the high lords, and the judges were afraid. They saw that none of the ruler's vestments of high nobility were on him. Then it was said that the ruler sickened because [the nobleman] no longer assumed the vestments of high nobility. Then he was looked at; they then saw that the nobleman was not a manly [warrior], that he did not in very dangerous places take captives in war.

Auh ixquich itech ca in ixquich ytech ca tlatoani niman ye nenonotzallo conilhuia yn tlatoani ma cocoliztli mitzmocuitilli yn telpuchtontli in amo ynemac in amo itlatqui moquicuitivetz, Auh ynin quen ticmitalhuia quen tlacava ỹ moyollotzin açon tlatlatitivi, aço comictitivi quen ticmitalhuia,

And there was conferring among all who were by the ruler's side.[3] They said to the ruler: "May the miserable youth who did not take up his gifts, his vestments, not make you sicken.[4] And further, what will you say? How is your heart inclined?" Perhaps they were to go to do away with him; perhaps they were to go to kill him. "What will you say?"

Auh niman ye quitoa, in tlatoani onechmocnelilique in tachcavã in pipiltin auh in

And then the ruler said: "Our valiant warriors, the noblemen and the lords, have done

2. *In tlacatecatl in tlacochcalcatl:* These titles were those borne by the two highest military commanders (Sahagún 1950–1982 Part IX [Book 8]: 77, 87; cf. Hassig 1988: 53, 278).

3. *Ixquich ytech ca* is repeated in the original text.

4. *Ma cocoliztli mitzmocuitilli:* A verb *cuitilia* (compulsive of *cui*) can be assumed, here in its vetative form. Perhaps it is also meant to be reverential.

tetecutli anca nechtlaçotla ioan, ca tel noçehoatl inic quipia in inchã yn imaltepeuh ma quimotlavcolilicã ma quimotlatlatilican,

Auh niman ye viloa, niman ye comictia auh yn ocomictique, niman ye vi in quinonotzazque

conilhuia totecue tlatoane tlacatle ca vticmotlatilli ym mumaçeval yn ocatca quivalitoa in pipiltin in tlatoque in machcavã ma quimucaquiti ca vquimutlalcauilli in imaçeoal yn ocatca ma mutlalli in iyollotzin yn inacayotzin:

niman ye quivalitoa ce ye qualli oquimucnelilique in imauh yn itepeuh in pipiltin in tlatoque otlacauhqui yn iyollotzin.

Auh anoço quitoz in tlatoani macamo nicã miqui niman ye yavtlatollo ma vmpa miqui yn yavc

auh ic mitoaya can ompa quinavalmictia auh niman ie muchiva yn yavyvtl yn çequi neltiaya vmpa miquia, auh in cequi avel miquia ye õpa oc ceppa vellamaya yn ivivi in quenin motetlaçaltiaya yn ivivi yn tlamaya, yn ovican, auh oc ceppa in yavtlatollo yn aço vel miquitiuh anoço oc ceppa tlamaz yn ovican tlama, Auh y ye iuhqui

me a service; so do they love me. Yet[5] also in this way they guard their homes, their city. Let them have pity on him. Let them do away with him."

And then they all departed. Then they killed him. And when they had killed him, they went to advise [the ruler].

They said to him: "Our lord, ruler, master, we have done away with him who was your commoner. The noblemen, the high lords, your valiant warriors say: 'May he hear; he who was his commoner has gone away. May his heart, his body find repose.'"

Then [the ruler] said: "It is well. The noblemen, the high lords have done their city a service. Its heart is inclined."

But perhaps the ruler would say: "Let him not die here. War is declared at once. Let him die in battle."

And it was said that they killed him there secretly. And then war was made. They ascertained that some had died and that some had not died. There, once, one with difficulty took a captive. In the same way as one was overpowered, with difficulty one took a captive in a dangerous place. And once more when war was declared, either he would go to die or again he would take a captive; in a dangerous place he took a captive. And similarly

[fol. 65v. col. A]

ynic napa y ye ipan yavtlatollo yn avelmiqui y ye izquipa tlama, Auh y yehoatl yc mocava in tlatoani ca vquinenevilli in tlatoani quin yeva yc necaco, auh ic necavallo avcac tle ipan quitotinemi.

Auh in çan quauhtli in oçelutl in çan tecutli in can tlatoquilia pilli:

yn anoço çivatl intla moxicoa ytech in tlatoani ca atlei, ytlatollo içiuhca cõmictia yn

when for the fourth time war was declared, he did not die; each time he took a captive. And the ruler left off; the ruler made him the equal of other [noblemen]. They no longer went saying anything about what a short while before was heard and the reason for [his] being abandoned.

And there was only the eagle warrior, the jaguar warrior; there was only the lord. They only[6] followed after the noblemen.

Or if the ruler became angry with a woman,
there was no accusing her. They killed her Paragraph 16

5. *Noçehoatl:* read *noço yehuatl.*

6. *Can:* read *çan.*

tlatvi ocommictique, o yehoa y, ynic mauhcamanca inic ayac itech muxicoz in tlatoani

ioã yn o yc temictiaya in çan quicuitivetzin, in itonal tlatoani ym maçevalli yn iuh tlaqua yn iv atli yn iuhca tlatoani y ye no iuh tlaqua y ye no iuh atli auh no tzacuiltiloya no mictiloya.

o ca iuhquin i ynic qualania yn tlatoani ỹ mitoaya yn tlatocacocolli yn tlatocatlavelli.

quickly; at dawn they killed her. By this, fear was established so that the ruler would not be angered by anyone.

And they killed people who took the ruler's rightful due. The commoner who ate [and] drank as the ruler ate [and] drank was also punished; he was also put to death.

Thus, there were the reasons for which the ruler became angry; for what was called the ruler's fury, the ruler's wrath.

PARAGRAPH 17
[fol. 65v col. B]

Jnic xvij parrapho ypan mitoaya inic tepapa tlavcoyaya in tlatoani.

Auh inic vntlamantli in ieliz in tlatoani inic tlavcoyaya in tlatoani ca ipampa ỹ maçeoalli in ixquich y novian y nican tlaocoyaya inic mitoaya motequipachotica yn ipampa yn amo quiavi in tlein quiquaz maçeoalli auh in atle nezi in itlaqual iquac mocavaya in tequitl avcmo quimacaya in tlacallaquilli yn aço ycal ytech nemi, quicavaya quivalivaya ypampa yc quintlavcoliaya yn aquiavi yn atle nezi in intlaqual in quezquixivitl in aço oxivitl in aço exiuitl yn aço nauhxivitl, in aquiaviz çenca ic motequipachoaya auh iquac conanaya yn itlaçopiltzin yn quĩ tepitzin in vmpa cõmictiaya in tepeticpac in mvteneoaya tlacatetevitl yc quitlavcoliaya ym maçeoalli, auh ic novian viya yn inextlaval inic novian quitzacutimani in tepeticpac i nextlavallo, Auh iuh muchivaya iquac vlinia in quiavitl, iquac patia in macevalli iquac celia in quiltzintli y nopaltzintli

Seventeenth paragraph, in which it is told how the ruler felt compassion for the people.[1]

And for the second characteristic of the ruler: The ruler felt compassion for all the commoners everywhere. He felt compassion here; so it was said that he was worried because [if] it did not rain [to produce] what the commoners would eat, and when their food did not appear, then tribute ceased; [the commoners] no longer gave tribute. Those who perhaps lived in their houses stopped [sending] what they had been sending.[2] Therefore he felt compassion for them when it did not rain, when their food had not appeared. For several years—perhaps two, perhaps three, perhaps four—it might not rain. For this reason he was very worried. And this was when they took away their precious children, when they later killed the little ones on the mountaintops. They were called human sacrificial papers.[3] Thus he showed compassion for the commoners. They went

1. Although Sullivan did not include this paragraph in her *huehuetlatolli* category, it constitutes an explicit follow-up, although much briefer, to the preceding one. As its title indicates, it is concerned with the reasons the ruler felt sadness and compassion for his subjects. Three are described: famine, war, and when his son and heir did not possess the leadership qualities necessary to successfully succeed him as ruler. The second is of particular interest. It eloquently expresses the notion that, in spite of the glorification of war in this aggressive, imperialistic society, it was attended by considerable anxiety on the part of the ruler who sent forth *in cuauhtli in ocelotl,* "the eagles, the jaguars," the warriors of his community who risked death and mutilation on the battlefield.

The illustration at the head of the paragraph shows a bearded ruler, his head *en face,* seated on a backed mat throne, his chin resting on the palm of his hand.

2. *Quicavaya quivalivaya:* Problematical translation; *iua* is usually used for persons; *ual-* usually implies direction toward the speaker.

3. *Tlacatetevitl (tlacatetehuitl):* literally, "human ritual papers." This term was applied to the infants who were sacrificed to the rain deity Tlaloc on hilltops and mountaintops.

iquac nezi, in itlaqual in maceoalli iquac paqui ỹ maceoalli. Auh in tlatoani no iquac moyollalia in tlaqua paqui in cochi paqui.

everywhere [to make] their payment [to the gods]; everywhere they covered[4] the mountaintops [with offerings], when payment was made [to the gods]. And when such was done, the rain stirred; at that time the commoners were restored; at that time the greens, the prickly pears sprouted. At that time the commoners' food appeared; at that time the commoners were happy. And at that time the ruler also rejoiced; when he ate he was happy, when he slept he was happy.

[fol. 66r]

oc centlamantli inic tlaocoyaya in itlatocatequiuh,

auh inic ontlamantli ynic tlaocoyaya iehoatl, in yavyutl yn oyavtlato yn cani motlalia yavyutl ytencopa. Auh niman ye eva in quauhtli yn oçelutl, auh iquac peva yn tlavcoxtimotlalia in quenin otlatoca in iquauh in iyoçeluh yn icuitlapil yn iatlapal in quenami quinamiquitiuh yn vmpa y yavc, cuix vel mochivaz cuix noço avelli, Auh y ye yquac y ye itlapoal ypan in iquac muchiva yavyutl amo cochi amo tlaqua cenca quica tlavcoyaya in iquauh yn ioçeluh yn que ye vetzin in itequiuh ca vmpa vnitztoc ça vmpa vntlacactoc çenca ic motequipachoa, ic tlavcoxtica, auh in iquac yn oalla in titlantli yn oconcac yn aço otlamaloc yn aço opuliuh in çe in altepetl yn oquicac iquac paqui iquac tlaqua iquac cochi ye quichia ym malli auh in iquac aziquivi mamalti çenca ic paq' auh in anoço vmpa oixpulivito in iquauh yn ioçeluh in icuitlapil yn iatlapal aço vmpa opulivito cenca yc tlaocoya cenca ic mutequipachoa yehoatl yc cocoya in tlatoani iehoatl ic peva in miqui in tlatoani miquiztli muchiva yc vntlamantli inic tlavcoyaya in tlatoani.

Other [reasons] for which [the ruler] was sad in his task of ruling.

And a second [occasion when] he was sad was when there was war, when he declared war; when, somewhere, by his orders war was established, and when the eagle warriors, the jaguar warriors went off. And this was when he began to be sad about how his eagle warriors, his jaguar warriors, his common folk advanced on the road, about how they would engage in battle. Could it be done? Was it impossible? And at the time of their reporting, when war was made, he did not sleep, he did not eat; he became very sorry[5] for his eagle warriors, his jaguar warriors. How was their work? There he just[6] lay awake all night; he lay listening. He was much worried about them; he was sad about them. But when messengers came, when he heard perhaps that captives had been taken, that perhaps a city had been destroyed, when he heard this, then he was happy; then he ate, then he slept. Now he waited for the captives [to arrive]. And when they went to take captives he was very happy. But if, perhaps, his eagle warriors, his jaguar warriors, his common folk had gone to perish, if they had perished, he was very sad about it, he was much worried about it. Because of this the ruler sickened, the ruler began to die, [his] death occurred. This was the second [occasion] when the ruler was sad.

Paragraph 17

4. *Quitzacutimani:* perhaps to be read *quitzacutimomana.*

5. *Quica tlavcoyaya:* perhaps to be read *quitlaocoliaya.*

6. *Ca:* probably to be read *ça.*

Jnic etlamantli inic tlavcoyaya in tlatoani iehoatl in itlaçopiltzin yn amo yyel yn amo otlacaqui in amo mozcalia yn ac quipiaz in atl in tepetl in iquac omic in tlatoani yehoatl yc tlavcoyaia yehoatl yc motequipachoa in ipiltzin yn amo oquichtli yn amo quimocuitlavia in yavyutl in que nemiz yn que yez in petlapan ycpalpan intla nemiz que mocaquiz ym maçeoalli o ca yehoatl i ynic tlaocoyaya in tlatoani, yn ac quipiaz in ac quipachoz yn icuitlapil yn iyatlapal

o ca ye ixquich yn inetequipachol yn tlatoani,

The third [occasion when] the ruler was sad was when his beloved son, the one who was to guard the city when the ruler died, was lazy, was stupid, was imprudent. For this reason he was sad, for this reason he was worried: his son was not a manly [warrior]; he did not care about war, about how he would live, how he would be on the mat, on the seat; whether the commoners would live; how they would be content. The ruler was sad, because [his son] was the one who was to guard, who was to rule his common folk.

These were all the afflictions of the ruler.

CHAPTER IV
THINGS RELATIVE TO MAN

PARAGRAPH 1
[fol. 82r]

Jnic. 4. capitulo ytech tlatoa yn tlacayutl.

Jnic. j. parapho ypã mitoa yn itoca in tlacamecayutl.

Mintotli
colli
tatli
nãtli
tepiltzin
teichpuch
teixviuh
tetla
teavi
/tatli.nãtli.
/tepilhoan.
/teixvioan.
/teteycaoã.
/teicutooan
/temintooã.

yn tepilhoã ytech quiça ỹ temach ỹ tepilo yoã ytech quiça ỹ tetla. ỹ teavi. yn tetla. ỹ teavi. ỹ qũichioa ỹpilhoa. auh ỹ temachoa yc monotza ỹ teycaoa yntla oquichti. auh ỹtla çioa yveltioa.

Fourth chapter, which tells of things relative to man.

First paragraph, in which are told the lineage terms.[1]

Great-grandfather.
Grandfather.
Father.
Mother.
One's son.
One's daughter.
One's grandchild.
One's uncle.
One's aunt.
Father, mother.
One's children.
One's grandchildren.
One's younger brothers.
One's younger sisters.[2]
One's great-great-grandchildren.[3]

One's children issue [from one]. One's nephew, one's niece[4] likewise issue from one's uncle, from one's aunt. One's uncle, one's aunt engender their children. And if the offspring of the aunt and uncle were male, they were called one's younger brothers, and if they were female, his older sisters.

1. This paragraph consists of a list of fifteen kinship terms, in both ascending and descending generations, plus a brief text that employs some of the terms in parentage statements. Sahagún collected similar data later in Tlatelolco, including the terms in the first chapter of Book 10 of the *Historia* (Sahagún 1950–1982, Part XI [Book 10]: 1–6; 1988, II: 584–587), in statements specifying the "virtues and vices" of each. Schultze Jena (1952: 4–5) first paleographized the paragraph and translated it into German; Giménez translated it into French in 1976. Rammow (1964) utilized its data to good advantage in her comprehensive study of the kinship system of the contact-period Central Mexican Nahua speakers—supplemented by Carrasco Pizana 1966.

2. *Teicutooan* (plural of *teicuton*): If in grammatical construction it is analogous to *teminton* (see note 3, this paragraph), it may signify one of a generation younger than younger sister, i.e., one's niece.

3. *Temintooã:* compare "*teminton, nieto o nieta tercera*" (Molina 1944, Part II: fol. 97v).

4. *Ỹ temach ỹ tepilo: Machtli* was the term used by a man when referring to a niece or a nephew; *pillotl* was the term used by a woman.

PARAGRAPH 2

Jnic. 2. parapho ypã mitoa yn intoca ỹ oquichti ỹ çioa çan oc tecemaxca etc.

oquichtli. tlatequipanoa. chicaoac.
çiuatl. tlacachioa / mopilhoatia

veve. tlamamana. teq'ti. tlavipana.

illama tlatlãtlaliã. calitic. yq'tiliztli. tzavaliztli etc.

telpuchtli. quauhteq'. tlaxeloa q'uhtla calaqui

ichpuchtli / tzava / monequi. atezi. momachtia yq'tiliztlj

telpuchtlapalivj. tlateq'panoa tlamama. veca yauh.

ichpuchtlapalivi. yq'ti. tzava. tlaqualchioa.

piltõtli. maviltia. tlaololoa. tzatzi.

conetõtli. quin otlacat. ayamo vel chichi.

piltzintli. ayamo tlacaq'. ayamo quimati

conetzintli ayamo tlachia. amo temauhcaytta

iyoloco nemi telpuchtli. tiachcauh chioa tlamamana motitlanj

yyoloco nemi çiuatl tlamachioa. etc.

çiuatlapalivi. tezi. tamaloa. tlaqualchioa.

ichpuchillama teixtlamachtia etc.

yyoloco nemi tlapalivi. çacamoa. elemiqui.

yyoloco nemi çioatlapalivi. tezi. atolchioa.

Second paragraph, in which are told male and female terms; they are still common to all.[1]

Man: He works, he is strong.

Woman: She has children, she procreates children.

Old man: He arranges things in order, he works, he puts things in order.

Old woman: She puts things in order in the house, [she concerns herself with] weaving, with spinning.

Youth: He cuts wood, he splits it, he goes into the forest.

Maiden: It is required that she spin. She does not grind maize. She learns to weave.

Youth of marriageable age: He works, he carries burdens, he goes far away.

Maiden of marriageable age: She weaves, she spins, she prepares food.

Small child [man's or woman's]: It amuses itself, it makes mud balls, it cries out.

Small child [woman's]: Right after it is born it cannot suckle.

Child [man's or woman's]: It does not yet understand, it knows nothing yet.

Child [woman's]: It needs guidance, it does not regard people with respect.

Grown youth: He becomes a master of youths,[2] he arranges things in order, he serves as a messenger.

Grown maiden: She embroiders, etc.

Young marriageable maiden: She grinds maize, she makes tamales, she prepares food.

Spinster: She instructs people, etc.

Grown youth of marriageable age: He clears the soil of vegetation, he cultivates the soil.

Grown maiden of marriageable age: She grinds maize, she makes atole.

1. This paragraph consists of an annotated list of terms for different categories of men and women. The annotations are in a different hand (including Sahagún's) and shade of ink from the terms themselves. The paragraph, as such, was not included in the *Historia*. However, some of the same terms appear in the data on age categories that Sahagún collected later in Tlatelolco and listed, with extensive annotations organized according to the "good vs. bad" characterizations of the different categories of the two sexes, in Chapter 3 of Book 10 (Sahagún 1950–1982, Part XI [Book 10] 11–13; 1988, II: 589–590). Schultze Jena (1952: 4–7) published a paleography, with German translation, of the paragraph; Giménez (1976) did the same, with French translation.

2. *Chio (chihua)*: read *mochihua*.

telpuchtepito. quaquavi. atlacui. etc.

Young youth:[3] He cuts wood, he draws water, etc.

ichpuchtõtli. quiquilpi. tlachpana tzava / momachtia / etc.

Young maiden:[4] She gathers edible plants, she sweeps, she spins, she learns, etc.

ye vel veve ocoliuh. aocmo tle iteq̃uh. aocmo tlacaq̃. aocmo vel aq' etc.

Very old stooped man: No longer does he work, no longer does he hear, no longer does he do things well.[5]

ye vel yllama ocoliuh. aocmo tlatequipanoa / aocmo mimati etc. aynyanj. vevezca, muyuma.

Very old stooped woman: She no longer works, she no longer thinks clearly, etc.; she does not go out,[6] she laughs, she shuffles along.

telpuchtlaveliloc, tecamanalhuya, tetaza

Wicked youth: He makes fun of people, he knocks people down.[7]

cuilonj. — Sodomite.
tecuilontianj. — Practicer of sodomy.
patlachpul. — Lesbian.
tetlanochilianj — Procurer (or procuress).[8]

PARAGRAPH 3

Jnic. 3. parrapho ypã mitoa yn intoca in oquichti çã teneixcavil etc.

Third paragraph, in which are told the names for men that are appropriate only to them.[1]

yautl — Enemy.
tochtli — Rabbit.
maçatl — Deer.
cuoatl — Serpent.[2]
xochitl — Flower.
cuetzpalli — Lizard.

3. *Telpuchtotli:* apparently corrected from *telpuchtontli.*

4. *Ichpuchtotli:* apparently corrected from *ichpuchtepiton.*

5. *Aq':* illegible, but read as *aq',* standing for *aqui.*

6. *Aynyanj:* read *a (mo) in yani.*

7. *Tetaza:* read *tetlaça.*

8. The last half-dozen lines are in Sahagún's hand. Reading of some terms (see notes 6 and 7, this paragraph) is problematical because they are almost illegible.

1. This paragraph lists names that were bestowed by the midwife and the parents on a newborn male child during the initial ritual bathing (cf. *Codex Mendoza* 1992, III: fol. 56v). Ten, possibly eleven, of these names are day signs in the 260-day divinatory cycle, the *tonalpohualli*—all except the uncertain one (Olin [Movement]?) are animals or birds. Nine or ten of the others are also animals or birds. It is somewhat puzzling to discover, in view of the fact that the title of the paragraph explicitly specifies that these names were given only to boys, two occurrences of the generic word for flower, *xochitl,* and another for a particular kind, *eloxochitl.* Personal names containing the element "flower" are usually considered to have been exclusively feminine. There is really nothing in the later *Historia* comparable to this paragraph. Schultze Jena (1952: 6–7) first transcribed it and translated it into German; in 1976 Giménez published a paleography of it with French translation.

2. *Cuoatl:* read *coatl* or *cohuatl.*

[fol. 82v]

çipac	Crocodile.
vlli	Rubber.[3]
xvchipepe	Flower-gatherer.
cuixtli	Kite.[4]
tototl	Bird.
tapayaxi	Toad.
vçomatli	Monkey.
quauhtli	Eagle.
oçelotl	Jaguar.
miztli	Mountain lion.
cuetlachtli	Wolf.
tecolutl	Horned owl.
vitzitl	Hummingbird.[5]
itzcujtli	Dog.[6]
coçatli	Weasel.
tlalli	Earth.
quimich	Mouse.
vitztecol	Dark brown.
eloxochitl	Magnolia.
nequametl	Maguey.
xuchitl	Flower.
vcuil etc.	Worm, etc.

ynin tocaytl yquac yn tlacati piltontlj yquac caltia quimaca yn itoca ỹ tiçitl yoã y pilhoaque y yaviltoca ypipiltoca.

These names [are given] when a baby is born. When the midwife bathes it, she and the parents give him his fun name, his child's name.

PARAGRAPH 4

Jnic. 4. parrapho ypã mitoa yn ītoca ỹ çioa çan teneixcavil etc.

Fourth paragraph, in which are told the names for women that are appropriate only to them.[1]

teyacapã	First born.
teicui	Younger sister.
xoco	Youngest sister.
papã	Flag.[2]

3. *Vlli:* perhaps to be read *olin* (movement), a day sign.

4. *Cuixtli:* read *cuixin* (*milano* in Molina 1944, Part II: 27v).

5. *Vitzitl:* read *huitzilin,* or possibly *huitztli* (thorn).

6. *Itzcujtli:* read *itzcuintli.*

1. This paragraph provides a relatively short list of names appropriate only for women. Over half are floral, or at least botanical. No day signs are included (unless *xochi (tl)* could be so considered). In addition, a short text, in a different ink, is added to explain the set of birth-order names, which were commonly borne by women. This paragraph, too, was not included in the later *Historia.* Schultze Jena (1952: 6–7) first paleographized it and translated it into German, and in 1976 Giménez did the same with French translation.

2. *Papã:* derived from *pamitl?*

tlacotl
xiloxoch
miyaoaxoch
eloxvch
mizquixaual
xochi
tomiyauh
chimalma, etc.

ça no yuhqui y cioa yquac ỹ tlacati yquac quitocayotia ytla achto tlacati y quinotza tecapa ynic ome tlacati tlacotl yoã teicui y ça tlatzaca tlacati xoco. auh yn oc cequi çaça quĩmaca ỹ tleyn intoca

Osier twig.
Calliandra.
Maize tassel flower.
Magnolia.
Mesquite face paint.
Flower.
Our maize tassel.
Shield-giver.

In the same way, when a woman is born, if[3] she is born first they name her, they call her *teyacapan;*[4] the second who is born [is called] *tlacotl* and also *teicui;* the one born last, *xoco.* And as for the rest, they give them any sort of name.

PARAGRAPH 5

Jnic. 5. parrapho ypã mitoa yn itotoca yn itech ca ỹ tonacayo ỹ pani neçi.

tonacayo titonacayotia
totzõteco toquavivixooa
totzon titlaveyaquilia
tixqua tlamama.
tixquamol
tixquatol.

Fifth paragraph, in which are told the names of [the parts] that are on our bodies, that appear on the surface.[1]

Our body: We become fleshy.
Our head: We shake our head.[2]
Our hair: We grow it long.
Our forehead: It carries things on the back.[3]
Our eyebrows.
Our eyelids.

[fol. 83r]

tixtelolo tlachia / cochi / naoalachia.
tocvchiya yc titixcuecueyonia
tocanaoacã
tonacaz / tlacaqui./ ycavaca
toxayac titixtlaça

Our eyes: They see, they sleep, they spy.[4]
Our eyelashes: With them we blink our eyes.
Our temples.
Our ears: They hear, they ring.[5]
Our face: We turn away our face in disgust or rage.

3. *Ytla:* read *intla.*
4. *Tecapa:* read *teyacapan.*

1. This paragraph consists of a lengthy list of exterior human body parts, with brief explanatory annotations in a different shade of ink. Sahagún later in Tlatelolco collected much more information on the same topic, which appears in Chapter 27 of Book 10 of the *Historia* (Sahagún 1950–1982, Part XI [Book 10]: 95–138). A paleography and German translation of this paragraph was first published by Gall (1940: 90–92), and López Austin later transcribed it and translated it into Spanish (1972: 132–134; 1980, II: 7–9, 73–75 [English translation: 1988, II: 1–3, 67–69]). These translations occasionally differ from those presented here.
2. *Toquavivixooa:* read *titocuahuihuixoah.*
3. *Tlamama:* that is, it sustains the tumpline.
4. *Naoalachia:* read *nahuallachia.*
5. *Tlacaqui./ycavaqui:* literally, they chirp, they sing (like a bird).

tixteliuhca
Our cheeks.

tocamatapal tlatlactic
Our palate: It is red.

toyac tlanecui / tlatzomiya
Our nose: It smells things; it is blown.

tocamac tlaqua / chicha
Our mouth: It eats, it spits.

tocopac yc titlavelmati
Our palate: By means of it we taste things.

tonenepil yc titlatoa/
Our tongue: With it we speak.

totlã tlaqua / yc titlaqua
Our teeth: They eat, with them we eat.

toquequetol
Our gums.

totexipal tlapachichina
Our lips: They suck.

tatliya
Our moustache.

totenchal
Our chin.

totẽtzõ muzcalttia. veyaquiya
Our beard: It grows, it becomes long.

toquechquavhyo yc titoloa
Our cervical vertebrae:[6] With them we bow our head.

tocvcvuh yc titlatoloa
Our esophagus: With it we swallow.

tacvlchimal
Our shoulder blade.

tacvl
Our shoulder.

tomolicpi yc titeoa yc titlatepiniya
Our elbows: With them we raise ourselves up, we poke things.

tomatzotzopaz tiquiyaoa
Our forearm: We offer it in dedication.

tomacpal yc titlaqua / tlatzitzquia
Our palm: With it we eat, it holds things.

tomapil mapiloa / tetlatitia / tlacuiloa / yc tzaoa
Our finger: It points,[7] it indicates something to someone,[8] it paints, with it one spins [cotton].

tozte muzcaltia / tlacotona / tlatzayana / tlaztecui
Our fingernails: They grow, they rip things apart, they tear things, they touch things.

totlac totlac cuechiniya
Our torso: Our torso sways.

telchiquiuh telchiquiuh eoa
Our chest: Our chest rises.

tomizicuil
Our ribs.

tite tite poçaoa / tite xaxaoaca/
Our abdomen: Our abdomen fills, our abdomen empties.

tomimiliuhca
Our loins.

tocuitlatetepo yc titlamama / nolivj.
Our spine: By means of it we bear things on our back, it curves.

totzintepitz yc ticate
Our ischium:[9] By means of it we are [on something].

totzintamal
Our buttocks.

toqueztepvl yc tinenemi / momalacachoa.
Our hip bone:[10] By means of it we walk, it rotates.

tometzquauhyo
Our thigh.

totlãqua ye titocototzoa / ye tomelaoa.
Our knees: By means of them we squat, we go straight.[11]

6. *Toquechquauhyo:* This word also appears in the annotation column, crossed out.

7. *Tiquiyaoa:* compare *iyaua* (Sahagún 1950–1982, Part III [Book 2]: 52, *coniavilia,* "raise in dedication"). López Austin (1988, II: 68) prefers "we hurt them."

8. *Tetlatitia:* read *telettitia,* or, better, *tetlaittitia.*

9. *Totzintepitz:* "ischial tuberosity" in Sahagún 1950–1982, Part IX (Book 10): 122.

10. *Toqueztepol:* López Austin (1988, II: 68): "the upper end of the femur."

11. *Tomelaoa:* read *titomelahua.*

totlanitz miyaoa / tiquiyaoa

Our shank: It is offered in dedication, we offer it in dedication.[12]

tocotzteuh viyoni

Our calf: It quivers.[13]

toxocpal yc tinenemi yc titoquetza^ ^nenemi / tlatelicça

Our feet: With them we walk, with them we stand;[14] they walk, they kick things.[15]

toquequeyol

Our ankle bones.

toxopil yc titlacça / yc titlamotzoloa / tlaxopeoa / motecuinja

Our toes: With them we run, with them we grasp things; they kick things, they trip.

tozte

Our nails.

toxvcpalixco. michiqui / miyaoa

Our foot sole: It is scraped, it is offered in dedication.[16]

tomimiyaoayo moquetza / quauhti

Our flank:[17] It stands upright,[18] it becomes stiff.

PARAGRAPH 6
[fol. 83v]

Jnic. 6. parrapho ypã mitoa yn itotoca yñ itic ca ỹ tonacayo yn amo ualneçj

Sixth paragraph, in which are told the names of the [parts of] the body that are within, that are not visible.[1]

toquaxical

Our skull.

toquatetexyo tlanemilia tlayoltevia

Our brain: It thinks, it predicts things.[2]

tezyo chichiltic / tlapaltic

Our blood: It is crimson, it is red.

tezteco

Our liver.[3]

ezcocotli viviconticac

Our blood vessels: They are climbers.[4]

toxvchiyo

Our fat.

totlaluayo tlalpia

Our tendons: They bind things.

toyollo teyolitia / tenemitia. tetecuinia

Our heart: It makes people live, it keeps people alive, it beats.

teltapach tezteco.

Our liver: Our blood container.

12. See note 7, this paragraph.

13. *Viyoni:* López Austin (1988, II: 68) prefers "travelers."

14. *Yc tinenemi yc titoquetza:* In the manuscript, the second word was also originally written *tinenemj;* subsequently, the *nenemi* was crossed out and *toquetza* was added. The ^ ^ which follows may indicate that *titoquetza* refers to *tocotzteuh,* above, and not to *toxocpal* (cf. López Austin 1988, II: 2).

15. *Nenemi/tlatelicça:* The ^ ^ before the first word may indicate that both words refer to *toxocpal,* above, rather than *toquequeyol.*

16. *Miyaoa:* See note 7, this paragraph.

17. *Tomimiyaoayo:* translated "lung" in Sahagún 1950–1982, Part XI (Book 10): 120, 130. The choice here, "flank," was also preferred by López Austin (1988, II: 69).

18. *Moquetza:* compare López Austin (1988, II: 69): "it suffers from exhaustion."

1. This paragraph is similar in format and basic subject matter to the preceding one but is concerned with internal human body parts. The topic, incorporating data Sahagún collected later in Tlatelolco, is covered in considerably more detail in the *Historia's* Chapter 27 of Book 10 (see note 1, Paragraph 5). Gall (1940: 93–82 [German]) and López Austin (1972: 134–136; 1980, II: 8–9 [Spanish]; 1988, II: 3 [English]) also paleographized and translated the paragraph.

2. *Tlayoltevia:* read *tlayolteouia.*

3. *Tezteco:* literally, "our vessel *(tecomatl)* of blood *(eztli).*" The term is repeated below, with *teltapach,* one of the more common terms for liver (cf. Molina 1944, Part II: fol. 71r).

4. *Viviconticac:* The reference is to climbing plants.

tochichi teyyomaca teyyotia	Our lungs: They give people breath, they make people breathe.
tochichicauh tequalantia	Our bile: It makes people angry.
totlatlaliaya quiyectiã tlaquallj quiyectilia	Our stomach: It cleans the food, it purifies it.
tocuitlaxcol mamina / tlanoquia	Our intestines: They have diarrhea, they have watery stools.
taxixteco	Our bladder.
tonenecoctetēcauh	Our kidneys.
tocecelica	Our cartilage.
omitl	The bones.

PARAGRAPH 7

Jnic. 7. parrapho ypã mitoa yn ītoca ỹ tlaca ỹ mauiztlililoni tlatoani pilli teuctli çiuapilli etc.	Seventh paragraph,[1] in which are told the designations for illustrious people: ruler, nobleman, lord, noblewoman, etc.[2]
tlacatl tlacaqui tetlaçotla	Person [of consequence]:[3] He comprehends, he loves people.
tlatoani tlatocati / tlavica	Ruler: He rules, he governs.
pilli pilti /	Nobleman: He becomes a nobleman.
teuctli tecuti	Lord: He becomes a lord.
tepiltzin momaviztlililanj	Offspring of noblemen:[4] He desires to be honored.
teixviuh mopoanj	Grandchild of noblemen: He is arrogant.
tetzon moquatlaça.	Hair[5] of noblemen: He tosses his head presumptuously.
teizte atlamati	Nail of noblemen: He is haughty.[6]
teixquamol movecapanoa	Eyebrows of noblemen: He exalts himself.
tevitzyo tetech atlamati	Thorn of noblemen: He becomes proud and haughty because he is protected by a powerful person.[7]

1. This paragraph provides an extensive list of terms for different categories of nobles, both male and female. Most are annotated in a different, lighter ink. Later in Tlatelolco Sahagún gathered more detailed information concerning the same theme, which he incorporated in Chapters 4–6 and 13 of Book 10 of the *Historia* (Sahagún 1950–1982, Part XI [Book 10]: 15–24, 45–50; 1988, II: 590–595, 602–604). The annotations conform to the usual pattern of the "good vs. bad" categories of the kinds of nobles enumerated in these chapters. Schultze Jena (1952: 30–31) also transcribed this paragraph and translated it into German.

2. To the right of the Nahuatl title of the paragraph is this heading, in Spanish, in a cursive handwriting (not Sahagún's) and a pale ink: *oficios y cōdiciones diversos de hobre y muger.* The reading of *diversos* is somewhat tentative (cf. Ballesteros-Gaibrois 1964, I: 105–27).

3. *Tlacatl:* A generic term for a man or woman of very high rank. There is no exact equivalent in English, but man, woman, or person (of consequence), or personage, may approximate the meaning in this context.

4. *Tepiltzin:* literally, someone's child; *te-* in this context means noble.

5. *Tetzon:* Things that issue from something, such as hair, nails, or thorns, in Nahuatl figuratively connote "descendant," "offspring."

6. *Atlamati:* literally, he is ignorant.

7. *Tetech atlamati:* compare Olmos 1875: 223.

teauayo mopilitoa	Prickle of noblemen: He claims to be a nobleman.
tetentzon mochachamaoa	Beard of noblemen: He is conceited.
tetzicueuhca amo tle ypã teita	Chip of noblemen: He thinks nothing of anyone.
tetlapãca motlaçotlalanj	Sliver of noblemen: He desires to be loved.
teezyo tetech quiz tlaçotlj	Blood of noblemen: He issues from noblemen; he is precious.
tetlapallo mopilnequi	Red ink of noblemen: He pretends to be a nobleman.
oquichtli moquichnequi. moq'chitoa	Man:[8] He pretends he is a man, he claims to be a man.
tiyacauh tlapaltic	Brave warrior: He is strong.
quachic. vej tiacauh / yaotlaveliloc.	Shorn one, great brave warrior: A rogue in war.
tequioa tlama	Valiant warrior: He takes captives.[9]
yautequioa tlama teyacana	Seasoned warrior: He takes captives, he leads people.
tlacatl tetlaçotla	Woman [of consequence]:[10] She loves people.
çiuapilli ixtlamati	Noblewoman: She is judicious.
çivateuctli mixtilia	Lady: She is vain.
conetl tecpilatoa	Child [woman's]: He speaks elegantly.
teichpuch teicnoitta	Daughter of noblemen: She feels pity for people.
tetzon temalhuia	Hair of noblemen: She treats people nicely.
teizte temaviztilia	Nail of noblemen: She honors people.

[fol. 68r]

teixquamol tetlaocolia	Eyebrows of noblemen: She is merciful to people.
tevitzyo yocoxca tlacatl	Thorn of noblemen: She is a tranquil woman [of consequence].
teauayo mocnoteca	Prickle of noblemen: She humbles herself.
tetẽtzon teymacaçi	Beard of noblemen: She respects people.
tetzicueuhca mopechtecanj	Chip of noblemen: She is one who bends her neck [humbly].
tetlapãca motlaçomatinj	Sliver of noblemen: She is appreciative.
teezo tlamauhcaytanj	Blood of noblemen: She is attentive to things.
tetlapalo toloanj	Red ink of noblemen: She is one who bows her head [humbly].

8. *Oquichtli:* In this context and in compounds that follow, *oquichtli* may signify "manly" (warrior) rather than merely "man." For this term and the titles of warriors following *moquichnequi* and *moq'chitoa,* compare Sahagún 1950–1982, Part III (Book 2 [1st ed.]): 102n3, and Part XI (Book 10): 23–24.

9. *Tlama* seems to be crossed out.

10. *Tlacatl:* see note 3, this paragraph.

PARAGRAPH 8A

Jnic 8 parrapho ypã mitoa yn ītlaviz yn ītlatqui y tlatoque ỹ capitanes.

Eighth paragraph, which tells of the military insignia [and] accouterments of the rulers [and] captains.[1]

Tlatoqz yn ītlatqui yn ītlaviz.

The accouterments [and] insignia of the rulers.

ychcavipilli

The padded cotton shirt[2]

ynic tlachiuhtli. ichcatlavitectli, tilmatica tlaquimiloli ypã tlaçotl tlatēcuetlaxyotilli no memecayo cuetlaxtica—

It is made in this manner: Unspun cotton is enveloped in cloth, to which it is stitched. It is edged with leather. It also has leather thongs.

teucuitlaquauhtētetl.

The golden eagle lip plug

ynic tlachiuhtli tlapitzali tlacuilolo yuhquī quauhtly ic tlatlali teocuitlatl—

It is made in this manner: The cast is designed like an eagle; thus the gold is shaped.

mayanacvchtli.

Green june beetle ear plugs

ynic tlachiuhtli tlatzacutli yca ỹ mayatl xoxocti—

Thus are they made: They are covered with [a mosaic of] green june beetles.[3]

1. This is undoubtedly Chapter IV's best-known paragraph. It is divided into two parts, which Francisco del Paso y Troncoso labeled A and B. The first consists of an annotated list of the military insignia and accouterments worn by the lords. The second provides the same type of list for the warrior captains. Paso y Troncoso, basing his decision on the similarity of subject matter, inserted illustrated folios 72–80 of the Real Academia de la Historia manuscript between the two folios, 68 and 69, that contain the text of Paragraph 8—thus, in effect, assigning them also to this paragraph although they did not belong to the integrated structure of the *Primeros Memoriales* as a whole, with its thematically organized sections sequentially numbered by chapter and paragraph. These inserted folios contain annotated pictorializations of three lords *(tlatoque pipiltin)* and three champion warriors *(tiacahuan)* in full battle gear, along with thirty-five battle standards, seven individual coyote battle suits, one feather tunic *(ehuatl)*, four headpieces, twelve feather shields, one gold necklace, and a pair of gold earspools. Later in Tlatelolco Sahagún collected a similar but somewhat briefer list, unillustrated, which he included as Chapter 12 of Book 8 of the *Historia* (Sahagún 1950–1982, Part IX [Book 8]: 33–35; 1988, II: 509–512).

Eduard Seler (1902–1923, II: 546–594 [English translation, Seler 1990–1993, III: 22–46]), in his comprehensive study of contact-period Central Mexican attire and insignia of social and military rank, first published the paleography of the Nahuatl text with German translation, line drawings of most of the illustrations, and comparative analyses of the data of this paragraph. In 1972, Thelma Sullivan transcribed the texts of the paragraph and translated them into English, with extensive notes, illustrated by copies of the black-and-white photographs of the pages of the original manuscript published by Paso y Troncoso. Her transcriptions and translations of the text of the second part of the paragraph were also published in *Codex Mendoza* 1992, I: Appendix K (pp. 249–254). These Sullivan versions, including many of the notes, are essentially repeated here.

Contact-period Central Mexican warrior costumes, accouterments, and insignia have recently been illustrated and discussed in detail, with appropriate utilization of the data of this *Primeros Memoriales* paragraph and other primary sources, in Anawalt 1977; 1981: 39, 46–52, 55–58, charts 3, 4; and in *Codex Mendoza* 1992, I: 112–131, Appendixes F, G, and H.

2. *Ychcavipilli (ichcahuipilli)*: Concerning this "quilted cotton armor," which apparently provided quite effective protection against indigenous weaponry, see the full discussion, with illustrations from primary sources, in Anawalt 1981: 48–51, 74–75, 194, 211, 217, and the more succinct one in Hassig 1988: 88, 97.

3. *Mayatl xoxocti: Hallorina dugesii.* See *mayate* in Santamaría 1959: 707–708. These ear plugs are worn by the second *tlatoani pilli* on fol. 72r but are not clearly visible.

maquavitl

The war club[4]

ynic tlachiuhtli auaquavitl tlapatlachxintli vel tlacẽcavali necoc tlacamacuicuitl vncã tlatectlj yn itztlj anoço tecpatl ayocuitlaticã tlaçaloli—

It is made in this manner: A piece of oak is cut into a board. It is well finished. Along both sides grooves are cut in which are set obsidian or flintstone [blades] glued with turtle dung.

xiuhnacvchtli

The turquoise ear plugs

ynic tlachiuhtlj. xiuhtica tlatzacutlj ca motquitica—

They are made in this manner: They are entirely covered with [a mosaic of] turquoise.

chimalli quetzalxicalcvliuhqui

The quetzal [feather] shield[5] with the stepped fret design

ynic tlachioalj otlatl ỹ tlatzayãtl.j ychicpatica tlavipãtli teotlatica tlaoapavilotili. yvã tlaçoivitica tlatzacutlj q̃tzaltica tlatlacuiloli

It is made in this manner: Split bamboo [pieces][6] are put together with maguey fiber. They are reinforced with heavy bamboo and covered with precious feathers. The design is of quetzal [feathers].

quetzalcuexyo. chimalli

The Huaxtec quetzal [feather] shield[7]

ynic tlatzacualj toztli quetzaltica tlacuiloli tentlapilolo—

It is covered with yellow parrot [feathers]. The design is of quetzal [feathers]. It has a hanging border [of feathers].[8]

tozmiquizyo chimalli

The yellow parrot [feather] death's head shield[9]

ynic tlatzacutli çã motquitica toztli xiuhtotoyvitica tlacuiloli nepa tzõtecomatl yuhqui

It is completely covered with yellow parrot [feathers]. In the center, in lovely cotinga

4. *Maquavitl (macuahuitl):* On this basic, close-quarter weapon of the contact-period Central Mexican warrior, see the discussion, with illustrations from primary sources, in Hassig 1988: 83–85, 289–290. According to him, the alleged "turtle dung glue . . . is apparently metaphorical and refers to the appearance of the substance, as actual turtle dung was not a Mesoamerican adhesive."

5. *Chimalli quetzalxicalvliuhqui:* This shield, featuring one of the commonest of the feather shield patterns, is carried by the first *tlatoani pilli* on fol. 72r. Seler (1902–1923, II: 551–552, Abb. 60, 80b, 88a, 89a, 100, 109a, 128, 161, 163a) discussed this shield and illustrated other examples in the *Matrícula de Tributos, Codex Mendoza,* and *Lienzo de Tlaxcala.*

6. *Teotlatica:* According to Hernández (1959–1984, II: 397), *teotlatl* was a species of bamboo that grew as thick as a man's arm and was used for staffs (cf. Santamaría 1959: 776). Seler (1902–1923, II: 551) read the word as *teocuitlatica,* "durch einem Goldrand verstarkt."

7. *Quetzalcuexyo chimalli:* This shield is carried by the second *tlatoani pilli* on fol. 72r. It displays another common pattern of the feather shields. Seler (1902–1923, II: 552, Abb. 59, 62, 78, 80a, 85, 89b, 127, 133, 141, 142, 165, 179) discussed the shield and illustrated other examples in the *Matrícula de Tributos, Codex Mendoza,* and *Lienzo de Tlaxcala.* He identified the crescent motifs that are a prominent feature of its decorative format with the *yacametztli,* "nose moon," the nasal ornament worn by the goddess Tlazolteotl/Ixcuina and other deities associated with the Huaxteca.

8. *Tentlapilolo:* literally, "it has a hanging border," i.e., of feathers.

9. *Tozmiquizyo chimalli:* This shield is carried by the upper *tiacauh* on fol. 72v.

miquiztli—.

feathers, is the representation of a skull like a death['s head.]

teucuitlaxapochimalli

The golden disc shield[10]

ynic tlatzaquali tlaçovitl nepātla mani teocuitlayavaltic teocuitlapepeyocyo yn iten tlapilolo.

It is covered with precious feathers. In the center is a gold disc; it is gleaming with gold. It has a hanging border [of feathers].

quauhtetepoyo chimalli

The eagle's foot shield[11]

ynic tlatzacutlj quavivitl yn itetepo mochiuhticac auh yn izte cuztic teocuitlatl tentlapilolo.

It is covered with eagle feathers. [The eagle's] foot is fashioned upright and its claws are of gold. It has a hanging border [of feathers].

teocuitlateteyo chimalli

The silver stones shield

ynic tlatzactli ça motquitica toztlj auh yn iztac tevcuitlatl macuiltemani ỹ inepātla teocuitlapepeyocyo yn itlapilolo.

It is covered entirely with yellow parrot [feathers], and there are five silver stones in the center; it is gleaming with silver. It has a hanging border [of feathers].

pvztequi chimalli

The cleft shield[12]

ynic tlatzaquali centlacol toztli cētlacol quezalli teçouhqui.

One half of it is covered with yellow parrot [feathers], one half with quetzal [feathers]. It has an open border [of feathers] around the edge.

cuztic tevcuitlaçuyanacvchtli

The gold palm ear plug[13]

ynic tlachiuhtla tlatzotzōtli teocuitlatecuepqui çoyatic.

It is made in this manner: It is of beaten gold. The border turns back like a palm.

10. *Teocuitlaxapochimalli:* This shield is carried by the lower *tiacauh* on fol. 72v. Seler (1902–1923, II: 553–554, Abb. 57, 67) noted and illustrated its presence also in the *Codex Mendoza* and the *Codex Telleriano-Remensis,* as well as its mention in the itemization of the battle accouterments of the lords in Book 8, Chapter 12, of the *Historia* (Sahagún 1950–1982, Part IX [Book 8]: 33–34; 1988, II: 509–510).

11. *Quauhtetepoyo chimalli:* This shield is the top illustration of fol. 75v. For the ideological connotations of this device, particularly as a symbol of various earth/fertility goddesses, see the discussions by Seler (1902–1923, II: 554–555, Abb. 72, 108) and, more recently, Nicholson (1994). Just below it is an illustration, appropriately annotated *oçelotetepoyo chimalli,* of a shield featuring the device of a jaguar's paw. This shield is omitted in the textual listings of fol. 68r.

12. *Pvztequi (poztecqui):* Seler (1902–1923, II: 556, passim) translated this term as "bicolored." The illustration of this shield, labeled *quetzalpuztecqui chimalli,* is the fourth from the top on fol. 75v. However, as Seler noted, this image differs from the textual description, which appears to describe a continuous edging of feathers attached to the entire border like that of the *ihuitezouhqui chimalli* on fol. 80r. Here it is clearly another version of the *tentlapilolo* (see note 8, this paragraph), the common feather fringe that edges just the lower border of the shield.

13. *Cuztic tevcuitlaçuyanacvchtli:* These gold earspools are illustrated as the lowermost item on fol. 75v.

cvzcapetlatl

ynic tlachiuhtli tlapitzali teocuitlatl tlatzatzaztectl epãtitla petlaçotl tencoyollo.

The mat necklace[14]

It is made in this manner: It is of cast gold. It is cut into strips and laid out in three rows like a fine mat. It has a border of round bells.

teucuitlacuzcatl temoltic

tlapitzali in teocuitlatl tlacuilolo yuhquĩ temoli ypã tlaq'xtili.

The golden beetle necklace[15]

Gold is cast. It is designed, it is formed like a beetle.

chayauac cvzcatl

ynic tlachiuhtli tlaçotl ỹ teocuitlatl chalchivitl tlaneloli nepãtla pilcac teocuitlatl tecoyolo.

The necklace of radiating pendants[16]

It is made in this manner: Gold [and] green stone [beads] are strung, mingled. In the center hangs [a green stone disc] with round gold bells around the edge.

chalchiuhcvzcatl ololiuhqui

ynic tlatlalili vel ololtic ỹ chalchivitl vel tomatic çã motq'tica

The necklace of round green stone beads[17]

It is fashioned entirely of perfectly round, very thick [pieces of] green stone.

xiuheuatl

ynic tlachiuhtli tilmatitech tlatectlj tlavipãtli ỹ xiuhtototl tẽtlapilolo.

The turquoise [blue] tunic[18]

It is made in this manner: On a piece of cloth lovely cotinga [feathers] are placed, set in rows. It has a hanging border [of feathers].

pillivieuatl

ynic tlachiuhtli. çã mochi pilivitl yn itech tlatectlj tilmatlj tẽtlapilolo.

The tunic of princely feathers[19]

It is made all of princely feathers which are placed on cloth. It has a hanging border [of feathers].

14. *Cvzcapetlatl:* The first *tlatoani pilli* on fol. 72r wears this necklace.

15. *Teucuitlacuzcatl temoltic:* This necklace is pictured as the item fifth from the top on fol. 75v. It is discussed by Seler (1902–1923, II: 550, Abb. 65, 66a/b), who noted that the illustration depicts a necklace composed only of globular beads, none in the shape of beetles. Citing two illustrations in Hernández (1651: 832), he also identified the *temolin* as "die bekannten Formen der tropischen Dynastidae oder Riesenkafer erkennen wird." It is identified as *Hallorina duguesi* in Sahagún 1950–1982, Part XII (Book 11): 100; 1988, II: 904.

16. *Chayauac cvzcatl:* The second *tlatoani pilli* on fol. 72r wears this necklace. Seler (1902–1923, II: 551, Abb. 15, 48) noted its inclusion in the list of dance accouterments of the rulers in Book 8, Chapter 9, of the *Historia* (Sahagún 1950–1982, Part IX [Book 8]: 28), on the picture of the mummy bundle of the Tenochca ruler Ahuitzotl (Durán 1967, II: Lám. 36), and on the portrait of the noble on fol. 55v that illustrates *Primeros Memoriales* Chapter III, Paragraph 5 (note 1).

17. *Chalchiuhcvzcatl ololiuhqui:* The third *tlatoani pilli* on fol. 72v wears this necklace.

18. *Xiuheuatl:* Molina (1944, Part II: 29v) defines *ehuatl* as "cuero por curar, o mondadura y caxcara de fruta." See Anawalt 1981: 50–52 for discussion of these warrior suits, with specification of the various English terms used by modern students for them.

19. *Pillivieuatl: Pillihuitl* may mean "chick feathers" rather than "princely feathers." See description of the *toznene* (young yellow-headed parrot; *Amazona ochrocephala* [Gmelin] in Sahagún 1950–1982, Part XII (Book 11): 22–23; 1988, II: 692–693. This tunic is worn by the second *tlatoani pilli* on fol. 72r.

tozeuatl

The yellow parrot [feather] tunic

ynic tlachivali çã mochi toztli yn itech tlatectli tilmatlj tẽtlapilolo.

It is made all of yellow parrot [feathers] placed on cloth. It has a hanging border [of feathers].

aztaeuatl

The white heron [feather] tunic

yn itech tlatectli tilmatlj çã motquitica aztayvitl tẽtlapilolo.

On an entire piece of cloth are placed white heron feathers. It has a hanging border [of feathers].

tozcvyotl

The yellow parrot [feather] coyote [insignia][20]

ynic tlachiuhtli colotli tlatlalili yn iuhqui ytzontecõ coyutl yc tlatzacuali toztlj yquetzaltemal.

It is made in this manner: A frame is fashioned like a coyote's head. It is covered with yellow parrot [feathers]. It has its crest of quetzal [feathers].

xiuhcoyotl

The blue coyote [insignia][21]

ynic tlachiuhtli ynic tlatzacutlj coyotzõtecomatl. xiuhtotoyvitl no yq̃tzaltemal.

It is made in this manner: The head of a coyote is covered with lovely cotinga feathers. It, too, has its quetzal [feather] crest.

quetzalquaquavitl

The quetzal [feather] horns [insignia][22]

ynic tlatlalili tlaçoyvitica tlatzacutli tzõtecomatl ocãpã mani q̃tzalj.

It is fashioned in this manner: A head is covered with precious feathers; on each side are [tufts of] quetzal [feathers].

quetzaltzitzimitl

The quetzal [feather] demon of the dark [insignia][23]

ynic tlatlalili colotlj yuhqui miquiztlj tzontacomatl çã motquitica quetzali yn itzõteco yuhquin i quatatapa.

A frame is fashioned resembling a death's head. It is covered entirely with quetzal feathers. Its head is as if unkempt.

20. *Tvzcoyotl:* This zoomorphic military suit is worn by the third *tiacauh* on fol. 73r. Seler (1902–1923, II: 557–558, Abb. 74, 76, 78) noted and illustrated its appearance in other primary sources *(Matrícula de Tributos, Codex Mendoza, Lienzo de Tlaxcala).* Compare notes 21, 73, 75, 77, 78, 86, 87, 90, this paragraph.

21. *Xiuhcoyotl:* A variant of the preceding battle dress, it is pictured as the lowermost item on fol. 74v. Seler (1902–1923, II: 560–561, Abb. 75) also noted and illustrated its appearance in the *Lienzo de Tlaxcala.* Compare notes 20, 73, 75, 77, 78, 86, 87, 90, this paragraph.

22. *Quetzalquaquavitl:* This battle headpiece is pictured as the third item from the top on fol. 73v. Seler (1902–1923, II: 561, Abb. 82, 83) noted its appearance also in the *Lienzo de Tlaxcala.* He suggested its connection with the goddess Xochiquetzal, whose principal iconographic feature was two bunches of quetzal feathers worn on her head.

23. *Quetzaltzitzimitl:* This headpiece is illustrated as the fourth item from the top on fol. 73r. As Seler (1902–1923, II: 562, Abb. 58. 85) recognized, the tribute sections of the *Matrícula de Tributos* and the *Codex Mendoza* include many examples of a complete *tzitzimitl* warrior suit. Concerning the significance of this macabre stellar demon, see Seler 1900–1901: 52–53.

quetzalquatlamoyaoalli

The quetzal [feather] bestrewn head [insignia][24]

ynic tlatzacutlj tzõtecomatl toztlj quetzalxixilqui momoyaoatiuh.

The head is covered with yellow parrot [feathers]. It has quetzal [feathers] stuck into it, going strewn [around it].

xiuhananacaztli

The blue water ears [insignia][25]

ynic tlatzcutli tzocalmatlatl xiuhtototl teocuitlaatoyatlatlacuiloli yn inacaztla.

A net of hair is covered with lovely cotinga [feathers]. There are representations of gold streams of water next to the ears.

quetzalpatzactli

The compressed quetzal [feathers insignia][26]

ynic tlachiuhtli colotlj tlatlalili nepapã ivitl ynic tlatzacutlj ocãpa mixnamiqui y quetzali yn icpac tlavipãtlj ça motquitica q̃zalj.

It is made in this manner: A frame is fashioned. It is covered with diverse feathers. On top, on each side, are rows of quetzal [feathers] which face each other; they are entirely of quetzal [feathers].

teucuitlavevetl

The gold drum [insignia][27]

ynic tlachiuhtlj colotli tlatlalili yn iuhqui vevetl teocuitlaatica tlatlacuiloli quetzalpayo.

It is made in this manner: A frame is fashioned like a drum. It has a design in gold[28] [and] a quetzal [feather] crest.

24. *Quetzalquatlamoyaoalli:* This headpiece is pictured as the lowermost item on fol. 73v.

25. *Xiuhananacaztli:* This headpiece is illustrated as the lowermost item on fol. 75r. As Seler (1902–1923, II: 565, Abb. 87) noted, Torquemada (1975–1983, IV: 330) described this device as the exclusive prerogative of the "Chichimec emperors" of Tetzcoco.

26. *Quetzalpatzactli:* This military standard is borne by the first *tlatoani pilli* on fol. 72r. As Seler (1902–1923, II: 565–566, Abb. 88. 89) noted, according to the account of the Tlatelolca merchants in Book 9 of the *Historia* (Sahagún 1950–1982, Part X [Book 9]: 5–8; 1988, II: 539–543), during the reign of Ahuitzotl (1487–1502) this device was captured by an armed force of Mexica *pochteca.* After capturing a place called Cuauhtenanco, they claimed to have withstood a four-year siege by a coalition of towns of Anahuac Ayotlan, including Tehuantepec and other communities to the east along the Chiapas coast (province of Xoconochco). This trophy, along with many others, was formally presented to the Tenochca *huey tlatoani.* Thereafter apparently incorporated into the standard military panoply of the Triple Alliance armies, it is illustrated in the tribute lists of the *Matrícula de Tributos, Codex Mendoza,* and *Lienzo de Tlaxcala.* Hassig (1988: 217–218, 347–348) considers the merchants' boasts of their single-handed conquest of the area improbable, but, citing numerous primary sources, he does attempt to reconstruct this final major military campaign of Ahuitzotl's reign, led by Ahuitzotl's nephew, the future Tenochca ruler, Motecuhzoma II.

27. *Teucuitlavevetl:* This standard is illustrated by the third figure from the top on fol. 74v. The *huehuetl* was the upright cylindrical drum with a drumhead of animal hide, usually beaten with the palms of the hands (see Castañeda and Mendoza 1933). Seler (1902–1923, II: 566, 594–597, Abb. 90, 91, 159, 160) noted that this type of drum, denominated in this context *yopihuehuetl,* was an element in the costume and insignia of the fertility deity Xipe Totec, which was adopted by Axayacatl, who ruled Mexico Tenochtitlan from 1469 to 1481, as his battle costume, as it was also by his son, Motecuhzoma II (1502–1520) (cf. Nicholson 1961). Seler also noted its presence on the military dress of the famed ruler of Tetzcoco, Nezahualcoyotl (Gemelli Careri 1699–1700, VI—derived from *Codex Ixtlilxochitl* 1976: 106r).

28. *Teotcuitlaatica:* read *teocuitlatica.*

tevcuitlapanitl

ynic tlachiuh tlatzotzõtlj teocuitlatl yuhqui panitl yc tlamatlj ome mani quetzaltzoyo.

The golden banners [insignia][29]

It is made of beaten gold in pieces like banners. There are two. They have quetzal [feather] tufts.

quetzalpanitl

ynic tlachiuhtlj tlapuztectli q̃tzali tlaixnepanoli no quetzaltzoyo.

The quetzal [feather] banners [insignia]

It is made of broken quetzal [feathers] fitted together. They, too, have quetzal [feather] tufts.

quetzalcopilli

ynic tlatlalili colotlj quavitztic qztzaltica tlatzacutlj quetzaltzoyo.

The quetzal [feather] conical headpiece [insignia][30]

A conical frame is fashioned. It is covered with quetzal [feathers]. It has a quetzal [feather] tuft.

çaquãpanitl

ynic tlachiuhtlj ça mochi çaquãyvitl y panitl q̃tzaltzoyo.

The [black and gold] troupial [feather] banners [insignia][31]

The banners are made all of [black and yellow] troupial feathers. They have quetzal [feather] tufts.

quetzalpapalotl

colotli tlatlalili papalotl quetzaltica tlatlacuilolo quetzaltzoyo

The quetzal [feather] butterfly [insignia][32]

A frame is fashioned; the butterfly is designed with quetzal [feathers]. It has a quetzal [feather] tuft.

29. *Tevcuitlapanitl:* The third *tlatoani pilli,* on fol. 72v, bears this standard. Seler (1902–1923, II: 567, Abb, 92, 93) also noted its appearance in the *Codex Telleriano-Remensis* and *Codex Vaticanus A.*

30. *Quetzalcopilli:* This standard is pictured as the item second from the top on fol. 75r. Seler (1902–1923, II: 572, Abb. 103, 104) believed that it was similar to one shown in the *Lienzo de Tlaxcala,* but there with yellow parrot feathers, hence a *tozcopilli.* He also suggested that there was a relationship between this standard and the *cuextecatl* (Huaxtec) warrior costume (discussed by him, pp. 604–610), which, among other elements, featured versions of the conical headpiece, the *copilli.* For *qztzaltica,* read *quetzaltica.*

31. *Çaquãpanitl:* This standard is pictured as the item second from the top on fol. 73v. Seler (1902–1923, II: 568, fig. 95) suggested that a version of it might be carried by the warrior of Xiquipilco in the *Codex Telleriano-Remensis* (1995: 37v).

32. *Quetzalpapalotl:* The second *tlatoani pilli* on fol. 72r bears this standard. Concerning the floral and igneous symbolic connotations of this and the four other butterfly standards included in this paragraph, see Seler 1902–1923, II: 572–574, Abb. 62, 105–106, 138–139. As he noted, these devices are also pictured in the tribute sections of the *Matrícula de Tributos* and the *Codex Mendoza* (Abb. 107, 108). Compare notes 33, 39, 64, 72, this paragraph.

xollopapalotl

The dark yellow parrot [feather] butterfly [insignia][33]

ynic tlatlalili colotlj yuhqui papalotl çã mochi xolo ynic tlatzacutlj q̃tzaltzoyo

A frame is fashioned like a butterfly; it is all covered with dark yellow parrot [feathers]. It has a quetzal [feather] tuft.

quetzaltototl

The quetzal bird [insignia][34]

ynic tlachiuhtli çã no colotlj tlatlalili yuhqui tototl q̃tzali yn iatlapal yoa yn icuitlapil quachichiq'le.

It is thus made: A frame is likewise fashioned like a bird. Its wings and tail are of quetzal [feathers]. It has a crest [of feathers].

tzatzaztli

The warping frame [insignia][35]

ça mochi quavitl yvitlatzavalj yn ite tlatectlj q̃tzali ypã manj.

It is all of wood. A hank of feather yarn is laid along the edge. On it is [a crest of] quetzal [feathers].

çaquãtonatiuh

The [black and yellow] troupial [feather] sun [insignia][36]

ynic tlatlalili colotlj yaoaltic çaquayvitica tlatzacutli tlatonatiuh ycuilolj.

Thus is it made: There is a circular frame. It is covered with [black and yellow] troupial feathers in the design of the sun.

ometochtlaviztli

The Two Rabbit insignia[37]

ynic tlatlalili colotlj yuhqui comitl yn i tlatzaquali pilivitl aztayvitl in icpac tlatlalili quetzalxixilqui.

A frame is fashioned like an earthenware vessel. It is covered with princely feathers[38] [and] heron feathers. On top are set quetzal [feather] spikes.

33. *Xollopapalotl:* This standard is pictured as the illustration second from the top on fol. 74r. Compare notes 32, 39, 64, 72, this paragraph.

34. *Quetzaltototl:* This standard is illustrated at the top of fol. 74r. Seler (1902–1923, II: 375, Abb. 109a) suggested that a similar device was illustrated in the tribute section of the *Codex Mendoza.*

35. *Tzatzaztli:* This standard is pictured at the top of fol. 74v.

36. *Çaquãtonatiuh:* This standard is pictured as the third item from the top on fol. 74r.

37. *Ometochtlaviztli:* This standard is illustrated as the lowermost item on fol. 74r. Ome Tochtli, Two Rabbit, was the calendric name of the *octli* gods in the aggregate. The device represents an *octli* (pulque) pot of a well-known type. The globular portion of the vessel displays the typical facial decoration of the *octli* deities, with the crescentic nose ornament, *yacametztli,* superimposed on the central area in red, which is flanked by dark green zones decorated with yellow lozenge-shaped elements. To the body of the pot are attached the typical winglike appendages bearing the same red and dark green colors. The foam of the beverage is represented by white heron plumage, garnished with green quetzal feathers. See Seler 1902–1923, II: 575; Bankmann 1984; Nicholson 1991; Anawalt 1993a.

38. *Pilivitl:* See note 19, this paragraph.

çaquāpapalotl

The [black and yellow] troupial [feather] butterfly [insignia][39]

ynic tlatlachiuhtli ça mochi çaquayvitl quetzaltzoyo.
ixquich i yn ītlauiz tlatoqz. pipilti, etc.

It is made all of [black and yellow] troupial [feathers]. It has a quetzal [feather] tuft.
All of these are the insignia of the rulers, noblemen, etc.

PARAGRAPH 8B
[fol. 68v]

Auh ynic ocuemitl tlaviztli yn ītlatqui yn ītlauiz tiyacaua.

And the second group of military insignia: the accouterments [and] insignia of the brave warriors.

ychcavipilli

The padded cotton shirt

ynic tlachiuhtli ichcatlavitectli tilmatica tlaquimiloli ypã tlaçotl tlatēcuetlaxvili velatlalpitl.

It is made in this manner: Unspun cotton is enveloped with cloth, to which it is stitched. It is edged with leather; it has good ties.

maquavitl

The war club

ynic tlachiuhtli avaq'vitl tlatilavacaxintli necoc tlacamacuicuitl ṽcã tlatectli im itztli ayocuitlatica tlaçaloli.

It is made of oak cut into a thick piece. On two sides there are grooves in which are set obsidian [blades] glued with turtle dung.

teutenacvchtli

The jet ear plugs

ynic tlachiuhtli teotetl tliltic velachictli ynic quitlalia tlatecque.

They are made of jet. They are black, highly polished. Thus the lapidaries fashion them.

quauhtentetl

The eagle lip plug

ynic tlatlalili tecpatl iuhq' nextecuili ynic quitlalia ypã quiquixtia tlateque.

A flintstone is fashioned like a grub. Thus the lapidaries fashion it; they made the likeness.

vevei cvzcatl

The great [shell] necklace

ynic tlachiuhtli tlapetlavali tecziztli vevey tlaçotl nepãtla mani yavaltic quapayahoaloli.

It is made in this manner: Large, polished shells are strung. In the center is a circle, a circle with a cross-piece.

39. *Çaquāpapalotl:* This standard is pictured as the item second from the top on fol. 74v. Compare notes 32, 33, 64, 72, this paragraph.

chipolcvzcatl

ynic tlachiuhtli ça mochi chipoli yn tlaçotl tlacozcatlalili tepitotõ.

The snail shell necklace[40]

It is made all of small snail shells that are strung together and fashioned into a necklace.

tezacanecuilli

ynic tlachiuhtli tecziztli chitecoltic ynic tlatectlj yztac.

The curved lip ornament

It is made of a conch shell cut in a curve. It is white.

ixcoloiuhqui chimalli

ynic tlachiuhtli otlatl ỹ tlatzayãtli ychicpatica tlavipãtli tlapalivitica tlatlacuilolo tẽtlapilolo.

The curved eye shield[41]

It is made in this manner: Split bamboo [pieces] are fitted together with maguey fiber. It is designed in red feathers. It has a hanging border [of feathers].

tepachiuhqui chimalli

ynic tlachiuhtli yvitica tlatzacutli tepuztlatzotzõtli ypã mamani yviteçouhqui.

The flattened shield[42]

It is made in this manner: It is covered with feathers; beaten copper is laid over it. It has an [open] border of feathers around the edge.

tlapalxapochimalli

ynic tlatzacutli toztli nepãtla mani chichiltic ynic nez ixapo.

The red disc shield[43]

It is covered with yellow parrot [feathers]. In the center appears a red disc.

tezacanecuilochimallj

ynic tlachiuhtli tliltic ỹ petlãqui yn ipã manj yztac y yn iuhq' tezacanecuili.

The shield with the curved lip ornament[44]

It is made in this manner: On a shiny black background is a white [design] like a curved lip ornament.

40. *Chipolcvzcatl:* This necklace, specified as being of gold, is worn by the first *tiacauh* on fol. 72r. It is composed of alternating gold and green globular beads, possibly in the form of shells.

41. *Ixcoliuhqui chimalli:* This shield is illustrated as the third item from the top on fol. 79v.

42. *Tepachiuhqui chimalli:* Seler (1902–1923, II: 578) preferred the translation "Der mit Kupferblechknopfen verzierte Schilde." It is not illustrated separately in the paragraph. He suggested that it represented the usual variety of the *quetzalcuexyo* or the *teocuitlateteyo* shield.

43. *Tlapalxapo chimalli:* No illustration of this shield is included in this paragraph, but two other shields that are pictured are very similar: the *teocuitlaxapochimalli,* carried by the first *tiacauh* on fol. 72v (see note 10, this paragraph), and the *texoxapochimalli,* pictured as the item second from the top on fol. 80r, where the central disk is blue.

44. *Tezacanecuilo chimalli:* This shield is pictured as the uppermost figure on fol. 80r. The tusklike lip plug, the *te(n)zacanecuilli,* was particularly but not exclusively a badge of the Tlaxcalteca warrior. Seler (1902–1923, II: 578) noted its occurrence on shields in the *Lienzo de Tlaxcala* (e.g., 1983: 13).

zitlallo chimalli

ynic tlachiuhtli cacalivitl ynic tlatzacutlj yztac yvitl yn ipã mamani zitlalpoi.

The star-studded shield[45]

It is made in this fashion: It is covered with crow feathers. On it are large stars[46] of white feathers.

ihuitezuvhqui chimalli

ynic tlachiuhtli tlil ỹ petlani apetzyo texotica tlacuilolo tezuuhqui.

The shield with the open feather border[47]

It is made of black [feathers] glistening with pyrites. It is designed in blue; there is an [open] border [of feathers] around the edge.

tlaavitectli chimalli

ynic tlachiuhtli ça motquitica tizatl ynic tlaavitectlj.

The whitened shield[48]

It is made in this manner: It is entirely covered with chalk; thus it is whitened.

chamolleuatl

ynic tlachivali çã motquitica chamolivitl yn itech tlatectli tilmatli tentlapilolo.

The red parrot [feather] tunic[49]

It is made entirely of red parrot feathers set on a piece of cloth. It has a hanging border [of feathers].

tlapallivieuatl

yn itech tlatectli tilmatli ça motquitica chichiltlapalivitl tentlapilolo.

The red feathered tunic[50]

On an entire piece of cloth bright red feathers are set. It has a hanging border [of feathers].

totollivieuatl

yn itec tlatectli tilmatli ça motquitica totolivitl çã pacoltic.

The turkey hen feather tunic

Turkey feathers are set on the entire piece of cloth—just the fine, curly ones.[51]

45. *Zitlallo chimalli:* This shield is illustrated as the lowermost item on fol. 79v.

46. *Zitlalpoi:* read *citlalpal.*

47. *Ihuitezuvhqui chimalli:* This shield is pictured as the fifth item from the top on fol. 80r. Seler (1902–1923, II: 578–579)—apparently basing his judgment principally on the shield's somewhat similar decorative scheme, featuring small white circles in a radial pattern, and its feather edgings—believed that this shield was a variant of the *zitlallo chimalli* (see note 45, this paragraph). The white ring in the center he identified as the *anahuatl,* the circular white shell pectoral with red leather wrapping on its upper segment that was particularly characteristic of the attire of the deity Tezcatlipoca.

48. *Tlaavitectli chimalli:* This shield is illustrated as the lowermost item on fol. 80r.

49. *Chamolleuatl:* Seler (1902–1923, II: 580) preferred the translation "Das Hemd aus dunkelvioletten Federn." This battle tunic is illustrated on fol. 76r., at the top.

50. *Tlapallivieuatl:* This battle tunic and the following one, *totolihuiehuatl,* were probably quite similar to the *chamolehuatl,* but they are not illustrated in this paragraph.

51. *Itec:* read *itech. Pacoltic:* read *paçoltic.*

tlapalquaxolotl

ynic tlachiuhtli colotli tlatlalili yaoaltic ynic tlatzacutli chamolivitl tẽtlapilolo ycpac ca ỹ miquiztli quetzaltzoyo pepeyocyo.

The red Xolotl head [insignia][52]

It is made in this manner: A round frame is constructed which is covered with red parrot feathers.[53] It has a hanging border [of feathers]. On top is a death['s head] with a tuft of quetzal [feathers]. It has bright [adornment].

iztac quaxolotl

ynic tlatlalili çã no iuhqui aztaiviticã tlatzacutli yn itẽtlapilolo teocuitlapepeyocyo ycpac ca ỹ miquiztli quetzaltzoyo.

The white Xolotl head [insignia]

It is thus fashioned: It is similarly covered with white heron feathers. It has its hanging border [of feathers and] bright gold adornments. On top is a death['s head] with a tuft of quetzal [feathers].

cueçalpatzactli

ynic tlatlalili colotli yuhquĩ tzontecomatl yvitica tlatzacutlj ycpac tlauipãtli cuezali çã motq'tica.

The compressed macaw [feather insignia][54]

A frame is fashioned like a head, which is covered with feathers. On top is a row entirely of macaw [feathers].

tlacvchpatzactli

ynic tlatlalili çã no iuhq' ça motquitica tlacochtli mitl mamazyo yn icpac tlavipãtli.

The compressed dart [insignia][55]

It is fashioned in the same way; it is entirely of darts, of arrows, made from quills in a row on top.

cacalpatzactli

ynic tlatlalili çã no iuhqui çã motquitica cacalivitl yn icpac tlavipantli.

The compressed crow [feather insignia][56]

It is fashioned in the same way; it is entirely of crow feathers in a row on top.

tlecocomoctli

ynic tlatlalili colotli yaoaltic yvitica tlatzacutlj çã motq'tica cuezali yn icpac tlamãtli

The crackling fire [insignia][57]

A circular frame is fashioned [and] covered with feathers. [The flames] on top are en-

52. *Tlapalquaxolotl:* This battle standard and the following one, *iztac quaxolotl,* are illustrated as the items second and third from the top, respectively, on fol. 76r. Another, called *tozquaxolotl,* is borne by the first *tiacauh* on fol. 72v. As Seler (1902–1923, II: 581–584, Abb, 127, 128, 129) noted, although here the heads atop these umbrella-like standards are skulls (and are so designated *[miquiztli]* in the texts), in illustrations of these devices in other sources *(Matrícula de Tributos, Codex Mendoza, Lienzo de Tlaxcala)* the head is that of the caninoid monster god, Xolotl—which fits the name of the standard.

53. *Chamolivitl:* Seler (1902–1923, II: 583) preferred the translation "mit dunkel rothen chamol-Federn belegt."

54. *Queçalpatzactli:* This standard is illustrated as the topmost item on fol. 76v. Seler (1902–1923, II: 584, Abb. 130, 133) noted its occurrence in the *Matrícula de Tributos,* and it also occurs on the cognate folios of the tribute section of the *Codex Mendoza.*

55. *Tlacvchpatzactli:* This standard is pictured as the lowermost item on fol. 76r.

56. *Cacalpatzactli:* This standard is illustrated as the item second from the top on fol. 76v.

57. *Tlecocomoctli:* This standard is illustrated as the item third from the top on fol. 76v.

tētlapilolo.

tirely of red macaw [feathers]. It has a hanging border [of feathers].

tlapallivitelolotli

ynic tlatlalili ololtic yn otlatl tlapitzaoacatzayātli ytech tlatectlȳ ȳ tlapalivitl pepeyocyo q̃tzaltzoyo.

The red feather ball[58]

A ball is fashioned of bamboo which was split into long, thin strips. On it are set red feathers. It has bright [adornments and] a quetzal [feather] tuft.

iztac ivitelolotli

ynic tlatlalili çāno iuhqui çā motquitica yztac yvitl pepeyocyo quetzaltzoyo.

The white feather ball[59]

It is thus fashioned: It is similarly entirely of white feathers. It has bright [adornments and] a quetzal [feather] tuft.

macuilpanitl

ynic tlachiuhtli macuili mani y panitl yuitica tlatzacutli quetzaltzoyo.

The five flag [insignia][60]

It is made in this manner: There are five flags that are covered with feathers. They have quetzal [feather] tufts.

aztatzũntli

ynic tlatlalili colotli yuhquī comitl yvitica tlatzacutli çā mochi iztac yvitl yn icpac yetiuh qztzaltzoyo.

The heron [feather] hair [insignia][61]

A frame is constructed like an earthenware vessel. It is covered with feathers. On top go all white feathers. It has a quetzal [feather] tuft.

copilli iztac

ynic tlatlalili colotli quavitztic aztaivitica tlatzacutli tentlapilolo quetzaltzoyo.

The white conical headpiece [insignia][62]

A conical frame is constructed. It is covered with heron feathers. It has a hanging border [of feathers and] a quetzal [feather tuft].

58. *Tlapallivitelolotli:* This standard is pictured as the lowermost item on fol. 76v.

59. *Iztac ivitelolotli:* This standard is illustrated as the topmost item on fol. 77r. Seler (1902–1923, II: 590, Abb. 145, 148) suggested that a version of it might be pictured in the *Lienzo de Tlaxcala.*

60. *Macuilpanitl:* This standard is pictured as the item second from the top on fol. 77r. Seler (1902–1923, II: 585–586, Abb. 134, 135) noted various occurrences of this device in the *Lienzo de Tlaxcala.*

61. *Aztatzvntli:* This standard is illustrated as the item third from the top on fol. 77r. As Seler (1902–1923, II: 589, Abb. 143, 147) noted, the device is also pictured in the *Lienzo de Tlaxcala* and constituted the standard headdress of the *octli* and rain gods. For *qtzaltzoyo,* read *quetzaltzonyo.*

62. *Copilli iztac:* This standard, labeled here *aztacopilli,* is pictured as the lowermost item on fol. 77r. This device is clearly a variant of the *quetzalcopilli,* which is discussed in note 30, this paragraph.

tozcololi

ynic tlatlalili colotli cocoltic çã mochi toztli ynic tlatzacutli cuezaltzoyo

tlapalitzmitl

ynic tlatlalili colotli quavitztic patlachtic ynic tlatzacutli yvitl cẽtlacol yztac cẽtlacol chichiltic.

itzpapalotl

ynic tlatlalili colotli yaoaltic ocãpã manj tepuztlatzotzõtli yn icpac tlapapalotectlj.

xacalli

ynic tlachiuhtli colotli yuhqui xacali yvitica tlatzacutlj tentlapilolo.

caltzaqualli

ynic tlatlalili colotli yuhquĩ cali çã no yvitica tlatzacutli tẽtlapilolo.

çacacalli

ynic tlatlalili yuhqui tlapevali colotli yztac yvitica tlatzacutlj.

The yellow parrot [feather] serpentine [insignia][63]

A serpentine frame is constructed. It is all covered with yellow parrot [feathers]. It has a red macaw [feather] tuft.

The red arrowhead [insignia][64]

A frame is constructed that is pointed at the top and broad [at the base]. Half of it is covered with white [feathers and] half with red.

The obsidian butterfly [insignia][65]

Thus is it constructed: There is a circular frame. On the two sides are [sheets of] beaten copper. On top is [a figure] cut in the form of a butterfly.

The straw hut [insignia][66]

A frame is constructed like a straw hut. It is covered with feathers [and] has a hanging border [of feathers].

The masonry house [insignia][67]

A frame is constructed like a [masonry] house. It is also covered with feathers [and] has a hanging border [of feathers].

The grass hut [insignia][68]

A frame is constructed like a trap. It is covered with white feathers.

63. *Tozcololi:* This standard is pictured as the topmost item on fol. 77v. Seler (1902–1923, II: 587, Abb. 140, 141, 142) noted its occurrences also in the *Matrícula de Tributos*, the tribute section of the *Codex Mendoza*, and the *Lienzo de Tlaxcala*.

64. *Tlapalitzmitl:* This standard is illustrated as the item second from the top on fol. 77v.

65. *Itzpapalotl:* This standard is illustrated as the second item from the top on fol. 78v. As Seler (1902–1923, II: 586–587) indicated, the cruciform elements of sheet copper that tip the butterfly's legs in the depiction of the Otomi igneous/mortuary deity Otontecuhtli in Chapter I, Paragraph 5A, are designated *itzpapalotl.* Itzpapalotl was also the name of a prominent "Chichimec" fertility goddess (discussion in Seler 1900–1901: 107–108). Compare notes 32, 33, 39, 72, this paragraph.

66. *Xacalli:* This standard is illustrated as the lowermost item on fol. 77v.

67. *Caltzaqualli:* This standard is pictured as the topmost item on fol. 78r.

68. *Çacacalli:* This standard is illustrated as the item second from the top on fol. 78r.

tzipitl

ynic tlachiuhtli quavitl tlaxintli yuhquī piltōtli tlatzotlanili ymac ca ytlamatzoval.

The fretful child [insignia][69]

It is made in this manner: Wood is carved like a child. It is varnished. In his hand is his rolled tortilla.

tlazimalvapalli

ynic tlachiuhtli colotli yuhqui vapali ic tlazimalo vnca ca yztapaltetl.

The maguey fiber pulling board [insignia][70]

A frame is constructed like a plank by means of which maguey fibers are pulled. A flat stone is there.

vexolotl

ynic tlatlali colotli yuhqui vexolotl tlayviyotili cacaxyo.

The turkey cock [insignia][71]

A frame is constructed like a turkey cock. It is covered with feathers [and] it has a carrying frame [as tail].

ixtlapalpanitl

ynic tlachiuhtli panitl çan ixtlapal onoc ocāpa tlapilolo.

The transverse banner [insignia][72]

It is made in this manner: A flag lies transversely. It has a tassel hanging on each side.

tlilpapalotl

ynic tlatlalili colotlj yuhquī papalotl cacalivitica tlatzacutli quetzalo.

The black butterfly [insignia][73]

A frame is constructed like a butterfly. It is covered with crow feathers. It has a quetzal [feather crest].

tlapalcvyotl

ynic tlatlalili colotli yuhq' coyutl ytzōteco tlapalivitica tlatzacutli no iuhquin ieoayo.

The red coyote [insignia][74]

A frame is constructed like a coyote. Its head is covered with red feathers, as well as its skin.

69. *Tzipitl:* This standard is illustrated as the third item from the top on fol. 78r. Molina (1944, Part II: 152v) defines *tzipitl* as "la criatura que esta enferma o desgañada a causa de estar su madre preñada." The corrupted form *chipil* is still in use today.

70. *Tlazimalvapalli:* This standard is pictured as the item third from the top on fol. 78v. The instrument it represents played a significant role in the preparation and utilization of the fiber of the maguey, one of the most useful cultigens of pre-Hispanic Central Mexico. The fibers, first soaked in water, were removed by abrading them with this wooden device and were then employed for various purposes, including weaving them into the coarse cloth that served for the clothing of the lower socioeconomic classes. See Anawalt 1981: 29; Museo Nacional de Culturas Populares 1988.

71. *Vexolotl:* This standard is illustrated as the fourth item from the top on fol. 78v. An aspect of the turkey cock, *huexolotl*, called *chalchiuhtotolin*, was one of the "Thirteen Sacred Birds" who served as patrons, along with the "Nine Lords" and the "Thirteen Lords," of sequent days of the 260-day divinatory cycle, the *tonalpohualli* (see Nicholson 1971: Table 2).

72. *Ixtlapalpanitl:* This standard is illustrated as the topmost item on fol. 79r.

73. *Tlilpapalotl:* This standard is illustrated as the third item from the top on fol. 77v. Compare notes 32, 33, 39, 64, this paragraph.

74. *Tlapalcvyotl:* This battle suit is illustrated as the second item from the top on fol. 79r. Compare notes 20, 21, 75, 77, 78, 86, 87, 90, this paragraph.

tlaq'miloli

The bundle [insignia][75]

ynic tlatlalili colotli yuhquī quimili nacazylpitica.

A frame is constructed like a bundle. The corners are tied.

iztac cvyutl

The white coyote [insignia][76]

ynic tlachiuhtli ça mochi iztac yvitl ynic tlatzacutli ytzōteco yoan yn ievayo.

It is made in this manner: Its head and skin are all covered with white feathers.

mexayacatl

The thigh-skin mask [insignia][77]

ynic tlatlalili colotli quavitztic yquanepâtla ycac yuhq'n chichiquiltic mixtexovi.

A conical frame is constructed. On the crown of its head is what is like a three-pronged harpoon. The face is painted blue.

[fol. 69r]

çitlalcoyutl

The star-studded coyote [insignia][78]

ynic tlachiuhtli ça mochi tliltic yvitl ynic tlatzacutlj ytzōteco no iuhq' ieoayo yztac yvitl ynic cuicuiltic.

It is made in this manner: Its head as well as its skin is all covered with black feathers. It has spots of white feathers.

tliltic cvyutl

The black coyote [insignia][79]

ynic tlachiuhtli çã motquitica totolivitl papaçoltic.

It is made in this manner: It is covered entirely with fine, [black] turkey-hen feathers.

maquavitzoctli

The pointed war club[80]

ynic tlaxintli avaquavitl nauhcāpa cuitlatetepone quavitztic

A piece of oak is cut. The four sides have sharp edges. It has a pointed tip.

75. *Tlaq'miloli:* This standard is pictured as the lowermost item on fol. 78r. The cult of the sacred bundle, the *tlaquimilolli*, was a significant aspect of indigenous Mesoamerican religion. See Stenzel 1970; Nicholson 1971: 409.

76. *Iztac cvyutl:* This military suit is not illustrated but must have been very similar to that pictured on fol. 75r as the item third from the top—sans the bunch of quetzal feathers. Compare notes 20, 21, 73, 77, 78, 86, 87, 90, this paragraph.

77. *Mexayacatl:* This standard is illustrated as the topmost item on fol. 78v. For *yquanepatla ycac yuhq' chichiquiltic*, Seler (1902–1923, II: 592) preferred the translation "auf der Scheitellinie eine Art (Zacken) kam." On the significance of this "thigh-skin mask," representing Itztlacoliuhqui, who was the son of the major earth/fertility goddess, Teteoinnan, and who played a significant role in the *veintena* ceremony of Ochpaniztli, see Seler 1902–1923, II: 592; Sullivan 1976b.

78. *Çitlalcoyutl:* This military suit is illustrated as the topmost item on fol. 79v. Compare notes 20, 21, 73, 75, 78, 86, 87, 90, this paragraph.

79. *Tliltic cvyutl:* This battle costume is illustrated as the item second from the top on fol. 79v. Compare notes 20, 21, 73, 75, 77, 86, 89, 90, this paragraph.

80. *Maquavitzoctli:* Molina (1944, Part II: 157v) defines *huitzoctli* as "palanca de roble puntiaguda para arrancar cespedes y abrir la tierra." The war club, which is not illustrated in this paragraph, was apparently somewhat similar in form to this agricultural tool. The latter, as Seler (1902–1923, II: 592) noted, served as the place sign for Huitzoco

tlavitolli

ynic tlaxintli tomavac vel atic ỹ mitl tlaxaltentlj

The bow[81]

It is wrought from a thick [piece of wood]. With it a polished arrow can be shot.

quauholloli

ynic tlaxintli avaquavitl çã quaololtic.

The ball of wood

Thus is it wrought: It is [a piece of] oak, just a wooden ball.

atlatl

ynic tlaxintli tomaoac veyac mamazyo tepoztli yn iquac ca quauhtica ỹ quitlaça.

The spear-thrower[82]

It is fashioned from a thick, long [piece of wood]. It [the dart] has flight feathers;[83] copper is at the tip. They hurled it with the piece of wood.

tematlatl

ynic tlachiuhtli mecatl ỹ tlamatlachioali vncã motlalia ỹ tetl ynic tlamotlalo tlatematlavilo.

The sling[84]

Thus is it made: It is of rope made into a net. A stone is placed in it. With it stones are hurled; there is hunting with a sling.

PARAGRAPH (8)
[fol. 72r]

Ce tlacatl tlatoani pilli yn itlatq' yn itlaviz

ychcavipil, yxiuheuauh. yteucuitlacuzcapetl. [illus.]

The accouterments [and] insignia of a personage, a ruler, a nobleman:[85]

His padded cotton shirt. His turquoise [blue] tunic. His gold mat necklace. His green

(*Codex Mendoza* 1992, III: fol. 37r). Seler translated the term for the club "Der Morgenstern," seemingly likening it—somewhat dubiously—to the medieval European club of that configuration (cf. Hassig 1988: 85, 290).

81. *Tlavitolli:* The bow and arrow was particularly associated with the seminomadic, more barbarous "Chichimec" lifestyle of the ancestors of many of the leading peoples of contact-period Central Mexico and with the hunters and gatherers of the arid northern Mexican steppes. It was also an important and effective weapon of the culturally more advanced Central Mexican groups at contact. See discussion in Hassig 1988: 79–80.

82. *Atlatl:* On this important indigenous Mesoamerican weapon, see Nuttall 1891; Seler 1902–1923, II: 368–369; Noguera 1945; Hassig 1988: 75–76.

83. *Mamaztli:* Compare Sahagún 1950–1982, Part XII [Book 11]: 55; an alternative translation would be "quills" (Molina 1944, Part II: 52r: *cañon con pluma*).

84. *Tematlatl:* On this important weapon of the contact-period Central Mexican armies, see Hassig 1988: 80–81, 288.

85. This text and all those following are contained on the nine folios (72–80) that Francisco del Paso y Troncoso inserted between fols. 68 and 69. All feature illustrations as well as text. As is evident from the notes up to this point, most of these illustrations can be directly connected to the textual terms listed and annotated on folios 68–69, which contain Paragraph 8 as it fits conformably within the integrated structure of Chapter IV. The first six texts on folios 72r–73r constitute substantial descriptions of the insignia and costumes of the lords, *tlatoque pipiltin* (fol. 72r/72v), and three warrior captains, *tiacahuan* (fols. 72v/73r), with all of the costume and insignia items rendered in the possessive form. The remainder of the texts on these folios consist of short labels for each illustration, all in the nominative form.

ychalchiuhtēteuh.
yteucuitlanacvch.
yquetzalpatzac. ychimal
quetzalxicalcvliuhqui.
ymaquauh. ytlaçomaxtli.
ytecpilcac.

Oc no çe tlacatl tlatoani
pilli yn itlatq' yn itlaviz
ychcavipil.
ypillivieuauh. yxiuhtēteuh. [illus.]
ymayanacoch.
ychayauac cuzqui.
yquetzalpapaluh. ychimal quetzalcuexyo.
ymaquauh. ytlaçomaxtli. ytlaçocac.

stone lip plug. His gold ear plugs. His compressed quetzal [feather insignia]. His quetzal [feather] shield with the stepped fret design. His war club. His precious breechcloth. His lordly sandals.

The accouterments [and] insignia of another personage, ruler, nobleman:

His padded cotton shirt. His tunic of princely feathers. His turquoise lip plug. His june beetle ear plugs. His necklace [of green stone and gold] with radiating pendants. His quetzal [feather] butterfly [insignia]. His quetzal [feather] Huaxtec shield. His war club. His precious breechcloth. His precious sandals.

[fol. 72v]

Jnic ei tlacatl pilli yn itlatq̃ yn itlaviz

ychcavipil. ytozeuauh. ychalchiuhtēteuh. [illus.] yxiuhnanacuch. yteucuitlapā. ychalchiuhcuzqui. ychimal tozmiquizyo. ymaquauh.
ytlaçomaxtli. ytecpilcac.

The accouterments [and] insignia of a third personage, a nobleman:

His padded cotton shirt. His yellow parrot [feather] tunic. His green stone lip plug. His turquoise ear plugs. His gold banner. His green stone necklace. His yellow parrot [feather] death['s head] shield. His war club. His precious breechcloth. His lordly sandals.

Auh ynic ōcuemitl
tiyacaoā yn ītlaviz
yn itlamamaltuzqua-
xolotl. ychcavipil. [illus.]
ytlapalivieuauh.
yteucuitlanacoch. yyacametz.
yteucuitlachipolcuzqui.
ychimal teucuitlaxapo.
yquāmaxtli. ytlaçocac—

And from the second group, the brave warriors' insignia:

His yellow parrot [feather] Xolotl head [insignia] carried on the back. His padded cotton shirt. His tunic of red feathers. His gold ear plugs. His crescent-shaped nose ornament. His necklace of gold snail shells. His gold disc shield. His eagle [feather] breechcloth. His lordly sandals.

[fol. 73r]

Jnic ome tlacatl yn itlatqui yn itlaviz

ychcavipil. yaztaeuauh. yxiuhnacoch. yteucuitlatempilol. [illus.]
yaztapatzac. ychimal texaxacalo. ytlaçomaxtli.

The accouterments [and] insignia of a second personage:

His padded cotton shirt. His heron [feather] tunic. His turquoise ear plugs. His gold lip pendant.[86] His compressed heron [feather insignia]. His shield with the thick lips design. His precious breechcloth. His war club. His precious sandals.

Paragraph (8)

86. *Yteucuitlatempilol:* This labret actually seems to be a *temalacatentetl,* "disk-shaped lip plug of fine turquoise in a gold setting." See Sahagún 1950–1982, Part IX (Book 8): 27.

ymaquauh. ytlaçocac.

The accouterments [and] insignia of a third personage.

Jnic ei tlacatl yn itlatqui yn itlaviz ychcavipil. ytuzcoyvuh. ytezacanecuil. ychimal tlilxapo. [illus.] yquāmaxtli. yztaccac. ymaquauh.

His padded cotton shirt. His yellow parrot [feather] coyote [insignia]. His curved lip ornament. His black disc shield. His eagle [feather] breechcloth. His white sandals. His war club.

[fol. 73v]

quetzalpanitl [illus.]

The quetzal [feather] banners [insignia].

Çaquāpanitl [illus.]

The [black and gold] troupial [feather] banner [insignia].

quetzalquaquavitl [illus.]

The quetzal [feather] horns [insignia].

quetzaltzitzimitl [illus.]

The quetzal [feather] demon of the dark [insignia].

quetzalquatlamoyaoallj [illus.]

The quetzal [feather] bestrewn head [insignia].

[fol. 74r]

quetzaltototl [illus.]

The quetzal bird [insignia].

xolopapalotl [illus.]

The dark yellow parrot [feather] butterfly [insignia].

çaquātonatiuh [illus.]

The [black and yellow] troupial [feather] sun [insignia].

ometochtlaviztli [illus.]

The Two Rabbit insignia.

[fol. 74v]

tzatzaztli [illus.]

The warping frame [insignia].

çaquāpapalotl [illus.]

The [black and yellow] troupial [feather] butterfly [insignia].

teucuitlavevetl [illus.]

The gold drum [insignia].

chamolcvyutl [illus.]

The red coyote [insignia].[87]

[fol. 75r]

xiuhcoyotl [illus.]

The turquoise [blue] coyote [insignia].

quetzalcopilli [illus.]

The quetzal [feather] conical headpiece [insignia].

iztac cvyutl [illus.]

The white coyote [insignia].[88]

ananacaztli [illus.]

The water ears [insignia].

87. *Chamolcvyutl:* This battle suit was not included in the textual listing of folios 68–69. Compare notes 20, 21, 73, 75, 77, 78, 87, 90, this paragraph.

88. *Iztac cvyutl:* This battle suit was not included in the textual listing of folios 68–69, but, as indicated in note 75, another of the same name, included among the insignia and accouterments assigned to the warrior captains, the *tiacahuan,* was probably nearly identical except for the absence of the quetzal feather plumage. Compare also notes 20, 21, 73, 75, 77, 78, 86, 90, this paragraph.

[fol. 75v]

quauhtetepoyo chimalli [illus.]	The eagle's foot shield.
oçelotetepoyo chimalli [illus.]	Jaguar foot shield.[89]
chimalli [illus.]	The silver stones shield.
teucuitlateteyo	
quetzalpuztecqui [illus.]	The cleft quetzal [feathers] shield.
chimalli	
teucuitlacuzcatl [illus.]	The golden beetle necklace.
temoltic	
teucuitlaçoyanacochtli [illus.]	The gold palm ear plug.
nicã tlami ỹ pillatquitl ỹ tlaviztli etc.	Here end the noblemen's accouterments [and] insignia.

[fol. 76r]

nica vmpeua ỹ [illus.] quauhtlaviztli	Here begin the eagle warriors' insignia.[90]
chamoleuatl [illus.]	The red parrot [feather] tunic.
tlapalquaxolotl [illus.]	The red Xolotl head [insignia].
yztac quaxolotl [illus.]	The white Xolotl head [insignia].
tlacvchpatzactli [illus.]	The compressed dart [insignia].

[fol. 76v]

Cueçalpatzactli [illus.]	The compressed macaw [feather insignia].
cacalpatzactli [illus.]	The compressed crow [feather insignia].
tlecocomoctli [illus.]	The crackling fire [insignia].
tlapallivitelolotli [illus.]	The red feather ball.

[fol. 77r]

yztac ivitelolotli [illus.]	The white feather ball.
macuilpanitl [illus.]	The five flag [insignia].
aztatzũtli [illus.]	The heron [feather] hair [insignia].
aztacopilli [illus.]	The heron [feather] conical headpiece [insignia].

[fol. 77v]

tozcocolli [illus.]	The yellow parrot [feather] serpentine [insignia].
tlapalitzmitl	The colored arrowhead [insignia].
tlilpapalotl	The black butterfly [insignia].
xacalli	The straw hut [insignia].

89. *Oçelotetepoyo:* See note 11, this paragraph.

90. This and the preceding annotation, both in a lighter colored ink, indicate the division of these illustrated folios into two sections: the first, which ends on fol. 75v, devoted to the accouterments and insignia of the nobles, the *pipiltin,* and the second, which begins on fol. 76r, concerned with those of the warriors of lesser social status, denominated "eagles," *cuauhtin.*

[fol. 78r]

caltzaqualli	The masonry house [insignia].
çacacalli	The grass hut [insignia].
tzipito	The fretful child [insignia].
tlaquimiloli	The bundle [insignia].

[fol. 78v]

mexayacatlaviztli [illus.]	The thigh-skin mask insignia.
ytzpapalotl [illus.]	The obsidian butterfly [insignia].
tlazimaluapalli [illus.]	The maguey fiber pulling board [insignia].
vexolotl. [illus.]	The turkey cock [insignia].

[fol. 79r]

yxtlapalpanitl [illus.]	The transverse banner [insignia].
tlapalcvyutl [illus.]	The red coyote [insignia].
tlecvyutl [illus.]	The fire coyote [insignia].[91]
chimallaviztli [illus.]	The shield insignia.[92]

[fol. 79v]

çitlalcvyutl [illus.]	The star-studded coyote [insignia].
tliltic cvyutl [illus.]	The black coyote [insignia].
ixcoliuhqui chimalli [illus.]	The curved eye shield.
çitlallo chimallj [illus.]	The star-studded shield.

[fol. 80r]

teçacanecuilo chimallj [illus.]	The shield with the curved lip ornament.
texoxapo chimallj [illus.]	The blue disc shield.
macpalo chimallj [illus.]	The hand shield.[93]
yhuiteteyo chimallj [illus.]	The shield with the feather border.
yhuiteteyo çouhqui [illus.] chimallj	The shield with the open feather border.
tlahavitectlj chimallj [illus.]	The whitened shield.

91. *Tlecvyutl:* This battle suit was not included in the textual listing of folios 68–69. Compare notes 20, 21, 73, 75, 77, 78, 86, 87, this paragraph.

92. *Chimallaviztli:* This standard was not included in the textual listing of folios 68–69. As Seler (1902–1923, II: 592, Abb. 99) recognized, it consists of a shield with a feather fringe that features a kind of *en face* grotesque visage. It is similar to the decoration on the shield carried by the second of the *tiacahuan* on fol. 73r, which is denominated *texaxacalo.* Seler compared it to a somewhat similar shield device in the *Lienzo de Tlaxcala.*

93. *Macpalo chimalli:* This shield was not included in the textual listing of folios 68–69. As Seler (1902–1923, II: 579, Abb. 1, p. 398, Abb. 2–3, pp. 400–401), noted, a shield with a somewhat similar device (arm and hand) is carried by the Tenochca ruler Axayacatl as part of his Xipe Totec battle costume at Tenochtitlan's conquest of Tlatelolco in 1473, as depicted in the *Codex Cozcatzin* and in a colonial oil painting of this ruler, probably related to the codex picture, now in the Handschriftensammlung Osterreichische Nationalbibliothek, Vienna (ex-Bilimek collection).

PARAGRAPH 9
[fol. 69r]

Jnic. 9. parrapho ypã mitoa yn izquitlamãtli cvcvliztli ypã mochiva ỹ tonacayo

Ninth paragraph, in which are told all the different diseases that occur in our bodies.[1]

allauac

Phlegm

ynic pati tzitzictic ytocã tlanelhuatl nica mochioa.

It is cured with a root called *tzitzictic*,[2] which grows here.

ezallauac

Bloody phlegm

ynic pati vaxquavitl amo nicã mochioani.

It is cured with *huaxcuahuitl*,[3] which does not grow here.

yztac allauac

White phlegm

ynic pati yn tlanelhoatl ololiuhqui nicã mochioa.

It is cured with the root *ololiuhqui*,[4] which grows here.

cuztic allauac

Yellow phlegm

ynic pati ỹ tlanelhuatl ytoca cocoztic çã no nicã mochioa.

It is cured with a root called *cocoztic*,[5] which also grows here.

tlailli

Bloody stool

ynic pati yzquican icac ỹ cẽtli tlatla ỹ mi yoã çoaeuatl.

It is cured with *centli tlatla*, which is everywhere; it is drunk with *zoaehuatl*.[6]

yztac tlailli

White bloody stool

ynic pati çã no iuhqui yoã amo tle zẽca ypayo çã tlatzivi.

It is cured in the same way [as bloody stool] and also there is not much that is its remedy; it just diminishes.

1. This paragraph lists a large number of human diseases, annotated with descriptions of the therapeutic techniques considered to have been appropriate for each, usually the application of medicinal herbs. Later in Tlatelolco Sahagún collected more extensive information on this topic (certified by eight "medicos mexicanos"), which he assigned to Chapter 28 of Book 10 of the *Historia* (Sahagún 1950–1982, Part XI [Book 10]: 139–163; 1988, II: 636–650). Gall (1940: 93–118) paleographized the chapter and translated it into German. López Austin (1972: 136–147) did the same, with Spanish translation.

2. *Tzitzictic:* unidentified herb. It should be noted that many of the medicinal herbs listed in this paragraph have not been reliably identified botanically, even some of those well known in the literature. Also, differences of opinion concerning botanical identifications are not uncommon, even among recognized authorities, a problem compounded by the fact that the same Nahuatl term was sometimes used for different—and variously identified—medicinal plants.

3. *Vaxquavitl (huaxcuahuitl):* probably *Acacia Crescencia alata* Colm., a *tierra caliente* tree (Santamaría 1959: 569).

4. *Ololiuhqui:* variously identified as *Rivea corymbosa, Ipomoea sidaefolia,* and/or *Datura metaloides* (Sahagún 1950–1982, Part XII [Book 11]: 129, 165, 170).

5. *Cocoztic: Thalicitrum hernandezi* Tauch. (Sahagún 1950–1982, Part XI [Book 10]: 144–65).

6. *Centli tlatla* and *çoaeuatl:* unidentified herbs.

apitzallailli

Bloody diarrhea

ynic pati tlanelhuatl ytoca tzipipatli. nicã mochiua.

It is cured with a root called *tzipipatli*,[7] which grows here.

apitzalli

Diarrhea

ynic pati coyotomatl çã no ynelhuyo nicã mochiua.

It is cured with *coyotomatl*,[8] as well as its root. It grows here.

cvoaçiviztli

Gout

ynic pati tlapatl yxiuhyo nicã mochiua. yoã moço.

It is cured with the leaves of *tlapatl*,[9] which grows here; also one is bled.

tlecouaçiviztli

Dysentery

ynic pati çã no iuhqui.

It is cured in the same way.

teucocoliztli

Leprosy

ynic pati. mopotonia ocotzotica moneloa ỹ patli ça ca ichpoli yoã ça ca tlepatli nicã mochiva.

It is cured thus: A plaster of pine resin[10] mixed with the medicine *ichpoli*[11] is applied, and also just with *tlepatli*, which grows here.

toçãpotzalli

Scrofula

ynic pati. motequi yoã patli motema ytzietl tenextlj.

It is cured by cutting, and the medication that is applied is tobacco [and] lime.

xvchiziviztli

Hemorrhoids

ynic pati.

They are cured by. . . .[12]

mexvaliztli

Abscess[13]

ynic pati tlanelhuatl cucuztic nica mochiua yoã iztatl.

It is cured with the root *cocoztic*, which grows here, and with salt.

7. *Tzipipatli:* unidentified herb.

8. *Coyotomatl: Vitex mollis* HBK (Sahagún 1950–1982, Part XII [Book 11]: 141, 144).

9. *Tlapatl: Datura stramonium* L. (Sahagún 1950–1982, Part XI [Book 10]: 129, 147).

10. *Ocotzotica: Ocotzotl* may be either pine resin or balsam of *Liquidambar styraciflua* L. (Sahagún 1950–1982, Part XI [Book 10]: 140–17).

11. *Ichpoli:* unidentified herb; *tlepatli* may be various species of *Plumbago* or *Tournifortia* (Santamaría 1959: 1056, 1059; Sahagún 1950–1982, Part XI [Book 10]: 157). Since each term is preceded by *ça ca*, perhaps they should be read *çacaichpoli* and *çacatepatli.* Santamaría 1959: 1040 lists a *zacatepatli.*

12. There is no further text.

13. *Mexvaliztli:* problematical translation. Perhaps it should be read *me (tztli)-hualiztli,* swelling or abscess of the thigh. The meaning of abscess is suggested by such terms as *tlaxhuiztli* (boil, abscess), *nenepillaxhualiztli* (tongue abscess), and so forth.

tlãquaallavaliztli

Swelling of the knee

ynic pati. moço vitzauhcatica. quiça yuhquī nopalalactlj.

It is cured by puncturing with a maguey thorn. [A liquid] resembling cactus water comes out.

[fol. 69v]

nanauatl

Pustules

ynic pati. nanauaxiuitl nicã mochiua yoã maçayacatzollj.

They are cured with *nanahuaxihuitl,*[14] which grows here, and with *mazayacatzolli.*[15]

totomoniliztli

Blisters

ynic pati. xoxouhqui ocotzotl ic mopotonia yoã cẽtli tlatla ṽmopachoa.

They are cured by applying a plaster of raw pine resin, and it is covered with *centli tlatla.*

çavatiliztli

Mange or itch

ynic pati cococ tlacotl ỹ tlanelhuatl itztic nicã mochiua.

It is cured with *cococ tlacotl,*[16] a root that is cold, which grows here.

tlaxviztli

Abscess

ynic pati tequixquitl calcuichtli ychcaychtlj yoã ocotzotl nicã mochiua.

It is cured with saltpeter, soot, cotton fiber, and pine resin, which are produced here.

qualocatl

Chiggers

ynic pati motequi yoa patli pizietl tenextli omopachoa.

They are cured by cutting, and [the cuts are] covered with tobacco [and] lime.

poçavaliztli

Swelling

ynic pati totoicxitl ytoca xivitl yoã ynelhuayo nicã mochiua.

It is cured with the herb called *totoicxitl,*[17] which grows here, and also its root.

quavaquiliztli

Drying up

ynic pati tlanelhuatl ylacatztic nicã mochiua.

It is cured with the root of the *ilacatztic,*[18] which grows here.

14. *Nanauaxiuitl:* unidentified herb. A *nanaguapacie (antivenérea y vulneraria—Solidago mexicana)* is listed in Santamaría 1959: 75.

15. *Maçayacatzollj:* unidentified herb.

16. *Cococ tlacotl:* unidentified herb.

17. *Totoicxitl:* unidentified herb.

18. *Ylacatztic:* unidentified herb.

tlapalanaltiliztli

ynic pati ocpatli otõtla mochiua yoã tlayapaloni ytlatla nicã mochiua.

Venereal disease

It is cured with *ocpatli,*[19] which grows in Otontlan, and with *tlayapaloni itlatla,*[20] which grows here.

atonaviztli

ynic pati xvmexiuitl yoã tlatzcaxiuitl. nicã mochiua.

Fever[21]

It is cured with *xomexihuitl*[22] and *tlatzcaxihuitl,*[23] which grow here.

tlanatonaviztli

ynic pati. tlaliyac. nacazcolotl. yoã tlalxocotl. tlalhuic mochiua.

Toothache

It is cured with copperas, *nacazcolotl,*[24] and lye, which are produced in Tlalhuic.

necaxaniliztli

ynic pati. tlatlauhcapatli yoã vvcholtic tlanelhuatl nicã mochiua.

Relapse

It is cured with *tlatlauhcapatli*[25] and the *oocholtic*[26] root, which grow here.

tzompiliviztli

ynic pati. tzompachquilitl yoã piçietl nicã mochiua.

Head cold

It is cured with the *tzompachquilitl*[27] and tobacco, which grow here.

tlatlaçiztli

ynic pati ololtatõti tlanelhuatl nicã mochiua. yoã tenexatl.

Cough

It is cured with the root *ololtatontli,*[28] and with lime water.

tlanqualiztli

ynic pati piçietl yoã poponelhuatl nicã mochiua.

Toothache

It is cured with tobacco and with *popotl*[29] root, which grows here.

19. *Ocpatli:* literally, "*octli* (pulque) medicine," roots or herbs of uncertain botanical identification that were added to the standard alcoholic beverage of pre-Hispanic Central Mexico to strengthen its intoxicating qualities (see Santamaría 1959: 768).

20. *Tlayapaloni ytlatla:* unidentified herb.

21. *Atonaviztli:* Apparently chills and fever. See Molina 1944, Part II: fol. 9r, "*atonaui,* tener calentura con frio; *atonauiztli,* calentura tal."

22. *Vxmexiuitl:* unidentified herb.

23. *Tlatzcaxiuitl:* unidentified herb.

24. *Nacazcolotl: Caesalpina coriacea* or *C. coriaria* (Sahagún 1950–1982, Part XII [Book 11]: 241).

25. *Tlatlauhcapatli:* variously identified as *Geranium carolinianum* L., *G. alchimilloides,* or *Achimaenes coccinea* Pers. (Sahagún 1950–1982, Part XI [Book 10]: 142, Part XII [Book 11]: 142; Santamaría 1959: 1060; Hernández 1942–1946, I: 62).

26. *Vvcholtic (oocholtic):* unidentified herb.

27. *Tzompachquilitl:* possibly *Sedum* sp. (Hernández 1942–1946, I: 140).

28. *Ololtatõtli:* unidentified herb.

29. *Popotl: Arundinella brasiliensis* Roddi; the term was also applied to various grasses (Santamaría 1959: 882).

nacazqualiztli

Earache

ynic pati. cuechtli michiqui motecã tonacazco yoã oxiayutl.

It is cured with the shell of the *cuechtli*,[30] which is scraped. It is placed in the ear together with liquid turpentine.

yvvallecatl

Night wind [disease]

ynic pati moxoxvtla itztica.

It is cured by making incisions with an obsidian knife.

ixcvcoliztli

Eye disease

ynic pati coayeli ynelhuayo yoã cuitlapatli yxiuhyo nicã muchiua.

It is cured with the root of the *coayeli* and with *cuitlapatli*[31] leaves, which grow here.

ixtamaçoliçiviztli

Crab lice

ynic pati mochichiqui yoã tequixquitl ṽmotema.

They are cured by scraping, and a sweat bath of saltpeter is taken.

yxpopoyotiliztli

Blindness

aocmo tle yc pati.

There is nothing by which it is cured.

ixpatzavaliztli

One-eyedness

çã no iuhqui aocmo no tle yc pati.

The same; there is likewise nothing by which it is cured.

yxcueponiliztli

Crossed eyes

aocmo tle ypayo.

Nothing is now its remedy.

axixcvcoliztli

Disease of the urinary tract

ynic pati coatli ynelhuayo yoã cucuc tlacutl. nicã mochiua.

It is cured with the root of the *coatli*[32] and *cococ tlacotl*, which grow here.

cuitlatexcalvaquiztli

Colic

ynic pati tequixquiatl yoã chillj.

It is cured with saltpeter water and chili pepper.

Paragraph 9

30. *Cuechtli:* probably a gastropod (*Oliva* sp.); see Sahagún 1950–1982, Part XI (Book 10): 141–22.

31. *Cuitlapatli:* unidentified herb.

32. *Coatli: Eysenhardtia polystachya* Ort., or possibly *Guayacum offininale, G. sanctum, G. planchoni*, etc. (Sahagún 1950–1982, Part XI [Book 10]: 150, 153; Santamaría 1959: 580).

ezquiçaliztli. ezvitomiztli

ynic pati eztetl yoã epaçotl ynelhuayo nicã muchiua. yoã çollj.

Menses

It is treated with blood stone and the root of *epazotl*,[33] which grows here, and quail.

neçivaquetzaliztli

amo tle ypayo ic miqui çiuatl yoã yn itic ca piltõtli vnca miqui.

Death in childbirth[34]

Nothing is its remedy, because the woman dies and the boy who is in the womb dies there.

nexvitiliztli

ynic pati chichiquavitl yeuayo tlalhuic muchiua.

Satiety

It is cured with the bark of the *chichicuahuitl*,[35] which grows in Tlalhuic.

tziyaliztli

ynic pati ylatziuhqui tlanelhuatl nica mochiua yoa chillj.

Pains in the side

They are cured with the *ilacatziuhqui*[36] root, which grows here, and chili pepper.

vapauiztli

ynic pati moçoço.

Muscular spasms

They are cured by bleeding.

quauhtiliztli

ynic pati colopatli yoã ololiuhqui tlanelhuatl nicã mochiua.

Pains in the flank

They are cured with *colopatli*[37] and the *ololiuhqui* root, which grow here.

totonqui

ynic pati cucuc tlacutl yoã tezezec nicã muchiua

Fever

It is cured with *cococ tlacotl* and with *tececec*, which grow here.

tletl

ynic pati eeloquilti xivitl yvã tlapaltetzmitl yvã tlachinoltetzmitl nicã muchiua.

Fever[38]

It is cured with *eloquilitl*[39] leaves and *tlapaltetzmitl* and *tlachinoltetzmitl*, which grow here.

33. *Epaçotl: Chenopodium ambrosioides* Linn. (Sahagún 1950–1982, Part XII [Book 11]: 193).

34. *Neçivaquetzaliztli:* "becoming a woman warrior."

35. *Chichiquavitl:* variously identified as *Contaria latifolia* Moc., *Cornus urbiniana* Rose, and/or *Garrya laurifolia* Hartw. (Sahagún 1950–1982, Part XI [Book 10]: 111, Part XI [Book 10]: 149).

36. *Ylatziuhqui:* read *ilacatziuhqui* (unidentified herb).

37. *Colopatli:* unidentified herb used for the treatment of scorpion and other poisonous insect stings (Santamaría 1959: 275).

38. *Tletl:* possibly high fever. Compare Molina 1944, Part I: fol. 23r, where *calentura grande tener* is followed by various verbs compounded with *tletl.*

39. *Eloquilitl:* variously identified as perhaps *Piper* sp., *Piperonia* sp., or *Iresine calea* (Sahagún 1950–1982, Part XII [Book 11]: 150).

tlallatonaviztly	Earth fever
Jnic pati tetzitzili yxiuhyo yoã xomexiuitl	It is cured with *tetzitzilin*[40] leaves and *xomexihuitl.*
yoallatonaviztli	Night fever
yn ipayo tzitzicaztlj yoã xomexiuitl nicã muchiua	Its remedy is nettles and *xomexihuitl,* which grow here.
cuetzpaliçiviztli	Lizard disease[41]
ynic pati. quiçoço. quitzatzapitza.	It is cured in this manner: They bleed [the patient]; they puncture him.
tlatlaçizmimiquiliztli	Chronic cough[42]
ynic pati. tlatemoviloni tlanelhuatl nicã muchiua.	It is cured with the *tlatemohuiloni*[43] root, which grows here.
quaxocociviztli	Head itch or mange
ynic pati motequi yoã tenextli. piçietl ṽmopachoa	It is cured by cutting, and it is covered with lime [and] tobacco.
mimiquiliztli	Loss of consciousness[44]
amo tle ypayo.	Nothing is its remedy.
tzontecococoliztli	Headache
ynic pati moço toyac yoã tzocuilpatli toyacac moteca.	It is cured by drawing blood from the nose and placing *tzocuilpatli*[45] in the nose
neçioacaxaniliztli	Dropped uterus
ynic pati quequexquic yoã matlalçaçalic yoã tlacameayutl.	It is cured with *quequexquic* and *matlalzazalic*[46] and the juice of the *tlacametl* maguey.

40. *Tetzitzili:* unidentified herb, the same as *tzompachquilitl.* Possibly of gourd family (Sahagún 1950–1982, Part XII [Book 11]: 197; Emmart 1940: 304–305).

41. *Cuetzpaliçiviztli:* problematical translation. It might be discomfort or sickness due to overeating.

42. *Tlatlaçizmimiquiliztli:* see note 44, this paragraph, on the possible meaning of *mimiquiliztli.*

43. *Tlatemoviloni:* unidentified herb.

44. *Mimiquiliztli:* Translation is problematical. Since *nacayomimiquiliztli* is *perlesia* (Molina 1944, Part I: fol. 95r), a kind of paralysis may be meant.

45. *Tzocuilpatli:* unidentified herb.

46. *Quequexquic* and *matlalçaçalic:* unidentified herbs.

netlavitequiztli

Being stuck by lightning

amo tle ypayo.

Nothing is its remedy.

elchiquiuhcocoliztlj

Chest ailment

ynic pati texocoyoli texcaltitech mochiua.

It is cured with *texocoyoli*,[47] which grows near crags.

totõcamoyavaliztlj

Spreading fever

ynic pati tlaltzitzicaztlj nica muchiua.

It is cured with *tlaltzitzicaztli*,[48] which grows here.

Quimopachivya. apvechale esta medicina
Amo qujmopachivia. no le apvecha esta medicina

[This remedy] is efficacious.
[This remedy] is not efficacious.[49]

PARAGRAPH (9)
[fol. 81r]

nacazpalaniliztli.

Ear suppuration[50]

Ypayo. õmotlatlalia cicimatic. totoltetl itevilotca. moneloa. ye mochi ypayo in tleĩ palãca patli in chichic. in tetelq'c in iuhq' chipili auacayollotli

Its cure is applying *cicimatic*[51] mixed with egg white. All the remedies for whatever is suppurating are medicines that are bitter, sharp to the taste, such as *chipili*[52] [and] the avocado stone.

câcamavaliztli.

Weakness

in ipayo. tlanoq'loni. itoca. oholoItic. tlanelvatl yoã ỹ caço tleĩ tlanoq̃loni. nimã qnoq'a ycamacpa. ỹ tlãpa. ỹ ye mamana yolatolli coni. amo tequixq'o. anoço totolayotl. oc q'valpachoz hi ỹ cocolli oc oppa expa q'valnoquiz. çatepã tlaq̃ auh inic huel valmimati oc q̃zquilvitl catli toztlapavaxtli patlj tlatlauhq' yn ica quavitl. auh vetzi in ixepeuallo

Its remedy is a purgative [using] the root called *oholoItic*,[53] as well as any kind[54] of purgative. Soon a purge is effective from the mouth and from below.[55] And when [the patient] is upset, he drinks a gruel of raw ground maize without saltpeter, or turkey broth. [In order] still to control the infirmity, he is to be purged two or three times more. Afterwards

47. *Texocoyoli: Oxalis* sp. (Sahagún 1950–1982, Part XII [Book 11]: 173–174).

48. *Tlaltzitzicaztli:* variously identified as perhaps a *Cucurbitacea, Urtica* sp., or a *Borraginacea (Wigandia kunthii)* Choisy)—Hernández 1942–1946, II: 388–389.

49. Read *aprovechale* and *aprovech.* The Spanish annotations are in Sahagún's own handwriting.

50. This is the first entry on the recto of folio 81, the sheet inserted by Francisco del Paso y Troncoso that features a text dealing with the same subject matter as Paragraph 9 on folio 69 but in a different script and format.

51. *Cicimatic: Carnavalia villosa* Benth. (Sahagún 1950–1982, Part XII [Book 11]: 184).

52. *Chipili: Crotalaria* sp. (Sahagún 1950–1982, Part XI [Book 10]: 140).

53. *Ohololtic:* perhaps *Euphorbia campestris* (Sahagún 1950–1982, Part XI [Book 10]: 141).

54. *Caco:* read çaça.

55. *Tlapā:* perhaps to be read *tlanipa.*

yeh in iyollo monequi.

he eats. And when he has been convalescing for a few more days, he drinks [the liquid of] the yellow-headed parrot stew [and] the remedy, the *tlatlauhqui* [tree],[56] with the wood; the bark comes off [and] the heart is used.

yxihicuixiliztli. yxatecuiliztli. yxyâyapaleualiztli.

Facial blemishes, face mutilations, blotches on the face

ynezca, hitla itic nemi. aço cana tlapalani yn iitic anoço xochicivitztli yitic nemi. anoço iitic nemi ỹ nanavatl. coniz yn itoca tletlemaitl. xoxouhq' ỹ coniz ỹ ye quẽ oppa expa quini tletlemaitl niman ipã motemaz. yni patli vmpa mochiva ỹ quauhchichinolla auh yni ỹ tleĩ iitic nemi cocolli ca quipatlaça. auh in opavetz. õmotlaliz. ỹ xixivitl itoca ihichcayo.

They are a sign that something exists internally; either there is putrefaction somewhere internally, or hemorrhoids exist internally, or pustules exist internally. [The patient] is to drink [an infusion of an herb] called *tletlemaitl;*[57] he is to drink it raw. After being a drinker of the [infusion of] *tletlemaitl* two or three times, he then bathes in it. This remedy grows in Quauhchichinolla. And when some internal ailment exists, it brings it to the surface, and when it comes out, the herb called *ihichcayo*[58] is applied.

yxaatemi. yxihicuici. yxyapaleua.

Swollen face, facial blemishes, blotches on the face

omocaxani. ynic pati. tlanechicolli yn itoca tlatlauhcapatli. tlaçaçaçalic. cotztematl. atepocapatli tlanelhva[tl] tochtetepo. tlamacazq' ipapa. auatoto. quachtlacalvaztli. cuicuitlapile. quau[h]patli. tlalpatli. nantzin mizquitlaxipeualli. tzatzayanalquiltic. motetzotzotzona. omilvitl elhuitl ciava. mopavaci.

One who has suffered a relapse is cured with a group [of herbs] called *tlatlauhcapatli, tlazazazalic,*[59] *cotztematl,*[60] *atepocapatli,*[61] the root[62] of the *tochtetepon,*[63] *tlamacazqui ipapa,*[64] *ahuatoto,*[65] *quachtlacalhuaztli,*[66] *cuicuitlapile,*[67] *quauhpatli,*[68] *tlalpatli,*[69] *nantzin,*[70] mesquite bark, *tzatzayanalquiltic.*[71]

56. *Tlatlauq' (tlatlauhqui):* Perhaps reference is to the mahogany tree (cf. Sahagún 1950–1982, Part XI [Book 10]: 142, Part XII [Book 11]: 9).

57. *Tletlemaitl: Plumbago* sp.? *Euphorbia* sp.? (Sahagún 1950–1982, Part XI [Book 10]: 142).

58. *Ihichcayo:* unidentified herb.

59. *Tlatlauhcapatli tlaçaçalic:* unidentified herb.

60. *Cotztematl:* Perhaps *cotztomatl* is meant (*Physalis coztomatl* Moc. et Sessé ex Dunal)—Sahagún 1950–1982, Part XI (Book 10): 142.

61. *Atepocapatli: Zexmenia aurea* or *Z. pringlei* (Sahagún 1950–1982, Part XI [Book 10]: 142).

62. *Tlanelhua[tl]:* The letters lost at the end of the page are supplied here and elsewhere in this paragraph in brackets.

63. *Tochtetepo(n):* unidentified herb.

64. *Tlamacazq' ipapa:* perhaps *Lycopodium dichotomum* Jacq. (Sahagún 1950–1982, Part XI [Book 10]: 143).

65. *Auatoto(n): Pernettia ciliata* Schlecht & Cham. (Sahagún 1950–1982, Part XI [Book 10]: 143).

66. *Quachtlacalvaztli: Mentzelia hispida* Willd.? *Phaseolus* sp.? (Sahagún 1950–1982, Part XII [Book 11]: 164).

67. *Cuicuitlapile: Valerianoides* sp. (Sahagún 1950–1982, Part XII [Book 10]: 141).

68. *Quau[h]patli:* perhaps *Baccharia* sp. or a member of the family Fabaceae (Sahagún 1950–1982, Part XI [Book 10]: 143; Santamaría 1959: 574).

69. *Tlalpatli:* perhaps *Datura* sp. (Sahagún 1950–1982, Part XI [Book 10]: 143).

70. *Nantzin: Byrsonima crossifolia* (L) DC (Sahagún 1950–1982, Part XI [Book 10]: 143).

71. *Tzatzayanalquiltic: Deanea tuberosa* Coult et N. (Sahagún 1950–1982, Part XI [Book 10]: 143).

necuvetzi. ipã motema.

They are soaked for two [or] three days. They are cooked; they form a syrup. With this one bathes.

yxchachaquachiviliztlj

Roughness of the face

yn ypayo. xivitl. ytoca. azpa. motzoyanja. yamãqui yc mixamia. miecpa ynic mixamia. yoã amo quiquaz ỹ chiava yoã ỹ xoquiyac. yoã coniz inic ceviz in iitic ca cocolli. ytoca. tlatlauhqui ỹ xivitl. çã itztic atl. quitinemiz. caxixaz ỹ cocolli. chichiltic. anoço xallo. yoan ma tlanoq'liz.

The remedy is an herb called *azpa.*[72] It is fried; [when] it is soft, the face is washed with it. The face is washed with it frequently and [the patient] is not to eat what is greasy and what is fetid. And in order to alleviate the sickness within, he is to drink an herb called *tlatlauhqui*[73] only in cold water. He is to go on drinking it. He will expel the disease with the urine; it is red or full of sand. And he is to be administered a purgative.

yxcocoliztli.

Eye disease

in ipayo. achi coniz in ixiuhyo in itoca xoxouhcapatlj yoã yc moquatzotzonaz.

As its remedy one is to drink a small amount of [an infusion of] the leaves called *xoxouhcapatli*[74] and to beat one's head with [the leaves].

ỹ ocuili tixtẽco moq̃tza.

Worms that appear on the eyelids

in cẽca cuecuetzoca. yc mochichiqui in tlanelvatl in itoca côcoztic. auh ỹ hiquac cochiz õmochichipiniz.

When they itch a good deal, they are rubbed with the root called *cocoztic,* and when [the patient] is to go to sleep, drops are applied.

yztac õmotlalia tixco, yoã ayauitl õmomana.

White [film] that settles on the eyes and mist that forms

in ipayo. chichiltic patli yuhqui ỹ azcatzõtecomatl. õmoteci. ytevilotca ỹ omochipinja. oppa expa cõchipinia. expa ỹ cemilvitl cõchipinia. yoã ỹ tlalayotlj ynelvayo ommochipiniz q'patla ỹ azcatzontecoma[tl] quitlacevilia auh ỹ hamo quitlacamati hj. mitzmina

Its remedy is a red medicine such as *azcatzontecomatl.*[75] It is ground up. Drops of its viscous part are applied; two [or] three times [the patient] applies the drops—three times a day he applies the drops. And drops [made from] the root of the *tlalayotli*[76] are to be ap-

72. *Azpa:* unidentified herb.

73. *Tlatlauhqui y xivitl:* unidentified herb.

74. *Xoxouhcapatlj:* unidentified herb.

75. *Azcatzotecomatl:* unidentified herb.

76. *Tlalalyotlj:* variously identified as *Gonolobus pedunculatus* Hemsl., *Asclepias linaria* Cav., *A. coulteri* de Caisne, *Marsdenia coulteri* id., *M. edulis* Wats., *M. Macrophylla* Fourn., *Metaselma barbigerum* Schl., *Rothrockia cordifolia* Grao., *Rouliniela ninfaria* Vail., and others (Sahagún 1950–1982, Part XI [Book 10]: 144; Hernández 1942–1946, I: 165; Santamaría 1959: 1057).

plied; they are a substitute for the *azcatzontecomatl* [drops]; they alleviate it. But when they do not alleviate it, [the patient] is bled.

yxnacapachiviztli

Growths on the eyes

yn ipayo, xivitl itoca ihiztaq'ltic ynelvayo õmochipinia. queva ỹ nacatl. q'palanaltia.

Their remedy is the root of an herb called *ihiztlaquiltic.* [77] Drops are applied. They lift the flesh; they disintegrate it.

yxtamaçoliciuiztlj.

Lice about the eyes

ipayo ỹ cocoztic tlanelvatl õmochipinia.

Their remedy is the *cocoztic* root. Drops are applied.

yxchichiticaviztli

Watering of the eyes

monequi moçoz. yoã mitzavavia. yoã õmochichipinia yn omoteneuh pâtli. monequi q'cavazq' ỹ octli. çã yevatl q'tinemiz ytoca iztac quavitl tonayã mochiva. yoã amo quiquaz ỹ chiava yoã ỹ xoquiyac. ynim patli q'cencevia ỹ tonacayo ỹ toyollo.

Bleeding is necessary and one is pricked with a thorn,[78] and drops are applied of what is called *patli.* [79] It is necessary that [the patient] abstain from *octli;* one is to go drinking what is called *iztac cuahuitl,* [80] which grows in the east. And one is not to eat what is greasy and what is fetid. This remedy soothes the body [and] heart completely.

yxcitlaliciviztli.

Film over the eyes

yn ipayo. cuetzpalin ycuitl tlillo. matlali tomayo.

Its remedy is lizard excrement with lampblack [and] *matlalin* [81] with tomato.

yxtezcaiciviztli

Glazing of the eyes[82]

hatle ipayo.

Nothing is its remedy.

77. *Ihiztaq'ltic:* unidentified herb.

78. The headings *yxtamaçoliciuiztli* and *yxchichiticaviztli* and two following words, *monequi moçoz,* are apparently crossed out.

79. *Yn ometeuh patli:* The meaning may be "the remedy [already] mentioned," referring to *cocoztic,* prescribed in the previous entry.

80. *Iztac quavitl:* perhaps one of the Mimosaceae or one of the Caesalpiniaceae (Sahagún 1950–1982, Part XI [Book 10]: 144).

81. *Matlali (matlalin):* copper rust? (Sahagún 1950–1982, Part XI (Book 10): 144); *Comelina pallida, C. erecta, C. tuberosa?* (Anderson 1963: 82).

82. *Ixtezcatl:* glazing of the eyes (Sahagún 1950–1982, Part II [Book 1]: 39. In Molina 1944, Part II: fol. 47v, the term is translated *anteojos para ver.*

Paragraph (9)

yxtototoliciviztli.

amo quittaz yn iztac

yxvauaciviztli

ypayo tlapaltequixquitl cēca mocuechoa. aquitō auhtic omotema yn iixco. anoço yztatl cēcan no auhtic ōmotema in iixco.

Cataracts

[The patient] is not to look at [anything] white. . . .[83]

Withering of the eyes

Its remedy is red saltpeter; it is finely ground. A small amount dissolved in water[84] is placed in the eyes, or else salt, also in a very watery solution, is placed in the eyes.

[fol. 81v]

tzōocuilqualiztlj.

ypayo. palli. tlilyamāq'. axi tlilaxi. axixtlj

quatequixquihiciviztli.

ypayo. avacatl. avacayolli / axi. pâlli. axixtlj

quatotomoctlj.

ypayo oxitl. ocotzotl. tlaaxnellolli.

quaxocociviztlj.

ypayo. motequi. motzoponia. tenextlj. mopaltevhtia. mopapalotēqui / mopotonia. ocutzotica

tzōtecōcocolli.

ic pati ecuxoliztli. yecoxo minecui. picietl minecuj neitzminaliztli neitzavaliztli. nepopochviliztli. nequaq̃miloliztlj.

Splitting of hair

Its remedies are black dye, a soft black; *axin*,[85] black *axin*; urine.

Dandruff

Its remedies are avocado, the avocado stone, *axin*, black dye, urine.

Scabies of the head

Its remedy is an unguent of turpentine[86] [and] liquidambar mixed with *axin*.

Abscesses on the head

Their remedy is to cut, to puncture, to dust with lime. A cut in the form of a cross is made [and] a plaster with liquidambar is applied.

Headache

It is cured by sneezing, by inhaling *ecoxo*, [87] by inhaling tobacco, by pricking with an obsidian blade,[88] by puncturing with an obsidian blade, by exposing one to incense, by wrapping the head.

83. The sentence is incomplete in the manuscript.

84. *Auhtic:* read *atic.*

85. *Axi (axin):* oily product of *Llaveia axinus* or *Coccus axin* (Santamaría 1959: 47).

86. *Ocotzotl:* or pine resin; see note 10, this paragraph.

87. *Yecoxo (ecoxo):* unidentified herb.

88. *Neitzavaliztli:* read *neitzahuailiztli.*

nequatzayanaliztlj.

Head injury

mîtzoma. tzõtica mitzoma. meolli õmotlalia. mexoxouhq' õmotlalia meçollatextli tlacoxonilli õmotema.

It is sewn; it is sewn with a hair. Maguey juice is applied; the ground green maguey leaf is applied dried. One takes a steam bath.

nequatlapanaliztli. quaxicalpatiliztlj.

Fractured skull, split skull

omitica motlamanilia, meolli ic motzaqua. anoço mexoxouhqui tlachichtli, anoço tlatextlj

It is set by inserting a piece of bone. It is covered with maguey juice or else with a grated, or ground, green maguey leaf.

nacazqualiztlj.

Earache

cuechtli michi õmoteca.

The *cuechtli* shell is scraped; [the scrapings] are applied.

nacazpalaniliztlj

Abscessed ear

ollachipilli õmoteca

Drops of liquid rubber[89] are applied.

nacazpalaniliztli

Abscessed ear

çã pani. mopotonia.

A plaster is applied to the outside.

yxyayapalevaliztli
ixahatemiliztlj.
yxchachaquachiviliztli.

Blotches on the face[90]
Swollen face[91]
Pitted face

ypayo totõqui axixtli. yc nexamilo oc yovac yoã schilcoztlj yc nexavalo ypã cochiva. oc yovac valmeva oc cepa axixtica nexamilo.

Its remedy is hot urine. The face is washed with it in the early dawn and painted with [ground] yellow chili at the time one goes to sleep. At dawn, upon arising, the face is washed once again with urine.

ixcocoliztli in tletl

Eye pains [like] fire

yn ipayo. mixitl cẽca auhtic yc neixteyayavaloloz. octli. otlaqualcauh cochoctli. õmochichipinia chichicaquilitl. tonalchichicaquilitl. õmochipinia. chicalotl imemeyalo õmochipi. tlachinoltetzmit[l].

Its remedy is *mixitl*[92] in a very watery solution. It is to be applied around the eyelids. Drops of *octli* that was left over, drops of leftover *octli,* are applied. Drops of *chichicaquilitl* [and][93] *tonalchichicaquilitl*[94] are ap-

89. *Ollachipilli:* read *ollachipinilli.*

90. *Yxyayapalevaliztli:* No annotation follows this heading; *cocamavaliztli,* the following heading, is crossed out in the manuscript.

91. *Ixahatemiliztlj:* No annotation follows this heading.

92. *Mixitl: Datura stramonium* (Sahagún 1950–1982, Part XI [Book 10]: 130; see also note 8).

93. *Chichicaquilitl:* variously identified as *Carraja mexicana, Sonchus siliatus,* and/or *Mimulus glabratus* (Sahagún 1950–1982, Part XII [Book 11]: 137).

94. *Tonalchichicaquilitl:* perhaps *Oenothera lacinata* Hill (Sahagún 1950–1982, Part XI [Book 10]: 143).

Paragraph (9)

yxcocoliztli yn iztac õmotlali ỹ mitoa ixcitlaliciuiztlj.

matlallo chichivalayotl õmochichipinia. tlilyamanqui. õmochipinia. olli õmotlalia

yxchichiticaviztli.

yn ipayo. mochichiq'. cochoctlj õmochipinia acaoxitl tixtẽco õmalava.

plied. Drops of *chicalotl* [95] milk [and] *tlachinoltetzmitl* [96] are applied.

Eye disease: a white [film] has settled [over the eyes] called *ixcitlalicihuiztli*

Drops of milk containing blue dye are applied. Drops of warm lampblack are applied. Rubber is placed [over the eyes].

Watering of the eyes[97]

Its remedy is rubbing. Drops of leftover [day-old] *octli* are applied. A reed unguent is smeared on the eyelids.[98]

PARAGRAPH 10
[fol. 70r]

Jnic. 10. parrapho ypã mitoa ỹ tlatolli ynic motlapaloa ỹ pipilti ỹ çioapipilti yoã ỹtlatolli ynic maoa.

yn iquac aca pilli tlatoanj ychã ca auh yn oc ce tlacatl çã no tlatoani pillj quilhuia nopiltzintzine ma vel xomeviltitie auh nimã quilhuia nopiltzintzine oticmihiyovilti ma ye nicã timovicatz.

Auh in otlica cana monamiqui quimolhuia ma nimitznotlaxillitzino nopiltzintzine / nimã quilhuia ma timovetzititzino nopiltzintzine nicauhtzine.

Auh i çivapipilti ynic motlapaloa yn iquac nepanotl ỹpã calaqui. quimolhiua. ma xvm-

Tenth paragraph, in which are told the words with which noblemen [and] noblewomen greet one another and the words with which they quarrel with one another.[1]

When some nobleman is in the house of a ruler and [there is] another personage who is also a ruler [or] a nobleman, he says to him: "My lord, be well seated." And then [the other] says to him: "My lord, you have undergone trials. Now be welcome here."

And when they meet somewhere on the road, one says to him: "Let me not upset you, my lord." Then [the other] says to him: "Do not let yourself fall, my lord, my younger brother."

And noblewomen thus greet one another when they enter one's house together; one

95. *Chicalotl: Argemone mexicana* or *A. ochroleuca* Sweet (Sahagún 1950–1982, Part XI [Book 10]: 143).

96. *Tlachinoltetzmitl:* perhaps *Kohleria deppeana* or *Croton draco* Schw. (Sahagún 1950–1982, Part XI [Book 10]: 143).

97. *Ixchichiticaviztlj:* Listed earlier in this paragraph with a different prescription (see notes 78–80).

98. Below this last item on the page (fol. 81v) is written, in another, bolder hand: *capitulo. ha,* and, below this: *Jnic cap. itech tlatoa,* with the line ending in an illegible word.

1. This paragraph presents a series of traditional, formalized greetings exchanged between rulers and noblemen and noblewomen, plus a parallel set of vituperative exchanges made when they quarreled. Useful for revealing certain attitudes and behavior patterns among the nobility of the contact-period Central Mexican Nahua speakers, the paragraph is also of value in its linguistic aspect, adding to our knowledge of the Nahuatl spoken by this elite sector of the society in different social contexts. There is an obvious relationship between the elegant, ritualized language of this paragraph and that typical of the *huehuetlatolli.* Schultze Jena (1952: 62–65) first paleographized the paragraph and translated it into German.

mevititie noconetzin toteco / nicã timovicatz notecuiyoçihoatl nochpuchticatzin.

auh in otlica monamiqui çivapipilti quimolhuia notecoçihoatl ma nimitznotlaxilitzino ma timococotzino nochpuchticatzin notecuiyoçioatl

ynic maoa pipilti quimolhuia yn iquac omoqualaniq̃. nicauhtzine tlẽ no ticmitalhuia ma çã no ximotlali xicaoã motlatol ma timococo oc xicaq' nicauhtzine y iehoatl tiquitoa ỹ motlatol camo tlachia çan iuhqũi tixtepetla taactiuetzi ça xitlamatinemj macamo xixtotomaoa ximimati ximixtili camo tonemiliz macamo xicui yn iztlactli ỹ tẽquallactli macamo xicaqui ỹ çivatlatolli tlein tiquitoa yequene cuix motlatoaya cuix amo çan atexatitla metlatitlan titlacat ma ça xipactinemi nicauhtzine anoçoc ytla ma oallani ỹ motlatol nicauhtzine oc xictlali moyollo ma oc ximocevi etc.

no yuh quitoa ỹ monamiqui etc.

Çivapipilti ynic maoa yn iquac tlein ic mopevaltia. quimolhuia noconetzin noçivapiltzin ma çã no ximovetziti noconetzin ma çã no ximotlamachtitinemi ma cocoliztli ticmocuiti tlein ticmitalhuja cuix mo totequiuh ỹ tlei ticmotenevilitzinoa ỹ tlein ticmitalhuitzinoa noçivapiltzin ma ça ximotlamachititinemi camo tinemiuhqui y tiçivapilli camo motechmonequi in ticmochivilia ma ximixtilli ma ximomaviztili nochpuchticatzin ma xictlalli moyollotzin anoçoc ytla mitzmococolhuiz ma oallanj etc.

auh ỹ monamiqui no iuh quitoa etc.

says to [the other]: "Be seated, my child, our lady." [The other says:] "You are welcome here, my lady, my maiden."

And when noblewomen meet on the road one says to [the other]: "My lady, let me not upset you." [The other says:] "Do not sicken, my maiden, my lady."

When noblemen quarrel with one another one says, when they have become angry: "My younger brother, what are you saying? Just seat yourself; leave off your words; do not sicken. Listen yet, my younger brother. What you say, your words, have no vision. It is as if you are blind; you are precipitate. Live wisely. Do not be stupid. Be prudent. Consider yourself. [This] is not our [sort of] life. Do not accept lies, trickery. Do not listen to women's talk. What are you saying? And is [this] your way of talking? Have you perhaps not just been born a slave's offspring?[2] Just be content, my younger brother; let your words perhaps yet end. My younger brother, be yet of good cheer. Rest yourself." Etc.

So also speaks the one whom he meets with. Etc.

Noblewomen thus quarrel when for some reason one is provoked. She says to [the other]: "My child, my lady, do not fall; my child, just consider. Let sickness not seize you. What are you saying? Is what you are stating, is what you are saying not our affair? My lady, just consider. You do not behave as if you were a noblewoman. What you are doing is not required of you. Consider yourself; respect yourself, my maiden. Be of good cheer. Perhaps something may injure you. Let this end." Etc.

And the one whom she meets also speaks thus. Etc.

Paragraph 10

2. Compare Olmos 1875: 218.

PARAGRAPH 11
[fol. 70v col. A]

Jnic. ii. parrapho ypã mitoa ỹ quenin motlapaloa yoã quenjm maoa ỹ maceoalti ỹ oquichti yoã ỹ çiva.

yn iquac ychã callaqui nepanotl quimolhuia / nicauhtze ma nimitzmauhti / q'lhuia. xioalmovica nicauhtze tlae nicã.

Auh in otlica yquac monamiqui quimolhuia ma timovetziti nicauhtze xivalmovica nicauhtzine ma nimitznotlaxilli.

Auh y çiva yquac ypã calaqui nepanotl quimolhuia noconetzin ma nimitznomauhtili xivalmovica noconetcatzin tlae nicã timovicatz.

Auh yn otlica yquac monamiq' quimolhuia ma timovetziti noconetzin. xivalmovica noconetcatzi. ma tomovetziti—

Oquichti maceualti ynic mava quimolhuia, ximiquani nocne tlapaltõtle ma nimitztopeuh nepa xiyauh itzcuimpolle chichipole ma nimitztelicça ma nimitzyacachaquani nepa xiyauh xvlopitle aquimamatie maceoaltotomacpole ycnopiltotomacpol ac tehoatl ac timomati totolpole amo ça ivi / nocne xolopitle nepa xiyauh tle tinechaitiz tlapaltõtle q̃ tinechivaz nocne cuix tinechquaz cuix tinechtoloz nicã tlamatinemi oyvuhtinemi tzatzitinemi mach nicã tixquiquiza tixtotomaoa xolopitanapole aocmo ticmati ahaque / chocholoque cuix otitlava xvcomicqz ocmixxicui ma topã tivetz tlavãque mac mitzcaoa ỹ noctli tatapacuitlapol tzo-

Eleventh paragraph,[1] in which it is told how male and female commoners greet one another and how they quarrel with one another.[2]

When they enter one's house together they say to one another: "My younger brother, let me not frighten you." [The other] says to him: "Come, my younger brother; be welcome here."

And when they meet one another on the road, one says to [the other]: "Do not fall, my younger brother. Come, my younger brother. Let me not upset you."

And when women enter their houses together they say to one another: "My child, let me not frighten you." [The other answers:] "Come, my child; you come welcomed here."

And when they meet one another on the road, one says to [the other]: "Do not fall, my child." [The other answers:] "Come, my child; do not fall."

When male commoners quarrel with one another, one says to [the other]: "Move aside, rascal, worthless man. Let me not hit you. Go to one side, cur, mongrel. Let me kick you. Let me not wet your nose. Go to one side, stupid lout, fat ungrateful wretch. Who are you? Who do you think you are? Dunghill fowl. There is nothing like [you], rascal, stupid. Go to one side. What will you do to me, worthless one? How will you send me away, rascal? Will you eat me? Will you swallow me? He goes hunting here; he goes howling; he goes yelling. It seems that here you are a fool, a mad-brain, a silly basket. You know nothing, stupefied one, senseless one.

1. *Jnic.* ii: read *Inic* 11.

2. This paragraph, the final one of the extant manuscript of the *Primeros Memoriales*, is parallel to the preceding one but focuses on expressions employed in similar exchanges by commoners. It is well established that most of the ethnographic and linguistic data collected by Sahagún and his assistants were supplied by educated members of the indigenous upper class. Although the information in this paragraph was probably also conveyed by a member of the elite, it purports to describe both the courteous and vituperative exchanges between members of the lower class—and in this respect it is probably unique in the Sahaguntine corpus. Noteworthy is the rich, colorful vocabulary of invective and insult used in the appropriate contexts by people of this societal level.

tzomacuicuitlapol quatatapapol cacalacapol tetlanēcapol tetlachocholpol ome ynenepilpol tetlatlatolçaçaca tetlatlatlatta ixmetlapilpol quatatacalpol yxpatzacpol ixpopoyopol tetlaxincapol no tlatoa / que no iuhqui / quatexamacçolpol ichtecapol tepā cacallacapol / iztlacapapol / xixipevipol tlacatecolopol / quen tjtechioaz / nocne / tle titechaitiz / cuix teoa tatiz titepetiz / ỹ timacevaltontli / ma nel cēca oc itla xiquito cuix i quē titechivaz / cuix ic titechpopoloz / / cuix tevatl titopil titotlatocauh ca ça no titzcutli titotoli / cuitlapā tlaçolpā / mocha monemiya ximocava nocne / valtzatzitivi neoā / etc. [fol. 70v Col. B] yn ixquich quitoa teaoa ça no ixqui ỹ quitoa ỹ monamiqui auh ça no ca yn amo tenāquilia çā choca.

Are you drunk, drunkard?[3] He takes Jimson Weed with *octli*. Don't fall on us, drunkard. Sober up. [His] clothing is dirty; [his] rags are filthy. He is a stone-head, a house-enterer, one who lives with others, an obstructor, a two-tongued one who exaggerates things to others, a people-watcher; gross-faced, of pitted head, one-eyed, blind, an adulterer. He also speaks. How, [when] he is also like a paper-brained one? He is a thief; he goes from house to house. He is a big liar, a flayed one, a man-owl. How will you send me away, rascal? What will you do with us? Will you rise to become a benevolent ruler?[4] You who are a little commoner? Say no more. How will you therefore send us away? Will you therefore subdue us? Are you our lord, our ruler? You are only a dog, a fowl. Your home, your existence is in the dung, in rubbish. Leave off, rascal." Both go shouting. They say all [this when] they abuse one; also they say all [this] when they confront each other. But also there is the one who does not answer; he only weeps.

[fol. 71r]

çiva ynic maoa.

Auh ynic maoa çiva macevalti quimolhuia / ay civato ma nachca quē tinechpevaltia / cuix tinonamic cuix tinoquichvi / ay / tlei / çivato / tētlatlatzicpol ma ximotlalli tlē tinechilhuia aviyanito / cuix tinochauh quē tinechpeoaltia cuix mopā nicacalactica cuix no ze mopal ninemi / cuix tinechtlaecoltia / cuix mopal notlatlaqua / ay / çivato quatzomapol / quatatapapol / ximocaoa tētlatlatzicpol ixtlaveliloc tlavelilocatontli / cacalacapol. xixipevi / atle quiquani / achilova / aizteyoa / tzincuecuetzocpol / tzinapizmiqui / ay / ma nachca / teixpā titlatlamatiznequi / quē titechivaz cuix teoa tatiz. titepetiz. tlavelilocatōtli tetla chochol ma nachca xoquiça ma nimitztopeuh / mach atle ipā titlatlachiya / mach nicā taatla-

Women quarrel with one another thus:

And when female commoners quarrel with one another, one says to [the other]: "Ah, little woman! Away! How will you dispute with me? Are you my husband? Are you my spouse? Ah! Little woman of some sort with the mouth stuck shut, sit down. What are you telling me, little pleasure girl? Are you my concubine? How do you dispute with me? Do I keep entering houses with you? Or do I live thanks to you? Do you give me what I need? Do I eat thanks to you? Ah, little woman with a mop of forehead hair, with disheveled hair, leave off. Her mouth is stuck shut. She is an impudent little wicked one, a house-enterer, a flayed one. She eats nothing. She has no chili; she has no salt. [She has] an itching rump, a starved rump. Ah, away! Paragraph 11

3. *Xocomicqz:* read *xocomicque.*

4. *Compare Olmos* 1875: 219.

matinemi / cuix tiçivapilli timocuepaznequi/ amo çã timaceualtõtli / mach nicã teixco tinemj / campa tivalla ma xiyauh aço iuhcã ỹ mochã / amo iuhca ỹ nicã ticteititiz / ticnopiltotomacpol ticnopillaveliloc cen / ca tzatzi ỹ nixquich quitoa ỹ teaoa çã no ixquich yn quitoa ỹ monamiqui tlacaolólooa mochi tlacatl quĩcaqui auh çan õca yn amo tenãquilia ça quicaquin tlatollj çã choca

Will you in public pretend to be a jester? How will you send us away? Do you rise to become the sovereign state? You are a wicked little one, inept with people. Away, go away! Let me not hit you. It seems that you disdain things; it seems that here you live in pride. Do you pretend to be a noblewoman? Are you not just a little commoner? It seems that here you lack respect for one. Where do you come from? Go away! Is perhaps your home that sort of place? What you will make it appear like is not like that. Ungrateful, miserable wicked one!" They yell a good deal. All this they say when they abuse one. Likewise they say all [this] when they confront one another. People gather around. Everyone hears them. But there are those who just do not answer; they only listen to the words; they only weep.

References Cited

Acosta Saignes, Miguel

1946 Los Teopixque: Organización sacerdotal entre los Mexica. *Revista Mexicana de Estudios Antropológicos* 8: 147–205.

Alcocer, Ignacio

1935 *Apuntes sobre la antigua México-Tenochtitlan.* Instituto Panamericano de Geografía e Historia, Tacubaya, Pub. 14.

1938 Comidas de los Mexicanos. In Sahagún 1938, III: 365–74.

Alvarado Tezozomoc, Hernando

1987 *Crónica Mexicana.* Edited by Manuel Orozco y Berra. 4th ed. Biblioteca Porrúa, 61. Mexico City: Editorial Porrúa.

Anawalt, Patricia Rieff

1976 The *Xicolli:* An Analysis of a Ritual Garment. *Actas del 41 Congreso Internacional de Americanistas, México, 2 al 7 de septiembre de 1974,* vol. 2: 223–235.

1977 What Price Aztec Pageantry? *Archaeology* 30: 226–233.

1981 *Indian Clothing before Cortés: Mesoamerican Costume from the Codices.* Norman: University of Oklahoma Press.

1990 The Emperor's Cloak: Aztec Pomp, Toltec Circumstance. *American Antiquity* 55(2): 291–307.

1992 A Comparative Analysis of the Costumes and Accoutrements of the *Codex Mendoza.* In *Codex Mendoza* 1992, I: 103–150.

1993a Rabbits, *Pulque,* and Drunkenness: A Study of Ambivalence in Aztec Society. In *Current Topics in Aztec Studies: Studies in Honor of Dr. H. B. Nicholson,* edited by Alana Cordy-Collins and Douglas Sharon, 17–38. San Diego Museum Papers, 30.

1993b Riddle of the Emperor's Cloak. *Archaeology* 46(3): 30–36.

Anders, Ferdinand

1970 Einleitung Summary und Resumen. In *Codex Magliabechiano* 1970.

Anderson, Arthur J. O.

1963 Materiales colorantes prehispánicos. *Estudios de Cultura Náhuatl* 4: 73–83.

1982a Aztec Hymns of Life and Love. *New Scholar* 8: 1–74.

1982b The Institution of Slave-bathing. *Indiana* 7: 91–92.

1988a A Look into Tlalocan. In *Smoke and Mist: Mesoamerican Studies in Memory of Thelma D. Sullivan,* edited by J. Kathryn Josserand and Karen Dakin, sections coordinated by H. B. Nicholson, Doris Heyden, Karen Dakin, and Nicholas A. Hopkins, part 1: 151–159. Oxford: BAR International Series, 402(i).

1988b Sahagún's Informants on the Nature of Tlalocan. In *The Work of Bernardino de Sahagún: Pioneer Ethnographer of Sixteenth-Century Aztec Mexico,* edited by J. Jorge Klor de Alva, H. B. Nicholson, and Eloise Quiñones Keber, 151–60. Studies on Culture and Society, vol. 2. Albany: Institute for Mesoamerican Studies, State University of New York.

1994 Los "Primeros Memoriales" y el *Códice Florentino. Estudios de Cultura Náhuatl* 24: 49–91.

Aveni, Anthony F.

1980 *Skywatchers of Ancient Mexico.* Austin: University of Texas Press.

Baird, Ellen Taylor

1979 *Sahagún's "Primeros Memoriales": A Structural and Stylistic Analysis of the Drawings.* Ph.D. dissertation, University of New Mexico, Albuquerque.

1983 Text and Image in Sahagún's *Primeros Memoriales.* In *Text and Image in Pre-Columbian Art,* edited by Janet C. Berlo, 155–79. Proceedings of the 44th International Congress of Americanists (Manchester, 1982). Oxford: BAR International Series, 180.

1988a The Artists of Sahagún's *Primeros Memoriales:* A Question of Identity. In *The Work of Bernardino de Sahagún: Pioneer Ethnographer of Sixteenth-Century Aztec Mexico,* edited by J. Jorge Klor de Alva, H. B. Nicholson, and Eloise Quiñones Keber, 211–227. Studies on Culture and Society, vol. 2. Albany: Institute for Mesoamerican Studies, State University of New York.

1988b Sahagún's *Primeros Memoriales* and *Codex Florentino:* European Elements in the Illustrations. In *Smoke and Mist: Mesoamerican Studies in Memory of Thelma D. Sullivan,* edited by J. Kathryn Josserand and Karen Dakin, sections coordinated by H. B. Nicholson, Doris Heyden, Karen Dakin, and Nicholas A. Hopkins, part 1: 15–40. Oxford: BAR International Series, 402(i).

1993 *The Drawings of Sahagún's "Primeros Memoriales": Structure and Style.* Norman: University of Oklahoma Press.

Ballesteros-Gaibrois, Miguel, ed.

1964 *Códices Matritenses de la Historia general de las cosas de la Nueva España de Fr. Bernardino de Sahagún.* 2 vols. Madrid: Ediciones José Porrúa Turanzas.

Bankmann, Ulf

1984 Ometochtecomatl: Ein altmexikanischen Pulquegefass im Museum zu Basel. *Verhandlungen der Naturforschungs Gesellschaft Basel* 94:307–320.

Barlow, Robert H.

1990 *Obras de Robert H. Barlow: Los Mexicas y la Triple Alianza,* vol. 3. Edited by Jesús Monjarás-Ruiz, Elena Limón, and María de la Cruz Paillés H. Mexico City: Instituto Nacional de Antropología e Historia and Universidad de las Américas, Puebla.

Barthel, Thomas

1964 Einige Ordnungsprincipien im Aztekischen Pantheon (zur Analyse der Sahagunschen Götterlisten). *Paideuma* 10(2): 77–101.

Bartholomaeus Anglicus

1529 *Libro de Proprietatibus Rerum en Romance.* Edited by Fray Vicente de Burgos. Toledo: Gaspar de Avila. (Original manuscript thirteenth century.)

Batres, Leopoldo

1902 *Archaeological Explorations in Escalerillas Street, City of Mexico, Year 1900.* Mexico City: J. Aguilar Vera and Co., Printers.

Baudot, Georges

1983 *Utopía e historia en México: Los primeros cronistas de la civilización mexicana (1520–1569).* Translated from the French by Vicente González Loscertales. Madrid: Espasa-Calpe. Original French version, Toulouse: Editions Edouard Privat, 1977.

Beyer, Hermann

1920 El Temalacatl: La "Piedra del Sacrificio Gladiatorio" del Museo Nacional de Arqueología. *Revista de Revistas,* year 11, no. 541 (September 19): 24. Reprinted in *El México Antiguo* 8: 87–94 (1956).

1921 El emblema de músicos y danzantes Aztecas. *Revista de Revistas,* year 12, no. 579 (June 12): 32–33. Reprinted in *El México Antiguo* 11:529–534 (1969).

Biondelli, Bernardino

1869 *Glossarium Azteco-Latinum et Latino-Aztecum, surâ et studio Bernardini Biondelli collectum ac digestum.* Milan: Valentiner et Mues.

Boone, Elizabeth Hill

1983 The *Codex Magliabechiano* and the Lost Prototype of the *Magliabechiano* Group. In *Codex Magliabechiano* 1983, Notes and Commentary volume. Berkeley: University of California Press.

1989 Incarnations of the Aztec Supernatural: The Image of Huitzilopochtli in Mexico and Europe. *Transactions of the American Philosophical Society,* vol. 79, part 2. Philadelphia.

1992 The Founding of Tenochtitlan and the Reign Dates of the Mexica Rulers According to Thirty-Nine Central Mexican Sources. In *Codex Mendoza* 1992, vol. 1, Appendix A.

Brinton, Daniel G.

1890 *Rig Veda Americanus: Sacred Songs of the Ancient Mexicans, with a Gloss in Nahuatl.* Philadelphia: Brinton's Library of Aboriginal American Literature, 8.

Briquet, C. M.

1985 *Les filigranes: Dictionnaire historique des marques de papier dès leur apparition vers 1282 jusqu'en 1600.* New York: Hacker Art Books. Reprint of second edition, Leipzig, 1923 (first edition, Geneva, 1907).

Brown, Betty Ann

1978 *European Influences in Early Colonial Descriptions and Illustrations of the Mexica Monthly Calendar.* Ph.D. dissertation, University of New Mexico, Albuquerque.

Burkhart, Louise

1989 *The Slippery Earth: Nahua-Christian Moral Dialogue in Sixteenth Century Mexico.* Tucson: University of Arizona Press.

Bustamante García, Jesús

1990 *Fray Bernardino de Sahagún: Una revisión crítica de los manuscritos y de su proceso de composición.* Mexico City: Universidad Nacional Autónoma de México, Instituto de Investigaciones Bibliográficas, Biblioteca Nacional, Hemeroteca Nacional.

Calnek, Edward E.

1992 The Ethnographic Content of the Third Part of the *Codex Mendoza.* In *Codex Mendoza* 1992, II: 81–91.

Carrasco, David

1982 *Quetzalcoatl and the Irony of Empire: Myths and Prophecies in the Aztec Tradition.* Chicago: University of Chicago Press.

Carrasco Pizana, Pedro

1950 *Los Otomíes: Cultura e historia prehispánicas de los pueblos mesoamericanos de habla otomiana.* Mexico City: Universidad Nacional Autónoma de México, Instituto de Historia, in collaboration with the Instituto Nacional de Antropología e Historia. Publications of the Instituto de Historia, First series, no. 15.

1966 Sobre algunos terminos de parentesco en el náhuatl clásico. *Estudios de Cultura Náhuatl* 5: 149–166.

Caso, Alfonso

1924–1927 Un antiguo juego mexicano, el patolli. *El México Antiguo* 2: 203–211.

1927 *El Teocalli de la Guerra Sagrada: Descripción e estudio del monolito encontrado en los cimientos del Palacio Nacional.* Mexico City: Publications of the Secretaría de Educación Pública; Monographs of the Museo Nacional de Arqueología, Historia e Etnografía.

1939 La correlación de los años azteca y cristiano. *Revista Mexicana de Estudios Antropológicos* 3: 11–45.

1956 Los barrios antiguos de Tenochtitlan y Tlatelolco. *Memorias de la Academia de la Historia* 15: 7–63.

1967 *Los calendarios prehispánicos.* Instituto de Investigaciones Históricas, Serie de Cultura Náhuatl, Monografías, 6. Mexico City: Universidad Nacional Autónoma de México.

1977–1979 *Reyes y reinos de la Mixteca.* 2 vols. Mexico City: Fondo de Cultura Económica.

Castañeda, Daniel, and Vicente T. Mendoza

1933 Los huehuetls en las civilizaciones precortesianas. *Anales del Museo Nacional de Arqueología, Historia y Etnografía,* 8(2): 288–311.

Castillo Farreras, Victor

1972 Unidades nahuas de medida. *Estudios de Cultura Náhuatl* 10: 195–223.

1974 Relación Tepepulca de los señores de Mexico Tenochtitlan y de Acolhuacan. *Estudios de Cultura Náhuatl* 11: 183–225.

Charlton, Thomas H.

1978 Teotihuacan, Tepepulco, and Obsidian Exploitation. *Science* 200(4347): 1227–1236.

Cline, Howard F.

1973 Selected Nineteenth-Century Mexican Writers on Ethnohistory. In *Guide to Ethnohistorical Sources, Part Two,* edited by Howard F. Cline and John B. Glass, 370–427. Handbook of Middle American Indians, vol. 13, Robert Wauchope, general editor. Austin: University of Texas Press.

Codex Aubin

1981 *Geschichte der Azteken: Codex Aubin und verwandte Dokumente.* Quellenwerke zur alten Geschichte Amerikas aufgezeichnet in den Sprachen der Eingeborenen, herausgegeben von

Ibero-Amerikanischen Institut Preussischer Kulturbesitz (Schriftleitung: Gerdt Kutscher +), Band 13. Berlin: Gebr. Mann Verlag.

Codex Borbonicus

1974 *Codex Borbonicus. Bibliothèque de l'Assemblée National, Paris (Y 120).* Vollstandige Faksimile Ausgabe des Codex im Originalformat. Kommentar: Karl Anton Nowotny, Herkunft und Inhalt des Codex Borbonicus. Jacqueline de Durand-Forest, Codex Borbonicus: Description Codicologique. Codices Selecti; Phototypice Impressi, vol. 44. Graz: Akademische Druck- u. Verlagsanstalt.

Codex Ixtlilxochitl

1976 *Codex Ixtlilxochitl. Bibliothéque Nationale, Paris (Ms. Mex. 65–71).* Reproduktion des Manuskriptes im Originalformat. Commentaire: Jacqueline de Durand-Forest. Graz: Akademische Druck- u. Verlagsanstalt, Fontes Rerum Mexicanarum, ed. Ferdinand Anders, vol. 9.

Codex Laud

1966 *Codex Laud (Ms. Laud Misc. 678). Bodleian Library, Oxford.* Introduction, C. A. Burland. Graz: Akademische Druck- u. Verlagsanstalt, Codices Selecti, Phototypice Impressi, vol. 11.

Codex Magliabechiano

1903 *The Book of Life of the Ancient Mexicans Containing an Account of Their Rites and Superstitions.* An Anonymous Hispano-Mexican Manuscript Preserved at the Biblioteca Nazionale Centrale, Florence, Italy. Reproduced in facsimile with introduction, translation, and commentary by Zelia Nuttall. Part 1, Introduction and Facsimile. Berkeley: University of California.

1904 *Codex Magliabecchiano XIII.* 3. Manuscrit mexicain post-colombien de la Bibliothéque Nationale de Florence reproduit en photochromographie aux frais de Duc de Loubat correspondant de l'institut. Rome.

1970 *Codex Magliabechiano. CL. XIII 3 (B. R. 232). Biblioteca Nazionale Centrale di Firenze.* Inleitung Summary und Resumen Ferdinand Anders. Graz: Akademische Druck- u. Verlagsanstalt, Codices Selecti, Phototypice Impressi, vol. 23.

1983 *The Book of Life of the Ancient Mexicans Containing an Account of Their Rites and Superstitions.* An Anonymous Hispano-Mexican Manuscript Preserved at the Biblioteca Nazionale Centrale, Florence, Italy. Reproduced in facsimile with introduction, translation, and commentary by Zelia Nuttall. Part 1, Introduction and Facsimile. Berkeley: University of California Press. Reprint of 1903 edition, with Boone 1983.

Codex Mendoza

1992 *The Codex Mendoza.* Frances F. Berdan and Patricia Rieff Anawalt, et al. 4 vols., including color photoreproduction. Berkeley: University of California Press.

Codex Ramírez

1987 *Códice Ramírez, manuscrito del siglo xvi intitulado: Relación del origen de los indios que habitan esta Nueva España según sus historias.* (Juan de Tovar) Edited by Manuel Orozco y Berra. With Alvarado Tezozomoc 1987. Biblioteca Porrúa, 61. Mexico City: Editorial Porrúa.

Codex Telleriano-Remensis

1899 *Codex Telleriano-Remensis.* Manuscrit Mexicain du Cabinet de Ch.-M. Le Tellier, Archevéque de Reims, a la Bibliothèque Nationale (Ms. Mexicain no. 385). Reproduit en photochromographie aux frais du Duc de Loubat et precedé d'une introduction contenant la transcription complete des anciens commentaires Hispano-Mexicains par le Dr. E.-T. Hamy. Paris.

1995 See Quiñones Keber 1995.

Codex Tudela

1980 *Códice Tudela.* José Tudela de la Orden. Con un prólogo de Donald Robertson y un epílogo de Wigberto Jiménez Moreno y la reproducción autorizada de tablas de Ferdinand Anders y S. Jeffrey K. Wilkerson. Madrid: Ediciones Cultura Hispánica del Instituto de Cooperación Iberoamericana.

Codex Vaticanus A

1979 *Codex Vaticanus 3738 ("Cod. Vat. A," "Cod. Ríos") der Biblioteca Apostolica Vaticana.* Farbreproduktion des Codex in Verkleinertem Format. Graz: Akademische Druck- u. Verlagsanstalt, Codices Selecti, Phototypice Impressi, vol. 65.

Coe, Michael D.
1975 Native Astronomy in Mesoamerica. In *Archaeoastronomy in Pre-Columbian America*, edited by Anthony F. Aveni, 3–31. Austin: University of Texas Press.
Couch, N. C. Christopher
1985 *The Festival Cycle of the Aztec Codex Borbonicus.* Oxford: BAR International Series, 270.
Dakin, Karen, and Doris Heyden
1988 Introduction: Thelma Dorfman Sullivan. In *Smoke and Mist: Mesoamerican Studies in Memory of Thelma D. Sullivan,* edited by J. Kathryn Josserand and Karen Dakin, sections coordinated by H. B. Nicholson, Doris Heyden, Karen Dakin, and Nicholas A. Hopkins, part 1: 3–9. Oxford: BAR International Series, 402(i).
Davies, Nigel
1977 *The Toltecs: Until the Fall of Tula.* Norman: University of Oklahoma Press.
1982 *The Aztecs: A History.* Norman: University of Oklahoma Press. Reprint of the edition published by Macmillan, London, 1973.
1987 *The Aztec Empire: The Toltec Resurgence.* Norman: University of Oklahoma Press.
Dennis, Bryan
1988 Proyecto Tlatelolco: New Opportunities at the Imperial Aztec Marketplace. *Ascent: The Journal of Undergraduate Research* (University of Colorado at Boulder) 1(2): 1–13.
Díaz del Castillo, Bernal
1960 *Historia verdadera de la conquista de la Nueva España.* Introducción y notas de Joaquín Ramírez Cabañas. Mexico City: Editorial Porrúa.
Dibble, Charles E.
1980 The Xalaquia Ceremony. *Estudios de Cultura Náhuatl* 14: 197–202.
1982 Sahagún's *Historia.* In *Florentine Codex: General History of the Things of New Spain, Fray Bernardino de Sahagún, Introductions and Indices,* edited and translated by Arthur J. O. Anderson and Charles E. Dibble. Monographs of the School of American Research, no. 14, part 1: 9–23. Salt Lake City: University of Utah Press.
1984 Sahagún's *Tonalpohualli. Indiana* 9 (Gedenkschrift Gerdt Kutscher, Teil I): 115–131.
Dressler, Robert L.
1953 *The Pre-Columbian Cultivated Plants of Mexico.* Harvard University, Botanical Museum Leaflets, vol. 16, no. 6.
Durán, Fray Diego
1967 *Historia de las indias de Nueva España e islas de la tierra firme.* Edición paleográfica del manuscrito autografo de Madrid, con introducciones, notas y vocabularios de palabras indígenas y arcaicas. La prepara y da a luz Angel Ma. Garibay K. 2 vols., Biblioteca Porrúa, 36–37. Mexico City: Editorial Porrúa.
1994 *The History of the Indies of New Spain.* Translated, annotated, and with an introduction by Doris Heyden. Norman: University of Oklahoma Press.
Durand-Forest, Jacqueline
1977 Description des divinités d'après les textes en Nahuatl et leur représentation dans les codices. *Journal de la Société des Américanistes* 66: 9–17.
Emmart, Emily Walcott
1940 *The Badianus Manuscript (Codex Barberini Latin 241), Vatican Library. An Aztec Herbal of 1552.* Baltimore: Johns Hopkins University Press.
Fewkes, J. Walter
1893 A Central American Ceremony which Suggests the Snake Dance of the Tusayan Villages. *American Anthropologist,* o.s., 6: 284–306.
Franco, José Luis
1969 Comments on articles by Hermann Beyer concerning musicians and their instruments. Reprinted in *El México Antiguo* 9: 597–608.
Friedmann, Herbert, Ludlow Griscom, and Robert T. Moore
1950–1957 Distributional Check-List of the Birds of Mexico. *Pacific Coast Avifauna,* nos. 29, 33. Berkeley, California: Cooper Ornithological Club.

Gall, August Freiherr von
1940 Medizinische Bücher (tici-amatl) der alten Azteken in der ersten Zeit der Conquista. *Quellen und Studien zur Geschichte der Naturwissenschaft und Medizin* 7: 4–5, 81–299.
Gallo, Joaquín
1955 Un ensayo: Identificación de las constelaciones de Sahagún. *Astronomía Popular* 1(1): 17–21.
García Granados, Rafael
1952–1953 *Diccionario biográfico de historia antigua de Méjico.* 3 vols. Mexico City: Publications of the Instituto de Historia, first series, 23.
Garibay K., Angel M.
1940 *Poesía indígena de la Altiplanicie.* Mexico City: Universidad Nacional Autónoma de México, Biblioteca del Estudiante Universitario, 11.
1944–1947 Parlipómenos de Sahagún. *Tlalocan* I(4): 307–313, II(2): 164–174, II(3): 235–254.
1948 Relación breve de las fiestas de los dioses. Fray Bernardino de Sahagún. *Tlalocan* II(4): 189–320.
1958 *Veinte himnos sacros de los nahuas (Fray Bernardino de Sahagún).* Fuentes indígenas de la cultura náhuatl, informantes de Sahagún, 2. Mexico City: Instituto de Historia, Seminario de Cultural Nahuatl, Universidad Nacional Autónoma de México.
1961 *Llave del Náhuatl: Colección de trozos clásicos, con gramática y vocabulario, para utilidad de los principiantes.* Segunda edición revisada y aumentada. Mexico City: Editorial Porrúa. First edition, 1940.
1965 *Teogonía e historia de los Mexicanos. Tres opúsculos del siglo XVI.* Mexico City: Editorial Porrúa, Colección "Sepan Cuantos . . . ," 37.
1971 *Historia de la literatura Náhuatl.* 2d. ed. 2 vols. Biblioteca Porrúa 1, 5. Mexico City: Editorial Porrúa. Originally published 1954–1955.
Gemelli Careri, Gio Francesco
1699–1700 *Giro del Mondo.* 6 vols. Naples.
Gibson, Charles
1964 *The Aztecs under Spanish Rule: A History of the Indians of the Valley of Mexico, 1519–1810.* Stanford, California: Stanford University Press.
Gibson, Charles, and John B. Glass
1975 A Census of Middle American Prose Manuscripts in the Native Historical Tradition. In *Guide to Ethnohistorical Sources, Part 4,* edited by Howard F. Cline, Charles Gibson, and H. B. Nicholson, 322–400. Handbook of Middle American Indians, vol. 15, Robert Wauchope, general editor. Austin: University of Texas Press.
Giménez, Iris
1976 L'élaboration de la *Historia General de las Cosas de Nueva España* de Fray Bernardino de Sahagún. Un exemple: les folios 82, 88m et 104 de l'Académie de l'Histoire de Madrid. *Caravelle, Cahiers du Monde Hispanique et Luso-Brésilien* 27: 171–87.
Gingerich, Willard
1988 Three Nahuatl Hymns on the Mother Archetype: An Interpretive Commentary. *Mexican Studies/Estudios Mexicanos* 4(2): 191–244.
Glass, John B.
1975 A Survey of Native Middle American Pictorial Manuscripts. In *Guide to Ethnohistorical Sources, Part 3,* edited by Howard F. Cline, Charles Gibson, and H. B. Nicholson, 3–80. Handbook of Middle American Indians, vol. 14, Robert Wauchope, general editor. Austin: University of Texas Press.
González Aparicio, Luis
1973 *Plano reconstructivo de la región de Tenochtitlan.* Mexico City: Instituto Nacional de Antropología e Historia.
González Rul, Francisco
1964 Trabajos en Tlatelolco. *INAH Boletín* 15: 17–18.
Hassig, Ross
1988 *Aztec Warfare: Imperial Expansion and Political Control.* Norman: University of Oklahoma Press.
Hernández, Francisco
1651 *Rerum medicarum Novae Hispaniae thesaurus.* Rome: Accademia dei Lincei.

1942–1946 *Historia de las plantas de Nueva España.* 3 vols. Mexico City: Instituto de Biología de la Universidad Nacional Autónoma de México.

1959–1984 *Obras completas.* 7 vols. Mexico City: Universidad Nacional Autónoma de México.

Heyden, Doris

1986 Xipe Totec: Dios nativo de Guerrero o hijo adoptivo? In *Primer Coloquio de Arqueología y Etnohistoria del Estado de Guerrero,* 373–387. Mexico City: Instituto Nacional de Antropología e Historia and Gobierno del Estado de Guerrero.

Hindman, Sandra, and James Douglas Farquhar

1977 *Pen to Press: Illustrated Manuscripts and Printed Books in the First Century of Printing.* Baltimore: Johns Hopkins University Press.

Historia de los Mexicanos por sus pinturas

1891 In *Nueva colección de documentos para la historia de México,* Joaquín García Icazbalceta, ed., vol. 3: 228–263.

Jiménez Moreno, Wigberto

1974 *"Primeros Memoriales" de Fray Bernardino de Sahagún.* Textos en Náhuatl, traducción directa, prólogo y comentarios por Wigberto Jiménez Moreno. Mexico City: Instituto Nacional de Antropología e Historia, Consejo de Historia, Colección Científico, Historia, 16.

Kelly, Isabel, and Angel Palerm

1952 *The Tajin Totonac. Part 1: History, Subsistence, Shelter, and Technology.* Washington, D.C.: Smithsonian Institution, Institute of Social Anthropology, Pub. 13.

Kirchhoff, Paul

1959 Las dos rutas de los Colhua entre Tula y Culhuacán. *Mitteilungen aus dem Museum für Völkerkunde in Hamburg,* 25 (Festband Franz Termer: Amerikanische Miszellen): 75–81.

Kubler, George, and Charles Gibson

1951 *The Tovar Calendar: An Illustrated Mexican Manuscript ca. 1585.* Reproduced with a commentary and handlist of sources on the Mexican 365-day year by George Kubler and Charles Gibson. New Haven: Memoirs of the Connecticut Academy of Arts and Sciences, vol. II.

Kutscher, Gerdt

1961 Ein Stammbaum des königlichen Geschichtes von Tetzcoco. *Baessler Archiv,* n.s., 9(2): 233–263.

León-Portilla, Miguel

1958 *Ritos, sacerdotes y atavíos de los dioses.* Introducción, paleografía, versión y notas de Miguel León-Portilla. Mexico City: Universidad Nacional Autónoma de México, Instituto de Historia, Seminario de Cultura Náhuatl, Fuentes Indígenas de la Cultura Náhuatl, Textos de los Informantes de Sahagún, 1.

Leopold, A. Starker

1959 *Wildlife of Mexico: The Game Birds and Animals.* Berkeley: University of California Press.

Lienzo de Tlaxcala

1983 *El Lienzo de Tlaxcala.* Edited by Mario de la Torre, texts by Josefina García Quintana, Carlos Martínez Marín. Mexico City: Edición Privada de Cartón y Papel de México, Colección Cultura y Pasado de México.

López Austin, Alfredo

1967 Cuarenta clases de magos del mundo Náhuatl. *Estudios de Cultura Náhuatl* 7: 87–117.

1972 Textos acerca de las partes del cuerpo humano y medicinas en los Primeros Memoriales de Sahagún. *Estudios de Cultura Náhuatl* 10: 129–154.

1974 The Research Method of Fray Bernardino de Sahagún: The Questionnaires. In *Sixteenth-Century Mexico: The Work of Sahagún,* edited by Munro S. Edmonson, 111–149. Albuquerque: University of New Mexico Press.

1979 El Xiuhpohualli y el Tonalpohualli de los Memoriales de Tepepulco. In *Mesoamérica: Homenaje al Doctor Paul Kirchhoff,* coordinación, Barbro Dahlgren, 41–51. Mexico: Instituto Nacional de Antropología e Historia.

1980 *Cuerpo humano e ideología: Las concepciones de los antiguos Nahuas.* 2 vols. Mexico City: Universidad Nacional Autónoma de México, Instituto de Investigaciones Antropológicas, Etnología/Historia, Serie Antropológica, 39.

1988 *The Human Body and Ideology: Concepts of the Ancient Nahuas.* Translated by Thelma Ortiz de Montellano and Bernard Ortiz de Montellano. 2 vols. Salt Lake City: University of Utah Press.

Martínez, Maximino

1936 *Plantas útiles de México.* Mexico City: Editorial Botas.

Matos Moctezuma, Eduardo

1982 *El Templo Mayor: Excavaciones y estudios.* Eduardo Matos Moctezuma, coordinador. Mexico City: Instituto Nacional de Antropología e Historia.

1988 *The Great Temple of the Aztecs: Treasures of Tenochtitlan.* Translated from the Spanish by Doris Heyden. London: Thames and Hudson.

1989 *The Aztecs.* Translated from the Italian by Andrew Ellis. New York: Rizzoli International Publications.

Matrícula de Tributos

1980 *Matrícula de Tributos (Códice de Moctezuma).* Museo Nacional de Antropología, Mexico (Cod. 35–52). Vollständige Farbreproducktion des Codex in Verkleinertem Format. Kommentar, Frances F. Berdan, Jacqueline de Durand-Forest. Graz: Akademische Druck- u. Verlagsanstalt, Codices Selecti, Phototypice Impressi, vol. 68.

Mena, Ramón

1926 *Filigranas o marcas transparentes en papeles de Nueva España del siglo XVI.* Mexico City: Monografías Bibliográficas Mejicanas, 5.

Mendieta, Fray Gerónimo de

1971 *Historia Eclesiástic Indiana.* Edited by Joaquín García Icazbalceta. 2d ed. Mexico City: Editorial Porrúa.

Molina, Fray Alonso de

1944 *Vocabulario en lengua Castellana y Mexicana.* Obra impresa en México, por Antonio de Spinola en 1571 y ahora editada en facsimil. Madrid: Ediciones Cultura Hispánica, Colección de Incunables Americanos, Siglo XVI, vol. 4.

Museo Nacional de Culturas Populares

1988 *El maguey: "Arbol de maravillas."* Mexico City: Museo Nacional de Culturas Populares/Gobierno del Estado de Hidalgo.

Neumann, Frank J.

1976 The Flayed God and His Rattlestick: A Shamanic Element in Pre-Hispanic Mesoamerican Religion. *History of Religion* 15(3): 251–263.

Nicholson, H. B.

1954 The Birth of the Smoking Mirror. *Archaeology* 7(3): 164–170.

1956 The Temalacatl of Tehuacán. *El México Antiguo* 8: 95–194.

1957 *Topiltzin Quetzalcoatl of Tollan: A Problem in Mesoamerican Ethnohistory.* Ph.D. dissertation, Department of Anthropology, Harvard University.

1961 The Chapultepec Cliff Sculpture of Motecuhzoma Xocoyotzin. *El México Antiguo* 9: 379–444.

1963 An Aztec Stone Image of a Fertility Goddess. *Baessler Archiv* 11(1): 9–30.

1967a A Fragment of an Aztec Relief Carving of the Earth Monster. *Journal de la Société des Américanistes* 56(1): 81–94.

1967b A Royal Headband of the Tlaxcalteca. *Revista Mexicana de Estudios Antropológicos* 21: 71–106.

1971 Religion in Pre-Hispanic Central Mexico. In *Archaeology of Northern Mesoamerica, Part One,* edited by Gordon F. Ekholm and Ignacio Bernal, 395–446. Handbook of Middle American Indians, vol. 10, Robert Wauchope, general editor. Austin: University of Texas Press.

1972 The Cult of Xipe Totec in Mesoamerica. In *Religión en Mesoamerica: XII Mesa Redonda,* 213–218B. Mexico City: Sociedad Mexicana de Antropología.

1973 Sahagún's *Primeros Memoriales,* Tepepolco, 1559–1561. In *Guide to Ethnohistorical Sources, Part Two,* edited by Howard F. Cline and John B. Glass, 207–218. Handbook of Middle American Indians, vol. 13, Robert Wauchope, general editor. Austin: University of Texas Press.

1974 Tepepolco, the Locale of the First Stage of Fr. Bernardino de Sahagún's Great Ethnographic Project: Historical and Cultural Notes. In *Mesoamerican Archaeology: New Approaches,* edited by Norman Hammond, 145–54. London: Duckworth.

1978 Western Mesoamerican Native Historical Traditions and the Chronology of the Postclassic. In *Chronologies in New World Archaeology,* edited by Clement W. Meighan and R. E. Taylor, 285–329. New York: Academic Press.

1979 Ehecatl Quetzalcoatl vs. Topiltzin Quetzalcoatl of Tollan: A Problem in Mesoamerican History and Religion. In *Actes du XLII Congrés International des Américanistes (Congrés du Centenaire), Paris, 2–9 Septembre, 1976,* vol. 6: 35–47.

1985 The New Tenochtitlan Templo Mayor Coyolxauhqui-Chantico Monument. *Indiana* 10 (Gedenkschrift Gerdt Kutscher, Teil 2): 77–98.

1987 Symposium on the Aztec Templo Mayor: Discussion. In *The Aztec Templo Mayor,* edited by Elizabeth Hill Boone, 463–484. Washington, D.C.: Dumbarton Oaks Research Library and Collection, Trustees for Harvard University.

1988a A Carved Teponaztli with the Representation of a Dancer in Fish Disguise. In *Memorias del 45°. Congreso Internacional de Americanistas, Universidad de los Andes, Bogotá, Colombia, Julio 1–7, 1985, vol. 2, Identidad y Transformación de las Américas,* compiled by Elizabeth Reichel, 320–333.

1988b The Iconography of the Deity Representations in Fray Bernardino de Sahagún's *Primeros Memoriales:* Huitzilopochtli and Chalchiutlicue. In *The Work of Fray Bernardino de Sahagún: Pioneer Ethnographer of Sixteenth-Century Aztec Mexico,* edited by J. Jorge Klor de Alva, H. B. Nicholson, and Eloise Quiñones Keber, 229–253. Albany and Austin: Institute for Mesoamerican Studies, SUNY-Albany, and the University of Texas Press.

1988c The Provenience of the *Codex Borbonicus:* An Hypothesis. In *Smoke and Mist: Mesoamerican Studies in Memory of Thelma D. Sullivan,* edited by J. Kathryn Josserand and Karen Dakin, sections coordinated by H. B. Nicholson, Doris Heyden, Karen Dakin, and Nicholas A. Hopkins, part 1: 77–97. Oxford: BAR International Series, 402(i).

1988d Recent Sahaguntine Studies: A Review. In *The Work of Fray Bernardino de Sahagún: Pioneer Ethnographer of Sixteenth-Century Aztec Mexico,* edited by J. Jorge Klor de Alva, H. B. Nicholson, and Eloise Quiñones Keber, 13–30. Albany and Austin: Institute for Mesoamerican Studies, SUNY-Albany, and the University of Texas Press.

1991 The Octli Cult in Late Pre-Hispanic Central Mexico. In *To Change Place: Aztec Ceremonial Landscapes,* edited by David Carrasco, 158–187. Niwot: University Press of Colorado.

1993 The Problem of the Identification of the Central Image of the "Aztec Calendar Stone." In *Current Topics in Aztec Studies: Essays in Honor of Dr. H. B. Nicholson,* edited by Alana Cordy-Collins and Douglas Sharon, 3–15. San Diego Museum Papers, 30.

1994 The Eagle Claw/Tied Double Maize Ear Motif: The Cholula Polychrome Ceramic Tradition and Some Members of the Codex Borgia Group. In *Mixteca-Puebla: Discoveries and Research in Mesoamerican Art and Archaeology,* edited by H. B. Nicholson and Eloise Quiñones Keber, 101–118. Lancaster, California: Labyrinthos Press.

Nicholson, H. B., and Eloise Quiñones Keber

1983 *Art of Aztec Mexico: Treasures of Tenochtitlan.* Washington, D.C.: National Gallery of Art.

Nicolau d'Olwer, Luis

1987 *Fray Bernardino de Sahagún (1499–1590).* Translated by Mauricio J. Mixco. Salt Lake City: University of Utah Press.

Noguera, Eduardo

1945 El atlatl o tiradera. *Anales del Museo Nacional de Arqueología, Historia y Etnografía (Mexico), Quinto Epoca,* 3: 205–238.

Nuttall, Zelia

1891 *The Atlatl or Spear-thrower of the Ancient Mexicans.* Archaeological and Ethnological Papers of the Peabody Museum 1(3). Cambridge: Harvard University.

Offner, Jerome A.

1983 *Law and Politics in Aztec Texcoco.* Cambridge Latin American Studies, 44. Cambridge: Cambridge University Press.

Olmos, Fray Andrés de

1875 *Grammaire de la langue Nahuatl ou Mexicaine composée en 1547 et publiée avec notes éclaircissements etc. par Rémi Siméon.* Paris: Imprimerie Nationale.

Orozco y Berra, Manuel
1960 *Historia antigua y de la conquista de México.* Con un estudio previo de Angel Ma. Garibay K. y biografía del autor, más tres bibliografías referentes al mismo, de Miguel León-Portilla. 2d ed. 4 vols. Biblioteca Porrúa, 17–20. Mexico City: Editorial Porrúa.

Paso y Troncoso, Francisco del
1898 *Descripción, historia y exposición del códice pictórico de los antiguos Náuas que se conserva en la biblioteca de la Cámara de Diputados de París (antiguo Palais Bourbon).* Florence: Tipografía de Salvador Landi.

Prem, Hanns J.
1988 Calendrical Traditions in the Writings of Sahagún. In *The Work of Fray Bernardino de Sahagún: Pioneer Ethnographer of Sixteenth-Century Aztec Mexico,* edited by J. Jorge KLor de Alva, H. B. Nicholson, and Eloise Quiñones Keber, 135–149. Studies on Culture and Society, vol. 2. Albany: Institute for Mesoamerican Studies, State University of New York.

Quiñones Keber, Eloise
1987 Ritual and Representation in the Tonalamatl of the Codex Borbonicus. *Latin American Indian Literatures Journal* 3(2): 184–195.
1988a The Annual Ritual Cycle in Mesoamerican Manuscripts. *Latin American Indians Literatures Journal* 4(2): 207–225.
1988b Deity Images and Texts in the *Primeros Memoriales* and *Florentine Codex.* In *The Work of Fray Bernardino de Sahagún: Pioneer Ethnographer of Sixteenth-Century Aztec Mexico,* edited by J. Jorge Klor de Alva, H. B. Nicholson, and Eloise Quiñones Keber, 255–272. Studies on Culture and Society, vol. 2. Albany: Institute for Mesoamerican Studies, State University of New York.
1988c Reading Images: The Making and Meaning of the Sahaguntine Illustrations. In *The Work of Fray Bernardino de Sahagún: Pioneer Ethnographer of Sixteenth-Century Aztec Mexico,* edited by J. Jorge Klor de Alva, H. B. Nicholson, and Eloise Quiñones Keber, 99–210. Studies on Culture and Society, vol. 2. Albany: Institute for Mesoamerican Studies, State University of New York.
1989a *Atl Tlachinolli:* A Verbal and Visual Metaphor in Aztec Art. In *Begetting Images: Studies in the Art and Science of Symbol Production,* edited by Mary B. Campbell and Mark Rollins (New Connections: Studies in Interdisciplinarity), 201–218. New York: Peter Lang.
1989b Mayahuel and Maguey: Sustenance and Sacrifice in an Aztec Myth. *Latin American Indian Literatures Journal* 5(2): 72–83.
1995 *Codex Telleriano-Remensis: Ritual, Divination, and History in a Pictorial Aztec Manuscript.* Foreword by Emmanuel Le Roy Ladurie. Austin: University of Texas Press.

Ramírez, José Fernando
1885 Códices mexicanos de Fray Bernardino de Sahagún. *Boletín de la Real Academia de la Historia* 6: 85–124.

Rammow, Helga
1964 Die Verwandschaftsbezeichnungen im klassischen Aztekischen. *Beiträge zur mittelamerikanischen Völkerkunde, Herausgegeben von Hamburgischen Museum für Volkerkunde und Vorgeschichte,* 6. Hamburg: Hamburgischen Museums für Völkerkunde und Vorgeschichte.

Robertson, Donald
1959 *Mexican Manuscript Painting of the Early Colonial Period: The Metropolitan Schools.* New Haven, Connecticut: Yale University Press.
1966 The Sixteenth-Century Mexican Encyclopedia of Fray Bernardino de Sahagún. *Journal of World History* 9(3): 207–225.

Sahagún, Fray Bernardino de
1905–1907 *Historia general de las cosas de Nueva España por Fr. Bernardino de Sahagún. Edición parcial en facsimile de los Códices Matritenses en lengua mexicana que se custodian en las Bibliotecas del Palacio Real y de la Real Academia de la Historia.* Edited by Francisco del Paso y Troncoso. 4 vols. Madrid: Hauser y Menet.
1938 *Historia general de las cosas de Nueva España.* Edited by Joaquín Ramírez Cabañas. 5 vols. Mexico City: Editorial Pedro Robredo.

1950–1982 *Florentine Codex: General History of the Things of New Spain,* translated and edited by Arthur J. O. Anderson and Charles E. Dibble. Monographs of the School of American Research, no. 14, 13 parts. Salt Lake City: University of Utah Press.
1956 *Historia general de las cosas de Nueva España.* Edited by Angel María Garibay K. 4 vols. Biblioteca Porrúa, 8–11. Mexico City: Editorial Porrúa.
1970 *Florentine Codex: General History of the Things of New Spain, Book 1: The Gods,* translated and edited by Arthur J. O. Anderson and Charles E. Dibble. Monographs of the School of American Research, no. 14, part 2. 2d ed., revised. Salt Lake City: University of Utah Press.
1975 *Historia general de las cosas de Nueva España.* 3d ed. Edited by Angel María Garibay K. Colección "Sepan cuantos . . . ," 300. Mexico City: Editorial Porrúa.
1978 *Florentine Codex: General History of the Things of New Spain, Book 3: The Origin of the Gods,* translated and edited by Arthur J. O. Anderson and Charles E. Dibble. Monographs of the School of American Research, no. 14, part 4. 2d ed., revised. Salt Lake City: University of Utah Press.
1979 *Códice Florentino.* El manuscrito 218–220 de la colección Palatina de la Biblioteca Medicea Laurenziana. Color photoreproduction. 3 vols. Florence and Mexico City: Giunti Barbera and Archivo General de la Nación.
1981 *Florentine Codex: General History of the Things of New Spain, Book 2: The Ceremonies,* translated and edited by Arthur J. O. Anderson and Charles E. Dibble. 2d ed., revised. Monographs of the School of American Research no. 14, part 3. Salt Lake City: University of Utah Press.
1988 *Historia general de las cosas de Nueva España.* Primera versión integra del texto castellano del manuscrito conocido como Códice Florentino. Introducción, paleografía, glosario y notas de Alfredo López Austin y Josefina García Quintana. 2 vols. Madrid: Alianza Editorial.
1993 *Primeros Memoriales by Fray Bernardino de Sahagún.* Facsimile edition, photographed by Ferdinand Anders. The Civilization of the American Indian Series, vol. 200, part one. Norman: University of Oklahoma Press.

Santamaría, Francisco J.
1959 *Diccionario de Mejicanismos.* Mexico City: Editorial Porrúa.

Schultze Jena, Leonhard, ed. and trans.
1950 Wahrsagerei, Himmelskunde und Kalender der alten Azteken aus dem Aztekischen Urtext Bernardino de Sahagún's. Quellenwerke zur alten Geschichte Amerikas aufgezeichnet in den Sprachem der Eingeborenen, IV. Herausgegeben von der Lateinamerikanischen Bibliothek, Berlin. Stuttgart: W. Kohlhammer Verglag.
1952 *Gliederung des alt-Aztekischen Volks in Familie, Stand und Beruf aus dem Aztekischen Urtext Bernardino de Sahagún's.* Quellenwerke zur alten Geschichte Amerikas aufgezeichnet in den Sprachen der Eingeborenen, V. Herausgegeben von der Lateinamerikanischen Bibliothek, Berlin. Stuttgart: W. Kohlhammer Verlag.

Seler, Eduard
1890 Ein Kapitel aus den in aztekischer Sprache geschriebenen, ungedruckten Materialien zu dem Geschichtswerk des Padre Sahagún (Göttertrachten und attribute). Altmexikanische Studien, I. *Veröffentlichungen aus dem Königlichen Museum für Völkerkunde,* I, Heft 4: 117–181.
1899a Die Achtzehn Jahrefeste der Mexikaner. Altmexikanische Studien, II. *Veröffentlichungen aus dem Königlichen Museum für Völkerkunde* VI, Heft 2–4: 67–209.
1899b Zauberei und Zauberer im alten Mexiko. Altmexikanische Studien, II. *Veröffentlichungen aus dem Königlichen Museum für Völkerkunde,* VI, Heft 2–4: 29–57.
1900 Die Ausgrabungen am Orte des Haupttempels in Mexiko. *Mittheilungen der Anthropologischen Gesellschaft in Wien* 31:113–137.
1900–1901 *The Tonalamatl of the Aubin Collection: An Old Mexican Picture Manuscript in the Paris National Library (Manuscrits Mexicains No. 18–19).* English ed. by A. H. Keane. London and Aylesbury: Hazell, Watson & Viney.
1902–1923 *Gesammelte Abhandlungen zur Amerikanischen Sprach- und Altertumskunde.* 5 vols. Berlin: Asher (vols. 1–2) and Behrend (vols. 3–5).
1904 Venus Period in the Picture Writings of the Borgian Codex Group. In *Mexican and Central American Antiquities, Calendar Systems, and History, Twenty-four Papers by Eduard Seler, et al.,*

translated from the German under the supervision of Charles P. Bowditch, 355–391. Bureau of American Ethnology Bulletin 28. Washington, D.C.: Smithsonian Institution.

1904–1909 *Codex Borgia: Eine altmexikanische Bilderschrift der Bibliothek der Congregatio de Propaganda Fide.* Herausgegeben auf Kosten Seiner Excellenz des Herzogs von Loubat. Erläutert von Dr. Eduard Seler. 3 vols. Berlin.

1927 *Einige Kapitel aus dem Geschichtswerke des Fray Bernardino de Sahagún aus den Aztekischen übersetzt.* Edited by Caecilie Seler-Sachs, with the assistance of Walter Lehmann and Walter Krickeberg. Stuttgart: Strecker und Schroeder.

1939 *Gessammelte Abhandlungen zur Amerikanischen Sprach- und Alterkumskunde,* vols. 1–5. Unpublished English Translations of German Papers in the Above Work Made under the Supervision of Charles P. Bowditch. Published with Permission of Peabody Museum, Harvard University, Owners of the Original Translation. With Slight Emendations to vols. 4 and 5 by J. Eric S. Thompson. Edited by J. Eric S. Thompson and Francis B. Richardson. Cambridge, Massachusetts: Carnegie Institution of Washington. Mimeographed.

1963 *Comentarios al Códice Borgia.* 3 vols. Mexico City: Fondo de Cultura Económica.

1990–1993 *Eduard Seler: Collected Works in Mesoamerican Linguistics and Archaeology.* English Translations of German Papers from *Gessamelte Abhandlungen zur Amerikanischen Sprach-und Alterthumskunde.* Made under the Supervision of Charles P. Bowditch. Published with the Permission of Tozzer Library, Peabody Museum, Harvard University, Owners of the Original Translation. With Slight Emendations to Volumes IV and V by Eric S. Thompson. Edited by J. Eric S. Thonpson and Francis B. Richardson and Illustrated with All the Original Figures, Maps, Plates, and Photographs. Second Edition. Frank E. Comparato, General Editor. Vols. I–IV. Culver City, California: Labyrinthos Press.

Standley, Paul C.

1920–1926 Trees and Shrubs of Mexico. *Contributions from the U.S. National Herbarium* 23: 1–1721.

Stenzel, Werner

1970 The Sacred Bundles in Mesoamerican Religion. In *Verhandlungen des XXXVIII. Internationalen Amerikanistenkongresses, Stuttgart-München, 12. bis, 18 August 1968,* Band I: 347–352.

Stresser-Péan, Guy

1971 Ancient Sources on the Huasteca. In *Archaeology of Northern Mesoamerica, Part 2,* edited by Gordon F. Ekholm and Ignacio Bernal, 582–602. Handbook of Middle American Indians, vol. 11, Robert Wauchope, general editor. Austin: University of Texas Press.

Sullivan, Thelma D.

1963 Nahuatl Proverbs, Conundrums, and Metaphors, Collected by Sahagún. *Estudios de Cultura Náhuatl* 4: 93–177.

1972a The Arms and Insignia of the Mexica. *Estudios del Cultura Náhuatl* 1: 156–193.

1972b Tlaloc: A New Etymological Interpretation of the God's Name and What It Reveals of His Essence and Nature. *Atti del XL Congresso Internazionale degli Americanisti, Roma-Genova, 3–10 Settembre, 1972,* vol. 2: 213–19.

1974 The Rhetorical Orations, or *Huehuetlatolli,* Collected by Sahagún. In *Sixteenth-Century Mexico: The Work of Sahagún,* edited by Munro S. Edmonson, 79–98. Albuquerque: University of New Mexico Press.

1976a *Compendio de la gramática náhuatl.* Mexico City: Universidad Nacional Autónoma de México, Instituto de Investigaciones Históricas.

1976b The Mask of Itztlacoliuhqui. *Actas del XLI Congreso Internacional de Americanistas, México, 2 al 7 de septiembre de 1974,* vol. 2: 252–262.

1982 Tlazolteotl-Ixcuina: The Great Spinner and Weaver. In *The Art and Iconography of Late Post-Classic Central Mexico: A Conference at Dumbarton Oaks, October 22nd and 23rd, 1977,* organized by Betty P. Benson, edited by Elizabeth Hill Boone, 7–35. Washington, D.C.: Dumbarton Oaks, Trustees for Harvard University.

1986 A Scattering of Jades: The Words of the Aztec Elders. In *Symbol and Meaning beyond the Closed*

Community: Essays in Mesoamerican Ideas, edited by Gary H. Gossen, 9–17. Studies on Culture and Society, vol. 1. Albany: Institute for Mesoamerican Studies, State University of New York.

1988 *Thelma D. Sullivan's Compendium of Nahuatl Grammar.* Translated from the Spanish by Thelma D. Sullivan and Neville Stiles. Edited by Wick R. Miller and Karen Dakin. Salt Lake City: University of Utah Press.

Taladoire, Eric

1981 Les terraines de jeu de balle (Mesoamérique et sud-ouest des Etats-Unis). *Mission Archeologique et Ethnologique Française au Mexique, Etudes Mesoaméricaines*, Serie II, 4.

Thompson, J. Eric S.

1966 Ayopechtli, an Aspect of the Nahua Goddess of the Maguey. In *XXXVI Congreso Internacional de Americanistas, España, Actas y Memorias* (Seville, 1964), vol. 2: 103–106.

Tonalamatl Aubin

1900–1901 See Seler 1900–1901.

Torquemada, Fray Juan de

1975–1983 *Monarquía Indiana.* 7 vols. Edición preparada por el Seminario para el estudio de fuentes de tradición indígena, bajo la coordinación de Miguel León-Portilla. Mexico City: Universidad Nacional Autónoma de México, Instituto de Investigaciones Históricas, Serie de Historiadores y Cronistas de Indias, 5.

Tudela de la Orden, José

1980 See *Codex Tudela* 1980.

Valls i Subirà, Oriol

1980 *La historia del papel en España, vol. 2, Siglos XV–XVI.* Madrid: Empresa Nacional de Celulosas.

Van Zantwijk, Rudolf

1963 Principios organizadores de los Mexicas. *Estudios de Cultura Náhuatl* 3: 101–136.

Vega Sosa, Constanza, coordinator

1979 *El Recinto Sagrado de Mexico-Tenochtitlan: Excavaciones 1968–69 y 1975–76.* Mexico City: Instituto Nacional de Antropología e Historia.

Zavala, Silvio

1939 *Francisco del Paso y Troncoso: Su misión en Europa, 1892–1916.* Mexico City: Departamento Autónomo de Prensa y Publicidad.

Zimmermann, Gunter, ed.

1970 *Briefe der indianischen Nobilität aus Neuspanien an Karl V und Philipp II um die Mitte des 16. Jahrhunderts.* Beiträge zur mittelamerikanischen Völkerkunde, herausgegeben vom Hamburgischen Museum für Völkerkunde und Vorgeschichte, 10. Munich: Klaus Renner.

Collaborators

ARTHUR J. O. ANDERSON (Ph.D., University of Southern California, 1940) had a long, active career as a teacher and research scholar, capped by his lengthy collaboration with Charles Dibble in producing the paleography of the Nahuatl text and an English translation of the twelve books of the *Florentine Codex* version of Fray Bernardino de Sahagún's *Historia General (Universal) de las Cosas de (la) Nueva España,* which incorporates portions of the *Primeros Memoriales.* For this landmark achievement and other important scholarly contributions to the field of Mesoamerican ethnohistory, Anderson was awarded the title of Commander, Order of the Aztec Eagle, by the government of Mexico, and that of Knight Commander, Order of Isabel la Católica, by the Spanish monarch.

CHARLES E. DIBBLE (Ph.D., Universidad Nacional Autónoma de México, 1942) is Emeritus Distinguished Professor of Anthropology at the University of Utah. His earliest major contributions to Mesoamerican ethnohistory were focused on the Aztec writing system; they included extensive commentaries on native-tradition pictographic histories from the Basin of Mexico. Dibble's scholarly career, like that of his collaborator, Arthur Anderson, was climaxed with the publication of the *Florentine Codex.* For this monumental project and Dibble's other valuable contributions to the field, he too was awarded the titles of Commander, Order of the Aztec Eagle, and Knight Commander, Order of Isabel la Católica.

ELOISE QUIÑONES KEBER (Ph.D., Columbia University, 1984) is Professor of Art History at Baruch College and at the Graduate School of the City University of New York. She has published extensively on the art of late pre-Hispanic and early colonial Central Mexico, including articles on Sahaguntine themes. She was a co-editor of *The Work of Bernardino de Sahagún: Pioneer Ethnographer of Sixteenth-Century Mexico* (1988). Most recently she published a commentary and color facsimile of the *Codex Telleriano-Remensis,* a prime source of our knowledge of the Aztec religious-ritual system, calendrics, and history, and she edited a tribute volume to Arthur Anderson and Charles Dibble, *Chipping Away on Earth* (1994).

H. B. NICHOLSON (Ph.D., Harvard University, 1958) is Emeritus Professor of Anthropology at the University of California at Los Angeles. He has undertaken considerable library and archival research in the ethnohistory of the Mesoamerican area co-tradition, as well as conducting field archaeological projects and publishing numerous articles and monographs in these fields. He was an associate editor for parts 3 and 4 of the *Guide to Ethnohistorical Sources,* volumes 14 and 15 of the *Handbook of Middle American Indians* (1975), and, with Quiñones Keber, he was a co-editor of *The Work of Bernardino de Sahagún.* He is director of the UCLA Aztec Archive, a computerized image storage and retrieval system for Late Postclassic Central Mexican aesthetic productions in public and private collections.

WAYNE RUWET (B.A., University of California at Los Angeles, 1967) has worked for many years in the College Library at UCLA, where he is Head of Operations, Circulation Department. He has a long-standing interest in the ethnographic, linguistic, and ecclesiastical writings of Sahagún and has conducted library and archival research on Sahaguntine and other Mesoamerican ethnohistorical themes in the United States, Mexico, and Europe, publishing various articles in this field. He is currently working on a comprehensive Sahaguntine biographical bibliography.

THELMA DORFMAN SULLIVAN (B.A., Hood College, Maryland, 1939) was one of the world's leading Nahuatl scholars. She studied philosophy and English literature at Hood College and Columbia University and subsequently began to write professionally for radio and theater. After her marriage to Dennis Sullivan, the two moved to Mexico City in the mid-1940s. In 1959 she began her study of Classical Nahuatl in the Seminario de Cultura Náhuatl of the Universidad

Nacional Autónoma de México, first with Miguel León-Portilla and soon also with Angel María Garibay K., founder of the *seminario.* During the next few years she became active in the field of late pre-Hispanic Central Mexican ethnohistory, publishing numerous articles and, especially, English and Spanish translations of Nahuatl texts, mainly Sahaguntine. Of particular value was her 1976 *Compendio de la Gramática Náhuatl* (revised English edition, 1988). Only her death in 1981 prevented her from completing her English translation of the *Primeros Memoriales.*

INDEX

www.ingramcontent.com/pod-product-compliance
Lightning Source LLC
Chambersburg PA
CBHW081327090726
47907CB00010B/2393

* 9 7 8 0 8 0 6 1 5 7 4 9 8 *